Advancing Education with Information Communication Technologies:

Facilitating New Trends

Lawrence A. Tomei
Robert Morris University, USA

Managing Director:	Lindsay Johnston
Senior Editorial Director:	Heather Probst
Book Production Manager:	Sean Woznicki
Development Manager:	Joel Gamon
Development Editor:	Michael Killian
Acquisitions Editor:	Erika Gallagher
Typesetters:	Jennifer Romanchak
Print Coordinator:	Jamie Snavely
Cover Design:	Nick Newcomer, Greg Snader

Published in the United States of America by
Information Science Reference (an imprint of IGI Global)
701 E. Chocolate Avenue
Hershey PA 17033
Tel: 717-533-8845
Fax: 717-533-8661
E-mail: cust@igi-global.com
Web site: http://www.igi-global.com

Library of Congress Cataloging-in-Publication Data

Advancing education with information communication technologies : facilitating
new trends / Lawrence A. Tomei, editor.
       p. cm. -- (Advances in information and communication technology
education series ; v. 6)
  Includes bibliographical references and index.
  Summary: "This book offers an overview of how research in ICT provides a new framework for education, focusing on the development and design of successful education programs"--Provided by publisher.
    ISBN 978-1-61350-468-0 (hardcover) -- ISBN 978-1-61350-469-7 (ebook) -- ISBN 978-1-61350-470-3 (print & perpetual access) 1. Educational technology. 2. Information technology. I. Tomei, Lawrence A.
  LB1028.3.A355 2012
  371.33--dc23
                         2011043676

British Cataloguing in Publication Data
A Cataloguing in Publication record for this book is available from the British Library.

All work contributed to this book is new, previously-unpublished material. The views expressed in this book are those of the authors, but not necessarily of the publisher.

Table of Contents

Detailed Table of Contents

Louis B. Swartz, Robert Morris University, USA
Michele T. Cole, Robert Morris University, USA
Daniel J. Shelley, Robert Morris University, USA

Our study presents the results of a satisfaction survey of business law instructors who have taught, or are teaching, online and/or onground. The authors used the framework suggested by Berge to examine the level of instructor satisfaction, using his four role categories: pedagogical, social, technical, and managerial. Their study found that for 73% of the categories' aspects, instructors were generally satisfied with online instruction. With regard to the classroom experience, instructors were generally satisfied across the board with regard to all aspects. In comparing the level of satisfaction with online and onground instruction, they found statistically significant differences between the two methods of instruction. In all four areas measured, instructors were more satisfied with classroom instruction than they were with online instruction of business law courses.

Arjan Raven, Kennesaw State University, USA
Elke Leeds, Kennesaw State University, USA
ChongWoo Park, Georgia Gwinnett College, USA

This paper reports the results of a confirmatory study of a Task Technology Fit (TTF) model. Three dimensions of fit: Task Match, Ease of Use, and Ease of Learning, are applied in the context of digital video tools use for oral presentation in a classroom environment. Students completed a digital video presentation that acted as a substitute for an in-class oral presentation. An existing survey instrument was adapted, and administered to the students to examine the impact on presentation skill and fit to task. Results confirm the adaptation of the TTF model and show significant relationships between variables. The model can be used in other task/technology combinations. Additional findings suggest that when there is a significant fit between digital video tools (technology) and improvement of oral presentation skills (task), student performance also improves. Digital video can be a useful alternative to in-class presentation when the goal is to improve presentation skill.

Chapter 3

Nwachukwu Prince Ololube, University of Education Port Harcourt, Nigeria
Andrew Egba Ubogu, Ahmadu Bello University, Nigeria
Daniel Elemchukwu Egbezor, University of Port Harcourt, Nigeria
Ugbomah Nwachukwu, NOVENA Univesity Ogume, Nigeria

The effective ways of teaching research methods to students is a process closely connected to socializing students towards writing an effective research project before graduation and determines how successful and effective they are in conducting individualized research. Several factors apart from setting up a successful learning community are essential, but competencies determine faculty effectiveness. This paper appraises students' evaluation of faculty (SEF). It evaluates students' perception of competencies required by faculty in teaching research methodology to undergraduate geography students at the Ahmadu Bello University in Nigeria. Using a questionnaire to gather data for the study, the paper argues that by evaluating the performance of faculty members, their knowledge, expertise, skills, and by applying certain adaptation mechanisms in teaching, the experience and effectiveness of teaching students' research methodology can be significantly improved. The authors use this medium to encourage colleges and universities, education planners and policy makers in Nigeria of the need to introduce and carry out SEF along side other evaluation techniques in determining faculty performances and effectiveness.

Chapter 4

Joseph Blankson, Carle Foundation Hospital, USA
Jared Keengwe, University of North Dakota, USA
Lydia Kyei-Blankson, Illinois State University, USA

In addition to possessing content knowledge required to teach students, today's teachers must be well equipped with appropriate technology skills and tools to guide and support student learning. The identification of this need has led teacher education programs to mandate all preservice teachers to enroll in technology courses as part of their teacher preparatory curriculum. Similarly, the International Society for Technology in Education (ISTE) has established the National Education Technology Standards for teachers (NETS- T) to help promote teacher technology competencies. The purpose of the study was to evaluate preservice teachers' self-assessed technology competency to determine whether preservice teachers perceived that their technology class enabled them to meet ISTE's required standards. Specifically, this paper explores the extent to which an educational technology course at a participating midwest college helped to improve preservice teachers' technology skills as well as to prepare them attain ISTE NETS- T.

Chapter 5

Pereware Aghwotu Tiemo, Delta State University, Nigeria.
O. T. Emiri, Delta State University, Nigeria
Adobi Jessica Tiemo, Delta State University, Nigeria

In order to bridge the digital gap and to facilitate the use of ICT in teaching and learning among lecturers and students in Nigeria universities, the Nigeria Communication Commission (NCC) organized a workshop to train lecturers in the use of ICT skill and knowledge. It was expected that 12,000 lecturers from various universities will be trained. It was discovered that the idea was welcomed since most of them find if difficult to integrate ICT in their academic work. As a result of this, the study seek to find out the success achieved among participants and their perception toward the programme.

Chapter 6

M. Erdal Balaban, University Istanbul, Turkey
Melih Kirlidog, University Istanbul, Turkey
Zerrin Ayvaz-Reis, University Istanbul, Turkey

Education is an expensive process and the quality of an education program is largely affected by resources devoted to it. Availability of qualified instructors and physical amenities such as labs are the most important resources that determine the educational quality. Based on the graduate Information Systems curriculum recommendation of Association for Computing Machinery (ACM) and Association for Information Systems (AIS) this article investigates the perceived importance of each course taught in graduate Information Systems programs in Turkey. The perceived importance is also compared with the availability of instructor and technological resources for each course to get an insight into educational resources and constraints.

Chapter 7

D. Scott Hunsinger, Appalachian State University, USA
Judy Land, North Carolina Central University, USA
Charlie C. Chen, Appalachian State University, USA

Many colleges and universities face the problem of recruiting and retaining students in information systems-related majors. The authors' study proposes a model to identify the primary factors leading to the retention of existing Computer Information Systems (CIS) majors. They identify four factors leading to student intention to remain a CIS major or to refer others to become a CIS major: (1) expectations, (2) perceived service quality, (3) satisfaction, and (4) regret. They discover that certain factors play a significant role in influencing a student's intention to remain a CIS major and/or to encourage others to major in CIS. By determining which factors impact students' intentions to remain a CIS major and to encourage others to major in CIS, we can focus our resources on these areas instead of spending time and money on those services which are not influential.

Chapter 8

Benjamin KS Khoo, New York Institute of Technology, USA

A major limitation in traditional class lectures that uses textbooks, handouts, transparencies and assignments is that students often are unable to "experience" user interface design. This limitation can be overcome by using the constructionist approach that allow students to experience user interface design by allowing them to "do" or "construct" so that they can understand and remember. This paper describes an Internet-based interactive case scenario that was developed, based on the constructionist approach, to teach students user interface design concepts in conjunction with the Questionnaire for User Interaction Satisfaction (QUIS). A proof of concept evaluation was conducted and the results indicate that this approach is effective in user interface design pedagogy.

Chapter 9
Albert Akyeampong, Ohio University, USA
Teresa Franklin, Ohio University, USA
Jared Keengwe, University of North Dakota, USA

This study explored one primary question: To what extent do student perceptions of various forms of instructional technology tools predict instructional quality? Participants for the study were drawn from a teacher education program in a large Midwest public university. Data were collected using a web-based survey with a total of 121 responses used in the final analysis. A multiple regression analysis was conducted to evaluate how well Productivity Tools, Presentation Tools, Communication Tools, and World Wide Web Tools predict Student Evaluation of Faculty Instructional Quality. The overall significant results of the regression model and the subsequent significant results of the t-test for Presentation Tools and Productivity Tools is an indication that Presentation and Productivity tools can be used by faculty to facilitate student and faculty interaction, promote cooperation among students, promote active learning techniques, give prompt feedback, emphasize time on task, communicate high expectation and respect diverse talents and ways of learning.

Chapter 10
Chia-Wen Tsai, Ming Chuan University, Taiwan

The vocational schools in Taiwan regard professional certifications as a badge of skills achievement. However, due to a national policy, pure online courses are not permitted. Moreover, it remains unclear whether every subject is suitable to be delivered via online courses. In this regard, the author conducted a quasi-experiment to examine the effects of applying blended learning (BL) with different course orientations on students' computing skills, and explored the appropriate combination for teachers who teach computing courses. Four classes in successive semesters, with a total of 195 students from the courses of 'Database Management System' and 'Packaged Software and Application', were divided into 2 (Design-oriented vs. Procedural-oriented) × 2 (BL vs. Traditional Learning) experimental groups. The results showed that students from both design-oriented and procedural-oriented courses delivered in BL environment, had significantly higher grades on the examination for certificates than those who learned in traditional learning environment.

Chapter 11
K. Giotopoulos, University of Patras, Greece
C. Alexakos, University of Patras, Greece
G. Beligiannis, University of Patras, Greece
A. Stefani, University of Patras, Greece

This paper presents a newly developed student model agent, which is the basic part of an e-learning environment that incorporates Intelligent Agents and Computational Intelligence Techniques. The e-learning environment consists of three parts, the E-learning platform Front-End, the Student Questioner Reasoning and the Student Model Agent. The basic aim of this contribution is to describe in detail the agent's architecture and the innovative features it provides to the e-learning environment through its utilization as an autonomous component. Several basic processes and techniques are facilitated through the agent in order to provide intelligence to the e-learning environment.

Chapter 12

This study assesses the factorial validity of the Computer Attitude Scale (CAS) using a sample (N=438) of students from Singapore. Developed by Selwyn (1997), the CAS is a four-factor scale that measures the perceived usefulness, affective, behavioral, perceived control components that were proposed to constitute the multidimensional construct known as computer attitude. The results of this study show an overall positive computer attitude among the students. However, factor analyses reveal multicollinearity among some items and these were removed from further analysis. A confirmatory factor analysis was performed on a proposed 15-item model of the CAS and it was found to have a good fit. Implications for education in the Asian contexts are discussed. Suggestions for future research are offered.

Chapter 13

Using technology tools in math instruction can help stimulate problem-solving skills and understanding of math concepts. However, teachers need to be confident in their abilities to use technology tools. This study investigated whether or not a four-week in-service professional development institute that addressed the use of technology in math education helped improved the teachers' attitude and confidence in applying technology. Findings indicated that as the teachers explored and used the available technology tools relevant to math instruction during the institute, the more proactive and motivated they became to continue their professional development in using technology for classroom instruction. They realized that they were able to use technology and desired to continue their education in this area.

Chapter 14

One way of identifying an effective materials-to-standards relationship (often defined educationally as "alignment") is through the use of metadata for books, visual media, computer software, educational kits, and manipulative materials. Embedded in the metadata is vocabulary containing standards-based terminology and other elements of educational pedagogy—evidence of an effective materials-to-standards relationship or alignment. This article attempts to define the materials-to-standards alignment process (as it relates to state standards) and its relationship to formative assessment and the use of learning objects—successful strategies being used in today's educational instruction and testing environment. The article also looks at two statewide examples of the use of metadata reflecting materials-to-standards alignment and identifies both current successes and future challenges associated with the broad use of each.

Chapter 15

This article intends to help educators interested in technology integration in the classroom acquire a firm theoretical foundation, pedagogical applications, and step-by-step technical procedures for infusing digital storytelling into the curriculum. Through illustrations of digital storytelling projects completed in the authors' undergraduate and graduate classes, this article discusses the benefits along with the challenges for using digital storytelling as a means of engaging students in reflective, active, and personally meaningful learning.

Chapter 16

One of the unprecedented benefits of campus-wide distance learning strategies has been the incorporation of more technology-based pedagogy into traditional classrooms, thus, increasing faculty and student teaching and learning opportunities. This "hybrid" or "blended" teaching has emerged largely due to a desire to widen access to educational opportunities, continuing education, and university resources (Curran, 2004; Garrison & Kanuka, 2004). However, a major challenge to this technologically enhanced pedagogy has been the training of higher education faculty. This article focuses on faculty technology literacy, the implementation of technology into traditional faculty pedagogy, and the need for effective faculty training to enhance appropriate technology integration into classroom instruction (Keengwe, 2007). In this paper, the authors recommend two tier training as a possible strategy to technology integration training challenges that instructors face in their pedagogical practices.

This paper presents a view of the effectiveness of teaching and learning systems by focusing on how courses using ICT can be designed based on educational theories and evaluated using student feedback. This study analyzes a distance learning project in which Thai and Japanese (grade 10) students studied how to use MX Flash software for the creation of animations. In designing the course prior to implementation, the theoretical framework was examined and the Constructivism theory and the Bloom's taxonomy were adopted. From these perspectives, effective learning-teaching methods are determined by course content, conditions of teaching processes, and media usage. The teaching processes were classified with the following three stages determined: (1) traditional lecture; (2) self-learning; and (3) collaborative learning. At the end of each class, the students were asked to respond to the course evaluation related to following the three domains: (1) comprehension; (2) cognitive load; and (3) motivation. These evaluations by the students were fully utilized in a regression analysis which examined whether the course design was appropriate for student understanding.

    Chetan S. Sankar, Auburn University, USA
    Howard Clayton, Auburn University, USA

For college graduates to be successful in today's global economy there has been an increasing demand for them to possess business knowledge as well as technical knowledge. To meet the demand, curriculum designers have sought to integrate new technologies, applications, data, and business functions into classrooms so that non-information technology (IT) majors can realize the benefits of IT. This paper discusses the results of research conducted on the use of multimedia case studies to address the curriculum designers' challenge. The authors have found that students, who are taught using multimedia case studies, perceived a comparatively greater improvement in their higher-order cognitive skills, ease of learning, team working skills, attitude toward information technology, and self-efficacy. This suggests a need for further research into adopting such instructional materials for teaching non-IT majors and for developing other innovative instructional materials.

    Nahed Kandeel, Mansoura University, Egypt
    Youssreya Ibrahim, Umm Al Qura University, Saudi Arabia

This paper investigates student nurses' perceptions of the impact of using information technology (IT) on teaching and learning critical care nursing. This study was conducted at the Faculty of Nursing, Mansoura University, Egypt. The sample included 163 of fourth year Bachelor of Nursing students enrolled in a critical care nursing course during the first semester of the academic year 2007-2008. The data was collected using a questionnaire sheet that gathered information about student nurses' IT skills and use, perception of the access to and use of IT at Faculty of Nursing, perception of the impact of using IT on teaching and perception, and on the impact of using IT on learning the critical care nursing course. The findings indicate that nursing students had a positive perception on the impact of using IT on teaching and learning the critical care nursing course. Students wanted access to IT at the Faculty, and expressed their need for more training on using Internet and Microsoft PowerPoint, and for IT resources in classrooms.

    Terry T. Kidd, Texas A & M University, USA
    Jared Keengwe, University of North Dakota, USA

With the call for educational reform in American public schools, various school districts have embarked on the process of reforming classroom instructional practices through technology to enhance quality education and student learning. This article explores the implications for educational technology practices within the context of urban schools. Additionally, this article highlights the need for administrators, policy makers and other educational stakeholders to reflect on effective ways to eliminate inequities and the gaps that exist between high and low Social Economic Status (SES) schools and teachers related to practices, resources, training, and professional development.

Chapter 21

This article is based on an exploratory study on the use of blogs to support learning in an online MBA school. In this paper, the authors examine students' perceptions toward blogs and their effectiveness. The study finds that although students are open to the idea of using blogs to enhance presentation and reflection of their learning, concerns exist on their suitability for threaded discussions in the presence of other platforms like threaded discussion boards. Therefore, what is less clear is the learning value and potential of blogs, especially that subset of learning that is orchestrated (and credentialed) by formal learning organisations.

Chapter 22

As mobile devices' use among consumers accelerates at an exponential rate, there is a need to examine how these mobile devices can be used as effective learning tools and not just a form of communication. In this paper, the authors use an empirical survey methodology to study various mobile learning tools that are currently available for use in higher education, their advantages and disadvantages in m-learning versus e-learning implementations, and to explore the current trends in m-learning.

Chapter 23

This study examines a sample (N=239) of pre-service teachers' self-reported intention to use technology. The Technology Acceptance Model (TAM) was used as a research framework in which findings contribute to technology acceptance research by demonstrating the suitability of the TAM to explain the intention to use technology among educational users. Using the structural equation modelling for data analysis, a good fit was found for both the measurement and structural models. Overall, the results of this study offer evidence that the TAM is effective in predicting pre-service teachers' intention to use technology. This paper concludes with a discussion of the limitations and recommendations for further study.

Chapter 24

Problem-based learning has been well-documented, from its early days in the teaching of medical professionals to its more recent use in other disciplines. It has been adopted in many educational institutions because it gives students a realistic problem and provides opportunities to translate knowledge into solutions. This article is a case study of this approach at a second-year technical course, in which members of the class were divided into groups and given a scenario concerning a fictitious organisation about to embark on a major upgrade to its existing and problematic networking infrastructure. The course consisted of two parts. The first group was provided with a set of virtual machines to upgrade, and the second group chose and implemented a major technology on this newly upgraded network. The authors outline how problem-based learning is used in this context in a way that informs the teaching of any technical computing course.

    Kittipong Laosethakul, Sacred Heart University, USA
    Thaweephan Leingpibul, Western Michigan University, USA
    Thomas Coe, Quinnipiac University, USA

A potential explanation for the decline of female participation in computing-related education and careers in the United States is the perception that computing is for males. In this regard, declining participation limits diversity in the IT workforce. Therefore, this paper investigates the impact of two psychological factors, computer anxiety and computer self-efficacy, on gender perception toward computing between American male and female students. The authors also investigate whether the same relationship is found in India, where, while computing is dominated by males, female participation is rapidly increasing due to global IT outsourcing.

    Manjit Singh Sidhu, University Tenaga Nasional, Malaysia
    Lee Chen Kang, University Tunku Abdul Rahman, Malaysia

Improving and enhancing education has been a prime goal for higher learning institutions that seek to provide better learning techniques, technologies, educators, and to generate knowledgeable students to fulfill the needs of industries. A significant area where improvements are required is in the engineering field. In this regard, one approach is to review the delivery and pedagogies used in current education systems. This paper examines the problems faced by staff and students in the field of Mechanical Engineering, which are found in the literature. Finally, the authors explore new technologies that could help enhance and promote the learning process of students experiencing problems.

    Solomon Negash, Kennesaw State University, USA

While the digital revolution has transformed the way many of us work and live, more than half the world's population lives in rural areas that have been shut-out of the digital transformation. Low-income countries have yet to realize the benefits from the digital revolution; therefore, a need exists for innovative and alternative models to overcome the lack of access to knowledge and learning. This paper examines the challenges faced by low-income countries in accessing ICT enabled content and proposes a Big-Small model where low-income countries can harness the ICT revolution. This paper concludes with a discussion on sustainability and future research directions.

The use of information technology to enhance classroom learning and deliver corporate training is the latest trend and focus of much research in the computer-mediated communication (CMC) and development industry. Technological advances continue to alter the various ways in which academic and organizational training is facilitated and conducted. This paper presents a review of the available literature and trends in CMC, specifically, CMC's theoretical approaches, types/roles, benefits/disadvantages, and contributions to academic institutions and corporate organizations. The authors also provide a discussion of future trends and implications in this subject.

Chapter 29

Educators have started incorporating iPods for academic purposes and a growing interest exists in using podcasting as an educational tool. However, it remains uncertain whether podcasting will hit the critical mass and become an indispensable teaching tool for the classroom. In this regard, it is critical to evaluate the adoption experience of the faculty and identify the benefits and challenges encountered in the process. This paper derives its theoretical framework from two threads, the original model of the diffusion of innovation and the modified model in the organizational setting, which will help explore the phenomenon of podcast use at universities. This paper examines factors that might have a significant role in the faculty's experiential use of podcasting.

Preface

Volume 6 in the AICTE series is actually two books in one. First, it is an examination of how teaching and learning has been advanced in the previous millennium and how it is likely to evolve into the 21st century. Second, this work will offer its readers a look at how new trends in pedagogy and technology have been influenced by recent advances in information and communications. Consider the following equation for successful student learning outcomes:

Teaching + Learning = Pedagogy + Technology

Effective teaching is inextricably linked to successful learning and is the result of an uncommon blend of two critical components: pedagogy – the study of teaching, and technology – the study of technical applications in the real world. Ignoring any of these four elements of the equation diminishes the others and ultimately places at risk the overall educational process.

So, let's look at each piece of this equation separately.

TEACHING

Effective teaching has consistently been associated with four elements: knowledge of the academic content, good organizational skills, interpersonal (including small and large group) skills, and passionate presentation. First and foremost, a teacher must meet the objectives of the curriculum and that calls for an unequivocal personal mastery of the content area. Stated objectives, modeled activities, guided practice, and assessment all hinge on the teacher's thorough understanding of the material. Knowledge of the subject and mastery of the teaching resources (including technology) are critical to effective teaching.

Good organization skills aid the teacher in planning effectively for instruction, designing materials that support the lesson, promoting interaction, and integrating appropriate methodologies appropriate for the context. Teachers must constantly acquire new techniques and keep abreast of the applied research that guarantees success.

Interpersonal skills allow teachers to monitor student progress, check student understanding, devote appropriate time to task, and scaffold lessons to previously learned material. Skilled teachers also establish and enforce consistent class rules, keep their class on target while avoiding departures from the subject, control potentially disruptive behavior, manage group work effectively, and, overall, make the best use of very limited time on task.

Finally, a passionate presentation is not restricted to a "fire and brimstone" delivery. The best teaching occurs when lessons are adjusted to fit the learning objectives, when they stimulate and encourage higher-order thinking, and when they simply communicate effectively with the learner. Great presentations offer content at a developmentally appropriate level and encourage student participation – especially in older children and adults. Often, technology integrated into instruction stimulates both the teacher and the learner – but not always. Sometimes it can be distracting, diverting the student's attention from essential content and established learning outcomes.

Effective teaching embraces a wide range of pedagogical abilities and technological skills that lead to an environment where all students can be successful, both academically and personally. This complex combination of abilities and skills is further integrated into a body of professional teaching standards that also include essential knowledge, dispositions, and commitments that allow educators to practice at a high level. (NBPTS, 1998)

LEARNING

The sum and substance of most educational psychology text books define learning in basic terms as a change in behavior. Certainly, earlier authors (at least prior to the 1990's) viewed learning in light of observable and measurable outcomes. Most, however, argued for their own brand of methodologies for producing the change whether it was in the real world or in the classroom. Often, learning was narrowly defined as a measure of capacity; for example, the amount of knowledge acquired, the quantity of information memorized that could be repeated, or the sum of facts and skills that could be demonstrated in practice. Too, a definition of learning was oftentimes relegated to the more abstract: articulating how interrelated parts affect the whole or expressing new knowledge (e.g., music) to produce wholly different results.

With the advent of more contemporary theories of learning, the focus shifted from discernible and quantifiable outcomes typically attributed to the teacher to schemata and personalization with the spotlight now on the learner. Under the later schools of educational thought, the student is actively involved and encouraged to participate in the learning process. The emphasis turns from the instruction and its delivery to the student. Learning is viewed from the perspective of the learner rather than the teachers. It does not occur only in classroom and it is not confined to the time frame of a lesson. Rather, learning is less formal, likely to occur anywhere, at any time (the eventual basis for distance education advocates).

Because students are actively involved in creating their own learning patterns and connections and because learning is just as likely to occur in informal settings outside the classroom, self-reflection is necessary to secure deeper learning and to ensure this learning is available in future situations; either in practice or as the scaffolding for even more knowledge.

PEDAGOGY

Pedagogy refers to a distinct set of skills used to impart content knowledge of a target subject matter area. Taken from the Latin, pedagogy is parsed to expose "peda" referring to children and "gogy" as the study of or process of teaching. In most contemporary educational applications, pedagogy most often refers to the general context of teaching and learning by adults as well as children, although the term "andragogy" has been expressly coined by Knowles and others to focus on adult learning.

On the other hand, technology has many references including, for our purposes here, a collection of tools and techniques for solving a particular problem, fulfill a specific need, or overcome a definitive challenge.

Pedagogy-based training begins by helping teachers understand the role of learning theory in the design and development of various classroom activities, and in the selection and use of appropriate instructional technologies. By far, a lack of (or deficiency in) pedagogical training is the most common cause of unsuccessful learning outcomes. To effectively use pedagogy, teachers must remain aware of the host of learning styles and corresponding instructional strategies.

Three so-called schools of educational psychology have evolved modern thinking and practice about how learning occurs and how instruction in the classroom ultimately affects that learning. Each has its own merits and shortcomings that may make them rewarding or inappropriate in certain learning situations. A basic understanding of the principles and assumptions of Behaviorism, Cognitivism, and Humanism is critical to any successful approach to classroom teaching.

Behaviorism

This oldest school of educational psychology (that remains viable in today's educational setting) focuses on the observable and measureable elements of the environment rather than mental or cognitive processes (which we will deal with later). According to the Behaviorist viewpoint, the environment provides the necessary stimulation to cause the learner to respond; and learner response is the behaviorist's definition of "learning." The environment changes the response in ways that increase or decrease the likelihood of its recurrence in the future. The Behaviorist view offers suggestions for managing the learning activities of students – suggestions that open the door to the infusion of technology in many cases.

Figure 1 represents, in its simplicity, the psychology of education that most clearly defines, for educators, several critical concepts of behavioral learning. For example,

- Reinforcement refers to consequences of responses that establish and maintain desirable behavior.
- Behavior comprises an immense body of activities; for the Behaviorist, the term includes only observable behaviors.
- Environment and environmental conditions are responsible for behavioral outcomes. By applying this view to learning, learners determine whether a particular behavior in a particular situation is appropriate or inappropriate.
- Interaction is the key: the interaction of the environment and behavior is a strong determinant of the appropriateness of a behavior.

Contemporary behaviorists view the environment as key to learning. Environment factors are seen in terms of stimuli and its resultant behavior or response. Teachers who claim a behaviorist bent view student behavior in light of external reward or reinforcement which they provide and their students with links to the stimuli presented. Teachers who accept the behavioral perspective of pioneers such as B. F. Skinner assume that the behavior of their students is a response to their past and present environment and that all behavior is learned. The ultimate teacher responsibility, according to the behaviorist, is to construct an environment in which the probability of reinforcing "correct" or proper student behavior is maximized; a goal best attained by careful organization and presentation of information in a designed sequence.

Figure 1. The Behavioral Model

Behavioral Theory of Learning

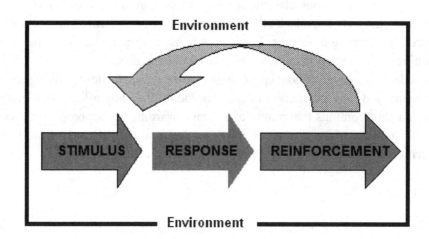

In practice, the behaviorist is defined by the traditional, teacher-centered, theory called instructivism that purports that knowledge is mastered passively by information transfer from an authority figure (i.e., the teacher) to a principally reflexive learner. Knowledge exists independent of, and external to, the learner; thus, an instructivist teacher assumes the responsibility for gathering knowledge and managing the distribution process in the classroom. Instructivism clearly places the burden for learning on the distributor of knowledge (i.e., teacher) and on choosing the most successful methods for dispensing learning. Traditionally, instructivists advocate for the lecture format; however, it takes very little imagination to see how technology has come to be embraced by the behaviorist teacher with its propensity to support the stimulus, response, reinforcement mandate. Several of the chapters in this volume of *Advancing Education with Information Communication Technologies* will fall within the behavioral pattern of pedagogy.

Cognitivism

Sprouting its roots from the behavioral perspective, Cognitivists perceive the student as an active participant in the learning process. They became interested in how people think, discover concepts, and solve problems and arrived at two conjoined perspectives: one emphasizes the acquisition of new knowledge; the second stresses its construction. The points of view advocate similar basic principles' for example, both:

- Stress helping students become independent learners by processing information in meaningful ways.
- Insist that less able students master appropriate learning strategies in an effort to become more successful in the classroom.
- Plan and implement lessons based on declarative and procedural learning tasks.

Those comfortable with the acquisition of knowledge bent embrace a model of learning depicted in Figure 2. Acquisition proponents employ the often-used information processing model to depict how learning occurs and how it can be enhanced.

Advocates of constructivism regard scaffolding as the prototype for explaining learning as a series of building blocks, as shown in Figure 3.

Adherents to cognitive psychology believe that effective teachers are those who seek out prior knowledge, knowledge that students already possess, and come to realize how each learner processes information and organize that knowledge in their own memory. Cognitive teachers use instructional strategies to help the learner acquire knowledge more effectively. They stress tools and techniques that include teaching students how to learn, remember, think, and motivate themselves.

Humanism

Humanists are concerned with making learning more responsive to the needs of their students; specifically, to the student's emotions, feelings, values, and attitudes. They are more accepting of the learner's needs and purposes for engaging in educational experiences and encourage programs that develop the learner's unique potential. Humanists view their role as one of facilitating the learner's sense of self-actualization (i.e., realizing one's full potential) and feelings of personal adequacy. Other characteristics of humanistic psychology include fostering the acquisition of basic skills and competencies (e.g., academic, personal, interpersonal, communicative, and economic) for living in a multicultural society; personalizing educational decisions and practice; and, recognizing the importance of human feelings, values, and perceptions in the educational process.

Figure 2. The Information Processing (Cognitive) Model

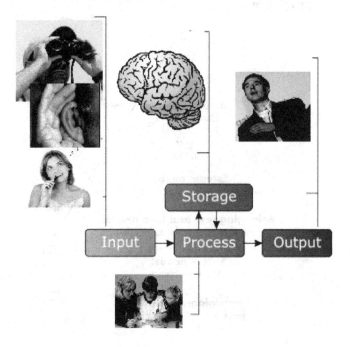

Figure 3. The Constructivist (Cognitive) Model

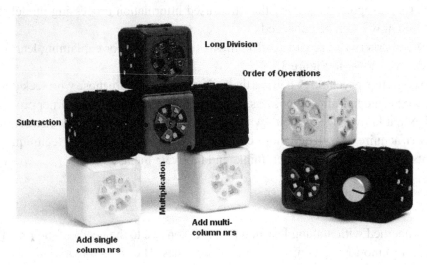

Humanistic teachers believe that how a person feels about learning is as important as how the person thinks or even behaves. Developing a learning climate that is challenging, understanding, supportive, exciting, and free from threat is of paramount importance in the classroom. They describe behavior not from the viewpoint of the teacher as do behaviorists but rather from the vantage point of the student who is performing the activity. Of highest regards is the development in learners of a genuine concern and respect for the worth of others and skill in resolving conflicts.

Of course, the preeminent model for humanism in the classroom (as well as the corporate office) is Maslow's hierarchy of human needs (Figure 4).

Figure 4. Maslow's Hierarchy of Human Needs (Cherry, 2011)

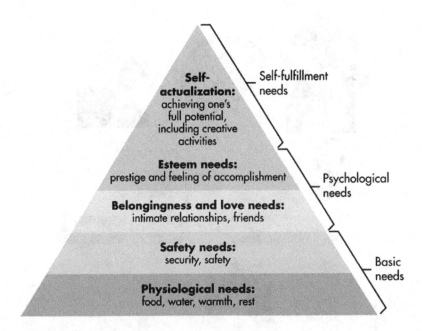

TECHNOLOGY

In 1996, Chickering and Ehrmann re-focused their highly successful work, *Seven Principles of Good Practice* created in 1987, to encompass the world of communication and information technologies – especially ICT resources for teaching and learning in higher education. Their premise was simple: "If the power of the new technologies is to be fully realized, they should be employed in ways consistent with the Seven Principles." Here they are:

Good Practice Encourages Contacts between Students and Faculty

Clear communication is one of the acknowledged keys to success in school. As the millennium advances, parents and students will continue to rely on technology to communicate with educators at all levels, but most importantly with teachers. Both students and parents have come to expect (some say demand) to be kept informed and involved in their child's education via some of the example technologies that follow.

- **Social networking sites:** Currently there are more than 650 million active Facebook users with Twitter, LinkedIn, and Skype adding millions more to the social networking milieu providing for so many possibilities for enhanced interpersonal communications venues using technology. Chances are good that the parents of children in elementary, secondary, and certainly post-secondary classrooms are online Facebook users who log in each day. With more than 250 million mobile device users, they probably retrieve messages on a real-time basis. Facebook is a quick and easy way to update parents on upcoming events or daily classroom happenings. Absences and tardiness can be reported instantly. Class activities and classroom celebrations are posted as they occur. Facebook can become a teaching tool for upper grade children in the hands of an effective teacher. Students can pose questions about homework and solicit help and assistance from other students, the teacher, or online tutoring sites. Students can even share their thoughts on an assignment and collaborate on a project – under the watchful eye of the teacher and following the rules of fair use and copyright.
- **Class Web Sites:**(teacher-made and commercial off-the-shelf). Scholastic's classroom web site builder is but one example of a simple and fantastic way to start communicating online. In minutes you can have a professional looking classroom Web page that parents and students can visit to get information as well as link to online activities. Using office productivity tools available on Window and Mac platforms, teachers can readily design and publish their own classroom web sites with little experience.
- **Synchronous and Asynchronous platforms:** A common, traditional visualization of a synchronous discussion entails students sitting in a classroom together examining the issues at hand. Using technology, students utilize conferencing systems (video, telephone, web-based conferencing tools) to receive instruction and interact with their teacher and peers at a distance. Some learning management systems (e.g., Blackboard and e-College) integrate synchronous environments and tools within their delivery platforms providing a traditional "feel" to the online classroom environment despite the participants being located remotely.

Asynchronous communication is by far the more popular technology-based communications model; barriers to implementation tend to be much lower as asynchronous tools typically demand minimal hardware and software expertise. For many applications, asynchronous technologies provide the desirable flexibility; access to the teaching material can occur at any time and any place. The educational uses of this technology allow the learner time to deliberate, seek additional references, refer to other materials, and prepare more thoughtful comments. Finally, it is cost-effective; asynchronous tools are typically free. Electronic mail, discussion groups, wikis and blogs, and social networking sites are currently the most popular implementations of asynchronous communications.

Good Practice Develops Reciprocity and Cooperation among Students

The increased opportunities for communication with faculty apply equally to student-student interaction. Group projects, study sessions, collaborative learning exercises, and group problem solving can be dramatically strengthened through technology-based communication tools that facilitate such activity.

In order to increase student satisfaction and learning effectiveness, students should be supported in both the development of collaborative technology tool use and their competencies as a collaborative group member. Some of the technologies reported in this volume explore ways in which students can participate in activities that require cooperation; assess the challenges and benefits of student cooperation using technological tools; discuss the role of group projects learning and how can technology can support the teacher; and, discuss technology-rich peer review process and how it can enhance student-student and student-teacher cooperation. They include:

- **Collaboration Suites:** Several companies have developed applications that address a range of collaborative needs encompassing tools that may be used autonomously as well as those that are optimized for group work. Collaboration tools include a host of applications (perhaps the widest scope of any of the technologies) ranging from traditional desktop applications for word processing, spreadsheets, communication, or calendaring to course management systems that offer work spaces for their students that embrace discussion boards, file sharing, and peer evaluation tools.
- **Project management solutions:** are multipurpose systems that often tools for collaborative aids for such project-related tasks as critical path, task management and scheduling, time tracking, resource allocation, collaborative writing or editing, communication, file sharing, and process documentation. Such tools are particularly useful for longer term projects where the teacher intends to track group interactions beyond the classroom and develop their students' work processes and communication skills.
- **Real-Time Communications:** Technologies in this category include web-based presentation tools, screen sharing applications, web, video or audio conferencing tools, and internet-based telecommunications (often called VoIP, or Voice over Internet Protocol. These tools are especially useful for project teams that are geographically separated or who are conducting a significant portion of their assignment at a distance. They allow teams to share work in progress, discuss concepts with the help of rich media, and exchange information and ideas in a manner that more closely approximates the face-to-face experience than traditional text-only communications. (Creative Commons, 2009).

Good Practice Uses Active Learning Techniques

Nothing speaks louder to active learning than the integration of instructional technology into the curriculum. The range of technologies that support active learning has increased geometrically over the past decade. The literature offers three categories of active learning technologies. They include tools and resources that encourage: learning by doing, learning by imitation, and learning by modeling. Digitized music is an excellent example of learning by doing. Software-based chemistry and biology lessons demonstrate learning by imitation, and simulation villages and communities allow students to create model cities and societies.

Good Practice Gives Prompt Feedback

Feedback is the name of the game when it comes to technology. The ways in which new technologies can provide feedback are limited only by one's imagination. For example, in this volume of *Advancing Education with Information Communication Technologies,* several chapters deal with such behavioral-oriented disciplines such as math education, engineering, problem-solving, and problem-based learning – each of which provide testimony to the value of prompt feedback and the proper use of technology to foster its application to ensure successful student learning outcomes.

Most distance learning environments promote feedback through the use of such tools as online assessment, grading, and results reporting; a grading center that summarizes each evaluated component of the course and provides a running tally of student progress toward established goals throughout the term; and, authentic assessment tools (e.g., electronic portfolios) that encourage students to critically self-evaluate their own progress, that of their peers, and accept the constructive comments of the teacher. Promptness is oftentimes built into the tools being used for feedback; feedback from an online examination, for example, occurs as soon as the testing period is over. Grades, correct answers, and item responses are made available to students immediately. Other times, prompt feedback is in the hands of the instructor. The tools may be available but the effectiveness of those tools remains in human hands.

Good Practice Emphasizes Time on Task

New technologies can dramatically improve time on task for faculty as well as students. Here are just a few examples.

- Turning in homework by electronic files to a file server that can be accessed from any location by either student or teacher.
- E-mailing assignments from a student's home provides more rapid distribution of assignments. Plus, going paperless allows teachers and students to use the computer to search for documents and files previously handled in filing cabinets and desk drawers.
- Posting assignments on the web or class site allows students to download materials just-in-time and prevents delays caused when students attempt to phone (or even email) their instructors regarding lost assignments and confusing written instructions.
- Utilizing available research materials now more prevalent in on-line and electronic databases than hard-copy library resources. Certainly, access to the Internet has changed the way students from elementary school through post-doctoral conduct research.

- Encouraging students to spend more time on-line in discussions or chats
- Limiting the need for students who live off campus to drive onto university grounds for classes and/ or appointments or to work in small or large groups.
- Using calendaring software promotes better planning by students and faculty and allows both to review their appointments and personal commitments in an effort to better control their most precious commodity: time.
- Offering technology (e.g., laptops) to students (or encouraging personal ownership with reduced purchase plans) promotes better use of time. For example, the time between classes on campus encourages students or faculty to check email, work on assignments, take notes in class, etc. Also, personal laptops reduce the learning curve that always comes into play when moving from one machine to another – even if they are the same make and model, the desktop, applications, and network connectivity are always unique.
- Finally, on the administrative side of instructional technology to enhance time on task, using an institution's web site to check transcripts, registration possibilities, and answer frequently asked questions has proven to be an impressive time on task saver.

Good Practice Communicates High Expectations

Under the general heading of "you get what you pay for," the use of new technologies often communicates higher expectations. Innovators in schools and companies are often the first to receive the latest technology not just so much in the veiled hope that the technologies will be accepted by the less inspired, but also as a means of confirming the anticipation that increases in productivity, quality, and overall academic excellence will be forthcoming. Working with students produces the same self-fulfilling prophecy. Technology can help establish and model high expectations by employing a variety of tools such as a well-written syllabus, a duly appointed calendar, or real-time assignment posts and grades found in most course management systems. High expectations necessitate setting high standards and learning goals grounded in realistic opportunities for the instructor, students, and the use of technology.

Good Practice Respects Diverse Talents and Ways of Learning

By some counts, there are at least four recognized schools of educational psychology that focus on how we teach and learn. There are another five educational philosophies concerned more with what we teach. Add these combinations to the diverse populations of learners (answering the who we are teaching question) and place all of this in the context of the history (i.e., the when question) of education and you have a considerable number of permutations and combinations of talents to consider. Technology, fortunately, offers modalities for teaching and learning that have come to address more distinct factions of learners than any other apparatus in the annals of educational practice. That said, technology resources are also limited by teachers and their personal preparation in its use. Powerful visuals and well-organized print are common in today's classroom; unfortunately, so are examples of how presentations have gone awry because the designer did not understand the pitfalls of using too many slides, constructed the text poorly, or violated artistic principles known to even the most novice media arts student.

Educational theory has advanced throughout the 20th century and will, most certainly, continue as we move soundly into the core of the new millennium.

Teaching + Learning = Pedagogy + Technology

Returning to the equation above, 7 chapters in *Advancing Education with Information Communication Technologies* focus on teaching; 8 chapters on learning; pedagogy is the key focus for 6 chapters; and, technology, appropriately, encompasses 8 chapters. Here is a recap of the 29 chapters.

Teaching is explored in the first series of chapters.

In **Chapter 3**, Ololube, Ubogu, Egbezor, and Nwachukwu seek to evaluate the tools appropriate for *Evaluating Faculty Teaching of Research Methodology to Undergraduate Geography Students in a Nigerian University*. Their chapter explores the competencies (and therefore the precise tools themselves) required to teach research methods.

Chapter 4, *Teachers and Technology: Enhancing Technology Competencies for Preservice Teachers* (Blankson, Keengwe, and Kyei-Blankson), reviews the content knowledge required for students to use appropriate technology. The chapter identifies the critical content subject matter and compares the related technology competencies with standards offered by the International Society for Technology in Education (ISTE).

Chapter 5, *Information and Communication Technology Training among Lecturers in the South-South Zone in Nigeria by the Nigerian Communication Commission* (Aghwotu, Emiri, and Tiemo) uncovered the ICT literacy skills required of lecturers and gathers them in a proposed training program that could be offered to higher education instructors.

Chapter 6, *Perceived Importance and Resource Constraints of Graduate Information Systems Courses in Turkey* (Balaban, Kirlidog, and Ayvaz-Reis) examines master's level information systems courses and the technology-based teaching resources used by faculty in one country. Authors consider the importance of these tools and offer a unique perspective into the strengths and limitations of technologies for teaching.

Chapter 13, *Improving Teachers' Self-Confidence in Learning Technology Skills and Math Education through Professional Development* (Hartsell, Herron, Fang, and Rathod). In this chapter, the authors spotlight math teachers and their use of technology for their own professional development for classroom instruction. As such, the chapter was placed under Teaching. Also discussed, however, was their examination of how technology helps students develop their problem-solving skills and math comprehension.

In *Faculty Training Strategies to Enhance Pedagogy-Technology Integration* (Keengwe, Georgina, and Wachira), **Chapter 16** focuses on faculty technology literacy and the integration of technology into traditional classroom instruction. A two-tier training program is introduced for your consideration.

Chapter 24, *Problem-Based Learning in a Technical Course in Computing: A Case Study* (Correia & Watson), outlines how problem-based learning is used in teaching technical computing courses; another example of the teaching with technology at work.

Learning. With its focus on the student, the next series of chapters examine a set of aptitudes that includes a host of technology based tools that were inconceivable just a decade ago.

In **Chapter 7**, *Enhancing Students' Loyalty to the Information Systems Major*, Hunsinger, Land, and Chen identify four factors leading to student retention in the IS major and investigate how collaborative tools impact of the success of these factors to recruit and retain top-notch candidates.

In **Chapter 9**, *Technology and Teacher Education: Student Evaluation of Faculty Instructional Quality*, by Akyeampong, Franklin, and Keengwe tie together technology-based tools and learning. The chapter excellently depicts various technologies for learning and how presentation and productivity tools can be used by students (as well as faculty) to promote successful learning outcomes.

In **Chapter 10**, *Facilitating Students to Earn Computing Certificates via Blended Learning in On-Line Problem-Solving Environment: A Cross-Course Orientation Comparison*, Tsai regards professional certifications in the country of Taiwan – a country where online courses are not yet permitted. Offering the reader some initial considerations of the effects of applying blended learning methodologies with various references on student computing skills, the author explored the most likely combinations of methodologies for learning computing content. The results are as might be expected: the addition of blended learning resulted in significantly higher grades. How they obtained those increases mark the truly important contributions of this paper.

Chapter 12, *A Cross-Cultural Validation of the Selwyn's Computer Attitude Scale*, written by Timothy Teo, scrutinizes the use of a widely accepted scale to discern attitudes toward the use of technology among students.

Student Nurses' Perception on the Impact of Information Technology on Teaching and Learning, **Chapter 19**, (Kandeel & Ibrahim) delves into the impact of an information technology-enhanced curriculum on critical care nursing. Candidate nurses found the need for more technology training using the Internet and presentation tools along with IT resources in their classrooms.

Chapter 21, *Evaluating Student Perceptions of Using Blogs in an Online Course* (Gullett & Bhanda) is a must read depiction of an online MBA program and its use of blogs to support student learning. The results of the study accompanying this chapter brings the reader a host of student perceptions that indicate their openness to the use of blogs coupled with serious concerns regarding their suitability as replacements for discussion groups and online discussion boards.

Chapter 23, *An Empirical Study to Validate the Technology Acceptance Model in Explaining the Intention to Use Technology among Educational Users*, also written by Timothy Teo, employs the TAM model to predict pre-service teacher's use of technology; in this case, predicting how, as learners in an educational preparation program, these students accept the adoption of technology as a viable instructional strategy.

Investigation into Gender Perception toward Computing: A Comparison between the US and India, **Chapter 25** (Laosethakul, Leingpibul, and Coe), probes the impact of computer anxiety and computer self-efficacy on gender decisions to pursue computing as an avocation. Females in particular are prone to increased participation in the discipline as a result of implementing some of the recommendations and suggestions found in this chapter.

Pedagogy. A look at pedagogy centers on identifying appropriate technology-based resources for the classroom from among the growing cache of computer hardware, educational software, electronic journals and publications, and Internet sites already available.

Chapter 1, *Instructor Satisfaction with Teaching Business Law: Online vs. Onground* (Swartz, Cole, and Shelley) offers the reader the results of an exhaustive survey of business law instructors who have taught online and on-ground, examining the level of instructor satisfaction against pedagogical, social, technical and managerial benchmarks. Here is one academic discipline that did not fare as well online than it did with the more traditional modality of classroom delivery.

Chapter 8, *User Interface Design Pedagogy: A Constructionist Approach*, by Khoo introduces the pedagogy associated with designing human interfaces and provides a solid argument that learning is best accomplished when students construct their own learning experiences. The chapter suggests technologies for teaching, taking such traditional, teacher-made tools as text and visual-based materials and preparing students to develop their own learning resources.

An Examination of the *Effectiveness of International Distance Education in High School Between Thailand and Japan* by Pavasajjanant deliberates on the value of courses using ICT and based on sound educational theory and student feedback. In **Chapter 17**, the author shares a review of a distance learning project based in these two countries integrated with traditional lecture, self-learning exercises, and collaborative learning pedagogies.

Chapter 18 by Sankar & Clayton, *An Evaluation of Use of Multimedia Case Studies to Improve an Introduction to an Information Technology Course*, looks at the integration of certain technologies, applications, data, and business activities to help non-IT students realize the benefits of technologies in their chosen career fields.

Closely akin to the research is **Chapter 20**, *Technology Integration and Urban Schools: Implications for Instructional Practices* (Kidd & Keengwe). In this chapter, readers will reflect on the inequities and disparities between various classes of schools with respect to technology-based practices, resources, training, and professional development.

Emerging Trends and Technologies for Enhancing Engineering Education: An Overview reveals some new technologies that can enhance pedagogy in the field of engineering (that also apply to many other hard science-related disciplines). In **Chapter 26**, Sidhu & Kang share some excellent examples of the problems faced by engineering faculty and students and some ways in which technology can help overcome those barriers to learning.

Technology. In his book, "*The Age of Spiritual Machines*," Ray Kurzweil (1999) purports how trends affecting humanity throughout the millenniums advanced arithmetically – at least initially, with new and evolving features doubling and tripling at first. After some time, nearly all trends take on geometric advances as they continue to grow and mature at a faster and faster rate. This theorem has been proven time and time again – the most prevailing trend, of course, being technology. Technology continues to advance at a now-geometric rate supported by the evolution of the Advances in Information and Communication Technology Education Series as it, too, has moved from Volume 1 to this newest body of work. It makes perfect sense that the majority of chapters accompanying this edition concern themselves with technology for teaching.

Chapter 2, *Digital Video Presentation and Student Performance: A Task Technology Fit Perspective*, explores today's video technologies in light of their task match (appropriateness to the classroom situation), ease of use (by teachers and students), and ease of learning (and, therefore, teaching as well). Research conducted by Raven, Leeds, and Park demonstrate a relationship between the effective use of digital video tools and improved oral presentation skills and, thereby, student performance in the classroom.

Serving as a "bridge" to our discussion of distance education, Giotopoulos, Alexakos, Beligiannis, and Stefani present *Bringing AI to E-Learning: The Case of a Modular, Highly Adaptive System* in **Chapter 11**. The chapter describes in detail the innovative contributions that artificial intelligence can make to distance education; in effect, making it more "intelligent" for the teacher and the learner.

Chapter 14, *Materials-to-Standards Alignment: How to "Chunk" a Whole Cake and Even Use the "Crumbs": State Standards Alignment Models, Learning Objects, and Formative Assessment-Methodologies and Metadata for Education*, Adamich examines statewide examples of the use of metadata reflecting materials-to-standards alignment and identifies current successes and future challenges.

Chapter 15, *Enhancing Teaching and Learning with Digital Storytelling*, explains the fruits of integrating digital storytelling into the curriculum. In their chapter, Want & Zhan present the benefits and challenges of this media as a means of winning students over to a program of reflective, active and personally meaningful study.

Chapter 22, *Applications of Mobile Learning in Higher Education*, employs an empirical study to survey the current uses of mobile technologies in higher education and their potential in e-learning environments.

In **Chapter 27**, Negash's research on *Accessing ICT Enabled Content in Low-Income Countries: Think Big, Start Small, and Scale Up*, examines how low-income countries can harness technology to tackle a host of issues including, but not limited to, a lack of access to knowledge and learning and sustainability.

The next chapter investigates *The Role of Computer-Mediated Communication: A Look at Methods for Delivering and Facilitating Training in Academic and Organizational Settings*. **Chapter 28** discusses how technological advances continue to alter the various ways in which educational and corporate training is conducted. CMC's theoretical approaches, types and roles, benefits and shortcomings, and contributions are explored.

Podcasting is spotlighted in **Chapter 29**, *Faculty Adopters of Podcasting: Satisfaction, University Support and Belief in Podcasting (Yang)*. In this chapter, the author examines the growing use of iPods for academic purposes. As an educational tool, podcasting is a fairly straightforward process providing ubiquitous benefits to students not unlike the printed text book.

CONCLUSION

Arguably, technology has already impacted the discipline of education to an extent not witnessed since the 15th century invention of the printing press. Technology is a literacy – a set of skills and competencies much like reading, writing, and grammar. It has become perhaps the most ubiquitous media for collaboration exceeded (at least for now) only by the printed text. We use technology to introduce the fundamentals of decision-making to our students in the hopes that they will apply these lower order skills to infuse technology-based resources into their own personal learning styles.

For teachers, technology has advanced our "bag of tricks;" the host of instructional teaching strategies used to address the various ways our students learn. Technology for teaching encourages faculty to stretch their inventory of tools used in the classroom, adding visual presentations, pre-selected text-based materials, web-enhanced content, and a plethora of media-rich resources.

Technology can also be considered its own academic discipline. Ponder for a moment how instructional technology has opened so many doors (while perhaps, closing others); destroyed former barriers to learning for many (while constructing impediments to others); and, created a culture that is certainly more inclusive than any we have experienced in prior generations (while leaving still others even further behind).

Books such as our *Advances in Information and Communication Technology Education Series* are imperative to the literature, providing readers with access to the latest trends and newest applications demanded in today's educational environment. In this Volume 6, we explored the fundamentals of teaching and learning on one side of our equation and key pedagogies and technologies on the other. The equation provides an organizational tool (an advanced organizer, if you will) for the discussions in the remainder of the book. Learn more about a host of instructional technology in the chapters that follow.

Lawrence A. Tomei
Robert Morris University, USA

REFERENCES

Cherry, K. (2011) Hierarchy of Needs: The Five Levels of Maslow's Hierarchy of Needs. About.com. URL: http:// psychology. about.com/ od/ theoriesofpersonality /a/ hierarchyneeds.htm

Chickering, A. W., & Ehrmann, S. C. (1996). Implementing the Seven Principles: Technology As Lever, "Implementing the Seven Principles: Technology as Lever," AAHE Bulletin, October, pp. 3-6.

Commons, C. (2009). Collaboration Tools: A Teaching with Technology White Paper, San Francisco, California. URL: http://www.scribd.com/doc/50133402/null

Kurzweil, R. (1999). *The Age of Spiritual Machines: When Computers Exceed Human Intelligence*. New York: Penguin Putnam, Inc.

Maslow's Hierarchy. (Downloaded 2011) http:// changingminds.org/ explanations/ needs/maslow.htm

National Board for Professional Teaching Standards. (1998). Washington, DC: Author. Available: http:// www.nbpts.org/

Tomei, L. A. (2005). *Taxonomy for the Technology Domain*. Hershey, PA: Information Science Publishing. doi:10.4018/978-1-59140-524-5

Chapter 1
Instructor Satisfaction with Teaching Business Law:
Online vs. Onground

Louis B. Swartz
Robert Morris University, USA

Michele T. Cole
Robert Morris University, USA

Daniel J. Shelley
Robert Morris University, USA

ABSTRACT

Our study presents the results of a satisfaction survey of business law instructors who have taught, or are teaching, online and/or onground. The authors used the framework suggested by Berge to examine the level of instructor satisfaction, using his four role categories: pedagogical, social, technical, and managerial. Their study found that for 73% of the categories' aspects, instructors were generally satisfied with online instruction. With regard to the classroom experience, instructors were generally satisfied across the board with regard to all aspects. In comparing the level of satisfaction with online and onground instruction, they found statistically significant differences between the two methods of instruction. In all four areas measured, instructors were more satisfied with classroom instruction than they were with online instruction of business law courses.

INTRODUCTION

While there have been a number of studies of student satisfaction with online instruction (Schulman & Sims, 1999; Russell, 1999; Ryan, 2000; Shelley, Swartz & Cole, 2007, 2008), there have been far fewer concerned with the topic of instructor satisfaction with online teaching; and, few, if any,

concerning instructor satisfaction with the online instruction of business law and the comparison to onground teaching of the same or similar course. Those studies that have been done tend to focus on the relationship of institutional supports to instructor satisfaction (Fredricksen, Pickett, Shea, Pelz, & Swan, 1999; Almeda & Rose, 2000; Hiltz, Kim, & Shea, 2007).

DOI: 10.4018/978-1-61350-468-0.ch001

To date, studies have demonstrated that, when instructors perceive that the institution where they teach values their online instruction; they too are satisfied with online instruction. Indicators that the institution values online instruction include the level of instructional technology available, the degree of peer support, academic recognition, and financial rewards. When these motivators are in place, instructors find the online experience to be flexible, more conducive to thoughtful and tailored instruction, more interactive, attractive to a more diverse student population, and generally more valuable as an instructional platform than classroom instruction.

Other studies which have looked at changing perceptions of the educational process on the part of the instructor in the online environment, have generally found corresponding increases in the level of satisfaction with the platform as the instructor becomes more accustomed to it (Conrad, 2004). Instructors who initially are resistant to teaching online become enthusiastic because the online format allows for the discovery and initiation of new learning tools; and, as a result, the instructor feels a renewed commitment to teaching. This is not unusual. Linda Harasim (2000) reported that experiences with the virtual learning environment gives instructors a renewed enthusiasm for teaching in part because of the student engagement in the online learning process. Some instructors also experience an improvement in onland (classroom) instruction because of the online experience. Shea, Pelz, Fredericksen, and Pickett (2002) surveyed two hundred and fifty-five faculty teaching online in the SUNY system and found general satisfaction with the online format and a belief that the online experience would improve classroom instruction.

Fjermestad, Hiltz and Zhang (2005) are among those who support the call for additional empirical studies of faculty satisfaction with online learning. The need to pursue an investigation of faculty use of, and satisfaction with, online learning tools in part led us to explore instructor satisfaction with teaching business law online. Our study looked at instructor satisfaction with online teaching, not only from the perspective of the instructor's evaluation of institutional facilitation of the experience, but also from the perspective of the instructor's evaluation of the students' learning experience.

In any comparison of online and traditional classroom instruction, there are obvious and fundamental differences. Traditional or classroom-based courses are taught in real time with the students and the instructor present. In the online format, the class is taught in a "cybernetic" environment, instruction does not have to be in real time, the students are not present in one place, and the instructor monitors most of the activity from a distance.

The fundamental differences between online and traditional instruction pose major challenges and concerns for course instructors and educational institutions. Online teaching forces the instructor to assume a new teaching role and necessitates a reappraisal, or at least a redefinition, of the traditional teacher-student relationship. In fact, online teaching requires the instructor to rethink and reorganize the existing teaching paradigm. The institution must develop new methods of monitoring the quality of instruction without interfering with that instruction.

In most cases, conveying the basic content to the students in the online format is straightforward, but in some ways more complex because the instructor cannot gauge the level of understanding at a particular moment using a particular delivery tool. The comment is often made by instructors that they can see when the "light comes on" from looking at a student's face. An even greater challenge is getting the instructional quality of the online course to match, or exceed, the instructional level of the traditional class. It is not sufficient for the online instructor to have an understanding of the technological skills and course development tools alone. He or she must have a strong sense of course design and an understanding of good pedagogy as well. Good pedagogy is generally accepted by educators to involve: 1) a high level of learner activity, 2) a high level of student interaction, 3) a format for motivation and, 4) a well-structured knowledge base.

Discussing the challenges to the instructor and developer of online law-related courses, Kathy Marcel noted that the best online courses were instructor-facilitated, student-centered and highly interactive (Marcel, 2002). The design of an online law course, as with the design of any online course, is critical. The instructor's responsibility is to design a learning experience and to guide the students through the process. Marcel found that, in fact, many law instructors tend to work very well with the facilitative aspect of good online course development. Marcel argued that because of the nature of their profession, law professors teaching online courses tended to expect students to be engaged and not merely passive consumers of information. The suitability of teaching law courses online was even more evident, she found, with regard to upper-level law courses, because these courses themselves often rely on case studies, projects and Socratic dialogue. (Not all respondents in our study would agree with Marcel's assessment, however.)

Rivera and Rice (2002) reported that while several studies have demonstrated that online and traditional courses were comparable with regard to the cognitive factors (learning, performance and achievement), the same could not be demonstrated consistently with regard to student and instructor perceptions and satisfaction with online learning.

To look at instructor perceptions and satisfaction with online education, we used Berge's (1995) role categories as our framework.

Research Questions

This study examined four research questions, each with a focus on one of the four categories used by Berge (1995).

RQ 1: How satisfied are instructors of business law courses with the pedagogical aspects of online course delivery versus onground course delivery

RQ 2: How satisfied are instructors of business law courses with the social aspects of online course delivery versus onground course delivery

RQ 3: How satisfied are instructors of business law courses with the technical aspects of online course delivery versus onground course delivery

RQ 4: How satisfied are instructors of business law courses with the managerial aspects of online course delivery versus onground course delivery

Methodology

Our study relied on satisfaction surveys to assess whether instructors of online and classroom-based courses in business law felt that online instruction was as satisfactory as traditional classroom-based instruction. Survey results were collected in Vovici, survey software which combines the features of Websurveyor with Perseus, and transferred to SPSS for analysis. We used independent samples t-tests to compare responses to the questions using "online v. onland" as the grouping variable.

We used the mean scores for each of the twenty-six aspect question responses to determine the level of satisfaction with online and onground instruction. There were eight aspect questions under the pedagogical category; six under the social category; eight under the technical category; and four under the managerial category. Each set of questions asked the participants to rate their level of satisfaction with a particular aspect. We used a five point Likert scale (0- "Very Satisfied", 1- "Satisfied", 2- "Does Not Apply", 3- "Dissatisfied", 4- "Very Dissatisfied").

Prior to running the independent samples t-tests, we deleted number 2 – "Does Not Apply" to be able to rely on the mean score to measure the level of satisfaction.

The survey was composed of twenty-two questions. The first eight were designed to measure the level of instructor satisfaction with online and onland instruction. The remaining questions were designed to develop a profile of the sample, asking for demographic as well as information on teaching experience, and instructional supports. Question 21 was open-ended asking for a comparison of the two types of instruction. The final question asked which platform was preferred.

Research Design

To examine instructor perceptions and satisfaction, we developed a survey that grouped questions around the four role categories that Berge (1995) identified in his discussion of moderation in computer conferencing. These are: *pedagogical*, which examines the role of the educational facilitator or instructor in expressing critical concepts, principles and skills; *social*, which focuses on the learning environment; *technical*, which enables the instruction to take place; and *managerial*, which centers on the organizational, procedural and administrative aspects of instruction (Berge, 1995).

The aspects under the pedagogical category in the survey instrument were:

- Student learning,
- Exam results,
- Effectiveness of assignments,
- Use of cases,
- Effectiveness of power point presentations,
- Discussion of course material,
- Use of group projects and,
- Effectiveness of lecture material.

Under the social category there were six aspects:

- Student participation,
- Interaction between students,
- Student motivation,
- Student-instructor relationship,
- Methods of communication, and,
- Enjoyment of instruction.

"Technology" included eight aspects:

- Suitability of the platform,
- Course resources available from the university,
- Course resources available from the textbook publishers,
- Ability to adapt instructional material to the class,
- Ongoing support services,
- Training in mode of instruction,
- Teaching environment, and,
- Instructional tools made available.

Under the fourth category, "managerial" there were four aspects:

- Ability to control cheating,
- ease of grading,
- Use of assurance of learning tools, and,
- Tools for student evaluation (of the instructor).

The four sets of questions (pedagogical, social, technical, and managerial) were presented twice, first to rate the level of satisfaction with *online* instruction (questions 1-4) and the second time (questions 5-8), to rate the level of satisfaction with *onground or traditional* classroom instruction.

Participant Sample

Of the one hundred and twelve respondents, forty-one did not respond to some of the demographic questions which accounts for the differing totals below. Seventy-five percent of the participant sample (68 of 91) had experience teaching both online and onground. Eighty-five percent taught at four year institutions (60 of 71), seven percent taught at two year institutions. The remainder answered "other". Seventy–one percent (52 of 73) taught at both the graduate and undergraduate level. Twenty-one percent taught undergraduates only, seven percent taught at the graduate level only.

The participants in the sample were 63% male and 37% female. Forty-one percent of the instructors were between the ages of 45 and 54, 33% were between the ages of 55 and 64. Forty-three percent were professors (31 of 72), 18% were associate or assistant professors. Ninety percent of 72 respondents were full-time faculty.

Of those who had experience with teaching online, 30% had from five to eight years of experience online, 27% had between one and four years experience. Remarkably, more than 17% had been teaching online for more than eight years.

Survey Instrument

The survey was developed in Vovici and first e-mailed to members of the Pre-Law Society as a pre-test. We modified the survey questions to correct for difficulty in responding to questions where more than one answer would be appropriate. We were able to have the survey posted on the website for the Academy of Legal Studies in Business, which is a forum for the exchange of ideas, and encourages support and cooperation among those who teach and do research in the field. The survey is appended at A.

RESEARCH RESULTS

Study results indicated that instructors were *more satisfied than not* (mean scores of equal to or less than 1.5) with online instruction with regard to 73% of the four categories' aspects. The exceptions were: discussion of course material under the pedagogical category (mean score of 1.62); interaction between students, student motivation, student-instructor relationship and enjoyment of instruction under the social category (mean scores of 1.60, 1.63, 1.58, and 1.67 respectively); and, ability to control cheating and use of assurance of learning tools under the managerial category (mean scores of 1.96 and 1.53 respectively).

Satisfaction with the aspects of instruction online contrasts sharply however, when compared to satisfaction with onground or classroom instruction. When asked to rate their satisfaction with onground instruction, instructors were *more satisfied than not* (means equal to or less than 1.5) *across the board in all* aspects of the role categories. In comparing the level of satisfaction with online and onground instruction, we found statistically significant differences between the two with regard to all aspects of instruction with the exception of course resources available from the university (t=.407) and ease of grading (t=.141).

Overall, in all four areas measured, instructors were more satisfied with classroom instruction than they were with online instruction of business law courses. Question 22 asked which method was preferred. Thirty-nine or 56.5% preferred teaching in the classroom; 19 or 27.5% said teaching partially online/partially in the classroom for the same course. Five or 7.2% answered, teaching both alternatively. Three people had no preference. Only one person preferred teaching online.

There were statistically significant differences between instructor satisfaction with the online and onland formats for instruction of business law in all aspects of the pedagogical category at the .001 level with the exception of "use of group projects" where significance was at the .005 level.

There were statistically significant differences between instructor satisfaction with the online and onland formats for instruction of business law in all aspects of the social category at the.001 level.

There were statistically significant differences between instructor satisfaction with the online and onland formats for instruction of business law in all technical aspects at the.005 level with the exception of "course resources available from the university" where there was no statistically significant difference between the two.

There were statistically significant differences between instructor satisfaction with the online and onland formats for instruction of business law in all managerial aspects at the.005 level with the exception of "ease of grading" where there was no statistically significant difference between the level of satisfaction with that aspect in online and onground instruction. Results of the independent samples t-tests are shown below.

RQ 1: How satisfied are instructors of business law courses with the pedagogical aspects of online course delivery versus onground course delivery

Mean scores for *online* satisfaction levels: 1.34, 1.29, 1.19, 1.35, 1.29., 1.62, 1.48, and 1.42

Mean scores for *onland* satisfaction levels:.70,.82,.53,.48,.74,.66,.88, and.46

RQ 2: How satisfied are instructors of business law courses with the social aspects of online course delivery versus onground course delivery

Mean scores for *online* satisfaction levels: 1.42, 1.60, 1.63, 1.58., 1.25, and 1.67

Mean scores for *onland* satisfaction levels:.86,.77, 1.14,.49,.41, and.33

RQ 3: How satisfied are instructors of business law courses with the technical aspects of online course delivery versus onground course delivery

Mean scores for *online* satisfaction levels: 1.32,.96, 1.22, 1.26, 1.19., 1.33, 1.48, and 1.31

Mean scores for *onland* satisfaction levels:.35,.83,.76,.44,.79,.95,.54, and.61

Table 1. *Instructor Satisfaction with Pedagogical Aspects Online v. Onground*

RQ. 1	t-test for Equality of Means	
	t	Sig. (2-tailed)
Student learning	4.963	.000
Exam results	3.366	.001
Effect assign.	5.664	.000
Use of cases	6.627	.000
Effect of ppts*	3.581	.000
Dissc. course mat	6.717	.000
Use of group proj.	3.909	.000
Effect. of lecture mat	7.605	.000

*Equal variances assumed. All others, equal variances not assumed

Table 2. *Instructor Satisfaction with Social Aspects Online v. Onground*

RQ. 2	t-test for Equality of Means	
	t	Sig. (2-tailed)
Student partici-pation	3.677	.000
Interaction btw. students	5.420	.000
Student motiva-tion*	3.255	.001
Stud. – inst. rel	7.247	.000
Meth. comm.	5.805	.000
Enjoy. instr.	8.982	.000

*Equal variances assumed. All others, equal variances not assumed

Table 3. Instructor Satisfaction with Technical Aspects Online v. Onground

RQ. 3	t-test for Equality of Means	
	t	Sig. (2-tailed)
Suitability of Platform	6.451	.000
Course resources univ*	.832	.407
Course resources pub	2.902	.005
Adapt mater*	6.447	.000
Ongoinsupp*	2.544	.012
Training	2.221	.029
Teach envir.	5.859	.000
Inst tools	5.090	.000

*Equal variances assumed. All others, equal variances not assumed

RQ 4: How satisfied are instructors of business law courses with the managerial aspects of online course delivery versus onground course delivery

Mean scores for *online* satisfaction levels: 1.96, 1.17, 1.53, and 1.38

Mean scores for *onland* satisfaction levels:.78,.93,.71, and.82

DISCUSSION AND CONCLUSION

Our study results are consistent with earlier studies of instructor satisfaction with regard to the technological supports for online and onground instruction, but diverge from other studies which found instructor satisfaction with various aspects of pedagogical, social and managerial categories to be more satisfactory in the online format (Shea, Pelz, Frederikson, & Pickett, 2002). Shea et al. were interested in how the online teaching experience would impact classroom teaching. While their focus was on instructional design,

Table 4. Instructor Satisfaction with Managerial Aspects Online v. Onground

RQ. 4	t-test for Equality of Means	
	t	Sig. (2-tailed)
Control cheating	7.052	.000
Ease of grading	1.486	.141
Use of Ass of Learn tools*	5.228	.000
Instr. Eval tools	3.201	.002

*Equal variances assumed. All others, equal variances not assumed

pedagogical reflection, differing ways to assess and teach, and the overall effect of online instruction on onground instruction (p. 104), their survey questions were comparative, asking in a sense which format was better. Ninety-six percent of their sample was satisfied with online instruction; 74% felt it was equal to or better than onground instruction. Significant percentages believed that interaction with students, interaction between students, and an instructor's knowledge of students was as good as, or better online (89%, 88% and 62% respectively). While 73% of our sample was generally satisfied with online instruction, we did not find that instructors were more satisfied with results in the online courses than with the results in onground courses.

Clay (1999) and later Hiltz et al. (2007) tied instructor satisfaction/motivation with the training and support made available to instructors. While we did see difference in the responses to questions on the level of satisfaction with training and support between online and onground instruction, in both formats instructors were generally satisfied with those two aspects.

While our study supports the continued role of online instruction as a valid educational tool, it is not yet the instructors' preferred tool. The comments section was consistent with the results of the SPSS analyses of the 26 aspects. For example, when asked "How would you compare online with classroom instruction?" of the eighty-five responses, most preferred the classroom; many appreciated the different roles each might play in higher education; some would prefer a combination – either a hybrid course or alternating between the two platforms. Of those who preferred the classroom experience, there were at least ten who expressed a decided disregard for online instruction as a valid mode of instruction.

The preference among instructors for the classroom format is not surprising when you consider that most people who like to teach, like to interact face-to-face with the student. It is also likely that the instructors themselves have had classroom-based educations and value that. While we have found a high level of satisfaction with online learning among students (Shelley et al., 2007, 2008), the same has not been true of instructors. Many, perhaps the majority of students who take advantage of online instruction are self-selected. Instructors by-and-large are responding to consumer demand. One respondent in our study noted that what makes online instruction work is" a motivated student base and a good platform". We would add to that, a motivated instructor and institutional supports.

If the demand for online instruction continues to grow, more faculty members will need to become more invested in making the medium a successful experience. If that happens and research expands in the area of online pedagogy, we can expect to find answers to what makes online education effective and satisfying for the student, instructor, and the institution.

Our institution, like many others is investing in online education to reach a more diverse and in some cases, isolated student population. The challenge will be to make online instruction and onground instruction work together to provide high quality instruction in both formats.

ACKNOWLEDGEMENT

We appreciate the help provided by Dr. Mary Hansen on the development of the survey (Appendix A) and the assistance provided by Ms. Beth Kampsen with the SPSS analysis.

REFERENCES

Almeda, M. B., & Rose, K. (2000). Instructor satisfaction in university of california extension's on-line writing curriculum. *Journal of Asynchronous Learning Networks, 4*(3), 180–195.

Berge, Z. L. (1995, January-February). Facilitating computer conferencing: Recommendations from the field. *Educational Technology*, 22–30.

Clay, M. (1999). Development of training and support programs for distance education instructors. *Online Journal of Distance Learning Administration, 11*(111). Retrieved June 19, 2008 from http://www.westga.edu/~distance/clay23.html.

Conrad, D. (2004). University instructors' reflections on their first online teaching experiences. *Journal of Asynchronous Learning Networks, 8*(2), 31–44.

Fjermestad, H. S. & Zhang, Y. (2005). Effectiveness for students: Comparisons of "in-seat" and aln courses. In S. Hiltz & R. Goldman (Eds.), *Learning Together Online: Research on Asynchronous Learning Networks* (pp. 39-79). London, UK: Lawrence Erlbaum Associates.

Fredricksen, E., Pickett, A., Shea, P., Pelz, W., & Swan, K. (1999). *Factors influencing faculty satisfaction with asynchronous teaching and learning in the suny learning network*. Retrieved June 19, 2008 from http://www.alnresearch.org/Data_Files/articles/full_text/fs-fredricksen.htm

Harasim, L. (2000). *Shift happens: Online education as a new paradigm in learning, internet and higher education special issue* (pp. 41-61). UK: Elsevier Science.

Hiltz, R. S., Kim, E., & Shea, P. (2007). Faculty motivators and de-motivators for teaching online: Results of focus group interviews at one university. In *Proceedings of the 40th Hawaii International Conference on System Sciences* (pp. 1-10).

Marcel, K. (2002, December). Can law be taught effectively online? *JURIST*. Retrieved May 5, 2005 from http://jurist.law.pitt.edu/lessons/lesdeco2.php

Rivera, J. C., & Rice, M. L. (2002). A Comparison of Student Outcomes and Satisfaction Between Traditional & Web Based Course Offerings. *Online Journal of Distance Learning Administration, 5*(3).

Russell, T. (1999). *The No significant difference phenomenon*. Office of Instructional Telecommunications, North Carolina State University Chapel Hill, N.C.

Ryan, R. C. (2000). Student assessment comparison of lecture and online construction equipment and methods classes. *T.H.E. Journal, 27*(6).

Schulman, A. H., & Sims, R. L. (1999). Learning in an online format versus an in-class format: An experimental study. *T.H.E. Journal, 26*(11), 54–56.

Shea, P. J., Pelz, W., Fredericksen, E. E., & Pickett, A. M. (2002). Online teaching as a catalyst for classroom-based instructional transformation. In J.R. Bourne & J.C. Moore (Eds.), *Elements of quality online education: learning effectiveness, cost effectiveness, access, faculty satisfaction, student satisfaction* (Vol. 3). Needham, MA: Sloan Consortium.

Shelley, D. J., Swartz, L. B., & Cole, M. T. (2007). A comparative analysis of online and traditional undergraduate business law classes. *International Journal of Information and Communication Technology Education, 4*(2), 10–21.

Shelley, D. J., Swartz, L. B., & Cole, M. T. (2008). Learning business law online vs. onland: A mixed method analysis. *International Journal of Information and Communication Technology Education, 3*(1), 54–66.

This work was previously published in International Journal of Information and Communication Technology, Volume 6, Issue 1, edited by Lawrence A. Tomei, pp. 1-16, copyright 2010 by IGI Publishing (an imprint of IGI Global).

APPENDIX A

47	0,	91

INSTRUCTOR SATISFACTION

The purpose of this research is to determine the level of instructor satisfaction with online instruction as compared with onground, or traditional classroom instruction. The survey will take only a few minutes to complete.

There are no foreseeable risks associated with this project, nor are there any direct benefits to you. This is a confidential questionnaire. Your responses will not be identifiable in any way. The anonymous responses will be analyzed by me and my research colleagues alone. Responses will be aggregated for purposes of dissemination to the academic community. Thank you in advance for your help. If there are any questions, please contact me at swartz@rmu.edu.

1. Please rate your level of satisfaction with ONLINE INSTRUCTION in your courses with regard to the following:

	Very Satisfied	Somewhat Satisfied	Somewhat Dissatisfied	Very Dissatisfied	Does Not Apply
Student learning	O	O	O	O	O
Exam results	O	O	O	O	O
Effectiveness of assignments	O	O	O	O	O
Use of cases	O	O	O	O	O
Effectiveness of Powerpoint presentations	O	O	O	O	O
Discussion of course material	O	O	O	O	O
Use of group projects	O	O	O	O	O
Effectiveness of lecture material	O	O	O	O	O

2. Please rate your level of satisfaction with ONLINE INSTRUCTION in your courses with regard to the following

	Very Satisfied	Somewhat Satisfied	Somewhat Dissatisfied	Very Dissatisfied	Does Not Apply
Student participation	O	O	O	O	O
Interaction between students	O	O	O	O	O
Student motivation	O	O	O	O	O
Student-instructor relationship	O	O	O	O	O
Method/s of communication	O	O	O	O	O
Enjoyment of instruction	O	O	O	O	O

3. Please rate your level of satisfaction with ONLINE INSTRUCTION in your courses with regard to the following:

	Very Satisfied	Somewhat Satisfied	Somewhat Dissatisfied	Very Dissatisfied	Does Not Apply
Suitability of the instructional platform for the subject matter	O	O	O	O	O
Course resources available from the university	O	O	O	O	O
Course resources available from the textbook publishers	O	O	O	O	O
Ability to adapt instructional material to the class	O	O	O	O	O
Ongoing support services available	O	O	O	O	O
Training in mode of instruction	O	O	O	O	O
Teaching environment	O	O	O	O	O
Instructional tools made available	O	O	O	O	O

4. Please rate your level of satisfaction with ONLINE INSTRUCTION in your courses with regard to the following:

	Very Satisfied	Somewhat Satisfied	Somewhat Dissatisfied	Very Dissatisfied	Does Not Apply
Ability to control cheating	O	O	O	O	O
Ease of grading	O	O	O	O	O
Use of assurance of learning tools	O	O	O	O	O
Student evaluation (of the instructor) tools	O	O	O	O	O

5. Please rate your level of satisfaction with ONGROUND OR TRADITIONAL CLASSROOM INSTRUCTION in your courses with regard to the following:

	Very Satisfied	Somewhat Satisfied	Somewhat Dissatisfied	Very Dissatisfied	Does Not Apply
Student learning	O	O	O	O	O
Exam results	O	O	O	O	O
Effectiveness of assignments	O	O	O	O	O
Use of cases	O	O	O	O	O
Effectiveness of Powerpoint presentations	O	O	O	O	O
Discussion of course material	O	O	O	O	O
Use of group projects	O	O	O	O	O
Effectiveness of lecture material	O	O	O	O	O

6. Please rate your level of satisfaction with ONGROUND OR TRADITIONAL CLASSROOM INSTRUCTION in your courses with regard to the following:

	Very Satisfied	Somewhat Satisfied	Somewhat Dissatisfied	Very Dissatisfied	Does Not Apply
Student participation	O	O	O	O	O
Interaction between students	O	O	O	O	O
Student motivation	O	O	O	O	O
Student-instructor relationship	O	O	O	O	O
Method/s of communication	O	O	O	O	O
Enjoyment of instruction	O	O	O	O	O

7. Please rate your level of satisfaction with ONGROUND OR TRADITIONAL CLASSROOM INSTRUCTION in your courses with regard to the following:

	Very Satisfied	Somewhat Satisfied	Somewhat Dissatisfied	Very Dissatisfied	Does Not Apply
Suitability of the instructional platform to the subject matter	O	O	O	O	O
Course resources available from the university	O	O	O	O	O
Course resources available from textbook publishers	O	O	O	O	O
Ability to adapt instructional material to suit the class	O	O	O	O	O
Ongoing support services available	O	O	O	O	O
Training in mode of instruction	O	O	O	O	O
Teaching environment	O	O	O	O	O
Instructional tools made available	O	O	O	O	O

8. Please rate your level of satisfaction with ONGROUND OR TRADITIONAL CLASSROOM INSTRUCTION in your courses with regard to the following:

	Very Satisfied	Somewhat Satisfied	Somewhat Dissatisfied	Very Dissatisfied	Does Not Apply
Ability to control cheating	O	O	O	O	O
Ease of grading	O	O	O	O	O
Use of assurance of learning tools	O	O	O	O	O
Student evaluation (of the instructor) tools	O	O	O	O	O

9. **I teach:**
   - O Online only, but have taught onground
   - O Onground only, but have taught online
   - O Online and onground
   - O Other (please specify)
   - If you selected other please specify: _____

10. **I teach:**
    - O At a 2 year institution
    - O At a 4 year institution
    - O Other (please specify)
    - If you selected other please specify: _____

11. **I teach:**
    - O At the undergraduate level only
    - O At the graduate level only
    - O At both the undergraduate and graduate levels
    - O Other (please specify)
    - If you selected other please specify: _____

12. **The primary instructional platform that I use is:**
    - O Blackboard
    - O ECollege
    - O WEB CT
    - O WEB CT VISTA
    - O MOODLE
    - O ANGEL
    - O First Class
    - O Classroom
    - O Lab
    - O Other (please specify)
    - If you selected other please specify: _____

13. **The instructional platform that I prefer is:**
    ○ Blackboard
    ○ Ecollege
    ○ WEB CT
    ○ WEB CT VISTA
    ○ MOODLE
    ○ ANGEL
    ○ First Class
    ○ Classroom
    ○ Lab
    ○ Other (please specify)
    If you selected other please specify: _____

14. **I use the following instructional supports:**
    ❑ Streaming video
    ❑ Online applets
    ❑ White boards
    ❑ Internet sites
    ❑ Overhead projection
    ❑ Video/television
    ❑ Chat rooms
    ❑ Threaded discussions
    ❑ Library resources
    ❑ Labs
    ❑ Course links
    ❑ Powerpoint with audio
    ❑ Simultaneous broadcasts
    ❑ Other (please specify)
    If you selected other please specify: _____

15. **I am**
    ○ Under 24
    ○ 25 – 34
    ○ 35 – 44
    ○ 45 – 54
    ○ 55 – 64
    ○ 65 or older

16. **I am**
    ○ Male
    ○ Female

17. **I am**
    ○ An Instructor
    ○ An Assistant Professor
    ○ An Associate professor
    ○ A Professor
    ○ Other (please specify)
    If you selected other please specify: _____

18. **My position is**
    ○ Full-time
    ○ Part-time
    ○ Other (please specify)
    If you selected other please specify: _____

19. **I have been teaching online for:**
    ○ Less than 1 year online
    ○ 1-4 years online
    ○ 5-8 years online
    ○ More than 8 years online
    ○ Other (please specify)
    If you selected other please specify: _____

20. **I have been teaching for:**
    ○ Less than 1 year
    ○ 1-4 years
    ○ 5-8 years
    ○ 8-12 years
    ○ 12-20 years
    ○ More than 20 years
    ○ Other (please specify)
    If you selected other please specify: _____

21. **How would you compare online with classroom instruction?**
    _____
    _____

22. **Which do you prefer?**
    ○ Teaching Online
    ○ Teaching in the Classroom
    ○ Teaching Partially Online/Partially in the Classroom for the Same Course
    ○ Teaching Both Alternately
    ○ No preference
    ○ Other (please specify)
    If you selected other please specify: _____

Chapter 2
Digital Video Presentation and Student Performance:
A Task Technology Fit Perspective

Arjan Raven
Kennesaw State University, USA

Elke Leeds
Kennesaw State University, USA

ChongWoo Park
Georgia Gwinnett College, USA

ABSTRACT

This paper reports the results of a confirmatory study of a Task Technology Fit (TTF) model. Three dimensions of fit: Task Match, Ease of Use, and Ease of Learning, are applied in the context of digital video tools use for oral presentation in a classroom environment. Students completed a digital video presentation that acted as a substitute for an in-class oral presentation. An existing survey instrument was adapted, and administered to the students to examine the impact on presentation skill and fit to task. Results confirm the adaptation of the TTF model and show significant relationships between variables. The model can be used in other task/technology combinations. Additional findings suggest that when there is a significant fit between digital video tools (technology) and improvement of oral presentation skills (task), student performance also improves. Digital video can be a useful alternative to in-class presentation when the goal is to improve presentation skill.

INTRODUCTION

In their 2006 study, Park and Raven proposed an adaptation of the traditional task-technology fit (TTF) model (Goodhue, 1995; Goodhue & Thompson, 1995). Park and Raven noted that the TTF model, despite its promise, was not used much in IS research. Other models, such as the Technology Acceptance Model (Davis, Bagozzi, & Warshaw, 1992) are much more extensively used. They identified several reasons why that might be the case. The original model had 12 dimensions of fit, but many of these dimensions seemed to not to be reflective of the fit concept.

DOI: 10.4018/978-1-61350-468-0.ch002

They redesigned the model, with 3 dimensions of fit that were derived from the work by Eason (1988): (1) Task Match (TM), Ease of Use (EOU), and Ease of Learning (EOL). They updated the model by including well-tested measures for performance (measured as usefulness). Park and Raven tested the revised model in the context of knowledge management systems, and confirmed that their revisions worked well in that context. In their discussion of possible future research they noted the need for replication of the study in other contexts.

This study seeks to provide such a replication of the Park & Raven model, in a different context, with a different type of technology. Fit is examined between the task of creating a digital video presentation and the technological use of digital video tools. The use of a digital video (DV) presentation in a course management system (CMS) is examined for its impact on student presentation skill and fit to task. The level of fit is then compared to performance by students.

Task, Technology, Fit and Performance

Information systems success has been examined through a series of studies, and several theories have been developed (Park & Raven, 2006). The theory that is of particular relevance here is task technology fit theory (Goodhue, 1995; Goodhue & Thompson, 1995). One of the key concerns in Information Systems (IS) research is to more thoroughly understand the relationship between information systems and user performance. TTF theory indicates that when technology and task fit together well, performance will be higher (see Figure 1). (Goodhue, 1995; Goodhue & Thompson, 1995; Zigurs & Buckland, 1998)

Goodhue and Thompson (1995) measured task-technology fit with 8 factors: quality, locatability, authorization, compatibility, ease of use/training, production timeliness, systems reliability, and relationship with users. A survey containing between two and ten questions for each factor was used with responses on a seven point Likert scale, ranging from strongly disagree to strongly agree. Park and Raven (2006), in their research, re-conceptualized fit. They identified three aspects of fit: Task Match, Ease of Use, and Ease of Learning as shown in Figure 2. These dimensions were subsequently applied to digital video technology and student presentation task.

Digital Video Technology and Student Presentation Task

Oral presentation ability is one of the seven most important oral communication skills required by entry-level workers (Maes, Weldy, & Icenogle, 1997). Oral presentation is required by most undergraduate business courses for workplace and career

Figure 1. The task-technology fit model adapted from Goodhue & Thompson (1995).

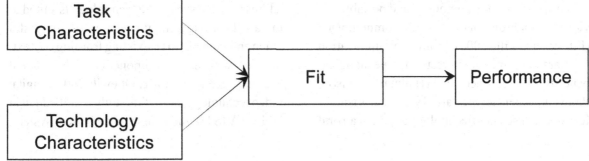

Figure 2. The Park & Raven (2006) re-configured task-technology fit model for Knowledge Management Systems

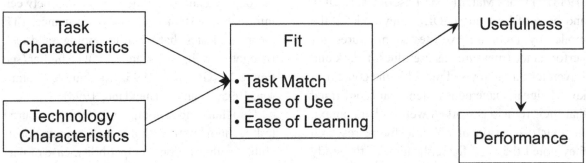

preparation (Campbell, Mothersbaugh, Brammer, & Taylor, 2001). It is increasingly recognized as an essential element in technical disciplines like engineering, biology, and mathematics (Darling & Dannels, 2003). In a typical university setting, courses provide feedback on relatively few oral presentations because of time constraints and the pressures of larger class sizes (Campbell, et al., 2001). Technology may provide one solution for higher education to transform educational processes (Leidner & Jarvenpaa, 1995) and to better address the need for oral communication skills in a time-constrained environment (Ober, 1987; Ober & Wunsch, 1983; Winsor, Curtis, & Stephens, 1997).

The use of technology by faculty and students has increased and placed growing importance on technology in the curriculum (Plutsky & Wilson, 2000). Technological developments in digital video technology are contributing to video-enhanced learning. Students are able to access a video as they were previously able to access a book. Video streaming to desktop computers and portable devices has made digital video access commonplace (Fill & Ottewill, 2006). While communication scholars have shown interest in the pedagogical benefits of video since 1970 (Hallmark, Hanson, Padwick, Abel, & Stewart, 1993), surprisingly few studies use video technology as part of an oral

communication skills based approach (Leeds & Maurer, 2009). Assessment of oral communication skills in the academic environment is necessary (Campbell et al., 2001; Maes et al., 1997; Reinsch & Shelby, 1997). Recent literature suggests that oral communication is of significant importance to organizational success and is a critical factor in graduate placement decisions (Aly & Islam, 2005; Campbell et al., 2001; Darling & Dannels, 2003; Ruchala & Hill, 1994; Sorenson, Savage, & Orem, 1990; Wardrope & Bayless, 1994). However, environmental needs for large class enrollments (Campbell et al., 2001; Geske, 1992) place a strain on universities to adequately teach and assess oral presentation delivery skills.

As technology usage is increasing, classroom size continues to increase, and the importance of oral presentation delivery skills remains paramount, it is important to examine how video technology fits with student presentation and how it can affect performance. The use of DV in a CMS to record and deliver oral presentation may address these issues if the technology is suited to the task. Learning technologies are most successful when embedded into an existing learning context; blended with other components of the student learning experience (Fill & Ottewill, 2006). Digital video technology use in this study is embedded in WebCT VISTA, the course management system.

RESEARCH QUESTIONS

The researchers investigated the following research questions:

1. Will the Park & Raven task technology fit model and instrument work with other technology/task combinations?
2. Does a better fit between the presentation improvement task and digital video technology result in better performance?

RESEARCH MODEL

Task, Technology

Goodhue and Thompson (1995) defined tasks as "…the actions carried out by individuals in turning inputs into outputs" (p. 216). They defined technology as "computer systems (hardware, software, and data) and user support services (training, help lines, etc.) provided to assist users in their tasks" (Goodhue & Thompson, 1995, p. 216). Finally, task technology fit was defined as "the degree to which a technology assists an individual in performing his or her portfolio of tasks" (Goodhue & Thompson, 1995, p. 216). In this study, the task is to improve presentation skill. The technology is the combination of digital video equipment and software, and the course management system.

Conceptualization of Task Technology Fit

IS researchers have used user evaluations of systems as a surrogate for IS success. A user evaluation means an assessment is made by a user about certain qualities of information systems (Goodhue, 1995). It is based on the assumption that users can evaluate a system service by comparing what they obtain with what they require to do their job. Eason (1998) argued that this is a 'match' or 'fit' evaluation where functionality is matched against task requirements, and usability is matched against user characteristics.

Task match was defined as "the ability of system functionality to serve user task needs" (Eason, 1988, p. 191). Ease of use (EOU) was defined by Eason (1988) as "the usability of system operating procedures" (p. 191). Eason (1988) defined ease of learning (EOL) as "the adequacy of the user support methods provided for user learning" (p. 191). For each of the constructs, Task Match, Ease of Use and Ease of Learning, Park and Raven (2006) developed measures for the context of knowledge management systems. The items used in their study were adapted for the digital video context of this research. The appendix displays the items.

Performance was measured by Park and Raven (2006) as usefulness, a construct first operationalized by Rai et al. (2002). In this study, two self-reported measures of performance have also been added. Usefulness was found to be directly affected by fit (Park and Raven, 2006). As shown in Figure 2, usefulness is expected to influence (self-reported) performance, rather than the other way around. Furthermore, usefulness is expected to have a mediating effect on the relationship between fit and performance.

RESEARCH METHODS

Sample

The fit between the task of creating a digital video presentation and the technological use of digital video tools was tested through the use of a purposive sample of two intact classes taught by one of the authors. Purposive sampling is nonprobability sampling where the investigator selects a subpopulation that is thought to be representative of the typical population (Singleton & Straits, 2005). This study focused on a particular group of students at a static point in time. "These designs are often used when the experimental treatment is administered to intact groups, such as school classes, making random assignment of individual subjects impossible" (Singleton & Straits, 2005, p. 207). A sample of 62 students was drawn from a population of 560 second year undergraduate business information systems course at a large southeastern state university in the fall of 2006.

Digital Video Technology Presentation

The students in the sample completed a digital video presentation that acted as a substitute for an in-class oral presentation. Classroom lectures on oral presentation planning, preparation, and delivery were presented in class. Students were assigned related reading, discussion, and video file analysis as part of their course work. They were placed into teams and asked to complete a twelve minute video presentation. Teams were trained on DV quality characteristics and DV editing software. Groups received training on capturing footage and editing tape; handouts and instruction were provided. Film clip examples that demonstrated the adequate or inadequate use of lighting, the importance of a tripod for steady filming, and the problems associated with background noise interference were shown. The same mini-DV cameras, equipment, and editing software were used for each team. Apple Macintosh iMovie© digital video editing software was used for the creation of the DV files. QuickTime© player was required for viewing. Students identified an appropriate location and acquired the necessary equipment from the campus presentation technology department. They filmed the oral presentation in one continuous take. If students wished to re-tape, they were required to start again at the beginning of the presentation. Inserting or editing footage was not permitted. Students then compressed video files and uploaded them to their associated course using the WebCT Vista course management system.

Students viewed the presentation through the CMS while faculty and independent study assessors evaluated student performance based on presentation and video quality characteristics. A preliminary study conducted by the researchers focused an investigation into public speaking and communication education literature to identify a set of delivery skills that are associated with successful oral presentation delivery (Leeds, Raven, & Brawley, 2007). Five primary traits were identified: (1) eye contact and the absence of reading, (2) vocal variety, (3) credibility and confidence, (4) absence of nervous mannerisms, and (5) gestures and the purposeful use of the body. These traits incorporated elements of oral communication delivery skill found in successful interactions.

Survey Instrument

Upon completion of the video presentation, surveys were distributed to students through WebCT Vista. Students received $ 10 in participant compensation and course bonus points equaling one-percent of their course grade for completing the survey. The survey instrument was adapted from items used in the Park and Raven (2006) study. Several items were dropped from the original instrument because they did not work in the digital video context, and most were rewritten to reflect the specific tasks and technologies of this study. The final survey consists of 4 demographic questions and 23 7-point Likert scale items (1 = very strongly disagree, 2 = strongly disagree, 3 = disagree, 4 = neutral, 5 = agree, 6 = strongly agree, 7 = very strongly agree). The specific constructs and measures in the survey questionnaire are listed in the appendix.

ANALYSIS AND RESULTS

Partial Least Squares Analysis

Partial Least Squares (PLS) analysis (with Smart PLS©) was used as the primary analysis tool in this study. PLS is an extension of the multiple linear regression model. It is also referred to as path analysis with composites, or soft modeling (Marcoulides & Saunders, 2006). PLS is a method for constructing predictive models versus causative models. It is an advanced statistical method that is based on the linear transition from a large number of descriptors to a smaller number of latent variables. PLS computes optimal linear relationships between latent variables in an attempt to account for as much of the manifest factor variation as possible (Tobias, 2007). It first estimates loadings of indicators on constructs and then iteratively estimates causal relationships among constructs (Fornell & Bookstein, 1982). In one analysis, an entire model such as the one shown in Figure 2 is analyzed.

PLS analysis was considered appropriate for this study because it places minimal demands on sample size and distributional assumptions (Chin, 1998; Fornell & Bookstein, 1982). PLS analysis is also appropriate for testing theoretical models in the early stages of development (Fornell & Bookstein, 1982). This study is a confirmatory study of an initial attempt to develop a theoretical model of task-technology fit in the KMS adoption context. It tests the same model in a blended technology context, using digital video tools and a course management system.

MEASUREMENT MODEL

Before testing the structural model, the measurement model was established by examining the psychometric properties of the measures.

Convergent Validity

Convergent validity was assessed through standardized loadings for each factor model. For convergent validity, the shared variance between each item and its associated construct should exceed the error variance. This translates into a loading of 0.707 or greater. Table 1 displays the loadings, which are all larger than the 0.707 threshold.

Three measures were used to assess internal consistency of each of the constructs: Cronbach's alpha, composite reliability, and average variance extracted (AVE). The Cronbach's alpha and composite reliability value are generally expected to be 0.7 or higher, indicating extensive evidence of reliability. Values of 0.80 or higher indicate exemplary evidence (Bearden, Netemeyer & Mobley, 1993; Yi & Davis, 2003). At the same time, a score between 0.60 and 0.70 may also be acceptable for exploratory research (Hair, Anderson et al., 1998; Nunally, 1967). Table 1 shows the Cronbach's alpha, composite reliability, and average variance extracted values for each construct. Four constructs have an alpha value of 0.8 or higher. Only Technology Characteristics has a low –but still acceptable - value at 0.671. Composite reliability values for all five constructs are .8 or higher, indicating exemplary composite reliability.

The third measure of construct reliability, average variance extracted, compares the amount of variance obtained from indicators with variance due to measurement error (Chin, 1998, p. 321; Fornell & Larcker, 1981). Acceptable levels for average variance extracted are 0.5 or higher (Chin, 1998). All constructs more than meet this criterion. Taken together, the three measures indicate that the constructs are very reliable.

Table 1. Construct analysis

Construct		Item	Standardized Loading	Cronbach's Alpha	Composite Reliability	Average Variance Extracted
Fit	Ease of Learning	EOL1	0.862	0.947	0.954	0.657
		EOL2	0.871			
		EOL3	0.710			
		EOL4	0.674			
	Ease of Use	EOU1	0.873			
		EOU2	0.824			
		EOU3	0.845			
		EOU4	0.826			
		EOU5	0.756			
	Task Match	TM2	0.833			
		TM3	0.813			
Performance Characteristics		PERFORM1	0.910	0.751	0.889	0.800
		PERFORM2	0.879			
Technology (System) Characteristics		SC2	0.775	0.671	0.815	0.594
		SC3	0.776			
		SC7	0.762			
Task Characteristics		TC4	0.915	0.811	0.914	0.841
		TC5	0.919			
Usefulness		USEFUL1	0.797	0.899	0.926	0.713
		USEFUL2	0.812			
		USEFUL3	0.898			
		USEFUL4	0.887			
		USEFUL5	0.824			

Discriminant Validity

To test for discriminant validity we investigated each indicator's loading on its own construct, and its cross-loadings on all other constructs were calculated. The results, displayed in Table 2, show that each indicator has a higher loading with its intended construct than its cross-loading with any other construct. Each block of indica-tors loads higher for its intended construct than for indicators from other constructs, establishing discriminant validity.

Structural Model

Figure 3 shows the structural model as it was tested in our study. The relationships between constructs are measured through the path coefficients and

Table 2. Construct loadings and cross loadings

Construct		Item	1	2	3	4	5
1. Fit	1-1. Ease of Learning (EOL)	EOL1	**0.862**	0.292	0.326	0.287	0.284
		EOL2	**0.871**	0.342	0.411	0.252	0.278
		EOL3	**0.710**	0.327	0.436	0.337	0.388
		EOL4	**0.674**	0.283	0.456	0.203	0.285
	1-2. Ease of Use (EOU)	EOU1	**0.873**	0.499	0.441	0.392	0.626
		EOU2	**0.824**	0.336	0.294	0.344	0.543
		EOU3	**0.845**	0.393	0.553	0.295	0.514
		EOU4	**0.826**	0.296	0.374	0.252	0.316
		EOU5	**0.756**	0.264	0.328	0.348	0.294
	1-3. Task Match (TM)	TM2	**0.833**	0.344	0.432	0.381	0.603
		TM3	**0.813**	0.309	0.330	0.373	0.449
2. Performance (PERFORM)		PERFORM1	0.318	**0.910**	0.299	0.560	0.521
		PERFROM2	0.451	**0.879**	0.339	0.466	0.454
3. Technology (System) Characteristics (SC)		SC2	0.278	0.071	**0.775**	0.020	0.142
		SC3	0.368	0.123	**0.776**	0.024	0.156
		SC7	0.461	0.515	**0.762**	0.412	0.592
4. Task Characteristics (TC)		TC1	0.361	0.457	0.252	**0.915**	0.501
		TC2	0.368	0.598	0.187	**0.919**	0.446
5. Usefulness (USEFUL)		USEFUL1	0.323	0.455	0.383	0.341	**0.797**
		USEFUL2	0.544	0.423	0.487	0.508	**0.812**
		USEFUL3	0.435	0.514	0.316	0.442	**0.898**
		USEFUL4	0.402	0.443	0.318	0.406	**0.887**
		USEFUL5	0.547	0.469	0.326	0.458	**0.824**

their significance levels, and the explanatory power of the model is expressed as R^2 values. The path coefficients were computed, and bootstrapping with 500 re-samples was used to determine the t-values for each of the relationships. A t-value of 2.58 or greater indicates a significance level of 0.01. All four relationships were positive and significant at the 0.01 level. This further confirms the findings of Park and Raven (2006).

The variance in the three dependent constructs; Fit, Usefulness, and Performance, was explained to varying degrees. The R^2 value of 0.33 for Fit means that 33% of the variance is explained by Task Characteristics and Technology Characteristics. For Usefulness, 29% of the variation is explained by Fit, and Usefulness in turn explains 30% of the variance in Performance. In the Park and Raven study, 48% of Fit was explained by Task Characteristics, Technology Characteristics, and Content Characteristics. The lower number in this study (33%) suggests that there may be additional constructs that would explain Fit.

DISCUSSION AND IMPLICATIONS

The primary research question of this study asked if the TTF model would work with other technology/task combinations. The Park & Raven (2006) study suggested three new dimensions of fit to simplify

Figure 3. The task-technology fit model showing the strength of relationship between constructs

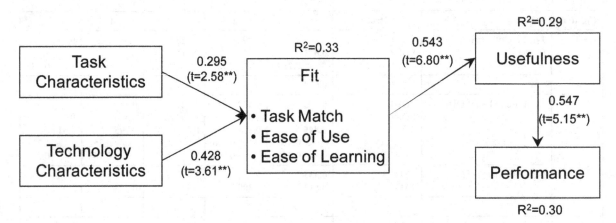

the fit measurements. Furthermore, they updated and developed measurements for all constructs of the TTF model. This study re-confirmed the Park & Raven study in the context of digital video tool use in the classroom. There were significant relationships between all four variables. The measurements used by Park and Raven were also shown to be applicable in this context.

The secondary research question asked if the fit between the presentation improvement task and digital video technology would lead to better student performance. When task and technology fit together, and when there is a significant fit between digital video tools (technology) and improvement of presentation skills (task), the student will perform better (improved presentation skills). The complexity of the task, and the reliability of the digital video tools are closely related to how well (1) the task matched the work, (2) how easy it was to learn how to use the DV tools, and (3) how easy it was to use the DV tools. These three in turn were closely related to the perceived improvement of presentation skills. Performance in the class does not only depend on how bright the student is, or how hard they work. If the technology and the task are not carefully matched then students won't learn. The implication is that digital video can be a useful alternative to in-class presentation when the goal is to improve

presentation skills. The strong relationships between fit, usefulness and performance indicate that fit is indeed important for performance, and that the fit between the presentation improvement task and the digital video technology does lead to better student performance

LIMITATIONS AND FUTURE RESEARCH

Any research study has limitations that derive from the need to focus, availability of data, and analysis methods used. As our study builds on the work of Park and Raven (2006), so other research can extend the findings of the work presented here. As the R-square values show, the variation in fit, usefulness, and performance is only partly explained (at levels of 33%, 29%, and 30% respectively. Other factors will likely have impacted the variation in these constructs, and future research might identify for instance what else impacts student self-reported measures of performance. The findings in this study confirmed the validity of the Park and Raven (2006) model in the context of digital video technology and oral presentation improvement. This in turn raises the question if there are task/technology combination for which this model would not work. Because of the limitations in the sample size, it was not possible to look at the three constructs that together form fit. With more data, it would be possible to explore the individual relationships that task match, ease of learning and ease of use have with task, technology, and performance. This would give more detailed insights into fit.

REFERENCES

Aly, I., & Islam, M. (2005). Factors affecting oral communication apprehension among business students: An empirical study. *Journal of American Academy of Business, Cambridge, 6*(2), 98–103.

Bearden, W. O., Netemeyer, R. G., & Mobley, M. F. (1993). *Handbook of marketing scales.* Newbury Park, CA: Sage.

Campbell, K. S., Mothersbaugh, D. L., Brammer, C., & Taylor, T. (2001). Peer versus self assessment of oral business presentation performance. *Business Communication Quarterly, 64*(3), 23–42. doi:10.1177/108056990106400303

Chin, W. W. (1998). The partial least squares approach to structural equation modeling. In G.A. Marcoulides (Ed.), *Modern Methods for Business Research* (pp. 295-336). Mahwah, NJ, USA: Lawrence Erlbaum Associates.

Darling, A. L., & Dannels, D. P. (2003). Practicing engineers talk about the importance of talk: A report on the role of oral communication in the workplace. *Communication Education, 52*(1), 1–16. doi:10.1080/03634520302457

Davis, F. D., Bagozzi, R. P., & Warshaw, P. R. (1989). User acceptance of computer technology: A comparison of two theoretical models. *Management Science, 35,* 982–1003. doi:10.1287/mnsc.35.8.982

DeLone, W. H., & McLean, E. R. (1991). Information systems success: The quest for the dependent variable. *Information Systems Research, 3*(1), 60–95. doi:10.1287/isre.3.1.60

DeLone, W. H., & McLean, E. R. (2003). The DeLone and McLean model of information systems success: A ten-year update. *Journal of Management Information Systems, 19*(4), 9–30.

Eason, K. (1988). *Information technology and organizational change.* Bristol, PA.: Taylor & Francis.

Falk, R. F., & Miller, N. B. (1992). *A primer for soft modeling,* Akron, OH: The University of Akron Press.

Fill, K., & Ottewill, R. (2006). Sink or swim: taking advantage of developments in video streaming. *Innovations in Education and Teaching International, 43*(4), 397–408. doi:10.1080/14703290600974008

Fornell, C., & Bookstein, F. L. (1982). Two structural equation models: LISREL and PLS applied to consumer exit-voice theory. *JMR, Journal of Marketing Research, 19*(4), 440–452. doi:10.2307/3151718

Fornell, C., & Larcker, D. F. (1981). Evaluating structural equation models with unobservable variables and measurement error. *JMR, Journal of Marketing Research, 18*(1), 39–50. doi:10.2307/3151312

Gefen, D., Straub, D. W., & Boudreau, M. C. (2000). Structural equation modeling and regression: Guidelines for research practice. *Communications of the Association for Information Systems, 4*(7), 1–30.

Geske, J. (1992). Overcoming the drawbacks of the large lecture class. *College Teaching, 40,* 151.

Goodhue, D. L. (1995). Understanding user evaluations of information systems. *Management Science, 41*(12), 1827–1844. doi:10.1287/mnsc.41.12.1827

Goodhue, D. L. (1998). Development and measurement validity of a task-technology fit instrument for user evaluations of information systems. *Decision Sciences, 29*(1), 105–138. doi:10.1111/j.1540-5915.1998.tb01346.x

Goodhue, D. L., & Thompson, R. L. (1995). Task-technology fit and individual performance. *MIS Quarterly, 19*, 213–236. doi:10.2307/249689

Hair, J. F., Anderson, R. E., et al. (1998). *Multivariate Data Analysis.* Upper Saddle River, New Jersey, USA: Prentice Hall.

Hallmark, J. R., Hanson, T. L., Padwick, G., Abel, D., & Stewart, P. (1993). *Communication apprehension remediation: The interaction effect of video self-observation and gender.* (Report No. CS508383) Miami, FL: Annual Meeting of the Speech Communication Association. (ERIC Document Reproduction Service No. ED363902).

Leeds, E., & Maurer, R. (2009). Using digital video technology to reduce communication apprehension in business education. *INFORMS Transactions on Education, 10*(1).

Leeds, E., Raven, A., & Brawley, B. (2007). Primary traits of oral business presentation: translatable use for assessment in a virtual learning environment. *College Teaching Methods & Styles Journal, 3*(4), 21.

Leedy, P., & Ormrod, J. (2001). *Practical research. Planning and design.* (7th Ed.) Upper Saddle River, NJ, USA: Merrill-Prentice Hall.

Leidner, D. E., & Jarvenpaa, S. L. (1995). The use of information technology to enhance management school education: A theoretical view. *MIS Quarterly, 19*, 265. doi:10.2307/249596

Maes, J. D., Weldy, T. G., & Icenogle, M. L. (1997). A managerial perspective: Oral communication competency is most important for business students. *Journal of Business Communication, 34*(67).

Marcoulides, G., & Saunders, C. (2006). PLS: A Silver Bullet? *MIS Quarterly, 30*(2), iii–ix.

Ober, S. (1987). The status of postsecondary business communication instruction--1986 vs. 1982. *Journal of Business Communication, 24*(49).

Ober, S., & Wunsch, A. P. (1983). The status of business communication instruction in postsecondary institutions in the United States. *Journal of Business Communication, 20*(5).

Park, C., & Raven, A. J. (2006). Knowledge Management Systems Success at the Individual Level: Task Technology Fit Perspective. In *proceedings of the 37th annual meeting of the decision sciences institute* (pp. 30911-30916), San Antonio, TX: Decision Sciences Institute.

Plutsky, S., & Wilson, B. (2000). Study to validate prerequisites in business communication for student success. *Journal of Education for Business, 76*(1), 15.

Reinsch, N. L. Jr, & Shelby, A. N. (1997). What communication abilities do practitioners need? Evidence from MBA students. *Business Communication Quarterly, 60*(4), 7–29. doi:10.1177/108056999706000401

Ruchala, L. V., & Hill, J. W. (1994). Reducing accounting students' oral communication apprehension: Empirical evidence. *Journal of Accounting Education, 1*(1), 41–50.

Singleton, R. A., Jr., & Straits, B. C. (2005). *Approaches to social research*. New York, NY: Oxford University Press.

Sorenson, R. L., Savage, G. T., & Orem, E. (1990). A profile of communication faculty needs in business schools and colleges. *Communication Education*, *39*(2), 148–160. doi:10.1080/03634529009378797

Tobias, R. D. (1995). An introduction to partial least squares regression. In *SUGI Proceedings*. Retrieved August 1, 2008 from http://support.sas.com/rnd/app/papers/pls.pdf

Wardrope, W. J., & Bayless, M. L. (1994). Oral communication skills instruction in business schools. *Journal of Education for Business*, *69*(3), 132–135.

Winsor, J. L., Curtis, D. B., & Stephens, R. D. (1997). National preferences in business and communication education: A survey update. *Journal of the Association for Communication Administration (JACA)* (3), 170-179.

Wold, H. (1982). Soft modeling: The basic design and some extensions. In K.G. Joreskog & H. Wold (Eds.), *Systems under Indirect Observation 2*. (pp. 1-54). North-Holland, Amsterdam.

Yi, M. Y., & Davis, F. D. (2003). Developing and validating an observational learning model of computer software training and skill acquisition. *Information Systems Research*, *14*(2), 146–169. doi:10.1287/isre.14.2.146.16016

Zigurs, I., & Buckland, B. K. (1998). A theory of task/technology fit and group support systems effectiveness. *MIS Quarterly*, *22*(3), 313–334. doi:10.2307/249668

This work was previously published in International Journal of Information and Communication Technology, Volume 6, Issue 1, edited by Lawrence A. Tomei, pp. 17-29, copyright 2010 by IGI Publishing (an imprint of IGI Global).

APPENDIX

Table 3. Constructs and measures

Construct	Item ID	Item
Ease of Learning	EOL1	Learning to use the digital video tools was easy for me.
	EOL2	It was easy for me to become skillful at using the digital video tools.
	EOL3	It was difficult to learn how to use the digital video tools for my assignment.
	EOL4	I took a long time to learn to use the digital video tools for my assignment.
Ease of Use	EOU1	The services provided by the digital video tools matched my requirements. I found it easy to get the digital video tools to do what I wanted them to do.
	EOU2	My interaction with the digital video tools was clear and understandable.
	EOU3	I found the digital video tools to be flexible to interact with.
	EOU4	I found the digital video tools easy to use.
	EOU5	The digital video tools were user friendly.
Task Match	TM2	The functionality of the digital video tools served my needs very well.
	TM3	The services provided by the digital video tools matched my requirements.
Performance Characteristics	PERFORM1	The quality of my work in the assignment has been excellent
	PERFORM2	My effectiveness in the assignment has been excellent
Systems Characteristics	SC2 (reversed)	The digital video tools were subject to unexpected or inconvenient down times which made it harder to do my assignment.
	SC3 (reversed)	The digital video tools were subject to frequent problems and crashes.
	SC7	I would rate the overall quality of the digital video tools to be excellent..
Task Characteristics	TC4 TC5	I had to collaborate with others in my assignment. My assignment required frequent coordination with the efforts of others.
Usefulness	USEFUL1	Using the digital video tools improved my performance in the assignment.
	USEFUL2	Using the digital video tools in my assignment increased my productivity.
	USEFUL3	Using the digital video tools enhanced my effectiveness in my assignment.
	USEFUL4	Using the digital video tools made it easier to do my assignment.
	USEFUL5	I found the digital video tools useful in my assignment.
Demographic Information	AGE	What is your age?
	GENDER	What is your gender
	RACE	Which best describes your race or ethnic group?

Chapter 3
Evaluating Faculty Teaching of Research Methodology to Undergraduate Geography Students in a Nigerian University

Nwachukwu Prince Ololube
University of Education Port Harcourt, Nigeria

Andrew Egba Ubogu
Ahmadu Bello University, Nigeria

Daniel Elemchukwu Egbezor
University of Port Harcourt, Nigeria

Ugbomah Nwachukwu
NOVENA Univesity Ogume, Nigeria

ABSTRACT

The effective ways of teaching research methods to students is a process closely connected to socializing students towards writing an effective research project before graduation and determines how success-ful and effective they are in conducting individualized research. Several factors apart from setting up a successful learning community are essential, but competencies determine faculty effectiveness. This paper appraises students' evaluation of faculty (SEF). It evaluates students' perception of competencies required by faculty in teaching research methodology to undergraduate geography students at the Ahmadu Bello University in Nigeria. Using a questionnaire to gather data for the study, the paper argues that by evaluating the performance of faculty members, their knowledge, expertise, skills, and by applying certain adaptation mechanisms in teaching, the experience and effectiveness of teaching students' re-search methodology can be significantly improved. The authors use this medium to encourage colleges and universities, education planners and policy makers in Nigeria of the need to introduce and carry out SEF along side other evaluation techniques in determining faculty performances and effectiveness.

DOI: 10.4018/978-1-61350-468-0.ch003

INTRODUCTION

The Ahmadu Bello University is dedicated to excellence in teaching. Excellence means the state or quality of excelling; it is effectively providing learning experiences that prepare students for the challenges of the multifaceted, ever varying, and diverse workplace in society. Ahmadu Bello University is the largest university in Africa, south of the Sahara. It is composed of 12 faculties - Arts, Science, Education, Engineering, Vet Medicine, Medicine, Pharmacy, Agriculture, Law, Administration, and Environmental and Social Sciences. Its geography department was established in 1962. It is a foundation department of the university. Presently, it has a student population of 453 students. The university handles both local and international students. The staff strength of the geography department is show in Table 1.

Geography is offered as part of a four-year program and as a major in faculties of science and education. The teaching of undergraduate geography is characterized as applied and vocational in nature and aims to produce graduates who are scientifically and technically skilled and who possess report writing skills. Skill areas such as literature searches and reviews, data collection and analyses, and communication are all set in a problem-solving context where students learn about the research planning and management process (University of New South Wales, 2003),

Table 1. Staff strength of the geography department

Ranks	Numbers
Professors	2
Readers	2
Senior lecturers	1
Lecturer 1	6
Lecturer 11	5
Assistant Lecturers	4
Total	20

The completion of an introductory course in research methods is a critical step for undergraduate students who will one day need to conduct their own original research. These courses are equally important for students who are not planning to conduct research in the future, because graduates still need to make informed decisions regarding research findings as part of their professional development. Consequently, research methods courses are an essential requirement of many undergraduate programs in the social and natural sciences. Research methods courses are challenging classes to teach because the technical complexity of the course material is quite high while student interest in this material can unfortunately be quite low (Ball & Pelco, 2006).

According to the University of New South Wales (2003), geography is the study of spatial and temporal variations of the phenomena that make up natural and human-dominated environments. The cultural significance of geography lies in its contribution to an understanding of the total environment. The geographer's skills also find practical application in the conservation and planned development of resources. Increasing numbers of geographers are employed as professionals in these applications. In the 21st century, geography is concerned with understanding the functioning of natural environments and human societies. Geographers study the natural processes, environmental problems, resource management systems, and social, cultural and economic processes that shape our interactions with nature.

Student-developed research projects involve original research conducted by a single student or a small group of students. Research projects provide a wonderful active-learning experience that students typically embrace with increased motivation and interest. Students learn first-hand the challenges of reviewing the relevant research literature when formulating research questions/hypotheses. Reading scientific research is much more purposeful when students direct this reading towards their own specific research goals and objectives. Students design their own studies and must make many challenging methodological decisions. These methodological decisions are more meaningful to the students as the consequences of their decisions are experienced first-hand rather than simply read from a textbook. Students use statistical analysis as a tool for turning raw data into answers for research questions the students themselves have formulated. The resulting findings are much more meaningful to the student than sample problems taken from a statistics text. Students gain valuable experience presenting research while getting immediate and specific feedback about their research efforts. Presenting research findings is much easier and more relevant when the student has been involved in each stage of the research process (Ball & Pelco, 2006).

The goal of the undergraduate geography degree program offered in the faculties of science and education of the Ahmadu Bello Universities is to equip students to conduct quality research as a prerequisite for graduation. The department of geography conducts research in the areas of hydrology, geomorphology, transportation, regional geography, rural geography, pedology, environmental resource management and planning, economic geography, GIS, population studies and medical geography. Undergraduate geography students in the college of education conduct research in any of the aforementioned areas and in the field education.

RESEARCH OBJECTIVES

This study evaluates student perception of faculty performance in their teaching methodology, material utilization, evaluation, interaction and instructional process competencies. This study also tries to find out if significant relationships exist in the relationship of respondents' demographic information (gender, age, level/years of study and faculty of study) and the perceived variables. This quantitative investigation can make a significant contribution to discussion amongst researchers, faculty, policy and decision makers, planners, and administrators in education. Thus, this study specifically and succinctly aims to:

- Theoretically and empirically measure how students perceive faculty teaching methodology aimed at improving or decreasing students' academic achievements in research methodology.
- Analyze the extent to which students perceive faculty instructional material utilization competencies.
- Evaluate the extent to which students perceive faculty instructional process competencies.
- Evaluate the degree to which students perceive faculty instructional evaluation competencies.
- Assesses the extent to which students perceive faculty interaction process competences (the degree to which teachers encourage and demonstrate effective familiarity with students).

Based on this study's five main research objectives the following research questions were formulated: (1) to measure how students perceive faculty teaching methodology (**RQ 1, RQ 2, RQ 3, and RQ 4**); (2) to evaluate the extent to which students perceive faculty instructional material utilization competencies (**RQ 5 and RQ 6**); (3) to analyze the extent to which students perceive faculty instructional process competencies (**RQ 7, RQ 8, RQ 9, RQ 10, RQ 11, RQ 12, and RQ 13**); (4) to evaluate the degree to which students perceive faculty instructional evaluation competencies (**RQ 14, RQ 15, RQ 16, RQ 17,** and **RQ 18**). And (5) to assess the extent to which students perceive faculty interaction process competences (**RQ 19**).

RQ 1: Is the problem-solving method effective during and after the research methodology course?

RQ 2: Is the adoption and use of individual student's instructional method effective?

RQ 3: Is the dramatization of instructional situations effective in research methodology course teaching?

RQ 4: Is the use of the lecture method of teaching effective during research methodology course tutoring?

RQ 5: Is the selection of appropriate research methodology course instructional materials done correctly?

RQ 6: Is the preparation and use of instructional research methodology course material effective?

RQ 7: Is the application and use of contemporary knowledge and ideas in teaching research methodology courses effective?

RQ 8: Is the use of questioning skills when teaching research methodology courses effective?

RQ 9: Is the development of research methodology course curricula effective?

RQ 10: Is the time management of research methodology courses effective?

RQ 11: Is the mastery of research methodology course material sufficient?

RQ 12: Is the classroom management of research methodology courses effective?

RQ 13: Is the clarity in the statement of research methodology course objectives effective?

RQ 14: Is the construction of various research methodology course evaluation instruments effective?

RQ 15: Is the employment of various research methodology course evaluation techniques effective?

RQ 16: Is the assessment of students' understanding of research methodology courses effective.

RQ 17: Is the use of evaluation data to improve instructional situations effective?

RQ 18: Is the keeping of records of individual research methodology course students accurate?

RQ 19: Is the interaction with research methodology course students respectful and effective?

REVIEW OF LITERATURE

Students' Evaluation of Faculty Teaching

Students' evaluations of faculty (SEF) teaching were started in the 1960's by enterprising college students. Since then, their use has spread so that now they are administered in almost all American colleges and universities and are probably the main source of information used for evaluating faculty teaching performance (Huemer, [n.d]). Today many colleges and universities in the United States demand their faculty members to treat the students as customers in their teaching practice. Using student evaluations of faculty performance (SEFP) or student evaluations of teaching effectiveness (SETE) has become increasingly common on college campuses across America. In a study that tracked the use of student evaluations of faculty in 600 colleges between 1973 and 1993, Seldin (1993 in Emery, Kramer & Tian, [n.d]) found that the use of SEFP/SETE increased from 29% to 86% during that period. Emery, Kramer and Tian (n.d) view the SEFP/SETE as a negative approach in terms of education quality control. They notice that with increased use the SEFP/SETE itself becomes increasingly controversial. The reasons for the controversy are not only in the student evaluations themselves, but also the way the student evaluations are often used.

Evaluation is a significant step for constructively improving the quality and role of faculty members. Evaluation is about using monitoring and other collected information to make judgments about progress. It is also about using the information to make changes and improvements.

Evaluation is an indicator of whether a faculty member's teaching exceeds, meets, or fails to meet a specified standard. The evaluation and the resulting performance measure are necessary for enhancing excellence in teaching through incentives and for achieving the objectives of a process (academic performance). It is accepted that the assessment of teaching is feedback about strengths and areas for improvement based on input from the faculty member being reviewed (University of Tennessee, [n.d]).

Students in developed countries complete evaluations of faculty members each semester; however, they do not receive greater weight than self or peer assessments during faculty evaluation processes. In contrast, student reviews of faculty teaching are not common in Nigeria as faculty members are not satisfied when feedback is negative. Another major finding of a study (Joshua & Joshua, 2004) conducted in Nigeria about students evaluating teachers' performances showed a significantly negative attitude irrespective of the use(s) to which the results of such evaluation would be put. This finding is quite unique and revealing in that Nigerian teachers, in this study, are not too different from their counterparts abroad.

Some researchers (Huemer, [n.d]; Dershowitz, 1992; Haskell, 1997) argue that SEF are a threat to academic freedom. Not only do SEF influence instructors' grading policies, teaching style, and course difficulty, but they may also restrict what a professor says in class. Faculty members may feel inhibited from discussing controversial ideas or challenging students' beliefs for fear that some students will express their disagreement through the course evaluation form. Suggestions are that SEF require faculty to think like politicians, seeking to avoid giving offense and putting style before substance. Thus some critics believe that teaching should be assessed by experts in the field, i.e., one's colleagues. Such measures, however, appear to be even less valid, as colleagues may influence fellow colleagues' ratings. Other methods of evaluating teaching effectiveness also appear invalid. Ratings by colleagues and trained observers are not even reliable (a necessary condition for validity)—that is, colleagues and observers do not even substantially agree with each other in instructor ratings (Huemer, [n.d])

According to Anomi (2007), in Nigeria, student evaluation of faculty (SEF) teaching has not yet been introduced in universities. Criteria for assessing academics for promotion in most Nigerian universities include qualifications, teaching, current research, publications, and service to the university/country. In addition, Anomi posits that university teachers are expected to possess content competence; pedagogical competence; the ability to deal with sensitive topics in an open, honest, and respectful way; the ability to contribute to the intellectual development of the student; the ability to treat students' grades, other academic records, and private communications with strict confidentiality; assessment of students that is valid, open, fair, and congruent with the course; and respect for the institution. These are ethical principles, which are conceptualized as general guidelines, ideals, or expectations that need to be taken into account along with other relevant conditions and circumstances in the design and analysis of university-college teaching. There is an enormous amount of literature on the subject of student evaluations of faculty (SEF) in the west, but they are lacking in African universities especially in Sub-Saharan Africa.

Research Methodology Courses

By research methods, we mean the range of approaches used in educational research to gather data, which is to be used as a basis for inference and interpretation for explanation and prediction (Miles & Huberman, 1994; Mouly, 1978). Traditionally, the word refers to those techniques associated with the positivistic model of eliciting responses to predetermined questions, recording measurements, describing phenomena and performing experiments (Cohen & Manion, 1994, p. 38). However, while the term methodology is sometimes applied to the methods and techniques used by social researchers, the methodological aspects of a study more accurately refer to the philosophy of science embedded both within these methods and within the researcher's approach to data collection and analysis (Pole & Lampard, 2002, p. 290).

Yin (1994) sees research methodology as a system of rules and principles that guide scientific investigation. Research methodology provides guidelines for collecting evidence about what takes place and for explaining why it takes place, and it does so in a way that enables other researchers to check the findings. Thus, research methodology is perceived as the organized method employed by a researcher towards the making and completion of a research goal. Generally, the method(s) used must be scientific and specific in relation to the questions and issues at hand, which should be straightforward and generalizable to the research, but relevant to future researchers. The idea here is that research methodology establishes a form and relation to the making of a research plan and contributing to the organized frame of a research goal.

On this basis, it might be inferred that the aim of a research methodology is to help students comprehend in the broadest terms possible the process of scientific inquiry as well as the product itself. Research methodology can best be perceived as the process of arriving at dependable solutions to problems through the planned and systematic collection, analysis, and interpretation of data. It is the most important tool for advancing knowledge, promoting progress, and enabling human being to relate more effectively to his/her environment, accomplish his/her purposes and resolve his/her conflicts. In summary, research methods in my opinion are merely the means of formulating the research data and outcomes.

Competencies and Good Teaching

According to Kautto-Koivula (1996) professional competence is often considered to involve at least two main domains: (1) proficiencies specific to a profession, discipline or organization. These include the discipline-specific knowledge-base, technical skills considered essential in the profession, and the ability to solve the types of problems encountered within the profession, and (2) general characteristics of the individual that facilitate the individual's development and maintenance of professional competence; these are intellectual ability, personality traits, motivation, attitudes and values. Kautto-Koivula further distinguished three cognitive domains of competence: (1) skills (either manual or intellectual); (2) knowledge, which is simply information committed to memory, and (3) the deeper learning variously described as understanding, conceptual learning or meaningful learning.

Campbell, et al. (2004) refer to faculty job competencies as the impact that factors (e.g. teaching methods, teacher expectations, classroom evaluation and organization and use of classroom resources) have on students' performance. In addition, they look at faculty efficacy as the power to realize socially valued objectives; especially, but not exclusively, the work concerned with enabling students to learn. According to them, four issues flow from this definition: the contexts and conditions for which students are enabled to learn can differ; the students can differ; the content of which objectives for learning are achieved can differ; and the values underlying learning and effectiveness can differ.

According to McCormick (1996, pp. 46-49) the best teachers captivate students with subject matter drawn out of themselves. Through effective instructional process students catch their excitement like the wake of a passing train. The very best teachers do not tie students down; they pull students along. They are sentimental and they are visionaries. Unlike being a great scholar, being a great teacher requires a passion for one's field of study and for one's students. After all, teaching is not just about ideas; it is about engaging hearts and minds in the process of learning. Teachers, like doctors and other professional workers, need essential tools to do their work best. Of course, it is true that the central figures in any learning situation are always the students and not the teachers, but it is equally true that learning may be greatly enhanced by the utilization of the many instructional materials available in the university and various agencies.

Brain (1998) asked the following questions in his search for what makes a good teacher: What are the qualities that combine to create an excellent, memorable teacher? Why do some teachers inspire students to work three times harder than they normally would while others inspire students to skip class? Why do students learn more from some teachers than others? For those who aspire to become better teachers, these are important questions. In addition, he identified the issue of "emphasis on teaching" as focusing on four essential qualities that distinguish exceptional teachers (1) knowledge, (2) communication skills, (3) interest, and (4) respect for students.

Quality teachers according to McCormick (1996) are the teachers who inspire students to compete against themselves, to take on tasks that seem to exceed their grasp, to discover and develop their real mettle as thinkers. At the same time, the very best teachers also seem to be the ones who never stop learning themselves; they are the folks who never quit reading new books, listening to new voices, or discussing new ideas, and whose quest for understanding is never finished. Biggs (2003) and Reiger and Stang (2000, pp. 62-64) asserts that the very best teachers are lifelong students, people who still know how little they really understand about life and how much they have left to learn about all the important questions. The classroom teachers need to be curious,

imaginative, empathetic, motivating, friendly and hardworking, thereby creating a learning environment that enhances and strengthens the learning disposition of the students

Methodology refers to the process of teaching and learning which brings the learner into relationship with the skills and knowledge that are specified and contained within the curriculum. According to Gutek (1988), methods are the means or procedures that a teacher uses to aid students in having an experience, mastering a skill or process, or acquiring knowledge.

In conclusion, the quality of good teaching is getting most students to use the higher cognitive level processes that the more academic students use spontaneously. It is teaching works by getting students to engage in learning-related activity that helps them attain the particular objectives set for the unit or course, such as theorizing, generating new ideas, reflecting, applying and problem-solving.

RESEARCH PROCEDURE

This study is based on the perceptions of students regarding faculty performance in their teaching methodology, evaluation, interaction, instructional process and the use of instructional material tools in teaching research method courses using a survey instrument. The research instrument (questionnaire) had 19 questions and measured on a likert-scale of 1 strongly disagree to 4 strongly agree. There were questions relating to demographic information: gender, age, level/year of study and faculty of study. During the distribution of the questionnaire, one of the authors who is a lecturer at the Ahmadu Bello University where the data was collected told the respondents the purpose of carrying out this research; in addition, the first page of the questionnaire stated reasons and the basis for the research and guidelines for answering the questions. The data were gathered using a simple random sample procedure among the 453 geography students in the faculty of science and education. Out of the 100 questionnaires distributed, 89 were returned. Three of the questionnaires were discarded because of errors in the way they were completed. Thus 86 questionnaires were used in the analysis. To find out the relationships between variables and faculty teaching research methodology and its effect on students, some statistical tests were conducted to validate the results. The statistical methods used were Frequency distribution, Mean and Standard deviation, Ch-square test, and ANOVA. The reason for using Mean is for the purpose of arriving at a single value that best describes the typicality and location of the distribution of all of the scores. Standard Deviation was used to indicate the extent to which the data disperse from one another. Ch-square test was applied to test the degree of association or difference in the variables. One-way-analysis of variance (ANOVA) was employed to test the relationship between variables and respondents' demographic information. The quality of this study is in its internal consistency. The coherence and reliability was examined using Cronbach's alpha reliability estimates to confirm the adequacy of the measures and the result was .812. The reliability shows a high level of internal consistency because it varies between 0 and 1, and the nearer

the result is to 1-, and preferably at or over 0.8- the more internally reliable the scale (Bryman & Cramer, 2001).

RESULTS

Participants

The first analysis conducted (see, Tables 2 to 5) was to find out the frequency distribution of respondents' demographic information. The majority of respondents, 56 (65.1%), were male while 30 (34.9%) were female. 48 (55.8%) of the respondents were 17-26 years old, 37 (43.0%) were 27-36 and 1 (1.2%) was 37 and over. Meanwhile, 61 (70.9%) of respondents were 300 level students while 25 (29.1%) were 400 level students. Additionally, 66 (76.7%) were faculty of science students and 20 (23.3%) were from the faculty of education.

Descriptive Analysis (Mean and Standard Deviation)

The second statistical analysis for this study began with an analysis of respondents' answers using mean and standard deviation. These reveal to what extent students perceive faculty compe-

Table 2. Frequency distribution tables for gender

		Frequency	Percent	Valid Percent	Cumulative Percent
Valid	Male	56	65.1	65.1	65.1
	Female	30	34.9	34.9	100.0
	Total	86	100.0	100.0	

Table 3. Frequency distribution tables for age

		Frequency	Percent	Valid Percent	Cumulative Percent
Valid	17-26 years	48	55.8	55.8	55.8
	27-36 years	37	43.0	43.0	98.8
	37-above	1	1.2	1.2	100.0
	Total	86	100.0	100.0	

Table 4. Frequency distribution tables for level/year of study

		Frequency	Percent	Valid Percent	Cumulative Percent
Valid	300 level	61	70.9	70.9	70.9
	400 level	25	29.1	29.1	100.0
	Total	86	100.0	100.0	

Table 5. Frequency distribution tables for faculty of study

		Frequency	Percent	Valid Percent	Cumulative Percent
Valid	Sciences	66	76.7	76.7	76.7
	Education	20	23.3	23.3	100.0
	Total	86	100.0	100.0	

tencies in the teaching of research methodology. Table 6 revealed that all the respondents agreed that faculty teaching of research methodology to students is effective. An overwhelming number of respondents felt that it is highly beneficial for students, especially students pursuing a professional certificate in geography.

We used Chi-square (X^2) analysis to determine whether relationships exist in faculty competencies and teaching of research methodology to undergraduate student. We found that the respondents show a significant relationship between the competencies variables and the effectiveness in teaching. All the competencies variables tested depict positive relationships *(p <.000)*. This does not mean that the probability is 0. It is less than *p <.0005* (Nworgu, 1991, p. 155; Marija, 1997, p. 230; Bryman and Cramer, 2001, p. 108). The highest X^2 value was *81.349* and the lowest was *16.512, Df = 3*. Thus, students are satisfied with faculty pedagogical competencies and were convinced of the benefit of studying and faculty effectiveness in teaching research methodology. (See Table 7).

The results from ANOVA analysis (Table 8) depicts that no significant differences were found in the variables and respondents' perception based on their gender, age, level/year of study and faculty of study at *F = 1.601, p >.209, F =.989, p >.376, F =.568, p >.453, F = 2.561, p >.113* respectively.

DISCUSSIONS AND CONCLUSION

This study showed that undergraduate students in Nigeria have the potential to evaluate faculty and recognize the importance of participating in SEF. It explored the contradictory view to SEF. The study supports the fact that students are relevant in faculty member evaluation and their input is a significant step for constructively improving the quality and role of faculty members. According to them, the teaching mode and methodology encourages students to foster interpersonal and individualized competencies in writing and developing research projects. The use of problem-solving methods, individual student's instructional methods, dramatization and demonstration of instructional situations and the effective use of the lecture method in teaching during research methodology course tutoring (**RQ 1, RQ 2, RQ 3,** and **RQ 4**) showed to advantage that faculty has competence and effectiveness in their teaching.

In evaluating the extent to which students perceive faculty instructional material utilization competencies we selected the following variables: selection of appropriate research methodology course instructional materials (**RQ 5**) and the preparation and use of instructional research methodology course materials effectively (**RQ 6**). The observation that comes to the fore is that despite the limited availability and access of technology tools to the faculty members and their lack of

Table 6. Results of descriptive (mean and standard deviation) analysis of variables

Variables	Mean	Std. D
METHODOLOGICAL COMPETENCIES		
RQ 1. Use problem-solving methods effectively	2.8721	.71614
RQ 2. Use of individual student's instructional method effectively	2.4767	.89083
RQ 3. Dramatize (Demonstrates) instructional situation effectively	3.0814	.61768
RQ 4. Effectively use the lecture method of teacher effectively	3.0233	.63202
MATERIAL UTILIZATION COMPETENCIES		
RQ 5. Select appropriate research methodology course instructional materials	3.0698	.66493
RQ 6. Prepare and use instructional research methodology course materials	2.8953	.71995
INSTRUCTIONAL PROCESS COMPETENCIES		
RQ 7. Apply the use of contemporary knowledge, ideas etc	3.0698	.62855
RQ 8. Use appropriate questioning skills when teaching	3.1163	.58246
RQ 9. Develop research methodology course curricula properly	3.1279	.73239
RQ 10. Ensure effective time management of their research methodology courses	2.6628	.83470
RQ 11. Show sufficient mastery of research methodology course	2.9535	.64911
RQ 12. Effectively manage their research methodology courses classroom	2.7093	.70069
RQ 13. Clearly state their research methodology course objectives correctly	3.0349	.69363
INSTRUCTIONAL EVALUATION COMPETENCIES		
RQ 14. Construct various research methodology course evaluation instruments	2.7674	.84956
RQ 15. Employ various research methodology courses evaluation techniques	2.8605	.75401
RQ 16. Assess students' understanding of research methodology course	2.6512	.83691
RQ 17. Use evaluation data to improve instructional situations effectively	2.5349	.86361
RQ 18. Keep records of individual research methodology students' accurately	2.4070	.80261
INTERRACTION PROCESS COMPETENCIES		
RQ 19. Interact with students respectfully and effectively	2.7209	1.06992

preference for instructional technology, they were still using the tools available to them to make their teaching more effective. Thus students found that there were significant relationships between the teaching and the effectiveness of pedagogy

The study also analyzed the extent to which students perceive faculty instructional process competencies (**RQ 7, RQ 8, RQ 9, RQ 10, RQ 11, RQ 12,** and **RQ 13**), which include effective use of contemporary knowledge and ideas, appropriate questioning skills when teaching, developing curricula properly, effective time management, sufficient mastery of course materials, effective management of the classroom and clear statement

of their research methodology course objectives. They showed positive relationship in faculty teaching and their learning outcome. In practical terms, the teaching entails verbalization by faculty in a cooperative classroom setting, which makes students acquire skills in oral communication, listening and ability to express themselves during lessons. The instruction modes activate students' motivation to actively participate in classroom activities.

Additionally, we assessed the degree to which students perceive faculty instructional evaluation competencies (**RQ 14, RQ 15, RQ 16, RQ 17,** and **RQ 18**). The construction of various evalu-

Table 7. Results of Chi-square analysis

Variables	X²	Sig. (2-tailed)
METHODOLOGICAL COMPETENCIES		
RQ 1. Use problem-solving methods effectively	49.907	.000
RQ 2. Use of individual student's instructional method effectively	18.651	.000
RQ 3. Dramatize (Demonstrates) instructional situation effectively	81.349	.000
RQ 4. Effectively use the lecture method of teacher effectively	28.558	.000
MATERIAL UTILIZATION COMPETENCIES		
RQ 5. Select appropriate research methodology course instructional materials	63.395	.000
RQ 6. Prepare and use instructional research methodology course materials	56.233	.000
INSTRUCTIONAL PROCESS COMPETENCIES		
RQ 7. Apply the use of contemporary knowledge, ideas etc	77.163	.000
RQ 8. Use appropriate questioning skills when teaching	40.837	.000
RQ 9. Develop research methodology course curricula properly	40.023	.000
RQ 10. Ensure effective time management of their research methodology courses	30.930	.000
RQ 11. Show sufficient mastery of research methodology course	78.279	.000
RQ 12. Effectively manage their research methodology courses classroom	53.070	.000
RQ 13. Clearly state their research methodology course objectives correctly	53.628	.000
INSTRUCTIONAL EVALUATION COMPETENCIES		
RQ 14. Construct various research methodology course evaluation instruments	25.349	.000
RQ 5. Employ various research methodology courses evaluation techniques	43.023	.000
RQ 16. Assess students' understanding of research methodology course	26.390	.000
RQ 17. Use evaluation data to improve instructional situations effectively	33.349	.000
RQ 18. Keep records of individual research methodology students' accurately	36.140	.000
INTERRACTION PROCESS COMPETENCIES		
RQ 19. Interact with students respectfully and effectively	16.512	.000

Table 8. Analysis of variance of variables and respondents' demographic information

Demographic Information	Groups	Frequency	Percentage	Mean	F Ratio	Significance
Gender	Male	56	65.1	3.1429	1.601	.209
	Female	30	34.9	2.9667		
Age	17-26 years	48	55.8	3.0000	.989	.376
	27-36 years	37	43.0	3.1892		
	37-above	1	1.2	3.0000		
Level/Year of study	300 level	61	70.9	3.0492	.568	.453
	400 level	25	29.1	3.1600		
Faculty of Study	Sciences	66	76.7	2.5606	2.561	.113
	Education	20	23.3	2.2000		

ation instruments effectively, employing evaluation techniques correctly, assessing students' understanding successfully, using evaluation data to improve instructional situations efficiently and keeping records of individual students accurately to assist them in further evaluative efforts was deemed positive by the students because students gain valuable experience presenting research while getting immediate and specific feedback from faculty about their research efforts. Presenting research findings is much easier and more relevant when the student has been involved in each stage of the research process (cf. Ball & Pelco, 2006).

Finally, this study evaluated the extent to which students perceive faculty interaction process competences (**RQ 19**) (encourage and demonstrate effective familiarity with students). Responses show that students acquire active interaction and leadership skills; these advantages are not far fetched because active learning and better academic achievement are fostered. Students who learn in a conducive environment as opposed to an unfriendly one tend to be more result oriented according to a study conducted by Ololube (2005a,b). According to Iyamu (2006), students learn more in a relaxed environment that gives them sufficient opportunities to ask questions, seek explanation and illustration than in strictly regimented environment.

The overall analysis of the results obtained showed that this study's findings regarding the intensity of the connection between methodological, material utilization, instructional, evaluation and interaction process competencies among faculty in teaching research methodology courses, showed a significant relationship; Tables 6 and 7 explain it all.

A further analysis (Table 8) to verify if significant differences exist in the respondents' opinion did not yield mixed results about the predictive value of demographic variables in students' evaluation of faculty competencies in teaching research methodology to undergraduate geography students. Students were not suspicious of faculty tendencies in their teaching competencies. Gender showed no significant difference in their opinions. The result portrays that both male and female students tend to be satisfied with faculty performances in their instruction. The difference in the respondents' age, level/year of study and faculty of study did not reveal any differences as well.

In spite of the outcome of this investigation, SEF is very questionable and yet most collages and universities in the west are fond of this practice as the means of educational control. Questions are always asked: does this practice encourage faculty to teach their students with future employers in mind, or does it encourage faculty to teach with their own student evaluations in mind? The answers to these questions are clear: if student evaluation of faculty performance and effectiveness are used for administrative control purposes, as "rational self-interested instructors" faculty definitely will alter their behavior to improve their performances and effectiveness. Examples of such behavior include lobbying to teach a course where better ratings are generally achieved, making a course less rigorous for students, relaxation of grading standards, or deciding against implementation of innovative instructional techniques (Emery, Kramer & Tian, [n.d]).

Researcher (Huemer, [n.d]) agree that SEF are highly reliable, in that students tend to agree with each other in their ratings of an instructor, and that they are at least moderately valid, in that student ratings of course quality correlate positively with other measures of teaching effectiveness. In one type of study, different instructors teach multiple sections of the same course, but there is a common final exam. The ratings instructors receive turn out to be positively correlated with the performance of their students on the exam. SEF also tend to correlate well with retrospective evaluations by alumni; in other words, former students rarely change their evaluations of their teachers as the years pass.

In closing, in our own commission as researchers, we deemed it fit to let us know that this study stands out as a search of the internet showed limited scientific research in determining the value and perception of SEF in higher education in Nigeria. We should bear in mind that this study was not conducted under the influence and control of the university in identifying whether faculty teaching of research methodology courses was effective. Rather it was a self-employed survey to determine students' perception of faculty preparedness in carrying out effective teaching.

In most industries, workers are used to evaluate their bosses; it is often used as one of several methods to ascertain the administrative ability and effectiveness of their managers (Ololube, 2000). Therefore, we use this medium to encourage colleges and universities in Nigeria of the need to introduce and carry out SEF alongside other evaluation techniques in determining faculty performances and effectiveness. Students should always be involved in faculty performance and effectiveness assessments, at least in the evaluation of faculty basic background in subject matter to reduce mediocrity. Finally, as a ground-breaking study, further research is required to compare the research finding of this study to ascertain if the research procedure and research questions used are in line with the outcome of this study. An extension of this type of study to other universities in Nigeria is highly recommended.

REFERENCES

Anomi, E. E. (2007). *Student expectations of faculty in a nigerian lis school.* Library Philosophy and Practice. Retrieved 15 January 2008, from http://www. webpages. uidaho.edu /~mbolin / adomi.htm

Ball, C. T., & Pelco, L. E. (2006). Teaching Research Methods to Undergraduate Psychology Students Using an Active Cooperative Learning Approach. *International Journal of Teaching and Learning in Higher Education, 17*(2), 147–154.

Biggs, J. B. (2003). *Teaching for Quality Learning at University* (2nd ed.). Buckingham, UK: SHRE and Open University Press.

Brain, M. (1998). *Emphasis on teaching. What is good teaching?* Raleigh, NC: BYG Publishing, Inc.

Bryman, A., & Cramer, D. (2001). *Quantitative data analysis with spss release 10 for windows: a guide for social scientists.* Philadelphia: Routledge: Taylor and Francis Group.

Campbell, J., Kyriakides, L., Muijs, D., & Robinson, W. (2004). *Assessing teachers job effectiveness: Developing a differentiated model.* London and New York: RoutledgeFalmer.

Cohen, L., & Manion, L. (1994). *Research methods in Education*. (4th ed.). London: Routldege.

Dershowitz, A. (1992). *Contrary to Popular Opinion.* New York: Pharos Books. Emery, C., Kramer, T., & Tian, R. (n.d). *Return to academic standards: challenge the student evaluation of teaching effectiveness.* Retrieved 10 January 2008, from http://www.bus.lsu.edu/ academics/accounting/ faculty/lcrumbley/stu_rat_of_%20instr.htm

Gutek, G. L. (1988). *Philosophical and Ideological Perspectives on Education.* Englewood Cliffs, NJ: Prentice Hall.

Haskell, R. E. (1997). Academic Freedom, Tenure, and Student Evaluation of Faculty: Galloping Polls in the 21st Century. *Education Policy Analysis Archives, 5*(6). Huemer, M. (n.d). *Student Evaluations: A Critical Review.* Retrieved 15 January 2008, from http://home.sprynet.com/~owl1/sef.htm

Iyamu, E. O. S. (2006). Promoting group-based learning. *Research on Learning, 8*(2), 27–35.

Jenkins, A., Blackman, T., Lindsay, R., & Paton-Saltzberg, R. (1998). Teaching and research: Student perspectives and policy implications. *Studies in Higher Education, 23*(2), 127–141. do i:10.1080/03075079812331380344

Joshua, M. T., & Joshua, A. M. (2004). Attitude of nigerian secondary school teachers to student evaluation of teachers. *Teacher Development, 8*(1), 67–80. doi:10.1080/13664530400200227

Kautto-Koivula, K. (1996). Degree-oriented adult education in the work environment. In P. Ruohotie & P. P. Grimmett (Eds.), *Professional Growth and Development: Direction, Delivery and Dilemmas* (pp. 149-188). Canada and Finland: Career Education Books.

Marija, J. N. (1997). *SPSS 6.1 Guide to Data Analysis.* New Jersey: Prentice Hall.

McCormick, P. (1996). There's no substitute for good teachers. *U.S. Catholic, 61*(6), 46–49.

Miles, M. B., & Huberman, A. M. (1994). *Qualitative data analysis.* Thousand Oaks, CA: Sage Publications.

Mouly, G. J. (1978). *Educational Research: the art and science of investigation.* Heinenmann. Boston: Allyn and Bacon.

Nworgu, B. G. (1991). *Educational Research: Basic issues and methodology.* Ibadan: Wisdom Publishers.

Ololube, N. P. (2000). *An appraisal of workers perception of academic and professional training on Managers' job effectiveness in the oil exploration industry, A case of Dec oil and Gas.* Unpublished PGD thesis, Federal University of Technology Owerri, Nigeria.

Ololube, N. P. (2005a). Benchmarking the motivational competencies of academically qualified teachers and professionally qualified teachers in nigerian secondary schools. *The African Symposium, 5*(3), 17-37.

Ololube, N. P. (2005b). School effectiveness and quality improvement: quality teaching in nigerian secondary schools. *The African Symposium, 5*(4), 17-31.

Pole, C., & Lampard, R. (2002). *Practical social investigation. Qualitative and quantitative methods in social research.* Harlow: Printice Hall.

Reiger, R. C., & Stang, J. (2000). Education productivity; Labor productivity; Motivation (psychology). *Employees—Training of. Education, 121*(1).

Robertson, I. T. (1991). *An evaluation of outdoor development as a management development tool.* MBA Dissertation. University of Edinburgh.

The University of New South Wales (UNSW). (2003). *School of Biological, Earth and Environmental Sciences.* Retrieved 23 December 2007 from http://www.fbe.unsw.edu.au/fbeguide/teaching&learning/resources/LearningCommunity_180803.pd

University of Tennessee. (n.d). *Ideas and best practices for evaluating faculty teaching.* Retrieved 10 January 2008, from http://www.utc.edu /Departments/ fcouncil/ FacultyHandbook/ Appen/Teaching.pdf

Yin, R. K. (1994). *Case Study Research: Design and Methods.* (2nd ed.). Thousand Oaks, CA: Sage.

This work was previously published in International Journal of Information and Communication Technology, Volume 6, Issue 1, edited by Lawrence A. Tomei, pp. 30-44, copyright 2010 by IGI Publishing (an imprint of IGI Global).

Chapter 4
Teachers and Technology:
Enhancing Technology Competencies for Preservice Teachers

Joseph Blankson
Carle Foundation Hospital, USA

Jared Keengwe
University of North Dakota, USA

Lydia Kyei-Blankson
Illinois State University, USA

ABSTRACT

In addition to possessing content knowledge required to teach students, today's teachers must be well equipped with appropriate technology skills and tools to guide and support student learning. The identification of this need has led teacher education programs to mandate all preservice teachers to enroll in technology courses as part of their teacher preparatory curriculum. Similarly, the International Society for Technology in Education (ISTE) has established the National Education Technology Standards for teachers (NETS- T) to help promote teacher technology competencies. The purpose of the study was to evaluate preservice teachers' self-assessed technology competency to determine whether preservice teachers perceived that their technology class enabled them to meet ISTE's required standards. Specifically, this paper explores the extent to which an educational technology course at a participating midwest college helped to improve preservice teachers' technology skills as well as to prepare them attain ISTE NETS- T.

INTRODUCTION

The integration of computer technology into instruction and its effect on student learning is of increasing interest to stakeholders such as policymakers, administrators, educators, students, and parents. Today, a major part of most school budgets are directed towards technology funding and implementation (Oppenheimer, 2003; Semich & Runyon, 2002). Further, as part of the 2001 No Child Left Behind Act, every student is required to be technologically literate by completion of middle school. To provide for the needs of the Net Generation learners (Oblinger & Oblinger, 2005) and to enhance effective instruction with

DOI: 10.4018/978-1-61350-468-0.ch004

technology, a National Educational Technology Plan was established in 2004.

As part of the national technology plan, teachers are required to meet national technology standards which require them to be technologically prepared for classroom instruction. Similarly, teachers are required to meet the International Society for Technology in Education (ISTE) National Education Technology Standards (NETS-T) established to help promote teacher technology competencies. Evidently, the national standards are in place in almost every state in the U.S. (U.S. Department of Education, 2006).

The ISTE standards are:

1. Teachers should be able to demonstrate a sound understanding of technology operations and concepts.
2. Teachers should be able to plan and design effective learning environments and experiences supported by technology.
3. Teachers should be able to implement curriculum plans that include methods and strategies for applying technology to maximize student learning.
4. Teachers should be able to apply technology to facilitate a variety of effective assessment and evaluation strategies.
5. Teachers should be able to use technology to enhance their productivity and professional practice.
6. Teachers should be able to understand the social, ethical, legal, and human issues surrounding the use of technology in PK-12 schools and apply those principles in practice.

When used appropriately, technology applications support the development of students' high-order thinking and problem-solving skills and help improve their attitudes toward and performance in their subjects (Wenglisky, 2006). As a result, ensuring technology competencies for teachers is critical to the success of the national technology plan. Semich and Runyon (2002) argue that, "It is becoming increasingly important for teachers to understand when and how to use technology to aid students' learning in classrooms and to understand and apply the concepts and information for various content areas" (p. 1433). Further, teachers should be given appropriate training that will allow them to become technology-proficient instructors (Smith, Smith, & O'Brien, 2002).

Teacher preparation programs have responded favorably to the national technology plan by integrating basic educational technology training in teacher education curricula. Preservice teachers are now required to enroll in instructional technology courses in partial fulfillment of graduation requirements. The primary objective of such technology classes is to introduce students to a wide range of basic computer concepts and skills mostly in the use of the Internet and the World Wide Web, Productivity Software, Presentation Software, and Multimedia and Educational Software.

Majority of students in colleges and universities across the U.S. are competent in basic computer technology applications (Keengwe & Anywanu, 2007). Not only are these students experts in word processing, emailing, and Power Point production, but often these students are also ahead of the educational curve in the use of technology tools such as ipods, wikis, blogs, and other applications which may have significant educational value (Bitter & Legacy, 2006; Dralle, 2007; Hoffner, 2007). Even so, other studies (Duhaney, 2000; Weisner & Salkeld, 2004) indicate that preservice teachers do not feel adequately prepared to integrate technology into their teaching. This instructional crisis might be attributed to instructors who do not promote technology use in a way that keeps up with the advances in how students are using technology (Project Tomorrow-NetDay, 2006).

Purpose of Study

National technology standards and guidelines were created by the National Council for Accreditation of Teacher Education (NCATE) and the International Society for Technology in Education (ISTE) to ensure adequate training of preservice teachers in instructional technology to enhance student learning. Being technologically literate, that is being "capable of understanding – with increasing sophistication – what technology is, how it is created, how it shapes society, and in turn is shaped by society" (NCATE/ITEA/CTTE Program Standards, 2003, p. 1) is no longer considered a viable option for preservice teachers.

ISTE recommends that teacher education programs provide diverse opportunities for teacher candidates to prepare them meet technology performance standards. However despite efforts by administrators and teachers to prepare quality teachers who can teach well with technology, results from previous research indicate that most preservice teachers do not meet the set technology standards and many do not even consider themselves competent enough to teach with technology (O'Bannon and Puckett, 2007; National Center for Education Statistics, 2000; Whetstone & Carr-Chellman, 2001). Educators and administrators are, therefore, charged with the responsibility of ensuring that, by the end of their program of study, all preservice teachers have the necessary skills to successfully incorporate technology into their instruction.

Bielefeldt (2001) and Brush et al. (2003) argue that although technology use has increased during the past decade, educators are still failing at keeping abreast of teachers' technology literacy. Further, although the advantages of technology use have been clearly documented (Keengwe, Onchwari, & Wachira, 2008), these advantages would not be fully realized if teachers are not trained to use technology effectively. Therefore to keep abreast of the technology standards, most teacher education programs have responded by offering educational technology courses as part of their teacher education curricula.

As colleges of education strive to integrate technology into teacher preparation programs, there is need to examine these technology programs and to determine whether they are having the necessary impact on students' perceived technology competencies, especially for the Net Generation students. Therefore, the purpose of the study was to evaluate preservice teachers' self-assessed technology competency to determine whether preservice teachers perceived that their technology class enabled them to meet ISTE's required standards.

Research Questions

The following research questions were investigated in the study:

A. Do the educational technology classes that preservice teachers enroll in offer technology skills over and above what students already know?

B. Do preservice teachers perceive that their technology competencies improve after enrollment in educational technology classes required by their colleges?

C. Are the technology modules covered in the classes appropriate and adequate to ensure that preservice teachers meet the necessary standards promulgated by ISTE?

Methodology

Setting and Participants

The study was conducted at a small private, four-year co-educational liberal arts college located in the Midwestern region of the United States. The college consisted of 650 students who were either residential students or local commuters.

The subjects of the study were 10 teacher candidates enrolled in the computer technology course offered as part of the teacher preparation curriculum. These candidates ranged from ages 20 to 25. All the preservice teachers were white. Seven were females and three were males.

Research Design and Data Collection

The study employed a pre-test post-test research design. Data sources used in this study comprised of a 5-point Likert scale (1=Not knowledgeable to 5= Expert) class survey administered to the students before and after the course, focus group discussions, observations, and student portfolios.

The Technology Course: ED410-Technology Integration into the Educational Curriculum

This course is designed for preservice teachers to integrate instructional technology into the educational curriculum. A major objective for the class was that, by the end of the course period, preservice teachers should be able to show evidence of meeting the ISTE National Educational Technology Standards for Teachers (NETS-T) at both the General Preparation level and the K-12 level.

Before enrolling in *ED 410-Technology Integration into Educational Curriculum,* students were expected to be already conversant with basic technology skills. The teacher education program required that students accurately and honorably complete a Computer Operations Competency Checklist designed according to NETS-T. Included in the checklist were a number of courses that student could complete to satisfy the requirement. As evidence of meeting the pre-requisite skills, students needed to obtain an approved signature from an instructor of the course in which the competency was demonstrated, a faculty advisor,

work program manager or a student worker in the computer lab who had been trained in various competencies and had witnessed the competencies performed. Students were also provided with self-paced modules that provided additional opportunities to meet the prerequisite for ED410.

Once the students met the prerequisite for the course, they were allowed enrollment. The course activities for *ED 410-Technology Integration into Educational Curriculum* were designed and implemented with reference to NETS-T. The instructional strategies for ED 410 were based on the constructivist philosophy of learning that requires individuals to construct knowledge or give meaning to a situation based on their experiences. The following proceedings describe the course topics, instructional strategies, and the extent to which the course met NETS-T.

Electronic Portfolio and "Integrating Technology into Education Curriculum"

It is essential for preservice teachers to become conversant with the NETS-T early in the course. To facilitate effective instruction, three instructional methods were used – presentations, discussions, and videos – that demonstrate how K-12 teachers might integrate technology into their lessons in various content areas and grade levels. To reinforce understanding, self assessment and attainment of the standards, the instructor provided students with an Electronic Portfolio template based on the standards.

Upon completion of each assignment, students were required to read the performance indicators, identify the standard(s) attained, write a reflection on how the assignment(s) meet that particular standard(s), create a hyperlink to the assignment as artifact and write about future learning goals. Grading rubrics were designed based on the performance indicators.

Integrating the Internet into the Curriculum

With reference to students' prior knowledge about the Internet, the instructional activities concentrated on:

1. How to evaluate a website using a web evaluation and
2. Conducting internet searches with Directories and Search Engines and refining searches using Boolean Logic (AND, OR and NOT).
3. Planning and presenting a lesson that integrated the Internet.

Topics covered included: Copyright and Internet Use, Plagiarism and the Internet, Equitable Access to Technology, Internet Etiquette (Netiquette), Student privacy, and Accuracy of Internet information. It was anticipated that these activities could support the students to master NETS-T standards 2, 5 and 6.

Integration of Multimedia and Hypermedia into Teaching and Learning

Three areas were covered: (A) Multimedia/hypermedia Software Packages; (B) Multimedia authoring tools; and (C) Web Authoring Tools.

A. **Multimedia/hypermedia Software Packages:** Multimedia is a combination of more than one type of media and media functions such as text, graphics, animations, audio and video to communicate a message. It was expected that teachers could be able to integrate multimedia resources such as instructional software, interactive books, ebooks, reference materials, and collections of developmental resources in their curriculum (Roblyer, 2006). The instructional activities comprised of a presentation on introduction to PK-12 educational software. Students were put into various groups based on their content areas and were asked to evaluate specific instructional software. A software evaluation rubric was provided. Students were also required to install and uninstall the software.

B. **Multimedia authoring tools:** Presentation software like *Microsoft PowerPoint* is widely available and used in education. Using information gathered on Integrating Technology Across the Curriculum from the course textbook, *Integrating Educational Technology into Teaching*(4th ed.) by Roblyer (2006), student were required to use PowerPoint to present topics relevant to their content area. Another program for multimedia presentation was *Windows Movie Maker*. The learning activity required students to create a 2-minute movie that could be used to teach a lesson in their content area. To assist with this project, the preservice teachers were introduced to the use of SnagIt for screen capture, flatbed scanner, digital cameras and digital video cameras.

C. **Web Authoring Tools:** Using *Microsoft Publisher*, students were instructed and guided to create personal webpages, educational websites to be used in their classes, or websites that inform their teaching profession. The students were permitted to sit together in class according to their content areas to facilitate collaboration. It was anticipated these activities students would help them to master NETS-T Standards 1, 2, 3, 5 and 6.

Integrating Productivity Software into Teaching and Learning

The activities under this area were aligned with NETS-T Standard 2, 3, 4 and 5. Different categories of productivity software were explored that included:

A. **Word Processing:** Students were introduced to a variety of ways by which the word processor could be integrated into teaching and student learning in the different content areas. These included activities such as journal-keeping, producing class newspapers, creating professional documents, using WordArt to design posters, using the Word Web Wizard to create a website, creating forms, creative writing, preparing graphs and charts, using the drawing tools to create basic shapes, writing and conducting surveys, quizzes and tests, writing story problems using the Microsoft Equation Editor, etc.

B. **Microsoft Publisher:** The learning activity required students to use Microsoft Publisher to create a school flyer to be used for a field trip, display information such as emergency numbers, permission signatures, etc.

C. **Database:** Using the GradeQuick Software, students were instructed to create end of Semester Grades and Attendance Report.

D. **Excel:** Students were instructed to use data provided to create a spreadsheet and then determine descriptive statistics such as the mean, mode, and median, and draw graphs and charts. Another activity required students to develop a lesson plan that incorporated spreadsheets into the curriculum for math, science, social studies, language arts or other content areas.

The final project required students to submit an Electronic Portfolio demonstrating the attainment of the NETS-T. The Portfolio process involved completing the NETS-T template by reflecting on how projects met the required standards, creating a hyperlink to the projects and discussing future learning goals. Students were also required to burn all projects on a CD and submit the finished product to the instructor.

Data Analysis

A paired t-test was applied to the class survey data to determine whether significant differences occurred in students' perceived technology competencies before and after the technology class and whether their acquired competencies ensured mastery of national technology standards set by ISTE. Data gathered from the focus group discussions, observations, and students portfolios were analyzed qualitatively.

RESULTS

The Cronbach alpha coefficient for the pre- and post-tests were 0.91 and 0.95, respectively. The results of the paired t-test results indicated that the overall post-test mean score ($M=75.2$, $SD=8.69$) was significantly greater than the overall pre-test mean score ($M=54.3$, $SD=8.71$), $t (14) =6.878$, $p<0.001$. The statistically significant results suggested an improvement in students' technological expertise and students' perception of attainment of NETS-T. The standardized effect size index, d, was 0.84, which represents a large value. Figure 1 shows pre- and post-test mean scores on the individual survey items.

Further comparison of the differences in pre- and post-test scores on the individual survey items also showed changes in student perception of their mastery of each standard. For example, a measure of students' perceived attainment of Standard 1 (teachers demonstrate a sound understanding of technology operations and concepts) indicated a change in pre-test and post-test scores from 3.50 to 4.20, respectively. The improvement could be attributed to students fully completing the checklist to learn the basic skills and concepts as a prerequisite to ED410 and an opportunity to focus on more advanced tools during the course.

In response to using the Internet to collect and evaluate information, the mean score changed from 3.5 on the pre-test to 4.5 on the post-test indicating

Figure 1. Pre-test and Post-test mean scores on survey to assess NETS-T

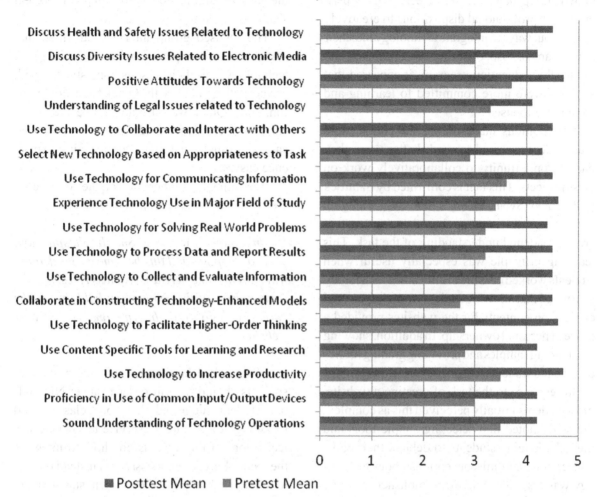

that students acquired simple and efficient strategies for conducting internet searches. Pre- and post test scores on understanding technology issues also improved from 3.3 to 4.1. Again, a noticeable change was observed for students using content specific tools for learning and research; the pre-test mean score was 2.8 and the post-test mean was 4.2. An examination of students' final electronic portfolios confirmed that the preservice teachers had indeed attained the NETS-T standards, especially standards 1, 2, 3, 5, and 6.

Although there was a significant difference in students' perception of attainment of the NETS-T, results from the study noted that students were still lacking in one area even after the course. Majority of the students had problems installing and uninstalling a program. Instructors of educational technology courses must allow preservice teachers the opportunity to practice such simple skills to discourage dependency on Instructional Technology staff.

The study also noted that the students enrolled were more comfortable and confident during class implying that it was better to offer technology courses to students after their completion of all methods courses applicable to their certification was mandated. By their senior year, preservice teachers would have acquired adequate content knowledge, pedagogical skills, technology experiences and professional dispositions to creatively think about ways to integrate technology into their content areas. Also, once they were accepted into the teacher education program, it appeared that students were more committed to learning and were more focused.

Observations made during the course were that students seemed to work better when they had the opportunity to collaboratively work on class projects. This fact is confirmed by Santrock (2008) and Swan, et. al. (2006). Encouraging students to work in groups based on their content areas broadened understanding of the task. This teaching principle was especially useful when students worked on QuickTime movies. The study also noted that allowing students to make personal choices on contents for the websites provided a sense of personal ownership. In addition, showing outstanding samples and providing grading rubrics challenged students to work beyond expectations.

In response to the task of creating a website, most students initially perceived this as complex; the study noted that selecting simple tools and then challenging students to debunk their naive conceptions and misconceptions about technology was essential. Microsoft Publisher provided excellent webpage templates and easy to create navigation buttons. Students were also provided with opportunities to learn from each other by requesting that students show their project for feedback and final grading.

Slavin (2006) describes Word Processor as a computer application for writing compositions that can be easily revised and edited and by far the most common application of technology in K-12 classrooms. It is not surprising that word processor is mostly used by teachers. The researchers noted that students' initial perception of Microsoft Word was just to write term papers. Student marveled at the different ways that Microsoft Word could be integrated into their instruction. One student said that "I have really learned a lot like using the basic programs, like word, using borders and shading and more ways to use word.

The focused group interview affirmed that students were competent and ready to integrate technology into their lessons. One student said, "Excel with graphs and the QuickTime movie was fun. GradeQuick was also a valuable exercise; I can now put students' grades into a computer and easy and quick, just make the teaching experience easy."

According to another student, the course covered a lot of skills and programs. The student stated:

I didn't know how to use SnagIt, Kidspiration, make a webpage and this become easier dealing with parents, like here are my class rules, and for some reasons if they cannot get hold of you, the parents can go to the Internet and look at your website.

When asked how many technology courses students should take in order to meet NETS-T, one student suggested that "one class should be enough to prepare preservice teachers to use technology if the focus is on "how to integrate the technology in our classrooms instead of how to use the technology." One student stated that in addition to technology integration, the preservice teacher should have some basic knowledge in "how to trouble shoot stuff, like on my computer if something goes wrong how I can fix this without running for help."

Majority of the students strongly agreed that trouble shooting should be part of technology courses for teachers. Hardware trouble shooting like connecting the computer to the projector and other accessories was also highly recommended. Even though students' competencies changed by the end of the class, the students were still concerned about how certain factors that were beyond their control could still affect their use of technology in teaching and learning.

According to one student:

Even though we now know how to use technology, factors such as the school district not having enough money for software and hardware, my lack of time to prepare, and scheduling computer lab hours in schools with one computer lab could hinder our efforts to use technology in teaching.

Motivating factors to use technology listed by students included access to hardware and software, incentives, appreciation, motivation, and excitement. Students also suggested that instructors model the use of technology in their courses to encourage them to use technology too. Modeling technology use and integration is a powerful way to get students to use technology in their future classrooms.

CONCLUSION

In summary, preservice teachers should be provided with the opportunities to use technology during their entire course of study to become more proficient. Instructors must be able to use good teaching and learning strategies to motivate students to learn and achieve course objectives. Instructors should also be able to effectively demonstrate how to effectively integrate technology, model appropriate use and provide guidance (Santrock, 2008).

The study confirmed that current students have adequate knowledge and technological experiences and therefore technology courses for preservice teachers should focus on "how to" integrate technology and less on "teaching technology" so that they can acquire considerable knowledge about current technology applications in their content areas (Roblyer, 2006). It is recommended that as part of their training, preservice teachers should enroll in technology courses after completing their methods courses and after their acceptance into the teacher education program. This ensures that students have adequate content knowledge to focus on how technology could be used in their content areas.

Implementing successful technology practices requires instructors who posses the required technology competencies. Further, these instructors need to model appropriate technology integration practices that include planning, designing and experimenting with sound learning environments and experiences supported by technology, and implementing curriculum technology integration plans and strategies to maximize student learning.

REFERENCES

Bielefeldt, T. (2001). Technology in teacher education. *Journal of Computing in Teacher Education, 17*(4), 4–15.

Bitter, G. G., & Legacy, J. M. (2006) Using technology in the classroom (Brief version). Boston, MA: Allyn & Bacon.

Brush, T., Glazewski, K., Rutowski, K., Berg, K., Stromfors, C., & Hernandez-Van Nest, M. (2003). Integrating technology in a field-based teacher training program: The PT3@ASU project. *Educational Technology Research and Development, 51*(1), 1042–1629.

Dralle, A. (2007). What instructional technology skills should new teachers possess? *VSTE Edge, 4*(7). Retrieved April 15, 2009, from http:// www. vste.org/ publications/ edge/ attach/ ve_0407/ edge_v4n7.htm.

Duhaney, D. C. (2000). Teacher Education: Preparing Teachers to Integrate Technology. *International Journal of Instructional Media, 29*(1), 23–29.

Hoffner, H. (2007). *The elementary teacher's digital toolbox.* Upper Saddle River, NJ: Prentice Hall.

ISTE. (2000). *National Education Technology Standards and Performance Indicators for Teachers.* Retrieved March 0, 2009, from http://cnets. iste.org/teachers/pdf/page09.pdf

Keengwe, J., & Anyanwu, L. (2007). Computer Technology-infused Learning Enhancement. *Journal of Science Education and Technology, 16*(5), 387-393.

Keengwe, J., Onchwari, G., & Wachira, P. (2008). The Use of Computer Tools to Support Meaningful Learning. *AACE Journal, 16*(1), 77–92.

National Center for Education Statistics. (2000). *Public school teachers' use of computers and the Internet*. Washington DC: U. S. Department of Education.

NCATE/ITEA/CTTE Program Standards. (2003). *Programs for the preparation of technology education teachers*. Retrieved April 9, 2008, from http:// www.ncate.org/ ProgramStandards/ ITEA/ ITEAStandards.doc

O'Bannon, B. W., & Puckett, K. (2007). *Preparing to use technology. A practical guide to curriculum integration*. Boston, MA: Allyn & Bacon.

Oblinger, D. G., & Oblinger, J. L. (2005). *Educating the Net Generation*. EDUCAUSE. E-book. Retrieved July 25, 2008, from http://www.edu-cause.edu/educatingthenetgen

Oppenheimer, T. (2003). *The flickering mind: The false promise of technology in the classroom and how learning can be saved*. New York, NY: Random House.

Project Tomorrow-NetDay (2006). *Our voices, our future. Student and teacher views on science, technology and education*. National Report on NetDay's 2005 Speak Up Event.

Roblyer, M. D. (2006). *Integrating educational technology into teaching* (4th ed.). Upper Saddle, NJ: Prentice Hall.

Santrock, J. W. (2008). *Educational psychology* (3rd ed.). Boston.MA: McGraw-Hill Learning Solutions.

Semich, G., & Runyon, L. (2002). Infusing technology in the classroom: Positive intervention makes the real difference in student learning. In C. Crawford et al. (Eds.), *Proceedings of Society for Information Technology and Teacher Education International Conference 2002* (pp. 1433-1437). Chesapeake, VA: AACE.

Smith, S. B., & Smith, S. J., & O'Brien, J. (2002). *Technology Innovation through Collaboration in a Teacher Education Program*. Retrieved August 11, 2008, from http:// thedigitalclassroom. com/ download/JCTESmith92604.pdf

Swan, K., Cook, D., Kratcoski, A., Lin, Y., Schenker, J., & Van't Hooft, M. (2006). Ubiquitous computing: Rethinking teaching, learning and technology. In S. Tettegah & Hunter (Eds.), *Educational and technology: Issues and applications, policy and administration,* (pp. 231-252). New York, NY: Elsevier.

U.S. Department of Education. (2006). *Education Technology Fact Sheet*. Retrieved August 29, 2008, from http://www.ed.gov/about/offices/list/os/technology/facts.html.

Weisner, J., & Salkeld, E. (2004). Taking Technology into Schools: A dialogue between a preservice teacher and a university supervisor. *TechTrends, 48*(3), 12–17. doi:10.1007/BF02763350

Wenglisky, H. (2006). Technology and achievement: The bottom line. *Educational Leadership, 63*(4), 29–32.

Whetstone, L., & Carr-Chellman, A. A. (2001). Preparing preservice teachers to use technology: Survey results. *TechTrends, 46*(4), 11–17. doi:10.1007/BF02784820

This work was previously published in International Journal of Information and Communication Technology, Volume 6, Issue 1, edited by Lawrence A. Tomei, pp. 45-54, copyright 2010 by IGI Publishing (an imprint of IGI Global).

Chapter 5

Information and Communication Technology Training among Lecturers in the South–South Zone in Nigeria by the Nigeria Communication Commission

Pereware Aghwotu Tiemo
Delta State University, Nigeria.

O. T. Emiri
Delta State University, Nigeria

Adobi Jessica Tiemo
Delta State University, Nigeria

ABSTRACT

In order to bridge the digital gap and to facilitate the use of ICT in teaching and learning among lecturers and students in Nigeria universities, the Nigeria Communication Commission (NCC) organized a workshop to train lecturers in the use of ICT skill and knowledge. It was expected that 12,000 lecturers from various universities will be trained. It was discovered that the idea was welcomed since most of them find if difficult to integrate ICT in their academic work. As a result of this, the study seek to find out the success achieved among participants and their perception toward the programme.

INTRODUCTION

The Nigeria Communication Commission (NCC) and the Digital Bridge Institute (DBT) Abuja, an arm of the NCC organized and co-sponsored their first zonal workshop on Advance Digital Apprecia-tion for lecturers from universities, polythenics and colleges of education in the south – south zone of Nigeria. The workshop took place between 16 and 20 October 2006 at the Federal Polythenic, Nekede, Owerri, Imo State (Okiy & Tiemo, 2007). Another phase of this excise took place in Delta

DOI: 10.4018/978-1-61350-468-0.ch005

State University, Abraka. One of the center in the South-South zone in Nigeria, between 14 and 18 April, 2008. The NCC, in a bid to ensure the application of ICT in Nigeria higher institutions, organized this workshop for lectures. According to Okiy and Tiemo (2007) the workshop is meant for lectures in higher institution with a view to equipping them with knowledge and skills of ICT which would facilitate the research and teaching in their various respective institutions. Ojeme (2007) quoting the Dean of the Faculty of Art University of Lagos Prof. Ayodeji Olukoju "that ICT had improve research and development in institution of higher learning and other agencies, that this ICT has eased the computerization of results and allowed for networking and accessibility of the internet. ICT has assisted in teleconferencing, reduced traveling and ensured safety and faster dissemination of information. A survey conducted by Olugbile (2006) revealed that many lecturers in Nigerian universities lack computer knowledge and that there is a high level of ICT literacy among the new breed of lecturers than old professor teaching in the nations various institutions. Various reasons such as lack of funds, inadequate ICT facilities, and lack of training programme was responsible for this trend. As a result of this the NNC organized this workshop for Nigeria institution to be given a good rating internally. Under the programme which is sponsored by NCC about 12,000 lecturers in Nigeria institutions will be trained in the next five years to expose them on a new methodologies of courses delivery so as to improve on their quality of products and reposition them for the current challenges of globalization.

Nwankwo (2006) quoting the Chief Executive Officer of DBI, that a report from the Federal Ministry of Education in Nigeria states that there are only 3,451 skilled ICT staff against 8,350 required in the next five years. This he said represented a human resources compliant deficit of 4,899 and if this problem is not properly addressed, could compound the global marginalization of Nigeria in the emerging digital economy.

This research will attempt to find out the success recorded among participant and their perception toward the programme. It also intends to find out whether the programe is meeting up to expectation.

Specific Purpose of the Study

The study seeks to address the following:

1. To find out the participant perception about the programme
2. To determine the level of ICT knowledge and skills before and after the programme.
3. To know the various ICT packages participants were exposed to.
4. To pin point the constraint encountered by participant during the programme.

Research Questions

The following research questions were formulated to guide the study:

1. What is the perception of the participants toward the programme
2. What is the level of ICT knowledge and skills before and after the programme.
3. What are the various ICT packages participants were exposed to during the programme.
4. What are the constraint encountered by the participants in the programme.

METHODOLOGY

Design of the Study

The study is a descriptive survey, this seeks to find out facts concerning existing phenomenon.

Location of the Study

The study was conducted in Delta State University, Abraka, South-South Zone in Nigeria.

Table 1.

S/N	Names of institution	No of expected participant	No. Of participant present
1	Cross River university of Technology, Calabar	10	9
2	Maritime Academy Of Nigeria, Oron	10	9
3	Abia State University, Uturu	10	9
4	School of Health Technology, Abia	10	10
5	Federal College of Education, Obudu	10	10
6	Abia State Poly, Abia	10	9
7	Akwu Ibom State Coll of Agriculture	10	8
	Total	70	64

Source: DBI Training Accreditation List (2008) in Delta State.

Population of the Study

The population of the study consisted of 70 lectures from 10 selected institutions in the South-south Zone in Nigeria. The entire numbers of present participants (64) were used for the study Table 1 shows the name of the institution and numbers of participants.

Instrument

A structured question with 13 items was developed and used as means of collecting data.

Method of Data Analysis

In analyzing the data collected the simple percentage was the main statistical tool used.

DATA ANALYSIS, INTERPRETATION AND DISCUSSION

Table 2 shows the distribution of respondents according to institutions and attendance from the attendance register.

Table 3 shows that 42 (65.6%) of respondents are males while 22(34.4%) are female. The means that majority of respondents are males.

Table 4 shows that 8(12.5%) are first degree holders (B.Sc, B.A., B.Ed.) while 40 (62.5%) of

Table 2. Distribution of participants by name of institution

Name of Institution	Frequency	%
Cross River University of Technology	9	14.1
Maritime Academic of Nigeria	9	14.1
Abia State University, Uturu	9	14.1
School of Health Technology, Abia	10	15.6
Federal College of education Obudu	10	15.6
Abia State Poly, Abia	9	14.1
Akwa Ibom College Of Agriculture	8	12.5
Total	64	100

Table 3. Distribution of participants by gender

Gender	Frequency	%
Male	42	65.6
Female	22	34.5
Total	64	100

Table 4. Distribution participants by higher academic qualification

Highest academic qualification	Frequency	%
B. Sc. /B.Ed/B.A	8	12.5
M.Sc./M.a/ M.Ed	40	62.5
Ph.D	16	25.0
Total	64	100

respondents are second degree holders (M.Sc./ M.A/ M.Ed) and 16(25%) are Ph.D holders. This means majority of respondents are master degree holders.

Table 5 shows that only 1 professor participated ion the programme, senior lecturer had 12 (18.8%), Lecturer I represented by 24(37.5%), Lecturer II represented by 16(25%), Assistant Lecturer represented by 6 (9.4%) and others had 5(7.8%).

SECTION B

Research Question One

What is the perception of participants towards the programme?

The analysed data in table 6 provides answer to this question.

Table 6 reveals that majority of participants 60(93.8%), 58(90.1%), 56(87.5%) strongly agreed that the programme is a welcomed development and necessary for academics in Nigeria. Also, from the table 58(90.1%), 54 (84.4%) strongly disagreed that the programme is not necessary or not compulsory.

Table 5. Distribution of participants by academic status

Academic Status	Frequency	%
Professor	1	1.6
Readers	-	-
Senior lecturer	12	18.8
Lecturer I	24	37.5
Lecturer II	16	25.0
Assistant lecturer	6	9.4
Graduate assistant	-	-
Others	5	7.8
Total	64	100

Research Question Two

What is the used of ICT knowledge and skills before and after the programme.

Data in Table 7 is used to answer this question.

Table 7 reveals that respondents represented by 44(69%) has no knowledge of ICT (were not ICT complaint) before the programmes while 5(8%) and 15(23%) of respondents had little knowledge of ICT's. However, after the programme a good percentage of respondents 50(78%), 4(6%) became ICT literate.

Research Question

What are the various ICT packages participants were exposed to during the programme.

Table 8 and Table 9 were used to answer this question.

From Table 8, it could be seen that Microsoft PowerPoint 64(100%), Microsoft word (64(100%), Microsoft Excel 64 (100%), and internet 64 (100%) are the packages participants were exposed to.

From Table 9, it would be seen that the following ICT facilities were made available for the programme computer 64(100%), 60(94%), internet 50(78%) and Compact Diskette 64(100%).

From Table 10, it could be seen that majority 50(78) are of the opinion that the ICT facilities made available for the programme are good. Also 6(9%) indicate facilities are very good.

From the Table 11, it was revealed that general cleanliness was represented by 60 (94%), good internet access /speed had 39 (61%) also indicate was good quick responds to faults 55 (86%), feeding had 40(63%) indicated good.

Table 12 indicates that for clarity majority 50 (78%) indicated good, expertise on various matters majority 50 (75%) indicated good, language power majority 40(63%) indicate fair, method of presentation/delivery had 40 (63%) indicated fair.

Table 6. Perception of participant

Perception of participants	SA		A		D		SD	
	F	%	F	%	F	%	F	%
The training has made me to understand more of ICT	60	93.8	4	6.2	-	0	-	0
Lecturers should be encourages to participate in the programme	58	90.1	6	9.4	-	0	-	0
It is a redcome development in Nigeria Educational system	56	87.5	8	12.5	-	0	-	0
The training is not necessary because it has been over taken by event	0	-	2	3.1	4	6.2	58	90.1
The training is not compulsory	0	-	0	-	10	15.6	54	84.4

Table 7. ICT knowledge and skills

How would you remark your ICT knowledge and skill proficiency.								
ICT status	Poor		Fair		Good		Very good	
	F	%	F	%	F	%	F	%
Before the programme	44	69	15	23	5	8	0	0
After the programme	0	0	10	16	50	78	4	6

Table 8. ICT packages /resources

ICT Package /Resources	Yes	%	No	%
Microsoft word	64	100	-	-
Microsoft Excel	64	100	-	-
Microsoft PowerPoint	64	100	-	-
Word pad	-	-	64	100
Front page	-	-	64	100
Internet	60	94	4	6
Web design			64	100
Database management	-	-	64	100
Programming	-	-	64	100
CorelDraw	-	-	64	100

SECTION D: CONSTRAINTS ENCOUNTERED IN PROGRAMME

What are the constraints encountered by participants?

Table 13 describes that the majority of participants encountered problem of accommodation 64 (100%) and insufficient time 60 (94%).

DISCUSSION OF FINDINGS

Research Question One

What is the perception of participants towards the programme

Most responds (Table 3) are of the opinion that the ADAPT programme for lecturers in Nigerian

Table 9. ICT facilities made available for the training

Which of the following ICT facilities were made available for your use during the programme.				
ICT Facilities	**Yes**	**%**	**No**	**%**
Computer	64	100	-	-
Printers	-	-	-	-
Diskette/flashes drive	-	-	-	-
Scanner	-	-	64	100
Projector and screen	60	94	4	6
Internet	50	78	14	22
Speakers	-	-	-	-
Compact Diskette	64	100	-	-

Table 10. Assessment of ICT facilities

How would you rate the facilities that were made available for the training?		
Assessment of ICT facilities	**Frequency**	**%**
Poor	-	-
Fair	8	13
Good	50	78
Very good	6	9

universities is a welcomed development and should be encouraged to go round all lectures in Nigeria universities. This is inline with the statement by Olugbile (2006) that many lecturers in Nigerian lack computer knowledge and that there is a high level of ICT literacy among the new breed of lecturers than old professors teaching in the nations various tertiary institution.

Nwankwo (2006) also quoting Chief Executive Officer of DBI that a report from the federal ministry of education in Nigeria stated that only 3,451 skilled ICT staff against 8, 350 required in the next five years.

However, with the impact this programme is making, it will bring to an end the fear or the future of Nigerian educational system in this information age.

Research Question Two

What is the level of ICT knowledge and skills before and after the programme.

From the findings (Table 7) it could be seen that majority of respondents became ICT literate after the ADAPT training. This finding confirms the assertion by Nwankwo (2006) that there are only 3451 skilled ICT staff against 8,350 required in the next five years. This he said represents a human resources complaint deficit of 4,899. the ADAPT training if properly encouraged will ameliorate the menace of ICT in tertiary institutions.

Research Question Three

What are the various ICT packages participants were exposed to during the programme.

From Table 8 and 9, it could be seen that the fundamental ICT programeme were exposed to participants. These include Microsoft word,

Table 11. Assessment of training environment

Training environment	Poor		Fair		Good		Very good	
	F	%	F	%	F	%	F	%
General cleanliness	-	-	4	6	60	94	-	-
Internet access/spend	-	-	25	39	39	61	-	-
Computer workstation	-	-	-	-	60	94	4	6
Noisy environment	-	-						
Quick respond to fault and abnormalities	-	-	4	6	5	8	55	86
Adequate training support materials	-	-	5	8	54	31	5	8
Feeding (quality, quantity and services)	-	-	20	31	40	63	4	6

Table 12.

How would you rank the instructor/lecturer?								
Training environment	Poor		Fair		Good		Very good	
	F	%	F	%	F	%	F	%
Clarity	-	-	14	22	50	78	-	-
Expertise in various matters	5	8	5	8	50	78	4	6
Language power	20	31	40	63	4	6	-	-
Method of presentation/ delivery	-	-	40	63	20	31	4	6

Table 13. Ranking of constraint

Perception of participants	SA		A		D		SD	
	F	%	F	%	F	%	F	%
Inadequate electricity	-	-	-	-	60	94	4	6
Accommodation	64	100	-	-	-	-	-	-
Inadequate resources personnel	-	-	-	-	60	94	4	6
Insufficient time	60	94	4	6	-	-	-	-
Inadequate ICT equipment	-	-	-	-	55	89	9	14
Unskilled instructor								
Slow response to fault	-	-	-	-	60	94	4	6
Inadequate instructional materials	-	-	6	8	58	91	-	-

Microsoft excel, micro power, PowerPoint, and internet use. And also all the facilities needed for effective training were made available. They include computer projector and screen and Compact Disk.

Research Question Four

What are the constraints encountered by participants?

From Table 13, the following constraints were encountered during the programme. They include accommodation and insufficient time.

SUMMARY OF FINDINGS

- The various institutions invited for the programme were duly represented (Table 1
- Majority of respondents are males (Table 2
- Majority of participants are master degree holders (Table 3)
- Lecturer I and Lecturer II had the highest number of participants (Table 4)
- Participant indicated that the programme is timely, important and be recommend for all lectures (Table 6)
- Majority participant were ICT illiterates before the programme (Table 7)
- Microsoft word, Microsoft PowerPoint, Microsoft excel and internet usage are the packages participant were expose to. (Table 8)
- Computer, projector screen, internet, and Compact Disk were the facilities made available for programme.
- The ICT facilities made available for programme were seen by participants as good. (Table 10)
- The environment of training was seen as generally good (Table 11)
- Participants assessment of lecturer/instructor revealed that for teaching was good, expertise on subject was also good, language power was fair, method of presentation was fair (Table 12).
- Lack of accommodation and adequate time were the problems encountered by respondents. (Table 13)

RECOMMENDATION

At the end of the programme laptop should be subsidize to lecturers in order to follow up their ICT skills and knowledge. In Higher institution in Nigeria their should be standard ICT centers. ICT should be integrated into the teaching and learning of higher institution and exchange programme of human resource among foreign and local institution should be welcomed.

REFERENCES

Nwankwo, B. (2006, September). NCC, DBI train 12,000 lecturers in ICT. *The Guardian, 27,* 35.

Ojeme, S. (2007, July 24). Don Calls for improved ICT development. *Punch Newspaper* (p. 20).

Okiy, R. B., & Tiemo, P. A. (2007). The Nigeria communication Commission and the Digital Bridge Institute First South-South Zonal Advance Digital Appreciation workshop for tertiary institution. *Library Hi. Tech New, 24*(3).

Olugbile, S. (2006, August 1). Old dons stum computer literacy. *Punch News* (p. 41).

This work was previously published in International Journal of Information and Communication Technology, Volume 6, Issue 1, edited by Lawrence A. Tomei, pp. 55-66, copyright 2010 by IGI Publishing (an imprint of IGI Global).

APPENDIX

Questionnaire

Dear Respondents, This is a questionnaire aimed at finding out the success among participant and their perception on Advance Digital Appreciation Programme for Lecturers in Higher Institutions in Nigeria. Your honest response to the items in this questionnaire will be highly appreciated. All data /information provided shall be used strictly for research purpose.

    Thanks

    Yours faithfully,

    Tiemo P. A. & Emiri O.T.

Section A: Bio Data

INSTRUCTION: Please thick were applicable and provided answer were necessary.

1.   Name of Institution _____
2.   Department _____
3.   Gender: Male () Female ()
4.   Highest Academic Qualification: HND () B.SC/B.Ed/ B.A () M.Sc/M.A. M. Ed. () Ph.D. ()
5.   Academic Status: Professor () Readers () Senior lecturer () Lecturer I () lecturer II () assistant lecturer () Graduate assistant () others please specify

Section B: Perception of Participant

Table 14.

S/N	Rank your perception toward the training programme. ITEM	SA	A	D	SD
1	The training has made me to understand more of ICT				
2	Lecturers should be encourage to participate in the programme				
3	It is a welcomes development in the national education.				
4	The training is not necessary because it has been over taken by event.				
5	The training is not compulsory				

Table 15.

S/N	How would you rank the instructor /lecturer? ITEM	Poor	Fair	Good	V.Good
1	Method of delivery /presentation				
2	Clarity				
3	Expertise on the various Subject matters				

Table 16.

S/N	How would you rank your ICT knowledge and skill proficiency?				
	ITEM	Poor	Fair	Good	V.Good
1	Before the programme				
2	After the programme				

ICT Packages/Resources

Table 17.

S/N	Which of the following ICT packages were you exposed to during the training?	YES	NO
	ITEMS		
1	Microsoft word		
2	Microsoft excel		
3	Microsoft PowerPoint		
4	Word pad		
5	Note pad		
6	Front page		
7	Internet		
8	Web design		
9	Database management		
10	Programming		
11	CorelDraw		

Table 18.

S/N	Which of the following ICT facilities were made available for your use during the programme?	YES	NO
	ITEMS		
1	Computer		
2	Printers		
3	Diskette /flash drive		
4	Scanner		
5	Projector and screen		
6	Internet		
7	Speakers		

Table 19.

How would you rate the facilities that were made available for the training.
Poor (), Fair (), Good (), Very Good ()

Table 20.

S/N	Rate the training environment in terms of the following.				
	ITEM	**Poor**	**Fair**	**Good**	**V.Good**
1	Gernal cleanliness				
2	Internet access/speed				
3	Computer workstation				
4	Noisy environment				
5	Quick respond to fault and abnormalities				
6	Adequate training support materials				
7	Feeding (quality, quantity and service)				

Table 21.

S/N	Rank the following problems you encountered during the progremme.				
	ITEM	**SA**	**A**	**D**	**SD**
1	Inadequate electricity				
2	Accommodation				
3	Inadequate resources personnel				
4	Insufficient time				
5	Inadequate ICT equipment				
6	Unskilled instructor				
7	Slow response to fault				
8	Inadequate instructional materials				

Chapter 6
Perceived Importance and Resource Constraints of Graduate Information Systems Courses in Turkey

M. Erdal Balaban
University Istanbul, Turkey

Melih Kirlidog
University Istanbul, Turkey

Zerrin Ayvaz-Reis
University Istanbul, Turkey

ABSTRACT

Education is an expensive process and the quality of an education program is largely affected by resources devoted to it. Availability of qualified instructors and physical amenities such as labs are the most important resources that determine the educational quality. Based on the graduate Information Systems curriculum recommendation of Association for Computing Machinery (ACM) and Association for Information Systems (AIS) this article investigates the perceived importance of each course taught in graduate Information Systems programs in Turkey. The perceived importance is also compared with the availability of instructor and technological resources for each course to get an insight into educational resources and constraints.

INTRODUCTION

Broadly speaking, Information Systems (IS) discipline investigates the effectiveness and efficiency of computers in an organizational setting where the level of investigation can be in micro level such as a commercial company or in macro level such as national ICT (Information and Communication Technologies) strategies. Since the discipline is at the cross-section of several technical and social disciplines, it borrows several theories and ideas from a diverse set of reference disciplines such as computer science and sociology. On the positive side, this diverse nature results in relatively

DOI: 10.4018/978-1-61350-468-0.ch006

easier obtainment of instructors for IS programs because some courses can be taught by instructors coming from other disciplines. However, the diversity has also some negative aspects which lead some researchers to regard the discipline as eclectic, lacking a theoretical base at the core, impractical, and merely following the advances in the industry (Benbasat & Weber, 1996; Benbasat & Zmud, 1999; Ciborra, 1998, Davenport, 1997). These critics to the nature of the IS discipline are opposed by a growing number of researchers who assert that IS is in the process of establishing itself as a mature discipline with theoretical and methodological soundness (Cheon et al., 1991; Cushing, 1990; Orlikowski & Baroudi, 1991) and with reputable journals and established conferences.

The requirement for a distinct IS education, however, is not debated anywhere. Today's penetration level of computers to all aspects of life and the relevant expectancy of efficiency and effectiveness evades such a debate.

Like the other computer-related education programs IS undergraduate and graduate programs are quite popular in Turkey. Unlike some industrialized countries where enrollment rates suffered after the dotcom crash there has been no decline of interest in computer-related programs in the country. However, the education system in Turkey has to struggle with severe constraints some of which has the potential to plague the long-term benefits supposed to be incurred by education. This article seeks to investigate the nature and severity of these constraints in IS graduate programs in Turkey. Since the severity of an educational constraint can only be meaningful with the relative importance attributed to the perceived importance of the relevant course, the perceived importance of each course are also investigated.

The remainder of this paper is organized as follows: The following section describes graduate IS programs in Turkey and it is followed by the theoretical framework section where resource-based

and outcome-based accreditation approaches in education are explained. The resource-based approach which is commonly used today is the essence of this paper where resource constraints are investigated. The next two sections elaborate the research methodology employed and data collection. Data are analyzed and results are discussed in the subsequent section which is followed by conclusion and future work.

IS GRADUATE PROGRAMS IN TURKEY

As of September 2008 there are 94 public and 36 private universities in Turkey. The private universities are run by foundations that have been established solely for educational purposes. Currently, there are 12 undergraduate and 13 graduate IS programs in the country. The 13 graduate programs are offered by four public and four private universities. Seven of the 13 programs are offered by the public universities. All students who want to have a postgraduate study have to sit an exam called ALES that is conducted all over the country twice a year. Three of the graduate IS programs in Turkey (all from the public universities) require some small tuition fees, but these programs usually require high ALES grades. Although the grade requirement of the remaining 10 programs is usually lower, they cost the students in excess of USD 10,000 for a two-year study and some institutions demand about twice that figure. This is quite high in Turkish standards and can be mainly be afforded by the students who are working in diverse areas and aiming an IS-related career.

There is a continuing debate about the education language in the country. In six of the 13 IS graduate programs the medium of instruction is English and in one of them German is used as the instruction language. The remaining six programs are either totally in Turkish or in Turkish-English mixed mode. Some prestigious universities have been using English as the medium of instruction since decades and they are followed by some new private and public universities. Although the opponents argue that using a foreign language in lectures is inappropriate for students and instructors whose native language is Turkish and foreign language should be only taught in foreign language lectures, there is a strong student demand for English based instruction. Teaching resources seem to be playing an important role for the instruction language. The universities that have adequate instructor and other resources for English-based instruction tend to teach in English.

Although the contents of the IS graduate programs in Turkey are rather close to each other, the program names are quite varied: Management Information Systems (4 programs), Management Information Systems and Engineering (1 program), Business Information Systems (1 program), Information Technologies (1 program), Organization Informatics (1 program), Communication Sciences-Informatics (1 program), Information Systems (1 program), Information Technology (1 program), Information Technologies in Management (1 program), and Informatics Online (1 program, e-Learning). This variety in program names reflects the situation in other parts of the world. For example, Gambill et al. (1989) made a survey study where the respondents were asked to provide the "exact name of the major" and ten different names were provided by the 69 responding institutions in the US. After statistically analyzing the courses offered by those programs the authors found that there were no major differences among them. They conclude that the reason for the difference in program names was totally independent of curriculum issues and it was partly affected by marketing concerns. The authors quote an anecdote of changing the program name from MIS to CIS in order to attract students who want to study "computers".

THEORETICAL FRAMEWORK

The quality of an education system is usually proportional to the resources devoted to it. A resource-rich teaching environment enables students to grasp concepts and relationships between concepts from several different points and encourage them to be active learners. The instructor evaluates the interests and capabilities of individual students and directs them to actively use relevant resources in the learning process. The flexibility that is inherent in this environment not only brings effectuality in learning, but also enables the efficient use of resources. Thus, resource-based learning has positive a connotation in the literature and usually regarded as an objective to be achieved (Fry et al., 2007; Hill & Hanafin, 2001).

Although resource-based learning and teaching is still popular, in the last few years a "bottom-line" approach to teaching is becoming prevalent. Unlike the resource-based learning where inputs or resources are emphasized, this new approach evaluates the merit of an education system according to the outputs or results. ABET's (Accreditation Board for Engineering and Technology) accreditation process is an example for this transformation. Until the 1990s ABET's accreditation process used to be input-based. In 1996, the organization shifted its focus in the accreditation process from input-based to output based where output meant to be what has actually been learned by students. In other words, instead of the resources devoted to the education program, educational "bottom-lines" which constituted outputs became the basis for the accreditation process. Goel (2006) reports that ABET is not alone in this paradigm shift and accreditation agencies in the UK, Australia, Japan, and Singapore have also transformed their accreditation process from the traditional resource-based approach to outcome-based approach. However, it must also be kept in mind that although this paradigm shift is an important step for fostering the effectiveness of education, ABET-accredited IS programs currently constitute only a tiny fraction of IS programs all over the world. Further, an important proportion of the IS programs are still shaped by the availability of resources such as instructors and physical amenities. This is particularly true for developing countries where there are large-scale structural problems such as comparatively lower level computerization, funding difficulties, and institutional weaknesses. Hence, availability of resources will determine education for the majority of the world in the foreseeable future. This is true for not only the general formation of education, but also its evaluation and accreditation. For example, the accreditation process in India by Indian institutions continues to be resource-based (*ibid*).

IS GRADUATE CURRICULUM RECOMMENDATION: MSIS 2000

Curriculum is the plan of education in a specific field. It determines the contents and the length of each component of an education program. Curriculum proposals have been developed for several disciplines. The efforts for developing IS curriculum began in the USA with the establishment of ACM (Association for Computing Machinery) Curriculum Committee on Computer Education for Management in 1970. The committee members issued a series of reports which paved the way to the development of the graduate IS curriculum model (Ashenhurst, 1972). The curriculum acknowledged the different educational requirements for technically trained systems designers and managerially oriented information analysts. The reports were complemented by the undergraduate curriculum model in IS the next year (Couger, 1973). Building on these two reports, in 1982 a committee of the ACM has developed an IS curriculum model for both undergraduate and graduate degrees (Nunamaker et al., 1982). Along with other computing disciplines' curriculum

recommendations, ACM, AIS (Association for Information Systems), and AITP (Association of Information Technology Professionals) have jointly developed the "IS'97 - Model Curriculum and Guidelines for Undergraduate Degree Programs in Information Systems" (Davis et al., 1997). These organizations have also issued the "IS 2002 Curriculum Guidelines for Undergraduate Degree Programs in Information Systems" (Gorgone et al., 2002) by further developing the 1997 report which had already become the basis for a guideline of the undergraduate IS programs in the Western world.

Besides these undergraduate curriculum reports, ACM and AIS jointly issued the "MSIS 2000 - Model Curriculum and Guidelines for Graduate Degree Programs in Information Systems" (Gorgone *et al.*, 2000). The report is mainly based on the typical IS degree structure in the Northern American universities and hence has no claim to be universally applicable. However, being aware of the conditions and constraints of different countries, the authors of the report maintain that the recommendations in the report can be a useful starting point for curriculum developers outside the US and Canada. The model incorporates four building blocks, namely *Foundations, Core, Integration,* and *Career Tracks* (Figure 1). At the *Foundations* level the model introduces the technical and business prerequisites of the IS skills to the students coming from diverse technical and non-technical backgrounds. *Core* courses incorporate the essential knowledge that an IS student should possess such as System Analysis and Design or Project Management. The *Integration* level aims to donate the students with a good comprehension of different technologies available and integrate these technologies with the material presented in the previous two levels. And finally, at the *Career Tracks* level the students are encouraged to deepen their knowledge in specific areas of the IS that they are particularly interested. The model is flexible not only in content, but also for the length of the study. The students with IS background should complete the program in one year if they study full-time. Other students should expect one additional year for graduation. The curriculum developers recommend borrowing the "sliding window" concept of some MBA programs. According to this concept, the first year of an MBA is devoted to learning the common business core that an undergraduate student would acquire in a business program. The second year builds on the first. In some business schools, a student with a previous business degree can skip over the first year and complete the MBA in one year. The sliding window concept that allows sliding from a total of 30 to 60 units (10 to 20 courses) gives the students flexibility to complete the program either with the essential IS requirements if they have a non-IS educational background, or further specializing in a career track if they have an undergraduate IS degree. A combination of these two can also be possible. The 30 units for well-prepared students can take 15 units of core courses, 3 units of integration, and 12 units in a career track. The 60 units for students without preparation can be as follows:

- 12 units of IS foundations
- 9 units of business foundations
- 15 units of core courses
- 3 units of integration
- 12 units of career track
- 9 units of electives or additional requirements

An important aspect of the MSIS 2000 is the emphasis on the requirement of the practical experience of the faculty members. Grounded on the fact that IS is a practice-oriented discipline, the MSIS 2000 emphasizes both the concept and the practice of IS, and it recommends that the "faculty should have both academic training and practical experience". Further, it recommends the appointment of adjunct faculty from the industry to cover specialized topics, particularly for the *Career Tracks* level. The 2002 report for the undergraduate IS curriculum also highlights the need for both academic training and practical experience in the faculty members.

Figure 1. The complete MSIS 2000 curriculum

IS Foundations	Business Foundations	IS Core		Career Electives
Fundamentals of IS	Financial Accounting	Data Management	Integration	Tracks (representative) • Consulting • Decision Making • Electronic Commerce • Enterprise Resource Planning • Globalization • Human Factors • Knowledge Management • Managing the IS Function • Project Management • Systems Analysis and Design • Technology Management • Telecommunications
IT Hardware and Software	Marketing (Customer Focus)	Analysis, Modeling and Design Data Communications and Networking		
Programming, Data and Object Structures	Organizational Behavior	Project and Change Management IT Policy and Strategy		
Pre-/Corequisite		Required		Elective
9-12 units	9 units	15 units	3 units	12 units

RESEARCH METHODOLOGY

Two methods were employed in this study. Firstly, course contents of the IS graduate programs were collected from the university web sites and a content analysis was performed on them. Holsti (1969) defines content analysis as "any technique for making inferences by objectively and systematically identifying specified characteristics of messages." Content analysis is a commonly employed qualitative research method that involves investigating texts for semantic tasks such as grouping or prioritizing items they contain. Several authors have either performed content analyses for several curricula or analyzed the process of conducting content analysis for the curricula (Goodson, 1988; Young, 1998; Reichgelt et al., 2002). Content analysis for curricula is typically conducted by examining the course contents in the syllabi (Ezer, 2005). This approach was employed in this research where each course taught in IS graduate programs in Turkish universities was grouped according to the classification in MSIS 2000. As a second step a quantitative analysis was performed for the answers collected by a survey instrument that was developed as an output of the first step.

In the first phase it was found that although most of the 13 programs showed some resemblance to the MSIS 2000, only two programs (from the same university) conformed to it at a significant degree. A personal communication with a faculty member who has been involved in developing those two programs revealed that the program developers spent deliberate efforts to comply with the MSIS 2000. That institution did not have much problem in its efforts to comply with the MSIS 2000, because it is an established university with abundant teaching resources in terms of instructors and physical amenities. The course names and contents in the other eleven programs had important deviations not only from the MSIS 2000 recommendations, but also from each other. An important reason for that diversity is the availability of teaching resources in designing the curriculum.

As a result of content analysis some courses which were deemed to be too specific (such as Computer Vision Techniques) were disregarded and a total of forty-four courses were identified to be relevant for an IS program. In cases where course names were synonymous but course contents were almost the same the most common course name was used. Additionally, four courses, namely Open Source Systems, Digital Divide, ICT for Development, and Community Informatics were identified which were regarded to be suitable for the conditions of Turkey. The list contained not only the course name, but also the course contents which were prepared according to the syllabi given in the web sites. These forty-eight courses were then located in the relevant group of the MSIS 2000. The structure of the first three groups, namely "IS Foundations", "Business Foundations", and "IS Core" were mainly kept intact with the exception of "Introduction to Management" which was inserted to "Business Foundations". That was regarded as necessary for students coming from disciplines such as engineering and having little or no exposure to business-related courses. The courses which could not be located in the first three groups were placed in the "Career Electives" group. In the placement process both course contents and course names in the program web sites were taken into consideration, replacing the course names proposed in the MSIS 2000. For example, "Fundamentals of IS" was replaced by "Introduction to MIS" which is the preferred course name in Turkish programs having mainly the same content.

DATA COLLECTION METHOD FOR THE SURVEY INSTRUMENT

Since the present research is about IS teaching in Turkey, data were collected from experts who are directly involved in the teaching process. A survey instrument which is based on the above-mentioned list was prepared to investigate the perceived importance of each course to be included in an ideal graduate IS program and available resources for it to be taught. In order to be clear about the courses the survey instrument contained not only the course names but also course contents. The instrument contained three questions for each course with Likert scale (1: strongly disagree, 5: strongly agree):

Q1: The course must be contained in the IS graduate program.

Q2: There are instructors available for the course to be taught.

Q3: There are physical amenities (such as software and labs) available for the course to be taught.

The survey instrument was prepared in the beginning of 2008 and was sent to thirty-five faculty members who are either program directors or actively teach in one or more of the thirteen graduate IS programs in Turkey. The carefully chosen potential respondents are seasoned faculty members who can be regarded as a focus group with abundant expertise in IS teaching in Turkey. However, this does not mean that IS is the main research or teaching area of all potential respondents. Contrary to some other computer-related disciplines such as Computer Engineering, there are very few independent Information Systems departments in Turkish universities and this is reflected in the academic community whose main interest is IS. Since there are quite few IS academics, some of the IS courses are taught by instructors coming from other disciplines. The background of the instructors was not taken into consideration when choosing the potential respondents.

Besides sending the survey instrument the potential respondents were also contacted personally or through telephone about the purpose of the study. Approximately one month after the sending process the potential respondents who have not returned the questionnaire were contacted again. As a result, thirty-one useable responses were received which makes 89% response rate.

DATA ANALYSIS AND DISCUSSION OF RESULTS

In order to calculate the relative intensity for perceived importance and resource constraints of each course (presented in Table 1) each number in the scale (1-5) was first multiplied by frequency for the number and then the result was divided by total number of respondents for that course. This weighted average approach prevented the bias that could result from missing values when calculating the average.

Table 2 presents the paired sample t-tests of the weighted averages of Question 1 and 2. The difference between these two groups is statistically significant whereas the difference between Question 1 and 3 is not.

The differences indicate that overall instructor resources in the country are in short supply compared to the perceived importance of courses in general. On the other hand, other types of resource constraints do not constitute important restrictions. On the contrary, these resources surpass the perceived importance of the courses. This can be expected because, as stated above, most of the investigated programs charge high tuition fees and program directors have abundant funds to be spent for the needs of these programs. However, these funds have little effect on providing the much needed instructor resources which is a long term issue. It must also be stated like other computer-related graduate programs, IS graduate programs are among the few lucky ones in the country which attract plenty of funds from the students. Many other programs which are not popular as IS graduate programs have to depend on the resources supplied by the Government which is much lower and it can be expected that

Table 1. Perceived importance and resources availability for each course

Group	Course Name	Q1:Course must be contained in the program				Q2: Instructors available		Q3: Phys. Resources available	
		We. Av.	S. De.	Mode	Med-ian	We. Av.	S. De.	We. Av.	S. De.
IS Fo.	Introduction to MIS	4.52	1.03	5	5	4.53	1.07	4.63	0.93
IS Fo.	ICT Hardware & Software	3.58	1.52	5	4	4.17	0.93	4.20	0.85
IS Fo.	Programming, Data, and Object Structures	3.67	1.32	4	4	3.86	1.41	3.97	1.16
Bus. Fo.	Financial Accounting	2.80	1.06	2	3	3.00	1.36	3.63	1.35
Bus. Fo.	Introduction to Marketing	2.87	1.28	2	3	3.33	1.42	3.63	1.30
Bus. Fo.	Organizational Behavior	3.07	1.08	3	3	3.13	1.25	3.77	1.19
Bus. Fo.	Introduction to Management	3.81	1.14	4	4	3.63	1.13	4.23	1.07
IS Core	Database Systems	4.48	0.85	5	5	4.50	0.82	4.62	0.73
IS Core	System Analysis & Design	4.73	0.64	5	5	4.47	0.90	4.33	0.96
IS Core	Data Communications & Networking	3.80	1.40	5	4	3.67	1.37	3.93	0.98
IS Core	Project Management	4.52	0.81	5	5	4.57	0.77	4.37	1.00
IS Core	IS Policy and Strategy	4.20	0.89	5	4	3.40	1.28	3.80	1.24
Car. El.	Decision Support Systems	4.48	0.68	5	5	4.33	0.88	4.27	0.94
Car. El.	E-Business	4.48	0.72	5	5	4.20	0.81	3.83	1.05
Car. El.	ERP Systems	4.23	0.96	5	4	3.90	1.09	3.90	1.12
Car. El.	Human-Computer Interaction	3.61	1.12	4	4	3.53	1.04	3.70	0.95
Car. El.	Globalization	2.71	0.74	3	3	2.97	0.93	3.40	1.07
Car. El.	Human Resources Management	2.52	0.93	2	2	2.87	1.14	3.30	1.26
Car. El.	Knowledge Management	4.32	0.87	5	5	4.03	1.00	4.03	1.03
Car. El.	Strategic Planning	3.58	0.81	3	4	3.53	1.01	4.03	1.07
Car. El.	Data Warehouses and Data Mining	4.65	0.71	5	5	4.20	1.00	4.03	1.13
Car. El.	ICT Governance & Regulatory Aspects	3.00	0.97	3	3	3.10	1.16	3.40	1.13
Car. El.	Analysis of Business Processes	3.77	1.09	4	4	3.47	1.01	3.70	0.95
Car. El.	Operations Management	3.58	0.92	4	4	3.70	1.02	3.93	1.05
Car. El.	Internet Applications Development	3.58	1.31	4	4	3.73	1.08	4.37	0.76
Car. El.	Emergency Information Systems	3.45	0.81	3	3	2.90	1.09	3.27	1.17
Car. El.	Organizational Impacts of ICT	3.90	0.98	5	4	3.43	1.07	3.77	1.07
Car. El.	Statistical Data Analysis	3.87	0.81	4	4	4.13	1.07	4.17	1.09
Car. El.	Finance Mathematics	2.42	1.18	2	2	3.13	1.43	3.40	1.50
Car. El.	Business Process Redesign	3.58	0.81	4	4	3.17	0.99	3.57	0.94
Car. El.	Entrepreneurship, Creativity & Innovation	3.19	1.05	3	3	2.87	1.01	3.43	1.33
Car. El.	Principles of Operating Systems	3.13	1.20	4	3	3.47	1.36	3.63	1.43
Car. El.	Research Methods in IS	4.35	0.84	5	5	3.93	1.05	4.00	0.91
Car. El.	Multimedia Information Systems	3.65	1.08	4	4	3.40	1.16	3.60	1.16
Car. El.	Information Theory	3.55	1.21	4	4	3.67	1.06	3.73	0.91
Car. El.	Computer Ethics & Law	4.16	0.93	5	4	3.40	1.19	4.13	1.07

continued on following page

Table 1. Continued

Group	Course Name	Q1:Course must be contained in the program				Q2: Instructors available		Q3: Phys. Resources available	
		We. Av.	S. De.	Mode	Med-ian	We. Av.	S. De.	We. Av.	S. De.
Car. El.	IS Security & Cryptography	4.26	0.82	5	4	3.53	1.22	3.50	1.07
Car. El.	Software Quality Management	3.84	1.04	4	4	3.30	1.32	3.77	1.14
Car. El.	Supply Chain Management	3.84	1.13	5	4	3.67	1.21	3.70	1.09
Car. El.	Customer Relationship Management	4.03	0.91	5	4	3.80	1.21	3.67	1.12
Car. El.	IT Auditing	3.71	1.16	5	4	2.87	1.55	3.57	1.38
Car. El.	Total Quality Management	3.23	1.20	3	3	3.53	1.25	3.60	1.22
Car. El.	E-government	3.58	1.12	4	4	3.33	1.18	3.77	1.14
Car. El.	Geographical Information Systems	3.52	0.93	4	4	3.10	1.16	2.93	1.17
Car. El.	Open Source Systems	3.30	1.06	4	3	3.13	1.36	3.13	1.28
Car. El.	Digital Divide	3.07	1.14	2	3	2.97	1.25	3.43	1.14
Car. El.	ICT for Development	3.71	1.16	5	4	3.50	1.04	3.93	0.92
Car. El.	Community Informatics	3.61	0.99	4	4	3.13	1.25	3.67	1.03

physical resource constraints in those programs are more severe.

Table 3 presents t-test results for comparing the perceived importance and resource availability for each course.

The results reveal that Turkish IS instructors attribute comparatively insignificant importance to the Business Foundations courses as a whole. The relative importance points that the four courses in this group (Financial Accounting, Introduction to Marketing, Organizational Behavior, Introduction to Management) receive (2.80, 2.87, 3.07, 3.81 respectively) is even less than several courses in the elective group. This could possibly be interpreted as an indication of high level of technical emphasis in the IS sphere in Turkey.

The t-test results reveal that there are instructor and physical amenity resources available for most of the courses. In other words, the availability of the resources is usually proportional to the perceived requirements. However, there are exceptions and it would be illuminating to investigate them for gaining an insight to balance of the requirements to the resources. Such an investigation would give valuable clues to the IS educators when planning their future programs.

One of the most critical shortcomings in the instructor resources are IT Policy and Strategy which is important due to the fact that the course belongs to the IS Core group. The MSIS 2000 recommends it to be instructed with the business executive's or senior IS executive's point of view

Table 2. Paired samples t-test results for comparing overall perceived importance with overall resource availability

	df	t	Sig. (2-tailed)
Question 1-2 difference	47	2.546	0.014*
Question 1-3 difference	47	-1.646	0.106

$p<0.05$*

Table 3. Paired samples t-test results for comparing the perceived importance of each course with its resource availability

Group	Course Name	Question 1-2 difference			Question 1-3 difference		
		df	t	Sig. (2-tailed)	df	t	Sig. (2-tailed)
IS Fo.	Introduction to MIS	29	0.00	1.00	29	-0.902	.375
IS Fo.	ICT Hardware & Software	28	-2.768	.010**	29	-2.354	.026*
IS Fo.	Programming, Data, and Object Structures	27	-1.536	.136	28	-1.781	.086
Bus. Fo.	Financial Accounting	27	-.862	.396	28	-2.853	.008**
Bus. Fo.	Introduction to Marketing	28	-2.020	.053	28	-2.560	.016*
Bus. Fo.	Organizational Behavior	28	-.367	.717	28	-2.669	.013*
Bus. Fo.	Introduction to Management	29	.947	.351	29	-1.795	.083
IS Core	Database Systems	29	-.254	.801	28	-.779	.442
IS Core	System Analysis & Design	28	1.758	.090	28	2.368	.025*
IS Core	Data Communications & Networking	28	.722	.477	28	-.812	.424
IS Core	Project Management	29	-239	.813	29	.867	.393
IS Core	IS Policy and Strategy	28	4.296	.000***	28	1.797	.083
Car. El.	Decision Support Systems	29	.891	.380	29	1.293	.206
Car. El.	E-Business	29	2.068	.048*	29	3.551	.001**
Car. El.	ERP Systems	29	1.361	.184	29	1.159	.256
Car. El.	Human-Computer Interaction	29	.403	.690	29	-487	.630
Car. El.	Globalization	29	-1.511	.142	29	-3.194	.003
Car. El.	Human Resources Management	29	-1.433	.163	29	-3.188	.003**
Car. El.	Knowledge Management	29	1.490	.147	29	1.188	.245
Car. El.	Strategic Planning	29	.278	.783	29	-2.149	.040*
Car. El.	Data Warehouses and Data Mining	29	2.904	.007**	29	2.902	.007**
Car. El.	ICT Governance & Regulatory Aspects	29	-.571	.573	29	-2.112	.043*
Car. El.	Analysis of Business Processes	29	.969	.340	29	.115	.909
Car. El.	Operations Management	29	-1.044	.305	29	-1.989	.056
Car. El.	Internet Applications Development	29	-1.044	.305	29	-2.887	.007**
Car. El.	Emergency Information Systems	29	2.898	.007**	29	.796	.433
Car. El.	Organizational Impacts of ICT	29	3.120	.004**	29	.660	.514
Car. El.	Statistical Data Analysis	29	-1.072	.293	29	-1.248	.222
Car. El.	Finance Mathematics	29	-2.137	.041*	29	-3.203	.003**
Car. El.	Business Process Redesign	29	2.091	.045*	29	.158	.876
Car. El.	Entrepreneurship, Creativity & Innovation	29	1.394	.174	29	-.955	.348
Car. El.	Principles of Operating Systems	29	-1.829	.078	29	-2.443	.021*
Car. El.	Research Methods in IS	29	1.838	.076	29	1.439	.161
Car. El.	Multimedia Information Systems	29	1.070	.293	29	.115	.909
Car. El.	Information Theory	29	-.680	.502	29	-.972	.339
Car. El.	Computer Ethics & Law	29	4.323	.000***	29	.177	.861

continued on following page

Table 3. Continued

Group	Course Name	Question 1-2 difference			Question 1-3 difference		
		df	t	Sig. (2-tailed)	df	t	Sig. (2-tailed)
Car. El.	IS Security & Cryptography	29	3.343	.002**	29	3.357	.002**
Car. El.	Software Quality Management	29	3.247	.003**	29	.235	.816
Car. El.	Supply Chain Management	29	.611	.546	29	.379	.708
Car. El.	Customer Relationship Management	29	1.278	.211	29	1.795	.083
Car. El.	IT Auditing	29	4.334	.000***	29	.680	.502
Car. El.	Total Quality Management	29	-1.137	.265	29	-1.242	.224
Car. El.	E-government	29	1.424	.165	29	-1.063	.297
Car. El.	Geographical Information Systems	29	2.562	.016*	29	3.458	.002**
Car. El.	Open Source Systems	28	1.070	.294	28	1.126	.270
Car. El.	Digital Divide	28	.367	.717	28	-1.487	.148
Car. El.	ICT for Development	29	1.030	.312	28	-1.158	.257
Car. El.	Community Informatics	29	2.454	.020*	29	-.372	.712

$p<0.05*$ $p<0.01**$ $p<0.001***$

in a case-based learning environment. Hence, instructors with Management background seem to be the ideal candidates to teach this course. Since this groups constitutes an important source for instructing IS courses in Turkey, some of the members of the groups should be encouraged to concentrate the IT Policy and Strategy course.

Computer Ethics and Law is another course where there is a significant gap between the perceived importance and available instructor resources. This is an elective course and requires specialized knowledge of ethics and law along with basic IS teaching skills. Since the intersection of these two areas does not constitute a wide sphere in the country it is not surprising that the gap is so wide. The required instructor resources for this course can be provided by encouraging people from either area to develop necessary skills for the other area.

Although perceived importance of IS Auditing is low, instructor resources for it is much lower resulting in a substantial gap. This is also not surprising because this course is occasionally taught as an elective only in one program and auditing of computer systems is not commonly practiced

in Turkish firms. Since auditing is an important part of the IS security and it will be much more common in future by the ever-increasing security threats and the sophistication of the IS practices, necessary instructor resources must be developed in the country.

Data Warehouses and Data Mining has the second highest importance attributed in the entire range of courses. Although it is an elective course in MSIS 2000 it is widely taught in the Turkish IS graduate courses as a compulsory one. The high level of importance can be possibly interpreted as the fairly mature level of IS in the country that leads to perceive the computer not simply as a record-keeping tool, but an analysis system that takes the advantage of the knowledge assets in the organization.

The statistically significant inadequacy of instructors compared to the perceived importance in the other courses (E-Business, Emergency Information Systems, Organizational Impacts of ICT, Business Process Redesign, IS Security and Cryptography, Software Quality Management, Geographical Information Systems, and Community Informatics) can be expected, because these courses are not widely taught in programs and there are not many instructors in the country who are experienced in them.

There are five courses where the perceived importance significantly exceeds the available resources (Systems Analysis and Design, E-Business, Data Warehouses and Data Mining, IS Security and Cryptography, and Geographical Information Systems). Requirements for specific software (e.g. CASE software in a lab environment for System Analysis and Design) seems to a prohibiting factor for teaching these courses. Nevertheless, System Analysis and Design and Data Warehouses and Data Mining are widely taught in the IS graduate courses in the country.

CONCLUSION WITH RECOMMENDATIONS AND FUTURE WORK

A graduate program's merit can ideally be gauged by the outcome, i.e., what the students have learned during their study. However, this is not an easy task and it seems that the majority of IS programs will be evaluated according to the contents and resources of teaching in the foreseeable future. The contents of teaching are determined by constraints of instructors, teaching material, and other physical amenities. This is particularly relevant for developing countries where constraints are usually more severe than developed countries.

This research has no claim to develop an IS graduate curriculum suitable for local conditions and necessities in Turkey other than introducing the four courses which were deemed to be suitable for Turkey. There is a growing body of literature for "ICT for development" and examining it thoroughly can be a useful starting point for IS graduate curriculum development that is optimum for local conditions and needs. The importance attributed to each course in this research could also be valuable for several countries which have similar problems and strive to overcome similar constraints. Such an endeavor could be the topic of future research and it could be important for drawing local attention away from a positivist mindset to a utilitarian insight as required by the practice-oriented and vocational nature of IS.

An important limitation in this study is the differentiation of compulsory courses and electives. Such a differentiation would be the basis of a detailed plan for an ideal IS graduate curriculum proposal based on the data collected in Turkey. Such a study would take local necessities, resources, and constraints into consideration and would be an alternative to MSIS 2000.

As stated above, there are only two IS graduate programs (from the same university) that conforms widely to MSIS 2000. Although it is a deliberate choice for these two programs to conform to MSIS 2000, the other programs' deviation from it is not deliberate. Rather, those programs have to offer to their programs the resources they have in hand. This is particularly true for instructor resources. This research shows that such a constraint is evident in both ways: Although some courses are regarded to be relatively unimportant they are taught since years, but some relatively more important courses cannot be taught due to the constraints.

Effective IS graduate programs that take the conditions of individual countries into account can be developed no matter how severe the constraints are. One of the first steps for realizing this is to have an insight to the constraints. This task can be regarded as a base of realistic self-evaluation and is crucially important for education planners. This article reveals that there is a shortage of qualified instructors for IS graduate programs in Turkey and other types of shortages are usually not significant. However, the instructor shortage can be overcome by several precautions one of which is the teaching outside one's institution. This is a widely-practiced routine in Turkey and it can possibly be practiced in other countries which suffer similar problems. Another precaution can be to attract qualified professionals from the industry to teach in IS courses. As noted above, this is recommended by the MSIS 2000 and is grounded by the practice-oriented nature of the discipline.

REFERENCES

Ashenhurst, R. (1972). Curriculum recommendations for graduate professional programs in Information Systems. *Communications of the ACM, 15*(5), 364–398. doi:10.1145/355602.361320

Benbasat, I., & Weber, R. (1996). Research commentary: Rethinking diversity. *Information Systems Research, 7*(4), 389–399. doi:10.1287/isre.7.4.389

Benbasat, I., & Zmud, R. W. (1999). Empirical research in Information Systems: The practice of relevance. *MIS Quarterly, 23*(1), 3–16. doi:10.2307/249403

Cheon, M. J., Choong, Lee, C., & Grover, V. (1991). Research in MIS-points of work and reference: A replication and extension of the Culnan and Swanson study. *Data Base for Advances in Information Systems Journal, 23*(2), 21–29.

Ciborra, C. U. (1998). Crisis and foundations: An inquiry to the nature and limits of models and methods in the Information Systems discipline. *The Journal of Strategic Information Systems, 7*(1), 5–16. doi:10.1016/S0963-8687(98)00020-1

Couger, J. D. (1973). Curriculum recommendations for undergraduate programs in Information Systems. *Communications of the ACM, 16*(12), 727–749. doi:10.1145/362552.362554

Cushing, B. E. (1990). Frameworks, paradigms, and scientific research in Management Information Systems. *The Journal of Information Systems, 4*(2), 38–59.

Davenport, T. (1997, April). Storming the ivory tower. *CIO Magazine* (pp. 38-41).

Davis, G. B., Gorgone, J. T., Couger, J. D., Feinstein, D. L., & Longenecker, H. E. (1997). *IS'97 model curriculum and guidelines for undergraduate degree programs in Information Systems.* Association for Computing Machinery. Retrieved September 1, 2008, from http://www.aisnet.org/Curriculum/Is97.pdf

Ezer, J. F. (2005). *The interplay of institutional forces behind higher ICT education in India.* Unpublished PhD dissertation, London School of Economics.

Fry, H., Pearce, R., & Bright, H. (2007). Reworking resource-based learning - a case study from a masters programme. *Innovations in Education and Teaching International, 44*(1), 79–91. doi:10.1080/14703290601081373

Gambill, S., Clark, J., & Maier, J. L. (1999). CIS vs MIS vs… : The name game. *Journal of Computer Information Systems, 39*(4), 22–25.

Goel, S. (2006). Competency focused engineering education with reference to IT related disciplines: Is the Indian system ready for transformation? *Journal of Information Technology Education,* (5): 27–52.

Goodson, I. F. (1988). *The making of curriculum: Collected essays.* London, UK: The Falmer Press.

Gorgone, J. T., Davis, G. B., Valacich, J. S., Topi, H., Feinstein, D. L., & Longenecker, H. E. (2002). *IS 2002 model curriculum and guidelines for undergraduate degree programs in Information Systems.* Association for Information Systems. Retrieved September 1, 2008, from http://www.acm.org/education/is2002.pdf

Gorgone, J. T., Gray, P., Feinstein, D., Kasper, G. M., Luftman, J. N., & Stohr, E. A. (2000). MSIS 2000 model curriculum and guidelines for graduate degree programs in Information Systems. *Communications of the Association for Information Systems,* (3): 1–51.

Hill, J. R., & Hannafin, M. J. (2001). Teaching and learning in digital environments: The resurgence of resource-based learning. *ETR&D-Educational Technology Research and Development, 49*(3), 37–52. doi:10.1007/BF02504914

Holsti, O. R. (1969). *Content Analysis for the Social Sciences and Humanities*. Reading, MA: Addison Wesley.

Nunamaker, J. F., Couger, J. D., & Davis, G. B. (1982). Information Systems curriculum recommendations for the 80s: Undergraduate and graduate programs. *Communications of the ACM, 25*(11), 781–805. doi:10.1145/358690.358698

Orlikowski, W. J., & Baroudi, J. J. (1991). Studying Information Technology in organizations: Research approaches and assumptions. *Information Systems Research, 2*(1), 1–28. doi:10.1287/isre.2.1.1

Reichgelt, H., Zhang, A., & Price, B. (2002). Designing an Information Technology curriculum: The Georgia Southern University experience. *Journal of Information Technology Education, 1*(4), 213–221.

Young, M. F. D. (1998). *The curriculum of the future*. London, UK: The Falmer Press.

This work was previously published in International Journal of Information and Communication Technology, Volume 6, Issue 1, edited by Lawrence A. Tomei, pp. 67-80, copyright 2010 by IGI Publishing (an imprint of IGI Global).

Chapter 7
Enhancing Students' Loyalty to the Information Systems Major

D. Scott Hunsinger
Appalachian State University, USA

Judy Land
North Carolina Central University, USA

Charlie C. Chen
Appalachian State University, USA

ABSTRACT

Many colleges and universities face the problem of recruiting and retaining students in information systems-related majors. The authors' study proposes a model to identify the primary factors leading to the retention of existing Computer Information Systems (CIS) majors. They identify four factors leading to student intention to remain a CIS major or to refer others to become a CIS major: (1) expectations, (2) perceived service quality, (3) satisfaction, and (4) regret. They discover that certain factors play a significant role in influencing a student's intention to remain a CIS major and/or to encourage others to major in CIS. By determining which factors impact students' intentions to remain a CIS major and to encourage others to major in CIS, we can focus our resources on these areas instead of spending time and money on those services which are not influential.

INTRODUCTION

Cultivating major loyalty is a more cost-effective solution than an expensive marketing effort to boost enrollment. Many business schools in the U.S. have been struggling with the decrease of enrollment in information systems majors due to the offshoring trend and economic downturns. About 76% of the surveyed universities in one study reported a decrease in the number of students enrolled in computer science, computer information systems, and management information systems majors (Pollacia & Lomerson, 2006). Computer science enrollments in the U.S. plummeted by more than 50% from 2000 to 2005 (Scarlatos & Lowest, 2007; Brookshire, 2006). A macro-level analysis shows that growth in IT careers will continue at a rate of higher than 30%

DOI: 10.4018/978-1-61350-468-0.ch007

through 2012 (Horrigan, 2004). Eight out of the eleven fastest-growing occupations through 2012 will require that a prospective employee hold a bachelor's degree in a computer-related field (Pollacia & Lomerson, 2006). The disparity between the demand and supply of IT professionals creates a timely, interesting and relevant topic for research on how to retain CIS majors by creating a positive major experience. Their satisfactory experience with the CIS major and the success of their career placement will inspire prospective students to pursue a CIS major, according to Social Cognitive Career Theory (Lent, Brown, & Hackett, 1994) and Major Choice Goals Model (Akbulut & Looney, 2007). The purpose of this study is to offer a fresh perspective on increasing CIS majors via examining primary factors leading to the retention of existing CIS majors.

LITERATURE REVIEW

A customer-oriented approach to students can increase their satisfaction with college life (DeShields Jr., Kara, & Kaynak, 2005). Students are internal customers, laborers, users, and products of the learning process (Sirvanci, 1996). Students need to pursue their own learning interests and enjoy the learning process. Aside from personal motivations of pursuing a discipline, a student's experience with academic, professional and extracurricular services provided by a major has a strong influence on increasing student satisfaction, thereby decreasing attrition rates. These experiences are particularly important for computer-related majors. The pattern of high attrition in computer-related majors has become a norm; drop rates of these majors are as high as 30% to 40% (Beaubouef & Mason, 2005).

Our study integrates research from several areas to examine the primary factors leading to students' satisfaction with the CIS major. A clear understanding of these factors can help us better understand how to alter today's trend of a con-

tinuous decrease in computer-related majors. The ability of doing so can create a win-win situation for several stakeholders, including IS students, employers, instructors, and academic institutions who have a growing need for IS talents. We identify four factors leading to student intention to remain a CIS major or to refer others to become a CIS major: (1) expectations, (2) perceived service quality, (3) satisfaction, and (4) regret. The following section will examine the causal relationships between these theoretical constructs and learn which relationships are useful at increasing student's loyalty to CIS major.

Expected Service Offerings of IS Major

It is commonly accepted that expectations are a key determinant for consumer satisfaction in the marketing field. Customers have different expectations, which can result in varying satisfactory experiences. Lack of clarity about different types of expectations when investigating customer satisfaction can easily jump to conclusions without understanding the real consumer behavior. One study classifies consumer expectations into three types: (1) predictive expectations, (2) normative expectations, and (3) comparative expectations (Prakash & Lounsbury, 1984). This study adopts the predictive expectation and comparative expectations to help understand how to increase a student's satisfaction with CIS major, thereby leading to major retention and referring intention.

Students of all majors expect quality delivery of academic, professional and extracurricular services from their departments. An effective IS department not only needs to provide common student services similar to other departments, but also needs to offer unique services to IS majors. Student services in demand by all business majors include student clubs, internship opportunities, curriculum design, teaching effectiveness, and job placement services. Unique services attracting CIS majors include (1) offering new technology courses, (2) providing hands-on experiences, and (3) participating in national and regional IS activities and clubs such as the Association for Information Technology Professionals (AITP) student chapter. We classify these services into academic, professional and extracurricular services, and organize them by IS major and all business majors (Table 1).

All majors need to receive academic, professional and extracurricular services such as advising, internship opportunities, and general student clubs. Unlike other majors, the IS major is a dynamic discipline dealing with the rapid advancement of information systems, and creative use of information systems in solving business problems.

The life span of a technical course is much shorter than that of a non-technical course because of rapid changes in the IT industry. Offshoring of IT jobs, the decline in students' analytical abilities and the dot.com failure have resulted in decreased enrollment in computer courses (Pollacia & Lomerson, 2006) and computer-related majors (Lenox et al., 2005). The number of IT professionals seeking employment decreased in 2004 and early 2005 (IT Labor Supply, 2007). CIS departments are under constant pressure to instill faculty with new technical skills and offer new courses to students. Many U.S. universities have experienced a decrease in the number of CIS majors (Lenox et al., 2005). The launch of new courses has the potential to attract new students and reduce student attrition (Sauer & O'Donnell,

2006). This academic service is essential to the sustained success of the IS major.

There is a growing need for IS students to seek professional services, including internships and job placement services, not just from their general advising center, but also from their respective IS department. Several external factors are driving this trend. The drop-out and attrition rates from colleges are increasing each year due to increased financial stress caused by the rising cost of living and student's lack of financial knowledge. About fifty percent of college students have loan debt of at least $10,000 according to a National Center for Education Statistics report (Williams, 2007). The increased pressure of staying in school to complete a four year degree program has driven CIS majors as well as other majors to seriously consider what job opportunities their major can provide. Also, many international firms have been outsourcing IS functions overseas. A Nasscom-McKinsey study (McKinsey Associates, 2005) foresees that the U.S. IT and BPO offshoring market will grow from $12.8 billion to $55 billion. As outsourcing activities continue to proliferate, the nature of IT jobs will be transformed from requiring purely technical skills to an increased focus on integrative skills. The CIS department provides an important role in readying students for such a demanding career. Integrating a hands-on component into the curriculum and providing IS certification training are two distinct professional services that are attractive to IS majors.

Table 1. Student services of IS major and all business majors

	IS Major	IS and Other Business Majors
Academic Service	Offerings of New Technology Courses Access to educational software	Curriculum Design Teaching Effectiveness Advising Service Independent Study
Professional Service	Hands-On Experiences IS Certification Training	Internship Opportunities Placement Services Resume Building
Extracurricular Service	IS-related clubs Specialized trips to IS-related companies	Student Clubs Study Abroad Trips

Especially notable is the smaller percentage of female students and faculty in the CIS major as compared to other majors. Women made up only 26.7% of computer and mathematical positions in 2006 according to the U.S. Bureau of Labor Statistics (Nobel, 2007). CIS majors need to cope with the challenge of having a disproportionate number of male students to female students. Extracurricular services provided by clubs such as AITP can potentially change the typical male-dominated IS profile and lead to higher student satisfaction.

Academic Service

Hypothesis 1a: The higher a student's expectation to receive academic services, the more satisfied the student will be with the CIS major.

Extracurricular Service

Hypothesis 1b: The higher a student's expectation to receive extracurricular services, the more satisfied the student will be with the CIS major.

Professional Service

Hypothesis 1c: The higher a student's expectation to receive professional services, the more satisfied the student will be with the CIS major.

Perceived Service Quality

Perceived service quality refers to customer expectations regarding the level of service that he/she will receive, and how well the delivery of service conforms to customer requirements. Students' satisfaction with their major experience is crucial to the continuing quality improvement (Sirvanci, 1996) of a CIS department. Unlike the measurement of product quality, service measurements are often intangible and performance-oriented.

Therefore, a uniform assessment of service quality based on precise specifications is harder to obtain (Kettinger & Lee, 1994). A student's experience with a major is hard to quantify, and needs to be based on the student's perceived service quality.

The perceived service quality in general is comprised of five dimensions: reliability, responsiveness, assurance, empathy and tangibles (Parasuraman, Zeithaml, & Berry, 1998). We further define these five dimensions for IS students' perceived service quality (Table 2). Teaching effectiveness, as part of perceived service quality, is an assurance element to bolster students' self-efficacy, expectations, and interests in staying in the IS major (Looney and Akbulut, 2007). The exemplary behaviors of instructors can create the effects of "role models" on students, particularly female students, when considering majoring in a science/engineering field (Sonnet, Fox and Adkins, 2007). A high degree of assurance of services offered by faculty and staff to students can lead to increased perceived service quality. Empathy refers to the individualized attention and caring that students can receive from faculty and staff of their IS department. A study that administered the Mehrabian's Balanced Emotional Empathy Scale (BEES) on 633 students found that majors and empathy levels are closely related to each other (Courtright, Mackey, & Packard, 2005).

The quality of physical facilities, such as classrooms and computer labs, and the appearance of faculty and staff are tangible elements of perceived service quality. The perceived quality of these tangible elements may affect the overall satisfaction of students within the CIS major. A previous study confirms the existence of a relationship between the type, size and age of a student's dormitory and student satisfaction levels (Ng, 2005). Service reliability is for faculty and staff to perform promised academic, professional and extracurricular services in terms of student expectations. The willingness of faculty and staff to respond to the demand of students has a strong influence on student satisfaction. A study

Table 2. Perceived service quality dimensions in the higher education context

Perceived Service Quality Dimensions	Definitions in IS Major Context
Assurance	Expertise and courtesy of department faculty and staff and their ability to inspire trust and confidence
Empathy	Caring, individualized attention the department provides its students
Tangibles	Physical facilities, computer equipment and appearance of staff and faculty
Reliability	Faculty, staff and Department Chair's ability to perform the promised academic, professional and extracurricular services dependably and accurately
Responsiveness	The willingness of faculty and staff to help students and provide prompt service

ranking the order of service quality finds that responsiveness is the fifth important factor leading to student satisfaction (LeBlanc & Nguyen, 1997).

Perceived service quality is one of the salient predictors for customer satisfaction and continuance usage. In order to reverse the downward trend of CIS enrollment, it is imperative to understand how to increase not only the enrollment of prospective students into the CIS major, but also the continued championing of the CIS major by existing students. A higher perceived service quality of the CIS major can lead to increased student demand (Palmieri, 2006) and a positive confirmation experience (Bhattacherjee, 2001). This research thus posits that there is a positive relationship between perceived service quality and satisfaction.

Academic Service

Hypothesis 2a: The higher a student's perceived quality about academic services, the more satisfied the student will be with the CIS major.

Extracurricular Service

Hypothesis 2b: The higher a student's perceived quality about extracurricular services, the more satisfied the student will be with the CIS major.

Professional Service

Hypothesis 2c: The higher a student's perceived quality about professional services, the more satisfied the student will be with the CIS major.

Impact of Satisfaction & Regret on Retention

Satisfaction is a salient independent variable for the intention of continued usage of various products and services, such as repurchase of automobiles (Oliver, 1993), camcorders and photographic products (Dabholkar et al., 2000), restaurant services (Swan & Trawick 1981), and business professional services (Patterson & Spreng, 1997). Customer satisfaction is a precursor to customer loyalty (Chiou & Droge, 2006), which can be measured with the intention to continue using the products and services. Customer satisfaction differs from attitude in its transitory nature (Anderson & Sullivan, 1993). The formation of an affective attitude towards a product or service indicates a high level of customer loyalty. By the same token, students' loyalty to their majors can be enhanced by the increased satisfaction of users with the services of a major. We posit that satisfaction can lead to students' intention to stay in the same major and recommend the major to other prospective students. Academic, professional and extracurricular services are antecedents of student satisfaction with a major. A positive major experience would be able to increase a student's intention to remain a CIS major throughout his/her college life.

Satisfaction to Retention

Hypothesis 3: Students who have higher satisfaction in the CIS major are more likely to intend to remain a CIS major.

Regret is an affective, but irrational anticipation (Sevdalis, Kokkinaki, & Harvey, 2008). The emotion can have negative impact on consumer decision-making process and eliminate the enjoyment of buying (Mandel & Nowlis, 2008). Buyers who switched to another brand or channel would have more regret than buyers who remained (Keaveney, Huber, & Hermann, 2007). Therefore, regret of purchasing a product or service can result in lower intention of using the same products, services, channels or brands.

Regret of choosing a major is similar to the regret of buying a product or service. Regret is a useful surrogate to understanding how much the existing students have enjoyed being with their major. According to the appraisal-tendency framework, regret is a negative emotion to mediate and conciliate the effects of consumers' appraisals about service failure (Bonifield & Cole, 2006). If a student were satisfied with his/her major, the negative emotion would not arise because his/her appraisals on using academic, professional and extracurricular services would be positive.

Students who have low regret of being a CIS major have a higher intention of remaining a CIS major. As such, regret is an antecedent to major retention and has a negative impact on major retention.

Hypothesis 4: Students who have lower regret about being a CIS are more likely to intend to remain a CIS major.

Impact of Satisfaction & Regret on Referral Intention

Happy customers would love sharing their positive experience with others. On the other hand, consumers share their negative emotion with friends and strangers if they are disappointed with services or products. The major reason of sharing and communicating the satisfactory experience or the regret of using a particular product or service is to strengthen social bonds or to warn others of using the same product or service (Wetzer, Zeelenberg, & Pieters, 2007). It is more cost-effective to recruit a referral prospect than a marketed prospect because of lower sales expenses, and higher return on investment (Cardis, 2006). One study divides customers into three categories: promoters, passively satisfiers and detractors based on their intention of providing referrals (Reichheld, 2006). This study finds that promoters account for 80% of referral rate and detractors account for 80% of negative word-of-mouth. A customer's satisfaction with a product or service has a positive and direct impact on the intention of providing referrals (Littlechild, 2007). Therefore, it is important to maximize the referral intention of the existing customers.

Working environment can affect job satisfaction of employees (Parish, Berry, & Lam, 2008). Physician humaneness and professionalism can improve patient's overall satisfaction and referral intention in the hospital environment (Lin & Guan, 2002). In the higher education context, a student's overall satisfaction with academic, extracurricular and professional services can increase the referral intention. A competitive school often relies on a strong alumni network to increase job opportunities for the existing majors, and thereby increasing the referral rate. This is a professional service. Sometimes, a university even pays referral fees to alumni if prospective students are recruited via the referral channel. A proper utilization of social network (e.g. alumni) is one of the effective selling strategies to increase the referral rate (Jun &

Kim, 2008). Improving the satisfaction of students with academic, extracurricular and professional services can lead to higher referral intention.

Hypothesis 5: Students who are more satisfied with the CIS major have a higher referral intention.

Hypothesis 6: Students who have less regret about being a CIS major have a higher referral intention.

Our proposed theoretical framework summarizes six hypotheses and is shown in Figure 1. Hypothesis 1 includes three sub-hypotheses to measure the correlations between expectation and satisfaction with respect to academic, professional and extracurricular services. Hypothesis 2 is used to measure the correlation between perceived service quality and satisfaction with respect to these three services.

Research Methodology

A survey was administered to 200 juniors and seniors majoring in Computer Information Systems. We sent an invitation email to these students, inviting them to participate in this study. In order to increase the participation rate, we raffled $10 gift cards to 10 participating students. A total of 68 students responded to our invitation email and filled out the online survey questionnaires. The response rate was 34%. However, 4 questionnaires were invalid, so we included data for 64 respondents in our analysis.

All survey questions were derived from theoretical constructs that have been statistically tested with respect to validity and reliability in previous studies. Table 3 summarizes operational definitions for all adopted constructs used in their original studies. The survey instrument is available upon request from the authors.

We conducted several linear regression analyses to determine the values of parameters studied for different dependent variables. The first func-

Figure 1. Theoretical Framework

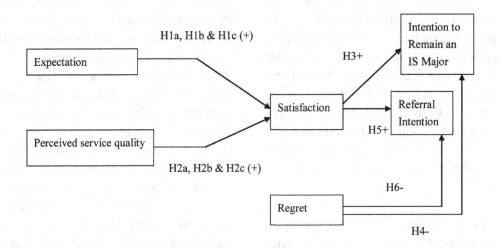

Table 3. Operational definitions of theoretical constructs

Theoretical Constructs	Operational Definition	How Measured
Expectation	Consumers form an initial expectation of a specific product or service prior to their first-time purchase.	Oliver (1977); Bhattacherjee (2001)
Perceived Service Quality	Users perceive that quality of the delivered goods and services conform to customer requirements, comprising of technical performance and functional performance. Five key metrics of perceived service quality are tangibles, reliability, responsiveness, assurance and empathy.	Kettinger and Lee (1994); Parasuraman, Zeithaml and Berry (1988)
Satisfaction	Satisfaction is a pleasurable or positive emotional state related to and resulting from a cognitive appraisal of the expectation-performance discrepancy.	Oliver (1977); Bhattacherjee (2001); Kettinger and Lee (1994)
Regret	The unpleasant experience of discovering that a forgone alternative would have led to a better outcome than the one chosen (Landman, 1987).	Tsiros and Mittal (2000)
Intention to stay in the Major	If the chosen alternative outperforms the chosen alternative, the students may well intend to stay in the CIS major.	Oliver (1977); Bhattacherjee (2001)
Referral Intention	If the chosen alternative outperforms the chosen alternative, the students may well intend to refer the CIS major to others.	Oliver (1977); Bhattacherjee (2001)

tion constructed for the linear regression analysis uses student satisfaction as the dependent variable, and expectations for academic, extracurricular and professional services as independent variables. We assume that a student's satisfaction level with the CIS major can be increased by an increase in expectations for academic, extracurricular and professional services. Statistical evidence indicates that this function has the best overall fit ($F=4.68$, $p<0.01$) (Table 4). A further examination of the value of parameters to cause the function to best fit shows that professional service expectations can lead to a student's satisfaction with the CIS major ($t=2.18$, $p<0.05$) (Table 5). On the other hand, academic and extracurricular services are not important determinants for major

satisfaction of a student based on the statistical evidence.

Dependent Variable: Student Satisfaction **($F=4.68$, $p<0.05$)

Independent variables: Academic, extracurricular and professional services expectations * $p < 0.05$

The second function constructed for the linear regression analysis has student satisfaction with CIS major as the dependent variable, and student's perceived quality for academic, extracurricular and professional services as independent variables. We assume that a student's satisfaction level with the CIS major can be increased by the increase of perceived service quality for academic, extracurricular and professional services. Statistical evidence indicates that this function has the best

Table 4. Analysis of variance for student satisfaction

Sum of Mean					
Source DF Squares Square F Value Pr > F					
Model 4 15.22470 3.80618 4.68 0.0023					
Error 60 48.77530 0.81292					
Corrected Total 64 64.00000					
Root MSE 0.90162 R-Square 0.2379					
Dependent Mean -3.1428E-16 Adj R-Sq 0.1871					
Coeff Var -2.86886E17					

Table 5. Expectation parameter estimates

Parameter Standard				
Variable DF Estimate Error t Value Pr > |t|				
Intercept 1 -0.00198 0.11184 -0.02 0.9859				
Academic 1 0.16059 0.12704 1.26 0.2111				
Extracur. 1 0.09533 0.13332 0.72 0.4774				
*Profess. 1 0.31119 0.14282 2.18 0.0333				

Table 6. Analysis of variance for perceived service quality & major satisfaction

Sum of Mean					
Source DF Squares Square F Value Pr > F					
Model 4 19.70794 4.92698 6.67 0.0002					
Error 60 44.29206 0.73820					
Corrected Total 64 64.00000					
Root MSE 0.85919 R-Square 0.3079					
Dependent Mean -3.1428E-16 Adj R-Sq 0.2618					
Coeff Var -2.73384E17					

overall fit (F=6.67, p <0.01) (Table 6). A further examination of the value of parameters to cause the function to best fit shows that perceived quality for academic services can lead to a student's satisfaction with the CIS major (t=4.13, p <0.01) (Table 7). On the other hand, perceived quality for professional (t=--1.05, p=0.299 > 0.05) and extracurricular (t=1.02, p=0.31 >0.05) services are not important determinants for major satisfaction of a student based on the statistical evidence.

The third function uses intention to remain a CIS major as the dependent variable, and satisfaction and regret as independent variables. We assume that a student's intention to remain a CIS major can be increased via the improvement of major satisfaction, and the lowering of regret. Statistical evidence indicates that this function has the best overall fit (F=8.23, p =0.00 <0.01) (Table 8). A further examination of the value of parameters to cause the function to best fit shows that improving satisfaction can lead to the increase of a student's intention to remain a CIS major (t=3.26, p<0.01) (Table 9). On the other hand, lowering regret (t=0.25, p=> 0.05) is not an important determinant in increasing a student's intention to remain a CIS major based on the statistical evidence.

The fourth function constructed for the linear regression analysis uses intention to refer others to major in CIS as the dependent variable, and satisfaction and regret as independent variables. We assume that a student's intention to refer others to major in CIS can be increased by improving satisfaction and lowering regret. Statistical evidence indicates that this function has the best overall fit (F=23.50, p < 0.01) (Table 10). A further examination of the value of parameters to cause the function to best fit shows that improving satisfaction (t=2.79, p< 0.01) and lowering regret (t=-3.0, p< 0.01) can lead to a student's referring intention (Table 11).

Discussion

The Computer Information Systems (CIS) major provides different kinds of services to students, including: (1) academic services, (2) professional services, and (3) extracurricular services. The quality and availability of these services to CIS majors can improve their satisfaction and decrease regret. These improvements can result in the increase of major retention and referring others to major in CIS. The presence of these relationships can increase the sustainability of CIS majors.

Table 7. Parameter estimates for perceived service quality

Parameter Standard					
Variable DF Estimate Error t Value Pr > |t|					
Intercept 1 -2.4932E-16 0.10657 -0.00 1.0000					
Academic 1 0.44353 0.10740 4.13 0.0001					
Extracurr. 1 0.10930 0.10740 1.02 0.3129					
Profess. 1 -0.11230 0.10740 -1.05 0.2999					

Table 8. Analysis of variance for major retention

Sum of Mean				
Source DF Squares Square F Value Pr > F				
Model 2 13.42489 6.71245 8.23 0.0007				
Error 62 50.57511 0.81573				
Corrected Total 64 64.00000				
Root MSE 0.90318 R-Square 0.2098				
Dependent Mean -4.727E-16 Adj R-Sq 0.1843				
Coeff Var -1.91068E17				

Table 9. Parameter estimates for intention to remain a CIS major, satisfaction and regret

Parameter Standard					
Variable DF Estimate Error t Value Pr > |t|					
Intercept 1 -3.1892E-16 0.11203 -0.00 1.0000					
Satisfaction 1 0.48118 0.14744 3.26 0.0018					
Regret 1 0.03744 0.14744 0.25 0.8004					

Table 10. Analysis of variance for referring intention, satisfaction & regret

Sum of Mean				
Source DF Squares Square F Value Pr > F				
Model 2 27.59761 13.79881 23.50 <.0001				
Error 62 36.40239 0.58714				
Corrected Total 64 64.00000				
Root MSE 0.76625 R-Square 0.4312				
Dependent Mean 7.17375E-17 Adj R-Sq 0.4129				
Coeff Var 1.068127E18				

Table 11. Parameter estimates for referring intention, satisfaction & regret

Parameter Standard					
Variable DF Estimate Error t Value Pr > |t|					
Intercept 1 1.55807E-16 0.09504 0.00 1.0000					
Satisfaction 1 0.34908 0.12509 2.79 0.0070					
Regret 1 -0.37528 0.12509 -3.00 0.0039					

One study suggests that academic services (e.g. faculty and class performance) should be motivators, and professional services (academic advising staff) are hygiene factors according to Hertzberg's theory (DeShields Jr., Kara and Kaynak, 2005). Faculty performance is influential to a student if a faculty member is considerate, accessible, professional and helpful. Class performance is high when a student can acquire skills and knowledge useful and applicable to the real life. Structured course scheduling is part of class performance. According to this study, the motivators are intrinsic satisfiers when the faculty performance and classes are fulfilled. The hygiene is an external dissatisfier if deficient.

Academic services studied in this paper belong to intrinsic motivators. Professional services fall into extrinsic motivators. Although these two kinds of services are closely related to each other in determining the major experience, this study provides additional insights based on the statistical evidence. First, it is important to increase a student's expectations for professional service that can be offered by the major. When a student has a higher expectation about the professional services, he/she is more likely to have a satisfying major experience. Professional services we studied include hands-on experiences in computer labs, IS certification training, internship opportunities, placement services, and resume advising. It is important to communicate clearly to students and increase their expectations about these services. CIS majors are concerned with job opportunities after graduation. Internship opportunities, place-

Table 12. Summary of hypotheses testing results

Hypothesis	P value	Supported (Yes/No)
Hypothesis 1a: The higher a student's expectation to receive academic services, the more satisfied the student will be with the CIS major.	0.2111	No
Hypothesis 1b: The higher a student's expectation to receive extracurricular services, the more satisfied the student will be with the CIS major.	0.4774	No
Hypothesis 1c: The higher a student's expectation to receive professional services, the more satisfied the student will be with the CIS major.	0.0333	Yes
Hypothesis 2a: The higher a student's perceived quality about academic services, the more satisfied the student will be with the CIS major.	0.0001	Yes
Hypothesis 2b: The higher a student's perceived quality about extracurricular services, the more satisfied the student will be with the CIS major.	0.3129	No
Hypothesis 2c: The higher a student's perceived quality about professional services, the more satisfied the student will be with the CIS major.	0.2999	No
Hypothesis 3: Students who have higher satisfaction in the CIS major are more likely to intend to remain a CIS major.	0.0018	Yes
Hypothesis 4: Students who have lower regret about being a CIS are more likely to intend to remain a CIS major..	0.8004	No
Hypothesis 5: Students who are more satisfied with the CIS major have a higher referral intention.	0.0070	Yes
Hypothesis 6: Students who have less regret about being a CIS major have a higher referral intention.	0.0039	Yes

ment services and resume advising can sharpen students' technical skills, and most importantly, improve their confidence in being a successful major. The accessibility and availability of these experiences in the professional area is essential to the increase of the satisfaction of CIS majors.

Second, perceived quality of academic services is the most important determinant for the increase of a student's major satisfaction. Extracurricular services seem to be irrelevant, and the least important service to CIS majors. This is probably due to the fact that this major is still being dominated by males which are more likely to be task-oriented, rather than relationship-oriented, in personality. Academic services surveyed in this study include: offering of new technology courses, access to educational software, course concentrations, teaching effectiveness of faculty, advising services, and independent studies. CIS majors judge the quality of their program primarily based on class experiences. An updated curriculum, the offering of elective courses, and teaching effectiveness of faculty are three cornerstones to

the success of improving a student's perceived quality of the CIS major.

The CIS department needs to place different emphases on expectations and perceived service quality depending on the objectives of major promotional events. For instance, our institution holds an Open House event each semester to increase prospective students' expectations about the CIS major and to recruit new students. At another event, the Majors Fair, highlighting the delivery of a quality program can be more effective at increasing the perceived quality of current majors than highlighting the delivery of extracurricular and professional services. In other words, academic services are a motivator and can increase the perceived service quality; professional services are a hygiene factor and can increase the major satisfaction.

When major satisfaction is increased, students are more likely to stay in the major rather than switching to other majors. Interestingly, it seems that the regret of being a CIS major does not substantially contribute to the increased intention of switching to another major. Major loyalty seems to be somewhat higher in the CIS major. Administrators and faculty need to direct their attention to improve the professional and academic services respectively in order to increase student satisfaction in the CIS major. In the long run, students would likely appreciate the efforts of administrators and faculty.

CONCLUSION

Bad news travels fast. The principles of consumer marketing research are also applicable to the behavior of students in the CIS major. A CIS major will try influencing others if they are satisfied or dissatisfied with their major experiences. In the short run, dissatisfied students are "stuck" in the program. In the long run, those students may affect the recruiting of prospective students and could do harm to the sustainability of the CIS major.

This study suggests the importance of extracurricular services is not as great as academic and professional services. It seems that the number of students who are attracted to extracurricular services is much fewer than those students who are attracted to other kinds of services. It is a great challenge for administrators, faculty, and student leaders to increase the perceived quality and expectations of students for these extracurricular services, including student clubs (e.g. Association for Information Technology Professionals and Project Management Clubs), study abroad trips and other extracurricular services.

Our study provides a theoretical foundation for future research in this area. Many CIS departments are facing the challenge of recruiting and retaining CIS majors. By determining which factors impact students' intentions to remain a CIS major and to encourage others to major in CIS, we can focus our resources on these areas instead of spending time and money on those services which are not influential.

REFERENCES

Akbulut, A. Y., & Looney, C. A. (2007, October). Inspiring Students to Pursue Computing Degrees. *Communications of the ACM, 50*(10), 67–71. doi:10.1145/1290958.1290964

Bonifield, C., & Cole, C. (2007, June). Affective responses to service failure: Anger, regret, and retaliatory versus conciliatory responses. *Marketing Letters, 18*(1-2), 85–99. doi:10.1007/s11002-006-9006-6

Business Editors/Technology, E. F. W. (1998, June 8). Regrets, They Have a Few -- College Grads Re-Think Majors, Career Choices. *Business Wire, 1.*

Cardis, P. (2006, July). Maximizing Referrals. *Professional Builder, 71*(7), 41–42.

Chorus, C. G., Arentze, T. A., & Timmermans, H. J. P. (2008, January). A Random Regret-Minimization model of travel choice. *Transportation Research, 42*(1), -18.

Courtright, K. E., Mackey, D. A., & Packard, S. H. (2005, April). Empathy among College Students and Criminal Justice Majors: Identifying Predispositional Traits and the Role of Education. *Journal of Criminal Justice Education. Highland Heights, 16*(1), 125–147.

DeShields, O. W. Jr, Kara, A., & Kaynak, E. (2005). Determinants of business student satisfaction and retention in higher education: applying Herzberg's two-factor theory. *International Journal of Educational Management, 19*(2/3), 128–139.

Hayashi, T. (2008, March). Regret aversion and opportunity dependence. *Journal of Economic Theory, 139*(1), 242. doi:10.1016/j.jet.2007.07.001

Horrigan, M. W. (2004, February). *Employment projections through 2012: Concepts and context.* Washington, DC: U.S. Bureau of Labor Statistics.

Jun, T., & Kim, J. (2008, May). A theory of consumer referral. *International Journal of Industrial Organization, 26*(3), 6623. doi:10.1016/j.ijindorg.2007.03.005

Keaveney, S. M., Huber, F., & Herrmann, A. (2007). A model of buyer regret: Selected prepurchase and postpurchase antecedents with consequences for the brand and the channel. *Journal of Business Research, 60*(12), 1207. doi:10.1016/j.jbusres.2006.07.005

LeBlanc, G., & Nguyen, N. (1997). Searching for excellence in business education: an exploratory study of customer impressions of service quality. *International Journal of Educational Management, 11*(2), 72. doi:10.1108/09513549710163961

Lent, R. W., Brown, S. D., & Hackett, G. (1994). Toward a unifying social cognitive theory of career and academic interest, choice, and performance. *Journal of Vocational Behavior,* (45): 79–122. doi:10.1006/jvbe.1994.1027

Lin, X., & Guan, J. (2002). Patient satisfaction and referral intention: Effect of patient-physician match on ethnic origin and cultural similarity. *Health Marketing Quarterly, 20*(2), 49. doi:10.1300/J026v20n02_04

Littlechild, J. (2008, May/Jun.). What Motivates Clients to Provide Referrals? *Journal of Financial Planning,* 10–12.

Looney, C. A., & Akbulut, A. Y. (2007). Combating the IS Enrollment Crisis: The Role of Effective Teachers in Introductory IS Courses. *Communications of the Association for Information Systems, 19*(1), 1–19.

Mandel, N., & Nowlis, S. M. (2008, June). The Effect of Making a Prediction about the Outcome of a Consumption Experience on the Enjoyment of That Experience. *The Journal of Consumer Research, 35*(1), 9. doi:10.1086/527339

Ng, S. L. (2005, March). Subjective Residential Environment and its Implications for Quality of Life Among University Students in Hong Kong. *Social Indicators Research, 71*(1-3), 467. doi:10.1007/s11205-004-8032-0

Parish, J. T., Berry, L. L., & Lam, S. Y. (2008, Feb.). The Effect of the Servicescape on Service Workers. *Journal of Service Research, 10*(3), 220. doi:10.1177/1094670507310770

Prakash, V., & Lounsbury, J. W. (1984). The Role of Expectations in the Determination of Consumer Satisfaction. *Academy of Marketing Science, 12*(3), 1–17. doi:10.1007/BF02739316

Reichheld, F. (2006). The Microeconomics of Customer Relationships. *MIT Sloan Management Review, 47*(2), 73.

Sarver, T. (2008, March). Anticipating Regret: Why Fewer Options May Be Better. *Econometric, 76*(2), 263.

Sauer, P. L., & O'Donnell, J. B. (2006). The Impact of New Major Offerings on Student Retention. *Journal of Marketing for Higher Education, 16*(2), 135–155. doi:10.1300/J050v16n02_06

Sevdalis, N., Kokkinaki, F., & Harvey, N. (2008). Anticipating a regrettable purchase; Implications of erroneous affective forecasting for marketing planning. *Marketing Intelligence & Planning, 26*(4), 375. doi:10.1108/02634500810879287

Sirvanci, M. (1996, October). Are students the true customers of higher education? *Quality Progress, 29*(10).

Sonnet, G., Fox, M. F., & Adkins, K. (2007, Dec.). Undergraduate Women in Science and Engineering: Effects of Faculty, Fields, and Institutions Over Time. *Social Science Quarterly, 88*(5), 1333–1356. doi:10.1111/j.1540-6237.2007.00505.x

Wetzer, I. M., Zeelenberg, M., & Pieters, R. (2007, August). Never eat in that restaurant, I did: Exploring why people engage in negative word-of-mouth communication. *Psychology and Marketing, 24*(8), 661. doi:10.1002/mar.20178

Williams, M. (2007). High cost of education. *Michigan Citizen, 30*(1), 47.

This work was previously published in International Journal of Information and Communication Technology, Volume 6, Issue 1, edited by Lawrence A. Tomei, pp. 81-95, copyright 2010 by IGI Publishing (an imprint of IGI Global).

Chapter 8
User Interface Design Pedagogy:
A Constructionist Approach

Benjamin KS Khoo
New York Institute of Technology, USA

ABSTRACT

A major limitation in traditional class lectures that uses textbooks, handouts, transparencies and assignments is that students often are unable to "experience" user interface design. This limitation can be overcome by using the constructionist approach that allow students to experience user interface design by allowing them to "do" or "construct" so that they can understand and remember. This paper describes an Internet-based interactive case scenario that was developed, based on the constructionist approach, to teach students user interface design concepts in conjunction with the Questionnaire for User Interaction Satisfaction (QUIS). A proof of concept evaluation was conducted and the results indicate that this approach is effective in user interface design pedagogy.

INTRODUCTION

The term user interface has been defined "as those aspects of the system that the user comes in contact with" (Moran, 1981, p.4). Systems were said to be "friendly" when users were able to seamlessly use or operate the complex systems through its well designed user interface. The term "user friendly" was coined to refer to a system that a user can easily interact through its interfaces. The field of user interfaces began to develop as systems developers and researchers spent more time and effort to enhance user interfaces to make

them more "user friendly." In the mid-1980s, the developing field of user interface design began to include other factors such as organizational issues, work practices, design, implementation and evaluation amongst others. As more factors were added, it became apparent that a more comprehensive term was needed to describe this field that was emerging. A broader term "human-computer interaction" (HCI) was then adopted to describe this new field. Today, HCI is taught as a course (or as part of a course) in the computer science and information systems curriculum of most universities. User interface designers try to

DOI: 10.4018/978-1-61350-468-0.ch008

satisfy the human requirements of a system by applying knowledge from many areas: cognitive psychology, input and output devices, guidelines and standards, dialogue types, and (because design knowledge is inadequate) prototyping methods. It is multidisciplinary (Preece et al., 1994).

The explosive growth of the Internet has resulted in a paradigm shift that has affected all aspects of our lives. The ease of use and accessibility to the Internet - any time and anywhere has helped propagate its growth. This paper describes an effort to harness the strengths of hypertext markup language (HTML) and utilize it to develop an interactive virtual menu systems based on a case scenario for user interface design using the constructionist approach (Papert, 1980a). The approach taken to teach students user interface design is to allow them to have a hands-on experience through the interactive virtual menu system. The interactive virtual menu system is the first prototype built. The constructionist approach uses constructive tasks to impart knowledge. The objective is to motivate learning through activity. In this way, learning is made more effective. The great Chinese sage Confucius once said "I hear and I forget. I see and I understand. I do and I remember."

LITERATURE REVIEW

Constructionism is a major principle in contemporary education theory and a strategy for learning. There are two facets to constructionism - that learning takes place as a result of actively constructing new knowledge and that learning is effective when "constructing" or "doing" activities that are personally meaningful. It is widely accepted in educational circles that an important part of the learning process consists of "hands-on" construction. Constructionism has been supported by the success of children educational activities based on building blocks (Resnick, 1991). It is a well-established methodology for learning

(Papert, 1991; Resnick, 1991). The constructionist approach uses constructive tasks to impart knowledge. Its goal is to develop creativity and motivate learning through activity. Constructionism asserts that knowledge is not simply transmitted from the teacher to students, but is actively constructed in the mind of the learner through various hands-on activities. In addition, it suggests that learners make their ideas by constructing their own knowledge structures. It has been shown that learning is more effective when it is activity-based rather than passively received (Brown, et al, 1989). The active "constructing" or "doing" tasks leads to discovery.

The concept of discovery learning is not new. Discovery learning can be described as experimentation with some extrinsic intervention -- clues, coaching, a framework to help learners get to a reasonable conclusion. It has appeared many times in educational philosophy, Dewey stated "there is an intimate and necessary relation between the processes of actual experience and education" (Dewey, 1938). It is also supported by learning theorists/psychologists such as Piaget, Bruner, and Papert, "Insofar as possible, a method of instruction should have the objective of leading the child to discover for himself." (Bruner, 1967). But it has never received overwhelming acceptance even though it has enjoyed a few positive swings of the educational-trend pendulum in American education (Jacobs, 1992).

The learner draws on his own experience and prior knowledge to discover the knowledge to be learned. This is embodied in a personal, internal, constructionist environment. Bruner stated that "Emphasis on discovery in learning has precisely the effect on the learner of leading him to be a constructionist, to organize what he is encountering in a manner not only designed to discover regularity and relatedness, but also to avoid the kind of information drift that fails to keep account of the uses to which information might have to be put." (Bruner, 1967)

MOTIVATION

In learning user interface design, students often are unable to grasp the full implications of the techniques found in textbooks. The knowledge found in the written text and in diagrams are static displays that do not fully illustrate the effects of a user interface on its users. User interfaces affects the user not only statically but also dynamically when the display changes through some form of direct manipulation of the metaphors on the display like a pushbutton. This is the navigational aspect of a user interface. The traditional mode of teaching user interface design did not allow the student to dynamically experience a user interface. A project to overcome this limitation was initiated with hypertext markup language which resulted in the development and use of an interactive virtual menu system prototype to teach user interface design.

The interactive virtual menu system was developed based on a case scenario for user interface design using the constructionist approach (Papert, 1980a). This project requires that the students interact and navigate through a virtual menu system on the Internet depending on what outcome is wanted and also provide a written quantitative evaluation of the interactive menu system based on a version of QUIS, Questionnaire for User Interaction Satisfaction (Slaughter, Harper & Norman, 1994). QUIS is a well-accepted evaluation tool for user interaction satisfaction. Its main role, to the students, is to serve as a guideline listing all the factors to consider when designing a user interface. In this way it serves as a teaching tool for the students. The quantitative evaluation exercise helps provide the students useful usability evaluation experience.

There are two motivations for this project. The first motivation pertains to the interactive virtual menu system on the Internet: To allow the student to interactively experience what a good (and/or bad) basic user interface for a menu system is like. The second motivation pertains to the use of a version of the user interaction satisfaction questionnaire based on QUIS: To clearly define to the students what basic criteria or features are required for a good user interface design or user interaction satisfaction and to provide usability evaluation experience.

APPROACH

The interactive virtual menu system allows the novice designers (students) to navigate the virtual menu system and to have complete control of the outcome. The user interface is usually understood to include things like menus, windows, the keyboard, the mouse, the "Beeps" and other sounds the computer makes, and in general, all the information channels that allow the user and the computer to communicate. In this project, the frills and thrills have been reduced to a minimum while the basics of user interface and menu system design are emphasized. The interactive virtual menu system is developed on the Internet and is used in conjunction with a version of the QUIS.

QUIS was developed by Kent Norman and his team at the HCI Laboratory in the University of Maryland, College Park. It is a usability testing tool designed to gauge the user's satisfaction with the user interface. The QUIS contains measures of user satisfaction in four specific interface aspects (screen factors, terminology and system feedback, learning factors, and system capabilities) and an overall measure of satisfaction. As the interactive virtual menu system is not a real fully functional interface, annotations were added to the questionnaire describing the relevance of each sub-section. QUIS is used in this project primarily as a teaching tool to illustrate to the students what basic design features to look for in a good interface design and also to provide usability evaluation experience.

As constructionism provided the approach to develop the interactive virtual menu system, a vehicle has to be chosen to deliver the system. The prevalence of the Internet and its technologies is an excellent candidate.

Internet

There are a few criteria that are necessary for the successful implementation of any new tool, in this case, for teaching the basics of good user interface design. One major criterion is that the students should be able to interact with a complete menu system, so as to experience the importance of navigation and structure in a menu system without having to develop a complete menu system by themselves. The menu system should be complete so that it mimics a real-life system that has options for inputs, for specific processes that perform different operations on the data and for generating specific outputs according to the user's choice. Another criterion is that the menu interfaces themselves should illustrate what is required from a user's perspective. The students should also be able to easily access this menu system wherever they are through the use of a computer. The success of the whole project actually depended on the students being able to access this menu system.

The global pervasion of the Internet has created a trend towards network centric computing. In this model, the content, communication, and computing converge on the network resulting in the network becoming the computer. Users can now access the Internet from almost anywhere and at any time. In addition, the constant reduction of hardware costs has expanded the user population. The Internet is now available to anyone who owns a computer with a modem and has access to an Internet Service Provider or to a university or college.

The Internet is the ideal vehicle to deliver the interactive virtual menu system. All the students have access to the Internet through their individual user accounts at the university. This project is an effort to harness the strengths of the Internet technologies, such as hypertext and image maps, to develop the interactive virtual menu systems based on a case scenario for user interface design using the constructionist approach. By using the

Internet, the linkage structures of hypertext and image maps can be utilized to create a virtual menu system that actually 'works' when the user performs a direct manipulation of the metaphors on the screen. It is a virtual menu system because even though the metaphors (such as pushbuttons) on the screens are activated when clicked, the environment is just a shell made up of a set of embedded image maps using the hypertext markup language.

In this virtual environment, users will be able to interact with the menu system and navigate via a direct manipulation paradigm. Each student is provided with a version of QUIS to help them identify the basic design features to look for in an interface design and for evaluating the virtual menu system. Through navigating the interactive menu system and "doing" the evaluation process (using QUIS) the student can gain an experiential knowledge of what basic features are required for a good user interface design and user interaction satisfaction.

Case Scenario

The Internet-based interactive virtual menu system had be one that mimics a real database management system. The scenario used to develop such a system is called a case scenario. A case scenario describes an actual situation that exists in the real world. Information for the case scenario is gathered by means of interviewing, reading and observing a real situation. Information from the case scenario is used to create and design the Internet-based interactive virtual menu system. The case scenario used for this project is described in the following paragraphs.

The case scenario is a real case of the Campus Safety (or Security) Department of a university in the USA. The Campus Safety Department of a university has the responsibility to keep the peace and maintain a safe environment for all personnel on the university campus. The department has always maintained records of all activities at the university. The existing data collection system at the Campus Safety Department is mainly manual. Legislations by the United States government stipulate that all students and potential students be given access rights to all statistics of criminal activities that occurred on any campus in the land. Thus, now there is an impetus to utilize a better data collection system.

The Campus Safety department maintains a record of all on-campus personnel and their vehicles, and also off-campus personnel and their vehicles that use the campus. The functional requirements can be defined as to maintain records of departmental employees, to monitor and control traffic violations, to monitor and control criminal incidents, and to record and monitor other incidents. The department keeps a record of its departmental employees. The department has to record and monitor other incidents, as seen in Table 1.

This department is also entrusted with the responsibilities to monitor and control traffic violations, as seen in Table 2.

It is also responsible to monitor and control criminal incidents, as noted in Table 3.

A computerized user-friendly information system is required to improve productivity and work efficiency. This information system must be user friendly and should encompass all data entry, report generation, administration, maintenance, and utility features that support the system. It should also be simple enough for the users to use and to maintain, yet provide all the features required for the day-to-day operations. The best application software that should be developed is a Database Management System (DMS).

The nature of the database at the Campus Safety Department requires that certain process functions be developed or coded. These process functions are needed to provide capabilities for:

Table 1. Incidents monitored and recorded by Campus Safety

1. Safety or Hazards Checks
2. Medical Assist
3. Lost and Found
4. Fire Alarm
5. Police Department Assists.

Table 2. Traffic Violations monitored and controlled by Campus Safety

1. Illegal parking (e.g. issuing parking tickets, moving tickets)
2. Speeding violation (e.g. issuing speeding tickets)
3. Traffic Accidents (e.g. generating accident reports)

Table 3. Criminal incidents monitored and recorded by Campus Safety

1. Larceny
2. Breaking and Entering
3. Malicious Destruction of Property
4. Disorderly or Uncooperative Conduct
5. Assault
6. Intrusion Alarm.

1. Security Control (e.g. System and User Login Control)
2. Editing Records (e.g. Add Records, Delete Records)
3. Searching Records (e.g. by ID Number, Name or Vehicle Registration Number)
4. Generating Reports (e.g. Standard or Ad Hoc Reports)
5. Database Back-up or Archive
6. Database Administration (e.g. Rebuilding a database)
7. Browsing the Database Records where students have the Right-To-Know.

The input or data entry process is mainly through screens that are designed called task interfaces. The transition between levels or menus can be made through screens designed called menu interfaces. Menus consist of a few pushbuttons for navigation between interfaces. The dialog box is used to prompt the user for action such as printing to a printer or to the screen.

When queries are executed, a result table is created based on the query. Reports are generated from these result tables. The system output or reports can be directed to the screen or to the printer. This is done through selecting the appropriate choice in the dialog boxes.

IMPLEMENTATION

The setting for the virtual menu system is framed in a 'Campus Safety Department Database System.' The Windows-based system employs standard Windows user interfaces. This project harnessed the strengths of Internet technologies, such as hypertext and image maps, to develop the interactive virtual menu system. By using the Hypertext Markup Language (HTML), the linkage structures of hypertext and image maps can be utilized to create a virtual menu system that actually 'works' when the user performs a direct manipulation of the metaphors on the screen. The graphical content of the interfaces can be developed by using most general drawing packages or using any Microsoft Office component software. Microsoft Office has a control toolbox that has all the main metaphors used in an interface, for example, pushbuttons. These metaphors can be easily embedded on an interface. When the interface design is completed, the interface has to be "captured" and saved as a.gif or.jpg file so that it is viewable by any Internet browser. There are a few free image capture software available through the Internet; the one that was used for this project is SnagIt32. Next, an image mapper is used to make the metaphors on the interface "active" or clickable. The image mapper that was used for this project is the Coffee Cup Image Mapper, which is also freely available from the Internet. The image maps allow the user to "click" on the active areas such as pushbuttons and loads the next predefined interface. In this way, the system allows the user to point at a "pushbutton" on the screen and clicks the mouse to execute commands.

As this tool is just a virtual environment, all the input features have been disabled. The overall depth structure of the menu system consists of three levels, with each level down providing a higher degree of detail. The first level basically serves as a main menu page and provides links for different options or tasks as well as more detailed information, found at the second level. The second level pages have links to other more detailed tasks in the third level that provides options to display different types of outputs or reports. See Figure 1. This context-structured approach allows the user to navigate between the levels easily as well as within a given level (so that the experienced user need not return to the top level to see other areas of information). This particular method of representation seemed best to capture the "inherent organization" of the displayed items (Norman, 1991, pp. 263-265).

Navigation among the pages is facilitated by different pushbuttons, which appear either vertically and/or horizontally aligned at the bottom of each successive screen or page, depending on the type of interface. Each interface has a title that shows the current context as well as serving as a reference point as to where the user is and where the user can go. The pushbuttons and its captions provide the user information as to what option each pushbutton will provide. These pushbuttons allow the user to "reposition to cognitive landmarks" (Norman, 1991, p. 230), avoiding the necessity to always return to the top level. In this way, the user can efficiently move from one area of interest to another. By providing a menu system, cognitive overload is avoided which minimizes the need for memorization and reduces the possibility of errors, two principles of good interactive design.

Figure 1. Menu Tree Diagram for the Campus Safety Information System

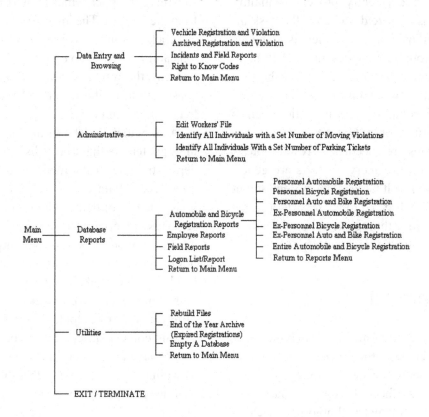

Interface Design

There are three main types of interfaces in the structure: the menu interface, the task interface and the dialog interface. The interface/screen images that were used were small in order to provide for fast downloading. Examples of interfaces can be seen in Figure 2, 3 and 4.

Graphic Design Components

Most of the features of the topography were chosen to promote a professional, simple image. The plain colored background was chosen for simplicity and clarity, as did the classic "white" background for the titles. Color was kept conservative, as per the "classic" professional look and also, so as not to overload the user (Shneiderman, 1992, pp.325-327). Pictures, Symbols, Signs, and Icons were kept to a minimum.

DISCUSSION

The complexity of both humans and computing systems makes their interaction less predictable than we would like. Even the best intentions can result in unusable systems or, more often, in systems with problems. A version of QUIS was provided for each student to provide feedback on the usefulness of this tool for teaching user interface design. This questionnaire requires the students to evaluate the interactive menu system based on four categories: overall user reactions, screen, terminology and system information, learning and system capabilities. Each of these categories contains questions that address specific issues within that category. The intent is for the students to evaluate the interactive menu system, and in the process, each category and its questions is expected to make plain to the students the basic requirements for a good interface design. There

Figure 2. Menu Options Interface

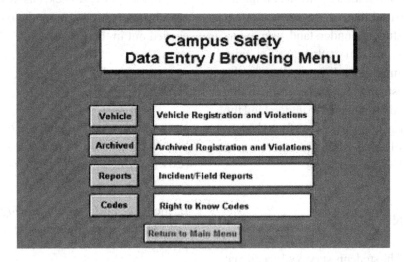

Figure 3. Task Options Interface

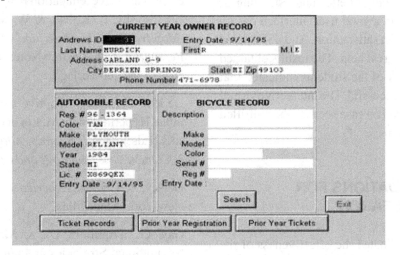

Figure 4. Dialog Interface

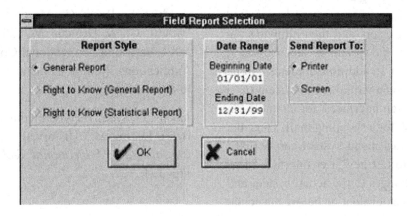

is also an additional question in the questionnaire to determine the usability of the menu system in assisting the students understand user interface design. Thus, the aim of this questionnaire survey is not so much in collecting data for the user interface satisfaction but to determine if this project has assisted the students to understand the basic features of a good user interface design. Feedback was collected from the student as a proof-of-concept of the prototype.

CONCLUSION

More than 90% of the students surveyed stated that the interactive menu system and the questionnaire has helped them gain a better understanding of what is required in a good user interface design and user interaction satisfaction. And 65% stated that it has been a great help. The results obtained from the feedback of the students indicated that this project was successful. The interactive virtual menu system based on case scenario has fulfilled both its motivations.

RECOMMENDATIONS FOR FUTURE RESEARCH

This research evaluated the effectiveness of the constructionist approach to user interface design pedagogy. The efficiency of the constructionist approach can be investigated in future where the interactive virtual menu system can be injected with navigational errors and then allowing the students to correct the system by reconstruction (as an assignment). In addition, students can be assigned to develop a virtual menu system (as a prototype) to design interfaces, for example, an information kiosk for a shopping mall. Thus, the concept of a virtual menu system can be used for prototyping to test new user interface ideas without major changes to the actual system and to get user feedback/evaluation before the actual system is fully developed.

As students' feedback, based on the prototype, have been positive, a more detailed study will be carried out in the future.

REFERENCES

Brown, J. S., Collins, A., & Duguid, P. (1989). Situated Cognition. In R. W. Lawler & M. Yazdani (Eds.), *Artificial Intelligence and Education, 2*, 254-268.

Bruner, J. S. (1967). *On Knowing: Essays for the Left Hand.* Cambridge, Mass: Harvard University Press.

Brusilovsky, P., & Henze, N. (2007). Open corpus adaptive educational hypermedia. In P. Brusilovsky, A. Kobsa, & W. Neidl (Eds.), *The Adaptive Web: Methods and Strategies of Web Personalization.* Lecture Notes in Computer Science. Springer-Verlag.

De Bra, P. (2004). Adaptive Web-based Educational Hypermedia. In M. Levene & A. Poulovassilis (Eds.), *Web Dynamics, Adaptive to Change in Content, Size, Topology and Use* (pp. 387-410).

Dewey, J. (1938). *Experience and Education.* New York: MacMillan.

Gay, G., Trumbull, D., & Mazur, J. (1991). Navigational Strategies and Guidance Tools for a Hypermedia Program. *Journal of Educational Computing Research, 7*(2), 189–202.

Gordillo, S., Rossi, G., Moreira, A., Araujo, J., Vairetti, C., & Urbieta, M. (2006). Modeling and Composing Navigational Concerns in Web Applications: Requirements and Design Issues. In *Proceedings of LA-Web.*

Jacobs, G. (1992). Hypermedia and Discovery-Based Learning: A Historical Perspective. *British Journal of Educational Technology, 23*(2), 113–121.

Karampiperis, P., & Sampson, D. (2005). Adaptive learning resources sequencing in educational hypermedia systems. *Educational Technology & Society, 8*, 128–147.

Masthoff, J. (2006). The User As Wizard. In *Proc. of the Fifth Workshop on User-Centred Design and Evaluation of Adaptive Systems* (pp. 460-469).

Nelson, W., & Palumbo, D. B. (1992). Learning, Instruction, and Hypermedia. *Journal of Educational Multimedia and Hypermedia, 1*(3), 281–299.

Norman, D. A. (1986). Cognitive engineering. In D. Norman & S. Draper (Eds.), *User Centered Systems Design*. Hillsdale, NJ: Lawrence Erlbaum Associates.

Norman, K. L. (1991). *The Psychology of Menu Selection*. Norwood, NJ: Ablex.

Papert, S. (1980a). Computer-based microworlds as incubators for powerful ideas. In R. P. Taylor (Ed.), *The Computer in the School: Tutor, Tool, Tutee*. New York: Teacher College Press.

Papert, S. (1980b). *Mindstorms: Children, Computers, and Powerful Ideas*. New York: Basic Books.

Papert, S. (1991). Situating Constructionism. In I. Harel & S. Papert (Eds.), *Constructionism*.

Preece, J., Rogers, Y., Sharp, H., Benyon, D., Holland, S., & Carey, T. (1994). *Human-Computer Interaction*. Workingham: Addison-Wesley.

Resnick, M. (1991). Xylophones, Hamsters, and Fireworks: The Role of Diversity in Constructionist Activities. In I. Harel & S. Papert (Eds.), *Constructionism*.

Rossi, G., Ginzburg, J., Urbieta, M., & Distante, D. (2007, July 16-20). Transparent Interface Composition in Web Applications. In *Proceedings of 7th International Conference on Web Engineering (ICWE2007)* (pp. 152-166), Como, Italy.

Shneiderman, B. (1992). *Designing the User Interface* (2nd. ed.). Reading, MA: Addison-Wesley.

Slaughter, L. A., Harper, B. D., & Norman, K. L. (1994). Assessing the Equivalence of Paper and On-line versions of the QUIS 5.5. In *Proceedings of the 2nd Annual Mid-Atlantic Human Factors Conference*, Washington, D.C.

Spiro, R. J., & Jehng, J. (1990). Cognitive Flexibility and Hypertext: Theory and Technology for the Nonlinear and Multidimensional Traversal of Complex Subject Matter. In D. Nix & R. Spiro (Eds.).*Cognition, Education, and Multimedia: Exploring Ideas in High Technology*. Hillsdale, NJ: Earlbaum.

This work was previously published in International Journal of Information and Communication Technology, Volume 6, Issue 1, edited by Lawrence A. Tomei, pp. 96-105, copyright 2010 by IGI Publishing (an imprint of IGI Global).

Chapter 9
Technology and Teacher Education:
Student Evaluation of Faculty Instructional Quality

Albert Akyeampong
Ohio University, USA

Teresa Franklin
Ohio University, USA

Jared Keengwe
University of North Dakota, USA

ABSTRACT

This study explored one primary question: To what extent do student perceptions of various forms of instructional technology tools predict instructional quality? Participants for the study were drawn from a teacher education program in a large Midwest public university. Data were collected using a web-based survey with a total of 121 responses used in the final analysis. A multiple regression analysis was conducted to evaluate how well Productivity Tools, Presentation Tools, Communication Tools, and World Wide Web Tools predict Student Evaluation of Faculty Instructional Quality. The overall significant results of the regression model and the subsequent significant results of the t-test for Presentation Tools and Productivity Tools is an indication that Presentation and Productivity tools can be used by faculty to facilitate student and faculty interaction, promote cooperation among students, promote active learning techniques, give prompt feedback, emphasize time on task, communicate high expectation and respect diverse talents and ways of learning.

INTRODUCTION

Technology permeates all sectors of human lives. While educational technology has been a focus of educational policy reform over the past two decades (U.S. Department of Education, 2006), the integration of technology into instruction and its effect on student learning is of increasing interest to stakeholders such as policymakers, administrators, educators, students, and parents (Keengwe, 2007). Even so, technology alone cannot realize many educators' vision for technology to im-

DOI: 10.4018/978-1-61350-468-0.ch009

prove education (Oppenheimer, 2003). Further, technology by itself cannot change the nature of classroom instruction unless teachers are able to evaluate and integrate the use of that technology into the curriculum (Geisert & Futrell, 2000).

Faculty in most teacher education programs are faced with the primary task of preparing graduates who are capable of incorporating technology in their lessons. The general expectation is that teacher education graduates would be both capable and committed to using technology as a tool for enhancing lessons plans that enhance student learning. Teacher educators are expected to be competent in using various technology tools in order to achieve this expectation. A U.S. Department of Education (2000) report indicates that:

Teachers must be comfortable with technology, able to apply it appropriately, and conversant with new technological tools, resources, and approaches. If all the pieces are put into place, teachers should find that they are empowered to advance their own professional skills through these tools as well (p. 39).

Preparing graduates who are capable and committed to using technology as a learning tool is a major task for teacher education programs (Howland & Wedman, 2004). Teacher preparation in higher education programs must prepare preservice teachers to incorporate technology effectively in their future K-12 classrooms. In the participating College of Education, technology is an integral part of the teacher education preservice program. At this college, technology's focus is to support student learning; faculty use technology tools to help teacher candidates explore various ways to integrate technology into their curricula, thereby adding value to the overall teacher preparation process. Given that technology integration is lacking throughout the educational curriculum (International Society for Technology in Education, 2000), integration of technology into existing teacher education programs would be the ideal step

toward integrating technology into the candidates' future K-12 classroom classrooms.

The growing interest in technology use in higher education by students or faculty is reflected in a number of recent studies on faculty or student technology use in higher education (Keengwe, 2007; Marwan, 2008). Technology has also opened new areas for instruction (Baylor & Ritchie, 2002) that are closely linked to student learning. Wepner, Tao, and Ziomek (2003) argue that:

If teacher education programs hope to keep up with the changes that are occurring as result of the new digital society, then it is imperative that we take a closer look at the role that technology can have in transforming teacher preparation (p. 72).

Teachers need to integrate computer skills into the content areas and recognize that computers are not ends in themselves (International Society for Technology in Education, 2000). In addition, for successful integration of technology in education, educational stakeholders must shift their focus from just providing more machines in the classrooms to investing in faculty. Fabry and Higgs (1997) state that:

If the integration of technology in the classroom in the next ten years is to look any different from the last ten, we must focus time, money, and resources in areas that can have the greatest impact for our students, our teachers (p. 393).

The Study

Technology has become an integral part of learning tools in most classrooms. Consequently, if the power of new technologies is to be realized, instructors need to employ instructional strategies consistent with the Seven Principles of Good Practice in Undergraduate Education and support preservice teachers to gain comfortable skills and ability in everyday technology use (Chickering

& Ehrmann, 1996). Therefore, this study sought to explore whether different forms of technology tools: Productivity Tools, Presentation Tools, Communication Tools, and World Wide Web Tools, reliably predict instructional quality using the Chickering and Gamson (1991) seven principles of good practice in undergraduate education, as a guide. The Seven Principles are a result of a review of 50 years of research on the way teachers teach and students learn (Chickering & Gamson, 1991). Good practice in undergraduate education according to the researchers:

1. Encourages student and faculty interaction,
2. Promotes cooperation among students,
3. Promotes active learning techniques,
4. Gives prompt feedback,
5. Emphasizes time on task,
6. Communicates high expectations and
7. Respects diverse talents and ways of learning (Chickering & Gamson, 1991, p. 5)

Purpose of Study

There is a call for evidence for the justification of huge investments into educational technology resources (Oppenheimer, 2003) and a critical need to quantify the use of educational technology to support student learning (Roblyer & Knezek, 2003; Strudler, 2003). Some researchers have explored the factors that enhance integration of technology into instruction (Bauer & Kenton, 2005; Keengwe, 2007) as well as the barriers to effective technology integration in the classroom (Keengwe, Onchwari, & Wachira, 2008). However, few studies are available on the perception of preservice teachers towards technology integration in the curriculum.

While public interest in the use and integration of technology in education is growing, research in this area is still in its infancy, especially that which focus on classroom instruction. Rapid improve-

ments in educational technologies also exceed the current knowledge of classroom technology practices (Allen, 2001) and imply the need for a study such as this. Therefore, the purpose of this study was to explore relationships between student perceptions of various forms of instructional technology tools and whether these forms of technology tools could predict instructional quality. The researchers also wanted to identify the variables that were more important than others in predicting instructional quality.

Research Question

The primary research question for this study was: To what extent do student perceptions of various forms of instructional technology tools predict instructional quality?

Significance of Study

Educators have consistently made various assumptions about the relationships between technology integration and instructional quality. For instance, teachers might assume that all different form of technology tools: Productivity Tools, Presentation Tools, Communication Tools, and World Wide Web Tools predict instructional quality. This study is intended to provide data to support or question that which is assumed. Secondly, examining the relationship among the various variables explored in the study will provide teachers with data to inform their classroom practices and to better facilitate student learning. For instance, based on the evidence from the study, productivity tools can be used by teachers to facilitate student and faculty interaction, promote cooperation among students, promote active learning techniques, give prompt feedback, emphasize time on task, communicate high expectation and respect diverse talents and ways of learning.

METHOD

Research Design

The study utilized a survey for data collection. A survey is an attempt to collect data from members of a population with respect to one or more variables (Gay & Airasian, 2003). The goal of a survey is to gain specific information about a representative sample of a particular group; a self-report measure is a strong method to provide great insight on an individual's perception. Close-ended surveys were administered to a sample of research participants and collected by the researchers after completion.

Participants

A convenient sample was drawn by purposefully selecting 8 undergraduate classes. The selection was based on classes which had a sizeable proportion of their students offering the listed majors under item 5 of Part I of the survey. This approach allowed a wide range of preservice students to be part of the study.

Instrument

The researchers employed an online survey method to collect, tabulate and analyze the data. Data were collected with an online questionnaire consisting of 52 items. The instrument site was located at the SurveyMonkey website (www.surveymonkey.com). This site linked the respondents to all the sections of the instrument hosted on the SurveyMonkey server. Email addresses of students in the College of Education at a large Midwest public university were obtained from the Office of Institutional Research. To improve the response rate, email reminders with links to the survey was sent out to all participants inviting those who may not have responded after two weeks of the first invitation to participate in the survey.

The instrument was developed following the literature on the Seven Principles of Good Practice in Undergraduate Education and the use of technology. Parts I of the instrument involved the academic and demographic information. The data on student academic and demographic helped the researchers to better describe the study participants. Part II of the instrument was designed to measure faculty instructional quality as perceived by students. This section was adapted from the questionnaire titled 'student evaluation of instruction' by the department of teacher education, College of Education in the participating university (Student Evaluation of Instruction, n.d.). Part III of the instrument relates to the various forms of technology and the seven principles of good practice in undergraduate education. The forms of technology tools included productivity tools, presentation tools, communication tools, and World Wide Web tools. The choice of these tools was informed by the literature.

An initial draft of the questionnaire that contained items to be included in the survey was reviewed by two faculty members knowledgeable in the field of education technology. Based on their comments and informed feedback regarding areas that required further clarification, the survey format was restructured, and several items in the survey were revised for improved clarity. Given that almost all the items on the instrument were modified to match the present study, reliability and validity of the instrument was determined through a pilot study.

A coefficient of .90 indicates a highly reliable instrument but coefficients ranging from .70 to .94 are acceptable for most instruments (McMillan & Schumacher, 1997). The researchers used Cronbach (α) reliability for item analysis. The analysis indicated to the researcher how reliable the items within each component and reliability for the whole scale were. From the main studies, overall reliability with Cronbach (α) of .968 was found. For instructional quality, Cronbach (α)

of.926 for instructional quality,.909 for productivity tools,.861 for presentation tools,.940 for communication tools and.948 for World Wide Web tools were found for the instrument. A summary of this information is provided in Table 1.

Validity of the Instrument

Validity tells a researcher how well a measure truly assesses what she or he wants it to; Validity is a relative concept that describes how appropriate or sound a measure is for the purpose for which it is meant. A measure is content valid if its individual items as a group cover all the different domains a researcher wants to measure (Light et al., 1990).

To ensure content validity in the study, the researchers distributed the instrument among three experts in the field to judge if the items are stated appropriately, the language used is appropriate and the items relate to each component. Suggestions from the experts were used to modify the instrument to ensure content validity.

A factor analysis was performed to support construct validity. Results of the factor analysis showed all questions loaded on 4 dimensions which together explained 72% of the variance. The items loaded well and appeared to measure the true construct for which it was intended. The results of the factor analysis supported the construct validity.

Table 1. Reliability analysis of the instrument

Subscale	Reliability: Cronbach's Alpha	N
O: Overall	.968	121
Q: Instructional Quality	.926	121
A: Productivity Tools	.909	121
B: Presentation Tools	.861	121
C: Communication Tools	.940	121
D: World Wide Web Tools	.948	121

Procedures

The researchers contacted the professors of the selected classes to request permission to administer the survey. The selection of 8 classes was informed by the pilot study response rate of 57%. The response rate of the main study was 56.6 percent. Given a class size of 25 to 30 students, the initial 8 classes provided enough participants for the survey. The researchers briefed students about the research prior to emailing them the survey hotlinks. After permission was granted to administer the survey, a specific date and time for the survey to be taken was determined by the researchers and the professor.

A Consent Form explaining the purpose of the study and soliciting the students' willingness to fill the survey and the survey instruments were also hand-delivered to the participants in their respective classes. Student and faculty names were not identified anywhere on the survey for confidentiality purposes. It was decided by the researchers that if any of the professors decided not to allow the research surveys to be conducted during class time, the researchers would seek 2 more classes with representative sample. However, all the professors contacted agreed to the researchers' request to conduct the study during regular class time.

The data were coded and prepared for analysis using the Statistical Package for Research Software Program (SPSS). Descriptive statistics was run to check for minimum and maximum values and compare the results to the ones in the data. Items found to be above maximum or minimum values than the original questionnaire were rechecked to ensure that the inconsistencies were not attributable to coding, recoding or data entry. The standardized Z scores tests was performed to capture any further errors and or extreme values that were not detected by the descriptive statistics. A total of 121 responses were used in the analysis. The Cook distance for all variables was examined and all values found to be within range. An influential point will have a Cooks value >1.

RESULTS

A multiple regression analysis was conducted to evaluate how well Productivity Tools, Presentation Tools, Communication Tools, and World Wide Web Tools predict Student Evaluation of Faculty Instructional Quality. The direct entry method was used. The model as a whole was significant, $F_{(4, 115)} = 38.543$, $p < .001$ (Table 2 and 3). An R^2 of .57 was obtained from the analysis indicating that approximately 57% of the variance of the student evaluation of Instructional Quality Scale can be accounted for by the linear combination of Productivity Tools Scale, Presentation Tools Scale, Communication Tools Scale, and World Wide Web Tools Scale.

The significant levels of the regression coefficients which were assessed through t statistics indicated that only two of the Independent variables, Productivity Tools Scale, Presentation Tools Scale, contributed significantly to the regression with t of 2.082 and 7.617 respectively. Presentation Tools Scale was more significant at predicting Instructional Quality. The prediction model was illustrated by Scatter plot of the residual ZRESID versus predicted values ZPRED.

The adjusted R^2 gives one an estimate of the shrinkage. The adjusted R^2 (from SPSS print out) estimates how much variance on y would be accounted for if we had derived the equation in the population from which the sample was drawn (Stevens, 1999). The adjusted R^2 for the regression model 1 was .558. A summary of these findings is provided in Table 2 and Table 3.

DEPENDENT VARIABLE: INSTRUCTIONAL QUALITY

Supplemental Analysis

Supplemental regression analysis was conducted to further explore the data. The predictors for the regression analysis were Faculty: Encourages student and faculty interaction scale – S1, Promotes cooperation among students scale – S2, Promotes active learning techniques scale – S3, Gives prompt feedback scale S4, Emphasizes time on task scale - S5, Communicates high expecta-

Table 2. Multiple regression analysis (N = 120) - Model one

R	R Square	Adjusted R Square	Change Statistics		
			df1	df2	Sig. F Change
.757	.573	.558	4	115	.000

Predictors (constant): D, B, C, and A.
A: Productivity Tools,
B: Presentation tools,
C: Communication tools,
D: World Wide Web tools.

Table 3. Multiple regression coefficients (N = 120) - Model one

Variable	B	Std. Error	Β	T
Constant	24.590	3.963	0	6.205
A_Sum Productivity Tools	.369	.177	.184*	2.082*
B_Sum Presentation Tools	1.521	.200	.668**	7.617**
C_Sum Communication Tools	-.144	.145	-.085	-.995
D_Sum World Wide Web Tools	.030	.115	.019	.262

* Significant at 0.05
* * Significant at 0.01
B - Unstandardized Coefficients
β - Standardized Coefficients

tions scale - S6 and Respects diverse talents and ways of learning scale – S7. Results from this analysis also indicated no statistically significant difference in the way female and male perceived Instructional Quality. Gender was therefore not a predictor of instructional quality.

DISCUSSION

The results indicated that productivity tools, presentation tools, communication tools, and World Wide Web tools were significant predictors of the dependent variable, instructional quality. Approximately 57% of the variance of the student evaluation of Instructional Quality Scale (I.Q.) was accounted for by its linear relationship with Productivity Tools Scale, Presentation Tools Scale, Communication Tools Scale, and World Wide Web Tools Scale. Two of the predictor scales, Productivity Tools Scale and Presentation Tools Scale were statistically significant in predicting the Instructional Quality; Productivity Tools Scale ($N = 120$, $\beta = 0.369$, $p < 0.05$) and Presentation Tools Scale ($N = 120$, $\beta = 1.521$, $p < 0.01$). In other words, an instructor who used the Presentation and Productivity tools would on average be perceived by students as exhibiting a high Instructional Quality. All 4 tools -Productivity Tools, Presentation Tools, Communication Tools, and World Wide Web Tools individually correlated significantly with Instructional Quality Scale.

Findings support research claims (Solvie & Kloek, 2007) that students learning needs could be addressed by technology tools. The results support past research that deployment of quizzes online, conversion of chalkboard content to PowerPoint slides and the broadcast of video lectures over the Internet for on-demand replay resulted in positive time utilization, and promoted learning and understanding of course material (Harley & Maher, 2003). All the four predictors individually correlated with Instructional Quality, an indication there was a relationship. The overall significant

results of the regression model and the subsequent significant results of the t-test for Presentation Tools and Productivity Tools was an indication that Presentation tool and Productivity tools could be used by faculty to facilitate student and faculty interaction, promote cooperation among students, promote active learning techniques, give prompt feedback, emphasize time on task, communicate high expectation and respect diverse talents and ways of learning. Among the four predictors, Presentation Tool emerged as the most important predictor of Instructional Quality.

The recognition of the benefits of Presentation Tool in instruction by students is well documented (Clarke, 2008). Evidence suggests students appreciate the benefits of Presentation Tools but are critical enough to discern the ability to use Presentation Tools in meeting teaching objectives versus using Presentation Tools as the main thrust of the lecture (Clarke, 2008). Using technology to promote good teaching involves using technology to deliver lectures, encouraging interaction among student and faculty, promoting cooperation among students and giving prompt feedback (Chickering & Gamson, 1991).

Students are diverse learners and learn through various means of instruction. The use of technology would better equip teachers with the means to diversify their instruction so that all students have a chance to learn in their own way. Consequently providing different potential pathways to learning through technology is important. Using a combination of all the various technologies – Presentation, Communication and the World Wide Web would help instructors to facilitate good instruction and enhance student learning. Where there are limited resources to cover all aspects of technology, committing resources towards Presentation and Productivity Tools appears to be a step in the right direction considering the current findings from this research. The researchers recommend equity of funding based on informed decisions to support Presentation and Productivity Tools

The results from main and supplementary regression support Chickering and Gamson (1991) that a good practice in undergraduate education involves the seven principles of good undergraduate education: it encourages student and faculty interaction, promotes cooperation among students, promotes active learning techniques, gives prompt feedback, emphasizes time on task, communicates high expectations and respects diverse talents and ways of learning. An effective instruction model should comprise of all these seven principles. The results also support Kvavik and Caruso (2005) findings that instructors perceived by students as integrating technology in the curriculum report more interest in the subject, more engagement, better understanding of the complex issue and improve learning. However, to make their teaching more effective, instructors should strive to integrate technology into the curriculum.

Limitations

The study used a self-reported questionnaire survey which is limited in nature by the accuracy of the participant's responses (Kerlinger & Lee, 2000). Although the researchers took methodological steps to facilitate accurate reporting such as confidentiality and voluntary participation, these procedures might have not ruled out the biases associated with self-report measures, including social desirability. Secondly, there are problems with individual responses; the responses collected represent only perceptions of participants. These responses may have been influenced by other variables not included in the study. Finally, the study was designed to focus on undergraduate students drawn from one College of Education at a participating large midwest public university. It is possible that results might not generalize to other colleges of education, types of institutions or private institutions.

CONCLUSION

The purpose of this study was to examine whether the various forms of technology tools: productivity tools, presentation tools, communication tools, and World Wide Web tools, reliably predict instructional quality. The study also examined various predictors: Productivity tools, Presentation tools, Communication tools, and World Wide Web tools and their ability to predict instructional quality.

The findings from the study and supplementary analyses demonstrated a statistically significant relationship between the predictors and Instructional Quality. Productivity and Presentation Tools emerged as significant predictors of Instructional Quality. Presentation Tools was more important in predicting Instructional Quality from the perception of the students than Productivity Tools.

Technology has the potential for changing the way teachers teach and students learn (Thompson, Schmidt, & Davis, 2003). The study provided baseline data to identify current faculty computer integration practices. These data could guide faculty in their classroom practices as well as provide them with evidence to guide them make sound classroom technology-related decisions that enhance and maximize student learning. The results also provide additional literature supporting the important role of technology in instruction. Based on the findings, administrators and instructors should strive to adopt and utilize technologies that students perceive as enhancing instructional quality.

REFERENCES

Allen, R. (2001, Fall). Technology and learning: How schools map routes to technology's promised land. *ASCD Curriculum Update, 1-3*, 6–8.

Bauer, J., & Kenton, J. (2005). Toward technology integration in the schools: Why it isn't happening. *Journal of Technology and Teacher Education, 13*(4), 519–546.

Baylor, A. L., & Ritchie, D. (2002). What factors facilitate teacher skill, teacher morale, and perceived student learning in technology-using classrooms? *Computers & Education, 39*(4), 395–414. doi:10.1016/S0360-1315(02)00075-1

Chickering, A., & Ehrmann, S. C. (1996, October). Implementing the seven principles: Technology as lever. *AAHE Bulletin*, 3-6. Retrieved February 7, 2008 from http://www.tltgroup.org/programs/seven.html

Chickering, A. W., & Gamson, Z. F. (Eds.). (1991). *Applying the seven principles for good practice in undergraduate education*. San Francisco, CA: Jossey-Bass Inc.

Clarke, J. (2008). PowerPoint and pedagogy maintaining student interest in university lectures. *Contemporary Issues in Technology & Teacher Education, 56*(1), 39–45.

Coley, R., Cradler, J., & Engel, P. K. (1997). *Computers and classrooms: The status of technology in U.S. schools. Policy Information Report*. Princeton, NJ: Educational Testing Service, Policy Information Center.

Fabry, D., & Higgs, J. (1997). Barriers to the effective use of technology in education. *Journal of Educational Computing, 17*(4), 385–395.

Gay, L. R., & Airasian, P. (2003). *Educational Research: Competencies for Analysis and Applications* (7th ed.). Upper Saddle River, NJ: Pearson Education.

Geisert, P., & Futrell, M. (2000). *Teachers, computers, and curriculum: Microcomputers in the classroom*. Boston, MA: Allyn and Bacon.

Harley, D., & Maher, M. (2003). Technology enhancements in a large lecture course. *EDUCAUSE Quarterly, 26*(3), 27–33.

Howland, J., & Wedman, J. (2004). A process model for faculty development: Individualizing technology learning. *Journal of Technology and Teacher Education, 12*(2), 239–262.

International Society for Technology in Education (ISTE). (2000). *National Educational Technology Standards (NETS) for teachers*. Retrieved November 15, 2008 from http://cnets.iste.org/teachers/

Keengwe, J. (2007). Faculty Integration of Technology into Instruction and Students' perceptions of Computer Technology to Improve Student Learning. *Journal of Information Technology Education, 6*, 169–180.

Keengwe, J., Onchwari, G., & Wachira, P. (2008). Computer technology integration and student learning: Barriers and promise. *Journal of Science Education and Technology, 17*(6), 560–565. doi:10.1007/s10956-008-9123-5

Kerlinger, F. N., & Lee, H. B. (2000). *Foundations of behavioral research* (4th ed.). Fort Worth, TX: Harcourt.

Kvavik, R. B., & Caruso, J. B. (2005). ECAR study of students and information technology, 2005: Convenience, connection, control, and learning. *EDUCAUSE Center for Applied Research (ECAR) publication, 6*.

Light, R. J., Singer, J. D., & Willett, J. B. (1990). *By design: Planning research on higher education*. Cambridge, MA: Harvard University Press.

Marwan, A. (2008). An Analysis of Australian Students' Use of Information and Communications Technology (ICT). *International Journal of instructional Technology and Distance Learning, 5*(11), 45-54.

McMillan, J. H., & Schumacher, S. (1997). *Research in education: A conceptual introduction* (4th ed.). Don Mills, ON: Longman.

Oppenheimer, T. (2003). *The flickering mind: The false promise of technology in the classroom and how learning can be saved.* New York: Random House.

Roblyer, M. D., & Knezek, G. A. (2003). New millennium research for educational technology: A call for a national research agenda. *Journal of Research on Technology in Education, 36*(1), 60–71.

Solvie, P., & Kloek, M. (2007). Using technology tools to engage students with multiple learning styles in a constructivist learning environment. *Contemporary Issues in Technology & Teacher Education, 7*(2), 7–27.

Stevens, J. (1999). *Intermediate statistics* (2nd ed.). Mahwah, NJ: L. Erlbaum.

Strudler, N. (2003). Answering the call: A response to Roblyer and Knezek. *Journal of Research on Technology in Education, 36*(1), 72–76.

Student Evaluation of Instruction. (n.d.). Athens, OH: Ohio University. *Teacher Education Department.*

Thompson, A. D., Schmidt, D. A., & Davis, N. E. (2003). Technology collaborative for simultaneous renewal in teacher education. *Educational Technology Research and Development, 51*(1), 73–89. doi:10.1007/BF02504519

U.S. Department of Education. (2000). *Teachers' tools for the 21st Century: A report on teachers' use of technology (NCES 2000-102).* Washington, DC: National Center for Education Statistics.

U.S. Department of Education. (2006). *Education Technology Fact Sheet.* Retrieved August 29, 2008 from http://www.ed.gov/about/offices/list/os/technology/facts.html.

Wepner, S. B., Tao, L., & Ziomek, N. M. (2003). Three teacher educators' perspectives about the shifting responsibilities of infusing technology into the curriculum. *Action in Teacher Education, 24*(4), 53–63.

This work was previously published in International Journal of Information and Communication Technology, Volume 6, Issue 2, edited by Lawrence A. Tomei, pp. 1-10, copyright 2010 by IGI Publishing (an imprint of IGI Global).

Chapter 10

Facilitating Students to Earn Computing Certificates via Blended Learning in Online Problem–Solving Environment:
A Cross–Course–Orientation Comparison

Chia-Wen Tsai
Ming Chuan University, Taiwan

ABSTRACT

The vocational schools in Taiwan regard professional certifications as a badge of skills achievement. However, due to a national policy, pure online courses are not permitted. Moreover, it remains unclear whether every subject is suitable to be delivered via online courses. In this regard, the author conducted a quasi-experiment to examine the effects of applying blended learning (BL) with different course orientations on students' computing skills, and explored the appropriate combination for teachers who teach computing courses. Four classes in successive semesters, with a total of 195 students from the courses of 'Database Management System' and 'Packaged Software and Application', were divided into 2 (Design-oriented vs. Procedural-oriented) × 2 (BL vs. Traditional Learning) experimental groups. The results showed that students from both design-oriented and procedural-oriented courses delivered in BL environment, had significantly higher grades on the examination for certificates than those who learned in traditional learning environment.

INTRODUCTION

Computing certification verifies that one is able to use a computer and apply common computer applications at a certain level of competence (Pfefer, 2002). These computing certifications, such as Microsoft Office Specialist (MOS), as-sist companies to increase the potential that a job candidate has the technical capabilities, skills, and other competencies to make a valuable employee (Anderson, 2007). These certifications exist to varying levels elsewhere in the world (McGettrick, Boyle, Ibbett, Lloyd, Lovegrove, & Mander, 2005), and are nationally or internation-

DOI: 10.4018/978-1-61350-468-0.ch010

ally standardized as they provide a unique measure of computer skills (Vakhitova & Bollinger, 2006). In this regard, many private vocational schools, facing the high pressure of market competition, often emphasize the proportion of students awarded technical/vocational certificates before they graduate. Teaching in this partition usually focuses on helping students to pass certification examinations (Shen, Lee, Tsai, & Ting, 2008). The quality and quantity of a student's certificates is an important criterion when applying for admission to universities or graduate schools. Therefore, how to help students enhance their professional skills and pass the examination for certificates is the major concern to many teachers in vocational schools in Taiwan.

In many educational settings, it may be inappropriate to ask students to work on actual problems in limited time, space, and context for evaluation. Thus, it is critical to find the evidence that students possess ability in solving particular classes of problems through a suitable assessment format (Wang, Chang, & Li, 2008). In the courses that target professional certifications, teachers usually focus their course content on problem-solving processes, and evaluate students' skills of solving simulated problems as examinations. That is, students have to learn and practice the problem-solving processes for earning professional certifications. Technological problem-solving skills provide students with the opportunity and facility to fulfill the various requirements of the technological design process, regardless of learning environment type (Walmsley, 2003). However, different certifications or courses may focus on design-oriented or procedural-oriented computing skills. For example, a course on Java or website planning may focus more on the design content and thinking, while those of Word or PowerPoint may emphasize more on manipulation. In this regard, the author attempted to explore whether courses of different natures are similarly appropriate to be conducted in online learning environment.

Universities and colleges across the United States have experienced an exceptional growth in the demand for online course instruction in the recent years (Ray, 2009). Nevertheless, the policy of e-learning in Taiwan is relative conservative in contrast with that in the U.S. For example, earning an academic degree entirely through online courses is still not allowed at present. Moreover, some universities only allow a teacher to deliver online classes for less than fifty percent of the whole semester's course. Thus, teachers in some nations with conservative institutions, such as Taiwan, have to adopt a mode of blended learning (BL) rather than pure online learning when implementing e-learning.

BL is a flexible approach to course design that supports the blending of different times and places for learning, offers the convenience of fully online courses without the complete loss of face-to-face contact. With regard to the effects of BL in previous research, a positive effect of blended e-learning on students' attitude toward computer and mathematics was found (Yushau, 2006). Moreover, students in a BL group attained significantly higher average scores than those in a traditional teaching group. The BL group had a significantly higher percentage pass rate than the traditional teaching group. It is believed that BL is more effective than traditional teaching (Pereira, Pleguezuelos, Merí, Molina-Ros, Molina-Tomás, & Masdeu, 2007). Therefore, BL is applied in this study to help students learn and develop their skills in using application software, and be examined as to its potential effects.

As more and more institutions of higher education provide online courses, the question remains as to whether they can be as effective as those offered in the traditional classroom format (Shelley, Swartz, & Cole, 2007). However, one of the main reasons for this real or perceived low impact of ICT-based tools on students' learning is that technology has often been introduced as an addition to an existing, unchanged classroom setting (De Corte, 1996; Bottino & Robotti, 2007).

There are some studies comparing the effectiveness between BL and traditional face-to-face learning (Castelijn & Janssen, 2006; Chen, Kinshuk, Wei, Chen, & Wang, 2007; Lee & Chan, 2007; Yushau, 2006). Nevertheless, it is necessary to further explore what kinds of subjects are more appropriately conducted in the online learning environment, and provide effective online instructional methods for vocational students. Therefore, the author redesigned two courses of 'Database Management System' and 'Packaged Software and Application' to integrate BL and innovative teaching technologies to help students learn and earn the related certificate. Specifically, this study investigated the potential effects of the different combinations of BL and course orientation on students' learning.

CONCEPTUAL FRAMEWORK

Course Type

Course type refers to the subject matter and nature (Benbunan-Fich & Hiltz, 2003). It is a critical variable in the online learning context, and many researchers have raised the importance of course type in online environment and explored the effectiveness of online learning in different courses (Abel, 2005; Benbunan-Fich & Hiltz, 2002, 2003; Carnwell, 2000). In the field of computer software education, there exists a difference in the natures of courses. In Benbunan-Fich and Hiltz's (2003) classification, courses are divided into two categories: more technical and less technical.

The research in this study was conducted in computing courses, which are technical courses; even so, the courses were still different in their subject matters. For example, the content and teaching styles in document processing (e.g., Microsoft Word) are much more procedural-oriented, while the teaching of programming (e.g., C++ or Java) and website planning are relatively more design-oriented. The more procedural-oriented course focuses more on imitation and operation. For example, students have to listen to the lecture and replicate the processes they learned; then they can master and perform the functions well. In contrast, design-oriented courses usually require students' higher-order thinking and teacher's interpretations and explanations.

It is indicated that design-oriented courses may help students acquire the various kinds of knowledge, thinking and actions (Young, Cole, & Denton, 2002), and lead to better learning effects. However, students' learning may be limited if students need more illustrations and higher-order thinking in the online courses without the teacher's on-the-spot explanation and assistance (Shen, Lee, Tsai, & Ting, 2008). However, there are few studies that have discussed effective teaching methods for different course orientations, particularly in the online environment (Shen, Lee, & Tsai, 2007). Therefore, the author explores whether both design-oriented and procedural-oriented courses are appropriate to be delivered in the online learning environment.

Blended Learning

BL is a form of technology-mediated learning that improves learning outcomes through an alternation of traditionally-delivered classes and Internet-delivered classes (Lai, Lee, Yeh, & Ho, 2005). BL not only offers more choices but also is more effective (Singh, 2003). Blending itself makes effective engagement in a range of situations possible, allowing students to fit their different activities together with more flexibility according to their particular circumstances (Aspden & Helm, 2004).

As for the effects of BL, previous research has found that performance as measured by the final mark of the course under the hybrid teaching method that incorporated both traditional face-to-face lectures and electronic delivery and communication methods is higher than when using a traditional teaching method (Dowling,

Godfrey, & Gyles, 2003). The effect of BL was potentially a more robust educational experience than either traditional or fully online learning (Rovai & Jordan, 2004). BL could add value when facilitated by educators with high interpersonal skills, and accompanied by reliable, easy-to-use technology (Derntl & Motschnig-Pitrik, 2005). Boyle, Bradley, Chalk, Jones, and Pickard's (2003) research indicated a generally positive evaluation of the main elements of BL, and widespread use of the new online features. Moreover, students in BL group attained significantly higher average scores than those in traditional teaching group. The BL group had significantly higher percentage pass rate than the traditional teaching group. It is concluded that BL was more effective than traditional teaching (Pereira, Pleguezuelos, Merí, Molina-Ros, Molina-Tomás, & Masdeu, 2007). Therefore, BL is applied in this study to help students learn and earn the related certificate.

METHODS

Participants

The participants in this study were 195 vocational students from four classes taking two compulsory courses titled 'Packaged Software and Application' and 'Database Management System' in a university of science and technology in Taiwan. None of them majored in information or computer technology.

Computing education is emphasized for students of all levels and disciplines, particularly in Taiwan's vocational education system. Even students in the departments of business administration or nursing still have to develop the required computing skills. Students at this university are expected to spend much more time and effort in mastering a variety of technological skills as compared to those in comprehensive universities in Taiwan.

Course Setting

The two involved courses ('Packaged Software and Application' and 'Database Management System') were semester-long, 2 credit-hour classes, and targeting first- and second-year college students from different major fields of study. Students received a study task dealing with the subject of Microsoft Word and Access. The major focus of the course of 'Packaged Software and Application' was to develop students' skills in using the tools and functions of Microsoft Word, while the emphasis in the course of 'Database Management System' was to develop skills in applying database via Microsoft Access. Moreover, these courses targeted helping students to earn the certificates of professional database application and document processing. That is, students had to take an examination for a certificate in Word or Access at the end of semester.

Course Content

Vocational schools in Taiwan often emphasize the proportion of students awarded such certificates before they graduate. As for the examinations, students are required to solve simulated problems. For example, in the course of Database Management System (design-oriented course), students may be asked to design and buildup databases for customers, and select those who live in Taipei City from the databases. Then, students have to present the records or data in printable reports or web pages. On the other hand, students in the procedural-oriented course of 'Packaged Software and Application' have to build documents such as autobiographies or circulars in Microsoft Word. The course content differed due to the different course orientation. However, teaching in both the courses focuses on the problem-solving processes students have to learn and practice they require to gain the skills to pass the certification exams. The content, learning processes and activities in these two courses are compared in Table 1.

Experimental Design and Procedure

In this study, the author explored whether students in the courses of 'Database Management System' and 'Packaged Software and Application' enhanced their skills in application software via e-learning. Based on reflection from our earlier experiments and research, we re-designed the course and conducted a series of quasi-experiments to examine the effects of BL, course orientation, and their combinations.

The experimental design is a 2 (Design-oriented vs. Procedural-oriented) × 2 (BL vs. Traditional Learning) factorial pretest-post test design (see Figure 1). There were four classes from two courses. The Design-oriented and BL group (C1, n=43), Design-oriented and Traditional group (C2, n=53), Procedural-oriented and BL group (C3, n=48) were experimental groups, while Procedural-oriented and Traditional group (C4, n=51) were the control group. Participants from the second-year students were randomly assigned to the two classes of 'Database Management System' (C1 and C2), while those first-year students were randomly assigned to the two classes of 'Packaged Software and Application' (C3 and C4).

Students in the two courses were asked to pass the examination to earn the certificate in Microsoft Access or Word. The examinations on these software applications were held right after the comple-

tion of teaching the course (the 16th week). The detailed schedule of the experiment is depicted in Figure 2:

Treatment of Blended Learning

It is suggested by Alonso, López, Manrique, and Viñes (2005) that an efficient blended learning solution includes the following ingredients: (1) An instructor who directs learning; (2) Email and telephone assistance for personalized learner support; (3) Virtual classes by means of computerized device; (4) Interaction between learners and the instructor and between the learners themselves through the chat to stimulate group learning; (5) Support for subjects related to learning management; (6) Assessment examinations; and (7) Certificate and diploma that certifies having taken or passed the course. In this study, the author adopted Alonso, López, Manrique, and Viñes' suggestions to design the treatment of BL.

In the BL environment, two software packages, Microsoft Access and Word, were taught separately in four classes (see Figure 1). The teacher lectured about how to solve simulated computing problems as mentioned in subsection '3.3 Course Content' through the Internet or in the classroom. In the beginning of the courses, students were encouraged to adapt to learn via a course website. The teacher audio recorded every

Table 1. Comparison of Design-oriented and Procedural-oriented courses

	Design-oriented	Procedural-oriented
Course involved	Database Management System	Packaged Software and Application
Application software used	Microsoft Access	Microsoft Word
Content focus	Developing students' skills in using database	Developing students' skills in applying the tools and functions of Microsoft Word
Learning processes and activities	Listening, thinking, understanding, and learning by doing	Simple step-by-step manipulation
Skills required	Higher-order thinking and know-how	Replicating what the teacher did
Problem-solving and tasks	Building and combining tables and queries Building queries according to simulated criteria Designing printable reports or web pages	Building documents such as business circulars or autobiographies Building worksheets with graphs

Figure 1. The Courses and interventions in this study

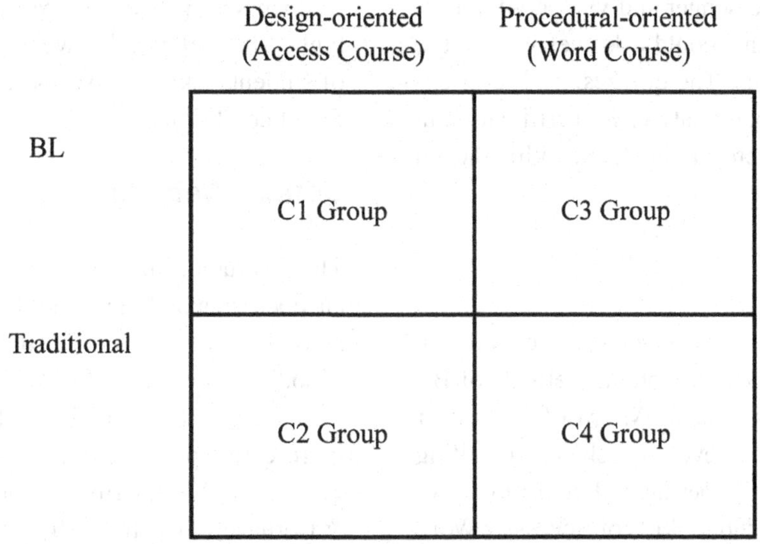

	Design-oriented (Access Course)	Procedural-oriented (Word Course)
BL	C1 Group	C3 Group
Traditional	C2 Group	C4 Group

session of his lecture, whether in the classroom or through Internet and later on translated lectures into HTML files with flash, video, and voice. These HTML files were then loaded into the course website. Students could preview and review the course sessions on this course website. Moreover, students had the opportunity to re-listen to the class at home if they faced problems. This course website also provided a channel and opportunity for students to review and practice before the certification examination.

Beginning in the third week, six weeks of coursework were moved onto the website. Within the first three weeks, the teacher adjusted students' learning gradually and smoothly. However, ten weeks of the coursework were still conducted in the traditional classroom. If students encountered questions, they could ask for help and chat with

Figure 2. The schedule of the course and skill tests in this semester (O: online classes; T: traditional classroom classes)

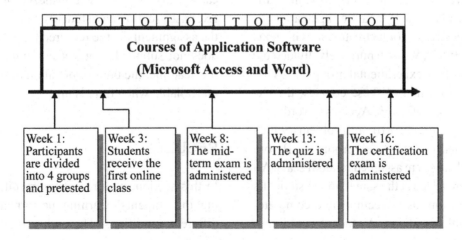

teacher and classmates in the online chatroom or through online messenger and videoconference. In addition, students could ask questions in the face-to-face classes. The quizzes, mid-term examinations, and examinations for certification in Word or Access were administered within the ten face-to-face classes.

Evaluation

A detailed evaluation of the project was conducted. The author explored the potential effects of BL on students' skills of using Microsoft Access or Word. To examine levels of change resulting from variations in experimental conditions, we first measured students' skills of Access or Word before they entered the class. In the first week, students in C1 and C2 built two databases, including tables and queries in Access, while those in C3 and C4 completed an autobiography and show bill in Word as pretests.

The pretest grades show that students' computer skills were uniformly low. None of the participants was able to answer any of the pretest questions correctly and completely. This confirms that the difference in students' skills of application software at the beginning stage among the four groups was not statistically significant. It is believed that the students had equal or no computer skills before they take this course. In addition, none of them had any experience in taking a web-based course. Therefore, the author ruled out initial differences as a plausible alternative explanation for the differences detected after treatments (Gribbons & Herman, 1997). We then purposely divided the students into four experimental groups.

At the conclusion of these courses, the examinations for certificate in Access or Word were conducted. There were two main problems, which each consisted of 7 to 9 sub-problems. Before testing, students were assigned random seats. All students were tested at the same time. A student's grade came from his correctness and completeness of problem solving. A student could earn

professional certification using DBMS (Access) or document processor (Word) if his grade was higher than 70. Finally, we tested the differences of students' skills in Access or Word under different conditions.

Course Website

The instructor in this study adopted Moodle, an open-source Learning Management System (LMS), as the platform for his teaching website. Moodle has been used for sharing useful information, documentation, and knowledge management in research projects (Martin-Blas & Serrano-Fernandez, 2009; Uribe-Tirado, Melgar-Estrada, & Bornacelly-Castro, 2007). The course website consists of five sections: Course Information, Course Content, Course Discussion, Students' System, and Assignments and Exercises. Course information provides course description, syllabus, assignments, grading and course-related information. Course Content includes lectures delivered and conversations that happened in the classroom and the computer files necessary for students' exercises. Students can download the files and listen to audio recordings to review or complete exercises, repeatedly. The teacher may ask questions on the Course Discussion board in order to promote discussion and interaction. Students' personal information and their logs are recorded in Students' System. Finally, the teacher can assign work to students in the Assignments and Exercises section and students have to complete the assignments in the required time. If a student does not submit his or her assignments before the deadline, the button for submission becomes unavailable when time is up.

RESULTS

In this section, we present the results concerning the students' learning performance under different conditions. The author first measured the effects of BL on students' grades for certification examinations. Independent sample t-test was used to compare grades between different groups. As shown in Table 2, students' grades for the design-oriented course in BL class (C1, mean=94.12) were significantly higher than those in the traditional class (C2, mean=81.94). That is, the effects of BL on students' skills of design-oriented computing skills are positive, resulting in higher grades than those who learned only in the traditional classroom.

Results from Table 3 show that students' grades for the procedural-oriented course in BL class (C3, mean=87.71) were also statistically higher than those in the traditional class (C4, mean=75.83). The effects of BL on students' procedural-oriented computing skills are positive, and higher than those who learn only in traditional classrooms. Furthermore, according to the data shown in Table 2 and Table 3, it is believed that BL helps students develop both design-oriented and procedural-oriented computing skills.

The results in the BL environment are compared in Table 4 and indicate that the difference between students' grades in the design-oriented course (C1, mean=94.12) and procedural-oriented course (C3, mean=87.71) were not statistically significant.

That is, students' learning of design-oriented computing skills seemed to not suffer in the BL environment, even without the teacher's on-the-spot assistance and monitoring.

Moreover, it is also revealed in Table 5 that the differences in students' grades for the design-oriented course (C2, mean=81.94) and procedural-oriented course (C4, mean=75.83) in the traditional learning environment were not statistically significant. Based on the data shown in Table 4 and Table 5, no matter in BL or traditional environment, the difference between students' grades for design-oriented course and procedural-oriented course were not statistically significant.

Finally, data from Table 6 shows that students from the design-oriented course who learned in the BL environment had the highest grades among four groups. The grades for certification examinations in C1 were significantly higher than C2 and C4, and also higher than C3, though insignificant. According to the study results, it is believed that the application of BL contributed to students' development of design-oriented and procedural-oriented computing skills.

Table 2. Independent samples t-test: Comparison of students' grades on certification examinations following design-oriented Course

Groups	N	Mean	S. D.	F	*t*-value	df	*p*-value
C1	43	94.12	15.426	8.549	2.482	94	.015 *
C2	53	81.94	28.986				

Note: *p* < 0.05

Table 3. Independent samples t-test: Comparison of students' grades on certification examinations following procedural-oriented course

Groups	n	Mean	S. D.	F	*t*-value	df	*p*-value
C3	48	87.71	16.663	12.604	2.518	97	.013 *
C4	51	75.83	28.388				

Note: *p* < 0.05

Table 4. Independent samples t-test: Comparison of students' grades on certification examinations following procedural- and design-oriented BL Courses

Groups	n	Mean	S. D.	F	t-value	df	p-value
C1	43	94.12	15.426	.625	1.897	89	.061
C3	48	87.71	16.663				

Note: $*p < 0.05$

Table 5. Independent samples t-test: Comparison of students' grades on certification examinations following procedural- and design-oriented traditional courses

Groups	n	Mean	S. D.	F	t-value	df	p-value
C2	53	81.94	28.986	.359	1.086	102	.280
C4	51	75.83	28.388				

Note: $*p < 0.05$

DISCUSSION AND IMPLICATIONS

The policy of e-learning in Taiwan is relatively conservative in contrast with that in the U.S. Teachers in this context have to adopt blended learning if they want to implement e-learning in their courses. It has not been clear whether all subjects are suited to be conducted in an online or blended learning environment. To improve our understanding of this issue, the author brought in and then tested rigorously a set of hypotheses between four experimental groups.

According to the findings of this study, we believe that our research has made some contributions to e-learning theory in three different ways. Firstly, our research contributed to the existing literature by specifying how teachers can help students develop computing skills and improve their grades in the examinations for certificates in a blended learning environment. Second, this study is one of the early attempts to investigate the learning effects for different course types in the online problem-solving environment. Third, our study clarified that not only a procedural-oriented course, but also a design-oriented course was suitable to be conducted and delivered in the blended learning environment.

The Effects of Blended Learning

The data shown in Table 2 illustrate a statistically significant difference ($p = 0.015$) for students' design-oriented computing skills between BL and Traditional classes. In addition, as the data in Table 3 shows, students' procedural-oriented computing skills in a BL class were also significantly higher than those in traditional classes ($p = 0.013$). That is, it can be concluded that BL and the related technologies contribute to students' development of computing skills. In the blended classes, the teacher audio-recorded every session of his lecture, whether in the classroom or through Internet, and later uploaded the audio files to the course website. From the log records, it is found that students logged in and re-listened to the course content, particularly before the quizzes and certification examination. The audio files and the arrangement of the blended course were found to play positive roles in helping students develop both design-oriented and procedural-oriented computing skills. The results in this study are similar to Yushau's (2006) study that shows a positive effect of blended e-learning on students' attitude toward computer and mathematics.

Table 6. One-way ANOVA: Students' grades on certification examinations

Dependent Variable	(I) Groups	(J) Groups	Mean Difference (I-J)	Std. Error	Sig.	95% Confidence Interval	
						Lower Bound	Upper Bound
Grades	C1	C2	12.173(*)	4.858	.013	2.59	21.76
		C3	6.408	4.971	.199	-3.40	16.21
		C4	18.285(*)	4.901	.000	8.62	27.95
	C2	C1	-12.173(*)	4.858	.013	-21.76	-2.59
		C3	-5.765	4.717	.223	-15.07	3.54
		C4	6.112	4.643	.190	-3.05	15.27
	C3	C1	-6.408	4.971	.199	-16.21	3.40
		C2	5.765	4.717	.223	-3.54	15.07
		C4	11.877(*)	4.760	.013	2.49	21.27
	C4	C1	-18.285(*)	4.901	.000	-27.95	-8.62
		C2	-6.112	4.643	.190	-15.27	3.05
		C3	-11.877(*)	4.760	.013	-21.27	-2.49

* The mean difference is significant at the .05 level.

Online learning provides flexibility and potential for applying innovative teaching and learning strategies (Chen, Wei, Wu, & Uden, 2009). However, it is not permitted and thus inapplicable to provide pure online courses to undergraduates in many nations. Moreover, it is also found that many students studying undergraduate programs, as well as many part-time graduate students, indicated their preferences for retaining some form of face-to-face teaching while at the same time taking advantages of e-learning (Lee & Chan, 2007). In Taiwan, students in the vocational system spend more time on part-time jobs, do not adequately get involved in their schoolwork, and don't care so much about their grades (Shen, Lee, & Tsai, 2007). In this specific context, teachers could adopt technologies and teaching websites to help students achieve better learning performance. For example, the blended course and audio-recorded content provide the flexibility and opportunities for students to attend class, review the course content, and practice what they learned at their convenient times, particularly before the examinations. The application of audio technologies and software could be effective and helpful to develop students' computing skills, and further lead to students' success in earning professional certifications. Therefore, it is suggested that teachers should adopt blended learning and related technologies to provide multiple channels and opportunities for students' learning.

Does The Course Type Matter in Blended Learning Environment?

In computer software education, different course types or certifications may have their own emphases, for example, design-oriented courses focus more on cognitive apprenticeship, while procedural-oriented courses emphasize replication. It still remains unclear which types are more suited to be conducted in online learning environments. In this study, it is found that students' grades in design-oriented skills are insignificantly higher than procedural-oriented computing skills ($p = 0.061$, see Table 4). That is, students' computing skills seem not to have suffered in the blended environment without the instructor's assistance and monitoring. On the contrary, the blended course and audio-recorded content provided the flexibility and opportunities for students to review and re-listen to course content, and practice their computing skills. The audio files and the arrangement of blended course may lessen the demand for teacher's on-the-spot assistance.

In this study, students from both design-oriented and procedural-oriented courses who learned in a BL environment had significantly better learning effects than those who learned in the traditional classrooms. Therefore, it is believed that both design-oriented and procedural-oriented courses are appropriate to be conducted and delivered in the blended learning environment, rather than in the traditional classrooms, particularly for those courses focused on earning professional certificates.

CONCLUSION

Increasing the effectiveness of e-learning has become one of the most practically and theoretically important issues in both educational engineering and information system fields (Lee & Lee, 2008). A further investigation of course orientations' fitness to online or blended learning environment is beneficial for improving the learning involved. Through analyzing students' learning outcomes, this study concludes that blended learning contributed to both design-oriented and procedural-oriented computing skills. Furthermore, although teachers who teach design-oriented computing courses may be concerned that students suffer and fail in the blended learning environment, this study also demonstrated that students in design-oriented computing courses could experience better learning effects than those in procedural-oriented computing courses, even though insignificant. This finding suggested that teachers of computing courses could take advantage of relevant technologies (e.g., course websites, audio technologies and software) to help their students

have more channels and opportunities to review and practice computing skills.

The analysis by blended learning with course orientations in this study provides a specific reference for educators and teachers in the context of vocational education, addressing how to enhance students' computing skills and pass an examination for professional certification. Finally, we look forward to future studies that replicate and modify the interventions, design, and arrangement of the blended course to fit curriculum needs, and further contribute to students' learning and skills development.

REFERENCES

Abel, R. (2005). Implementing best practices in online learning: A recent study reveals common denominators for success in Internet-supported learning. *EDUCAUSE Quarterly, 28*(3), 75–77.

Alonso, F., López, G., Manrique, D., & Viñes, J. M. (2005). An instructional model for web-based e-learning education with a blended learning process approach. *British Journal of Educational Technology, 36*(2), 217–235. doi:10.1111/j.1467-8535.2005.00454.x

Anderson, C. (2007). *Preventing bad hires: The value of objective prehire assessment*. Retrieved April 13, 2009 from http:// download. microsoft. com/ download/f/2/b/ f2bde3bb-c982-4c5a-ae41-9300b6b8d413/Preventing_bad_hires.pdf

Aspden, L., & Helm, P. (2004). Making the connection in a blended learning environment. *Educational Media International, 41*(3), 245–252. doi:10.1080/09523980410001680851

Benbunan-Fich, R., & Hiltz, S. R. (2002). *Correlates of effectiveness of learning networks: The effects of course level, course type, and gender on outcomes*. Paper presented at the 35th Annual Hawaii International Conference on System Sciences.

Benbunan-Fich, R., & Hiltz, S. R. (2003). Mediators of the effectiveness of online courses. *IEEE Transactions on Professional Communication, 46*(4), 298–312. doi:10.1109/TPC.2003.819639

Bottino, R. M., & Robotti, E. (2007). Transforming classroom teaching & learning through technology: Analysis of a case study. *Educational Technology & Society, 10*(4), 174–186.

Boyle, T., Bradley, C., Chalk, P., Jones, R., & Pickard, P. (2003). Using blended learning to improve student success rates in learning to program. *Learning, Media and Technology, 28*(2-3), 165-178.

Carnwell, R. (2000). Pedagogical implications of approaches to study in distance learning: developing models through qualitative and quantitative analysis. *Journal of Advanced Nursing, 31*(5), 1018–1028. doi:10.1046/j.1365-2648.2000.01394.x

Castelijn, P., & Janssen, B. (2006). *Effectiveness of Blended Learning in a Distance Education Setting.* Retrieved April 13, 2009 from http:// www.ou.nl/ Docs/ Faculteiten/ MW/MW%20Working%20 Papers/gr%2006%2006%20castelijn.pdf

Chen, N. S. Kinshuk, Wei, C. W., Chen, Y. R., & Wang, Y. C. (2007). Classroom climate and learning effectiveness comparison for physical and cyber F2F interaction in holistic-blended learning environment. In *Proceedings of the 7th IEEE International Conference on Advanced Learning Technologies* (pp. 313-317).

Chen, N. S., Wei, C. W., Wu, K. T., & Uden, L. (2009). Effects of high level prompts and peer assessment on online learners' reflection levels. *Computers & Education, 52*(2), 283–291. doi:10.1016/j.compedu.2008.08.007

De Corte, E. (1996). Changing views of computer supported learning environments for the acquisition of knowledge and thinking skills. In Vosniadou, S., De Corte, E., Glaser, R., & Mandl, H. (Eds.), *International perspectives on the designing of technology-supported learning environments* (pp. 129–145). Mahwah, NJ: Lawrence Erlbaum.

Derntl, M., & Motschnig-Pitrik, R. (2005). The role of structure, patterns, and people in blended learning. *The Internet and Higher Education, 8,* 111–130. doi:10.1016/j.iheduc.2005.03.002

Dowling, C., Godfrey, J. M., & Gyles, N. (2003). Do hybrid flexible delivery teaching methods improve accounting student learning outcomes? *Accounting Education: An International Journal, 12*(4), 373–391. doi:10.1080/0963928032000154512

Garrison, D. R., & Kanuka, H. (2004). Blended learning: Uncovering its transformative potential in higher education. *The Internet and Higher Education, 7*(2), 95–105. doi:10.1016/j.iheduc.2004.02.001

Gribbons, B., & Herman, J. (1997). True and quasi-experimental designs. *Practical Assessment, Research & Evaluation, 5*(14). Retrieved April 13, 2009 from http://PAREonline.net/getvn.asp?v=5&n=14

Lai, S. Q., Lee, C. L., Yeh, Y. J., & Ho, C. T. (2005). A study of satisfaction in blended learning for small and medium enterprises. *International Journal of Innovation and Learning, 2*(3), 319–334. doi:10.1504/IJIL.2005.006373

Lee, J. K., & Lee, W. K. (2008). The relationship of e-Learner's self-regulatory efficacy and perception of e-Learning environmental quality. *Computers in Human Behavior, 24*(1), 32–47. doi:10.1016/j.chb.2006.12.001

Lee, P. W. R., & Chan, F. T. (2007). Blended learning: Experiences of adult learners in Hong Kong. In J. Fong & F. L. Wang (Eds.), *Blended Learning* (pp. 79-87). Retrieved April 13, 2009 from http://www. cs.cityu.edu.hk/ ~wbl2007/ WBL2007_Proceedings_HTML/ WBL2007_PP079-087_Lee.pdf

Martin-Blas, T., & Serrano-Fernandez, A. (2009). The role of new technologies in the learning process: Moodle as a teaching tool in Physics. *Computers & Education, 52*(1), 35–44. doi:10.1016/j.compedu.2008.06.005

McGettrick, A., Boyle, R., Ibbett, R., Lloyd, J., Lovegrove, G., & Mander, K. (2005). Grand challenges in computing: Education-A summary. *The Computer Journal, 48*(1), 42–48. doi:10.1093/comjnl/bxh064

Pereira, J. A., Pleguezuelos, E., Merí, A., Molina-Ros, A., Molina-Tomás, M. C., & Masdeu, C. (2007). Effectiveness of using blended learning strategies for teaching and learning human anatomy. *Medical Education, 41*(2), 189–195. doi:10.1111/j.1365-2929.2006.02672.x

Pfefer, J. (2002). Merging IT training with academia. In *Proceedings of the 30th annual ACM SIGUCCS conference on User services* (pp. 95-98).

Ray, J. A. (2009). An Investigation of online course management systems in higher education: Platform selection, faculty training, and instructional quality. *International Journal of Information and Communication Technology Education, 5*(2), 46–59.

Rovai, A. P., & Jordan, H. M. (2004). Blended learning and sense of community: A comparative analysis with traditional and fully online graduate courses. *International Review of Research in Open and Distance Learning, 5*(2). Retrieved April 13, 2009 from http://www.irrodl.org/index.php/irrodl/article/view/192/274

Shelley, D. J., Swartz, L. B., & Cole, M. T. (2007). A comparative analysis of online and traditional undergraduate business law classes. *International Journal of Information and Communication Technology Education, 3*(1), 10–21.

Shen, P. D., Lee, T. H., & Tsai, C. W. (2007). Applying web-enabled problem-based learning and self-regulated learning to enhance computing skills of Taiwan's vocational students: A quasi-experimental study of a short-term module. *Electronic Journal of e-Learning, 5*(2), 147-156.

Shen, P. D., Lee, T. H., & Tsai, C. W. (2008). Enhancing skills of application software via web-enabled problem-based learning and self-regulated learning: An exploratory study. *Journal of Distance Education Technologies, 6*(3), 69–84.

Shen, P. D., Lee, T. H., Tsai, C. W., & Ting, C. J. (2008). Exploring the effects of web-enabled problem-based learning and self-regulated learning on vocational students' involvement in learning. *European Journal of Open, Distance and E-Learning*, (1). Retrieved April 13, 2009 from http://www. eurodl.org/ materials/contrib/ 2008/ Shen_Lee_Tsai_ Ting.htm

Singh, H. (2003). Building effective blended learning programs. *Educational Technology, 43*(6), 51–54.

Uribe-Tirado, A., Melgar-Estrada, L. M., & Bornacelly-Castro, J. A. (2007). Moodle learning management system as a tool for information, documentation, and knowledge management by research groups. *Profesional de la Informacion, 16*(5), 468–474. doi:10.3145/epi.2007.sep.09

Vakhitova, G., & Bollinger, C. R. (2006). *Labor market return to computer skills: Using Microsoft Certification to measure computer skills*. Retrieved April 13, 2009 from http://gatton.uky.edu/faculty/Bollinger/Workingpapers/MSwagepaper11_06.pdf

Walmsley, B. (2003). Partnership-centered learning: The case for pedagogic balance in technology education. *Journal of Technology Education, 14*(2). Retrieved April 13, 2009 from http://scholar.lib.vt.edu/ejournals/JTE/v14n2/walmsley.html

Wang, H. C., Chang, C. Y., & Li, T. Y. (2008). Assessing creative problem-solving with automated text grading. *Computers & Education, 51*(4), 1450–1466. doi:10.1016/j.compedu.2008.01.006

Young, A. T., Cole, J. R., & Denton, D. (2002) Improving technological literacy. *Issues in Science and Technology*. Retrieved April 13, 2009 from http://findarticles.com/p/articles/mi_qa3622/is_200207/ai_n9115217

Yushau, B. (2006). The effects of blended e-learning on mathematics and computer attitudes in pre-calculus algebra. *The Montana Math Enthusiast, 3*(2), 176–183.

This work was previously published in International Journal of Information and Communication Technology, Volume 6, Issue 2, edited by Lawrence A. Tomei, pp. 11-23, copyright 2010 by IGI Publishing (an imprint of IGI Global).

Chapter 11
Bringing AI to E-Learning:
The Case of a Modular, Highly Adaptive System

K. Giotopoulos
University of Patras, Greece

C. Alexakos
University of Patras, Greece

G. Beligiannis
University of Patras, Greece

A. Stefani
University of Patras, Greece

ABSTRACT

This paper presents a newly developed student model agent, which is the basic part of an e-learning environment that incorporates Intelligent Agents and Computational Intelligence Techniques. The e-learning environment consists of three parts, the E-learning platform Front-End, the Student Questioner Reasoning and the Student Model Agent. The basic aim of this contribution is to describe in detail the agent's architecture and the innovative features it provides to the e-learning environment through its utilization as an autonomous component. Several basic processes and techniques are facilitated through the agent in order to provide intelligence to the e-learning environment.

1. INTRODUCTION

One of the main characteristics of e-learning is user-centricity. Thus seeking effective user-centered design and implementation techniques is a significant goal. User-centricity has many forms; one of the most important is adaptation to

user behavior. Recommender techniques are the spearhead of adaptation research; they have been applied to numerous application areas with significant success, especially in e-commerce. Although, recommender techniques have been considered in a wide range of recent research efforts, they are mainly focused on lessons learned from the

DOI: 10.4018/978-1-61350-468-0.ch011

e-commerce domain. The same techniques, with minor variations are being used in e-learning. The analogy is not as straight forward as it is widely accepted since many concepts are fundamentally different. E-learning has many common characteristics with e-commerce applications and many differences as well: a learner does not behave always as a buyer does.

One of the main goals of e-learning adaptation is how to improve learning efficiency. One possible solution is to promote a personalized learning experience –which could be used as reinforcement to the foundations laid by the linear structured text books and the on-line and off-line lectures. The classic information transfer paradigm used in most e-learning applications is well understood and well supported by existing practice. In order to advance effective learning we will promote another paradigm that focuses on the learner and on new forms of learning. In our approach the learner has an active and central role in the learning process. Learning activities are aimed at facilitating the construction of knowledge and skills in the learner, instead of the memorization of information. Information transfer still exists in the new paradigm, but only as a simple component, not the main goal.

In this paper we describe an innovative web-based Intelligent Tutoring System (ITS) that introduces Artificial Intelligence (AI) techniques and agents technology in order to enhance the performance and the effectiveness of the e-learning system. In section 2 there is a structured presentation of the main issues related to the concept of an e-learning system, the state-of-the-art concerning the functionalities of an e-learning environment and the scientific subjects that the proposed solution focuses on. In section 3 the description of the proposed system is presented, while in section 4 the innovative features of the agent's integration are described and specified. In section 5 the student model agent architecture of the proposed system is described, while in section 6 the rule optimization module (concerning the updating procedure

of the student model and the Bayesian Network's decision rules) is presented. Finally in section 7 conclusions and future work are presented.

2. STATE OF THE ART

Adaptive e-learning systems often employ models of the user. A user model is a representation of the user's properties and characteristics. Before a user model can be used it has to be constructed. This process requires much effort especially for gathering the required information and for generating a model of the user.

The behavior of an adaptive system varies according to the data from the user model and the user profile. In (Koch, 2000) there is a description of the necessity of applying user models as follows: "Users are different: they have different background, different knowledge about a subject, different preferences, goals and interests. To individualize, personalize or customize actions a user model is needed that allows for selection of individualized responses to the user."

In the context of e-learning, adaptive systems are more specialized and focus on the adaptation of the learning content and its presentation. According to (Mödritscher et al., 2004), an adaptive system focuses on how the knowledge is learned by the student and pays attention to learning activities, cognitive structures and the context of the learning material.

In Figure 1, the structure of an adaptive system, according to (Brusilovski & Maybury, 2002) with three stages during the process of adaptation is shown. It controls the process of collecting data about the user, the process of building up the user model (user modeling) and the adaptation process.

The system proposed in this contribution is also three staged, it is an Intelligent Tutoring Systems (ITS). ITSs are adaptive instructional systems applying artificial intelligence (AI) techniques.

Figure 1. The structure of an adaptive system

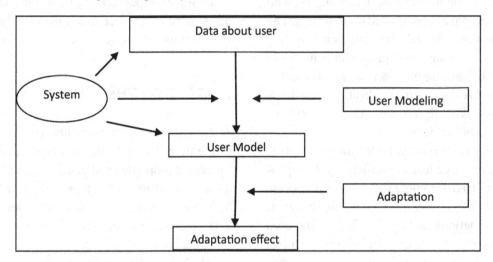

The goal of an ITS is to provide the benefits of one-on-one instruction automatically and cost effectively (Shute & Psotka, 1996). Similarly, in other instructional systems, ITS consist of components representing the learning content, teaching and instructional strategies as well as mechanisms to understand what the student does or does not know. In ITS, these components are arranged into the expertise module, the student-modeling module, the tutoring module and a user interface module (Brusilovsky, 1994). The expertise module evaluates the performance of the student and generates instructional content. The student-modeling module represents the user's current knowledge and estimates reasoning strategies and conceptions. This information is used by the ITS to determine, how the teaching process should continue. The tutoring module holds information for the selection of instructional material. This information describes how this material should be presented and when. The user interface module is the communication component that controls interaction between the student and the system.

A variety of AI techniques are used to represent the learning and teaching process. For example, some ITS capture topic related expertise in rules. We focus on Intelligent Agents (Hill, 2003). The Intelligent agents are tools that can manage the

information overload, serve as academic experts, and create programming environments for the learners. Intelligent agents should be able to model the user in order to remember his/her knowledge, skills and learning style. The primary function of an e-learning intelligent agent is to help a user to interact with a computer application that corresponds to a learning domain (Gâlea et al., 2003). Intelligent agents have three main educational potentials: they can manage information overload, they can serve as pedagogical experts and they can even create knowledge (Baylor, 1999).

3. SYSTEM DESCRIPTION

Our approach to ITS design is centred on the extension of current educational content interchange formats (e.g. the Content Packaging Specification currently under extension by international e-learning bodies such as the IEEE LTSC (IEEE, 2009), CEN/ISSS LTW (CEN/ISSS LTW, 2009), IMS (IMS, 2009), ADL (ADL, 2009) and SCORM (SCORM, 2009) to facilitate the definition of adaptive and conditional navigation rules taking into account user characteristics (user profiles, testing sessions, etc). These navigation rules will be described together with the learning assets within a single content packaging format. The aim of such a notation is to enable instructional designers to describe (in a common, reusable, interoperable and machine readable way) navigational logics which define how knowledge packages (i.e., educational courses, sets of learning assets, etc.) can be disaggregated and presented, in a different way, according to different learner characteristics. As a result, e-learning applications and services can provide different knowledge routes to each individual learner, according to his/her characteristics and needs. The aforementioned format will be used as the interchange format between the specific architectural modules developed, which addresses the needs of all envisaged players of the e-learning arena, namely learners and educational content and/or applications and service providers. The main objectives of the proposed system are to provide the necessary means to the e-learning users to achieve the specific learning goals and complete the e-learning process. This is happening by taking into account the specific and personal needs and interests of each learner.

There is a need for the implementation of a new specific business model that is compliant to the learning needs and goals of the system. The new business model highlights a process with three main roles and two main control flows, while delivering learning material to learners by means of effective and efficient learning experiences.

The most important aspects of the business model are efficiency, personalization features and user modeling issues. The overall idea is to use AI techniques in order to provide the necessary infrastructure to achieve the specific targets. More specifically, to integrate intelligent agent technologies together with Bayesian networks (Pearl, 1998; Charniak, 1991) in order to provide (to the end user) a personalized guidance within the e-learning process and a necessary tool to model the knowledge of the learner based on interactions between the learner and the system. Bayesian Networks have been used and proved very efficient in many Intelligent Tutoring Systems, including (Conati &

VanLehn, 2000; Gen & Cheng, 1997; Martin & VanLehn, 1995; Mayo & Mitrovic, 2000; Mislevy & Gitomer, 1996; Zapata-Rivera & Greer, 2001). Much of their use so far, however, has been for knowledge assessment (Mayo & Mitrovic, 2000; Mislevy & Gitomer, 1996).

In this contribution special focus is given to the fact that knowledge is dynamic and continuously updated. In order to support this dynamicity, it is necessary to provide an infrastructure that initializes the model of the learner and also maps the interaction to a specific model tree, based on the interactions of the learner with the system during a specific course. The teacher supports this procedure by all available means. First of all, the teacher establishes the basic models for the knowledge and provides the initial rules for the decision making policy of the agent based on the input of the Bayesian network. This process is not automated because it is extremely difficult for a system to decide with high precision the individual educational needs of a learner. Based on these rules the system will identify the basic models for the knowledge and guide the mapping procedure between the knowledge model and the student model.

The role of the Bayesian Network within the system is mainly to support the process of the *Student Questioner Reasoning module*. The input to this module is an XML file containing the answers to each particular questionnaire given by students and the weights (probability of the student to answer correct in a given question) given by the teacher. Using these weights, a Bayesian Network is created where leafs present the questions (Conati et al., 2002). According to the answers of each student, the student modeling algorithm is activated in order to balance the network. The result of the algorithm's execution is the possibility of each student to answer correct or wrong the remaining questions of the questionnaire.

Furthermore, the Bayesian Network interacts continuously with the agent in order to populate the user model and establish the basis for the decision making process of the agent (Giotopoulos et al., 2005). The models are continuously communicated from the Bayesian network to the agent and vice versa. Each model is associated to a specific learner.

4. INNOVATIVE FEATURES OF THE AGENT'S INTEGRATION

The role of the agent in the e-learning environment is twofold:

- To provide a wrapper of the "intelligent" functionalities that formulate the core services of the e-learning environment
- To support the provision of dynamic content for the learning process of a specific student

4.1. "Intelligent Wrapper"

Concerning the first aspect of the agent's role it is important to mention that the target and basic aim of the e-learning environment is to provide concrete functionalities to the users of the system. The most important aspect is to be able to provide personalized services to each user. The reason for this is based on the fact that e-learning systems anticipate each user (student) to behave in a different way according to the user model that has been constructed by the modeling procedure. Each user model is defined by specific criteria and it is dynamic. The interaction of the user with the system is constantly updating the user model and the system requires a continuous interaction with the modeling procedures in order to extract the appropriate information for the balanced reaction of the learning process. In the specific system, the agent retrieves the information from the modeling procedures and according to specific rules "decides" and plans the next steps of the learning process for each specific user at each specific time.

4.2 Dynamic Content Provision

The agent is able to access personal information that is stored in the e-learning environment and is strictly related to the modeling procedure of the environment. But how can an intelligent e-learning environment exploit the utilization of such information in order to enhance the quality of the learning services provided and when? Actually the business model supports not only a single content provider, but a network of content providers, in order to reimburse a multi point source of content for the educational aspects of the learning process.

The role of the agent in the specific procedure is also twofold.

1. Based on the user model and the educational interests of the user, it provides a list of relative content sources. These sources are related with the subject's content at each specific session, the user's interests, based on the user profile, and the interactions of the user with the system (user modeling procedure).

2. Furthermore, the role of the agent in the e-learning environment supports a continuous interaction of the specific e-learning system with other e-learning systems based on web service technologies. The goal is to provide alternative resources for the educational structure of the learning process.

5. STUDENT MODEL AGENT ARCHITECTURE

The Student Model Agent is designed to receive information from e-learning systems in order to process it, according to evolutionary rule-based techniques, and take decisions about the next step of the learning process for a student. In addition, the agent is capable of rebuilding the set of rules, based on the results of the decision making, utilizing an evolutionary algorithm. The agent must provide a scalable implementation that makes it possible to add different student models and decision making routines in order to update the student model in different stages of the learning process.

The Student Model Agent is empowered with an interface supporting the SOAP and WSDL protocols in order to communicate and exchange data with the e-learning platforms via XML-based messages. The utilization of web services for the integration of the Student Model Agent increases reusability, whereas different e-learning systems can be benefited from the usage of the services provided by the agent. The web services based implementation enables seamless communication with other internet based systems that provide useful information for the e-learning process such as digital libraries and/or web search engines. This feature provides the e-learning systems, supported by the agent, with additional functionalities in order to help the learning process.

The Student Model Agent is implemented according to the architecture depicted in Figure 2.

The consists of three repository subsystems and three functional modules.

The three repositories are:

- Rule Processes Repository where, the rule-based decision making processes for examining a particular student model and exporting the appropriate training task, are stored. These processes can be applied in different cases according to the information that are sending to the agent. These processes are implemented in executable format as Java packages and can be executed dynamically from the Execution Module.

- Models Repository is a repository of the various student models that are used for the agent in order to take the decisions about the training process of a particular student. The scheme of the student models varies. The student models are presented by a specific custom XML scheme in order to be utilized by the agent functionalities.

Figure 2. Student Model Agent architecture

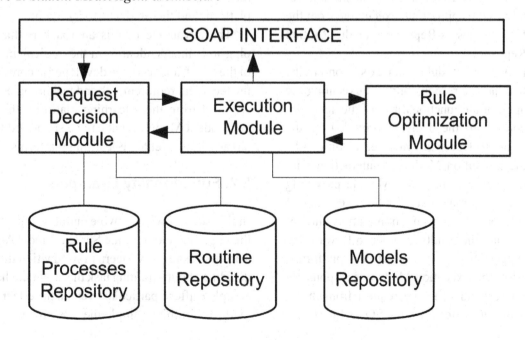

- Routine Repository is the third repository of the agent which contains routines that can be executed in order to invoke external services from other learning supporting systems. These routines are implemented as executable classes that include a SOAP client in order to communicate with external systems.

The functional modules are executable components that implement specific internal and external functionalities of the agent:

- Request Decision Module is used for processing the input information provided to the agent via the SOAP interface and decides the appropriate function that has to be executed from the agent. There are four categories of functions: Insert New Student Module, Update Student Module, Execute Rule-Based Decision Process and Execute External Routine. The Request Decision Module is parsing the input and decides which of the four functionalities has to be executed. In the case of execution of a decision process or an external routine, the Request Decision Module retrieves the appropriate executable from the Rule Processes Repository or the Routine Repository.

- Execution Module is an execution engine that has the responsibility of executing the appropriate functionalities of the agent according to the decision provided by the Request Decision Module. Additionally, the Execution Module is interacting with the Rule Optimization Module providing the appropriate data for the execution of rule based decision optimization and retrieving the results in order to forward the suggestions to the e-learning platforms. Also, the Execution Module is responsible for responding to the request from the e-learning platform via the SOAP Interface.

- Rule Optimization Module is empowered with an evolutionary algorithm in order to validate and optimize the rule based decision processes according to the student behaviors that are described in the student models.

5.1. Collaboration with E-Learning Platforms

The Student Model Agent is implementation independent from the e-learning platform. In order the two systems to be able to collaborate efficiently an additional plug-in must be implemented in the e-learning platform so as to install the appropriate interaction control functions with the Student Model Agent. This plug-in is consisted of two functional modules. The first module includes the functions with the appropriate mechanisms exposing the functionalities of the agent to the e-learning platform. These functions implement the interface for defining rules according to the decision procedures that are supported by the agent and the collection of data in order to send it to the agent for processing. The second module is a SOAP interface that implements the communication and data transfer between the e-learning platform and the Student Model Agent.

The advantage of this approach is that the plug-in is independent from the implementation of the agent, and has to be developed according to the technical requirements and technologies that are used from the e-learning platform; thereby the Student Model Agent can be supported from already implemented e-learning platforms.

5.2. Functionality Examples

In this section we use two examples to describe the implementation of the Student Model Agent. The first example concerns the functionality of deciding about a training task that a student has to complete after a particular event in the e-learning platform. In this example the rule process' optimization procedure is also described. The second example concerns the execution of an external routine.

5.2.1. The Decision Function Example

The first step in the *Decision Function Example* includes the initialization of the rules from a tutor for a specific training task. For simplicity, we assume that the tutor is defining rules concerning the answers of a questionnaire for a specific course. These rules that are defined by the tutor are not abstract, but are declared according to the decision making methods that are supported by the Student Model Agent. These rules are forwarded to the Model Agent and are stored to the Rule Processes Repository with the associated decision processes.

In the next step of the example, we assume that the model of a particular student is stored in the Models Repository. This student according to his learning process answers the corresponding questionnaire. The e-learning platform is gathering the answers and forwards them to the Student Model Agent with the request of executing the decision procedure for suggesting the next learning task to the student.

The request and the information are transferred over the SOAP interface to the Request Decision Module. The module processes the request and "realizes" that it is an Execute Rule-Based Decision Process request; it retrieves the corresponding process from the Rule Processes Repository and forwards it to the Execution Module.

The student model is retrieved by the Execution Module from the Models Repository and the decision making procedure is initiated. The results are transferred back to the e-learning platform via the SOAP interface and the student model is updated with the new information.

In the next step, the optimization of the rules that have been defined by the teacher, is taking place. The Rule Optimization Module retrieves

the decision rules and the associated information from the Execution Module. The Module calls an evolutionary algorithm which optimizes the given set of rules evaluating the associated students models that are built according to these rules. Finally, the results are sent to the Execution Module which forwards the suggested rule set to the e-learning platform in order for them to be accepted or rejected by the tutor.

5.2.2. External Routine Example

The second example is describing the functionality of the Student Model Agent to execute an external routine in order to provide additional information to the student to help him in the learning process. Our example is based on the assumption that a tutor has defined rules specifying that according to a series of answers in a questioner, the student has to read additional learning material that is provided from a digital library located somewhere in the web. The execution of this functionality requires that the specific routine, which includes the invocation script of the web service methods of the digital library needed to retrieve the appropriate material, has to be stored in the Routine Repository.

The first part is similar to the first example. The student answers the questionnaire and the answers are fed as input to the Student Model Agent. The agent is processing the data and according to the defined rules decides that the user wants additional learning material. The next step is the creation of a request from the Execution Module to the Request Decision Module that includes a functionality of "Execute External Routine" type. The Request Decision Module locates and retrieves the routine from the Routine Repository and forwards it to the Execution Module. While the routine is executed the Execution Module invokes the corresponding web services method (for example get_publications_for_physics) of the external digital library in order to retrieve the requested learning material. Finally, the material is sent via the SOAP interface to the e-learning platform for presentation to the student.

6. THE RULE OPTIMIZATION MODULE

The Rule Optimization Module uses two Evolutionary Algorithms (EAs) (Mitchel, 1996; Michalewicz, 1990) in order to validate and optimize, according to the student behavior, the rule based decision processes that are described by the student models. The first EA is applied to each specific student in order to update his/her student model and the category he/she is assigned to, while the second is applied in order to evolve the decision rules used by the Bayesian Network and update its structure and contents.

6.1. Updating Student Models

At the beginning of the learning process, each student is requested to answer a specific questionnaire related to the specific course he/she is attending. According to his/her answers the student is set to a specific category (knowledge level). After that, the student is requested to answer some questions/exercises about the specific course according to his/her category. His/her specific answers as well as all information concerning his answering process are monitored and stored in the system. This information includes, for each student, his/her specific answer in each question/exercise, the time spent by the student in each question/exercise and whether and how many times he/she asked for hints. This information is used as input in the first EA, which evolves and results in a vector (student interaction pattern) describing as well as possible the knowledge level of each specific student. This vector is compared to the knowledge category

Figure 3. The student model updating process

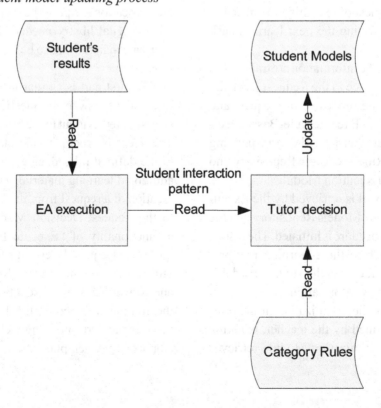

rules defined by the tutor of each specific lesson and the student is newly categorized according to the comparison's results. The student model updating process is shown in Figure 3.

The steps of the first EA are presented in Figure 4. The EA used is a classic one (Vose, 1998; Gen & Cheng, 1997). The initial population is generated using a set of random binary strings (genomes). The objective function estimates the goodness (fitness) of each individual (genome) in the population. The fitness of each individual is based on how many student interaction patterns it can satisfy. A student interaction pattern has the following structure:

<correctness time tries hints>

that represents whether the student answered correctly, how much time the student spent on an exercise, the number of tries and how many hints he asked for. A pattern is satisfied if correctness equals ''yes, 'time' belongs to [T1, T2], 'tries' belongs to [E1, E2] and 'hints' belongs to [H1, H2].

Next, we describe a specific student model updating case in order to make it more clear. Suppose that a student belongs to category three (3) and the rule for category three, defined by the tutor, is as follows:

(80%<correctness<100%) and
(60sec<time<180sec) and (1<times<2) and
(1<hints<2)

Suppose that after the completion of the student updating process the interaction pattern for this student is the following:

(60<correctness<80%) and
(60sec<time<180sec) and (1<times<2) and
(3<hints<5)

The tutor compares the student interaction pattern with the rule describing category three and decides to set the specific student to category two.

One open issue is to incorporate another EA in the system whose aim will be to evolve and update the category rules at the end of each semester for each specific course and set the respective comparison's criteria. If another EA is incorporated in the system the tutor will be relieved from the difficult task to define the most appropriate category rules and comparison's criteria. This will be one of the main subjects of our future work.

6.2. Updating Bayesian Network's Decision Rules

The second EA is applied in order to evolve the decision rules used by the Bayesian Network and update its structure and contents. These rules, which are initially defined by the tutor, have, in general, the following form:

If the answer in the previous question is correct (wrong), then go to the next question; else go to first question whose probability to be answered correctly (wrongly) is smaller (bigger) than a specific threshold.

The second EA based on the "answering" history of each student or group of students is evolving these rules trying to optimize the values of their thresholds. In order to better explain the updating process of the Bayesian rules we present the following example. Suppose that a specific rule of the Bayesian network is the following: "If the student answers correctly question five then he/she proceeds to question six; else he/she proceeds to the first question whose probability to be answered correctly is smaller than 0.75". The first question, after question five, whose probability to be answered correctly is smaller than 0.75, is question 9. So each student, after answering question five, he goes either to question six, if he has answered question five correctly, or to question

Figure 4. The structure of the EA

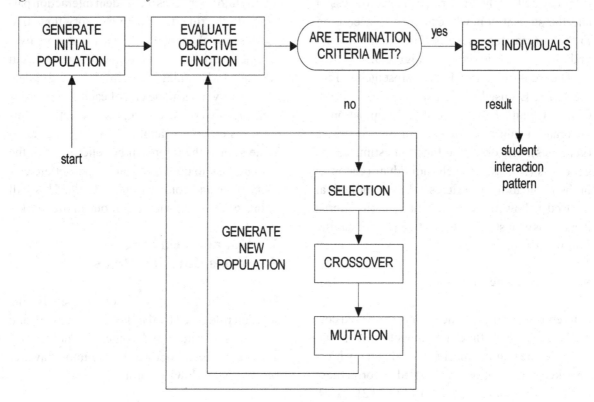

9, if he has answered question five wrongly. After all students of a specific semester have completed answering all questions, this answering history is put as input in the EA. Based on this history, the EA evolves the above rule together with many other rules and, let us assume, that it results in a rule with threshold value equal to 0.7. This newly defined rule is evaluated by the tutor, who compares it with the previous one and decides whether the rule will be updated or not.

One open issue is to incorporate another EA in the system whose aim will be to evolve and update the initial rules at the end of each semester for each specific course and set the respective decision's criteria. If another EA is incorporated in the system the tutor will be relieved from the difficult task to define the most appropriate initial rules and decision's criteria. This will be one of the main subjects of our future work.

7. CONCLUSION AND FUTURE WORK

We presented a system that uses Artificial Intelligence techniques and agent's technologies in order to enhance the performance and the effectiveness of an e-learning system. A new business model that is compliant to the learning needs and goals of the system was identified in order to proceed with the design and implementation of the system. The most important aspect of the proposed solution is the integration of intelligent agent technologies together with Bayesian Networks and Evolutionary Algorithms in order to provide (to the end user) a personalized guidance within the e-learning process and a necessary tool to model the knowledge of the learner based on interactions between the learner and the system. The personalization procedure is implemented by specific rules that are provided by the teacher and specific modules are responsible for the optimization of the learning process of the student.

The main focus of our future work will be the integration of ontologies to support not only the user modeling procedures, but also the procedures concerning the knowledge modeling. The basic idea is to try and identify all common features of the knowledge models in all international standards and design an ontology that will facilitate the common use in all e-learning systems. Furthermore, specific focus will be given to the design and implementation of new intelligent agents that will automate more aspects of the learning process based on learning standards acceptable by the learning theory too.

REFERENCES

ADL. (2009). Retrieved from http://www.adlnet. org

Baylor, A. (1999). Intelligent agents as cognitive tools for education. *Educational Technology, 39*(2), 36–41.

Brusilovski, P., & Maybury, M. T. (2002). From adaptive hypermedia to the adaptive web. *Communications of the ACM, 45*(5), 30–33.

Brusilovsky, P. (1994). The Construction and Application of Student Models in Intelligent Tutoring Systems. *Journal of Computer and Systems Sciences International, 32*(1), 70–89.

CEN/ISSS LTW. (2009). Retrieved from http://www.cenorm.be/isss

Charniak, E. (1991). Bayesian networks without tears. *AI Magazine, 12*(4), 50–63.

Conati, C., & VanLehn, K. (2000). Toward computer-based support of meta-cognitive skills: a computational framework to coach self-explanation. *International Journal of Artificial Intelligence in Education, 11*, 389–415.

Conati, C. A., Gertner, S., & VanLehn, K. (2002). Using Bayesian Networks to Manage Uncertainty in Student Modeling. *User Modeling and User-Adapted Interaction, 12*, 371–417. doi:10.1023/A:1021258506583

Conati, C. A., Gertner, S., VanLehn, K., & Druzdel, M. J. (1997). On-line student modeling for coached problem solving using Bayesian networks. In A. Jameson, C. Paris, & C. Tasso (Eds.), *Sixth International Conference on User Modeling* (pp. 231-242). New York: Springer.

Gâlea, D., Leon, F., & Zaharia, M. H. (2003). E-learning Distributed Framework using Intelligent Agents. In M. Craus, D. Gâlea, & A. Valachi (Eds.), *New Trends in Computer Science and Engineering* (pp. 159-163). ISBN 973-9476-40-6

Gen, M., & Cheng, R. (1997). *Genetic Algorithms and Engineering Design*. New York: John Wiley & Sons.

Giotopoulos, K. C., Alexakos, C. E., Beligiannis, G. N., & Likothanassis, S. D. (2005). Computational Intelligence Techniques and Agents' Technology in E-learning Environments. *International Journal of Information Technology, 2*(2), 147–156.

Hill, L. (2003). *Implementing a Practical e-Learning System*. Retrieved January 18, 2009 from http://agora.lakeheadu.ca/pre2004/december2002/elearning.html

IEEE. (2009). *LTSC*. Retrieved from http://ieeeltsc.org

IMS. (2009). Retrieved from http://www.imsproject.org

Koch, N. (2000). *Software Engineering for Adaptive Hypermedia Systems*. Unpublished doctoral dissertation, Ludwig-Maximilians-University, Munich, Germany. Retrieved from http://www.pst. informatik.uni-muenchen.de/ personen/ kochn/ PhDThesisNoraKoch.pdf

Martin, J., & VanLehn, K. (1995). Student assessment using bayesian nets. *International Journal of Human-Computer Studies*, *42*, 575–591. doi:10.1006/ijhc.1995.1025

Mayo, M., & Mitrovic, A. (2000). Using a probabilistic student model to control problem difficulty. In G. Gauthier, C. Frasson, & K. VanLehn (Eds), *the Fifth International Conference on Intelligent Tutoring Systems* (pp. 524-533). Berlin: Springer.

Michalewicz, Z. (1990). *Genetic Algorithms + Data Structures = Evolution Programs*. Berlin: Springer-Verlag.

Mislevy, R. J., & Gitomer, D. H. (1996). The role of probability-based inference in an intelligent tutoring system. *User Modeling and User-Adapted Interaction*, *5*(3-4), 253–282. doi:10.1007/BF01126112

Mitchel, M. (1996). *An Introduction to Genetic Algorithms*. Cambride, MA: MIT Press.

Mödritscher, F., Manuel Garcia-Barrios, V., & Gütl, Ch. (2004). The Past, the Present and the future of adaptive E-Learning. In *Proceedings of the International Conference Interactive Computer Aided Learning*.

Pearl, J. (1998). *Probabilistic Reasoning in Intelligent Systems*. Los Altos, CA: Morgan Kaufmann.

SCORM. (2009). Retrieved January 5, 2009 from http://www.adlnet.org/Technologies/scorm/

Shute, V. J., & Psotka, J. (1996). Intelligent tutoring systems: Past, Present and Future. In *Handbook of Research on Educational Communications and Technology* (pp. 1–99). New York: Scholastic Publications.

Vose, M. F. (1998). *The Simple Genetic Algorithm: Foundations and Theory*. Cambridge, MA: MIT Press.

Zapata-Rivera, J. D., & Greer, J. E. (2001). SModel server: Student modeling in distributed multi-agent tutoring systems. In J. D. Moore, C. L. Redfield, & W. L. Johnson (Eds.), In *Proceedings of the 10th International Conference on Artificial Intelligence in Education*, San Antonio, TX (pp. 446-455).

This work was previously published in International Journal of Information and Communication Technology, Volume 6, Issue 2, edited by Lawrence A. Tomei, pp. 24-35, copyright 2010 by IGI Publishing (an imprint of IGI Global).

Chapter 12
A Cross–Cultural Validation of the Selwyn's Computer Attitude Scale

Timothy Teo
Nanyang Technological University, Singapore

ABSTRACT

This study assesses the factorial validity of the Computer Attitude Scale (CAS) using a sample (N=438) of students from Singapore. Developed by Selwyn (1997), the CAS is a four-factor scale that measures the perceived usefulness, affective, behavioral, perceived control components that were proposed to constitute the multidimensional construct known as computer attitude. The results of this study show an overall positive computer attitude among the students. However, factor analyses reveal multicollinearity among some items and these were removed from further analysis. A confirmatory factor analysis was performed on a proposed 15-item model of the CAS and it was found to have a good fit. Implications for education in the Asian contexts are discussed. Suggestions for future research are offered.

1. INTRODUCTION

Technology has become an integral part of teaching and learning. With increased usage of instructional technology, web-based instructional resources like the electronic textbooks are slowly making their way into the higher education system. Given its increased use, it is important to understand the influence that computers has on students' attitudes toward learning. An important aspect in the successful implementation of technology in teaching and learning is user acceptance, which is influenced by users' attitude towards computers (Teo, 2008). Various studies have addressed the issue of students' attitude toward instructional technology and specifically toward computer technology and technologically-enriched learning environments (Drennan, Kennedy, & Pisarski, 2005; Hahne, Benndorf, Frey, & Herzig, 2005). For this reason, students' attitudes toward computers have been studied with different samples and instruments by many researchers since the 1980s. Attitude

DOI: 10.4018/978-1-61350-468-0.ch012

has been found to be a predictor of the adoption of new technologies by users at various levels, such as young students (Teo & Noyes, 2008), post-secondary school students (Teo, 2006), and pre-service teachers (Teo, Lee, & Chai, 2008).

Over the last few years a considerable body of literature has been written to explain the numerous variables found to have an influence on computer attitudes. These included computer anxiety, computer stress, perceptions of computers, and computer proficiency (Crable, Brodzinski, & Scherer, 1991; Gardner, Discenza, & Dukes, 1993; Hudiburg, Brown, & Jones, 1993; Igbaria & Chakrabarti, 1990; Kay, 1993; Loyd & Gressard, 1984; Maurer, 1994; Nickell & Pinto, 1986; Pope-Davis & Twing, 1991; Teo & Noyes, 2008; Woodrow, 1991). This broad array of research is multi-disciplinary and incorporates a wide variety of perspectives and topics. However, at its foundation, the above research was directed at examining the effect of attitude in influencing a person's ability to use a computer efficiently.

The attitudes and feelings involved with computers are difficult to identify. As the role of the computer expands and increases in our education system, it is crucial that educators are aware of how attitudes toward computers affect the way our students learn with computers. Recent years, researchers have found close relationships between computer attitudes and other variables. Of these, the most crucial is the positive relationship between computer attitudes and computer usage. No matter how sophisticated and powerful the state of technology is, the extent to which it is implemented depends on users having a positive attitude toward it (Huang & Liaw, 2005). This is consistent with Teo (2006) who suggested that negative attitudes toward computers may exist, and could be a deterrent to using computers in the learning environment. When students respond positively to computers, they tend to master the necessary skills quickly. Conversely, for students who find the using the computer to be an unpleasant and anxious experience, mastering the appropriate skills could

prove to be difficult. This anxiety may take the form of hostility, fear, and/or resistance; these are attitudes, which may inhibit the acquisition of computer skills much as mathematics anxiety can inhibit achievement in this subject (Yildirim, 2000). It appears that, students' attitudes towards and acceptance of computer technology, as well as learning about computers, may be important in the integration of electronic technologies in the classroom, workplace, and home.

Research has suggested that computer attitudes play an influential role in determining the extent to which students use the computer as a learning tool (Teo, 2006) and future behaviors towards the computer such as using it for further study and vocational purposes (Huang & Liaw, 2005). Among others, Sankaran, Sankaran, and Bui (2000) found a positive correlation between a student's attitudes toward course format and his or her performance in the course. Specifically, it was found that students who favored web-based courses had performed better than those students who had completed the course through the lecture format. This was corroborated by Pan, Sivo, and Brophy (2003) who found that, among other variables such as subjective norm, computer self-efficacy, and perceived usefulness, attitude toward WebCT was the only variable that was significant in predicting the students' final grade. On the influence of attitude on future behaviors, Sanders and Morrison-Shetlar (2001) found that, among other variables, attitude towards web-based materials play a significant role in influencing the future use of the web management system (e.g., WebCT).

1.1. Measuring Computer Attitudes

From much of the published research, Likert-type attitude scales have been developed and validated to measure computer attitudes. For example, the Loyd and Gressard's (1984) Computer Attitude Scale (CAS) is the most extensively used scale with three affective dimensions: computer anxiety, computer confidence, and computer liking. At a later stage, Loyd and Loyd (1985) added a fourth dimension, computer usefulness to the CAS. Nash and Moroz (1997) combined computer confidence and computer anxiety subscales and formed one computer confidence/anxiety subscale, then added one more factor, academic endeavours, which was associated with computer training. In the end, the CAS became a 34-item scale covering computer liking, computer usefulness, computer confidence/anxiety and attitude toward academic endeavours associated with computer training. Other computer attitude scales were developed by Bear, Richard, and Lancaster (1987), Chen (1986), Jones and Clarke (1994), Mitra (1998) and Reece and Gable (1982).

Although these computer attitude scales and measures have been credited for providing researchers with insights into the nature of computer attitudes and its relationship to computer use, these were mainly designed for older students and there is a paucity of scales relating to younger people. As computers are used extensively across all levels in education, there is certainly a need for researchers to gain access to an instrument that is developed for use among younger students. An attempt was made by Selwyn (1997) who developed a computer attitude scale (CAS) for the 16-19 year-olds. In the CAS, four subscales were included: affect toward the computer, perceived usefulness of computers, perceived control of computers, and behavioral attitudes towards computers.

While the above instruments have been useful to facilitate a greater understanding of computer attitudes, few have attempted to use a scale in its entirety in a non-Western country with English as a working language, such as Singapore. The purpose of this study is to examine the factorial validity of the CAS for use by young students in Singapore.

2. METHOD

2.1. Participants

The participants in this study were 438 students recruited from two primary schools in a multi-cultural country in the South-East Asia region. These are co-educational schools each with a student population of over 1500. At the request of the participating schools, intact classes were used. The mean age of the participants was 10.96 (SD= 0.76) and 49.5% were female. Among the participants, 91.6% reported that they have access to a personal computer at home. Overall, the length of daily computer usage was 4.15 hours (SD= 1.72).

2.2. Procedures

The participants were briefed on the aim of this study and completed the CAS in school before the start of the lesson. The researcher administered the CAS in both schools and each session took about 20 minutes. At all times, the researcher was present to answer queries and clarify doubts. The CAS was completed in English using the original items.

2.3. Measure

The Computer Attitude Scale (CAS) is a 21-item instrument developed by Selwyn (1997). Based on a sample of 266 students in UK, Selwyn reduced an original 49-item scale to 21 items. Using principal component analysis with varimax rotation, Selwyn identified four components of computer attitudes. The first component, *Affective*, consists of six items that measured feelings towards computers. The second component, *Perceived Usefulness*, consists of five items that measured the extent to which the computer is believed to be able to enhance job performance. The third component, *Perceived Control*, consists of six items that measured the perceived ease, or difficulty, of using the computer. The fourth component, *Behavioral*, consists of four items that measured behavioral intentions and actions regarding computers. Participants responded to the 21 items on a 5-point Likert scale ranging from strongly disagree (0) to strongly agree (4). Ten of the CAS items were reversed scored so that higher scores indicated more positive attitudes towards computers. Potential scores on the CAS ranged from 0 to 84. Internal consistency for each component and the CAS as a whole was calculated using Cronbach's Alpha and these were *Affective* (.93), *Perceived Usefulness* (.82), *Perceived Control* (.88), *Behavioral* (.79), and CAS (.90). For this study, the scoring

was re-scaled to strongly disagree (1) to strongly agree (5) to match the scale that the participants in this study was familiar.

3. RESULTS

3.1. Overall Computer Attitudes

Table 1 shows the mean and SD for the CAS and each individual items. The range of means is between 2.17 to 3.33, suggesting that most participants either agreed or strongly agreed

Table 1. CAS Items, means, and standard deviations (N=438)

No	Item	Mean	SD	Skewness	Kurtosis
1	If given the opportunity to use a computer I am afraid that I might damage it in some way.+	3.21	.89	-0.88	0.02
2	Computers help me to organize my work better.	3.17	1.08	-1.26	0.77
3	I could probably teach myself most of the things I need to know about computers.	2.82	1.09	-0.72	-0.24
4	I would avoid taking a job if I knew it involved working with computers.+	3.23	.91	-0.78	-0.38
5	I hesitate to use a computer in case I look stupid.+	3.51	.82	-1.62	2.21
6	Computers can enhance the presentation of my work to a degree which justifies the extra effort.	2.89	1.19	-0.90	-0.05
7	I am not in complete control when I use a computer.+	3.07	.96	-0.77	-0.13
8	I don't feel apprehensive about using a computer.	3.20	1.26	-1.48	0.94
9	I can make the computer to do what I want it to do.	2.66	1.29	-0.67	-0.63
10	I only use computers in school when told to.+	3.00	1.20	-1.17	0.51
11	I need an experienced person nearby when I use a computer.+	3.20	.94	-1.17	1.16
12	Using a computer does not scares me at all	3.20	1.23	-1.44	0.90
13	Most things that a computer can be used for I can do just as well myself.+	2.73	1.08	-0.58	-0.10
14	I avoid coming into contact with computers in school.+	3.12	1.00	-0.86	0.11
15	If I get problems using the computer, I can usually solve them in one way or the other.	2.65	1.17	-0.57	-0.52
16	I hesitate to use a computer for fear of making mistakes I can't correct.+	2.99	.97	-0.68	0.08
17	Computers can allow me to do more interesting and imaginative work.	3.33	1.05	-1.70	2.24
18	I will use computers regularly throughout school.	2.17	1.33	-0.18	-1.09
19	I do not need somebody to tell me the best way to use a computer.	2.41	1.35	-0.30	-1.10
20	Computers make me feel uncomfortable.+	3.51	.85	-1.95	3.86
21	Computers make it possible to work more productively.	3.06	1.15	-1.06	0.24

+ indicate item that was reversed scored

with the items in the CAS. However, this view is mitigated with the fairly wide spread of score for most items. The standard deviations for fourteen (66%) of the items were higher than 1.00, indicating a wide spread of responses among the participants. Following the recommendations of Kline (2005) recommendations that the skew and kurtosis indices should not exceed $|3|$ and $|10|$ to ensure normality of the data, the data in this study is regarded as normal for further analysis.

The means and SD for the components of are shown n Table 2. The means *Affective* and *Perceived Use* are higher than *Perceived Control* and *Behavioral* although all standard deviations were similar. Internal consistency was calculated using Cronbach's alpha for each component and the CAS. Results showed that, while the reliability index for the CAS as a whole acceptable (.72), those of the separate component fell below the minimal level of .70 suggested by Sax (2001).

Selwyn (1997) reported that CAS scores falling below 35 could be interpreted as a relatively negative attitude towards computers whereas scores above 51 represent participants who hold relatively positive attitudes towards computers. Using these criteria, only 1 (0.2%) of the participants in the present study could be considered as having negative attitudes toward computers, while a sizable majority (91.1%) were considered to have positive attitudes toward computers. The remaining 8.7% (38) were considered to possess normal attitudes toward computers.

Table 2. Means and Standard Deviations for CAS Components

		Mean	SD	Alpha
1	Perceived Use	3.03	.62	.45
2	Affective	3.27	.57	.57
3	Behavioral	2.90	.66	.38
4	Perceived Control	2.80	.58	.44
	CAS	3.00	.43	.72

3.2. Factorial Validity

To examine the factorial validity of the CAS, a principal component analysis with varimax rotation was conducted on the 21 items. Visual inspection of the scree plot and the eigenvalue-greater-than-1 rule were used to determine the number of components to retain. On assessing the factor loadings for item retention, Hair, Black, Babin, Anderson, and Tatham (2006) suggested values greater equal or greater than .50 generally possess practical significance. An inspection of the scree plot and factor loadings suggested the existence of four interpretable factors. This resulted in the removal of six items (4, 5, 8, 12, 18, & 20) from further analysis. Table 3 shows the retained items and their loadings on the four factors.

3.3. Confirmatory Factor Analysis (CFA)

In recent years, many researchers have used CFA to examine the factorial validity of measures. Some reasons for the popularity of CFA as method for assessing scale validity are firstly, CFA provides a strong test of a model. Instead of testing one model, CFA tests various models against one another. These models are variations of one another, also known as nested models (Maruyama, 1998). Hence, instead of confirming a model through one test, CFA tests a variety of conceptualizations of the data and allow a comparison of different models in order to identify the model of best fit for retention. Secondly, CFA provides additional information about the dimensionality of a scale (e.g., Rubio, Berg-Weger, & Tebb, 2001). When models are tested against each other, further details about how the items and constructs of a scale are related to one another are uncovered. The researcher may rely on such information to decide on the appropriate uses of a scale, alternative versions of a scale, or to further theory in a particular area. In this study, CFA was used to examine the factorial structure of the CAS using

Table 3. Principal components analysis for the 15-item four-component CAS (N=438)

CAS		PU	A	B	PC
17	Computers can allow me to do more interesting and imaginative work.	.70			
6	Computers can enhance the presentation of my work to a degree which justifies the extra effort.	.66			
2	Computers help me to organize my work better.	.64			
21	Computers make it possible to work more productively.	.55			
3	I could probably teach myself most of the things I need to know about computers.	.51			
10	I only use computers in school when told to.+		.73		
13	Most things that a computer can be used for I can do just as well myself.+		.70		
14	I avoid coming into contact with computers in school.+		.56		
9	I can make the computer to do what I want it to do.			.71	
15	If I get problems using the computer, I can usually solve them in one way or the other.			.64	
19	I do not need somebody to tell me the best way to use a computer.			.52	
1	If given the opportunity to use a computer I am afraid that I might damage it in some way.+				.75
7	I am not in complete control when I use a computer.+				.60
11	I need an experienced person nearby when I use a computer.+				.52
16	I hesitate to use a computer for fear of making mistakes I can't correct.+				.52
	Percentage of variance explained	13.66	11.37	9.45	12.02

Note: Figures less than .50 were excluded. PU= Perceived Usefulness; PC= Perceived Control; A=Affective; B=Behavioral

the maximum likelihood estimator with AMOS 7.0 (Arbuckle, 2006).

A variety of fit indices are used to test for model fit. Hair et al. (2006) suggested using fit indices from various categories: absolute fit indices that measure how well the proposed model reproduces the observed data, parsimonious indices that is similar to the absolute fit indices but take into account the model's complexity, and incremental fit indices that assess how well a specified model fit relative to an alternative baseline model. To this end, the Tucker-Lewis index (TLI), comparative fit index (CFI), root mean square error of approximation (RMSEA), and standardized root mean residual (SRMR) are used in this study. Because the χ^2 has been found to be too sensitive to an increase in sample size and the number of observed variables (Hair et al. 2006), the ratio of χ^2 to its degree of freedom (χ^2/df), was used, with a range of not more than 3.0 being indicative of

an acceptable fit between the hypothetical model and the sample data (Carmines & McIver, 1981).

Several models were computed as part of the CFA to allow comparisons of different conceptualization of the factor structure to be made. First, a null model that assumes all the factors to be unrelated. Second, a one-factor model that tests whether all the factors load on one overall factor. A support for the one-factor model suggests that the respondents in this study do not differentiate among the factors and that all items are representative of a unidimensional construct. Third, an uncorrelated factor model that tests whether all the four factors in the model are independent. A support for this model suggests that these four factors are not related to one another and are indeed four different constructs. Fourth, a correlated factor model that tests whether the four factors are related to one another. Support for this model indicates that participants had discriminated between the

Figure 1. Final Model of the 15-item Computer Attitude Scale (Selwyn, 1997)

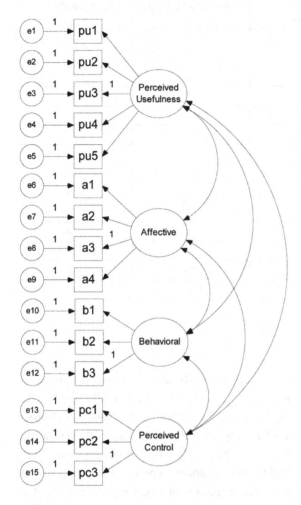

four factors but they are intercorrelated with one another. Finally, a hierarchical model that represents a second-order factor structure to account for the relationships among the four factors. Support for this model suggests that while all five factors are related, they are also related to a higher-order factor. A series of CFA were conducted (Table 4) to test the five models described above. Results indicate that the correlated model (model 4) has the best fit and on this basis, it was the retained as the model of best fit.

Table 5 shows the standardised and unstandardised parameters estimates for all 15 items. All are significant at the .001 level. In addition, the t-values, or critical ratio for each of the items are significant as well. These values support the *a priori* hypothesis of the relationships between the assigned items and their latent constructs. The final model of the 15-item CAS is shown in Figure 1.

4. DISCUSSION

This study serves to examine the overall computer attitudes of young students in Singapore, and to validate Selwyn's CAS for use among young students in Singapore. From the above analysis, the revised 15-item Selwyn's (1997) CAS is a fairly reliable instrument for use by 11 to 12 year olds in Singapore.

Table 4. Confirmatory Factor Analysis of alternative models

Model	χ^2	df	χ^2/df	TLI	CFI	RMSEA	SRMR
Null	741.32	105	7.06	---	---	.12 (.11,.13)	---
One-factor	363.14	90	4.04	.50	.57	.08 (.07,.09)	.09
Uncorrelated factor	252.35	90	2.80	.70	.75	.06 (.06,.07)	.09
Correlated factor	123.78	84	1.47	.92	.94	.03 (.02,.05)	.04
Hierarchical	146.26	86	1.70	.88	.91	.04 (.03,.05)	.05

*p <.001

Table 5. Parameter estimates of the 15-item CAS (4-correlated factors)

Factor	Item	unstandardised estimate	standardised estimate	t-value**
Perceived Usefulness	pc1	1.00*	.57	---
	pc2	.73	.45	6.23
	pc3	.73	.46	6.31
	pc4	.79	.51	6.69
	pc5	.87	.51	6.71
Affective	a1	1.00*	.43	---
	a2	1.17	.50	5.87
	a3	1.07	.49	5.81
	a4	1.43	.59	6.27
Behavioural	b1	1.00*	.55	---
	b2	1.06	.54	6.64
	b3	1.24	.56	6.74
Perceived Control	pc1	1.00*	.26	---
	pc2	1.78	.53	3.18
	pc3	1.57	.42	3.14

* This value was set at 1.00 to set the metric for estimation purpose. ** $p < .001$

The results show that a large majority of the sample possessed an overall positive attitude towards computers. Such positive attitudes are likely to be influenced by the Singapore government who, in 1997, began a national drive to equip schools with computers in order that teachers and student could be exposed to educational technology (Ministry of Education, 1997). This is cconsistent with current research that found greater usage and experience for the computer would lead to more positive computer attitudes (Garland & Noyes, 2004; Shashaani, 1997). Furthermore, using computers more frequently and developing a variety of computer-related skills and techniques increase one's knowledge of the computer as a whole thus widening one's learning environment and potential that in turn promotes a positive feeling towards the computer (Houtz & Gupta, 2001; Masoud, 1991).

At the exploratory factor analysis stage, items 4, 5, 8, 12, 18, and 20 were removed. Of these, items 4, 5, and 20 were negatively-worded items and it was possible that this may have created difficulties to the respondents. Research has shown that negatively-worded questions may cause problems in comprehension. This is especially so when using such items with non-native speakers (Marsh, 1986). Borgers, Hox, and Sikkel (2004) reported that using negatively-worded statements on young children (11 years and younger) was inconsistent with Piaget theory of cognitive development as they have not developed their formal thinking ability that is necessary to understand logical negation. Consequently, using negatively-worded survey items among children at aged 11 and below may result in response unreliability (Borgers & Hox, 2000). This, in part, explains the relatively low alphas for each of the subscales of the CAS even though the CAS as a whole is fairly internally consistent (0.72).

4.1. Implications for Asian Educational Contexts

From the above discussion, the CAS is a fairly valid measure for use by the sample in this study. In addition, there is scope for the CAS to be used in the Asian education contexts because of the construct that in the CAS: perceived usefulness, perceived control, affective, and behavioral. These constructs overlap with other measures of computer attitude such as those that have been used by researchers who have employed participants in the Asian region in their studies. For example, using the TAM, Teo, Lee, and Chai (2008) found that the computer attitudes among pre-service teachers in Singapore were significantly predicted by perceived usefulness, perceived ease of use, subjective norm, and facilitating conditions, with an R^2 of .42. Among these variables, perceived usefulness was the strongest (β =.48) predictor of computer attitudes. In another study using a Malaysian sample, Teo, Wong, and Chai (in press) found that the computer attitudes of pre-service teachers in Malaysia were significantly predicted by perceived usefulness and perceived ease of use. Additionally, attitude was a significant predictor of the Malaysian pre-service teachers' intention to use computers ((β =.88).

Further research into the CAS could examine the impact of negatively-worded items on different sample of various age groups. Researchers could re-consider the six removed items and re-validate the original 21-item scale using another sample. Finally, it would be worthwhile to establish the measurement invariance of the CAS across cultures and sub-samples e.g. gender, cultures, and age to widen our understanding of the utility of the CAS.

REFERENCES

Arbuckle, J. L. (2006). *Amos (Version 7.0) (Computer Program)*. Chicago: SPSS.

Bear, G. G., Richards, H. C., & Lancaster, P. (1987). Attitudes towards computers: validation of a computer attitudes scale. *Journal of Computing Research, 32*(2), 207–219. doi:10.2190/1DYT-1JEJ-T8J5-1YC7

Borgers, N., & Hox, J. J. (2000). *Reliability of responses in questionnaire research with children*. Paper presented at the Fifth International Conference on Logic and Methodology, Cologne, Germany.

Borgers, N., Hox, J. J., & Sikkel, D. (2004). Response effects in surveys on children and adolescents: the effect of number of responses options, negative wording, and neutral mid-point. *Quality & Quantity, 38*, 17–33..doi:10.1023/B:QUQU.0000013236.29205.a6

Carmines, E. G., & McIver, J. P. (1981). *Analyzing models with unobserved variables: Analysis of covariance structures*. Thousand Oaks, CA: Sage.

Chen. (1986). Gender and computers: the beneficial effects of experience on attitudes. *Journal of Educational Computing Research, 2*, 265-282.

Crable, E. A., Brodzinski, J. D., & Scherer, R. F. (1991). Psychology of computer use: XXII. Preliminary development of a measure of concerns about computers. *Psychological Reports, 69*, 235–236. doi:.doi:10.2466/PR0.69.5.235-236

Drennan, J., Kennedy, J., & Pisarski, A. (2005). Factors affecting student attitudes toward flexible online learning in management education. *The Journal of Educational Research, 98*(6), 331–338..doi:10.3200/JOER.98.6.331-338

Gardner, D. G., Discenza, R., & Dukes, R. L. (1993). The measurement of computer attitudes: an empirical comparison of available scales. *Journal of Educational Computing Research, 9*, 487–507. doi:10.2190/DXLM-5J80-FNKH-PP2L

Garland, K. J., & Noyes, J. M. (2004). Computer Experience: a poor predictor of computer attitudes. *Computers in Human Behavior, 20*, 823–840.. doi:10.1016/j.chb.2003.11.010

Hahne, A. K., Benndorf, R., Frey, P., & Herzig, S. (2005). Attitude towards computer- based learning: determinants as revealed by a controlled interventional study. *Medical Education, 39*, 935–943..doi:10.1111/j.1365-2929.2005.02249.x

Hair, J. F. Jr, Black, W. C., Babin, B. J., Anderson, R. E., & Tatham, R. L. (2006). *Multivariate data analysis* (6th ed.). Upper Saddle River, NJ: Prentice-Hall International.

Houtz, L. E., & Gupta, U. G. (2001). Nebraska high school students' computer skills and attitudes. *Journal of Research on Computing in Education*, *33*, 316–325.

Huang, H. M., & Liaw, S. S. (2005). Exploring user's attitudes and intentions toward the web as a survey tool. *Computers in Human Behavior*, *21*(5), 729–743..doi:10.1016/j.chb.2004.02.020

Hudiburg, R. A., Brown, S., & Jones, T. M. (1993). Psychology of computer use: XXXIX. Measuring computer users' stress: the computer hassles scale. *Psychological Reports*, *73*(1), 923–929. doi:10.2466/pr0.1993.73.3.923

Igbaria, M., & Chakrabarti, A. (1990). Computer anxiety and attitudes towards microcomputer use. *Behaviour & Information Technology*, *9*(3), 229–241..doi:10.1080/01449299008924239

Jones, T., & Clarke, V. A. (1994). A computer scale for secondary students. *Computers & Education*, *22*, 315–318..doi:10.1016/0360-1315(94)90053-1

Kay, R. (1993). An explanation of and practical foundations for assessing attitudes toward computers: the Computer Attitude Measure (CAM). *Computers in Human Behavior*, *9*, 371–386..doi:10.1016/0747-5632(93)90029-R

Kline, R. B. (2005). *Principles and practice of structural equation modeling* (2nd ed.). New York: Guilford Press.

Loyd, B. H., & Gressard, C. (1984). Reliability and factorial validity of computer attitude scales. *Educational and Psychological Measurement*, *44*, 501–505..doi:10.1177/0013164484442033

Loyd, B. H., & Loyd, D. E. (1985). The reliability and validity of an instrument for the assessment of computer attitudes. *Educational and Psychological Measurement*, *45*, 903–908.. doi:10.1177/0013164485454021

Marsh, H. W. (1986). Negative item bias in rating scales for preadolescent children: a cognitive phenomenon. *Developmental Psychology*, *22*(1), 37–49..doi:10.1037/0012-1649.22.1.37

Maruyama, G. (1998). *Basics of structural equation modelling*. Thousand Oaks, CA: Sage Publications.

Massoud, S. L. (1991). Computer attitudes and computer knowledge of adult students. *Journal of Educational Computing Research*, *7*, 269–291. doi:10.2190/HRRV-8EQV-U2TQ-C69G

Ministry of Education. (1997). *Masterplan for Information Technology*. Singapore: Ministry of Education.

Mitra, A. (1998). Categories of computer use and their relationships with attitudes toward computers. *Journal of Research on Computing in Education*, *30*(3), 281–295.

Nash, J. B., & Moroz, P. A. (1997). An examination of the factor structures of the computer attitude scale. *Journal of Educational Computing Research*, *17*(4), 341–356. doi:10.2190/NGDU-H73E-XMR3-TG5J

Nickell, G. S., & Pinto, J. N. (1986). The computer attitude scale. *Computers in Human Behavior*, *2*, 301–306..doi:10.1016/0747-5632(86)90010-5

Pan, C., Sivo, S. A., & Brophy, J. (2003). Students' attitude in a web-enhanced hybrid course: A structural equation modeling inquiry. *Journal of Educational Media and Library Sciences*, *41*(2), 181–194.

Pope-Davis, D. B., & Twing, J. S. (1991). The effects of age, gender, and experience on measures of attitude regarding computers. *Computers in Human Behavior, 7,* 333–339..doi:10.1016/0747-5632(91)90020-2

Reece, M. J., & Gable, R. K. (1982). The development and validation of a measure of general attitudes toward computers. *Educational and Psychological Measurement, 42,* 913–916.. doi:10.1177/001316448204200327

Rubio, D. M., Berg-Weger, M., & Tebb, S. S. (2001). Using structural equation modeling to test for multidimensionality. *Structural Equation Modeling, 8*(4), 613–626..doi:10.1207/S15328007SEM0804_06

Sanders, D. W., & Morrison-Shetlar, A. I. (2001). Student attitudes toward web- enhanced instruction in an introductory Biology course. *Journal of Research on computing in Education, 33*(3), 251-262.

Sankaran, S. R., Sankaran, D., & Bui, T. X. (2000). Effect of student attitude to course format on learning performance: An empirical study in web vs. lecture instruction. *Journal of Instructional Psychology, 27,* 66–74.

Sax, G. (2001). *Principles of educational and psychological measurement and evaluation* (5th ed.). Belmont, CA: Wadsworth.

Selwyn, N. (1997). Students' attitudes toward computers: validation of a computer attitude scale for 16-19 education. *Computers & Education, 28,* 35–41..doi:10.1016/S0360-1315(96)00035-8

Shashaani, L. (1997). Gender differences in computer attitudes and use among college students. *Journal of Educational Computing Research, 16,* 37–51..doi:10.2190/Y8U7-AMMA-WQUT-R512

Teo, T. (2006). Attitudes toward computers: A study of post-secondary students in Singapore. *Interactive Learning Environments, 14*(1), 17–24.. doi:10.1080/10494820600616406

Teo, T. (2008). Assessing the computer attitudes of students: an Asian perspective. *Computers in Human Behavior, 24*(4), 1634–1642..doi:10.1016/j.chb.2007.06.004

Teo, T., Lee, C. B., & Chai, C. S. (2008). Understanding pre-service teachers' computer attitudes: applying and extending the Technology Acceptance Model (TAM). *Journal of Computer Assisted Learning, 24,* 128–143..doi:10.1111/j.1365-2729.2007.00247.x

Teo, T., & Noyes, J. (2008). Development and validation of a Computer Attitude Measure for Young Students (CAMYS). *Computers in Human Behavior, 24*(8), 2659–2667..doi:10.1016/j.chb.2008.03.006

Teo, T., Wong, S. L., & Chai, C. S. (in press). A cross-cultural examination of the intention to use technology between Singaporean and Malaysian pre-service teachers: an application of the Technology Acceptance Model (TAM). *Journal of Educational Technology & Society.*

Woodrow, J. E. J. (1991). A comparison of four computer attitude scales. *Journal of Educational Computing Research, 7*(2), 165–187. doi:10.2190/WLAM-P42V-12A3-4LLQ

Yildirim, S. (2000). Effects of an educational computing course on pre-service and in- service teachers: A discussion and analysis of attitudes and use. *Journal of Research on Computing in Education, 32*(4), 479–495.

This work was previously published in International Journal of Information and Communication Technology, Volume 6, Issue 2, edited by Lawrence A. Tomei, pp. 36-46, copyright 2010 by IGI Publishing (an imprint of IGI Global).

Chapter 13

Improving Teachers' Self-Confidence in Learning Technology Skills and Math Education through Professional Development

Taralynn Hartsell
The University of Southern Mississippi, USA

Houbin Fang
The University of Southern Mississippi, USA

Sherry S. Herron
The University of Southern Mississippi, USA

Avinash Rathod
The University of Southern Mississippi, USA

ABSTRACT

Using technology tools in math instruction can help stimulate problem-solving skills and understanding of math concepts. However, teachers need to be confident in their abilities to use technology tools. This study investigated whether or not a four-week in-service professional development institute that addressed the use of technology in math education helped improved the teachers' attitude and confidence in applying technology. Findings indicated that as the teachers explored and used the available technology tools relevant to math instruction during the institute, the more proactive and motivated they became to continue their professional development in using technology for classroom instruction. They realized that they were able to use technology and desired to continue their education in this area.

INTRODUCTION

Technology is a tool that could be used in the mathematics classroom to enhance learning (NCTM, 2000). There are many forms of technology that can assist in teaching mathematics, supplement instruction, and remediate mathematical skills that require reinforcement. Tools such as spreadsheets, databases, educational software programs, drill-and-skills programs, scientific calculators, interactive whiteboards, and other applications are appropriate methods to teach mathematical concepts. The problem lies in that some teachers do not know how to use the technology tools

DOI: 10.4018/978-1-61350-468-0.ch013

or feel that they possess the ability to integrate technology effectively. Hence, teachers need to obtain the knowledge and skills that would help improve their self-confidence in using the technology at hand (ISTE, 2008). Mitchem, Wells, and Wells (2003) state that, "Research on schools and teaching has suggested for decades that student success and achievement are intricately associated with students' interactions with effective teachers" (p. 1). If this is true, then mathematic s teachers are the key agents to bringing out reform toward technology integration (Garofalo, Drier, Harper, & Timmerman, 2000). But, the way to effectively prepare teachers to become change agents is another issue. Professional development is a primary factor toward helping teachers become self-adept in learning the knowledge and skills required of them when teaching math content. This study investigates whether professional development could promote math education teachers' self-confidence in using and applying the technology tools learned back to the classroom. In-service teachers participating in a Math Summer Institute are the participants in this particular study, and the researchers explore whether completing a four-week intensive professional development institute has improved the participants' knowledge, skill sets, attitude, and self-confidence in applying what they have learned.

Literature Review

The effective preparation of teachers to teach mathematics in K-12 education is recognized as a vital factor toward students' academic success. In conjunction with the curriculum, teachers are the key in assisting students to learn required information necessary to succeed in the mathematics curriculum (Schmidt et al., 2001). Several professional organizations note the importance of teacher preparation and professional development as a means toward improving the aptitudes of math education teachers, especially in regards to technology integration. The National Council of Teachers of Mathematics (2000) considers technology as being essential "in teaching and learning mathematics; it influences the way mathematics that is taught and enhances students' learning" (p. 2) as one of their six principles of school mathematics. Furthermore, the Association of Mathematics Teacher Educators (2006) goals includes one to promote the recognition of the ever-increasing impact of technology on mathematics teacher education and has made a position statement on the importance of preparing math teachers to meet the current standards of integrating technology. If one reviews the Association of Mathematics Teacher Educators newsletter called *Connections* (2008), the content solely concentrates around technology and why these tools should be utilized in the math classroom. If organizations such as these recognize the importance of technology, then teacher preparation and professional development need to include a demonstration that goes beyond just the "how to use technology," but how to integrate.

Reasons behind using technology in the mathematics curriculum are numerous. Heid (1997) cites that technology when used in conjunction to teaching math could (a) make learning more student-centered, (b) give students the experience of being mathematicians themselves, (c) provide an avenue for reflection, and (d) make available constant access to the instruction, meaning that the instruction is no longer restricted when the teacher teaches. Contextual learning in constructive environments is critical when applying technology in math education. Students need to apply learning in novel and authentic situations so that they can practice skills, knowledge, and decision-making, while experiencing the implications or repercussions of certain decisions (Dyer, Reed, &Berry, 2006). Constructive or contextual learning environments actively engages the students as they (a) relate learning to one's life experience, (b) experience and learn by doing or through exploration and discovery, (c) applying the concepts to actual scenarios, (d) cooperate with others in terms of sharing, responding, and communicating with others, and (e) transfer the knowledge to a new context or novel situation that has not been covered in the classroom (Crawford, 2001). In short, technology in math education provides students with an opportunity to explore, reflect, and discover the consequences of learning math concepts.

The issue toward successful implementation of technology in math education is professional development. A large body of literature cites that the major obstacle toward teachers using technology in the classroom is the lack of proper teaching training (VanFossen, 1999; Veen, 1993; Whetstone & Carr-Chellman, 2001; Wild, 1996). Teachers today are often behind in meeting current challenges of the rapid expansion of technology in education. Many technology tools are available to teachers, but the application of these tools to teach content areas can be foreboding, especially when training is not present. Other studies on the effectiveness of teaching technology in pre-service and in-service courses reveal some positive results such as the participants improving their likelihood to use technology in the classroom and altering their perspectives toward technology as an obstacle (Lee & Hollebrands, 2008). Although some studies indicated that certain technology tools are more likely to be used than others, an introduction to technology in math education is important (Franz, Pope, & Fredrick, 2005). Thus, professional development is critical when expecting teachers to use technology in the math classroom. With more practice, teachers' self-assurance increases.

Problem Overview

Educators in math education should integrate technology tools as a means to assist students to learn mathematical concepts and principles. Technology can become an interactive supplement to the standard form of math instruction through paper-and-pencil methods to stimulate higher order problem-solving skills in novel situations. In addition, technology is a tool that could be applied in classrooms to assist students with diverse needs and learning styles to approach math and problem-solving scenarios more effectively (Kurz, Middleton, & Yanik, 2005). Students are not a homogeneous group of individuals in which everyone learns at the same pace and in the same method. Hence, math instruction should be individualized to cater diverse learning styles. One classroom teacher cannot design and develop personalized math curricula for thirty-three distinct students. But, the teacher could use different instructional tools and strategies that could accommodate individual learning characteristics (Cohen, 2001). With the availability of technology in schools, homes, libraries, and other public spaces, using technology as instructional tools to teach mathematical concepts and problem-solving skills seems to be the logical approach. However, the teacher is the central cornerstone toward successful implementation and integration of technology. The teacher is the one who selects and evaluates which technology tool to use at specific times. Without access and knowledge concerning technology hardware and software, successful integration of technology will not occur. In addition, not only do classroom math teachers need constant instruction and assistance in using various hardware and software application tools, personal self-aptitude and esteem are also essential criteria toward effective integration. The teacher has to know what he/she is doing in the classroom, along with embracing a positive outlook toward using technology as a means to instruct math. Thus, attitude and confidence are key criteria when trying to integrate technology into the mathematics curriculum.

For teachers who are currently in the classroom, in-service professional development conducted during the summer is a way in which they can obtain instruction concerning available technology tools. In addition, these in-service institutes can provide teachers with practice in using and adapting technology into their curriculum. The goal of these in-service institutes is to foster a positive reinforcement on part of the teacher's ability to take the knowledge back to the classroom. The researchers in this study were involved in such an in-service Summer Math Institute to help teachers in the surrounding area to learn, explore, utilize, and practice different technology tools that could be applied to math instruction. The researchers wanted the participating teachers to understand that alternative instructional tools were available that could be successfully utilized in the math curriculum. Improving the participating teachers' self-confidence was a primary objective of the in-service math institute.

This study tried to assess whether participating in a four-week Summer Math Institute concerning the integration of technology into the math curriculum helped improve teachers' skills, knowledge, ability, and willingness to apply what they learned. To examine this research problem, four research questions were investigated:

1. Does participating in an in-service training session concerning technology integration into math instruction help teachers learn how to apply and use their knowledge and skills in the classroom (RQ1)?
2. Does participating in an in-service training session concerning technology integration into math instruction help develop teachers' interest in using technology and self-confidence to apply what has been learned (RQ2)?
3. Do teachers who complete a technology-oriented in-service training session focus more on learning to use the technology during the professional development, as opposed to applying the technology in teaching (RQ3)?
4. Do teachers who complete a technology in-service training session have a more positive attitude and outlook toward technology after completing the professional development (RQ4)?

Methodology

Participants

Participants for the research study involved public school mathematics teachers in grades 5 – 8 from South Mississippi. A total of 75 teachers (24 in 2005, 24 in 2006, and 27 in 2008) participated in the Summer Math Institute. Between five to nine high-needs schools were represented each year (5 of 9 in 2005, 9 of 12 in 2006, and 5 of 12 in 2008). In this case, high-needs schools were those that served not less than 20 percent of the children from families with incomes below the poverty line. The vast majority (80%) of the teachers had more than 3 years of teaching experience; 12% had over 25 years. The Institute provided four-weeks of professional development on the integration of technology into math instruction including: strategies involving the scientific graphing calculator, Microsoft PowerPoint, Microsoft Excel, MS Paint, MathType Equation Editor, and the Internet. Instruction occurred in a computer lab equipped with an interactive whiteboard and enough computers for each teacher to work individually. Each teacher was provided a USB flash drive and TI graphing calculator to use during the institute and for classroom instruction.

Instrumentation

Methods of data collection for this study involved teachers completing a pre- and post-survey and completing a weekly reflection instrument. An instrument for the in-service institute derived from The Concerns-Based Adoption Model was developed by the researchers (Hall & Loucks, 1979). The model describes a hypothesized sequence of seven stages that individuals experience as they adopt a new practice. Professional development strategies may then be tailored for the predominant stage of a group. The Stages of Concern instrument, consisting of 35 items, was developed for assessing concerns of teachers as they adopt new practices (Hall, George, & Rutherford, 1979). Teachers respond using a scale of 0 – 7 with 0, indicating that the concern is irrelevant and 7 indicating that the concern is very true. Bailey and Palsha tested this version with a shorter, 15-item instrument (1992). Using multiple statistical tests, these researchers demonstrated enhanced psychometric properties with the shortened version and made the argument for a five-stage model. The correlation between total concerns on both the long and short versions of the questionnaire was .92. Along with a brief description of each level of concern, the Cronbach's Coefficient Alpha for each factor is provided below.

- **Awareness:** The individual has little concern or involvement with the innovation, but wants to learn more about it. Cronbach's α long version .74; short version .74.
- **Personal:** Individuals are concerned with how the innovation will affect them, with a specific focus on required changes in roles and tasks. Cronbach's α long version .76; short version .83.
- **Management:** Individuals are concerned with time management, organization, and prioritizing responsibilities. Cronbach's α long version .55; short version .60.
- **Impact:** Individuals focus on the innovation's effects. Cronbach's α long version .73; short version .81.
- **Collaboration:** Individuals are concerned about working with others to implement the innovation. Cronbach's α long version .78; short version .79.

The survey developed specifically for this institute consisted of 24 items based on a four-point Likert scale: 4=Strongly Agree, 3=Agree, 2=Disagree, and 1=Strongly Disagree (see Appendix). Modifications included changing the statements from generic to more specific terms.

For example, the statement "I am concerned about not having enough time to organize each day using this innovation," was changed to "I am concerned about not having enough time to organize each day when it comes to combining math and technology." There were sixteen items (1-16) of this nature. In addition, 8 statements (items 17 – 24) required teachers to indicate their perceived level of proficiencies in specific technologies (e.g., Microsoft PowerPoint, Microsoft Excel, graphing calculators, MathType Equation Editor, the Internet). Following the initial orientation session, the survey was administered during the first day of the 2005, 2006, and 2008 institutes. The questionnaire was administered again four weeks later at the end of the last regularly scheduled working day.

The second method of data collection consisted of prompted responses. The instrument consisted of five prompts on a one-page reflection paper. Each prompt was positioned within a large circle with room provided for teachers to record their responses. Prompts included: (a) I expected, (b) I got, (c) A thing of value, (d) I wish, and (e) Next I will or Next I need. In this regard, Krathwohl's affective domain taxonomy (1964) helped frame the effectiveness of a professional development institute by taking into account prior expectations. If participants' expectations are incongruent with the goals of a professional development program as indicated by responses in the "I expected" circle, then teachers may be dissatisfied with the experience despite the quality of the program. The prompts served as a means of formative assessment and enabled instructors to make modifications if needed. The prompts also facilitated the process of metacognition. Metacognition is the process of monitoring one's own learning progress and making changes to improve learning strategies (Winn & Snyder, 1998). Ways to facilitate metacognitive approaches to instruction, including the use of prompted responses, have been described in *How People Learn* (NRC, 2000). On the Friday of each week of the Institute, time was set aside at the end of the day for completing the prompted response instrument. Following the Institute, the researchers listed each teacher's responses to each prompt in an Excel document.

Findings

The presentation of findings is organized into one of the four categories developed for this study: (1) technology integration, (2) hardware, (3), software, and (4) confidence. These categories emerged as the researchers reviewed and analyzed the prompted reflections. Initially, the researchers began with six categories, but later immersed two categories into one of the four. The following discussion addresses the results from the survey, supported with responses given by the participants in the prompted reflections.

Survey Instrument

The survey consisted of 24 items (see Appendix). The researchers anticipated that scores for some items would *decrease* from pre to post, because it was hypothesized that teachers would demonstrate greater concerns about using technology in teach-

ing mathematics at the beginning of the institute than at the end of the institute. Thus, numbers 1, 2, 5, 6, 8, 9, 15, and 16 were coded as negative items. All the negative worded statements were recoded (reversal of responses) during analysis of the survey. The researchers anticipated that scores for other items would *increase* from pre- to post-test, because it was hypothesized that teachers would demonstrate less confidence about using various technology tools at the beginning of the institute and greater confidence at the end. Positive items included numbers 3, 4, 7, 10 - 14, and 17 - 24. Overall, the survey included 16 positive and eight negative statements. The eight negative items are italicized in the Appendix. Two of the positive items overlapped among categories. Item number 7 combined integration, hardware, and software; number 17 combined integration and confidence. All the hardware and software questions were positively worded. While analyzing the overall confidence, the researchers considered all 24 items, including those designated as confidence. As shown in table 1, six positive items (4, 7, 10, 13, 14, and 17) and four negative items (1, 5, 9, and 16) were categorized as *integration*;

Table 1. Classification of survey items for data analysis according to category and coding

	Integration	Hardware	Software	Confidence
Positive	4,7,10,13,14,**17**	3,7,21,23	7,18,19,20,22,24	11,12,**17**
Negative	1,5,9,16			2,6,8,15

Table 2. Minimum and maximum scores in each category

	Total number of items	Scale	Minimum Score	Maximum Score
Positive integration	6	1-4	6	24
Negative integration	4	1-4	4	16
Hardware	4	1-4	4	16
Software	6	1-4	6	24
Total positive Confidence	16	1-4	16	64
Total Negative Confidence	8	1-4	8	32

four positive items for *hardware* (3, 7, 21, and 23), six for *software* (7, 18, 19, 20, 22, and 24); three positive (11, 12, and 17) and four negative (2, 6, 8, and 15) for *confidence*.

Descriptive statistics (means and standard deviations) were used to describe the central tendency and dispersion on all measures. Table 2 provides the minimum and maximum scores for each category. The participant's responses over technology integration, hardware, software and confidence at the beginning and end of the program were compared by using two-tailed paired sample t-test. The 0.05 level of significance was set for the rejection of all null hypotheses.

Technology Integration

The first category to be discussed is technology integration. Participants were asked to rate their capabilities and knowledge for incorporating technology into math instruction. Results from this particular area helped answer the research questions RQ2 and RQ4. The analysis revealed that teachers' concerns decreased over the course of the institute each year. The analysis revealed significant changes in participants' attitudes toward the integration of technology in math instruction in 2005 and 2008, positive changes though not significant in 2006 (see Table 3). These results indicated teachers' confidence levels in using technology in their math instruction increased as well as their knowledge about the use of technology. They had more confidence in both their

capabilities and knowledge needed for integrating technology into math instruction.

Participants' improved attitude toward technology integration also emerged in the prompted reflections. The following statements demonstrate how the institutes altered teachers' attitudes toward the use of technology in teaching mathematics.

As a result of this workshop, I expect to become a more efficient user of technology and use calculators and computers in my classroom.

A thing of value from this experience is the benefit of being able to learn to use a variety of strategies for various technologies in mathematics instruction for the classroom.

Next I need to go observe a computer discovery class (7th grade) in my school to learn more about how technology can be used.

Next I will take back to my classroom all the information that I have learned in this workshop. I want to carry all my skills back to the classroom to help instruct my students.

Hardware

In the hardware items, teachers were asked to rate their proficiency in the use of a graphic calculator (T1-83 or T1-84) and other technology materials. Results from this particular area helped answer the research questions RQ1 and RQ3. Paired

Table 3. Attitude toward integration of technology in mathematics instruction

Year	Pre-Survey		Post-Survey		Change of Score		t	p[1]
	N	(Mean±SD)	N	(Mean±SD)	N	(Mean±SD)		
2005	18	27.50±2.12	17	30.35±3.52	15	2.20±3.53	2.41	0.0300
2006	16	28.69±2.85	17	30.71±2.93	10	0.40±3.03	0.42	0.6857
2008	22	30.23±2.14	24	32.04±3.91	20	2.30±4.08	2.52	0.0208

Note: [1] by paired *t* survey.

Table 4. Attitude toward hardware use in mathematics instruction

Year	Pre-Survey		Post-Survey		Change of Score		t	p[1]
	N	(Mean±SD)	N	(Mean±SD)	N	(Mean±SD)		
2005	18	9.50±1.58	21	12.52±1.50	16	3.00±2.22	5.40	<0.0001
2006	21	10.62±1.88	20	12.65±1.93	17	2.12±2.50	3.50	0.0030
2008	24	9.67±1.95	26	12.69±2.43	23	3.00±2.65	5.44	<0.0001

Note: [1] by paired *t* test.

t-tests revealed significant and positive changes in self-confidence in the knowledge and use of hardware across the three years (see Table 4). These findings show that participating in the summer mathematics institutes had a positive impact toward the attitudes of using hardware in math instruction. Researchers could also see that the participants obtained greater confidence in using hardware and became more aware of institutional support for hardware. This confidence not only made these teachers believe they were better able to use hardware, but also helped them become future leaders in their schools to advocate technology access and availability.

Participants' attitude toward the utilization of technology hardware to teach math concepts also changed for the better in the prompted reflections. The following statements demonstrate how the institutes improved teachers' attitudes toward the use of related technology hardware in teaching mathematics.

I got a lot of information on the calculator skills this week and how to graph the information in tables. I am feeling reasonably safe and competent with calculator use.

Wish I can learn more ways of implementing all this into my classroom. I would like to use this and see how the Smart Board and the Smart View software (in conjunction with the graphing calculator) can be used in the classroom.

I wish our district would use the graphing calculator presentation as part of our staff development. This technology can really help us teach math skills.

I expect to continue learning about Excel and the graphing calculator. So far, I have learned many things such as creating graphs and random number generators in the calculator that I had no knowledge of prior to this workshop.

I wish we were reviewed more on using the Smart-Board. We do not know all of its features and what it can do in the classroom

I wish I had a SmartBoard in my classroom. But, now I know how to ask for it (from my principal) because of what it could do for the classroom.

Software

The third category is the application of various software programs in education. Results from this particular area helped answer the research questions RQ1 and RQ3. Teachers' attitudes toward related software programs used in mathematics instruction are revealed in Table 5. Teachers were asked to rate their knowledge of software programs that included Excel, PowerPoint, Equation editor, and the Internet. Researchers found significant and positive differences between the pre- and post-surveys in all three years. From these results, researchers believe that teachers became

Table 5. Attitude toward software use in mathematics instruction

Year	Pre-Survey		Post-Survey		Change of Score		t	p[1]
	N	(Mean±SD)	N	(Mean±SD)	N	(Mean±SD)		
2005	20	13.25±3.34	21	19.57±3.33	18	6.50±3.43	8.03	<0.0001
2006	20	15.50±3.03	21	19.81±3.93	17	3.88±5.81	2.76	0.0141
2008	23	15.65±4.15	26	20.54±4.66	22	4.73±4.97	4.46	0.0002

Note: [1] by paired *t* test.

Table 6. Overall confidence in incorporating technology in mathematics instruction

Year	Pre-Survey		Post-Survey		Change of Score		t	p[1]
	N	(Mean±SD)	N	(Mean±SD)	N	(Mean±SD)		
2005	11	56.27±3.00	17	70.76±6.72	10	15.10±5.17	9.23	<0.0001
2006	14	62.79±6.14	16	72.56±6.07	9	7.33±7.58	2.90	0.0199
2008	21	59.62±6.93	23	71.30±9.23	19	12.05±8.86	5.93	<0.0001

Note: [1] by paired *t* test.

more prepared for using the software programs available, and this increased confidence will have a positive impact on the usage of software programs in their teaching process.

Teachers also changed in their perspective toward using different software application programs to teach math concepts in the prompted reflections. The following statements demonstrate how the institute helped teachers positively perceive the use of software in teaching mathematics.

I want to continue learning various functions in Excel and use special features of PowerPoint so that I can use these programs when creating lesson plans.

A thing of value is learning how to make spreadsheets, creating charts and graphs, and using clipart. I also enjoyed creating PowerPoint for teaching math lessons and using animations.

A thing that I valued the most was using spreadsheets to create gradebooks. Learning how to create a gradebook from scratch and putting formulas into cells to get operations performed was useful. I know how to make the spreadsheet more for "my taste."

Confidence

The fourth category involves an increase in confidence, attitude, and a desire to continue using technology to teach math concepts in math classrooms.. Results from this particular area helped answer the research questions RQ1, RQ2, and RQ4. The results revealed significant improvement in their concerns regarding the use of technology across all years (see Table 6). According to these results, the researchers believed that the participants acquired greater confidence regarding technology integration and their knowledge of hardware and software compared to before attending the institutes. The significant changes between the scores of pre- and post-survey also indicate that the teachers were more prepared to utilize the technology available in schools. The institutes not only gave teachers knowledge of hardware and software, but also helped them gain confidence to integrate technology into their curriculum. This confidence would help teachers utilize the available technology in schools and in math classrooms. In turn, the improved confidence would help teachers explore more concepts and applications in this area.

The responses in the prompted reflections also indicate an increase in self-confidence and willingness to learn more about technology integration. The following statements demonstrate how the in-service training led by the Institute's instructors assisted in improving teachers' confidence and continuing their desire to use technology. Most of these comments with reference to confidence emerged in the *Next I will* or *Next I need* prompt.

I will continue to learn all that I can in order to be an asset to my students and my school. I also want to pass this information to my fellow co-workers.

I will continue to practice experimenting and using what I have learned. I want to take these skills into my own classroom.

I will continue to work harder in understanding the various formulas in Excel and work on my own!

I am getting a SmartBoard this coming year. So, I need to go in and play with it. I also need to begin creating PowerPoint's for certain math skills taught this coming school year while this is still fresh on my mind. I would also love to set up a master Excel sheet with formulas already set in it for students to use.

I will try and take time to find places/topics in the curriculum standards to insert Excel and PowerPoint. I also need to continue building my confidence in what I am doing.

I want to take all this information back to my classroom to make it a more exciting and productive environment for learning.

I got 50000000 much more from all this. My brain was exercised greatly with the math concepts to go along with the technology skills.

An interesting finding from the prompted reflections was the issue of time, in addition to technology access. The teachers wanted to keep learning and using these technology tools in the classrooms. But, time and access were a reoccurring concern as exemplified in these statements, "I wish I had more time with colleagues to develop in-depth math lessons for my class and have more computers in my class to implement the lessons," and "I wish I had more time and access to integrate all of this into my daily schedule."

CONCLUSION AND DISCUSSION

The research questions asked for this particular study have been answered. First, offering an in-service professional development institute concerning technology integration into math instruction can help teachers learn how their knowledge and skills could be used in the classroom. Teachers not only learned about the technology hardware and software per se, but also the practical skills that they could use in instruction. By modeling appropriate uses of technology in the institute, teachers could envision how instruction can be carried out. Second, participating in an in-service professional development institute concerning technology integration into math instruction helped develop teachers' self-confidence to apply what they learn. Many teachers who had never used a computer before voiced their aspirations to continue learning and using technology beyond the institute. Some expressed interest in becoming leaders in their schools to help others learn to use the technology tools. Third, the teachers who completed this technology-oriented institute not only focused on learning to use the technology, but also on the application of technology in teaching. The questionnaire and prompted reflections indicate that although teachers valued the how-to-use-technology instruction they received, the teachers also began thinking about how they could use the technology in their math lessons and how to make it part of their school culture. This information reveals that the institute was successful in taking teachers from the initial "awareness" level all the way to the final "collaboration" level in Bailey and Palsha's five-stage model of concern (1992). Finally, the teachers who completed this institute developed a more positive attitude and outlook toward technology. Most were excited to continue their exploration of the possibilities that technology tools could provide in the classroom and how to obtain them.

This study does have its limitations. First, the sample population is not representative of teachers in South Mississippi. They were selectively chosen to participate in the Institute through an application process. Second, the administration of the prompted reflection instrument was not always consistent. In some years, the weekly reflections were administered on Thursday rather than Friday and the content schedule fluctuated that affected how the participants responded to the prompts (e.g., for one year the topic of grants was predominant, but not in another). Although this factor did not affect the data findings, not all the participants completed both the pre- and post-surveys. Nonetheless, the findings from this study address the effectiveness of conducting an intensive, four-week professional development institute focused on the integration of technology in teaching mathematics and how this could enhance teachers' attitude, confidence, and skills acquisition.

Teachers' perceptions, attitudes, and concerns should be addressed during any professional development workshop or institute. Simply administering a questionnaire before and after an event bypasses the rationale for a concerns-based survey, and, other than providing institutional assessment, serves as a fruitless exercise. Feedback from the weekly reflections enabled instructors to address teachers' struggles with certain technologies or mathematical concepts immediately. Instructors provided personal attention and instruction was modified accordingly. As revealed by this study and others (Atkins & Vasu, 2000; Rakes & Casey, 2002), future studies should continue to be performed in the tradition of Hall and Loucks (1978) in order to examine the effectiveness of professional development in improving teachers' confidence and attitude. However, a survey is only useful if the professional development staff uses the initial analysis to design the professional development experiences. That said, however, a survey alone is not sufficient to determine all areas of concerns that teachers may have. Prompted reflections, administered daily during a workshop or weekly during an institute, provide a simple and effective way to obtain additional feedback and take immediate steps to address teachers' concerns. However, an even more thorough qualitative approach could be performed that includes interviews, observations, and document analyses. This type of examination would bring a further in-depth perspective of how professional development sessions can change the environmental culture and people's perspectives.

Professional development helps teachers become the key agents they need to be. If anyone expects change to occur in the classroom, teachers need to be well-informed, skilled, ready, and possess the correct tools for change to take place. Without this help and support, change in the mathematics classroom will not occur. The Summer Math Institute provided teachers with the professional development needed to integrate technology into the math classroom. However, this professional development model is just not limited to mathematics. Schools, colleges, and universities can adopt similar types of extended professional development to help facilitate the acquisition of not only content material (e.g., math, science, language arts), but technology skills and pedagogical applications as well. In addition, professional development requires to be delivered over a longer period of time in order to be effective in changing the confidence level of teachers. A one-time, daylong workshop is not sufficient enough to initiate change in terms of attitude and confidence. Participants in such shorter professional development sessions may acquire specific technology skills or content knowledge, but the application of such skills and knowledge may not be fully recognized. A long-term professional development model is required to help stimulate continuing interest among the participants and increase confidence. A final observation that emerged from this study is that time and access to technology must be provided to mathematics teachers. This access to technology needs to be ensured in order for change to occur in instruction. Comments made by the participants in this study emphasized the need for extra time to assimilate all the information and skills learned into their actual teaching. Furthermore, the participants were concerned that the technology used in the professional development workshop may not be available back at their schools. They believed that , in order to fully integrate what had been learned from the Summer Math Institute, extra time to practice using the technology tools was required. This is an area in which educational institutions need to consider if change is to occur. In short, effective professional development is one way to stimulate interest that would extend beyond the constraints of the workshop itself and lead toward greater self-confidence in one's ability.

REFERENCES

Association of Mathematics Teacher Educators. (2008)... *Connections, 18*(1), 1–16.

Atkins, N. E., & Vasu, E. S. (2000). Measuring knowledge of technology usage and stages of concern about computing: A study of middle school teachers. *Journal of Technology and Teacher Education, 8*(4), 279–302.

Bailey, D. B., & Palsha, S. A. (1992). Qualities of the Stages of Concern Questionnaire and implications for educational innovations. *The Journal of Educational Research, 85*(4), 226–232.

Cohen, V. L. (2001). The name assigned to the document by the author. This field may also contain sub-titles, series names, and report numbers. Learning styles and technology in a ninth-grade high school population. *The entity from which ERIC acquires the content, including journal, organization, and conference names, or by means of online submission from the author.Journal of Research on Technology in Education, 33*(4). Retrieved March 5, 2009 from http://206.58.233.20/jrte/33/ 4/abstracts/ cohen.html

Crawford, M. (2001). *Teaching contextually research, rationale, and techniques for improving student motivation and achievement in mathematics and science.* Retrieved March 5, 2009 from http:// www. cord.org/ uploadedfiles/ Teaching%20 Contextually%20 (Crawford).pdf

Dyer, R. D., Reed, P. A., & Berry, R. Q. (2006). Investigating the relationship between high school technology education and test scores for algebra I and geometry. *Journal of Technology Education, 17*(2), 7–17.

Franz, D., Pope, M., & Fredrick, R. (2005). Teaching preservice teachers to use mathematic-specific technology. In C. Crawford et al. (Eds.), *Proceedings of Society for Information Technology and Teacher Education International Conference 2005* (pp. 3462-3466). Chesapeake, VA: AACE.

Garofalo, J., Drier, H., Harper, S., & Timmerman, M. A. (2000). Promoting appropriate uses of technology in mathematics teacher preparation. *Contemporary Issues in Technology and Teacher Education, 1*(1). Retrieved March 9, 2009 from http://www. citejournal. org/vol1/ iss1/ currentissues/ mathematics/article1.htm

Hall, G., George, A., & Rutherford, W. (1979). *R & D Report No. 3032.* Austin, TX: University of Texas, Research and Development Center for Teacher Education.

Hall, G. E., & Loucks, S. (1978). Teacher concerns as a basis for facilitating and personalizing staff development. *Teachers College Record, 80*, 36–53.

Heid, K. M. (1997). The technological revolution and the reform of school mathematics. *American Journal of Education, 106*(1), 5–61. doi:10.1086/444175

International Society for Technology in Education. (2008). *National Educational Technology Standards (NETS•T) and Performance Indicators for Teachers*. Retrieved March 5, 2009 from http://www.iste.org/AM/Template.cfm?Section=NETS

Krathwohl, D. R., Bloom, B. S., & Masia, B. B. (1964). *Taxonomy of educational objectives: Handbook II: Affective domain*. New York: David McKay Co.

Kurz, T. L., Middleton, J. A., & Yanik, H. B. (2005). A taxonomy of software for mathematics instruction. *Contemporary Issues in Technology & Teacher Education, 5*(2), 123–137.

Lee, H., & Hollebrands, K. (2008). Preparing to teach mathematics with technology: An integrated approach to developing technological pedagogical content knowledge. *Contemporary Issues in Technology & Teacher Education, 8*(4), 326–341.

Mitchem, K., Wells, D. H., & Wells, J. G. (2003). Effective integration of instructional technologies (IT): Evaluating professional development and instructional change. *Journal of Technology and Teacher Education, 11*(3), 399–416.

National Council of Teachers of Mathematics. (2000). *Executive summary: Principles and Standards for School Mathematics*. Retrieved March 5, 2009 from http://www. nctm.org/ uploadedFiles/ Math_Standards/12752_exec_pssm.pdf

National Research Council. (2000). *How people learn: brain, mind, experience, and school*. Washington, DC: National Academy Press.

Rakes, G. C., & Casey, H. B. (2002). An analysis of teacher concerns toward instructional technology. *The International Journal of Educational Technology, 3*(1). Retrieved March 8, 2009 from http://www.ed.uiuc.edu/IJET/v3n1/rakes/index.html

Schmidt, W. H., McKnight, C. C., Houang, R. T., Wang, H. C., Wiley, D. E., Cogan, L. S., & Wolfe, R. G. (2001). *Why schools matter: a cross-national comparison of curriculum and learning*. Indianapolis, IN: Jossey Bass Publishing.

VanFossen, P. (1999, November 19-21). *Teachers would have to be crazy not to use the Internet!": Secondary social studies teachers in Indiana*. Paper presented at the Annual Meeting of the National Council for the Social Studies, Orlando, FL.

Veen, W. (1993). The role of beliefs in the use of information technology: implications for teacher education, or teaching the right thing at the right time. *Journal of Information Technology for Teacher Education, 2*(2), 1390–153.

Whetstone, L., & Carr-Chellman, A. (2001). Preparing preservice teachers to use technology: Survey result. *TechTrends, 45*(4), 11–17. doi:10.1007/BF02784820

Wild, M. (1996). Technology refusal: rationalizing the failure of student and beginning teachers to use computers. *British Journal of Educational Technology, 27*(2), 134–143. doi:10.1111/j.1467-8535.1996.tb00720.x

Winn, W., & Snyder, D. (1996). Cognitive perspectives in pyschology. In Jonassen, D. H. (Ed.), *Handbook of research for educational communications and technology* (pp. 112–142). New York: Simon & Schuster Macmillan.

APPENDIX

Survey for (SM)^2 I Summer Math Institute Participants

The purpose of this questionnaire is to determine your current concerns regarding the integration of mathematics and technology into your classes. The items were developed from typical responses of teachers who ranged from no knowledge at all about the ideas to many years experience in using them. **Therefore, a good part of the items on this questionnaire may appear of little relevance to you at this time.** For completely irrelevant items, please circle **"NA"** on the scale. Other items will represent those concerns that you *do* have, in varying degrees of intensity, and should be marked higher on the scale. Please respond to the items in terms of your present concerns about your involvement, or how do you feel about your involvement with **integrating mathematics and technology into your classes.** We do not hold to any one definition of this innovation, so please think of it in terms of your own perceptions of what it involves in your teaching situation.

1 = completely disagree
2 = somewhat disagree
3 = somewhat agree
4 = completely agree
NA = Irrelevant

1.	*I am concerned about my ability to integrate mathematics with technology.*	1 2 3 4 NA
2.	*I am concerned about not having enough time to organize each day when it comes to combining math and technology*	1 2 3 4 NA
3.	I am concerned about availability of technology materials at my school.	1 2 3 4 NA
4.	I would like to help other faculty in their attempts to blend technology into their subject areas.	1 2 3 4 NA
5.	*I have a very limited knowledge about integrating mathematics and technology.*	1 2 3 4 NA
6.	*I am concerned about the students' abilities in technologies exceeding my own.*	1 2 3 4 NA
7.	I would like to how what resources are available if we decide to integrate mathematics and technology.	1 2 3 4 NA
8.	*I am concerned about my inability to manage all that integrating math with technology requires.*	1 2 3 4 NA
9.	*I would like to know how my teaching or administration is supposed to change when integrating these subjects.*	1 2 3 4 NA
10.	I would like to revise the instructional approach for integrating technology into the mathematics classroom.	1 2 3 4 NA
11.	I would like to have more information on time and energy commitments required for integrating these subjects.	1 2 3 4 NA
12.	I would like to know what other faculty are doing in this area.	1 2 3 4 NA
13.	I would like to determine how to supplement, enhance, or replace the mathematics teaching that I use to integrate technology.	1 2 3 4 NA
14.	I would like to use feedback from students to change my integration of the two subjects.	1 2 3 4 NA
15.	*. I would like to know how my role in the classroom will change when I am using this approach.*	1 2 3 4 NA

16.	*Coordination of tasks, grading, and equipment is taking too much of my time with regards to integrating math and technology.*	1 2 3 4 NA
17.	I would like to know how using this approach is better than what I have been doing in my classroom.	1 2 3 4 NA
18.	I am proficient in the use of Powerpoint in my classroom.	1 2 3 4 NA
19.	I am proficient in the use of Microsoft Excel in my classroom	1 2 3 4 NA
20.	I am proficient in the use of integrating Microsoft Excel into Word documents.	1 2 3 4 NA
21.	I am proficient in the use of graphing calculators (ex: TI-83) in my classroom.	1 2 3 4 NA
22.	I am proficient in using MathType Equation Editor to create documents.	1 2 3 4 NA
23.	I am proficient in using the graphing calculator to perform spreadsheet applications.	1 2 3 4 NA
24.	I consider my knowledge of the Internet to be very proficient.	1 2 3 4 NA

Note: Items in italics were coded as negative statements for the purpose of item analyses (e.g, the researchers anticipated that scores for these items would go down from pre- to post-test).

This work was previously published in International Journal of Information and Communication Technology, Volume 6, Issue 2, edited by Lawrence A. Tomei, pp. 47-61, copyright 2010 by IGI Publishing (an imprint of IGI Global).

Chapter 14

Materials–to–Standards Alignment:
How to "Chunk" a Whole Cake and Even Use the "Crumbs": State Standards Alignment Models, Learning Objects, and Formative Assessment – Methodologies and Metadata for Education

Tom Adamich
Visiting Librarian Service, USA

ABSTRACT

One way of identifying an effective materials-to-standards relationship (often defined educationally as "alignment") is through the use of metadata for books, visual media, computer software, educational kits, and manipulative materials. Embedded in the metadata is vocabulary containing standards-based terminology and other elements of educational pedagogy—evidence of an effective materials-to-standards relationship or alignment. This article attempts to define the materials-to-standards alignment process (as it relates to state standards) and its relationship to formative assessment and the use of learning objects—successful strategies being used in today's educational instruction and testing environment. The article also looks at two statewide examples of the use of metadata reflecting materials-to-standards alignment and identifies both current successes and future challenges associated with the broad use of each.

INTRODUCTION

As a result of the "No Child Left Behind" (NCLB) Act of 2001, state-based educational agencies have made standardized testing a priority in their respective jurisdictions. America's public and private schools have adapted by analyzing their teaching strategies and curriculum delivery methods to find ways to better address the issues often associated with standardized testing (i.e., inadequate understanding of individual, test-related concepts by students, difficulty teaching

DOI: 10.4018/978-1-61350-468-0.ch014

individual, test-related concepts by students, lack of educator preparation time and often misdirected use of instructional materials).

Several questions arise:

- "How can educators teach individual, test-related concepts effectively?"
- "Are there strategies and materials available to "teach" individual, test-related concepts that are available, reliable, and pedagogically sound?"
- "How can these materials (and their reliable connection to standards-based test concepts) be identified and made available to educators (and, for that matter, students)?"
- "What are the current successes and future challenges associated with describing these materials and providing access to their description for educator/student evaluation?
- How can instructional technology be used to make these important details available to educators/students?

Several states (including Ohio and California, which will be featured here) have taken steps to develop what is known as metadata-based materials-to-standards alignment tools that address the relationship of instructional materials to individual, test-related concepts. In the case of the former (Ohio), the metadata-based alignment process is "strict and humanistic", using rubrics and human collaboration to analyze the materials, extract evidence of successful test/standard alignment, and use descriptive terminology (known as curriculum-enhanced cataloging) to create metadata for the alignment. In the case of the latter (California), the metadata-based alignment process is broad and facilitated", using existing curriculum-enhanced metadata and enhancing it with additional uses of terminology and automation. Both alignment processes rely heavily on information technology networks and IT design to function.

This article – presented in two parts – attempts to illustrate that materials metadata containing materials-to-standards alignment-based descriptive elements which are distributed electronically to educators/students can be an effective tool for both groups to use when making sound instructional/learning and materials purchasing decisions. Part one is a general overview of the current standards-based learning environment, including a discussion of basic formative assessment concepts and practices as well as a brief overview of the elements of theory associated with the learning object – an entity which can also be described as a "chunk" of information or the "smallest teachable concept. Part two features two metadata-based materials-to-standards alignment creation and distribution case studies – "The Ohio Alignment Concept" and California's "Linking your Library Collection to the California State Content Standards" initiative. Additionally, part two discusses the role that the school library and library resources (both print and electronic) play in the creation and maintenance of materials-to-standards alignment-based metadata, as well as related technology-based content delivery and preservation issues.

PART ONE

Formative Assessment and Learning Objects: The "Chunk" and Their Relationship to the "Smallest Teachable Concept"

In this article's title, a discussion of the comparison of curriculum standards alignment, formative assessment and learning objects to a cake (i.e., "whole cake", "chunk" and "crumb") has direct significance to understanding learning in today's standards-based learning environment. Educators tend to identify the "whole cake" as standardized testing, a summative form of assessment which includes a variety of concepts from several curricular areas. Additionally, the "chunk" portion of the cake, educationally speaking, refers to an individual question or group of questions that relate, either directly or indirectly, to demonstrating an understanding of a concept (and is often assessed using a variety of testing strategies including free response, essay, multiple choice selection, etc.). Furthermore, the educational "crumb" part of the cake analogy is connected either to one element or several elements that form a core concept. It is in this context that the discussion of the "learning object" begins. Let's examine each of these concepts in more detail, beginning with formative assessment.

Formative Assessment

According to Schwarz and Sykes' *Psychometric foundations of formative assessment* (Schwartz & Sykes, 2004), formative assessments are frequent and evaluate a "small number of data points (items)." Other favorable characteristics of formative assessment include providing information to accomplish the following:

- Identify current student knowledge levels at a "highly granular level"
- Support prescriptive teaching information at multiple levels (student, class, school)
- Align content and materials to state standards*
- Promote instructional effectiveness
- Predict how well students are prepared to meet state standards and annual summative state assessments(Schwarz & Sykes, 2004)

Another key feature of formative assessment is the "diagnostic" nature of the basic concept. While summative assessments like standardized testing incorporate a "comprehensive" approach to testing (i.e., using single, paper-based tests populated with a preponderance of concrete, single-response

test questions covering a wide array of topics and often administered on a "one-time-only" basis), formative assessments are more specific and differ fundamentally in several ways:

- Content contains high levels of technical rigor
- Assessments are deep and broad, often incorporating constructed-response items
- Assessments are given at multiple times for progression tracking
- Both traditional and non-traditional (i.e., electronic) modes of assessment are available
- Local educators can "customize" some aspects of the formative assessment (FA) system
- Fine-grain alignment to content standards
- FA system is dynamic and improves over time (Schwarz & Sykes, 2004).

Once again, the strong relationship of alignment to formative assessment is clearly evident. According to Schwarz and Sykes, alignment is a form of "validation" in the formative assessment model and involves an examination of the "items that comprise the assessment and an alignment of that test content to standards, obtaining item and test statistical characteristics and may even involve steps such as ascertaining the usability of score reports (Schwarz & Sykes, 2004)

One may ask the question, "How does formative assessment's "diagnostic characteristics" relate to the learning object "chunk" and the smallest teachable object "crumb" discussed earlier?" Simply stated, since formative assessment involves frequent testing of concepts -- ideas which are often highly-technical, granular and directly aligned to standards -- the learning object (particularly the electronic-based interactive variety) and the smallest teachable concept are the "core elements" of formative assessment.

Another question, "How does one identify and locate instruction materials which teach specific concepts – the "chunk" and the ""crumb" – that are also "standards friendly"? Hopefully, part 2 of this paper and its discussion of the creation of metadata to reflect materials-to-standards alignment will answer that question.

Learning Object

According to the Learning Technology Standards Committee of the Institute of Electrical and Electronics Engineers (IEEE), a learning object is any entity, digital or non-digital, that may be used for learning, education, or training (Learning Technology Standards Committee, 2002). An additional definition identifies the learning object as "any digital resource that can be reused to support learning" (Wiley, 2001). Yet another definition talks about the learning object as "web-based interactive "chunks" of "e-learning" designed to explain a stand-alone learning objective (Centre for Excellence in Teaching and Learning in Reusable Learning Objects, 2005). In every case, these definitions are a direct link to both a standardized test's individual questions and groups of question categories respectively. They also form the basis for the discussion on both formative assessment/Bayesian Inference Models theory and the materials-to-standards alignment models being profiled in this article.

The instructional goal behind the use of the learning object is to attempt to define how the "smallest teachable concept" can contribute to a better understanding of that concept – both individually and in context with other concepts. The additional derived benefit of using a learning object is to promote the "diagnostic and probability-based" benefits of teaching smaller, more specific pieces of information.

Now that we have a fundamental understanding of the use of formative assessment and how it incorporates learning objects as the "chunks" and "crumbs" of standardized testing and summative assessment (i.e., the "cake"), let's look at several examples of successful utilization of these concepts in the education context (using the creation/delivery of materials metadata to reflect materials-to-standards alignment).

PART TWO

Metadata Containing Materials-to-Standards Alignment-Based Description: Creation and Distribution

While it can be said that the Internet's ability to share location/identification information associated with materials-to-standards aligned instructional materials (which reflect the material's relationship to both individual, item-level concept understanding and the use of formative assessment teaching strategies/learning objects) is relatively new, the creation of metadata incorporating materials-to-standards alignment concepts is not. This type of metadata creation – known as curriculum-enhanced cataloging – traces its origins back to the early 1990s.

The Birth of Materials-to-Standards Alignment Metadata: CEMARC

Murphy, in "Curriculum-enhanced MARC (CE-MARC): a new cataloging format for school libraries", describes the origins of the CEMARC as a means of describing school library materials labeled as "curriculum materials" using descriptive terminology associated with what Murphy labels "descriptive detail" including a summary note, reading level of the item, book pagination or film running time, or name of illustrator. The intended audience – school librarians and educators – are familiar with both the context and relationship of the descriptive elements included in the metadata and how their connection to the materials in question enhances the understanding of the item's content and effective use (Murphy, 1994).

According to Murphy, CEMARC was developed by Roger Minier and the Northwest Ohio Educational Technology Foundation (NWOET) (Murphy, 1994). It uses the MARC metadata standard as its foundation and was intended to represent the relationship—through description – of a material's content to a variety of education-based concepts. CEMARC was also designed to promote the concept of alignment in that the user – accessing the metadata by searching the school library card catalog --- would retrieve the descriptive metadata using key curriculum-enhanced elements of the description that had been indexed and made searchable in the library catalog database by programming protocol. At the time, the concept of free-text searching or keyword searching had not yet been developed, and the library catalog database's structure relied on indexed field access for information retrieval.

At the time, CEMARC cataloging followed the following methodology (Figure 1).

These fields are noteworthy in that they contain many of the same item-level specificity elements associated with teaching a concept via formative assessment (elements of Bayesian predictability; evidence of identification as a learning object). Some of the notable CEMARC indexed fields (again, utilizing the MARC metadata standard, MARC Standards, n.d.) include the following:

- MARC 520 (summary note containing descriptive subject and pedagogy-related terminology)
- MARC 521 (incorporating indicators for special learner characteristics and motivation/interest level)
- MARC 658 (curriculum objective)

An example of the MARC 521 special learner characteristics and motivation/interest level tag is as follows:

521 ##$aJunior high school through college students and adults (MARC Standards, n.d.)

The MARC 658 indexed field contains an even greater level of subject and pedagogically-relative terminology. Its use facilitated the potential for applying the concept of materials-to-standards alignment. Below is an example of the MARC 658 curriculum objective:

658 ##$aReading objective 1 (fictional)$bunderstanding language, elements of plots, themes, motives, characters, setting by responding to the multiple-meaning word$cNRPO2-1991$dhighly correlated.$2ohco (MARC Standards, n.d.)

A comprehensive listing of CEMARC fields can be found in my article *CE MARC: the educa-*

Figure 1.

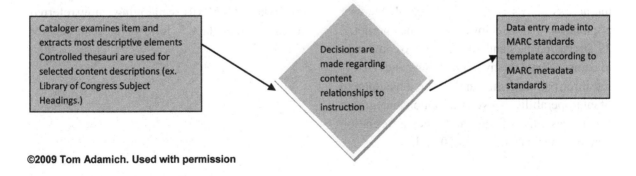

tor's library receipt (Adamich, 2006). Another good source of CEMARC explanation and theory relative to its use in assessment in education is another article I wrote -- *CE cataloging and the school library as language set repository: using a MARC record for assessment* (Adamich, 2006). There are numerous examples of current applications of materials-to-standards alignment as well as reference to other CEMARC resources.

While the overall concept of embedding the actual standards that aligned a particular instructional material item to the learning object it represents is sound, there have been many obstacles to the universal application of this technique. One obstacle has been the dynamic nature of state standards, which have been changed and modified over time. Metadata, without proper maintenance either via human intervention or using algorithms, tends to remain static.

Another obstacle facing the widespread creation of materials-to-standards alignment metadata has been access. While this methodology has generated some useful metadata for evaluation, in the early days of CEMARC cataloging, the data had limited access coverage and required the installation of specialized searching software. The concepts associated with the Internet and the "virtual library" (i.e., the library without walls) coupled with limited use of the ANSI/NISO Z 39.50 operating standard -- the American National Standard Information Retrieval Application Service Definition and Protocol Specification for Open Systems Interconnection – did not allow for access outside of individual libraries and/or document repositories. There was certainly not the access across education and/or library user populations that we enjoy today via the Internet. Z 39.50 created the standard way for two computers to communicate relative to searching and retrieving information; it encouraged the development of interoperability between and among integrated library systems software and other information delivery mechanisms (Z 39.50, n.d.).

Materials-to-Standards Alignment Metadata Creation Today

Today's materials-to-standards alignment metadata creation still incorporates many of the same entry conventions and content features of past. Evaluation of materials in context is still primarily accomplished via human intervention. If standards are embedded in the metadata, the process is still somewhat manual (however, the online access to state standards has increased exponentially, so the availability of standards for cut/paste application via word processing protocol has vastly improved). Furthermore, standard thesauri are still used for many of the subject analysis entries. Again, subjectivity is still the primary creation focus.

However, the exponential development of technology application via the Internet relative to interoperability of metadata with HTML-based software, file manipulation, and open source software application has expanded the potential for materials-to-standards alignment applications. Instead of being restricted to using the MARC metadata standard for entry, other metadata standards such as Dublin Core, MODS, PBCore, and a host of others are being used. These metadata standards also afford numerous crosswalk opportunities for communication between and among standards to promote metadata access in a variety of electronic applications and venues. Please refer to my overview of metadata standards types in Curriculum-based cataloging and the new metadata: cataloging beyond the world of MARC for an expanded discussion of current interoperability uses of metadata standards (Adamich, 2007).

Today's CEMARC cataloging – now referred to as CE-metadata – follows these processes (Figure 2).

Figure 2.

©2009 Tom Adamich. Used with permission.

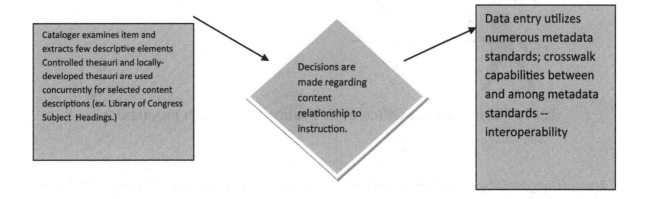

EXAMPLES OF SUCCESSFUL MATERIALS-TO-STANDARDS ALIGNMENT APPLICATIONS: TWO CASE STUDIES AND TWO STRATEGIES

With the goal of supporting formative assessment's item-level strategies (including incorporation of Bayesian psychometric probability and the extensive use of learning objects in teaching), CEMARC cataloging used to create metadata-based materials-to-standards alignments for instruction materials and resources has evolved since its inception in the early 1990s. While its use is not widespread, the core concepts have been successfully applied in several contexts – primarily education based.

The following case studies profile two successful examples of materials-to-standards alignment applications. Both are based on a large degree to a combination of technology-based access and utilizing materials evaluation techniques relative to the assignment of state standards, contextual descriptions, pedagogy-based terminology, and other descriptive elements to metadata for each material and/or material group.

While their approaches to assignment and utilization differ slightly, the goal of each – to identify key content elements that may support greater understanding of a concept or idea at a highly-granular item level – exist. The other key component of each application is a strong advocacy and training program for users – emphasizing the fact that each system acts as a teaching tool, not as an end to itself:

Case Study #1: Classroomclicks. com and the California Academic Content Standards

In 2001, Elainea Scott, Program Manager for the Tulare County (California) Educational Resource Services (ERS) Program of the Tulare County Instructional Services Division had the formidable task of converting the cataloging for the program's 7,700 book titles and nearly 9,000 video titles from a records-based system with no subject description to incorporating Library of Congress Subject Headings as descriptive elements (Tulare County (Calif.) Office of Education, 2001-2002). When Scott heard of the difficulty teachers had been having finding materials to use when teaching the specific content found in the California Academic Content Standards (CACS), she saw it as an opportunity to link or "map" the vocabulary of the standards to the newly-added

Figure 3. Classroomclicks.com

Library of Congress Subject Headings vocabulary. Thus, the core concept behind Classroomclicks. com was born (Figure 3).

Scott and her Standards Resource Team – Steve Woods, Judi Hopper, Nathan Wills, and Marjorie Denham – mapped each CACS to a group of Library of Congress Subject Headings. They then utilized Mr. Woods information technology expertise to design Classroomclicks.com that presents the standards in electronic format and allows users to then search the Tulare County ERS program library catalog for related items that correspond to the resulting CACS/LCSH mapping (Tulare County (Calif.) Office of Education, 2001-2002).

The methodology used by the Standards Resource Team to "align" materials to standards is based on the use of "inter-indexer consistency" in subject cataloging techniques. Chan defines inter-indexer consistency as the consistency associated with how individual cataloging records are indexed with subject headings which are obtained from a subject thesaurus (in this case the Library of Congress Subject Headings) (Chan, 1989). Chan's study examined five hundred cataloging records for the same material item originating from the Library of Congress and from participating libraries to determine if the participating libraries' records indeed included LCSH headings and if those headings were entered according to LCSH entry conventions (Chan, 1989). Chen's argument

is that, while the subjective nature of cataloging makes it difficult to predict whether or not a subject heading will be included in the metadata (either from the LCSH thesaurus or another thesaurus), the use of "controlled vocabulary" like LCSH will increase the percentages of consistency if a term/group of terms becomes a part of the metadata (Chan, 1989).

Since Scott and the Standards Resource Team converted the Tulare County (California) Educational Resource Services (ERS) Program's library catalog to LCSH, they had a consistent base of terms from which to work. Thus, the task of mapping the specific terminology of each CACS to an LCSH became much easier. Since Scott and her team assigned each LCSH to the records in the ERS catalog, they controlled the process of validating whether an "LCSH-to-CACS match" would occur. Therefore, the team includes the selected subject headings in the resulting online search. According to Scott, the functionality of Classroomclicks.com is based upon whether or not there are "hits" that result from the inclusion of LCSHs in the metadata that will "map" to the CACS standards terms they determined - through group analysis and professional, pedagogically-based collaboration – had either a direct or closely-related connection to a particular LCHS. Of course, Scott concedes "…the resource [being] only as good as the cataloging of the materials; if there is poor cataloging, the result will be fewer hits (Scott, 2007).

Upon further analysis, it is evident that there is validity in the Classroomclicks.com model of mapping Library of Congress Subject Headings to California Academic Content Standards terms and hoping that "good subjective cataloging" takes place to have a particular LCSH contained in the metadata for a particular item (or the "learning objects" discussed earlier which may be contained within or associated to that item). Classroomclicks. com is currently licensed in seven California counties where the system interacts dynamically with each county's ERS library catalog (Tulare County (Calif.) Office of Education, 2007).

Case Study #2: The Ohio Model of Alignment

Another model that incorporates "good subjective cataloging", state academic standards, and materials alignment with standards at a higher level of complexity and human intervention is The Ohio Model of Alignment. Developed via a cooperative effort between the U.S. Department of Education's Institute of Educational Sciences, the Ohio Department of Education, INFOhio – The Information Network for Ohio's Schools, and the Northwest Ohio Educational Technology Foundation (Figures 4 and 5), the Ohio Model of Alignment features collaborative interaction between a content specialist (initially, teachers who teach social studies) and a teacher-librarian who act as

an "educational team" to identify components of books, media, and other resources that directly address or "align" to a particular academic content standard. These educational teams then take the identified content and interact with technology to create metadata for the material that specifically addresses both the standard and the material's aligned segment.

The Ohio Model of Alignment's connection to the U.S. Department of Education's Institute of Educational Sciences is the result of the Ohio Model of Alignment's relationship to the Data Drive Decisions for Academic Achievement (D3A2) Initiative, a U.S. DOE grant-funded program developed by the Ohio Department of Education to improve ODE's data exchange system to point Ohio's educators to specifically-aligned resources that address Ohio Academic Content Standards and the needs of individual students (Ohio Department of Education, 2007).

D3A2 (available at http://www.d3a2.org) uses an electronic resource exchange containing metadata for Ohio Academic Content Standards-aligned lesson plans, activities, and assessment items, all of which are have electronic origins. Additionally, training and other professional development opportunities are utilized to provide Ohio educators and students an opportunity to, as discussed earlier by Schwarz and Sykes in their discussion of formative assessment, align materials to state standards, promoting an environment of assessment that is highly-technical and frequent. According to the project's overview,

Figure 4. NWOET

©2009 Northwest Ohio Educational Technology. Used with permission.

Figure 5. INFOhio

THE INFORMATION NETWORK FOR OHIO SCHOOLS

©2009 INFOhio. Used with permission.

one of D3A2's primary goals is to "contribute a sustainable infrastructure to promote and enhance information-based education practice and content alignment across the state (Ohio Department of Education, 2007)."

The Ohio Model of Alignment incorporates some of the same D3A2-based alignment and infrastructure-based goals into its effort – concentrating primarily on aligning portions of books, media and other materials found currently in Ohio's school libraries to the Ohio Academic Content Standards. The unique aspect of the Ohio Model of Alignment, as mentioned earlier, is its use of an "education team" – composed of an educator who is a content specialist and a teacher-librarian – who interact to identify the parts of the material being aligned and create/distribute the metadata created for the alignment using a highly-automated and interactive process.

Steps in the Ohio Model of Alignment

Much like the Classroomclicks.com search engine – which uses computer technology to create a searchable database of aligned materials mapped to the California Academic Content Standards -- The Ohio Model of Alignment attempts to create searchable metadata of materials whose segments are aligned to the Ohio Academic Content Standards. Also, like Classroomclicks.com, the process is highly automated and attempts to encourage

multiple catalog access for the nearly 2,000 Ohio schools who participate in the INFOhio School Library Automation Network and in the open access environment via the INFOhio Curriculum Resources Catalog (link available at http://www. infohio.org/UC/UCrev.html).

However, unlike Classroomclicks.com, The Ohio Model of Alignment does not map the standards to existing metadata content (i.e., the Library of Congress Subject Headings link used in the former) but relies instead on educator collaboration to identify searchable alignment elements (including portions of the actual standard) which will be collocated electronically and, eventually, inserted in to the metadata by a teacher-librarian to create a modified record.

According to the INFOhio Alignment Standard, a library item in any format is eligible for alignment if the material's content (or portion thereof – i.e., the "learning object" described earlier) adheres closely to the following statement:

Content aligned to Ohio's Academic Content Standards should result in a measurable increase in students' understanding of concepts or ability to perform skills in the benchmark and/or grade level indicators identified (INFOhio, 2007).

Listed below is an outline and graphical representation of The Ohio Model of Alignment (Figure 6):

Figure 6. The Ohio Model of Alignment

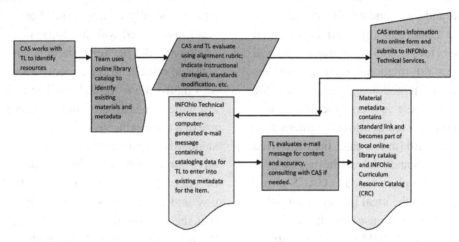

- Content area specialist (CAS) works with teacher-librarian (TL) to identify resources.
- CAS evaluates material according to the evaluation rubric (See App. A) and enters identified information into Alignment Submission Form (See App. B.)
- E-mail message generated which displays specific information to be entered into the existing metadata for the item (including MARC – Machine Readable Cataloging – Standard coding)
- TL evaluates the e-mail message and either enters the fields (via cut/paste) into an existing metadata record or contacts the CAS for further consult (i.e. content may require editing, etc.)
- The TL-modified metadata then becomes part of the library's online card catalog; the record is also to be loaded into INFOhio's Curriculum Resource Catalog (CRC), where it will become the "master metadata record" for the title and be available for inclusion in another INFOhio- automated school's library catalog or for use by a non-INFOhio-automated school in a stand-alone automated library automation system (LAS).

Classroomclicks.com and the Ohio Model of Alignment: Similarities and Differences - Implications for Replication in the Classroom and the Business World

As mentioned earlier, The Ohio Model of Alignment and Clasroomclicks.com differ structurally with regard to the elements used to connect metadata and a state's academic content standards (i.e., The Ohio Model of Alignment's "metadata-embedded standards and instructional strategies vs. Classroomclicks.com's external mapping to standards via Library of Congress Subject Headings and technology). The tools also differ in their approach to collaboration (i.e., statewide participation from multiple stakeholders – content area specialists and teacher-librarians with The Ohio Model of Alignment vs. local collaboration among library managers and curriculum specialists – with the approval of the California Department of Education using Classroomclicks.com).

Nevertheless, both Classroomclicks.com and The Ohio Model of Alignment share two important design elements which contribute to their success; both tools rely on training (both on-site and virtually) and technology applications (search engines, online forms, computer-generated messages, etc.) to carry out their missions.

In the Classroomclicks.com training process, Elainea Scott and the Standards Resource Team of the Tulare County (California) Educational Resource Services (ERS) Program featured earlier conduct informational training sessions which discuss the methodology used to create the research tool. In these sessions, they also identify the technology used to allow the interaction between the standard (in this case, the California Academic Content Standards) and the metadata for the resource to take place (a.k.a. a CACS portal that links content to the local library automation system's metadata warehouse) (Scott, 2007).

In contrast, The Ohio Model of Alignment uses statewide collaborative training sessions conducted by INFOhio and the Northwest Ohio Educational Technology Foundation to introduce participants to The Ohio Model of Alignment (including the alignment criteria/process, alignment tools, content area specialist and teacher-librarian role definitions, and hands-on concurrent sessions for teachers on alignment and teacher-librarians on materials selection and cataloging) (INFOhio, 2007). Roger Minier, NWOET Executive Director, Lois Lequyea, INFOhio Curriculum Resource Catalog & Alignment Cataloging Specialist, Paula Deal and Mimi Bogard, both INFOhio Program Consultants developed the sessions and serve as session moderators. Additionally, The Ohio Model of Alignment's technology references mirror Classroomclicks.com with identification of the use of computer-generated e-mail and metadata import/export of both the original metadata and the Ohio Academic Content Standard/instructional strategies-modified metadata, respectively.

Furthermore, both Classroomclicks.com and The Ohio Model of Alignment share an understanding of the important role that materials-to-standards alignment can play in promoting formative assessment training techniques that reinforce the model's use of technically rigorous, frequent assessments that may be presented in both traditional and non-traditional (i.e., electronic) formats. Both tools also foster the use of Bayesian psychometric approaches such as benchmarking and probability to determine both competency levels associated with a standard and diagnostic strategy to identify remediation elements and associated remediation frequency ratios.

Finally, the fact that both The Ohio Model of Alignment and Classroomclicks.com promote the use of a comprehensive strategy for materials-to-standards alignment that "operates in a dynamic environment where evaluation and modification of associated strategies and tools (both technology and training-based) is encouraged" means that these designs can be adapted and serve as "best practices" models for both education and business practices. As the need for accountability increases in education and business, the use of such tools as Classroomclicks.com and The Ohio Model of Alignment – coupled with a thorough understanding of the rationale behind their design and functionality – will prove to be a valuable investment in both human and financially-based resources.

CONCLUSION AND SPECULATIONS: THE FUTURE OF METADATA-BASED MATERIALS-TO-STANDARDS ALIGNMENT

As has been presented in this treatise, the idea of using metadata rich in context-based description (which is pedagogically sound and content specific) to support the formative assessment testing needs of both education and business has definite merit. While it's true that the widespread application of both the technology and methodology associated with materials-to-standards alignment has yet to take place, the potential for such utilization – enriched by the data accessibility and portability opportunities provided by the Internet – exists.

One of the major challenges which have limited the successful creation of materials-to-standards alignment metadata has been the access to standards information (both educational and business-based) which has been codified and made available in electronic form for easy access. Another limitation has been a lack of advocacy in both the educational and business communities to accept a more dynamic approach to metadata creation that, while still adhering to standard entry conventions and the development of entry policy, must also allow for interpretation and modification at the local level to better adapt to local workflows and economic realities.

One promising source of future study and potentially widespread use of state (and national) standards is the research and business model implementation being carried out by AcademicBenchmarks (AB). AB is a firm which has developed identification protocol to connect content and products to standards in both education and business. Their client list includes notable education-based organizations and companies such as Scholastic, Annenberg, and the American Education Association as well as businesses including Super Duper, Inc. (grocery store chain) and Datawise. A number of state schools and educational service agencies are also AB clients.

Another potential source of ideas for materials-to-standards metadata creation comes from the Gateway to 21st Century Skills Project. Sponsored by the National Education Association, the Gateway project hosts a variety of project resources including the Gateway to Educational Materials (GEM), a searchable catalog of over 50,000 educational resources that have been aligned to national academic standards (ex. NETS). The database may be searched by lesson type, grade level, keyword, mediator, beneficiary and price-Code. A searchable glossary for each category is included. Additionally, the GEM search engine may retrieve successful searches by matching terms in the entire text of the resource's metadata, its title, the description, and/or keywords. As was mentioned earlier with Classroomclicks.com and The Ohio Model of Alignment, GEM's advantage

is its ability to work successfully within a dynamic, changing materials and standards environment.

It is this potential to adapt to changes in both standards and to the materials themselves that may encourage the further exploration of how materials-to-standards metadata can provide item level identification and validation of content to assist educators and workers alike in their efforts to utilize formative assessment and instructional materials evaluation needs.

REFERENCES

Adamich, T. (2006). CE MARC: the educator's library 'receipt'. *Knowledge Quest, 35*(1), 64–68.

Adamich, T. (2006). CE cataloging and the school library as language set repository: using a MARC record for assessment. *Knowledge Quest, 35*(2), 73–78.

Adamich, T. (2007). Curriculum-based cataloging and the new metadata: cataloging beyond the world of MARC. In *Knowledge Quest, 35*(5), 66-71.

Centre for Excellence in Teaching and Learning in Reusable Learning Objects. (2005). *CETL FAQs*. Retrieved October 5, 2007 from http://www.rlo-cetl.ac.uk/faqs.htm

Chan, L. M. (1989). Inter-indexer consistency in subject cataloging. In *Information technology and libraries, 8*(4), 349-357.

INFOhio – The Information Network for Ohio's Schools and the Northwest Ohio Educational Technology Foundation. (2007). Overview of Social Studies alignment training (PowerPoint presentation). *Social Studies Alignment Training Resources, 1*(1), 9.

INFOhio -The Information Network for Ohio's Schools and the Northwest Ohio Educational Technology Foundation. (2007). Alignment criteria and process (PowerPoint presentation). In *Social Studies Alignment Training Resources, 1*(1), 6.

Learning Technology Standards Committee. (2002). *IEEE Standard for Learning Object Metadata. IEEE Standard 1484.12.1.* New York: IEEE.

Murphy, C. (1994, July 17-22). Curriculum-enhanced MARC (CEMARC): a new cataloging format for school librarians. In *Proceedings of the 23rd Annual Conference of the International Association of School Librarianship,* Pittsburgh, Pennsylvania (pp. 79-80).

Ohio Department of Education. (2007). *Data Driven Decisions for Academic Achievement (D3A2).* Retrieved October 15, 2007 from http://www.ode. state.oh.us/ GD/Templates/ Pages/ODE/ODEDetail.aspx?Page=3&TopicRelationID=55&Content=34940

Ohio Department of Education. (2007). *D3A2 overview.* Retrieved October 15, 2007 from http://www.d3a2.org/about.asp

Schwarz, R. D., & Sykes, R. (2004, June). *Psychometric foundations of formative assessment* (pp. 1-4). Paper presented at the National Educational Computing Conference, New Orleans, LA. Retrieved October 5, 2007 from http:// www. iste.org/ Content/ NavigationMenu/ Research/ NECC_Research_Paper_Archives/NECC_2004/Schwarz-Richard-NECC04.pdf

Scott, E. (2007). *No library resource left behind: linking your library collection to the Academic Content Standards (PowerPoint presentation). Tulare County.* Calif.: Office of Education.

Scott, E. (2007, July 12). *Follow-up questions - use of ClassroomClicks in Calif. Districts.* Personal e-mail correspondence.

Standards, M. A. R. C. (n.d.). *Network Development and MARC Standards Office - Library of Congress.* Retrieved June 15, 2009 from http://www.loc.gov/marc

Standards, M. A. R. C. (n.d.). *Network Development and MARC Standards Office - Library of Congress.* Retrieved June 15, 2009 from http://www.l oc.gov/ marc/ bibliographic/ bd521.html

Standards, M. A. R. C. (n.d.). *Network Development and MARC Standards Office - Library of Congress.* Retrieved June 15, 2009 from http://www.loc.gov/ marc/bibliographic/ bd658.html

Tulare County. (Calif.) Office of Education. (December 2001- January 2002).Just a click away – Educational Resource Services Program Manager Elainea Scott and the new on-line Standards Resource Guide. In *The news gallery.* Retrieved October 12, 2007 from http://www.tcoe.k12.ca.us/PressRoom/NG2001_12/index.shtm

Tulare County. (Calif.) Office of Education. (December 2001- January 2002).Just a click away – Educational Resource Services Program Manager Elainea Scott and the new on-line Standards Resource Guide. In *The news gallery.* Retrieved October 12, 2007 from http://www.tcoe.k12.ca.us/PressRoom/NG2001_12/index.shtm

Tulare County. (Calif.) Office of Education. (2007) *Standards resource guide.* Retrieved October 12, 2007 from http://www.Classroomclicks.com/

Wiley, D. A. (Ed.). (2001). Connecting learning objects to instructional design theory: a definition, a metaphor, and a taxonomy. In *The Instructional Use of Learning Objects: Online Version.* Retrieved October 5, 2007 from http://reusability.org/read/chapters/wiley.doc

Z 39.50. (n.d.). *Network Development and MARC Standards Office - Library of Congress.* Retrieved June 15, 2009 from http://www.loc.gov/z3950/agency/

This work was previously published in International Journal of Information and Communication Technology, Volume 6, Issue 2, edited by Lawrence A. Tomei, pp. 62-75, copyright 2010 by IGI Publishing (an imprint of IGI Global).

Chapter 15
Enhancing Teaching and Learning with Digital Storytelling

Shuyan Wang
The University of Southern Mississippi, USA

Hong Zhan
Embry-Riddle Aeronautical University, USA

ABSTRACT

This article intends to help educators interested in technology integration in the classroom acquire a firm theoretical foundation, pedagogical applications, and step-by-step technical procedures for infusing digital storytelling into the curriculum. Through illustrations of digital storytelling projects completed in the authors' undergraduate and graduate classes, this article discusses the benefits along with the challenges for using digital storytelling as a means of engaging students in reflective, active, and personally meaningful learning.

1. INTRODUCTION

Since the early days of civilization, storytelling has been important for the distribution of knowledge and preservation of heritage from generation to generation in world cultures. From the Egyptian age to the 21st century, storytelling has changed from oral fables and tales to utilizing digital images to display events/plots in multimedia ways. Regardless of the story-telling format, a common element identified in the storytelling is its educational nature—to distribute knowledge and share understanding among people across different cultures.

This article begins with a review of the traditional formats of storytelling in education, continues to introduce digital storytelling including its definition, educational advantages, theoretical foundations, and the research findings of digital storytelling in education, and is followed by procedures of digital story production as well as tools selection. This article also shares the experiences

DOI: 10.4018/978-1-61350-468-0.ch015

of implementing digital storytelling in the authors' graduate and undergraduate curricula. Challenges in using storytelling as a new pedagogical tool are addressed with suggestions of balancing technical and pedagogical preparation in order to optimize this innovative tool in education.

2. TRADITIONAL FORMATS OF STORYTELLING IN EDUCATION

Prior to the advent of the writing systems, storytelling was the only tool available by which individuals within their communities could pass down their beliefs, traditions, and historical culture to future generations. After the invention of the printing press in 1450, storytelling became even more important to society because printed stories became more available and accessible to many people who could learn from the historical stories and pass down their knowledge and heritage to future generations (Abrahamson, 1998).

As the oldest form of education, storytelling contributes uniquely to children's language and literacy development in speech and written composition, as well as language development in both reading and listening (Trawick-Smith, 2003). Therefore, as an instructional strategy and learning tool, storytelling was initially implemented mainly in early childhood education. By creating and narrating personal stories or fables, young learners can acquire content knowledge and develop language skills in the process of plotting, writing, revising, and narrating their stories. Abrahamson (1998) observed that, in addition to language and literacy development, literature also shows that storytelling, as an instructional strategy or a learning tool, has been applicable to other disciplines such as communication, social studies, and even math.

Nowadays, the power of storytelling has been widely recognized as an effective, meaningful, enjoyable, and creative way to enhance teaching and learning. Storytelling is found in all types of teaching, thus storytelling is viewed as the

foundation of the teaching profession (Abrahamson, 1998). By telling stories of what happens in the world, teachers expose learners to the existing world of knowledge where learners can learn, construct, and further develop their own knowledge by organizing complex elements in a given context, and by reflecting on their learning processes and life experience.

Storytelling is not only effective in early child education, but also effective in all areas of higher education. When applying storytelling in higher education, McDrury and Alterio (2003) presented a five-stage model on Reflective Learning through Storytelling, which involves both tellers and listeners of the stories in connecting the story with their own experiences. Each of the five stages (i.e., story finding, story telling, story expanding, story processing, and story reconstructing) engages students by encouraging them to reflect on learning processes and experiences of their lives. Through these five stages, students can improve their learning because storytelling, as a pedagogical tool in higher education, seriously takes the needs of students to make sense of experiences and seek meaning from their lives (Wells, 1986, cited in McDrury & Alterio, 2003).

3. DIGITAL STORYTELLING AS A NEW PEDAGOGICAL TOOL

Although storytelling as an instructional tool is not new in education, digital storytelling has become a new pedagogical endeavor that emerged from the proliferation of digital technologies including digital cameras, photo editing software, authoring tools, and Web 2.0 technologies such as Flickr and Myspace (Meadow, 2003; Alexander & Levine, 2008). As with practical applications of the traditional forms of storytelling, digital storytelling as an instructional medium has also been used by educators in many ways across the curriculum, not only in arts and humanities, but also in mathematics and science. The across-curriculum application of digital storytelling is because that this medium facilitates the convergence of four student-centered learning strategies: (1) student engagement, (2) reflection for deeper learning, (3) project-based learning, and (4) the effective integration of technology into instruction (Barrett, 2005). A comprehensive review in this paper of studies related to educational uses of digital storytelling and an illustration of the integration of digital storytelling into different classes will help educators perceive the pedagogical potentials for this new medium and learn the best practices for engaging students in reflective and active learning by producing meaningful products.

4. WHAT IS DIGITAL STORYTELLING?

According to Porter (2005), digital storytelling is the combination of the ancient art of oral storytelling with a palette of technical tools to weave personal stories using digital images, graphics, music, and sound mixed together with the author's own story voice. Different from traditionally linear narratives, digital storytelling shapes its power by integrating digital technologies, thereby giving a deeper dimension and vivid color to characters, situations, experiences, and insights (http://electronicportfolios.org/digistory/).

As with the traditional storytelling, telling stories digitally also involves plotting a personal narration about self, family, ideas, achievements, disappointments, or learning experiences. However, by using any of the available multimedia tools, including graphics, audio, video, animation, and Web publishing, digital stories may become short movies that can be made on computers with basic hardware and software by people relatively unfamiliar with high technology so as to narrate personal stories enhanced with written or spoken text, still images, video, and background music. It is the digital technology that changes storytelling into a modern form. Digital storytelling can be an

instructional, persuasive, historical, and reflective action. Digital storytelling, in this paper, refers to its educational application of using the movies created in the classroom, where students use still images or video clips accompanied by narratives or music to create a movie to report their understandings and/or findings on any subject area.

5. WHY DIGITAL STORYTELLING IN EDUCATION

Educational use of digital storytelling has undergone a process from involving mainly self-discovery to sharing knowledge with learning communities. The early use of digital storytelling was to utilize a new set of digital media tools for self-reflection and for investigating issues of identity (Boase, 2008). Because of the potentials of digital storytelling for reflective, active, emancipative, and enjoyable learning, digital storytelling has been applied in the classroom as both a teaching tool and a learning tool in many innovative ways. Teachers can use digital stories to deliver instructional content, including the presentation of an idea, illustration of a procedure, reinforcement of understanding, and a review of materials. Students can create a story to share their experiences, report their findings, reflect on their understandings, and the like. Most specially, since Web 2.0 platform has been well-established and enriched with various social learning software applications, storytelling has emerged as a new genre in Web 2.0 applications in education (Alexander & Levine, 2008).

The increased interest in integrating digital storytelling into the curriculum can be seen in many theoretical and applied areas within higher education (Abrahamson, 1998). Two application forms of digital storytelling (including its innovative version of Web 2.0 storytelling) in higher education have been identified: a composition platform and a curricular object (Alexander & Levine, 2008). As a composition platform, teachers and students write in different genres (that may be shared in blogs or other Web 2.0 tools) to share personal experiences, conduct research, present ideas, and distribute knowledge in an individual and meaningful way. At an object platform, teachers and students "better communicate an important subject" (Alexander & Levine, 2008, p. 52) including arts, humanities, mathematics, and science. In addition, due to the digital features of the storytelling, the completed stories can be easily archived and subsequently made available as future learning objects. These educational practices are grounded in learning theories and encouraged by research findings in illustrating the effectiveness of digital storytelling on instruction and students' learning processes and end-products.

6. THEORIES SUPPORT EDUCATIONAL USE OF DIGITAL STORYTELLING

Constructionism (Papert, 1993) and narrative paradigm (Fisher 1985, 1989) are the two fundamental theories supporting various and innovative uses of digital storytelling in education. Theoretically, constructionism is developed from Piaget's doctrine that knowledge simply cannot be "transmitted" or "conveyed ready make" to another person. Papert interprets constructionism in contrast with constructivism and instructionism. Constructionism, in Papert's words, is the "personal reconstruction of constructivism" that emphasizes the role of construction of knowledge in the "world" rather than purely in the "mind" (Papert, 1993, p. 142-143). Papert asserts that learning occurs "most felicitously" when learners are engaged in constructing a meaningful and sharable "public entity." One distinguishing feature of constructionism is "learning by making," which is different from constructivist "learning by doing." The notion of "learning by making" places

special emphasis on the learning that takes place when learners are engaged in building external and sharable objects or artifacts (p. 3), such as creating and sharing their stories enhanced by still images, voices, and background music.

Constructionism suggests that children will be more involved in learning if they are doing or constructing something that can be seen or used by others. Through two kinds of constructions, the construction of knowledge and the construction of personally meaningful artifacts, learners can achieve the best learning. By emphasizing reflection and sharing/learning in communities, the constructionist approach supports whole processes and end-products of teaching and learning via the medium of digital storytelling (Solidoro, 2007).

In addition to constructionism, the narrative paradigm, a well-known theory in human communication, supports the use of digital storytelling in education, a lifelong learning process which takes place mainly via communications. The narrative paradigm claims narration as a theory of "symbolic actions—words and/or deeds—that have sequence and meaning for those who live, create, or interpret them" (Fisher, 1984, p. 2). Because "man is in his action and practice, as well as in his fictions, essentially a story-telling animal" (MacIntyre, 1981, as cited in Fisher 1984, p. 1), narration has relevance to his stories in the real world, in fictive contexts, in life, or in the imagination. The narrative paradigm assumes that all forms of human communication can be seen fundamentally as stories, as interpretations of aspects of the world occurring in time and shaped by history, culture, and character (Fisher, 1985). The interpretations and explanations of symbolic messages used in communication normally consist of creation, composition, adaptation, presentation, and reception.

Narrative stories are effective as educational tools because they are believable, rememberable, and entertaining (Neuhauser, 1993). Digital storytelling becomes an even more effective means of communication because narration is enhanced by visual aids, still images, music, and the authors' voice which expresses emotions. By digitally telling stories of different genres, learners may learn from, about, and through stories, and learn by reflecting on the experience of narrating and the narrating of experience (Cortazzi & Jin, 2007). Because various educational applications of digital storytelling are in compliance with how human beings learn, researchers have found that digital storytelling has played an effective role in many aspects of education.

7. STUDIES OF DIGITAL STORYTELLING IN EDUCATION

Many studies have found that digital storytelling in various ways positively affects and supports students' learning by encouraging them to organize and express their ideas and knowledge in an individual and meaningful way (Robin, 2005). Morehead, Li, and LaBeau (2007) used digital storytelling as an effective approach in teacher preparation programs for developing personal narrative into a powerful and emotional tool for employability portfolio development. Schiro (2004) integrated digital storytelling into teaching students algorithms and problem-solving through several stages of learning in order to help them develop mathematical skills. Papadimitriou (2003) applied digital storytelling to computer science and programming. More (2008) even used digital stories to increase social skills for children with disabilities. Bull and Kajder (2004) included digital storytelling in the language arts classroom and Royer and Patricia (2009) increased students' reading comprehension with digital storytelling.

Digital storytelling has gained its popularity in foreign language classrooms where digital storytelling promotes target language development and formation of socio-cultural identities. Skinner and Hagood (2008) conducted a case study to explore the intersection of socio-cultural identities,

existing foundational literacy, and new literacy practices in the form of digital storytelling of two English language learners: a 7-year old, America-born, male Mexican-American kindergartener and a 16-year old, female Chinese-American junior in high school. Data were collected from individual interviews with the two language learners and from an analysis of their digital story artifacts—*Spider-man* by the kindergartener and *Third Culture Kid* by the high school junior. The interviews revealed the two learners' textual preferences and digital storytelling design processes. The study found that digital storytelling is a promising instructional strategy for scaffolding young English language learners' development in story comprehension, decoding of print-based texts, reading fluency, vocabulary acquisition, and writing processes involving drafting, editing, and revising on the computer. In addition, digital storytelling allowed the two learners to use English to make sense of their lives as inclusive of intersecting cultural identities and literacy, thus further promoting the development of empowering critical literacies for English language learners.

Digital storytelling not only helped promote students' learning interests in different subjects, but also helped build learning communities. Banaszewski (2002) asked his fourth and fifth graders to build a community through storytelling. He created a positive classroom environment by sharing the students' stories about an important place within the classroom where students saw themselves as authors with a purpose and an audience. According to Banaszewshi (2002), sharing a story about an important place involved many risks for students. The teacher needed to take those same risks by sharing a place story of his own. Banaszewshi shared with his students how he saw the classroom as a place where he always felt at home and showed them pictures he had drawn to help convey some of the feelings about his place. He used the digital story he created about his place in the classroom to help students practice the story-coaching model.

Many successful cases have found that digital storytelling is a promising instructional strategy. Gils (2005) summarized the advantages of using digital storytelling in education into five categories: (a) providing more variation than traditional methods in current practice; (b) personalizing the learning experience; (c) making the explanation or the practice of certain topics more compelling; (d) creating real life situations in an easy and affordable method; and (e) improving the involvement of students in the process of learning. These identified advantages further encourage more educators to utilize digital storytelling in their instructional practice.

8. HOW TO CREATE DIGITAL STORYTELLING?

In general, the creation of digital storytelling includes two steps: story composition and technology integration. Digital story composition follows the same process as any type of composition: analyzing the writing situation including considerations for audience analysis, purpose, and voice and tone; drafting to generate ideas for the story; developing the stories to connect the plot with content; and revising and editing the stories. When the story is finalized, the story is digitized using carefully selected technology tools. Although digital storytelling differs for different educational purposes, considerations of the seven elements to a digital story help with the overall creative process (Lambert, 2002). According to Lambert, these elements include point of view, dramatic question, emotional contact, the gift of your own voice, the power of sound tracks, economy, and pacing.

Whenever creating a digital story, students have to make a story plan before they start. They need to define the purpose of the story, analyze the audience, and decide what tools are to be used. Once the purpose is defined and the audience is clear, they should plan a storyboard and write an initial script, which needs to be revised according to the images collected. Then, they should collect images and music. They can take pictures with a digital camera, scan old images, or download images from Internet. They can videotape an event and digitize it. All images and video clips as well as music should be saved in one folder. Their story project will be saved in this folder to make sure the project works properly before the project is converted into a movie. Once all materials are ready, students can start working on their stories. After importing images, video clips, and music into the software program they chose, they can create the storyboard of the project. Then, students should add effects to the slides, title to the story, give credits of images and music, and/or captions for different parts if needed. Then, they can record and save their narratives according to their scripts, which can be done to an individual slide or to the entire story. Students can always evaluate and modify their stories in the movie project mode (.MSWMM if Windows Movie Maker is used). If they are satisfied with the story, they can convert it to a movie format (.WMV) so that the movie can be viewed from a jump drive, CD, or a website. However, they can only revise their story in the project mode. Therefore, they need to keep their projects in case something needs to be changed later.

9. TOOLS FOR CREATING DIGITAL STORYTELLING

Most digital storytelling programs are designed for users with little or no technical background to make sure everybody should be able to create digital stories. In addition to the movie-editing applications, a user also needs a recording device and microphone, hardware and software to manipulate images and video, or devices to take pictures and videos.

A number of simple applications are available for free download from the Internet or come with the operation system. Avid Free DV works with both Windows and Mac operating systems. It has basic video- and-audio-editing capabilities. Microsoft Photo Story 3 is a free downloading software program but it only works with Microsoft Windows XP Operating System. Users can use images and video clips to easily make a movie with Photo Story 3. Windows Movie Maker is an efficient storytelling tool because it is user-friendly and functionally effective. The software allows users to create, edit, and share movies with still images and/or video clips. Users can easily add special effects, transitions, titles/credits, background music, and narration to their movies. The most important aspect of the software is the free download which is already included in recent versions of Microsoft Windows. Apple iMovie comes as a part of the Apple OS X Operating systems. It works in a way similar to Windows Movie Maker and has many advanced features and add-ons. Unlike the free Windows Movie Maker that can be downloaded if not include in the XP Operating system, iMovie is only free when you purchase a new Mac system and cannot be downloaded from the Internet for free. There are more complex video-editing applications such as Ulead, Adobe Premiere Pro, and others, which provide more flexibility for advance users to create sophisticated stories.

The following table (Table 1) summarizes the most important and popular tools for creating digital storytelling:

In addition to the above programs which are specially used for creating videos, students can also use Microsoft PowerPoint to create their stories and save the file as PowerPoint Show instead of PowerPoint Presentation. Then their PowerPoint slides will be shown automatically as a movie. This program is better for those teachers and students who do not have time to learn a new application but are very familiar with the MS PowerPoint program.

10. EXPERIENCES OF USING DIGITAL STORYTELLING IN THE CLASSROOM

The authors of this paper have been using digital storytelling over the past few years in four different types of classes with positive experiences.

The first course, *Computer Applications in Education,* was an undergraduate course designed to help future professional education students learn how to integrate computer technologies into the classroom. The course supported the ISTE's standards for training future teachers to apply technology in the areas of student learning and student assessment. One of the assignments was to create a two-minute story with Windows Movie Maker. The purpose of this assignment was to promote students' interests in using technology in curriculum development and strengthen their technology skills. The story could be a self-intro, about family, or anything around a particular theme (e.g., nature, music, a historical event, or a book). The story movie was required to have a title slide, an ending slide, and at least five pictures on a specific theme. Students narrated the movie according to the pictures of the theme. They were encouraged to add background music while they were speaking. Most students took pictures with a digital camera while some students scanned hard copy photos and then saved them to a USB jump drive. After finishing their movie projects, students shared their completed stories with the class. Among the movies they created, most were stories about themselves, their family, their friends, and activities they attended. They were very excited about the skills they learned in this project. Many students indicated that creating stories provided them with more opportunities to communicate meaningfully with their friends and fellow students. Compared to other course-related projects required for this class, students showed the most interest in storytelling and were willing to revise the movie until they felt satisfied with

Table 1. Tools for creating digital storytelling

		Use	Platform	Cost (Approx)
Hardware				
	Digital camera	Create still images	Windows/Mac	$80-$500
	Digital video camera	Create video clips	Windows/Mac	$100-$500
	Flip	Create video clips	Windows/Mac	$90-$300
	Webcam	Record and create digital images or video clips	Windows/Mac	$40-$100
	Microphone	Record narration	Windows/Mac	$20-$150
	Scanner	Digitize photos	Windows/Mac	$30-$350
Software				
	Avid Free DV	Edit videos and audios	Windows/Mac	Free
	Movie Maker	Create digital stories from still images and video clip; add audios	Windows	Free
	Photo Story 3		Windows	Free
	Image Blender 3			$50
	iMovie		Mac	Free
	Adobe PhotoShop Element	Modify images used in digital stories	Windows/Mac	$30-$60
	Goldware	Audio editor, recorder, and converter	Windows	Free evaluation version available; $45 for full version
	Audacity	Audio editor and recorder	Windows/Mac	Free
	Ulead	Video editing	Windows	$60
	Adobe Premiere Pro	Professional video editing software	Windows/Mac	$299-799
Shareware				
	CD-ROM	Share and publish stories	Windows/Mac	20 cents
	DVD		Windows/Mac	50 cents
	Website		Windows/Mac	Free site available

their stories. They said that they felt more interested in integrating technology into their future classroom with such technology.

Another course was *Computers in Education.* This was a 3-credit hour online graduate course. This course not only provided students with theories of teaching and learning with technology, but also created a technology-enhanced learning environment where they experienced how these technologies could help them learn. In addition to reading and researching, students were asked to finish eight technology projects according to a teaching scenario: to report the students' learning

activities to their parents in a parent meeting. One project was to create a movie about the kids in class, an activity, or anything which they thought would help the parents understand what the students did in class. The purpose of this assignment was to provide students with opportunities where they could master technology skills and apply these technology skills to the real life practices.

Some students created a story describing how he/she taught in class or the activities he/she conducted to teach the subject content. For instance, a student took pictures of the activities conducted in his math class to demonstrate how he taught math. Another student told her audience how she taught her language arts class. After creating their stories, all students indicated that this assignment was fun and beneficial. Most of them stated that they would "use this feature for parent nights and end-of-the-year parties throughout my career." All in-service teachers wanted to teach their students Windows Movie Maker program so that their students might use storytelling for class projects and presentations. Some students mentioned that they would use this program to stream together many of their old vacation photos or family photos. As one student indicated in her reflection, "I just cannot say enough how grateful I am for knowing that this program exists and how easy it is to use."

In-service teachers appreciated the opportunity they had when collecting materials for their stories. As one student described the experience in creating her story with her class,

Including my students in that project brought us to a different level in our relationship. When I asked them to give me their permission to take pictures and include them in my own class project, they understood that I knew where they were coming from when pressured with school work. Most of them were "camera hogs" and delighted in being photographed and videoed. They also could not wait to see the end result. When I showed them the final project they were astounded at my technological abilities. Using this tool introduced me to a wide arrange of possibilities for future use in the classroom. In the coming semester, I am going to video them doing their class projects and make copies for the students to keep for themselves. As I teach seniors, it is a component they can include in their senior memory books and be able to enjoy for years to come.

Most students mentioned that digital storytelling was especially a useful tool for online classes because students were able to get to know their peers, to put a person's name with a face, and to see what others were doing. Through this project, they shared personal experiences of what worked and some things that did not work. Students learned from each other and gained confidence in using technology.

Digital storytelling was used as a reflection and assessment tool in *Networks in Education*. This course was a graduate course providing students with an overview of classroom electronics, computer hardware, software, and networking. The emphasis was on understanding classroom electronics, how computers work, and how they interface with other computers as well as with peripheral devices. Topics covered included selecting computers and peripherals for personal and school use, network topologies, upgrading hardware, operating systems, diagnosis and troubleshooting, network specifications, and applications of networks in school settings. In the previous years, students had mid-term and final exams to be evaluated. Students were tired of remembering technical terms and their functions. They also forgot those terms easily after the exams. Instead of having the regular examinations, students were asked to create a reflective story in which they showed their audience how to install a computer from scratch. They took pictures for each part and explained the term and usages in their narratives. According to these students, this project was meaningful and memorable because it provided opportunities to examine and learn from complex and professional situations. Every student was satisfied with their stories. Compared with the standard tests, students felt that storytelling helped them remember the content in a meaningful way that they could use in the future. After sharing different stories they had created, they asked for each others' permission to keep a copy of their project because they thought those stories would help them review what they learned in class.

Digital storytelling was also experimented in a second year mandarin Chinese course, *Mandarin Chinese IV*. This course was an undergraduate course emphasizing the students' development in the basic communicative abilities in listening, speaking, reading, and writing for real communication purposes. In this course, students were required to create an artifact to demonstrate their target language proficiency. Students were allowed to select topics of their own interest for their stories, but they were required to use learned Chinese vocabulary and sentence structures in the stories. Students were also encouraged to explore new words and structures by themselves to compose a meaningful and coherent story. During the creation process, students started writing the story scripts in the target language. Then the instructor met each student individually to help the student revise the scripts in ways such as clarifying meanings, correcting wrong characters and word usage, and improving sentence structures. The individual instructor-student conferences, which involved students in listening, speaking, reading, and writing, provided an opportunity for students to practice all four language skills in an authentic way when students were working on the project. After the script was finalized, students assembled still images or video clips that could be reflected in the stories. Before recording, students practiced reading the scripts over and over again, so their pronunciations and intonations would be at their best. Students became more fluent in using the vocabulary and sentence structures that they practiced in their stories.

From our own experiences of integrating digital storytelling into these four classes, we thought that incorporating storytelling into learning and assessment processes not only helped our students learn the subject and master technology skills but also motivated their learning interests and practice their problem-solving skills. Undoubtedly, educators are using storytelling to stimulate students' critical thinking skills, encourage self-review, and convey practice realities across and within disciplines (McDrury, 2003).

11. CHALLENGES IN USING DIGITAL STORYTELLING

Although younger students are technology natives and younger educators are capable users of technology, using digital storytelling as an effective learning strategy and pedagogical strategy is still challenging because this type of storytelling involves many different skills, both creative and technical, some of which may also be new to "older" students and teachers.

Neither the graduate nor the undergraduate students in our classes had problems in mastering the skills of creating digital stories with Windows Movie Maker; however, they did have problems involving such as the large image file size, fuzzy images in the movie, losing image files in the project storyboard, and incorrect file format. Several students used images directly downloaded from a digital camera. Those images had very high resolutions so that the file size was very large. A 2-3 minute movie (with 5-10 images) might gain 80 – 190 MB in file size due to the high resolution images. As a result, some students encountered pauses and stops while playing their large file size movies to the class. One student could not even download her movie from the server. When checking her file size, her movie was 186 MB, which caused her movie downloading time to be much longer than others. Once they reduced their image size and recreated their stories, they did not have the same problem. In contrast, some other students used images downloaded from the Internet, which had low resolution. The story file size was small, but the pictures in the movie were fuzzy and blurred. Therefore, making the right resolution and dimensions of the image was important to creating a good movie.

Narrative recording was a second problem for some students, who did not like their voices when played on the computer. If there was a choice, they would use music and text to replace their voices in the movie. The third problem was how to use music properly. First of all, students used music that matches the content of the story. Then, students had to make sure the length of the music fit the length of the story. A few students complained that their story did not stop after all images were displayed and their file size was larger than expected. Checking their stories, they found that the story was 2 minutes but the music was 5 minutes. They solved the problems by cutting the music to fit their stories. The last problem students encountered was that their projects would not display correctly if they reopened the movie projects on another computer. This problem was caused by students' inexperience with technology. Although they were told to save all the images, narration, and music in the same folder with their movie project and take the whole folder to other computers if they could not finish the project and/ or did not have time to convert the project into a movie in class, some students only saved the movie project to their USB drives. As a result, the images on the storyboard in their project did not show when they worked on other computers. The storyboard was only a placeholder for the images which would not show if the whole folder did not go with the project. The same thing happened when students submitted their movies. Instead of submitting their movie files (.WMV), some students submitted their projects (.MSWMM) which meant that the project was not converted to a movie. Therefore, the movie (in fact, the project) did not play on the instructor's computer.

All problems mentioned above were related to the basic knowledge of technology usages. These problems were easy to solve once students were experienced. To use digital storytelling effectively in the classroom, teachers should be well-prepared technically and pedagogically. We agree with Boase (2007): "the challenge that digital storytelling in education poses is how to harness the massive potential of the story form, with its possibilities to inspire, engage, transform, through a process that will endow it with opportunity for reflection, critical thinking, and problem solving" (p.10).

12. CONCLUSION

This article provides an overview of digital storytelling in education and how the medium can be integrated into the curriculum. Some functional samples were discussed to help educators understand how digital storytelling can be used in instructional settings. Overall, digital storytelling is a valuable learning tool and plays an important role in education, and thus should not only be considered as a multimedia element separate from the actual teaching and learning processes. Educators are discovering that digital storytelling has the potential to become a valuable educational tool for students when taught in an effective manner (Royer & Richards, 2007).

REFERENCES

Abrahamson, C. (1998). Storytelling as a pedagogical tool in higher education. *Education, 118*. Retrieved June, 27 2009 from http://www.questia.com

Alexander, B., & Levine, A. (2008, November/ December). Web 2.0 storytelling emergence of a new genre. *EDUCAUSE Review*, 40–56.

Banaszewski, T. (2002). Digital storytelling finds its place in the classroom. *Information Today*. Retrieved February 12, 2009 from http://www.infotoday.com/MMSchools/jan02/banaszewski.htm

Barrett, H. (2005). Storytelling in higher education: A theory of reflection on practice to support deep learning. In *Proceedings of the Technology and Teacher Education Annual Conference 2005* (pp. 1878-1883). Charlottesville, VA: Association for the Advancement of Computing in Education. Retrieved February 12, 2009 from http://electronicportfolios.com/portfolios/Kean.pdf

Barrett, H. (2006). *Researching and evaluating digital storytelling as a deep learning tool.* Retrieved February 12, 2009 from http:// electronicportfolios.com/ portfolios/ SITEStorytelling2006.pdf

Boase, K. (2008). *Digital storytelling for reflection and engagement: A study of the uses and potential of digital storytelling.* Retrieved February 12, 2009 from http://resources.glos.ac.uk/tli/lets/projects/pathfinder/index.cfm

Bull, G., & Kajder, S. (2004). Digital storytelling in the language arts classroom. *Learning and Leading with Technology, 32*(4), 46–49.

Cortazzi, M., & Jin, L. (2007). Narrative learning, EAL and metacognitive development. *Early Child Development and Care, 177,* 645–660. doi:10.1080/03004430701379074

Fisher, W. (1985). The narrative paradigm: An elaboration. *Communication Monographs, 52,* 347–367. doi:10.1080/03637758509376117

Fisher, W. (1989). Clarifying the narrative paradigm. *Communication Monographs, 56,* 55–58. doi:10.1080/03637758909390249

Gils, F. (2005, February 17-18). *Potential applications of digital storytelling in education.* Paper presented at the 3rd Twente Student Conference on IT, University of Twente, Faculty of Electrical Engineering, Mathematics and Computer Science, Enschede, The Netherlands.

Kajder, S., & Swinson, J. (2004). Digital images in the language arts classroom. *Learning and Leading with Technology, 31*(8), 18-9, 21, & 46.

Lambert, J. (2007). *Digital storytelling cookbook.* Retrieved March 1, 2009 from http://www.storycenter.org/cookbook.html

McDrury, J., & Alterio, M. (2003). *Learning through Storytelling in Higher Education.* London: Kogan Page.

Meadow, D. (2003). Digital storytelling: Research-based practice in new media. *Visual Communication, 2*(2), 189–193. doi:10.1177/1470357203002002004

More, C. (2008). Digital stories targeting social skills for children with disabilities. *Intervention in School and Clinic, 43*(3), 168–177. doi:10.1177/1053451207312919

Morehead, P., Li, L., & LaBeau, B. (2007). Digital storytelling: Empowering prospective teachers' voices as future educators. In C. Crawford et al. (Eds.), *Proceedings of Society for Information Technology and Teacher Education International Conference 2007* (pp. 634-635). Chesapeake, VA: AACE

Neuhauser, P. C. (1993). *Corporate Legends and Lore: The Power of Storytelling as a Management Tool.* New York: McGraw-Hill.

Papadimitriou, C. (2003, July 2). MythematiCS: In praise of storytelling in the teaching of CS and Math. In *Proceedings of the International Conference on CS Education, ITICSE,* Thessaloniki, Greece.

Papert, S. (1993). *The children's machine: Rethinking school in the age of computer.* New York: Basic Books.

Porter, B. (2005). *Digitales: The art of digital storytelling.* Denver, CO: Bernajean Porter Consulting.

Robin, B. (2005). *Educational uses of digital storytelling. Main directory for the educational uses of digital storytelling* (Tech. Rep.). Houston, TX: University of Houston, Instructional technology Program. Retrieved February 12, 2009 from http://www.coe.uh.edu/digitalstorytelling/default.htm

Royer, R., & Richards, P. (2007). Increasing reading comprehension with digital storytelling. In C. Montgomerie & J. Seale (Eds.), *Proceedings of World Conference on Educational Multimedia, Hypermedia and Telecommunications 2007*(pp. 2301-2306). Chesapeake, VA: AACE.

Schiro, M. (2004). *Oral storytelling and teaching mathematics*. Thousand Oaks, CA: SAGE Publications.

Skinner, E., & Hagood, M. (2008). Developing literate identities with English language learners through digital storytelling. *The Reading Matrix, 8*(2), 12–38.

Solidoro, A. (2007). *The digital storytelling: Multimedia creative writing as a reflective practice.* Retrieved February 12, 2009 from http:// www. filografia.org/ documents/ 1.%20Theoretical%20 introduction/ 1.4%20Digital%20Storytelling.pdf

Trawick-Smith, J. (2003). *Early childhood development: A multicultural perspective.* Upper Saddle River, NJ: Pearson Education, Inc.

This work was previously published in International Journal of Information and Communication Technology, Volume 6, Issue 2, edited by Lawrence A. Tomei, pp. 76-87, copyright 2010 by IGI Publishing (an imprint of IGI Global).

Chapter 16
Faculty Training Strategies to Enhance Pedagogy–Technology Integration

Jared Keengwe
University of North Dakota, USA

David Georgina
Minnesota State University, Mankato, USA

Patrick Wachira
Cleveland State University, USA

ABSTRACT

One of the unprecedented benefits of campus-wide distance learning strategies has been the incorporation of more technology-based pedagogy into traditional classrooms, thus, increasing faculty and student teaching and learning opportunities. This "hybrid" or "blended" teaching has emerged largely due to a desire to widen access to educational opportunities, continuing education, and university resources (Curran, 2004; Garrison & Kanuka, 2004). However, a major challenge to this technologically enhanced pedagogy has been the training of higher education faculty. This article focuses on faculty technology literacy, the implementation of technology into traditional faculty pedagogy, and the need for effective faculty training to enhance appropriate technology integration into classroom instruction (Keengwe, 2007). In this paper, the authors recommend two tier training as a possible strategy to technology integration training challenges that instructors face in their pedagogical practices.

INTRODUCTION

Universities and colleges across the globe have focused upon creating Information Technology (IT) infrastructures to enhance the quality of teaching and learning, especially one that is provided though e-learning or distance education platforms.

State of the art technology, access to the Internet, asynchronous learning tools (teaching platforms), and teacher training facilities are present in many institutions of higher education around the world. Additionally, efforts to meet the demands of the 21st century learner have led to dramatic increase in the number of online courses offered by many institutions of higher learning across the nation.

DOI: 10.4018/978-1-61350-468-0.ch016

In the United States, almost 64 percent of all institutions offer at least one online course and 55 percent of all institutions offer at least one blended course (Allen, Seaman, & Garret, 2007). Distance education technology programs are seen as a means to broaden enrollment and increase gross margins. As a result, at some point in their teaching career, university instructors will consider teaching their classes either partially or fully online (Clark-Ibanez & Scott, 2008). However, the move from traditional to online teaching has created additional responsibilities for participating faculty members as well as students.

The pathway of course migration to online learning environments often begins with the assumption that instructional designs, grading procedures, and other methods that typically work in the traditional classroom would remain the same in online settings. However, that is not the case – the major challenge to this technology-enhanced pedagogy remains that of providing training to faculty to ensure transition of this process. Specifically, there is need for professional development activities and support programs that will help faculty successfully teach online.

Faculty need to prepare graduates who can effectively use technology as a learning tool, yet the faculty themselves are new to various technology uses and have no personal experiences as students themselves in technology-infused classrooms (Jacobsen, Clifford, & Friesen, 2002). Further, while it is evident that university and department sponsored trainings are often employed to create a more technology literate faculty, the question remains whether or not these training opportunities are effective. The focus on pedagogy and technology is crucial since instructors have a primary role of preparing graduates who will use technology in their workplaces. According to the International Society for Technology in Education (2000):

Today's classroom teachers must be prepared to provide technology-supported learning opportunities for their students…being prepared to use technology and knowing how that technology can support student learning must be integral skills in every teacher's professional repertoire (p. 2).

Technology Literacy

Technology literacy is the ability of an individual to responsibly, appropriately, creatively, and effectively use appropriate technology tools to communicate; access, collect, manage, integrate, and evaluate information; build and share knowledge; and improve and enhance learning in all subject areas and experiences. Technology literacy is different from information literacy; The American Library Association's (ALA) Association of College and Research Libraries (2006) states that technology literacy is concerned solely with understanding technology and the skillful use of it.

Brandt (2001) suggests that it is not enough that students and faculty "have rudimentary skills in using a given technology—instruction could be given one day in how to use a system, but the interface or underlying technology could change overnight" (p. 74). Therefore, to help students incorporate technology into their lessons requires that faculty use technology beyond their office; faculty must design courses that require their students to use technology themselves (Wetzel, 2001). Given that a majority of students enrolled in our colleges and universities have grown up in the digital environments, Evans (2005) warns:

To view technology in terms of an autonomous tool is to ignore the fact that one's use of technology is wrapped up in a sense of identity and in the social contexts that shape both technologies and identities (p. 15).

There is a sort of commonality present in the different technology tools, instructional design strategies, and hybrid course creation. This commonality is the learning object in the form of a media asset or digital object. Polsani (2003) states that in order for a digital object to become a learning object, it should be "wrapped in a Learning Intention" (p. 5). The learning intentions comprise of two elements: form and relation. Form is the framework in which the digital object is embedded; and relation is the understanding "through which an object becomes an object of knowledge… through a reasoned organization of sensibility" (p. 6).

Instructors could use, for instance, a digital picture of Picasso's Guernica to explore art or the history of Spain. Instructors might access this digital image at anytime, for any reason. Students are not left to simply ponder an image upon a screen if they possess the ability and the technology to interact with the image (web quests, personal searches or similar web sites). Some instructors considering creating learning objects may find that this activity requires advanced technology skills than creating a power point. This begs a new question: if faculty need to learn new technology-based pedagogical skills, how are they to be taught and, more importantly, how are they to be measured?

Defining User Levels of Technology

Spotts (1999) conducted one of the first studies to determine and define user levels of technology. His results identified three categories: high level users, medium level users, and low level users. Responses from the interview questions revealed that "five primary areas (variables) influence the process by which a higher education faculty member becomes aware of, evaluates, and decides to use or not to use a newer instructional technology" (p. 95). The study concluded that, for faculty members to effectively use technology, they should receive technological support, academic recognition (promotion and tenure considerations), release time, and appropriate training (Spotts, 1999).

Novitzki (2000) devised a related study aimed at recognizing levels of user proficiency in asynchronous learning tools (ASL). Novitzki's study revealed that the high level usage or extensive use of the ASL "resulted in the most consistent improvement of all the raw data" (p. 15). Although Novitzki's sample size was too small for any statistically valid general inferences to be made, Novitzki's user level scales (low use, moderate use, high use) provides a starting point for describing technology literacy proficiency (as ascribed by the user) as well as serves to validate Spotts's (1995-96) study. Both studies provide a credible tool for recognizing and categorizing user levels or proficiencies in technology literacy. A collection of essays written by college faculty, IT workers, and administration (Brown, 2003) also support the above studies.

Hybrid or Blended Learning

Garrison and Kanuka (2004) suggest that a truly blended learning environment "represents a fundamental reconceptualization and reorganization of the teaching and learning dynamic, starting with various specific contextual needs and contingencies…" (p. 97). If this suggestion is true, then the role played by technological literacy is crucial in teaching and learning within blended courses. Perhaps the most successful approach to integrating technology into pedagogy is the creation and utilization of the blended course. But the questions remain how these courses are defined and used successfully.

A simple definition of blended courses is that they combine face-to-face learning experiences with web-based learning experiences (Curran, 2004; Derntl & Motschnig-Pitrik, 2005; Garrison & Kanuka, 2004). Within this deceptively simple definition lies a multitude of learning environments and approaches to teaching and learning (project-based learning environments, research-based learning environments, asynchronous learning networks, web-enhanced teaching platforms, digital online learning tools, etc.).

A study by Olapiriyakul and Scher (2006) reviewed three internal studies conducted at Jersey Institute of Technology and provided three main technological components required for a hybrid course; Technology infrastructure, Instructional technology, and Technology in learning. Further, they suggest that developing and designing web-based learning (hybrid) courses is an iterative process, which includes five main phases: course content design, course development, course implementation, course evaluation, and course revision. The study also explored the relationships between hybrid course creation, implementation, and evaluation. The results suggested the need for an establishment of a creative balance between pedagogy and technology that will support faculty to design, deliver, and support course design and content.

The five phases identified by Olapiriyakul and Scher (2006) are very similar to what Gustafson and Branch (2007) refer to as—ADDIE: analyze, design, develop, implement, and evaluate (pp. 11-12). Olapiriyakul and Scher's phases are as follows:

1. **Course content design:** Concerned with needs of the instructor, student learning outcomes, course requirements, and course goals. This step includes determination of course management tools, identifying students, details of course materials, and coordinating materials for face to face and online delivery.

2. **Course development:** Concerned with course materials delivery, presentations software, web design, teaching supporting systems, and administrative systems.

3. **Course implementation:** Divided into two components – face to face and online. Appropriate communication technologies should support a high level of student participation.

4. **Course evaluation:** Deals with reviewing course goals and objectives in order to determine the effectiveness of the course design, content, and delivery system as it relates to student learning outcomes.

5. **Course revision in hybrid learning:** A continuous process which reviews effectiveness of technological tools and efficacy of course materials (p. 297-300).

FACULTY TECHNOLOGY TRAINING

The arguments to invest and build Information Technology (IT) infrastructures may have subsumed the notions of usability for traditional pedagogy; in the early stage of educational IT movement, little consideration was given to authentic faculty training. The assumption seems to be that faculty will learn to use the system(s) to accommodate their instructional needs; faith in faculty's ability outweighs the reality of learning a new paradigm. However, technology alone does nothing to enable the integration of technology-based pedagogies.

The primary task of technology infrastructure is to support both instructional technology and student learning. This includes technology tools to enhance and support communication between student and instructors. Since many universities have technological infrastructures that support Internet and database technologies (such as online registrations, student financial aid or online directories), the crucial issues remains accessibility (capacity and speed of network) and security networks. Additionally, the technology needed to support pedagogy focuses on web-based instructional platforms (such as Blackboard, Desire2Learn, and WebCT) and incorporates digital learning objects. Learning-support technology goals consist of creating communities (Olapiriyakul & Scher, 2006). An example of this technology is the creation of an online community that assists the self-acquisition of knowledge and enables students to share common values, expertise, and understanding (multi-user software, online student help, and course tutorials).

There are many approaches and strategies for faculty training. Brown, Benson, and Uhde (2004) describe three fictional case studies which address a primary component missing in faculty development opportunities—technology training. These case studies could improve technology literacy and provide a systematic support framework for professional development. Each case study reviews the professors' (Dr. Sage, Dr. Wise, and Dr. Smart) technology literacy and identifies areas of technological weakness. Brown, Benson, and Uhde (2004) offer possible training solutions that can be modeled to assist instructional practices. Their suggestions regarding workshops or training forums focus on the following areas of emphasis:

1.   Limiting the number of participants per workshop to allow for more individualized instruction.
2.   Encouraging participants to leave the workshop with an immediate goal to implement the new skill in practice.
3.   Providing the opportunity for follow-up workshops in which participants share their successes, failures, learning processes.
4.   Providing technical support to individual faculty members. [technology infrastructure]
5.   Reducing advising loads or committee assignments (release time) for trainees.

In order to effectively enable learning, Brown, Benson, and Uhde (2004) also suggest that university sponsored workshops provide "technical

experts who are sensitive to the technologically challenged, facilitate communication, sharing, coaching between colleagues [mentors], create avenues of communication for technical needs, develop individualized action plans, and provide opportunities to access the necessary resources from the institution" (p. 104). Recent studies indicate that technology literacy training should be as uniquely individual as is the constituent faculty; individual departmental cultures should be considered before faculty training is provided (Brown, 2003: Ertmer, 2005; Mayo, Kajs, & Tanguma, 2005).

Zhoa and Cziko (2001) argue for a credible argument that accounts for actual learning during faculty technology training. Their research examines teacher reluctance or reticence in adopting technology into their pedagogy. Their results support other studies which suggest that while low level use of technologically enhanced pedagogy is wide-spread, high level use is more sporadic (Ertmer, 2005, p. 26).

Zhoa and Cziko (2001) provided a Perceptual Control Theory (PCT) framework to help understand why teachers choose to incorporate technology into their pedagogy. The PCT framework considers the "goals of the teachers and how the use of technology might help or hinder their goals" (p. 9). The researchers argued that certain assumptions exist on why teachers do not use technology despite the lack of empirical studies. This untested set of assumptions function as:

The theoretical base underlying many efforts to help teachers integrate technology with their teaching.... [T]he assumption that the lack of teacher involvement in technology has been caused by the lack of suitable training and thus providing more opportunities to develop technological skills of teachers will lead to more technology integration (p. 7).

Zhoa and Cziko (2001) argued that some teachers (even when afforded the technology and training) refused to integrate technology into their pedagogy. The missing element of these assumptions is the recognition that teachers are active living organisms. PCT recognizes that humans have higher-level internal goals and they endeavor to bring these goals into fruition by varying lower-level goals. Another way to view this would be, "lower level goals serve as a means to achieve higher-level goals" (p. 9). According to the authors, the following three PCT conditions are necessary for teachers to use technology:

1. The teacher must believe that technology can be more effective in achieving high-lever goals than what was previously used.
2. The teacher must believe that using technology will not cause disturbances to other high-level goals.
3. The teacher must believe that they have the necessary user proficiencies and resources to use technology (p. 21).

An interesting aspect of PCT's effect upon technological training is that learners (trainees) are less likely to distance themselves from technical experts. One of the most popular training approaches, according to Zhoa and Cziko (2001), "is having experts 'sell' to teachers the mighty power of technology" (p. 25). Teachers may feel that their trainers are not as interested in the pedagogical effects of the technical tools. The perception is that the trainers have different goals than the teachers—focusing upon technology rather than pedagogy. PCT offers three ways to reduce potential disturbances in technology training that include:

A. Pedagogical changes are secondary when promoting the use of technology; once technology is integrated into the curriculum, it will facilitate new pedagogical approaches on its own.
B. Develop easy to use tools – easy access, common graphic-interfaces, web-based tools

C. Provide on-site support so that teachers will feel confident that when they have a problem, there will be assistance (p. 26).

Schrum (1999) also address the real-time problems that teachers face and offers four useful points relating to teacher technology training: one, it takes considerably longer to learn about technology for personal or pedagogical use than learning a new teaching model; two, access to the new technology at school and at home is essential; three, fear of the unknown must be addressed; four, the use of new technology may require teachers to reconceptualize the ways in which they teach. Perhaps Schrum's most important perception is that forced or mandated change from the administration may result in "tenuous acceptance, without real change" (p. 85).

Integrating technological literacy and practice into a traditional classroom course design (in order to enhance learning), creates changes on a fundamental level. Changes in pedagogy shift from teacher-centered to learner-centered (Huba & Freed, 2000), and "the class becomes less a conduit for information, in Paolo Friere's sense of a 'banking' mode, than an active 'making' mode, where information and skills are generated by active participation" (Burch-Brown & Kilkelly, 2003, p. 168). Faculty members are being challenged by their institutions to embrace new pedagogical technologies, and continue with their extensive teaching, advising, curriculum development/ assessment, and committee workloads. Since, according to Schrum, Burbank, Engle, Chambers, and Glassett (2005), most faculty members have little training in pedagogy, "teaching expertise is not a requirement for employment" (p. 279).

One training solution is a module-based approach which combines learning theory, motivational research, blended and online courses. Creating Optimum Learning Environments (CREOLE) was developed as an online training program for college faculty, based on the principles of teaching and learning and on developing online teaching skills. Schrum et al. (2005) conclude that this, and similar programs, "create faculty online learning opportunities that may help change the way teaching and learning occurs. By undergoing training through online modules, faculties gain an experiential understanding of the nature of web-based learning; they may be better able to integrate what they learned into their pedagogy" (p. 288).

Garrison and Kanuka (2004) suggest that technology and blended pedagogy require:

A. Creation of clear institutional direction and policy
B. Framing the potential, increase awareness, and commit
C. Establishment of a single point of support, quality assurance, and project management
D. Creation of an innovation fund to provide the financial support and incentives to faculty and departments
E. Strategic selection of prototype projects
F. Development of formal instructional design support
G. Systematic evaluation (teaching, learning, technology, and administration of courses)
H. Creation of a task group to address issues, challenges and opportunities as well as communicating and recommending new directions (p. 103).

TWO TIER TRAINING

The greatest challenge for administrators is how to provide successful training to support faculty integration of technology into their pedagogy to enhance student learning. Technological literacy training is dependent upon the institution's technology infrastructure. Luke (2000) states: "Unless educators take a lead in developing appropriate pedagogies for these new electronic media and forms of communication, corporate experts will be the ones to determine how people will learn, what they learn, and what constitutes literacy (p. 71).

Tier One: Mentors

The first tier of the Two-Tier training session requires department volunteer faculty members (referred to as faculty mentors) who are willing to undergo the first round of training. These are faculty who have been the most active in the department's technology integration efforts and will already be using forms of technology in their teaching. The idea behind this first tier mentor training is to open up a dialogue between colleagues. While the mentors may not agree with the particular type of software or teaching platform being used by the IT trainers, this may become the first of many learning opportunities for the IT trainers and the faculty. In some cases, instructors might feel intimidated by the trainers' expert technology as well as trainers feel that instructors will simply regard them as technology "geeks." Evidence from a recent study suggested that one of the most frequent complaints about training was that IT trainers had no teaching experience; they were trained in technology, not in pedagogy—the tools were more important than the instruction (Georgina, 2008). Training IT trainer in the use of the new infrastructure or teaching platform first, will accomplish three ends: a. The IT trainers will be able to adjust training to facilitate faculty by simply allowing the faculty to have input into the training techniques (summative assessments); b. The faculty mentors will be able to assist at larger training sessions within their departments and (hopefully) will become agents for further pedagogical integration; and c. The mentors will become the go-to people in the department when other faculty members have immediate questions (mentors may also be the first to provide IT support to others in the faculty center for teaching excellence). Employing faculty mentors may ease the techno-fear for other faculty trainees. Training suggestions for the First-Tier training trainers include: 1. Scheduling at least two training sessions; 2. Listening to what the faculty mentors are saying, take notes, and address their concerns;

3. Suggesting that the mentors create discipline related lessons using the technology; 4. Scheduling second meetings two to three weeks after the initial training and address any new concerns; and 5. Asking mentors to bring along samples of integrated pedagogical technology used for their specific lessons. This simple process will assist the trainers in modeling workshops or training sessions for larger groups and will also allow for specific departmental technology practices (an English or Humanities department will have much different technology software requirements than an Aerospace or Chemistry department). It is crucial that the trainers understand the concerns raised and the practices used by the mentors. Remember, the mentors learn by doing, experimenting with software and teaching platforms on their own. If possible, the trainers should try and implement ways that incorporate the mentor's technology use into the integration scheme. For example, some mentors may use and create web pages as a means of actively integrating technology. Others may incorporate wikis, web discussions, Power Point, etc. into their classrooms. Trainers should embrace this as an opportunity to reveal and educate how their platforms or software modules can, should, and do allow for these individualized technologies.

Tier Two: Small Departmental Workshops

The second tier of the Two-Tier training practice is for faculty and graduate students within an individual department. If the University or College deems it necessary to hold large faculty forums, then these forums should be the precursors to the actual faculty workshops. The key to successful faculty training is to facilitate small workshops—no larger than 15 and no fewer than 5 faculty or student members. This may require more time to train than the entire faculty, but it could guarantee more successful training sessions. Graduate students and teaching assistants should be encouraged to attend the workshops. The

Graduate students may be more technologically savvy than most faculty members and could be a real bonus to the department's move towards integrating technology into pedagogy.

Ideally, these workshops will have one to two IT trainers and at least one departmental faculty mentor. Effective workshops include the following characteristics:

A. Limiting the number of participants per workshop (5-15);

B. Including first-tier faculty mentors as trainers;

C. Demonstrating technology with pedagogical examples;

D. Encouraging participants to leave the workshop with an immediate goal to implement the new skill in practice;

E. Instructing trainees on the software/teaching platform assessment methods available;

F. Providing opportunity for feedback, reactions, and questions by scheduling follow-up workshops (at least one) in which participants share their successes, failures, and learning processes;

G. Offering IT or department sponsored technical support to individual faculty members between each official training session. (This is where faculty mentors can be extremely beneficial to the department.); and

H. Encouraging, as part of the workshop process, departmental forums and other workshops. These can initially be facilitated by the faculty mentors and should include showcases of faculty and student technology use.

CONCLUSION

The answers to questions about pedagogy and technology integration partially lie in the in the various strategies for the integration of technology throughout college courses including: the instigation of college-wide teacher trainings on instructional technologies, the development of e-learning environments and departmental level research on effective e-learning strategies, technology skills, and instructional development centers. Faculty should strive to implement technology tools as part of their own repertoire of tools in courses they are assigned to teach.

Blended (hybrid) courses include strategies and practices that require the student to interact with subject matter using digital tools, and this interaction becomes an additional component to learning (Derntl & Motschnig-Pitrik, 2005; Garrison & Kanuka, 2004). A primary concept to understanding technology training might be that instructors prefer technology training that successfully integrates their pedagogy, not technology training that simply reveals how the instructional technology tools work. Therefore, the manner in which technology training is conducted is crucial.

Faculty training in the integration of technology into pedagogy is critical; faculty must be trained in the use of the tools—not just given access to the tools—integrating new software and hardware as part of their interactive teaching and learning strategies. Technology alone does nothing to enhance pedagogy; successful integration is all about the ways in which technology tools are used and integrated into the teaching and learning process to enhance student learning. According to Jacobsen et al. (2002), the real challenge is to "develop fluency with teaching and learning with technology, not just with technology, itself" (p. 44).

Technology has tremendous potential to support blended learning if used appropriately. Additionally, students are arriving into colleges each year with more and more techno-abilities.

However, rather than viewing technology as merely a tool for delivery, it should be seen as a means to improve learning. Grabe and Grabe (2008) conclude: "it seems reasonable that teachers will be more likely to help their students learn with technology if the teachers can draw on their own experiences in learning with technology" (p. 4).

REFERENCES

10-16). Upper Saddle River, NJ: Merrill-Prentice Hall.

Allen, I. E., Seaman, J., & Garret, R. (2007). *Blending in. The extent and promise of Blended Education in the United States*. Needham, MA: The Sloan Consortium.

American Library Association. (2006) *Information literacy competency standards for higher education*. Chicago: American Library Association. Retrieved June 25, 2009, from http://www.ala.org/ala/acrl/acrlstandards/informationliteracycompetency.htm#iltech

Brandt, D. (2001). Information technology literacy: Task knowledge and mental models. [from the Academic Search Premier database.]. *Library Trends*, *50*(1), 73. Retrieved July 20, 2009.

Brown, A. H., Benson, B., & Uhde, A. P. (2004). You're doing what with technology? An exposé on "Jane Doe" college professor. *College Teaching*, *52*(3), 100–104.

Brown, D. (2003). Fitting workshops into faculty mores. In Brown, D. G. (Ed.), *Developing faculty to use technology: programs and strategies to choices and challenges*. Madison, WI: Atwood Publishing.

Burch-Brown, C., & Kilkelly, A. (2003). Creative high-tech/low-tech teaching in an integrated teaching environment. In Brown, D. G. (Ed.), *Developing faculty to use technology: Programs and strategies to choices and challenges* (pp. 167–171). Madison, WI: Atwood Publishing.

Clark-Ibanez, M., & Scott, L. (2008). Learning to teach online. *Teaching Sociology*, *36*, 34–41. doi:10.1177/0092055X0803600105

Curran, C. (2004) Strategies for e-learning in universities. *National Distance Education Centre and Dublin City University*. Retrieved June 15, 2009 from http://repositories.cdlib.org/cshe/CSHE-7-04/

Derntl, M., & Motschnig-Pitrik, R. (2005). The role of structure, patterns, and people in blended learning. *The Internet and Higher Education, 8*(2), 111–130. doi:10.1016/j.iheduc.2005.03.002

Ertmer, P. (2005). Teacher pedagogical beliefs: The final frontier in our quest for technology integration? *Educational Technology Research and Development, 53*(4), 25–39. doi:10.1007/BF02504683

Evans, E. (2005). Autonomous learning or social practice? Students' construction of technological literacy. *Journal of literacy technology, 5*(1), Retrieved July 20, 2009 from http://www.literacyandtechnology.org/v5/ellen_evans_05.pdf

Garrison, D., & Kanuka, H. (2004). Blended learning: Uncovering its transformative potential in higher education. *The Internet and Higher Education, 7*(2), 95–105. doi:10.1016/j.iheduc.2004.02.001

Georgina, D. A. (2008). *Technology Integration in Higher Education Pedagogy: Faculty Perceptions of Integration Skills*. Saarbucken, Germany: VDM & Co. KG, Org.

Grabe, M., & Grabe, C. (2008). *Integrating technology for meaningful learning* (5th ed.). Boston, MA: Houghton Mifflin Company.

Gustafson, K. L., & Branch, R. M. (2007). What is instructional design? In R. Reiser & J. V. Dempsey (Eds.), *Trends and issues in instructional design and technology* (2ⁿᵈ ed., pp.

Huba, M., & Freed, J. (2000). *Learner-Centered assessment on college campuses: Shifting the focus from teaching to learning*. Boston: Allyn and Bacon.

International Society for Technology in Education (ISTE). (2000). *National Educational Technology Standards (NETS) for teachers*. Retrieved March 25, 2008, from http://cnets.iste.org/teachers/

Jacobsen, M., Clifford, P., & Friesen, S. (2002). Preparing teachers for technology integration: Creating a culture of inquiry in the context of use. *Contemporary Issues in Technology and Teacher Education, 2*(3). Retrieved July 15, 2009, from http://www.citejournal.org/vol2/iss3/currentpractice/article2.cfm

Keengwe, J. (2007). Faculty Integration of Technology into Instruction and Students' Perceptions of Computer Technology to Improve Student Learning. *Journal of Information Technology Education, 6*, 169–180.

Luke, C. (2000). Cyber-schooling and technological change: Multiliteracies for new times. In Cope, B., & Kalantzis, M. (Eds.), *Multiliteracies: Literacy learning and the design of social futures* (pp. 69–91). New York: Routledge.

Mayo, N., Kajs, K., & Tanguma, J. (2005). Longitudinal study of technology training to prepare future teachers. *Educational Research Quarterly, 29*(1), 3–15.

Novitzki, J. (2000). Asynchronous learning tools in the traditional classroom: A preliminary study on their effect (IR No. 058-617). In *Proceedings of the International Academy for Information Management Annual Conference*, Brisbane, Australia.

Olapiriyakul, K., & Scher, J. M. (2006). A guide to establishing hybrid learning courses: Employing information technology to create a new learning experience, and a case study. *The Internet and Higher Education, 9*(4), 287–311. doi:10.1016/j.iheduc.2006.08.001

Polsani, P. (2003). Use and abuse of reusable learning objects. *Journal of Digital Information, 3*(4), 2–19.

Schrum, L. (1999). Technology professional development for teachers. *Educational Technology Research and Development, 47*(4), 83–90. doi:10.1007/BF02299599

Schrum, L., Burbank, M. D., Engle, J., Chambers, J., & Glasset, K. (2005). Post-Secondary educators' professional development: Investigation of an online approach to enhancing teaching and learning. *The Internet and Higher Education, 8,* 279–28. doi:10.1016/j.iheduc.2005.08.001

Spotts, T. (1999). Discriminating factors in faculty use of instructional technology in higher education. *Educational Technology & Society, 2*(4), 92–99.

Wetzel, K. (2001). Toward the summit: Students use of technology. *AACTE Briefs, 22*(6), 5.

Zhoa, Y., & Cziko, G. (2001). Teacher adoption of technology: A perceptual control perspective.

This work was previously published in International Journal of Information and Communication Technology, Volume 6, Issue 3, edited by Lawrence A. Tomei, pp. 1-10, copyright 2010 by IGI Publishing (an imprint of IGI Global).

Chapter 17
Effectiveness of International Distance Education in High School between Thailand and Japan

Natcha Pavasajjanant
University of Hyogo, Japan

ABSTRACT

This paper presents a view of the effectiveness of teaching and learning systems by focusing on how courses using ICT can be designed based on educational theories and evaluated using student feedback. This study analyzes a distance learning project in which Thai and Japanese (grade 10) students studied how to use MX Flash software for the creation of animations. In designing the course prior to implementation, the theoretical framework was examined and the Constructivism theory and the Bloom's taxonomy were adopted. From these perspectives, effective learning-teaching methods are determined by course content, conditions of teaching processes, and media usage. The teaching processes were classified with the following three stages determined: (1) traditional lecture; (2) self-learning; and (3) collaborative learning. At the end of each class, the students were asked to respond to the course evaluation related to following the three domains: (1) comprehension; (2) cognitive load; and (3) motivation. These evaluations by the students were fully utilized in a regression analysis which examined whether the course design was appropriate for student understanding.

INTRODUCTION

In accordance with wide development of Information and Communication Technologies (ICT) related to distance learning for higher education, the effort to improve learning and teaching quality using ICT support has been reshaping traditional classroom environments for school education. Computers seem to be the most common ICT tool for distance learning. ICT develops distance learning in two directions; one is the so-called e-learning type, and the second is the broadcasting type (Bates, 1986). Much learning contents through PCs has been developed. As for the broad-

DOI: 10.4018/978-1-61350-468-0.ch017

casting type, ordinary classroom lectures can be transmitted information or even images to other classrooms in different campuses or universities via online-communications.

International distance education is one of the most efficient methods of transferring cutting-edge knowledge and technology, even though it has more problems than traditional face-to-face education (Tsuji, 2004, 2006; Tsuji et al., 2002). ICT has enabled the connection of educational institutions in different countries, and has promoted globalization in education. Many prominent universities in the U.S. and Europe have already established campuses in Asian counties and offer the same lectures though the Internet. This is part of their global strategy to cope with increasing competition among them, and some counties have undertaken to transfer educational know-how to developing countries. Developing countries, on the other hand, are looking for a way to satisfy insufficient educational infrastructure and teaching staff as a means of coping with growing demand for higher education. International distance learning thus meets the desires of both developing and developed counties.

Previous Studies

Distance learning offers a range of research topics. According to technological development, some educators (e.g., Hasegawa, 2006) attempted to develop the lecture environment in the university level with the high technological support system from the aspect of reliability, stability and interactivity. In case of international distance learning, many innovative educators attempted to raise teaching and learning quality to the level of face-to-face traditional classroom learning. Cho (2006), for example, studied communication by using e-mail in the class of social study subject between Japan and Korea. Different backgrounds such as culture and language were focuses on the teaching design, and presents actual problems such as the

imbalance of communications among students, the language barrier and student's ICT knowledge. Some research viewed the implementation of educational media as supplementary sources to approach learning. Yun (2003) attempted to use various media such as the video conference system, school homepage, and web board in teaching Japanese for foreigners. Few students, however, used ICT media. This situation usually occurs in many case studies, and accordingly it is difficult to identify factors and reasons of successful usage of ICT.

The most of distance education projects therefore seem to be designed according to teachers' individual experiences, rather than to the vigorous analysis of the effective combination of ICT in order to improve students' learning performance. Gagne (1987) believed that the conditions of effective learning include not only important issue relate to how technology used in teaching, but also the capacities and qualities of an individual learner. Moreover, a variation of learners' characteristics from different cultures and backgrounds is difficult to obtain any substantial result of learning effectiveness only by the studying of previous case studies. Learning effectiveness should be analyzed from the viewpoint of educational concepts of teaching and the actual feedback of learning. A few studies, however, have investigated focusing on learners, such as studies of the possibilities and appropriateness of learners receiving knowledge within the limits of technology, variations in teaching method, students' knowledge background, cultural difference, etc.

Objective of this Paper

In order to improve the quality of education through the use of technology and to accommodate the needs, knowledge and characteristic of students, the aims of this study are thus summarized as follows: (i) To design and manage an international distance learning program which focuses on teaching as well as learning based on educational theories; and (ii) To identify the effectiveness of the course design by analyzing students' learning performance. A second purpose was to examine how the original aims of course design were achieved during implementation; that is, how deeply students acquired knowledge, and how smoothly they perceive course contents, instructional methods and media usage. The results and the relationship among these perceptions were investigated using a regression analysis.

FRAMEWORK OF DISTANCE LEARNING COURSE

An Experimental International Distance Course

This course was conducted with participation from 201 grade 10 students of Kyoto University of Education Affiliated High School in Kyoto, Japan and 211 grade 10 Thai students of Chulalongkorn University Demonstration School in Bangkok, Thailand. The course was conducted once a week for about 50 minutes for 3 months (October-December 2005). They learned how to use MX Flash, a software application for the creation of animations, and since the software were new to them, leaning content and resulting ICT media were carefully designed. Both Thai and Japanese students shared the same curriculum and teaching contents which provided in School homepage.

The classes started at the introductory level and advanced to the completed level, at which students were supposed to be able to create a short animation in English. Both students were required to improve their knowledge and skills by employing media available in-class and by accessing related information out of class.

Theoretical Basis of Course Designing

Here, we discuss the educational theories behind this experimental distance learning course; in particular it was based on two foundations.

The Constructivism theory was initiated by Piaget (1954) and Vygotsky (1987), and developed by Camborne (1988, 1995) who suggested "Condition of Learning". This concept outlined a sequence of interactive processes to enhance students understanding. Since ICT was introduced in education, Jonassen et al. (1994) complemented Constructivism in the ICT environment. They proposed a model of learning environments by focusing on the collaboration of learning and the use of ICT to employ the learning experience (Jonassen et al., 1999).

In designing this course, based on constructivism knowledge is thought to be constructed by learners through two processes; namely (i) connecting new and old information and (ii) interrelating the learning style and the stage of students' learning achievements. This course then outlines three styles of learning and related factors; 1) traditional lecture, 2) self-learning and 3) collaborative learning. Constructivism thus transforms the student from a passive recipient of information to an active participant in the learning process.

Effective learning requires a clear perspective of how well students can access desirable knowledge. Bloom's taxonomy (Bloom, 1956) offers a promising approach to learning objectives in each step of experiences that promote constructivist approaches to learning. Learning objectives were identifies as four levels: (i) the first provides students the ability to acquire facts and information, and then to recall them (Recognition); (ii) following this, students can understand the basic use of the acquired knowledge (Understanding);

(iii) in the third, they then can use this knowledge in application to other situations; that is, students can break down knowledge into its integrated elements and apply it to other thing (Application); and (iv) in the final stage, students can construct their own new knowledge based on knowledge and information obtained so far (Analysis).

Based on the above two theories, the following three stages of teaching processes were pedagogically arranged in our experiment project: (a) traditional lecture; (b) self-learning; and (c) collaborative learning. The relationship of this arrangement of teaching processes with those of Constructivism and Bloom's taxonomy is indicated in Figure 1. Details of important requirements concerning teaching contents, communication platform among teachers and students, and media selection, are provided in Table 1.

Three Stages of the Learning Process

A. **Traditional lecture.** Students were lectured a basic knowledge of MX Flash animation software by a teacher in a traditional way. To familiarize students with ICT media dur-

ing this first stage, simple ICT media such as hyper text, on-line text, on the school's homepage was utilized.

B. **Self-learning style.** Students were expected to apply their basic knowledge by learning in practice via direct experience. Students were instructed the target of learning, namely, the production of a motion animation, and then students learned by WBT on the school's homepage. Students were taught the guidelines required to complete assignments for about 10 minutes at the beginning of the class, and then had to complete the assignment within the class period by applying the basic knowledge gained from the traditional lecture and by exploring the new learning content from the provided homepage or elsewhere by themselves. The teachers approached students individually to provide advices. Students send completed tasks via the school intranet at the end of class. Students were asked to form teams of about 4 or 5 persons to create short cartoon animations. As preparation, the students were taught how to use ICT media, such as the WBT, as well as in related information

Table 1. Course design - three stages of the learning process

learning method	Traditional lecture	Self-learning	Collaborative learning
Class time			
Thailand	1st - 2nd lesson	3rd - 4th lesson	5th - 6th lesson
Japan	1st - 3rd lesson	4th - 6th lesson	8th - 10th lesson
Learning content	Basic usage of MX Flash	Workshop in making a simple animation using MX Flash	Grouping to create a animation
	ICT media used as online text posted on the school website	Introduce how to use WBT/BBS	Match each group as team partners.
			Inter-group communication via BBS
Role of teacher	Instructor	Advisor	Advisor
Communication direction	Teacher to students	Students in the same classroom	Students in the same classroom and in a different classroom
ICT Media	On-line Text	WBT, BBS	Video conference, BBS
Media	Oral, Print-out,	Oral, Print-out,	Oral, Print-out,

Figure 1. Learning styles, and objectives based on educational theories

Constructivism learning	(Passive) Learning → → → Experiencing (Active)		
	Learning basic knowledge	Leaning by experiencing and being advised	Learning by experiencing at the more explicit level
Bloom's taxonomy	Recognition-Understanding	Application	Analysis
	↓	↓	↓
Learning style	**Traditional lecture**	**Self-learning**	**Collaborative learning**
Learning objectives	Understand basic concept of MX Flash	Learn to use MX Flash to create animation by themselves	Exchange idea and create a short animation story for presentation.

and computer literacy. They were informed about the collaborative learning style which would be conducted later with the foreign students of another school.

C. **Collaborative learning style.** Students analyzed and developed their knowledge by learning in a collaborative way. Students exchange their knowledge with friends not only in their own class but also with the partner teams in the other country. Students formed teams, which were then matched with foreign student teams as team partners. They were instructed to communicate which each other under the condition that the animations thereby created had to contain at least one idea from the partner team. Students were required to exchange and obtain knowledge or techniques from friends or teachers in both countries via a BBS (Bulletin Board System) to create their own animations. During the class, students spend time mainly on creating animation with their teams and accessed BBS to find comments from the partner teams and made a discussion. At the end of every class, they were asked to show their posting comment to teacher.

Other Factors in Course Design

A. **Teaching content and corresponding ICT media.** Teaching content was arranged to match the learning goals in each stage. However, this content is not only about academic knowledge or content coverage, but also the acquisition of related skill such as mastering ICT media such as hypertext, WBT (Web-based Training), BBS (Bulletin Board System), etc.

B. **Role of teachers.** In the self-learning style, students are required to take an active role in the learning process. The teacher took the role of advisors. Practically, however, classroom learning discipline and time limitations causes teachers to rush to finish their lecture in passive way. It is therefore necessary to remind both teachers and students to be aware of maintaining an appropriate role, consistent with the characteristic of the particular learning styles.

C. **Communication direction.** In international distance learning environment, Turoff (1995) pointed out that, even students utilize various kinds of interactive technologies, They more often learned passively by one-way communication from the teacher to students. It is necessary to balancing of passive and active communication direction. The key component in generating higher achievement of learning is to identify the direction of communication, and to remind all participants to balance the proportion of communication (Hiltz, 1997).

D. **Learning media.** Provide media which suit the teaching contents and communication context will assist students to achieve the intended learning outcome (Spark, 1983). However, students with a lack of ICT skill and unfamiliarity with new learning environment may feel that ICT media is inefficient or inadequate. Besides adding ICT usage to learning content, traditional media such as paper print-outs and oral presentations were utilized simultaneously with ICT media.

Based on the above discussion, the course design can be summarized as shown in Table 1.

LEARNING FEEDBACK AND EVALUATION

Evaluation of Course

The purpose of this activity was to identify the effect of this course design on the learning performance of students. According to Chandler and Sweller (1994), high cognitive performance which promotes effective learning outcomes is related to the following three factors: (i) comprehension; (ii) cognitive load; and (iii) motivation. Comprehension implies how deeply students understand; cognitive load means how comfortable students feel about the acquisition of course content, instructional method and media usage (Klemm, 2003); and motivation implies how spontaneously

students want to learn. We adopted these three evaluation items in this paper to evaluate the course. This experimental project was conducted as a voluntary activity, and the collection of concrete evaluations, such as test scores, is difficult. To grasp the actual results of the learning outcome as comprehensively as possible, students were asked to answer a questionnaire on their self-evaluation of their understanding at the end of each class.

A. **Comprehension:** Comprehension is the capacity and qualities of the individual student in identifying how much they have developed their knowledge, which corresponds to Question 1 in the questionnaire.

B. **Cognitive Load:** Cognitive load refers to the load placed on working memory during the learning process. It is natural that people learn those items that they have already understood better and faster. On the other hand, the more difficult the item, the longer the time they need for understanding in the learning process. Effective learning methods with a low rate of cognitive load can therefore enhance student understanding.

Klemm (2003) noted that the contents and the way to deliver knowledge are the important key components in effective on-line learning. According to this guideline, our present survey consisted of the two factors: (1) cognitive load in the teaching content; and (2) cognitive load in the teaching method of each class. Q2 "Cognitive load in the teaching content" is related to the difficulty in learning of the subject contents, which is MX Flash software application for creating animations. Q3 "Cognitive load in the teaching method" of each class is directed at the difficulty of the teaching and learning process for each period of the class.

C. **Motivation:** "Motivation" is another important factor in promoting "Comprehension". In ICT-based distance learning environ-

Figure 2.

Q1. Do you understand today's class?

    ④ Very much, ③ Quite understand, ② Not really, ① Not at all

Q2. Do you feel difficult in learning today's content, Flash MX?

    ④ Not at all, ③ Not quite difficult, ② A bit difficult, ① Very difficult

Q3. Is today's class activity difficult?

    ④ Not at all, ③ Not quite difficult, ② A bit difficult, ① Very difficult

Q4. Do you want to learn more about Flash MX?

    ④ Want to learn more very much, ③ Want to learn more, ② Not quite much, ① Not at all

Q5. Do you want to search for related information from the Internet or any other on-line sources?

    ④ Want to learn more very much, ③ Want to learn more, ② Not quite much, ① Not at all

---

ments, it is necessary to ensure that students exert sufficient effort to sharing what they are learning and pass on their knowledge to other participants by mastering the technology. Students were therefore asked their motivation in "teaching contents" and "the media and information literacy," as presented in Question 4 and 5.

Referring to the principle for instructional design of Swellers et al. (1998), improvement in "Comprehension" in learning requires that "Cognitive load" be diminished and "Motivation" be maximized.

Student feedback at each step of the learning process was collected at the end of each class. We made the above five questions as simple as possible since students had to fill replies right after each class and they did not have enough time to answer lengthy and detailed questions. The question which lengthy and many questions made them to rush to answer in an ambiguous way. The total of approximately 1,700 answers was analyzed to identify the effectiveness of the course design, identify significant factors and recommend effective approaches to promoting learning.

D.   **Questionnaire (see Figure 2)**

RESULTS OF REGRESSION ANALYSIS

Models for Estimation

"Comprehension" is affected by the two concepts of "Cognitive load" and "Motivation" under the different learning styles of traditional, self-learning and collaborative. Comprehension was thus set as a dependant variable, while cognitive load with regard to learning contents, cognitive load with regard to learning methods, motivation towards learning contents, and motivation towards media information literacy were independent variables. This estimation was done using the following equation:

Comprehension $= \beta_0 + \beta_1 x_1 + \beta_2 x_2 + \beta_3 x_3 + \beta_4 x_4 + u_i$

where i denotes a particular student and x_is are as follows:

x_1:   Cognitive load with regard to learning contents

x_2:   Cognitive load with regard to learning methods

x_3:   Motivation towards learning contents

x_4:   Motivation towards media and information literacy

The summary statistic is shown in Table 2. The results are expected to identify which factors or components enhance students' comprehension which varies in each learning style.

Results of Estimations

A.   **Traditional Lecture Style:** In Table 3 for Japanese students and Table 4 for Thai students, the most important factor for both countries to achieving comprehension was Q3 "Cognitive load in teaching method." Coefficients for the both countries were at the 1% significance level. These findings indicate that in the traditional lecture,

Japanese and Thai students understood well when the contents were properly delivered by the explicit teaching method.

With regard to the Q2 "Cognitive load in teaching contents" of Japanese students, from Table 3, this factor was not significant, and this implies that the difficulty of contents was irrelevant to their Q1"Comprehension". The teacher's lecturing and communication skills seemed more important for face-to-face study. In contrast, Table 4 indicates that Thai students perceived a relatively high Q2," with a coefficient of 0.2154 at the 5% significance level. Thai students understand better when teaching contents are easy to understand, in turn suggesting that courses aimed at Thais should

Table 2. Summary of statistics

	Japanese students			Thai Students				
Traditional lecture	Obs	Mean	Stan. Div.	Obs	Mean	Stan. Div.	t-test	
Q1 Comprehension	270	3.26	0.65	254	2.88	0.64	-6.79	***
Q2 Cognitive load in teaching contents	270	2.41	0.75	253	2.28	0.70	-2.05	***
Q3 Cognitive load in teaching method	270	2.49	0.75	254	2.44	0.76	-0.67	
Q4 Motivation towards teaching contents	270	3.14	0.62	253	2.77	0.77	-5.98	***
Q5 Motivation towards media and information literacy	267	1.96	0.95	253	2.03	0.84	0.83	
Self learning	Obs	Mean	Stan. Div.	Obs	Mean	Stan.Div.	t-test	
Q1 Comprehension	380	3.14	0.67	245	2.56	0.67	-10.49	***
Q2 Cognitive load in teaching contents	379	2.20	0.74	244	2.26	0.77	0.96	
Q3 Cognitive load in teaching method	380	2.40	0.76	241	2.27	0.78	2.11	***
Q4 Motivation towards teaching contents	380	3.09	0.66	245	2.52	0.84	-9.51	***
Q5 Motivation towards media and information literacy	378	2.39	1.08	245	2.00	0.82	-4.80	***
Collaborative learning	Obs	Mean	Stan. Div.	Obs	Mean	Stan. Div.	t-test	
Q1 Comprehension	349	3.10	0.73	204	2.54	0.81	-8.44	***
Q2 Cognitive load in teaching contents	349	1.90	0.66	204	2.17	0.78	4.29	***
Q3 Cognitive load in teaching method	348	2.13	0.70	203	2.16	0.84	0.50	
Q4 Motivation towards teaching contents	349	3.08	0.74	201	2.57	0.95	-7.00	***
Q5 Motivation towards media and information literacy	349	2.79	0.97	203	2.08	0.91	-8.45	***

***, ** and * indicate 1%, 5% and 10% significance level, respectively.

Table 3. Comprehension of Japanese students in traditional lecture style

Dependent variable: Q1- Comprehension	Coef.	Std. Err.	t-value	p-value	
Q2 Cognitive load in teaching contents	0.0568	0.0722	0.79	0.432	
Q3 Cognitive load in teaching methods	0.3689	0.0736	5.01	0.000	***
Q4 Motivation towards teaching contents	0.1931	0.0570	3.39	0.001	***
Q5 Motivation towards media and information literacy	0.0542	0.0369	1.47	0.143	
Constant	1.4965	0.2014	7.43	0.000	***
No. of sample	267				
R2 adjusted	0.2962				

***, ** and * indicate 1%, 5% and 10% significance level, respectively.

Table 4. Comprehension of Thai students in traditional lecture style

Dependent variable: Q1- Comprehension	Coef.	Std. Err.	t-value	p-value	
Q2 Cognitive load in teaching contents	0.2154	0.0615	3.50	0.001	***
Q3 Cognitive load in teaching methods	0.3078	0.0556	5.54	0.000	***
Q4 Motivation towards teaching contents	0.1050	0.0461	2.28	0.024	**
Q5 Motivation towards media and information literacy	0.0916	0.0413	2.22	0.028	**
Constant	1.1659	0.1453	8.02	0.000	***
No. of sample	244				
R2 adjusted	0.4189				

***, ** and * indicate 1%, 5% and 10% significant level, respectively.

be designed with close attention to the level and volume of contents of each session.

Regarding motivation, Q4 "Motivation towards teaching contents" and Q5 "Motivation towards media and information literacy" in Table 4, results showed that Japanese students understood only the former with a 1% significance level. This finding suggests that they understood the lesson much better if they found the contents interesting. Significance level for the Thai students regarding Q4 was smaller than that for the Japanese, whereas Q5 had greater effect on the comprehension than for the Japanese. In other words, Thai students had greater interest in PCs, for example, and this enhanced their "Comprehension".

B. **Self-learning Style:** Table 5 indicates that Q4 "Motivation towards teaching contents"

was the most important item to the Japanese students, followed by Q2 "Cognitive load in teaching contents". Teaching contents had a strong influence on the Japanese students. They will understand well if the contents are able to stimulate an eagerness to learn and easy access to knowledge. Q3 "Cognitive load in teaching methods" also affected understanding. Observation of the class revealed that the Japanese students remained focused on completing the assignments by themselves within the limited class period time. These results indicate the teaching methods which are easy to practice and possibly finish within the class period being recommended.

The reason why Q5 "Motivation towards media and information literacy" in Table 5 has a negative sign is that Japanese students showed less interest in related technology for learning, such as computer skills, in this teaching style, and this led to lower their comprehension for this lesson. Media and information literacy is related to the ability to extend this literacy from knowing how to use computers to being able to access information on various applications such as provided by technical infrastructure, social, cultural, and philosophical contexts. From this result, we infer that the students realized that media and information literacy played an important role to support what they were learning, but to understand this lesson is required to be investigated other factors in further details.

The result of Thai students in Table 6 shows that Q2 "Cognitive load in teaching contents" and Q3 "Cognitive load in teaching methods" had a strong influence on understanding, with a coef-

ficient of 0.3199 and 0.2460, both at the 1% significance level. These results show that Thai students felt difficulty with activities in the self-learning style.

The difficulty of teaching method and contents could possibly affect their comprehension in self-learning. Observation of classes indicated that Thai students appeared unfamiliar with the self-learning style, and the Thai teachers found it difficult to maintain advisory roles. Indeed, on several occasions they were forced to return to the traditional style of teaching in order to complete the tasks on time.

C. **Collaborative Learning Style:** For Japanese students, in Table 7, Q4 "Motivation towards teaching contents" became the greatest influence on understanding, with a coefficient of

Table 5. Comprehension of Japanese students in the self-learning style

Dependent variable: Q1- Comprehension	Coef.	Std. Err.	t-value	p-value	
Q2 Cognitive load in teaching contents	0.1729	0.0634	2.72	0.007	***
Q3 Cognitive load in teaching methods	0.1382	0.0626	2.21	0.028	**
Q4 Motivation towards teaching contents	0.2806	0.0485	5.78	0.000	***
Q5 Motivation towards media and information literacy	-0.0663	0.0294	-2.25	0.025	**
Constant	1.7139	0.1841	9.31	0.000	***
No. of sample	377				
R2 adjusted	0.2114				

***, ** and * indicate 1%, 5% and 10% significant levels, respectively.

Table 6. Comprehension of Thai students in the self-learning style

Dependent variable: Q1- Comprehension	Coef.	Std. Err.	t-value	p-value	
Q2 Cognitive load in teaching contents	0.3199	0.0583	5.48	0.000	***
Q3 Cognitive load in teaching methods	0.2460	0.0596	4.13	0.000	***
Q4 Motivation towards teaching contents	0.1234	0.0425	2.9	0.004	***
Q5 Motivation towards media and information literacy	0.0639	0.0437	1.46	0.146	
Constant	0.8319	0.1168	7.12	0.000	***
No. of sample	237				
R2 adjusted	0.5256				

***, ** and * indicate 1%, 5% and 10% significant levels, respectively.

Table 7. Comprehension of Japanese students in the collaborative learning style

Dependent variable: Q1- Comprehension	Coef.	Std. Err.	t-value	p-value	
Q2 Cognitive load in teaching contents	0.2234	0.0679	3.29	0.001	***
Q3 Cognitive load in teaching methods	0.1112	0.0651	1.71	0.089	*
Q4 Motivation towards teaching contents	0.3552	0.0468	7.58	0.000	***
Q5 Motivation towards media and information literacy	-0.0286	0.0356	-0.80	0.422	
Constant	1.4269	0.1959	7.28	0.000	***
No. of sample	348				
R2 adjusted	0.2570				

***, ** and * indicate 1%, 5% and 10% significant level, respectively.

0.3552 at the 1% significance level, followed by Q2 "Cognitive load in teaching contents". This result implies that the importance of teaching contents tended to become much stronger than in the self-learning style.

Table 8 shows the results for Thai students. Understanding was strongly influenced by "Cognitive load in teaching contents (Q2) and teaching methods (Q3). Neither of the motivations affected the Thai students in this teaching style; rather, low cognitive loads for contents and process were necessary to their understanding. On this basis, collaborative learning for Thai students should adopt easily understood contents and less complicated activities.

Regarding to the estimations of coefficient above, even students realized that the design of the "Teaching method" is important, but greater attention should be paid to considering how to deal with obstacles which produce learning unpleasantness or difficulty. This was hampered by

Table 8. Comprehension of Thai students in the collaborative learning style

Dependent variable: Q1-Comprehension	Coef.	Std. Err.	t-value	p-value	
Q2 Cognitive load in teaching contents	0.4185	0.0759	5.51	0.000	***
Q3 Cognitive load in teaching methods	0.2972	0.0692	4.29	0.000	***
Q4 Motivation towards teaching contents	0.0601	0.0494	1.22	0.225	
Q5 Motivation towards media and information literacy	0.0613	0.0526	1.17	0.245	
Constant	0.7140	0.1454	4.91	0.000	***
No. of sample	200				
R2 adjusted	0.5137				

***, ** and * indicate 1%, 5% and 10% significant level, respectively.

unfamiliarity with ICT skills in the exchange of data, but also language, since the students had to communicate in English.

Appropriateness of Course Design

Another goal of this study is to identify the effect of the course design used on the learning performance of students in order to examine the appropriateness of the course design, as presented in Table 1. This can be checked by examining the estimated results related to "Cognitive load in teaching methods" in the three teaching styles. If the coefficients of this variable in the estimation are not significant or negative, then student comprehension in each teaching style would not meet the aim of the course design. From Tables 3 to 8, all coefficients associated with this variable in the six estimations were positive and significant with at least 10% level. It can therefore be concluded that the course design had a positive effect on students.

DISCUSSION

Effect of Learner Characteristics

Comprehension for Japanese students was primarily influenced by both cognitive load and motivation. For Thai students, in contrast, cognitive load was more important than motivation. In terms of comprehension among Thai students, cognitive load had the strongest influence on comprehension, whereas motivation had the least influence in the same teaching styles with Japanese students. Closer investigation of this interesting result should identify whether the lack of motivation among Thai students is derived from the variation in learning cultures, or from a failure in teaching methods.

Effect of in-School Classroom Discipline

A class period of 50 minutes seems not enough for self-learning and collaborative learning. Class observation showed that students experienced difficulty in completing their assignments in time. On several occasions, the teachers of both countries found it difficult to maintain advisory roles in the limited class time and this forced them to return to the traditional style of teaching. Moreover, both Thai and Japanese students lost about 10-15 minutes in transferring to the computer classroom, leaving only 35-40 minutes for the class itself. We recommend the adjustment of times to better match actual classroom conditions, such as by providing a shorter period for each class session and longer term for the whole course.

Experience with the ICT Learning Environment

Unfamiliarity with teaching methods was a learning obstacle. Although the Japanese students had some experience with technology-enabled distance education, the present study was the first time for the Thai students to experience such a teaching or learning environment. Although the subject contents were new to all students and their background knowledge level at the beginning of the class was the same, Thai students required the contents with a much lower cognitive load. This in turn suggests that the lower level of experience with ICT learning environments tended to discourage the adoption of a positive learning attitude. The readiness of students to utilize an ICT-based teaching or learning environment should therefore be considered. They should be provided with sufficient experience or information by showing a video clip, for instance, of a former class or conducting a trial mock-up.

International Learning Barrier of Language

Students had to learn all activities in the English language. This requirement was to provide students with a good opportunity to integrate their knowledge of English with computer skills. In practice, it increased the difficulty in learning. Although an on-line English dictionary or translation software was available, students rarely used it. Observation showed that students of both countries had problems in composing sentences for communication, rather than vocabulary problems. Lack of communicative skill seemed a more serious impediment to learning than their actual English level. Promotion of communication skills would therefore be the key to lowering the language barrier.

CONCLUSION

This paper presents a view of the effectiveness of learning-teaching systems in international distance education between Thailand and Japan by focusing on the design of the course and the qualities of learning performance.

In course design, the Constructivism theory provided a learning architecture which promoted a more interactive acquisition of knowledge through experiences such as self-learning or collaborative learning. Moreover, this course also proposes requirements for the success of distance learning. Our results indicate that Constructivism can be considered a new paradigm for distance education. Bloom taxonomy was adopted not only to range appropriate learning targets and intended learning outcome, but in actual practice, it also helped teachers to estimate student readiness at each step of their learning and to rapidly validate the appropriateness of the instructional strategies and media selection.

The empirical results indicate that for the same learning environment, Thai and Japanese students had different perceptions of the effect of learning processes and contents on their comprehension. Such variation, particularly in "Teaching Method," is strengthened in the more complex setting of self-learning and collaborative learning. Moreover, when we examined estimated coefficients divided by country, Japanese preferred contents which promoted high motivation, while Thai students preferred content which was more easily understood. We can therefore state that "Teaching Content" should be considered as an additional major factor. Contents should be more strongly simplified than for normal traditional learning. Our study will be of benefit in the development of guidelines for prioritizing teaching and learning factors such as contents, processes, materials and ICT media.

The combination of various teaching methods supported by technology reveals the possibilities of enhancing effective learning in school education. This study found that course design should place greater emphasis on interactive communication. Most students used the WBT and BBS only in the classroom, and only students who were their group representative participated in the BBS. The number of teacher as advisors was also insufficient, because many of the students required direct advice from teachers. We therefore offer several suggestions which may enhance interaction communication.

- Discussion via the BBS should be made compulsory when interactive communication is considered to be essential, particularly in collaborative learning.
- The real-time interaction of between teachers and students with technology support in the classroom environment will assist when teacher manpower in the advisor role is insufficient.

Finally, this study attempted to analyze the major potential promoters of learning in practical and consistent manner. However, learning impact is subject the particular characteristics of each country and understanding the actual effects of course design require further studies.

ACKNOWLEDGMENT

The author expresses her deep thanks to Professor Masatsugu Tsuji, University of Hyogo, who guided this research as an adviser and to Mr. Tomonari Yamada and Mr. Amponpong Amarin for cooperating as in-class teachers in Japan and Thailand. Special thanks are also due to Dr. Yuji Akematsu, JSPS Research Fellow, University of Hyogo, for his valuable advice on the statistical analysis.

REFERENCES

Bates, T. (1986). Computer Assisted Learning or Communication: Which Way for Information Technology in Distance Education. *Journal of Distance Education, 1*(1), 41–57.

Bloom, B. S. (1956). *Taxonomy of Educational Objective*. New York: Longmans.

Cambourne, B. (1995). Towards an Educationally Relevant Theory of Literacy Learning: Twenty Years of Inquiry. *The Reading Teacher, 49*(3), 182–190. doi:10.1598/RT.49.3.1

Cambourne, B. L. (1988). *The Whole Story: Natural Learning and the Acquisition of Literacy*. Auckland, New Zealand: Ashton-Scholastic.

Chandler, P., & Sweller, J. (1994). Cognitive Load Theory, Learning Difficulty and Instructional Design. *Learning and Instruction, 4*, 295–312. doi:10.1016/0959-4752(94)90003-5

Cho, K. (2006). Analysis of Intercultural Competency in the e-mail Exchange between Elementary School Students of Japan and Korea. *Journal of Japan Society for Educational Technology, 30*(1), 59–66.

Gagne, R. M. (1987). *Instructional Technology: Foundation*. Hillsdale, NJ: Lawrence Erlbaum.

Hasegawa, J. (2006). Practices for Real-time Distance Lecture Environments with Multimedia Supports. *Journal of Research Center for Distance Learning, 2*(2), 79–91.

Hiltz, S. R., & Wellman, B. (1997). Asynchronous Learning Networks as a Virtual Classroom Communication. *Journal of the Association for Computing Machinery, 40*(9), 44–49.

Howell, C. D. (2006). *Statistical Method for Psychology* (6th ed.). New York: Thomson Wadsworth Press.

Jonassen, D. H., Campbell, J. O., & Davidson, M. E. (1994). Restructuring the Debate: Learning with Media. *Educational Technology Research and Development, 42*(2), 31–39. doi:10.1007/BF02299089

Klemm, E. B. (2003). Cognitive load Criteria for Critical Evaluation and Selection of Web-Based Resources for Science Teaching. In *Proceedings of the Annual Meeting Report of National Association for Research in Science Teaching* (pp. 2-9).

Natcha, P., Sasaki, N., & Yamada, T. (2006). Development of Self-learning and Collaborative Learning with Media-mix Utility. In *Proceedings of the Japanese Association for Education of Information Studies, 22nd Conference* (pp. 190-1).

Spark, J. J. (1983). *Distance Education: International Perspective*. London: St. Martin Press.

Sweller, J., Van, J. M., & Paas, F. (1998). Cognitive Architecture and Instructional Design. *Educational Psychology Review, 10*, 251–296. doi:10.1023/A:1022193728205

Tsuji, M. (2004). Issues of International Distance Learning. *International Journal of Computer, the Internet and Management, 12*(2), 201-8.

Tsuji, M. (2006). A Comparative Analysis of Distance Learning Methods: Lessons Learned from the Experiences of Osaka University. In K. Fukui (Ed.), *ESP e-Learning for Global Competency* (Frontiers Science Series No. 51, pp. 55-67). Tokyo: Universal Academy Press.

Tsuji, M., Taoka, F., & Teshima, M. (2002). A Comparative Analysis of International Distance Learning: ISDN VS. The Internet. In Murphy, D., Shin, N., & Zhang, W. (Eds.), *Advancing Online Learning in Asia* (pp. 201–210). Hong Kong: Open University of Hong Kong Press.

Turoff, M. (1995). Designing a Virtual Classroom. In *Proceedings of the International Conference on Computer Assisted Instruction* (pp. 1-13).

Vygotsky, L. S. (1978). *Mind in Society: Development of Higher Psychological Processes.* Cambridge, MA: Harvard University Press.

Yun, J. H. (2003). Implementation of Video Conferencing System in Japanese Language Lesson for Distance Learning. In *Proceedings of the 2003 Conference proceedings, Society for Teaching Japanese as a Foreign Language* (pp. 189-94).

This work was previously published in International Journal of Information and Communication Technology, Volume 6, Issue 3, edited by Lawrence A. Tomei, pp. 11-24, copyright 2010 by IGI Publishing (an imprint of IGI Global).

Chapter 18
An Evaluation of Use of Multimedia Case Studies to Improve an Introduction to Information Technology Course

Chetan S. Sankar
Auburn University, USA

Howard Clayton
Auburn University, USA

ABSTRACT

For college graduates to be successful in today's global economy there has been an increasing demand for them to possess business knowledge as well as technical knowledge. To meet the demand, curriculum designers have sought to integrate new technologies, applications, data, and business functions into classrooms so that non-information technology (IT) majors can realize the benefits of IT. This paper discusses the results of research conducted on the use of multimedia case studies to address the curriculum designers' challenge. The authors have found that students, who are taught using multimedia case studies, perceived a comparatively greater improvement in their higher-order cognitive skills, ease of learning, team working skills, attitude toward information technology, and self-efficacy. This suggests a need for further research into adopting such instructional materials for teaching non-IT majors and for developing other innovative instructional materials.

INTRODUCTION

Need for Development of Context-Based Collaborative Skills

For today's graduates to achieve success as professionals in a global world, they must acquire a new set of skills, many of which have yet to become a major part of traditional educational pedagogies.

Curriculum designers are increasingly called upon to create a suitable balance between technical knowledge and business knowledge (Trauth, Farwell, & Lee, 1993; Kirsch, Braun, Yamamoto, & Sum, 2007). To fulfill such a demand, graduates must gain strong leadership skills, which are required for job advancements, as well as become proficient in information technology (IT) concepts (Glyer-Culver, 2003). IT refers to anything related

DOI: 10.4018/978-1-61350-468-0.ch018

to computing technology, such as networking, hardware, software, systems, the Internet, or the people that work with these technologies.

Another unprecedented requirement is for students to acquire stronger soft skills and cognitive skills (Kirsch et al., 2007). Critics of traditional IT programs claim that IT graduates demonstrate "brilliant" technical expertise but severely lack social skills (Slater, McCubbrey, & Scudder, 1995). As those needs of business and industry expand and evolve, IT curricula should integrate new technologies, applications, data, and business functions into both IT and non-IT classrooms (Trauth, Farwell, & Lee, 1993; Savander-Ranne, Lunden, & Kolari, 2008). Unfortunately, in today's information-driven environment these essential ingredients rapidly become obsolete.

Forgues and Koskela (2009) demonstrate that traditional procurement processes in companies reinforce socio-cognitive barriers that hinder team efficiency. They also illustrate how new procurement modes can transform the dynamic of relationships between the client and the members of the supply chain, and have a positive impact on team performance. Their paper demonstrates first that problems with integrated design team efficiency are related to *context* and not process - they are not technical but socio-cognitive; second that fragmented transactional contracting increases socio-cognitive barriers that hinder integrated design team performance; third that new forms of relational contracting may help to mitigate socio-cognitive barriers and improve integrated design team performance, fourth that changing the *context* through procurement does not address the problem of obsolete design practices. Taber (2008) argues for emphasis on collaborative learning for preparing people to deal with stressful and challenging situations in their work. Pittaway and Cope (2007) argue that experiential, work-based learning is needed to simulate contexts similar to those in which entrepreneurs learn.

Kirsch et al. (2007) further pointed out that students, who lack context-based collaborative

skills (such as team working, positive attitude, and self-efficacy), find more difficulty in obtaining and retaining employment. They added that at the same time cognitive skills give students a foundation upon which future learning and skills development can occur.

Types of Interventions Available to Teach These Skills

In recent years, an increasing number of programs have required students to participate in teamwork assignments and presentations and to "solve business problems experientially through a cross-functional approach" (Slater, McCubbrey, & Scudder, 1995). Some educational institutions have been successful at extending their curricula beyond the traditional lecture method by incorporating information technologies, including online discussions and field experiences into their teaching methods (Leidner & Jarvenpaa, 1995; Moffett, 2001; Sudzina & Suzina, 2003; Santhanam, Sasidharan, & Webster, 2008). Other methods focus on the use of hands-on projects, service projects that benefit communities (Turner & Grizzaffi, 2003), or other forms of problem-based learning (Franz, Hopper, & Kritsonis, 2007), to better facilitate practical learning experiences. Leidner and Jarvenpaa (1995) suggested that integrating more IT elements into classrooms does not inherently improve the required skills of today's students. They stress that the IT elements need to be used innovatively to enable educators to effect changes in teaching and learning processes at their institutions. However, only a few studies have measured what types of interventions are likely to alter students' perception.

Case studies have greatly succeeded in improving the learning experiences of undergraduates because they help students make connections between theory and its actual practice (Mizukami, 2002; Butler, Lee, & Tippins, 2006) and greatly aid in teaching critical thinking skills (Lee, 2007). Case-based instructional methods have also been used successfully in other disciplines to train students for the professional world (Koh & Branch, 2004). Furthermore, adding various forms of media (such as video, photos, and audio) to the case studies allows students to learn about information technologies while having a more hands-on, real-world experience. Such technologies in IT classrooms might enable the effective acquisition of constructive, cognitive, collaborative, and socio-cultural models of learning (Leidner & Jarvenpaa, 1995).

Although the use of multimedia case studies has been growing in popularity in recent decades (Fasko, 2003) and is generally met with positive responses from students (Razvi & Allen, 2005), there is an apparent need for additional research and empirical data regarding the usefulness of teaching with multimedia case studies (Fasko, 2003). In response, this paper studies the potential impact of multimedia case-study method on

altering student perceptions. The authors pose the following research question for this paper: Controlling for students' gender, ethnicity, work experience, class seniority, and GPA, as well as for instructor experience, when compared to traditional methods does the use of the multimedia case study method in an introductory class enhance students' mastery of the skills and possession of the attributes that are increasingly required of graduates? These skills and attributes include perceived improvement in learning concepts (higher-order cognitive skills and ease of learning) and soft skills (team-working, attitude, and self-efficacy).

Research Model

The authors created the research model shown in Figure 1. In this section, the model is described, the terms used in the model are defined, and hypotheses are formulated.

Figure 1. Research model: variables influencing perceived improvement in learning concepts and soft skills

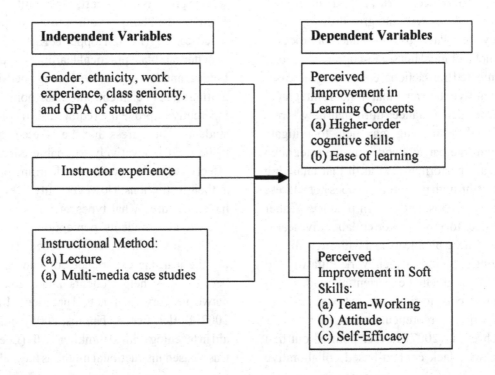

- **Gender/ethnicity/work experience/class/ GPA:** These personal qualities were designated as control variables. They needed to be taken into account because each characteristic has the potential to affect the outcome by virtue of its effect on how a student learns and perceives instruction in the classroom as well as the body of knowledge the student has already acquired.
- **Instructor experience** was an attribute with two levels (present vs. absent) based on the number of years of teaching of the instructor. This was included as a control variable because it is believed it could affect students' perceptions of the material being taught.
- **Instructional Method:** Two instructional methods were compared: (a) lecture method and (b) use of multi-media case studies.
  - The lecture format is a traditional classroom setup in which the instructor leads the class through material from textbooks, etc. Knowledge is transmitted from the expert (here, the instructor) to the learner.
    Multimedia case studies, on the other hand, base learning on both individual and group interactions with the materials. The teacher discusses the theory in class then conducts sessions in a computer laboratory in which the students analyze the multimedia case study to apply the theories to solve practical problems.
- **Perceived Improvement in Learning Concepts:** The students' perceptions on learning the introductory IT concepts were measured by two variables: higher-order cognitive skills and ease of learning.
  - **Higher order cognitive skills** relates to the perception that an individual has acquired an adequate portfolio of skills to make a decision within a specified period of time. It im-

plies an improved ability to identify, integrate, evaluate, and interrelate concepts within the case study, and hence make the appropriate decision in a given problem-solving situation (Hingorani, Sankar, & Kramer, 1998).
  - **Ease of learning** is simply the student's understanding of how learning works for her or him, and her or his role in the learning process. They include emotional response to learning, confidence in learning new materials, responsibility, accomplishment, and understanding of cross-disciplinary work, all of which contribute to team working skills and higher order cognitive skills (Santhanam, Sasidharan, & Webster, 2008).
- **Soft Skills:** This research studied students' perceptions on acquiring three major soft skills: team working, attitude, and self-efficacy.
  - **Team working skills** are the set of interpersonal and communications skills that help individuals function in a team decision-making environment. These skills include listening, interpersonal relations, idea sharing, and consensus making.
  - The **attitude** of the student encompasses both the student's attitude toward the subject being taught and whether the student believes she or he will be able to learn the material. Many employers consider the employee's attitude toward work an important measure of how well she or he can contribute to the company (Shuman, Besterfield-Sacre, & McGourty, 2005).
  - **Self-efficacy** is regarded as part of the deep learning process because it is related to students' plans to persist in

their field of study (Marra, Rodgers, Shen, & Bogue, 2009). Self-efficacy refers to individuals' beliefs in their capabilities to plan and take the actions required to achieve a particular outcome (Bandura, 1986).

Based on the research model, the authors developed the following hypotheses:

- **Hypothesis 1**: The change in students' perceived cognitive skill learning will be greater for students who are instructed using lecture plus multimedia case method than for students who are instructed using lecture only.
- **Hypothesis 2:** The change in students' perceived ease of learning IT will be greater for students who are instructed using lecture plus multimedia case method than for students who are instructed using lecture only.
- **Hypothesis 3:** The change in students' perceived team working skills will be greater for students who are instructed using lecture plus multimedia case method than for students who are instructed using lecture only.
- **Hypothesis 4:** The change in students' attitude toward IT will be greater for students who are instructed using lecture plus multimedia case method than for students who are instructed using lecture only.
- **Hypothesis 5**: The change in students' self efficacy will be greater for students who are instructed using lecture plus multimedia case method than for students who are instructed using lecture only.

Experimental Design

The authors decided to test the hypotheses in an *Introduction to Information Technology* course offered to business students in a southeastern U.S. university. During a particular semester, this course was taught in three sections by three different instructors. The objective of this course was to give the introductory students an overview of the management of computer-based systems and their role in business through the study of systems, information technology components (hardware, software, data, procedures, people, and telecommunications), various types of information technology, system development approaches, and the strategic nature of information technology. The students in these sections represented both IT and non-IT majors. Although the course content and objectives of the course were similar across the sections, the method of delivery varied.

The experimental section was taught by a professor with more than 25 years of industrial and university teaching experience. The control sections, which employed the traditional lecture method, were taught by an experienced professor with more than 30 years of experience and by a graduate student with four years of teaching and industrial experience. Owing to the nature of student registration for courses at the university, instructor names not being announced at time of registration, and the fact that the introduction to information technology course is offered every semester, the students in each section can be assumed to be random samples from the population of students in an introduction to information technology class at a typical university in the United States. Furthermore, assignment of which students received which experimental "treatment" can also be regarded as random and not subject to any bias.

Teaching Methodologies Used in Experimental and Control Classes

The teaching methodology used in the experimental class involved a three-phase approach shown in Figure 2. Students were provided theoretical materials related to an information technology topic using lecture sessions in the first week (2 class sessions). They then analyzed a case study related to the lecture session in a computer laboratory (2 class sessions). The case study presented a business and IT problem and provided multiple alternatives to solve the problem. A sufficient number of teams were created among the students so that each alternative could be assigned to one team to defend. In addition, one team was designated to take the perspective of the management to act as jury/ judge. During the third week, the students defended their solutions to the problem. The management team questioned them and then, in the next class period, selected a solution for implementation and presented it to the class. The control classes involved traditional lectures with the aid of a textbook (Turban, Rainer, & Potter, 2003) and occasional guest lectures by industry executives. Student learning was evaluated using tests and individual assignments scheduled at regular intervals.

Measures

The authors developed a survey instrument (available from www.litee.org) that gathered students' background information and measured their perceptions on the constructs that were hypothesized. Respondents were asked to indicate the extent of their agreement with 36 evaluatory statements on a 5-point Likert scale. The scale ranged from 1, "strongly disagree," to 5, "strongly agree." The questionnaire was modified to incorporate two versions: pre and post. The pre-questionnaire was implemented at the start of the course and the post-questionnaire was implemented at the end of the course.

Procedures Used in the Experimental and Control Sections

In the experimental section, electronic journals (available from authors) were collected at three different times during the course. The journals provided an opportunity for students to present a formative evaluation of their learning in the course and for the instructor to refine the course content based on the feedback. In the experimental section, three tests were given, while four tests were given in the control sections.

Course grades for students in the experimental section were allocated in the following manner: 30% for the case study analysis, 20% for individual assignments, and 50% for tests and quizzes. For student in control section I, grades were allocated as follows: 8% for class preparation and participation, and 23% for each of four exams. Allocation of course grades for students in control section II was 20% for assigned homework, and 20% for each of four exams.

DATA ANALYSIS

The survey data were scrutinized to check for obvious cases of invalid or useless responses given by students bubbling in the same response to every item. Less than 5% of the total number of cases were deemed of a suspicious nature fitting this description and were eliminated. Cronbach Alphas were computed for each of five previously established constructs and were deemed close enough to the 0.70 criterion signifying an acceptable level. These constructs, along with the Cronbach Alpha measure of their internal consistency/reliability are described in Table 1.

Five summated scales corresponding to the five constructs were formed by averaging the scores on the survey items identified with each construct. For as many students as possible, these scores, along with the demographic data (gender, ethnicity, work experience, etc.) were matched for those who filled out the pre-treatment and post-treatment surveys. The authors had a final total of 119 usable cases. The change (post-treatment − pre-treatment) in the summated scores were calculated and employed as the dependent variables in five separate regression models that

Figure 2. Course map for the experimental class

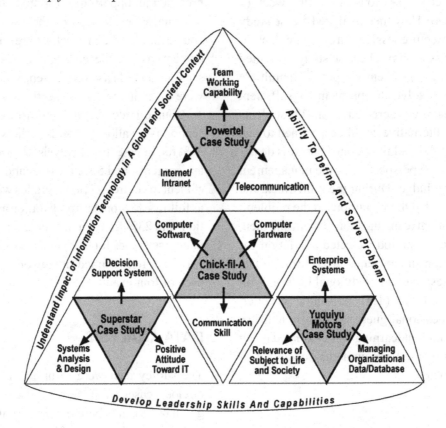

were estimated to test the five research hypotheses.

Model Implementation

A generic regression model was developed to test the research hypotheses. The regression model is expressed as:

$$\text{Delta} = \beta_0 + \beta_1 \text{ CaseMeth} + \beta_2 \text{ Instructor} + \beta_3 \text{ GPAScl} + \beta_4 \text{ WorkExp} + \beta_5 \text{ Female} + \beta_6 \text{ Minority} + \beta_7 \text{ Senior},$$

where

Delta = post-treatment – pre-treatment summated score for each construct (higher-order cognitive skills, ease of learning, team-working, attitude, and self-efficacy).

CaseMeth = 1 if course instructed via multimedia cases and = 0 otherwise

Instructor = 1 if instructor has less than 5 years of teaching experience and = 0 otherwise

GPAScl = 1 if student GPA is 2.0 – 2.5, = 2 if GPA 2.51 – 3.0, = 3 if GPA 3.01 – 3.5, = 4 if GPA > 3.5

WorkExp = 1 if student work experience <= 1 year, = 2 if exp 1 – 2 years, = 3 if exp 2 – 3 years, = 4 if exp > = 4 years.

Female = 1 if student is female, = 0 otherwise

Minority = 1 if student is an ethnic minority, = 0 otherwise

Senior = 1, if student is a senior, = 0 otherwise

Table 1. List of constructs and items used to measure them

Construct	Survey Items	Cronbach Alpha
Higher-Order Cognitive Gains	15, 16, 17, 18, 19	0.87
Ease of learning subject	1, 2 (rev), 3, 7, 8 (rev)	0.75
Team Working Benefits	26, 27, 28, 29, 30	0.84
Attitude towards IT	4, 10, 11, 13, 14, 20, 21, 25	0.67
Self-Efficacy	22, 23, 24, 31, 32, 33, 34, 35	0.69

RESULTS

Table 2 shows the means and standard deviations for the differences between the post- and pre-surveys for the five dependent variables for the three sections. A relatively high mean value implies a substantial difference between the post and pre values, whereas a low mean value implies a minimal difference between the post and pre values. Results from each of the five regression models are shown in Table 3 and the resulting conclusions about the related hypotheses are shown in Table 4.

DISCUSSION

There was extremely strong support for all hypotheses. It appears that the multimedia case method was able to bring about many important benefits to students. The findings can be summarized as follows:

A. Use of multimedia case study method leads to perceived improvement in higher-order cognitive skills

B. Use of multimedia case study method leads to perceived increase in ease of learning about IT

C. Use of multimedia case study method leads to perceived improvement in team working skills

D. Use of multimedia case study method leads to perceived positive attitude toward information technology

E. Use of multimedia case study method leads to perceived improvement in self-efficacy

The highly significant linkage between use of multi-media case studies and perceived improvement in higher-order cognitive skills (Tables 3 and 4) might be attributed to the opportunity for students to make presentations of their case analyses. The process involved in presenting required students to identify relevant information, analyze it, and provided support for their recom-

Table 2. Means and standard deviation of the dependent variables

	Constructs	Higher-Order Cognitive Skills	Ease of Learning	Teamwork	Attitude	Self-Efficacy
Experimental Section n = 37	Mean	0.71	0.65	0.72	0.32	0.47
	Std. Dev.	0.74	0.56	0.91	0.69	0.59
Control Section 1 n = 42	Mean	0.22	0.35	-0.23	-0.08	-0.17
	Std. Dev.	0.63	0.53	0.51	0.56	0.49
Control Section 2 n = 40	Mean	0.06	-0.07	-0.24	-0.08	-0.11
	Std. Dev.	0.83	0.85	0.71	0.67	0.64

mendations. A possible implication is that, for an introductory class, students should be required to break down a problem, analyze it, and create possible solutions.

The results in Tables 3 and 4 show that the students perceived that both the case study methodology and the instructor experience had a significant influence on increasing the ease of learning about IT. As shown in Table 2, students taught by an experienced instructor (experimental section and Control Section I) had positive means for ease of learning compared to a negative mean for the section taught by an inexperienced instructor. This evidence supports the finding from the regression model that the students perceived that experienced instructors were influential in perceived ease of learning about IT. However, the mean value was 0.65 for the experimental section, whereas it was

0.35 for Control Section I. This shows that even among experienced instructors, the perceived ease of learning is higher for the students taught using multi-media case studies. The students in the experimental section also commented about their fears about learning IT decreasing. A possible implication from these comments is that some students have a fear of IT because it is perceived to be intimidating and unforgiving. It is critical for instructors to understand this fear and take steps to make the technology friendlier to the students in introductory classes.

Tables 3 and 4 show that the use of multimedia case studies had a highly significant impact on perceived improvement in team working skills. The role-playing exercises by the students (acting as technical specialists, consultants, and managers in a company) may have made the teams work

Table 3. Key summary statistics from regression models to test the hypotheses

Dependent Variables	Regression Stats.	Independent Variables						
		CaseMeth	Instructor	GPAScl	WorkExp	Female	Minority	Senior
Higher-Order Cognitive Skills	Coefficient	0.485	-0.188	0.008	0.045	0.102	-0.132	-0.168
	t-value	2.781	-1.116	0.107	0.721	0.722	-0.617	-1.152
	p-value	0.006	0.267	0.915	0.473	0.472	0.539	0.252
Ease of Learning	Coefficient	0.351	-0.377	-0.008	-0.023	0.174	0.244	0.002
	t-value	2.253	-2.5	-0.13	-0.405	1.371	1.276	0.012
	p-value	0.026	0.014	0.897	0.686	0.173	0.205	0.99
Teamwork	Coefficient	0.952	0.004	-0.049	0.057	-0.096	0.159	-0.198
	t-value	5.637	0.022	-0.705	0.945	-0.698	0.767	-1.402
	p-value	0.000	0.983	0.482	0.347	0.487	0.445	0.164
Attitude	Coefficient	0.414	-0.019	-0.072	0.032	0.153	-0.098	0.011
	t-value	2.747	-0.128	-1.153	0.591	1.25	-0.531	0.088
	p-value	0.007	0.898	0.252	0.556	0.214	0.596	0.93
Self-Efficacy	Coefficient	0.624	0.090	-0.064	-0.028	-0.063	0.113	-0.052
	t-value	4.587	0.685	-1.127	-0.572	-0.571	0.679	-0.460
	p-value	0.000	0.495	0.262	0.568	0.569	0.499	0.647

Table 4. Results of testing each hypothesis

Hypothesis	p-value	Conclusion
Hypothesis 1	.006	Very strongly supported
Hypothesis 2	.026	Strongly supported
Hypothesis 3	.000	Overwhelmingly supported
Hypothesis 4	.007	Very strongly supported
Hypothesis 5	.000	Overwhelmingly supported

well together. The experimental class also used a personality profile (Olson, 2003) to inform their students about their personalities. The students were allowed to choose their own teammates and were requested to discuss their personality profiles and how they would add value to the team. The methodology and teaching pedagogy possibly helped the students improve their team working skills. Based on both the quantitative and qualitative evidence presented here, we believe it is reasonable to suggest that instructors in Introduction to Information Technology courses should require team-working among their students.

As seen in Tables 3 and 4, it appears that the use of multimedia cases had a strong influence on perceived positive attitude toward IT. A positive attitude toward IT has become very important because the enrollment of students in IT and computer science has significantly dropped over the past few years (Lomerson & Pollacia, 2005; Perez & Murray, 2008). The students in our study commented that the multi-media case study methodology made them link the theories learned with practice and made them realize the importance of IT in other subject areas, such as finance, accounting, marketing, and human relations.

A possible implication from the comments is that students need to be informed of how much they are using IT in their day-to-day life so that their attitudes change toward the technical materials in IT. During the early decades of introducing IT in organizations, the emphasis on technical matters might have been appropriate since most students did not use computers. With the current widespread availability of computers and use of IT systems, an introductory course must now focus on changing the students' attitudes rather than dwelling on the technical terminologies. The linkage between use of multi-media case studies and positive attitude toward IT suggest an important role for this methodology in Introduction to Information Technology courses.

Results in Tables 3 and 4 show that the use of multimedia cases was strongly associated with perceived improvement in self-efficacy. The comments by students support the finding that perceived improvement in self-efficacy might have been obtained through the use of the experimental methodology.

Based on these comments, one might generalize that the students need to be informed of the major role of IT in their lives. It is also important for students to understand that the specific technology they learned in class might be irrelevant in a couple of years but the concepts they mastered will help them adapt to newer technologies more quickly (Einarsson, 1972; Kilov & Sack, 2009; Castro-Schez, Castillo, Hortolano, & Rodriguez, 2009). Taken together, the claims made by these researchers and the shown linkage between perceived self-efficacy and use of multi-media case studies emphasizes the need for use of such case studies in introductory IT courses.

LIMITATIONS

The results are based on analyzing data obtained in one semester. The generalizability of the results would be enhanced if the experiment were to be repeated over several semesters and utilize several instructors. Moreover, longitudinal tracking of students could add value to the study. Another limitation is that the reported results are based on perceptions of the students. A common test across the experimental and control sections might help remedy this. Another possibility is to track the students' career choices and employment offers after graduation. Furthermore, there might be other factors such as time invested by students, methods of assessment, student major, and technology comfort that have to be included in the measures.

In the future, it may be possible to develop a causal model that links the acquisition of different skills to the overall course performance. It may be also possible to test this model across different campuses by obtaining data on implementation in several experimental and control classes.

CONCLUSION

Weber (2004) discussed students' difficulty in obtaining a deep understanding of and facility with higher-level skills without having first acquired a good knowledge of fundamental IS/IT concepts. He emphasized the need for a broad, long-term perspective. The multimedia case study methodology as reported in this paper seems to have addressed the issue that Weber discusses. We have shown a linkage between the use of multimedia cases and perceived acquisition of higher-level skills while having a reasonable knowledge of fundamental IS/IT concepts. This suggests the need for further research into adopting these instructional materials in other schools and for developing other innovative instructional materials. Even though administrators see the pervasiveness of IS/IT across the universities and society, they are reluctant to increase investment in faculty and research facilities in IS/IT. Indeed, several universities have decreased investment in their IT departments and programs due to the decrease in enrollment in those disciplines. It is imperative that administrators in universities and other policy makers in private and public grant agencies invest substantial resources to researching the effects of multimedia case studies and other instructional materials.

ACKNOWLEDGMENT

We greatly appreciate the contribution of Dr. Nelson Ford and Dr. Barry Cumbie at Auburn University who worked with us in evaluating the methodology. This paper was developed with support from the National Science Foundation Grant # 0736997 and 0934800. Any opinions, findings, and conclusions or recommendations expressed in this paper are those of the authors and do not necessarily reflect the views of the National Science Foundation.

REFERENCES

Bandura, A. (1986). *Social Foundations of Thought and Action: A Social Cognitive Theory*. Englewood Cliffs, NJ: Prentice-Hall.

Butler, M. B., Lee, S., & Tippins, D. J. (2006). Case-Based Methodology as an Instructional Strategy for Understanding Diversity: Preservice Teachers' Perceptions. *Multicultural Education*, 20–26.

Castro-Schez, J. J., Castillo, E., Hortolano, J., & Rodriguez, A. (2009, February). Designing and Using Software Tools for Educational Purposes: FLAT, a Case Study. *IEEE Transactions on Education*, *52*(1), 66–74. doi:10.1109/TE.2008.917197

Einarsson, G. (1972, August). An Advanced Course in Communication Systems Based on Case Studies. *IEEE Transactions on Education, 15*(3), 156–160. doi:10.1109/TE.1972.4320748

Fasko, D. J. (2003, April). *Case Studies and Methods in Teaching and Learning.* Paper presented at the annual meeting of the Society of Educators and Scholars, Louisville, KY.

Franz, D. P., Hopper, P. F., & Kritsonis, W. A. (2007). National Impact: Creating Teacher Leaders Through the Use of Problem-Based Learning. *National Forum of Applied Educational Research Journal, 20*(3), 1–9.

Glyer-Culver, B. (2003). *A Survey of Former Business Students (General Business, Management, Marketing, Real Estate). Summary Findings of Respondents District-Wide.* Sacramento, CA: Los Rios Community College, Office of Institutional Research.

Kelly, G. (2008). A Collaborative Process for Evaluating New Educational Technologies. *Campus-Wide Information Systems, 25*(2), 105–113. doi:10.1108/10650740810866594

Kilov, H., & Sack, I. (2009). Mechanisms for Communication between Business and IT Experts. *Computer Standards & Interfaces, 31*, 98–109. doi:10.1016/j.csi.2007.11.001

Kirsch, I., Braun, H., Yamamoto, K., & Sum, A. (2007). *America's Perfect Storm: Three Forces Changing Our Nation's Future.* Princeton, NJ: Educational Testing Service.

Koh, M. H., & Branch, R. M. (2004, October). *Online Learning Environments: A Report of an Instructional Design Case Event.* Chicago: Association for Educational Communications and Technology.

Lee, K. (2007). Online Collaborative Case Study Learning. *Journal of College Reading and Learning, 37*(2), 82–100.

Leidner, D. E., & Jarvenpaa, S. L. (1995, September). The Use of Information Technology to Enhance Management School Education: A Theoretical View. *Management Information Systems Quarterly, 19*, 265–291. doi:10.2307/249596

Lomerson, W. L., & Pollacia, L. (2005, October). Declining CIS Enrollment: An Examination of Pre-College Factors. In *Proceedings of ISECON on EDSIG*, Columbus, OH (Vol. 22).

Marra, R. M., Rodgers, K. A., Shen, D., & Bogue, B. (2009). Women Engineering Students and Self-Efficacy: A Multi-Year, Multi-Institution Study of Women Engineering Student Self-Efficacy. *Journal of Engineering Education, 98*(1), 27–38.

Maxwell, J. R., Gilberti, A. F., & Mupinga, D. M. (2006). *Use of Case Study Methods in Human Resource Management, Development, and Training. Terre Haute.* IN: Indiana State University.

Meyer, E., & Land, R. (2003). *Threshold Concepts and Troublesome Knowledge: Linkages to Ways of Thinking and Practicing within the Disciplines, ETL Project Occasional report 4.* Retrieved October 27, 2008, from http://www.ed.ac.uk./etl/publications.html

Mizukami, M. D. (2002, July). *Learning from Cases and Bridging Some "Theory-Practice" Gaps.* Paper presented at the annual world assembly of the International Council on Education for Teaching, Amsterdam.

Moffett, D. (2001). *Using the Internet to Enhance Student Teaching and Field Experiences.* Paper presented at the annual meeting of the Mid-Western Educational Research Association, Chicago.

Olson, G. B. (2005). Team-Working in the Real-World. In Sankar, C. S., & Raju, P. K. (Eds.), *Introduction to Engineering through Case Studies* (4th ed., pp. 221–266). Anderson, SC: Tavenner Publishers.

Perez, J., & Murray, M. (2008, August). Keep Your IS Program Viable by Offering an IT Literacy Service Course: One Department's Response to Declining Enrollments. In *Proceedings of the AMCIS Conference*, Toronto, Canada.

Pittaway, L., & Cope, J. (2007, April). Simulating Entrepreneurial Learning: Integrating Experiential and Collaborative Approaches to Learning. *Management Learning, 38*(2), 211–233. doi:10.1177/1350507607075776

Razvi, S., & Allen, J. D. (2005, April). *The meaningfulness of case studies in an educational psychology class: Students' perspectives.* Paper presented at the annual meeting of the American Educational Research Association, Montreal, Canada.

Santhanam, R., Sasidharan, S., & Webster, J. (2008). Using Self-Regulatory Learning to Enhance E-Learning-Based Information Technology Training. *Information Systems Research, 19*(1), 26–47. doi:10.1287/isre.1070.0141

Savander-Ranne, C., Lunden, O.-P., & Kolari, S. (2008, November). An Alternative Teaching Method for Electrical Engineering Courses. *IEEE Transactions on Education, 51*(4), 423–431. doi:10.1109/TE.2007.912500

Shuman, L. J., Besterfield-Sacre, & McGourty, J. (2005). The ABET Professional Skills – Can They be Taught? Can they be Assessed? *Journal of Engineering Education, 94*(1), 41–56.

Slater, J. S., McCubbrey, D. J., & Scudder, R. A. (1995, September). Inside an Integrated MBA: An Information Systems View. *Management Information Systems Quarterly, 19*, 391–410. doi:10.2307/249601

Sudzina, M. R., & Sudzina, C. M. (2003, June-July). *Insights into Successfully Teaching with Cases On-Line: The View from Both Sides of the 'Net.* Paper presented at the annual meeting of the World Association for Case Method Research and Case Method Application, Bordeaux, France.

Taber, N. (2008). Emergency Response: Elearning for Paramedics and Firefighters. *Simulation & Gaming, 39*(4), 515. doi:10.1177/1046878107306669

Trauth, E. M., Farwell, D. W., & Lee, D. (1993, September). The IS Expectation Gap: Industry Expectations Versus Academic Preparation. *Management Information Systems Quarterly*, 293–307. doi:10.2307/249773

Turban, E., Rainer, K. R., & Potter, R. (2003). *Introduction to Information Technology*. New York: John Wiley & Sons.

Turner, R. M., & Grizzaffi, K. (2003, May). *Creative Alternatives for Service Learning: A Project-Based Approach.* Paper presented at the annual meeting of the Campus Compact National Center for Community Colleges, Scottsdale, AZ.

Weber, R. (2004). Some Implications of the year-2000 Era, Dot-com Era, and Offshoring for Information Systems Pedagogy. *Management Information Systems Quarterly, 28*(2), iii–xi.

This work was previously published in International Journal of Information and Communication Technology, Volume 6, Issue 3, edited by Lawrence A. Tomei, pp. 25-37, copyright 2010 by IGI Publishing (an imprint of IGI Global).

Chapter 19
Student Nurses' Perception on the Impact of Information Technology on Teaching and Learning

Nahed Kandeel
Mansoura University, Egypt

Youssreya Ibrahim
Umm Al Qura University, Saudi Arabia

ABSTRACT

This paper investigates student nurses' perceptions of the impact of using information technology (IT) on teaching and learning critical care nursing. This study was conducted at the Faculty of Nursing, Mansoura University, Egypt. The sample included 163 of fourth year Bachelor of Nursing students enrolled in a critical care nursing course during the first semester of the academic year 2007-2008. The data was collected using a questionnaire sheet that gathered information about student nurses' IT skills and use, perception of the access to and use of IT at Faculty of Nursing, perception of the impact of using IT on teaching and perception, and on the impact of using IT on learning the critical care nursing course. The findings indicate that nursing students had a positive perception on the impact of using IT on teaching and learning the critical care nursing course. Students wanted access to IT at the Faculty, and expressed their need for more training on using Internet and Microsoft PowerPoint, and for IT resources in classrooms.

INTRODUCTION

The current revolution in technology plays a major role in recent transformation of nursing education. IT raised the expectations of both students and teachers. Chalk and blackboard are no longer

DOI: 10.4018/978-1-61350-468-0.ch019

enough for nursing students' education. The traditional approach of education, which assumes that the teacher is the sole source of knowledge and deposits it into passive students is no longer accepted (Freire, 1994).

Technology is seen as a catalyst for teaching and learning, and a driving force of shifting towards an open learning (Sandholtz et al., 1997). It affects the way teachers teach and students learn (Thompson et al., 2003). IT creates new ways of thinking, learning and solving problems for students (Girl & Chong, 1998). It allows students to be more independent and responsible learners, and more interactive in communication with their colleagues (Schoech, 2000). It also encourages teachers to develop their skills and use computer technology to maximize student learning (Keengwe, 2007). Hence, IT is rapidly becoming an integral part of nursing education.

Literature highlighted the need for integrating IT into nursing education (Clark, 1998; Lowry & Johnson, 1999). In fact, IT has been extensively used in nursing education in the United States of America and Europe (Birx et al., 1996; Clark, 1998; Connolly & Elfrink, 2002; Rhodes, 2005; Wilson, 2002). In 1992, the American Nursing Association (ANA) recognized nursing informatics as a distinct specialty area within nursing. In 1994 the ANA defined nursing informatics as *"the specialty that integrates nursing science, computer science, and information science in identifying, collecting, processing and managing data and information to support nursing practice, administration, education, research and the expansion of nursing knowledge" (p. 3).* In Britain, the NHSIA (2001) has emphasized the importance of technology integration in preregistration education, and has listed computer knowledge and IT competencies required of nurses. Similarly, the Australian Nursing Federation, together with Royal College of Nursing Australia recommended the development of national information technology and information management competency standards for nurses, and the adoption of a competency model (Hegney et al., 2007). This actually emphasizes the importance of IT skills for nurses' professional development and advancement (Fetter, 2009).

IT is considered as an important part of contemporary health care service delivery and professional nursing practice (Kenny, 2002). Hence, integrating IT into nursing education and developing nursing students IT skills were seen as a means for improving the quality of nursing care.

Increasingly, IT is playing a very important role in daily nursing practice. The use of computerized patient documentation systems is important to patient operations and safety, particularly in an environment that relies on IT (Ornes & Gassert, 2007). For example, in the intensive care unit which is a high technology environment, nurses need to be competent in dealing with machines that sound an alarm when their patients' vital signs go in dangerous directions (McBride, 2005). In order for nurses to be able to deal with such technology effectively and safely, they need to develop their IT skills (Bond, 2007).

The use of IT in nursing education has received increasing attention over the recent years in Egypt. In response to the recommendations of the Ministry of Higher Education to improve the quality of education through adoption of new teaching methods and advanced technology, Critical Care Nursing Department (CCND) at Faculty of Nursing, Mansoura University was one of the pioneers in using IT as a tool for teaching and learning critical care nursing course (CCNC). Educators used IT as a means for improving learning, enhancing student engagement and making critical care nursing education more interesting and convenient.

According to the literature, positive IT outcomes in education depend greatly on teachers, students and availability of technology resources. Teachers' IT skills, teaching style and attitude influence the effective use of IT in classroom (Webster & Hackley, 1997). Additionally, the success of using IT depends at a considerable extent on students' acceptance and use of IT in learning (Van Raaij & Schepers, 2008). Students' perception of the impact of IT is central to the educational process, and shapes the direction of its future use. Understanding the impact of IT informs us about its value for students, and suggests ways in which technology implementation can be enhanced and supported (Price & Oliver, 2007). In the absence of published information about the impact of using IT in nursing education in Egypt, this study was designed to address this area.

PURPOSE OF THE STUDY

The main purpose of this study was to investigate student nurses' perception of the impact of using IT on teaching and learning of critical care nursing.

METHODS

Study Design

The study had a cross sectional descriptive design.

Setting

This study was carried out at Faculty of Nursing, Mansoura University, Egypt.

Sample

The sample included all fourth year Bachelor of Nursing students enrolled in CCNC during the first semester of the academic year 2007-2008, who accepted to participate in the study (n = 163 out of 180). The response rate was 90.5%.

The Study Tool

The research instrument used in this study was a questionnaire developed from *et al* relevant literature (Girl & Chong, 1998; Draude & Brace, 2000; Gupta & Houtz, 2000; Chao et al., 2003; Valdez, 2006). It is composed of four sections. The first section (Table 1) collects information about student nurses' IT skills and use. The second section (Table 2) focuses on student nurses' perception of the access to and use of IT at Faculty of Nursing. The third section (Table 3) assesses student nurses' perception of the impact of using IT on

Table 1. Student nurses' IT skills and use

Item	Frequency	%
Since when you are using IT?		
Never	16	9.8
Less than one year	86	52.8
From 1-2 years	30	18.4
More than 3 years	14	8.6
What are your sources to access IT?		
None	12	7.4
Home	43	26.4
College	22	13.5
Friends	17	10.4
Internet Café	69	42.3
Which of the following IT skills do you possess?		
None	43	26.4
Word processing	40	24.5
PowerPoint	15	9.2
Internet	40	24.5
Electronic mail	8	4.9
All of the above	15	9.2
Others (computer games)	2	1.2
How did you gain computer skills?		
Computer classes at Faculty	20	12.3
Friends & relatives	63	38.6
Self learning	35	21.5
All of the above	6	1.2
Others: no computer skills	39	26.4

teaching CCNC, and the fourth section (Table 4) addresses student nurses' perception of the impact of using IT on learning CCNC. The second, third and fourth sections included 22 items, structured as statements, in the form of a 5-point likert scale from 1 to 5, where 5 refers to "strongly agree", 4 refers to "agree", 3 for "uncertain", 2 for "disagree" and 1 refers to "strongly disagree". For these three sections, students were asked to indicate the degree to which they agree or disagree with the proposed statements by checking one of five alternatives ranging from strongly disagree to strongly agree.

The questionnaire was reviewed by three experts in the filed of education technology from the Communication and Information Technology Center. Based on their comments and feedback, some items were revised and rephrased to improve clarity. The tool was developed in English and translated into Arabic. To ensure the validity of the translation, back translation technique was used (Honig, 1997; Birbili, 2000). The translated questionnaire was reviewed by a lecturer from Faculty of Education, English Department.

Alpha Crombach test (Cronbach, 1951, 1970) was used to test the reliability of the tool. The closer the alpha is to 1.0, the more reliable the test is. In this study, Alpha score for the 22 items of the tool (sections 2, 3 & 4) was 0.80 which confirms the tool reliability.

Table 2. Student nurses' perception of access to and use of IT at Faculty of Nursing

Item	Frequency	%
1- All students should have access to computers at the Faculty		
Strongly disagree	0	0
Disagree	0	0
Uncertain	1	0.6
Agree	29	17.8
Strongly agree	133	81.6
2- Students should have access the Internet at Faculty to collect information for their assignments		
Strongly disagree	0	0
Disagree	0	0
Uncertain	5	3.1
Agree	40	24.5
Strongly agree	118	72.4
3- Computer advisor should be available all the time to assist students when needed		
Strongly disagree	0	0
Disagree	0	0
Uncertain	3	1.8
Agree	45	27.6
Strongly agree	115	70.6
4- Training programs must be arranged for students on how to use the Internet and Microsoft Power-Point		
Strongly disagree	0	0
Disagree	1	0.6
Uncertain	4	2.5
Agree	35	21.5
Strongly agree	123	75.5
5- Each classroom must be equipped with IT equipment and resources		
Strongly disagree	1	0.6
disagree	2	1.2
Uncertain	2	1.2
Agree	35	21.5
Strongly agree	123	75.5
Overall mean scores X ± SD	23.3±1.4	

Table 3. Student nurses' perception of the impact of using IT on teaching Critical Care Nursing Course

Item	Frequency	%
1- Using IT in classroom enhances teaching CCN		
Strongly disagree	0	0
Disagree	1	.6
Uncertain	4	2.5
Agree	84	51.5
Strongly agree	74	45.4
2- Using IT in classroom allows teachers to present information in a variety of formats		
Strongly disagree	0	0
Disagree	0	0
Uncertain	3	1.9
Agree	74	45.4
Strongly agree	85	52.1
3- Using IT in classroom helps students to visualize critical care lecture materials which makes learning more interesting		
Strongly disagree	0	0
Disagree	0	0
Uncertain	7	4.3
Agree	59	36.2
Strongly agree	97	59.5
4- IT provides more opportunities to interactions between students and teachers		
Strongly disagree	3	1.8
Disagree	17	10.4
Uncertain	38	23.3
Agree	76	46.6
Strongly agree	29	17.8
5- Using IT at classroom saves teachers' time and effort		
Strongly disagree	1	.6
Disagree	3	1.8
Uncertain	10	6.1
Agree	71	43.6
Strongly agree	78	47.9
6- IT is a useful tool only if the teacher is able to master technology		
Strongly disagree	2	1.2
Disagree	2	1.2
Uncertain	12	7.4
Agree	85	52.1
Strongly agree	62	38.0
7- Using IT is ineffective when the teacher uses it only as a mean for reading the lecture		
Strongly disagree	9	5.5
Disagree	22	13.5
Uncertain	14	8.6
Agree	72	44.2
Strongly agree	46	28.2
Total mean score X ± SD	28.5±5.7	

Data Collection

For the purpose of this study, IT was used in teaching CCNC in a form of PowerPoint presentations in the classroom, videos of critical care nursing procedures, access to the Faculty Electronic lab, and access to relevant web sites. Students were divided into fourteen groups, each group included from 12 to 13 students. Each group was assigned to prepare a project relevant to critical care procedures or topics using IT. The proposed activities involved developing a Maquette, providing

Table 4. Student nurses' perception of the impact of using IT on learning Critical Care Nursing Course

Item	Frequency	%
1- Using IT in critical care nursing course classes attracts students' attention and enhances receiving of information		
Strongly disagree	0	0
Disagree	6	3.7
Uncertain	2	1.2
Agree	109	66.9
Strongly agree	46	28.2
2- Using IT in presenting critical care subjects in classroom stimulates students' critical thinking & imagination		
Strongly disagree	2	1.2
Disagree	10	6.1
Uncertain	31	19.0
Agree	87	53.4
Strongly agree	33	20.2
3- IT encourages students' active participation in their learning		
Strongly disagree	1	0.6
Disagree	25	15.3
Uncertain	37	22.7
Agree	80	49.1
Strongly agree	20	12.3
4- Using IT provides students with a variety of learning styles		
Strongly disagree	0	0
Disagree	18	11.0
Uncertain	18	11.0
Agree	101	62.0
Strongly agree	26	16.0
5- IT allows students to exchange ideas and information with other colleagues		
Strongly disagree	12	7.4
Disagree	49	30.1
Uncertain	44	27
Agree	37	22.7
Strongly agree	21	12.9
6- Using IT allows access to large amount of information at low cost		
Strongly disagree	21	12.9
Disagree	64	39.3
Uncertain	25	15.3
Agree	40	24.5
Strongly agree	13	8.0
7- Using IT in classroom is a useful mean for students in preparing their assignments and presenting them in a variety of formats		
Strongly disagree	2	1.2
Disagree	13	8.0
Uncertain	22	13.5
Agree	95	58.3
Strongly agree	31	19.0
8- IT allows students to be creative in preparing their assignments		
Strongly disagree	2	1.2
Disagree	10	6.1
Uncertain	15	9.2
Agree	86	52.8
Strongly agree	50	30.7

continued on following page

Table 4. Continued

Item	Frequency	%
9- IT encourages students to be producers of information and not only passive receivers		
Strongly disagree	2	1.2
Disagree	12	7.4
Uncertain	27	16.6
Agree	85	52.1
Strongly agree	37	22.7
10- Mastering IT enhances student's confidence when presenting their assignment		
Strongly disagree	0	0
Disagree	9	5.5
Uncertain	20	12.3
Agree	94	57.7
Strongly agree	40	24.5
Total mean score X ± SD	**41.4±8.3**	

a PowerPoint presentation or designing a Poster presentation. Considering the fact that not all students were competent in using computers and Internet, a facilitator from critical care faculty staff was assigned to supervise and instruct each group. Students were given 5 weeks to complete the assignments and provide a presentation for their product. Each project was evaluated by a three- member committee from critical care nursing department.

The questionnaire was piloted on 10 nursing students. The aim of the pilot study was to assess the clarity of the statements and make necessary amendments prior to the main study. Students of the piloting group were asked to read the statements carefully, complete the questionnaire and highlight statements that require more clarification. Based upon students' comments, some of the statements were rephrased. For the main study, the questionnaire was handed out to students during the last lecture in CCNC in January 2008 by an assistant lecturer who was not involved in teaching fourth year program. Students were given 20 minutes to fill in the questionnaire. The completed questionnaires were collected by the assistant lecturer.

Ethical Considerations

A permission to conduct the study was obtained from the Dean of Faculty of Nursing, before inviting students to participate in the research. Students were provided with information about the study. They were assured that participation in the study was purely voluntary, and that those who declined involvement in this research would not be penalized or affected in any way. Data were collected anonymously.

Data Analysis

Data were analyzed using the SPSS Version 9.0. Statistical methods used included frequency, percentage, mean and standard deviation.

RESULTS

Student Nurses' IT Skills and Use

Results in Table 1 show that about half of participants (52.8%) reported using IT for less than one year, 8.6% used IT for more than 3 years and 9.8% did not use it at all. The primary source of access to IT was the Internet Café (42.3%). Other sources, in order of ranking, were home (26.4%), college (13.5%) and friends (10.4%), and 7.4% reported having no IT access. Students reported having different IT skills, such as word processing (24.5%), Internet use (24.5%), PowerPoint (9.2%) and Electronic mail (4.9%), and 26.4% of students reported having no IT skills. Students acquired IT skills from a variety of sources including friends and relatives (38.6%), self taught (21.5%) and computer classes (12.3%).

Student Nurses' Perception of the ACCESS to and Use of IT at the Faculty

Results in Table 2 illustrate that the majority strongly agreed or agreed that all students must have access to computers (99.4%) and Internet at Faculty of Nursing (96.9%). Students emphasized the need for the availability of a computer advisor all the time to assist students when needed (98.2%). They also highlighted the need for more training on using Internet and Microsoft PowerPoint (97%), and IT equipment and resources in each classroom (97%). For interpretation, the total score for the second section (student nurses' access to and use of IT at Faculty of Nursing) is 25. Positive perception is reflected by 70% (17.5) or above, 50% (12.5) neutral and below 50% negative perception. Overall, student nurses' perception of the use of and access to IT at Faculty of Nursing is positive (with the total mean score X ± SD 23.6±1.4).

Students Nurses' Perception of the Impact of Using IT on Teaching CCNC

Results in Table 3 show that the majority of students strongly agreed or agreed that using IT enhanced teaching CCNC (96.9%), allowed teachers to present information in a variety of formats (97.5%) and helped students to visualize lecture materials which made learning more interesting (95.7%). Students believed that IT was useful in

teaching only when the teacher was able to master technology (90.1%) and was ineffective when the teacher used it only as a means for reading the lecture (72.4%). Despite most students (64.4%) strongly agreed or agreed that IT provides more opportunities for interaction between students and teachers, a considerable number of students were either uncertain (23.3%) about this issue, or disagreed with this statement (10.4%). The total score of the third section (student nurses' perception of the impact of using IT on teaching CCNC) is 35. Positive perception is reflected by 70% (24.5) or above, 50% (17.5) neutral and below 50% negative perception. In general, IT has a positive impact on teaching CCNC from student nurses' perspectives (with the total mean score X ± SD 28.5±5.7).

Student Nurses' Perception of the Impact of Using IT on Learning CCNC

Table 4 illustrates that most students strongly agreed or agreed that using IT in classroom attracts students' attention and enhances receiving of information (95.1%), stimulates critical thinking and imagination (73.6%), and provides a variety of learning styles (78%). The majority reported that IT was a useful tool for collecting information for their assignments (77.3%) and preparing them in a creative way (83.5%), and for enhancing students' confidence when presenting their work (82.2%). Despite the general agreement about the impact of IT on learning CCNC, there was a considerable uncertainty concerning whether IT encourages students' active participation in their learning (22.7%), allows students to exchange ideas and information with other colleagues (27%), or stimulates students' critical thinking (19%). About half of students (52.5%) believed that using IT was costly. The total score for section D (the impact of IT on learning CCN) is 50, positive perception is reflected by 70% (35) or above, 50% (25) or above neutral and below 50%

Table 5. Correlation between students' years of experience of using IT and the perception of the impact of IT on teaching and learning Critical Care Nursing Course

Years of experience		Impact of IT
P	r	
.013	.194*	Using IT in classroom enhances teaching CCNC
.036	.164*	Using IT in classroom allow teachers to present information in a variety of formats
.092	.132	IT provides more opportunities to interactions between students and teachers
.023	.178*	IT is a useful tool only if the teacher able to master technology
.911	.009	Using IT is ineffective because the teacher depends on it as a mean for reading the lecture
.006	.215**	Using IT at classroom attracts students' attention and enhances receiving of information
.028	.173*	Using IT in presenting subjects in classrooms stimulates students' critical thinking & imagination
.222	.096	IT encourages students active participation in their learning
.000	.273**	Using IT provides students with a variety of learning styles
.001	.260**	IT allows students to exchange ideas and information and web sites with other colleagues
.865	.013	Using IT allows access to large amount of information at low cost
.036	.164**	IT allows students to be creative in preparing their assignments
.062	.146	IT encourages students to be producers of information and not only passive receivers
.000	.329**	Mastering IT enhances student's confidence when presenting their assignment

(less than 25) negative perception. In general, IT has a positive impact on students' learning of critical care nursing course from student nurses' perspectives (with the total mean score X ± SD 41.4±8.3).

The total score of sections 2, 3 and 4 is 110. Positive perception is reflected by 70% (77) or above, 50% (55) or above neutral and below 50% (less than 55) negative perception. Overall, the use of IT in teaching CCNC has a positive impact on the process of teaching and learning from student nurses' perspectives (with the total mean score X ± SD 89.4±8.9).

Results show a positive correlation between students' years of IT experience, and their perception of the impact of IT on the process of teaching and learning (Table 5). Moreover, students' IT skills had a positive significant correlation with students' perception of the impact of IT on enhancing teaching, exchanging ideas and information with colleagues, preparing and presenting assign-

ments, creativity in preparing assignments and enhancing students' confidence when presenting their work (Table 6).

DISCUSSION

The results of this study reveal that using IT in classroom has a positive impact on the process of teaching and learning from student nurses' perspectives. Students strongly expressed the need to access computers and Internet at the Faculty for preparing their assignments. They demanded training programs on using the Internet and Microsoft PowerPoint. This could indicate that the current computer classes at the Faculty are inadequate for developing students' IT skills. Student nurses also emphasized the need for IT resources in all classrooms. The data pointed to an important fact, that is, the ability of nursing faculty to master technology made IT a useful

Student Nurses' Perception on the Impact of Information Technology on Teaching and Learning

Table 6. Correlation between student nurses' IT skills and their perception of the impact of IT on teaching and learning Critical Care Nursing Course

Students' IT skills		Impact of IT
P	r	
.013	.194*	Using IT in classroom enhances teaching CCN
.052	.153	Using IT in classroom allows teachers to present information in a variety of formats
.355	.073	Using IT in classroom helps students to visualize lecture materials and make learning more interesting
.222	.096	IT provides more opportunities to interactions between students and teachers
.982	.002	IT is a useful tool only if the teacher able to master technology
.378	-.070	Using IT is ineffective because the teacher depends on it as a mean for reading the lecture
.640	.037	Using IT in classroom attracts students' attention and enhances receiving of information
.602	-.041	Using IT in presenting subjects classrooms stimulates students' critical thinking & imagination
.482	.055	IT encourages students' active participation in their learning
.068	.144	Using IT provides students with a variety of learning styles
.032	.168*	IT allows students to exchange ideas and information an web sites with other colleagues
.571	-.045	Using IT allows access to large amount of information at low cost
.025	.175*	Using IT at classroom is a useful means for students in preparing their assignments and present them in a variety of formats
.002	.243*	IT allows students to be creative in preparing their assignments
.686	-.032	IT encourages students to be producers of information and not only passive receivers
.000	.304**	Mastering IT enhances student's confidence when presenting their assignment

teaching tool. This is in the same line with Fetter's (2009) findings which illustrated student nurses' belief that faculty should possess IT skills to be proficient teachers and role models. It actually reflects the importance of developing teachers' IT skills on the outcome of students' learning. This supports Fabry and Higgs (1997), and Keengwe (2007) suggestion of investing time, money and technology resources in teachers who have greatest impact on student education. Ornes and Gassert (2007) also highlighted the need to increase faculty staff knowledge and understanding of nursing informatics competencies required from beginning nurses.

The results showed the benefits of using IT from student nurses' perspective. Using IT enhanced teaching CCNC, allowed teachers to present information in a variety of formats and made CCNC more interesting. Besides, it attracted students' attention in classroom, enhanced their reception of information, stimulated their critical thinking and imagination, and provided them with a variety of learning style. IT was also a useful tool for students in preparing their assignments and presenting them confidently. These findings are congruent with the results of other studies which examined students' perceptions and attitude towards computer technology and Internet in education (Schoech, 2000; Havelka, 2003; Kvavik & Caruso 2005; Li & Kirkup, 2007; Sagin Simsek, 2008). In Turkey, Sagin Simsek (2008) found that students were satisfied with the application of information and communication technologies in their reading courses and had positive attitudes towards online courses. Schoech (2000) found that on line courses helped students to be more independent and responsible learners and using the Internet made them more interactive with their colleagues.

Interestingly, the primary source for students' access to IT was the internet Café and only 13.5% of students used the college IT resources. It could be partly due to the limited IT resources located for students at Faculty which made them pay to use the IT in internet Café. This actually explains why half of students considered IT costly. Unexpectedly, 26.4% of students had no computer skills at all, only 12.3% gained computer skills from attending computer class at the Faculty and 21.5% were self taught. These are very interesting findings considering the fact that Faculty of Nursing students do study computer sciences in the first, second and third year for four semesters.

CONCLUSION

This study contributes to the body of research that provides evidence for the benefits of IT for nursing students' teaching and learning. The findings show that nursing students have positive perception of the impact of using IT in teaching and learning CCNC. It was surprising to see such positive attitudes towards IT despite students' inadequate access to IT at the Faculty. The study highlights the need for computer courses that develop nursing students' IT skills and meet their needs. Successful use of IT in classroom can not only be achieved by students' positive perception of IT, but also by nursing faculty's mastery of technology, and availability of computer technology in classrooms.

RECOMMENDATIONS

1. Improvement of IT resources at Faculty of Nursing to meet students' needs.
2. More integration of IT in teaching and learning.

3. More attention to computer courses aims, content and practical applications.
4. While this study investigated the impact of IT on the quality of teaching and learning from the perspectives of students, future research could consider adoption of IT from the perspectives of teachers.

LIMITATIONS OF THE STUDY

This study used a self report questionnaire which is a strong tool for providing insight on individuals' perception, attitude, feelings and other information that can not easily be observed (Talbot, 1995). However, this method may limit participants' responses into specific choices, and may not give an opportunity to determine why people perceive things in a certain way.

REFERENCES

American Nurses Association. (1994). *Scope of Practice for Nursing Informatics*. Washington, DC: American Nurses Publishing.

Birbili, M. (2000). *Translating from one language to another. Social Research Update, 31*. Surrey, UK: University of Surrey.

Birx, E., Castleberry, K., & Perry, K. (1996). Integration of laptop computer technology into an undergraduate nursing course. *Computers in Nursing, 14*, 108–112.

Bond, C. (2007). Nurses' requirement for information technology: a challenge for educators. *International Journal of Nursing Science, 44*, 1075–1078. doi:10.1016/j.ijnurstu.2007.01.009

Chao, T., Bulter, T., & Ryan, P. (2003). Providing a technology edge for liberal arts students. *Journal of Information Technology Education, 2*, 331–347.

Clark, D. (1998). Course redesign. Incorporating an Internet web site into an existing nursing class. *Computers in Nursing, 16,* 219–222.

Connolly, P. M., & Elfrink, V. L. (2002). Using Information Technology in Community-Based Psychiatric Nursing Education. *Home Health Care Management & Practice, 14,* 344–352. doi:10.1177/1084822302014005006

Cronbach, L. J. (1951). Coefficient alpha and the internal structure of tests. *Psychometrika, 16,* 297–334. doi:10.1007/BF02310555

Cronbach, L. J. (1970). *Essentials of psychological testing* (3rd ed.). New York: Harper & Row.

Draude, B., & Brace, S. (2000). *Assessing the impact of technology on teaching and learning: student perspectives.* Murfreesboro, TN: Middle Tennessee State University. Retrieved May 21, 2007, From http://www.mtsu.edu/~itconf/proceed99/brace.html

Fabry, D., & Higgs, J. (1997). Barriers to the effective use of technology in education. *Journal of Educational Computing, 17*(4), 385–395.

Fetter, M. (2009). Curriculum Strategies to Improve Baccalaureate Nursing Information Technology Outcomes. *The Journal of Nursing Education, 48*(2), 86–90. doi:10.3928/01484834-20090201-05

Freire, P. (1994). *Pedagogy of the oppressed.* London: Continuum.

Girl, T., & Chong, L. (1998). Student teachers' perception of information technology and creativity. In Waas, M. (Ed.), *Enhanced learning: Challenge of integrating thinking and Information Technology into the Curriculum* (*Vol. 2,* pp. 584–591).

Gupta, U., & Houtz, L. (2000). High school students' perceptions of information technology kills and carrers. *Journal of Information Technology, 14*(4), 2–8.

Havelka, D. (2003). Students' beliefs and attitudes towards information technology. In *Proceedings of the ISECON,* San Diego, CA.

Hegney, D., Buikstra, E., Eley, R., Fallon, T., Gilmore, V., & Soar, J. (2007). *Nurses and information technology. An Australian Nursing Federation project funded by the Australian Government Department of Health and Ageing.* Commonwealth of Australia. Retrieved February 2, 2009, from http://www.anf.org.au/it_project/PDF/IT_Project.pdf

Honig, H. (1997). Positions, power and practice: functionalist approach and translation quality assessment. *Current Issues in Language and Society, 4*(1), 15–19.

Keengwe, J. (2007). Faculty integration of technology into instruction and students' perceptions of computer technology to improve student learning. *Journal of Information Technology Education, 6,* 169–179.

Kenny, A. (2002). Online learning: enhancing nurse education? *Journal of Advanced Nursing, 38*(2), 127–135. doi:10.1046/j.1365-2648.2002.02156.x

Kvavik, R., & Caruso, J. (2005). *ECAR study of students and information technology: convenience, connection, control and learning.* Boulder, Co: Educause Center for applied Research. Retrieved May 5, 2007, from http://www.educause.edu/LibraryDetailPage/666?ID=ERS0506

Li, N., & Kirkup, G. (2007). Gender and culture differences in Internet use: a study of China and the UK. *Computers & Education, 48,* 301–317. doi:10.1016/j.compedu.2005.01.007

Lowry, M., & Johnson, M. (1999). Computer assisted learning: the potential for teaching and assessing in nursing. *Nurse Education Today, 19,* 521–526. doi:10.1054/nedt.1999.0390

McBride, A. (2005). Nursing and the informatics revolution. *Nursing Outlook*, *53*(4), 183–191. doi:10.1016/j.outlook.2005.02.006

NHSIA. (2001). Health informatics competency profiles for the NHS. In *Proceedings of the NHS Information Authority, Ways of Working with Information Programme*, Winchester, UK.

Ornes, L., & Gassert, C. (2007). Computer Competencies in a BSN Program. *Research Briefs*, *46*(2), 75–78.

Price, S., & Oliver, M. (2007). A framework for conceptualizing the impact of technology on teaching and learning. *Educational Technology & Sociology*, *10*(1), 16–27.

Rhodes, M. L., & Curran, C. (2005). Use of the human patient simulator to teach clinical judgment skills in a baccalaureate program. *Computers, Informatics, Nursing*, *23*, 256–262. doi:10.1097/00024665-200509000-00009

Sagin Simsek, C. (2008). Students' attitudes towards integration of ICTs in a reading course: a case in Turkey. *Computers & Education*, *51*, 200–211. doi:10.1016/j.compedu.2007.05.002

Sandholtz, J. H., Ringstaff, C., & Dwyer, D. (1997). *Teaching with technology: Creating student-centered classroom*. New York: Teachers College Press.

Schoech, D. (2000). Teaching over the internet: results of one doctoral course. *Research on Social Work Practice*, *10*(4), 467–487.

Talbot, L. (1995). *Principles and practice of nursing research*. St. Louis, MO: Missouri.

Thompson, A. D., Schmidt, D. A., & Davis, N. E. (2003). Technology collaborative for simultaneous renewal in teacher education. *Educational Technology Research and Development*, *51*(1), 73–89. doi:10.1007/BF02504519

Valdez, G. (2006). *Critical Issue: Technology: a catalyst for teaching and learning in the classroom. Learning Point Associate*. Retrieved June 12, 2007, from http://www.ncrel.org/sdrs/areas/issues/methods/technlgy/te600.htm

Van Raaij, E. M., & Schepers, J. J. (2008). The acceptance and use of a virtual learning environment in China. *Computers & Education*, *50*, 838–852. doi:10.1016/j.compedu.2006.09.001

Webster, J., & Hackley, P. (1997). Teaching effectiveness in technology-mediated distance learning. *Academy of Management Journal*, *40*(6), 1282–1309. doi:10.2307/257034

Wilson, S. (2002). Development of a personal digital assistant (PDA) as point-of-care technology in nursing education. PDA cortex. *The Journal of Mobile Informatics*. Retrieved June 27, 2007, from http://www.pdacortex.com/pda_nursing_education.htm

This work was previously published in International Journal of Information and Communication Technology, Volume 6, Issue 3, edited by Lawrence A. Tomei, pp. 38-50, copyright 2010 by IGI Publishing (an imprint of IGI Global).

Chapter 20
Technology Integration and Urban Schools:
Implications for Instructional Practices

Terry T. Kidd
Texas A & M University, USA

Jared Keengwe
University of North Dakota, USA

ABSTRACT

With the call for educational reform in American public schools, various school districts have embarked on the process of reforming classroom instructional practices through technology to enhance quality education and student learning. This article explores the implications for educational technology practices within the context of urban schools. Additionally, this article highlights the need for administrators, policy makers and other educational stakeholders to reflect on effective ways to eliminate inequities and the gaps that exist between high and low Social Economic Status (SES) schools and teachers related to practices, resources, training, and professional development.

INTRODUCTION

The restructuring of the educational learning environments within the past decade has produced a growing emphasis on a type of learner that has been characterized as the urban learner. The urban learner is best defined in the context of socially-related problems including poverty, structural and institutional racism, class, and gender bias (Obiakor & Beachum, 2005). These learners tend to fall behind socially, developmentally, economically and academically (Obiakor & Beachum,

2005). While public urban schools have realized some success in Internet access and technology resources (Parsad & Jones, 2005), evidently, over time, it is far easier to acquire hardware, software, and access than it is to capture the potential of technology to bring about significant student learning outcomes (Cuban, 2001; Keengwe, 2007; Oppenheimer, 2003).

The major challenge facing teachers is how to integrate technology to help students learn well and become actively involved in the teaching and learning process (Bauer & Kenton, 2005;

DOI: 10.4018/978-1-61350-468-0.ch020

Keengwe, 2007; Tulloch, 2000). For technology to have a greater impact within the public educational system, teachers and students alike must not only have access to technology, but also have access to technology in a contextual matter that is culturally relevant, responsive, and meaningful to their educational practices. To this end, technology tools have great potential to narrow the achievement gap of selected student groups in the US educational system (Kulik, 2003; Magolda, 2006).

Amidst the euphoria and craze over the power and potential of educational technology to transform the way students learn, communicate, and the ways in which societies function, there is an increasing debate as to who has access and the consequences of that access. This debate has serious implications for classroom instruction, specifically for teachers and students who work and learn in the low Social Economic Status (SES) school contexts. Students from higher income families have been found to use computers in school and in their homes more frequently than students from economically disadvantaged families (Becker, 2001; Fulton & Sibley, 2003; Jin & Bagaka, 2005). This trend continues to put low SES teachers and students who belong to racially diverse or economically disenfranchised communities at an educational disadvantage.

The educational and academic underachievement of students in low SES schools has been well-documented (Council of Great City Schools, 2008; Johnson, 2002). Despite the constraints on public school funding in most states, schools continue to devote an increasing percentage of their annual budgets to technology resources (Oppenheimer, 2003). However, evidence of digital divide, parallel to historical disparities, continues to distinguish low SES schools from their affluent counterparts (Guttentag & Eilers, 2004; National Center for Education Statistics, 2004). Further, although there are on-going government initiatives to help bridge the information

and technological divide, there exist disparities in the ability of American school-children to access and use modern educational technologies.

A historical measure of digital equity has been based on the ratio of the number of computers divided by the number of students. However, a more recent measure involves determining levels and quality of Internet access, quality in equipment, and quality of use. A different dimension of this problem relates to questions about differences in home access to technology that might impact low SES student achievement. Studies conducted by Bauer and Kenton (2005); Becker (2001), and Finneran (2000) established that low SES schools are more likely to use technology for drill and practice, whereas high SES schools use technology in innovative teaching strategies. Further, high SES students are more likely to use technology for school assignments, e-mails, and relevant educational programs. Pinar (2004) reports that computer technology is often used for remediation, to drill, and to demoralize students into passing standardized test, contrary to promoting quality teaching and active student learning. Further, the current use of technology such as computer tools in low SES schools generally helps its users (students) to become disengaged and alienated subjects, lowering their motivation to learn. Additional supply of computer tools and software cannot change the face of learning; many questions remain unanswered as to whether or not the large financial investments in technology has impacted student learning (Burnham, Miller, & Ray, 2000). Therefore, there is need to motivate, train, and equip educators with the skills necessary to enhance proper use and integration of computer tools into instruction (Keengwe, 2007).

A National Consideration of Digital Equity report prepared by International Society for Technology in Education (ISTE, 2007) in collaboration with Macro International suggests that when considering the role of technology in development of the 21st-century learner, digital equity is more than a comparable delivery of goods and services, but a fair distribution based on students' needs. The report offers suggestions for addressing the issue of digital issue such as technology training workshops for teachers. The report also recommends the following five strategies toward digital equity:

A. Legitimize the significant role culture plays in students' educational experience
B. Continue to challenge perceptions about the role of technology in education
C. Encourage others to recognize the critical link between technology, professional development and classroom practice
D. Create opportunities for students to access technology outside the classroom
E. Continue to seek funding for technology and training in spite of challenges.

PURPOSE OF STUDY

Although previous studies have established a pattern for questioning technology use and possible disparities in the past, most of these studies rely on data collected in the mid to late 1990's. As a result, there is need to explore current practices related to technology use and digital equity. Effective use of technology in schools cannot be fulfilled by providing more hardware and software as is the case in most low SES schools that are provided with tools and not strategies for use (Kidd, 2009). Indeed, schools need to equip teachers with the skills necessary for effective use of educational related technologies in their classroom practices.

The purpose of this study was to examine technology practices in relation to how teachers utilize technology to support quality teaching in both lower and higher SES schools and the components that support or hinder such practices.

Evidence from this study highlights the need for major educational stakeholders to reflect on effective ways to eliminate inequities and the gaps that exist between high and low Social Economic Status (SES) schools and teachers related to practices, resources, training, and professional development.

METHODOLOGY

The data for the study was drawn from the base year of the Educational Longitudinal Survey of 2002-2006 (ELS: 02). The ELS: 02 is a national survey administered by National Center for Educational Statistics to provide an overall picture of current educational experience of secondary (9-12) students and teachers in the U.S. The survey has four sub components completed by students, teachers, parents and school administrators. The survey included 1,052 public and private schools representing about 12,000 students across the country.

For this study, the teacher and administrator survey data were used. The total number of teachers that participated in the survey was about 7,322. The teacher survey provided items used to measure how much training teachers had received in technology use. These items were used to measure teacher training: (a) received training in basic computer skills, (b) received training in the use of the Internet, (c) received training in integrating technology in the curriculum, (d) received training in software applications, e) received training in use of Internet, (f) received training in use of other technology and, (g) received follow-up or advanced training. The outcome measures for these items were dichotomous, yes or no.

The teacher survey also measured Internet and Technology use in Instructions. The item provided on the teacher survey to measure this outcome were: (a) how often do you use the computer to create class presentations, (b) how often do you use WWW sites to plan lessons, (c) how often do you access model lesson plans from internet, (d) how often do you do research teaching on the internet, (e) how often do you take professional development courses on the internet, (f) how often do you download instructional software from the internet, (g) how often do you use the computer to give class presentations and, (h) how often do you use the computer to prepare multimedia presentations. The outcome measures for these items were on a four point Likert scale, ranging from "never" to "more than once a week."

Finally, the teacher survey measured how often teachers used technology to communicate between parents, students, and for administrative duties. The item provided on the teacher survey to measure this outcome were: (a) how often do you take professional development courses on the Internet, (b) how often to you use the computer to communicate with colleagues, (c) how often to you use the computer to communicate with parents, (d) how often to you use the computer to communicate with students, (e) how often do you use the computer for administrative records and, (f) how often to you use the computer to post homework and other information. The outcome measures for these items were also a four point Likert scale, ranging from "never" to "more than once a week."

In order to measure the socioeconomic level of the schools involved, the administrator survey was

used. School administrators were asked the report the percent on students at their schools that were eligible for a free lunch program. School percentages were then ranked according to eligibility. The distribution of these percent values were divided into three quartiles, ranging from lowest to high SES schools. They were about 3933 teachers from low SES schools, 2324 from middle SES schools and about 1065 teachers from high SES schools. A Pearson's chi-square test was used to determine if there was an association between technology training and use by teachers in the school with different socioeconomic status,

RESULTS

Eight three per cent (83%) of the teachers indicated they had received training in basic computer skills while 78.7% of the teachers indicated they had received training on software applications. The most frequent use of the computer by classroom teachers was to create class presentations. About eighty one percent (80.7%) of the teachers indicated that they used computers to create instructional materials more than several times a week. Few teachers (7%) indicated they used computers to prepare multimedia presentations more than once a week while others (6.5%) indicated they used computers to give class presentations as well as prepare multimedia presentations more than

Table 1. Percentage of teachers receiving training

Teacher Training N= 7322		
	Yes	No
Received training in basic computer skills	83.0%	17.0%
Received training in software applications	78.7%	21.3%
Received training in the use of Internet	78.6%	21.4%
Received training in the use of other technology tools	45.7%	54.3%
Received training in integrating technology in curriculum	76.4%	23.6%
Received follow-up or advanced training	43.2%	56.8%

once a week. Table 1 provides a summary of the percentage of teachers who received training on technology preparation and the ability to integrating technology in the curriculum they taught.

The most frequent use of the Internet was to use World Wide Web (WWW) sites to plan lessons. Forty five percent (44.5%) of the teachers indicated they used a www site more than a week. About sixteen percent (15.5%) of the teachers indicated that they used the Internet to access model lesson plans more than once a week. Similarly, some teachers (12.9%) indicated that they used the Internet more than once a week to research teaching. Finally, less than 10% of the teachers indicated they used the internet more than once a week for other items such as downloading instructional software and taking development courses on the Internet. Table 2 provides a summary of how often Internet and computers were used by classroom teachers.

The most frequent use of the computer in communication was for administrative purposes. A majority of the teachers (78.7%) reported using the computer for administrative purposes more

than once a week. Almost fifty three percent (52.9%) of the teachers indicated that they used the Internet for colleague discussions more than once a week. A similar number of the teachers (52.6%) indicated that they used the Internet for colleague discussions and to communicate with colleagues more than once a week. Some teachers (26%) indicated that they used the computer to communicate with students more than once a week. One fifth of the teachers (20.8%) indicated that they used the computer to post homework/information more than once a week. Finally, less than twenty percent of the teachers (18.8%) indicated that they used the computer to communicate with parents. Table 3 provides a summary of the teachers' reported use of the computers and Internet.

The results indicated that several differences (p<.001) exist in technology training teachers have received in high, median and low SES schools. Teachers from high SES school indicated a larger percent of them had received training in basic computer skills. Eighty four percent (84.1%) of the teachers from high SES school

Table 2. Reported internet and computers use by classroom teachers

Internet and Technology Use in Instructions N= 7322				
How often do…	Never	Less Than Once a Month	Between one a week and once a month	More than once a week
You use computers to create class presentations	2.4%	3.3%	13.6%	80.7%
You use the WWW sites to plan lessons	6.3%	16.1%	33.0%	44.5%
You access model lesson plans from the Internet	28.7%	30.8%	25.0%	15.5%
You research teaching on Internet	25.4%	34.3%	27.4%	12.9%
Teachers take professional development courses on the Internet?	88.5%	8.5%	2.0%	1.1%
You download instructional software from the Internet	59.1%	26.5%	11.9%	2.5%
You use computer to give class presentations	37.1%	33.7%	22.7%	6.5%
Students use computers to prepare multimedia presentations	38.2%	34.1%	20.7%	7.0%

Table 3. Teachers' use of the computers and internet

How often do you use...	Communication N = 7322			
	Never	Less Than Once a Month	Between once a week and once a month	More than once a week
The Internet for colleague discussions	17.5%	14.6%	15.0%	52.9%
Computer to communicate w/colleagues	18.3%	14.3%	14.8%	52.6%
Computers to communicate w/parents	41.9%	17.0%	22.3%	18.8%
Computers for administrative records	10.7%	4.6%	6.0%	78.7%
computers to communicate w/students	43.6%	16.5%	14.0%	25.9%
Computers to post homework/information	63.6%	9.4%	6.2%	20.8%

reported receiving training in basic computer skills compared to seventy nine percent (78.6%) of the teachers from low SES school.

There was a significant difference (p<.001) exist on the percent of teachers that received training on software applications across the three SES environments. Teachers from Middle level SES schools had the highest percent (85.3%) compared to 80.6% and 80.9% for Low and high SES teachers respectively. When asked if they had received training in the use of the Internet there was a significant difference (p<.001). Majority (83.7%) of the teachers from high SES schools reported they had received training compared to about seventy seven percent (77.2%) of the teachers from low SES schools.

A little over eighty percent (82.4%) of the teachers from middle SES school reported receiving training. When asked if they had received training in integrating technology in curriculum, teachers from middle class schools indicated they had received the most. In this case, 77.1% of the teachers from middle class schools compared to 75.6% and 72.6% for teachers in high and low SES schools. There were no other significant differences across the three SES groups on if teachers had received follow-up or advanced training. Table 4 provides a summary of teacher training on computers and technology uses reported across socioeconomics school levels.

The results indicated that several differences exist (p<.001). The highest use of computers across all three SES groups was how often the use computer to prepare multimedia presentations (e.g., video, graphics, animation, and audio to deliver lecture). Teachers from middle SES schools reported the highest percent usage. Eighty percent (80.4%) of these teachers reported using computer to prepare multimedia presentations more than once a week. Seventy seven percent (76.8%) of the high SES teachers and seventy five percent (75.3%) of the low SES teachers reported using computer to prepare multimedia presentations more than once a week. Teachers from high SES school indicated a larger percent of them use computers to create class presentations (i.e. graphics, audio, or video in isolation). Sixty four percent (64.4%) of the teachers from high SES school reported using computers to create class presentations more than once a week. Regarding teachers from low SES school about fifty eight percent (57.9%) of the teachers reported using computers to create class presentations more than once a week.

Fifty eight percent of the teachers from middle class schools reported using computers to create class presentations more than once a week. The group that reported using WWW sites to plan lessons the most were teachers from high SES schools. Nearly thirty eight percent (37.9) of the

Table 4. Teacher training on computers and technology uses

Professional Development and training in basic computer skills N=7322			
	Yes	No	Chi-Square
Received training in basic computer skills SES N = 3933 Low N = 2324 Middle N = 1065 High	78.6% 81.7% 84.1%	21.4% 18.3% 15.9%	24.5***
Received training in software applications SES N = 3933 Low N = 2324 Middle N = 1065 High	80.6% 85.3% 80.9%	19.4% 14.7% 19.1%	28.1***
Received training in the use of Internet SES N = 3933 Low N = 2324 Middle N = 1065 High	77.2% 82.4% 83.7%	22.8% 17.6% 16.3%	45.2***
Received training in the use of other technology SES N = 3933 Low N = 2324 Middle N = 1065 High	41.2% 42.2% 42.0%	58.1% 57.8% 58.0%	.4
Received training in integrating technology in curriculum SES N = 3933 Low N = 2324 Middle N = 1065 High	72.6% 77.1% 75.6%	27.4% 22.9% 24.6%	10.2*
Received follow-up or advanced training SES N = 3933 Low N = 2324 Middle N = 1065 High	45.5% 45.1% 44.4%	54.4% 54.9% 55.6%	.7

teachers from High SES schools reported using WWW sites more than once a week. Nearly thirty one percent of the middle school teachers indicated they used WWW sites more than once a week. Thirty three percent (33.4%) of the teachers from low SES schools reported using WWW sites more than once a week.

When asked how often they accessed model lesson plans from the Internet, teachers from low SES schools were less likely to do so. Over fifty percent (51.5%) reported never accessing model lesson plans from the internet. Forty seven percent (47.1%) of the teachers from middle SES schools and forty six percent (46.4%) of the teachers

from high SES schools reported never accessing model lesson plans from the Internet. Almost fifty percent (47.9%) of the teachers from low SES schools compared to thirty nine percent (38.5%) of the teachers from high SES school reported never doing research teaching on Internet. Forty three percent of the teachers from middle SES schools reported never doing research teaching on Internet. There was a ten percent decrease in usage of the computer to give class presentations when comparing teachers from High and low SES schools. Close to sixty percent (59.7%) of the Low SES teachers and forty nine percent of the teachers from high SES schools reported never

Table 5. Internet and technology use for instruction

Internet and Technology Use for Instruction N=7322					
How often do you...	Never	Less Than Once a Month	Between once a week and once a month	More than once a week	
Use computers to create class presentations SES N = 3933 Low N = 2324 Middle N = 1065 High	6.1% 4.3% 4.3%	11.2% 9.8% 8.9%	24.8% 27.8% 22.4%	57.9% 58.1% 64.4%	52.1**
Use WWW sites to plan lessons SES N = 3933 Low N = 2324 Middle N = 1065 High	27.9% 21.7% 19.7%	34.8% 39.3% 35.3%	33.4% 30.6% 37.9%	3.9% 8.4% 7.1%	58.5***
Access model lesson plans from Internet SES N = 3933 Low N = 2324 Middle N = 1065 High	51.5% 47.1% 46.4%	34.6% 34.8% 38.1%	11.6% 15.9% 19.0%	2.3% 6.4% 4.4%	75.8***
Research teaching on Internet SES N = 3933 Low N = 2324 Middle N = 1065 High	47.9% 43.0% 38.5%	35.8% 34.8% 38.1%	12.8% 15.8% 19.0%	3.5% 6.4% 4.4%	91.0***
Take professional development courses on Internet SES N = 3933 Low N = 2324 Middle N = 1065 High	88.1% 86.1% 87.3%	9.6% 10.2% 10.1%	.9% 1.9% 1.2%	1.4% 1.8% 1.1%	11.9
Download instructional software from Internet SES N = 3933 Low N = 2324 Middle N = 1065 High	77.5% 74.2% 75.5%	11.1% 12.8% 11.9%	4.8% 7.5% 6.8%	6.6% 5.5% 5.8%	16.5
Use computers to give class presentations SES N = 3933 Low N = 2324 Middle N = 1065 High	59.7% 56.5% 49.3%	29.9% 30.2% 34.9%	9.0% 11.4% 12.6%	1.4% 1.9% 3.2%	65.7***
Students use computers to pre-pare multimedia presentations SES N = 3933 Low N = 2324 Middle N = 1065 High	13.5% 10.5% 9.6%	4.7% 3.1% 3.8%	6.5% 6.0% 9.8%	75.3% 80.4% 76.8%	63.9***

used the computer to give presentations. Fifty seven percent (57.3%) of the teachers reported never using the computer to give presentation. There were no other significant differences for the remaining usages of the computers. Table 5 provides a summary of Internet and technology use for instruction across socioeconomics levels.

The results indicated that several differences exist (p <.001). There was a significant difference in the using the computer to communicate with colleagues. Fifty-five percent (54.7%) of the teachers from high SES school and forty seventy percent (47.3%) of the teachers from low SES schools reported using computer to communicate with colleagues more than once a week. Similar, nearly half (53.8%) of the teachers from middle SES schools reported using computer to communicate w/colleagues more than once a week. There was a significant difference in the using the computer to communicate with parents.

Almost three times as many teachers located at High SES schools reported using the computer to communicate with parents more than once a week compared to teachers in low SES schools. The percentages were 26.7% and 9.4% respectively. Thirteen percent (13.4%) of the middle SES teachers reported using computer to communicate with parents more than once a week. There was a significant difference in the using the computer to communicate with students. Thirty percent (30.4) teachers from high SES schools compared to twenty five of the teachers from low SES schools reported they used computers to communicate with students more than once a week. Twenty one percent (20.8%) of the teachers from middle SES schools reported using the computers to communicate with students more than once a week.

Finally, there was a significant difference in the using the computer to post homework and information. About twenty two percent (21.7%) of the teachers from high SES schools compared to twenty percent (20.4%) of the teachers from Low SES schools used computers to post homework and information. Eighteen percent (18.2%) of the teachers from middle SES schools reported using computers to post homework and information.

The results indicated several significant differences existing at the .05 level. For instance, there was a significant difference in the using the computer for administrative records. Seventy nine percent (78.6%) of the teachers from high SES school and seventy five percent (75.2%) of the teachers from low SES schools reported using computers for administrative records more than once a week. Similarly, eighty percent of the teachers from middle SES schools reported using computers for administrative records more than once a week. Table 6 provides a summary of the Internet and technology use for communication across socioeconomics levels.

DISCUSSION

The data reveals differences between high SES and low SES school relating to technology, professional development, communication, and integration ability. Previous research (Bailie, 2007; Finneran, 2000; Pinar, 2004; Teclehaimanot, 2006; Vonderwell & Peterman, 2008) indicated that lower SES schools used technology for drill practices while higher SES schools used technology for innovative teaching and learning practices. Based on data from this study, there is evidence to suggest that more work is needed to close the technology use gap in low and high SES school settings.

The data revealed that teachers were more likely to use the computer to create class presentations. However the data also suggests that teachers are less likely to allow their student to use the technology to create or give a multimedia presentation. As a result, there is need for high quality training related to technology use. This training might include software applications, digital tools such as digital video, graphics, animation, and peripherals. Scheduling follow-up sessions to monitor the progress of their professional development is equally critical to ensuring effective use and integration of technology in the classroom.

There is need for equal access to the technology, support both technical and instructional, and teachers equipped with knowledge and skills to utilize these technology tools. Further, curriculum

Table 6. Teacher internet and technology use for communication

How often do you...	Communication Through Technology N=7322				
	Never	Less Than Once a Month	Between once a week and once a month	More than once a week	
Take professional development courses on Internet SES N = 3933 Low N = 2324 Middle N = 1065 High	90.6% 90.2% 84.4%	7.0% 8.0% 12.8%	1.8% 1.1% 2.6%	.6% .7% .20%	57.3***
Use computers to communicate w/colleagues SES N = 3933 Low N = 2324 Middle N = 1065 High	17.3% 14.9% 18.0%	16.3% 13.8% 14.5%	19.1% 17.5% 12.8%	47.3% 53.8% 54.7%	53.7***
Use computers to communicate w/parents SES N = 3933 Low N = 2324 Middle N = 1065 High	67.0% 42.0% 33.0%	13.0% 19.5% 14.3%	10.6% 25.1% 25.8%	9.4% 13.4% 26.9%	707.8***
Use computers to communicate w/students SES N = 3933 Low N = 2324 Middle N = 1065 High	45.2% 49.3% 36.2%	18.4% 12.7% 19.7%	11.4% 17.2% 13.7%	25.0% 20.8% 30.4%	177.6***
Use computers for administrative records SES N = 3933 Low N = 2324 Middle N = 1065 High	13.3% 10.1% 10.3%	4.3% 4.2% 5.3%	7.2% 5.4% 5.8%	75.2% 80.3% 78.6%	16.8*
Use computers to post home-work/ information SES N = 3933 Low N = 2324 Middle N = 1065 High	66.7% 67.3% 60.6%	8.8% 7.4% 11.1%	4.1% 7.1% 6.6%	20.4% 18.2% 21.7%	52.3***

and content area training, and pedagogical skill training in connection to technology integration and instructional practices. Scheduling follow-up sessions to monitor the progress of their professional development is equally critical to ensuring effective use and integration of technology in the classroom. Providing equal access to quality professional development, and current research based instructional strategies might help to bridge the gap between technology disparities affecting its use, its integration and impact on student academic achievement.

Evidence from the study indicates that socioeconomic status of the school still plays an important role in how well teacher are trained and their ability to integrate technology in the classroom. In this case, teachers from low SES schools are less likely to receive training in basic computer skills, and Internet use compared to teachers from high SES schools. This could lead to fewer opportunities for teachers at lower SES schools to allow students the opportunity to engage at the higher levels of Bloom's taxonomy to create educational products related to the curriculum content, thus fostering critical thinking skills. Finally, teachers from low SES schools are less likely to use technology for communication purposes. This includes communication between teacher and student, along with teacher-parent communications.

RECOMMENDATIONS

The increasing demand for research-based evidence for the effectiveness of specific instructional practices has created renewed interest in educational research (Edyburn, Higgins, & Boone, 2005; Flowers & Flowers, 2008). As a result, recent research (Kidd, 2009) offers various strategies to integrate technology in low SES schools such as building collaborative partnerships for professional development, training, and enrichment programs on their campuses to effectively equip both veteran and novice teachers to use technology within their specific content domain areas.

Strategies that have proved successful in influencing student academic performance includes project and inquiry based learning opportunities, students working in pairs through computer assisted instruction, and through social interactions and teamwork (Kidd, 2009); using digital video, audio, and graphics to supplement instruction (Boster, Meyer, Roberto, & Inge, 2002); curricula focusing on analysis of real-world situations supported by computer assisted instructional software program (Kidd, 2009); and application software that utilizes higher order thinking skills (Kulik, 2003).

Teachers in either lower SES or high SES should familiarize themselves with current technology tools and trends, become active in understanding and designing learning objectives and activities at the higher levels of Blooms taxonomy, practice integrating technology into their daily instructional practices, transition to a reorientation phase where they realign their teaching and student learning outcomes with the technology, and finally become revolutionized in their teaching practices where technology usage is evident and the process facilitates high academic achievement through quality teaching and active student learning.

Effective use of technology occurs when the application directly: (a) supports the curriculum objectives being assessed; (b) provides opportunities for student collaboration and project/inquiry based learning; (c) adjusts for student ability and prior experience, and provides feedback to the student and teacher about student performance; (d) is integrated throughout the lesson; (e) provides opportunities for students to design and implement projects that extend the curriculum content being assessed; and (f) is used in an environment where organization leadership supports creative teaching innovation (Boster, Meyer, Roberto, & Inge, 2002; Kidd, 2009; Kulik, 2003).

As district administrators, educators, and major stakeholders rethink curricular and instructional reform for student achievement, they must also rethink their ideas for professional development and how technology integration fits within the broader context of quality teaching and student engagement. This way both teachers and students have the opportunity to become full participants in their pursuits toward educational equality, while integrating technology and meeting achievement standards, thus bridging the educational and technological gap.

REFERENCES

Bailie, F. (2007). How a Technology Grant from the National Academy Foundation Has Begun to Make a Difference for Minority Students in an Urban High School. In C. Crawford et al. (Eds.), *Proceedings of Society for Information Technology and Teacher Education International Conference* (pp. 762-769). Chesapeake, VA: AACE.

Bauer, J., & Kenton, J. (2005). Toward technology integration in the schools: why it isn't happening. *Journal of Technology and Teacher Education, 13*(4), 519–546.

Becker, H. J. (2001). *How are teachers using computers in instruction?* Paper presented at the meeting of the American Educational Research Association. Retrieved May 25, 2008, from http://www.crito.uci.edu/tlc/FINDINGS/special3/ Boster, F. J., Meyer, G. S., Roberto, A. J., & Inge, C. C. (2002). *A report on the effect of the united streaming application on educational performance.* Farmville, VA: Longwood University.

Burnham, L., Miller, A., & Ray, L. (2000, March). *Putting the pieces together.* Paper presented at the International Conference on Learning with Technology, Does Technology Make a Difference? Temple University, Philadelphia.

Council of Great City Schools. (2008). *Raising the Achievement of English Language Learners in the Seattle Public Schools.* Retrieved August 20, 2008, from http://www.cgcs.org/Pubs/Seattle_Bilingual.pdf

Cuban, L. (2001). *Oversold and underused: Computers in the classroom.* Cambridge, MA: Harvard University Press.

Edyburn, D., Higgins, K., & Boone, R. (2005). *Handbook of special education technology research and practice.* Whitefish Bay, WI: Knowledge by Design, Inc.

Finneran, K. (2000). Let them eat pixels. *Issues in Science and Technology, 1*(3), 1–4.

Flowers, T. A., & Flowers, A. L. (2008). Factors affecting urban African American high school students' achievement in reading. *Urban Education, 43*(2), 154–171. doi:10.1177/0042085907312351

Fulton, K., & Sibley, R. (2003). Barriers to equity. In Solomon, G., Allen, N., & Resta, P. (Eds.), *Toward digital equity: Bridging the divide in education* (pp. 14–24). Boston: Allyn & Bacon.

Guttentag, S., & Eilers, S. (2004). *Roofs* or *RAM? Technology in urban schools.* Retrieved on October 26, 2008, from http://www.horizonmag.com/4/roofram.htm

International Society for Technology in Education. (2007). Retrieved August 23, 2008, from http://www.iste.org/Content/NavigationMenu/Professional_Development/Programming_at_NECC/Summits1/20078/Digital_Equity_Summit/national-consideration-DE.pdf

Jin, S., & Bagaka, J. (2005). The role of teacher practices and classroom characteristics on the "digital divide" in students' usage of technology tools: A multilevel analysis. *Contemporary Issues in Technology & Teacher Education, 5*(3), 318–329.

Johnson, R. S. (2002). *Using data to close the achievement gap: How to measure equity in our schools.* Thousand Oaks, CA: Corwin Press.

Keengwe, J. (2007). Faculty Integration of Technology into Instruction and Students' perceptions of Computer Technology to Improve Student Learning. *Journal of Information Technology Education, 6,* 169–180.

Kidd, T. T. (2009). The dragon in the schools backyard: A review of literature on the uses of technology in urban schools. *The International Journal of Information and Communication Technology, 5*(1), 88–102.

Kulik, J. (2003). *Effects of using instructional technology in elementary and secondary schools: What controlled evaluation studies say.* Arlington, VA: SRI International.

Magolda, P. (2006). Critical fusion-technology and equity in secondary education. *AACE Journal*, *14*(3), 287–311.

Obiakor, F. E., & Beachum, F. D. (2005). *Urban education for the 21st century: Research, issues, and perspectives*. Springfield, IL: CC Thomas Publishing.

Oppenheimer, T. (2003). *The flickering mind: The false promise of technology in the classroom and how learning can be saved*. New York: Random House.

Parsad, B., & Jones, J. (2005). *Internet access in U.S. public schools and classrooms: 1994-2003 (NCES 2005-015). U.S. Department of Education*. Washington, DC: National Center for Education Statistics.

Pinar, W. (2004). *What is Curriculum Theory?* New York: Lawrence Erlbaum Associates.

Teclehaimanot, B. (2006). Technology Use in an Urban Setting: Implications for Schools Change. In C. Crawford et al. (Eds.), *Proceedings of Society for Information Technology and Teacher Education International Conference* 2006 (pp. 1837-1847). Chesapeake, VA: AACE.

Tulloch, J. B. (2000). Sophisticated technology offers higher education options. *T.H.E. Journal*, *2*(4), 58–60.

Vonderwell, S., & Peterman, F. (2008). Technology Integration and Community Mapping in Urban Education. In C. Crawford et al. (Eds.), *Proceedings of Society for Information Technology and Teacher Education International Conference* 2008 (pp. 2257- 2260). Chesapeake, VA: AACE.

This work was previously published in International Journal of Information and Communication Technology, Volume 6, Issue 3, edited by Lawrence A. Tomei, pp. 51-63, copyright 2010 by IGI Publishing (an imprint of IGI Global).

Chapter 21
Evaluating Student Perceptions of Using Blogs in an Online Course

Evelyn Gullett
U21Global, Singapore

Mamata Bhandar
U21Global, Singapore

ABSTRACT

This article is based on an exploratory study on the use of blogs to support learning in an online MBA school. In this paper, the authors examine students' perceptions toward blogs and their effectiveness. The study finds that although students are open to the idea of using blogs to enhance presentation and reflection of their learning, concerns exist on their suitability for threaded discussions in the presence of other platforms like threaded discussion boards. Therefore, what is less clear is the learning value and potential of blogs, especially that subset of learning that is orchestrated (and credentialed) by formal learning organisations.

INTRODUCTION

There are many definitions of blogs, as they have intrigued many in the education field.

A blog is a read-write web educational application in which a target audience can freely share insights, experiences, recommendations, or comments on the topic or blog post of another peer in that audience group. In other words, a blog needs to be treated as an active participant in the discursive process (Cameron & Anderson, 2006).

While there have been studies on blogging and its use with learning communities, sharing of resources, and ideas (Oravec, 2003; Williams & Jacobs, 2004), it seems that little focus has been given to how students perceive blogging in

DOI: 10.4018/978-1-61350-468-0.ch021

the context of online education. Williams (2004) suggested in his paper that blogging can be a transformational technology for teaching and learning, and so universities should consider setting up blog facilities within their learning management system (LMS).

Blogs are one of the many applications provided by Web 2.0, a latest technology being talked about today in the field of education and learning. Web2.0 allows for vivid networks of participation (O'Reilly, 2005), with value added by user action (Jones, 2006). Realising that Web2.0 technologies bring wonderful networking, collaborative, and support opportunities to Higher Education (Instone, 2005; Weller et al., 2005), we felt that using Blogs, next to Discussion Boards, as an additional pedagogical tool may just be another way to enhance and enrich student participation, as well as enable deep reflective learning for our students.

Blogging isn't just a part of the recent Web 2.0 technology, but also an element of Enterprise 2.0, enterprise social software that is used in various organisations and includes wikis, and collaboration/groupware to name a few (Zhang et al., 2009). A blog does not restrict the reader or writer to time (Flately, 2005), it is as asynchronous as DBs and like in DBs; everyone has an equal voice in the blogging forum.

Blogs have also been considered communication tools (Flately, 2005; Poling, 2005) and as online journals enhancing online classroom comprehension (Poling, 2005).The nature of blogging engines allows for the creation of a legitimate warehousing of captured knowledge, and archiving for later retrieval (Bausch et al., 2002).

BACKGROUND

Apart from the obvious benefits that blogs allow for more expressive and informal writing, it has also been lauded as a knowledge management tool in organizations. They provide the potential for relatively undifferentiated articles of information that pass through an organisation to be contextualized, in a manner that adds value hence generating 'knowledge' from mere 'information' (Williams & Jacob, 2004). Comment systems and democratic posting privileges allow employees in an organisation to give voice to ideas and provide feedback on procedures in a manner not previously possible in a distributed office environment.

Further, personalised responses to news and messages are a simple means of developing an understanding of the collective knowledge of an organisation. It is a means of broadening that knowledge, thus creating 'intelligence' from 'knowledge' (Pór & Molloy, 2000). Therefore, in a business context, blogs provide a forum for learning. It logically follows that the experience of collective knowledge generation can and should be applied to traditional educational environments.

Another observation one might make of the existing academic literature on blogging is related to educational applications of blogs. This literature tends to be concentrated in the areas of teacher training and other professions. Here, the use of reflective journals as a learning tool is an accepted custom and practice. As a consequence, there is an increased likelihood of a favourable disposition to blogs in these communities (e.g., Stiler & Philleo, 2003; Wagner, 2003).

Despite the fact that both students and faculty, over the years, have become very comfortable with the use of discussion boards (DBs), we thought it would be a good idea to introduce blogs as a new pedagogical element into some of our online classes. This article will address the questions of how students who are used to communicating and discussing through DBs in the Learning management system (LMS) would perceive the use of blogs in their learning. Specifically, how its use would enrich their learning and knowledge creation. The article will also examine whether or not they would like to use blogs in their classes.

Context and Setting: About U21Global

U21Global is a joint venture between a network of Universitas 21 and Manipal Education, which delivers a number of online learning graduate programs. The U21 affiliated universities participating in U21Global are the University of Virginia, Tecnológico De Monterrey, University of Birmingham, The University of Edinburgh, University of Glasgow, The University of Nottingham, University College Dublin, Lund University, The University of Melbourne, The University of Queensland, National University of Singapore, The University of Hong Kong, Shanghai Jiao Tong University, Fudan University, Korea University, University of Delhi and Waseda University.

Unlike traditional universities, the representation of international learner presence at U21G is nearly 100%, making cross-cultural approaches to virtual teams an important pedagogical issue. With all courses being conducted entirely online and with more than 6,000 enrolled students from more than 72 countries, which include China, India, the United Arab Emirates, New Zealand, Australia, Germany, England, North and South America, the need to cater to different cultures in each class, or virtual community of practice, is evident. This is ensured by employing professors from across the globe to develop the online course content in a cross-culturally sympathetic manner (as opposed to a mono-cultural approach) and also by ensuring that professors from all over the globe facilitate the classes. On an average, students in this MBA program are in their mid 30s with at an average of 10 years of work experience.

Participant Course Setting

The students were enrolled in MBA online courses, namely MBA601 Organisational Behaviour, MBA 770 Information Technology Systems for Business and MBA 751, Enterprise Knowledge Management. The average number of students enrolled in each class was 26.

MBA 601 Organisational Behaviour (5 Classes)

The Blog for classes in MBA601 Organisational Behaviour were set up during the end of the course, namely for week 9-12. The thought behind this was that students were able to already get a feel of the online class room setting, get comfortable with their peers and facilitator, and get used to the DB tool. There were 2 blog topics set up for this blog. The first was called "Contemporary Organisational Behaviour Issues". Here the students were asked to post their observations, experiences, possibly articles they have read in this space. They were also asked to engage with their peers by giving their reactions to the findings and thoughts they post on this topic.

They were advised to post, read, and engage throughout week 9 and 12 of the course. This will be added on as 10% of their grade. The second blog topic was called "Your Reflection". Here the students were asked to post their reflections on some of the contemporary issues they have shared and have learned about from their peers. How does this relate to their organisational work environment at the moment? What learning have they taken away from some of the contemporary issues in Organisational Behaviour? What learning have they taken away from this blogging for the past 4 weeks?

MBA 770 Information technology Systems in Business and MBA 751 Enterprise Knowledge Management (5 Classes)

Participants in four MBA770 Information technology Systems in Business and two MBA 751 Enterprise Knowledge Management classes were surveyed. The blogs for two classes were used for discussion of exploratory questions in the first week of the class. The question asked was to explore latest IT trends and explain at least one such technology/software/hardware. The blog was to be graded like a regular discussion topic. For the remaining three classes the blog was used for reflective postings at the end of every month when they would complete four discussion assignments. This is similar to "Your Reflection" in the MBA 601 classes. Here the students were asked to post their reflections on the learning over the discussions during the past four weeks. Students are asked to conceptually synthesize their learning, highlight their contributions and nominate best posts of classmates as well.

The above data collections details are summarised in the table below (Table 1).

METHODOLOGY

The data in this empirical qualitative analysis is derived from an online questionnaire that included five closed statements (this was an objective type questionnaire, where the participant was to select one choice of yes or no) and 13 open-ended questions. 72 students from across the three subjects and 11 classes responded to the data on the questionnaire. The questionnaire included questions/items on three broad areas:

A. Respondents background
B. Items pertaining to the use of blogs as a learning tool in an online course
C. Open ended questions.

The questionnaire was seeking respondents' perception using a Blog instead of a Discussion Board during a four-week period of a course, as well as their learning experience after making use of a Blog. The combination of yes/no questions and open-ended questions enabled gathering of views on suitability and effectiveness of blogs in the setting. The data enabled themes to emerge and allowed researchers to make assertions about the study as did Stake (1995). Coding sampling units were defined syntactically by using words, sentences, or paragraphs of the data/texts. Analysing content allowed the distillation of a large amount of raw qualitative data into themes. The categorical-content method (Lieblich et al., 1998) was applied for analysis of participant answers given to the open ended questions, as it allowed for the identification of distinct themes that become visible when reading raw qualitative data.

The main idea of this exercise and paper was to get an idea of student perceptions on the use of blogs and this particularly in the context of online management /business education. The context is important since students in different settings may have different perceptions towards such online tools; not to mention the nature of students and nature of the course structure and design. The questions ranged from simple demographics(please see attached sample questionnaire) to their views on blogs in general, comparison between blogs and DBs in terms of quality, ease of use etc. and their views on its use in online education. Questions were left open-ended to source breadth of views and perceptions vs getting yes/no answers as the study was also aimed at improving use of blogs through a qualitative approach and did not wish to restrict to yes/no.

Table 1. Data collection details

Subject	No. of classes	Responses	Implementation
MBA 601	5	52	Exploratory questions on contemporary issues and reflective posts during the last 4 weeks of the course.
MBA 770	4	16	Exploratory question on contemporary IT/technology trends during the first week of the class and reflective posts
MBA 751	2	4	Reflective posts
TOTAL	11	72	

Data Analysis

Participants were a mix of females and males ranging between the age group of 35 and 49. Educational backgrounds included BA and MA level. The demographics indicated that participants were from Germany, Qatar, Singapore, Egypt, India, Malaysia, Vietnam, Dubai and China. There were three categories of blog users. One section had never used blogs; another had a very basic blog reading exposure while yet another section was new to blogging. This observation was made before blogs were to be introduced in the classes.

The closed question portion of the questionnaire gave us an initial insight on what students thought of blogs (how they perceived them versus DBs, which is what they were used to and was also given as an educational tool along with the blog). This data is summarised in the table below (Table 2)

The open ended portion of the questionnaire focused on the perceptions derived when students used blogs in place of DBs as a pedagogical tool in online learning.

For data analysis, all responses were collated and coded separately by both researchers. The themes that emerged were combined. This was to allow for different interpretations to be brought into the analysis. After reading through the student responses the following conclusions/ themes emerged:

Blogs as a Supplementary Tool Should Not Replace DBs

The study showed that the majority of participants agreed that blogs should be used for sideline or related issue discussions. Although a handful felt they were good even for core discussions, the majority indicated that they are better for informal discussions, hence should be used as a supplementary tool and should not replace the DBs as a prime mode of discussion.

Topics that respondents find useful for Blogs included reflective posts, protocols or jargon related to the module, topics needing more clarification, general issues outside the scope of the course material, latest happenings and news in the field to get global perspectives from students all over the world. Overall, students felt that Blogs should not replace DBs and that they may be more suitable for sharing knowledge with much larger audience. The majority responded that Blogs should only be used as a learning supplement.

Blogs vs DBs for Threaded Discussions

Poling et al. (2005), found that by using blogs, students could delve further into topics discussed in class during a time of day where they normally are working quietly and independently. This again is not applicable in the context of this study, since here students work online and direct their own learning. The study also suggested that students can

Table 2. Perception of blogs vs DBs

	YES	NO	Unsure/undecided
I find it easy to use blogs	20	5	1
Blogs are easier to use than DBs	7	13	2
It is easier to follow the discussion in blogs than in DBs	6	18	
I feel my posts have more quality in blogs than in DBs, considering the informal nature of blogs	13	11	1
I strongly believe blogs should be adopted as a standard communication tool in online education	12	9	4 as a supplementary tool

direct their own learning as the computer brings them in contact with information (and people) not available in print; again in the current setting this is always the case.

Poling (2005) also revealed that as students communicate in the blog, they question and challenge each other's thinking, leading to deeper and more meaningful interaction than previously afforded during individual journaling. In our case however, this kind of meaningful interaction was confirmed by some students who were really comfortable using blogs. For the rest though they said the DBs were a much better form of interaction.

While we had some students who were familiar with blogs and some who had never been exposed to blogs, most participants felt that blogs were not as user-friendly as compared to DBs, mainly because it is difficult to track new posts made in a blog. Blogs are not threaded the way DBs are, which made it frustrating for some participants and discouraged some to participate in blog postings all together. In other words, it is harder to follow the thread on the blog since we are not being informed who has added the new posting to that particular thread since our last visit. This is unlike DBs, where the students are informed of how many postings are yet to be read and also how many postings are in reply to their own post/thread.

Such problems with blogs was also reported by Krause (2004) who identified some of the problems with blogging, referring to them as "haphazard contributions to blogs, minimal communication between students through their blogs and poor or inadequate quality reflection on the course materials as evidenced in blog content". The participants did express that both pedagogical tools have their pros and cons and support learning in their own way.

Overall, this leads us to believe that it is important to identify for which tasks Blogs should be used without compromising on the learning objective.

Blogs as a Tool for Free Self Expression and Generating Additional Knowledge

Just as (Zhang et al., 2009) found that blogs are effective in expressing and sharing ideas and are a facilitating tool for discussions and brainstorming within an organisation, the respondents of this study also expressed the same opinions. Some students found blogs to be less formal and allowed for more expression.

Students seemed to like the fact that graphics and range of formats could be used in a Blog as against DBs, which are limited in this respect. One student clarified:

I liked the fact that graphics and range of formats could be used. Discussion boards are limited in this respect. The ability to use multiple formats – graphics /sound / PPT slides in the body of the text to reinforce the points.

However blogs may not be effectively used for discussions and brainstorming in an organisational setting (Zhang et al., 2009). The reason of course is tracking in threads, which students need to do and the presence of DBs is a more convenient way for conducting discussions. In line with Zhang et al. (2009) though, most students agreed that blogs do facilitate knowledge sharing. The study showed that Blogs also contribute to self-learning, and allow for greater self expression, as well as creative learning.

Additional knowledge is created, as students add Blog posts on the topics of their choice, unlike DBs that ask specific questions around a certain topic or subject. Further, they then follow the Blog topic that interests them most. As a participant put it:

...posts in Blogs have a very wide scope whereas posts on DBs are confined to some aspects/issues only.

Some students felt that with blogging "it became easier to converse as we had the liberty to centralise the topic around a point of our choice". Others felt that "Blogs are like public diary notes; you can write anything about what you like, dislike and express it freely". The student adds, "I think the blog allows me to express better, esp[ecially] thru graphics and pictures, than just mere words."

The free flow of conversation and creation of additional knowledge was something that clearly stood out.

General Acceptance on using a New Pedagogical Tool

It was essential to get an idea of how perceptive students are in this context to new technologies, considering students are accustomed to using threaded DBs as a pedagogical tool in this online course setting. It was surprising to see that, to a very large extent, students were very positive towards the idea of using blogs, and in general were open to the idea of new pedagogical tools being introduced in online learning.

Providing guidance through 'How-to' notes helped those using the Blog feature. Although some of the participants who were new to Blogs had difficulties initially, most said that the guidance helped them to overcome their initial apprehension. A handful of them claimed it was not really easy. As expected, this was mainly for those who were first timers.

There could be a limitation in the software as we used wordpress, which was integrated with WebCT. Public blog sites are probably easier for such editing. However, when integrated with the learning platform certain features/tools may be unavailable and this may have caused the difficulty.

There were blog lovers who disapproved with threaded discussions and interactive discussions. They like blogs because they can sort posts based on authors, related comments and based on archives etc. Overall, barring a few students who

resisted the idea of blogs, most agreed that blogs can and should be a part of online education. The study shows that students were pleased and appreciated the exposure to Blogs for reasons ranging from exposure to new tools to adopting a tool to enhance presentation/writing and quality of posts.

Student Recommendations on 'How-to Improve' the use of Blogs

Students were more than eager to make suggestions on what features need to be included and also on what topics could be blogged about. On the technology front they had several suggestions. Some of the tools suggested including Digg to make the blog more interesting as they can not only comment but can also vote for the post that they like, something they do in all their reflective posts; nominate two best posts on that topic. Almost all noted the importance of RSS and it is also evident through many comments that the main difficulty is due to tracking inability, which can be solved by RSS. In this case RSS could not be enabled within the WebCT platform.

They also wanted the blog to be within the U21 learning environment. Although this was largely the case, the blog opened in a separate page. What students would have liked is a similar interface with the ability to blog. Students did want the blog editor to be more user friendly and easier to format. Many said that although blogs were easy to use, to get around formatting took them a lot of time and some felt the tools/features were limited. Since the blog was integrated with WebCT, when students posted their blogs, their students IDs were displayed. It was however hard to identify the author, unless they signed their posts. So they said they should be able to modify their profiles so as to display their names and not only IDs. They also expressed that comments are not shown until they are clicked, a minor point but something that can add to the inconvenience and making thread management difficult.

Some requested for more sophisticated functionalities such as building in more search capabilities apart from the keyword tagging already present and allow for threaded discussions. As can be guessed, these suggestions were from those that supported blogging and who were frequent bloggers. Some suggested using blogs for team collaboration, as they felt that current team collaboration was static.

Flately (2005) also indicated that using blogs to facilitate group work is clearly appropriate and an excellent medium for student-centered learning. This is true and students agree, but the critical element here is the kind of discussions and presence of other media. Students found DBs better for threaded discussions, although some agreed they blogs do help in presenting their thoughts more effectively.

The fact that students came forward with suggestions in an open-ended questionnaire may indicate that they are excited about this tool and are willing to use it believing it increases their creating, gaining and sharing of knowledge when taking an online class.

One suggestion that came up and, in effect reflects the thoughts of most, is blending the two tools. Blogs are welcome and appreciated but lack of certain features make it inconvenient for using blogs for threaded discussions. The solution then will be to ensure that elements of DB exist to make the blog more productive for a formal learning environment. In which case, it can also be used for core discussions. Likewise, learning can be made effective if RSS and email notification and marking of read/unread post can be incorporated.

CONCLUSION

This study explored how students perceive the use of Blogs in an online management education scenario. Although such studies have been conducted before, none were in the setting of an online MBA class. This study showed that participant perceptions are mainly positive and confirm that over time, students become better readers, writers and self - directed learners through the use of blogs. Concerns regarding blogs were expressed in certain areas such as interactivity, ease tracking of Blog posts and most importantly in thread management. Furthermore, the study shows that Blogs should be a supplemental pedagogical tool, next to DBs.

Results indicate that DBs focus on creating knowledge pertaining to theory and application due to effective participation and thread management. This is a more formal pedagogical approach. Participants felt that this was also important. Further, results indicate that Blogs create additional knowledge in a free-flow kind of way, allowing for creative expression by adding pictures, posting what they feel passionate about, and deciding which Blog post to follow and engage in. Thus, this is considered a more informal pedagogical approach. Overall, the sense was that as bloggers and participants will reap the benefits of their use of Blogs over time.

Recommendation based on student views then, is to use blogs in combination with DBs such that each is used for tasks appropriate for that medium. This should also make them assessable and provide an opportunity to gain knowledge in their life-long learning journey. The possible solution is then on having a blended approach; implementing blogs to address the concerns while balancing faculty perceptions and pedagogical issues.

This study has initiated research on use of blogs, specifically in the online management education area. Although this is a preliminary study on student perceptions, the other half of this study, which will be treated in another paper, will focus on the faculty perceptions on use of blogs. Another area to be addressed, as is reflected from some of the surveys comments of this study, is on whether the blogging space is really important. Or is it the idea of blogging that should be incorporated in existing learning management systems? Finally, another area that can be explored is whether perhaps their ubiquitous use indicates they are a disruptive technology, and if so, how can this be addressed.

REFERENCES

Bausch, P., Haughey, M., & Hourihan, M. (2002). *We Blog: Publishing Online with Weblogs.* New York: John Wiley & Sons.

Cameron, D., & Anderson, T. (2006). Comparing Weblogs to Threaded Discussion Tools in Online Educational Contexts. *Instructional Journal of Instructional technology and Distance learning, 2*(11). ISSN 1550-6908

Downes, S. (2004). Educational Blogging. *EDUCAUSE* Review, *39*(5), 14-26. Retrieved October 26, 2009, from http://www.educause.edu/pub/er/erm04/erm0450.asp

Farmer, J. (2004). *Communication dynamics: Discussion Boards, weblogs and the development of communities of inquiry in online learning environments.* Retrieved October 26, 2009, from http://incsub.org/blog/2004/communication-dynamics-discussion-boards-weblogs-and-the-development-of-communities-of-inquiry-in-online-learning-environments-of-inquiry-in-online-learning-environments

Flately, M. E. (2005). Blogging for enhanced teaching and learning. *Business Communication Quarterly, 68*(1), 77–80. doi:10.1177/108056990506800111

Garrison, D. R., & Anderson, T. (2003). *E-Learning in the 21st century, A framework for research and practice.* New York: Routledgefalmer. doi:10.4324/9780203166093

Godwin-Jones, B. (2003). Emerging technologies Blogs and Wikis: Environments for on-line collaboration. *Language Learning & Technology, 7*(2), 12-16. Retrieved October 26, 2009, from http://llt.msu.edu/vol7num2/emerging/default.html

Instone, L. (2005). Conversations beyond the classroom: Blogging in a professional development course. In *Proceedings of ASCILITE conference,* Brisbane, Australia.

Jones, G. (2006). The Skinny on Web 2.0. *InformationWeek.* Retrieved October 26, 2006, from http://www.informationweek.com/story/showArticle.jhtml?articleID=193001026

Krause, S. D. (2004). When blogging goes bad: A cautionary tale about blogs, email lists, discussion, and interaction. *Kairos, 9*(1). Retrieved October, 2009, from http://english.ttu.edu /kairos/9.1/binder.html?praxis/krause/index.html

Lamshed, R., Berry, M., & Armstrong, L. (2002). *Blogs: Personal e-learning spaces.* http://www.binaryblue.com.au/docs/blogs.pdf

Lieblich, A., Tuval-Mashiach, R., & Zilber, T. (1998). *Narrative research: Reading, analysis and interpretation.* Newbury Park, CA: Sage.

O'Reilly, T. (2005). *Compact definition. O'Rielly Radar.* Retrieved October 26, 2009, from http://radar.oreilly.com/archives/2005/10/web_20_compact_definition.html

Oravec, J. A. (2003). Blending by blogging: Weblogs in blended learning initiatives. *Journal of Educational Media, 28*(2-3), 225–233. doi:10.1080/1358165032000165671

Poling, C. (2005). Building communication and collaboration among staff and students. *Leading & Learning with Technology, International Society for Technology in Education, 32*(6).

Pór, G., & Molloy, J. (2000). *Nurturing Systemic Wisdom Through Knowledge Ecology.* Systems Thinker.

Richardson, W. (2004). *Reading and blogging, Weblogg-Ed.* Retrieved October 26, 2009, from http://www.weblogg-ed.com/2004/03/31

Weller, M., Pegler, C., & Mason, R. (2005). Use of innovative technologies on an e-learning course. *The Internet and Higher Education, 8,* 61–71. doi:10.1016/j.iheduc.2004.10.001

Williams, J., & Jacobs. (2004). Exploring the use of blogs as learning spaces in the higher education sector. *Australasian Journal of Educational Technology, 20*(2), 232–247.

Williams, J. B. (2004). Exploring the use of blogs as learning spaces in the higher education sector. *Australasian Journal of Educational Technology, 20*(2), 232–247.

Zhang, A. M., Zhu, Y., & Hildebrandt, H. (2009). Enterprise Networking Websites and Organizational communication in Australia. *Business Communication Quarterly, 72*(1), 114–119. doi:10.1177/1080569908330381

APPENDIX

Survey on Student Perception of using blogs in online education

As you all know, online education is a very popular trend now and we as faculty at U21 Global are constantly striving to incorporate newer and better tools that can make online learning more effective. As part of that initiative we have prepared a questionnaire on the use of blogs n this section. We would welcome your comments as they are instrumental in the development of using this tool for online learning. Please feel free to add in if you have anything else to say.

Many thanks for your time and comments!

	Demographics	
1	Name (optional)	
2	Age	
3	Gender	
4	Country/city residing in?	
5	Prior usage of blogs?	
	Perceptions of using blogs (Please provide comments in addition to yes/no answers for the following questions)	
6	How easy/difficult was it for you to use the blog in the section to read/write/comment?	
7	Does the informal nature of blogs increase the quality of your post? What about frequency of posts?	
8	What kinds of blogs appeal to you the most with regards to using it for online learning?	
9	If your blogs were not graded and yet part of the section, how much do you think you would use the blog (for reading/writing/commenting)?	
10	Would you advocate using blogs in online education? Why/Why not?	
11	What is the best way you think blogs can be incorporated in our online courses and why?	
12	Can blogs be used for core discussions or are they more suitable for side discussions or reflective postings?	
13	Now that you have used blogs in this section, are you more likely to use blogs in others sections or external blogs?	
	Blogs vs DBs	
14	How convenient are blogs for writing your reflective posts as compared to DBs?	
15	How convenient are blogs for carrying out threaded discussions like in the DBs?	
16	Do you think the quality of your and others posts are better when in the blog or on the DB? Why?	
17	Which do you think is more interactive; blogs or DBs and why?	
18	Do you think blogs can replace DBs as main learning in online education OR they can best be used as a supplementary tool? Why?	
19	In terms of knowledge creation; do blogs or DBs allow for more/better knowledge creation? Why?	
20	In terms of knowledge sharing; do blogs or DBs allow for more/better knowledge sharing? Why?	

This work was previously published in International Journal of Information and Communication Technology, Volume 6, Issue 3, edited by Lawrence A. Tomei, pp. 64-74, copyright 2010 by IGI Publishing (an imprint of IGI Global).

Chapter 22
Applications of Mobile Learning in Higher Education:
An Empirical Study

Babita Gupta
California State University, USA

Yangmo Koo
California State University, USA

ABSTRACT

As mobile devices' use among consumers accelerates at an exponential rate, there is a need to examine how these mobile devices can be used as effective learning tools and not just a form of communication. In this paper, the authors use an empirical survey methodology to study various mobile learning tools that are currently available for use in higher education, their advantages and disadvantages in m-learning versus e-learning implementations, and to explore the current trends in m-learning.

INTRODUCTION

Development of information technology and use of internet has brought about major changes to the traditional educational paradigm, with electronic learning (e-learning) using the Internet is emerging as an alternative channel of education to the traditional face-to-face education. E-learning plays an important role at the different levels of education settings. E-learning provides advantages in terms of time and space compared to the traditional classroom type of education (Weekes, 2006; Slevin, 2000). It is expected that e-learning providing remote or distance learning capability could be a viable alternative to the traditional face-to-face education.

Recent advances in mobile technology have enabled a variety of mobile technology applications to learning. Mobile devices include cellular phones, personal digital assistants (PDAs), MP3 players, smart phones, portable game devices, handhelds, tablets, and laptops (Wagner, 2005).

DOI: 10.4018/978-1-61350-468-0.ch022

Figure 1. Active users of mobile internet in the United States (in millions)

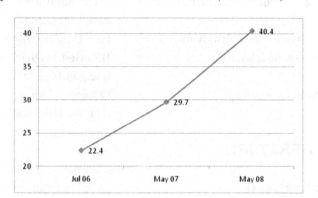

More and more people from all ages use mobile devices, and it appears that they are familiar with using these devices (Wagner, 2005). It is estimated that the mobile phones are currently used by 50 percent of world population and is expected to grow to 80 percent in 2013, which would be about 5.8 billion people worldwide, compared to 1.5 billion people in 2004 (IBM Study Finds, 2008; Prensky, 2004). This number is considered to be at least three times more than that of PCs (Muyinda, 2007). In the U.S., in one year between January 2008 and January 2009, the number of people who used web-enabled mobile devices such as smart phones *every day* grew from 10.8 million to 22.4 million (Kolakowski, 2009). In 2008, the United States had 15.6% active mobile Internet usage penetration rate with 40 million mobile subscribers who use these services at least once in a month (Figure 1), of these about 39.2% are in age group of 18-34 years (Nielsen Mobile, 2008).

In today's society, there is a constant influx of new information. Therefore, having the ability to learn by making use of technology that is better suited to deliver knowledge and resources in real-time is a becoming a necessary skill in itself. By adding the mobile technologies that enable capability to learn "anytime, anywhere, e-learning is transformed into mobile learning (m-learning). For this reason, m-learning can be used as an effective tool to support classroom material, introduce new ways of learning, and help enhance study skills. Moreover, with younger populations becoming acquainted with technology at an earlier age, its effects on learning may have a powerful impact.

One of the major advantages using technology in education is its effect on raising learners' motivation to learn. This phenomenon is more evident for the younger generations who grew up using computers in their daily lives. Since this generation is used to the fun activities and various learning tools available in digital realm, traditional ways of learning sometimes does not appeal to them. However, with the use of technology, learning process does not have to be boring. In the e-learning context, interactive and fun activities are possible to implement. Moreover, since a young learner's attention span is usually very short, fun and interactive activities that invite learners' active participation are more effective (Koo, 2008).

This research examines how these mobile devices can be used as effective learning tools. Also, we explore the various kinds of learning tools that use mobile technology are currently available. In particular, the current trend and people's awareness about m-learning is surveyed. This study focuses on the following research questions:

1.   What kinds of learning tools using mobile technology are currently available?

2. Are learners (students) familiar with the mobile learning tools?
3. What are the advantages and disadvantages of implementing m-learning versus e-learning?
4. What are the trends in m-learning?

REVIEW OF THE LITERATURE

What is Electronic Learning (E-Learning)?

According to Slevin (2000), people can easily access the online education using a personal computer or laptop computer. One of the major advantages we gain from this technological development is overcoming limitations of time and space. One consequence of e-learning globalization is that it facilitates global educational knowledge management across national and cultural boundaries. Virtual reality and information and communication technologies (ICT) open a new world to us. New business models are emerging with higher education taking a more e- commerce approach with educator-to-consumer (E2C), educator-to-educator (E2E), educators-to-business (E2B), and business-to-educators (B2E) e-learning models.

Electronic learning, online learning, and distance learning are all ways to identify the delivery of education using computer supported digital technology without requiring physical presence of the student at the site of instruction. The definitions of this concept vary but all share the same idea - use of technology to eliminate the traditional classroom setting. Obringer (2001) defines e-learning as self paced, hands-on learning, which could be CD-ROM based, network-based, intranet-based, or internet based. Allen and Seaman (2007) identify online courses as those in which at least 80 percent of the course content is delivered online:

- **Web Facilitated:** Courses that use web based technology to what is essentially a face-to-face course.
- **Blended/Hybrid:** Course that blends online and face-to-face delivery.
- **Online:** Course where most of the content is delivered online (no face-to-face meetings).

As internet use widens across disciplines, it also has an impact on education. According to the Center for Adult Learning and Education Credentials of the American Council on Education distance learning means "a system and a process that connects learners with distributed learning resources, for example, the Internet, computer- based training, satellites, virtual reality, or teleconferencing" (Barclay, 2001, p. 12).

Oh (2003) briefly characterized e-learning in three major categories:

1. Separation of time and/or place between instructor and learner, among learners, or between learners and learning resources;
2. Interaction between instructor and learner, among learners or learners and learning resources conducted through one or more media, especially through the use of ICT; and
3. A teaching and learning process not limited by time and/or place (Cardenas, 1998; Holmberg, 1998; Keegan, 1986; Porter, 1997).

As Rosenberg (2001) mentioned, e-learning enhances problem-solving strategies, builds e-learning communities on the web and connects pre- and post-learning process. There are two different concepts regarding e-learning depending on the technical realization: computer based training (CBT) and web base training (WBT). Rosenberg (2001) posits that instructional options and technological realization of WBT are usually more complex than those of CBT. E-learning products and handheld devices such as laptops or personal digital assistants (PDA) are tools for mobile learning. These are classified as mobile based training (MBT) which is classified as a subgroup of CBT (Hoppe & Breitner, 2003).

E-learning facilitates collaboration among students and faculty separated by time and distance and is driving its success. E-Learning technologies provide greater opportunities for richer student-faculty interactions that amplify collective knowledge possessed by each actor (Hill & Roldon, 2005). E-learning can enhance the student and faculty educational experience and provides the promise of accessible and affordable higher education for everyone.

What is Mobile Learning (M-Learning)?

More people become comfortable with using smart mobile devices that are web enables (see Figure 1). This creates opportunities to use wireless technologies to enhance e-learning model by introducing the "anytime anywhere" concept. This allows learners to be in the field or outdoors greatly expanding the reach of e-learning to disciplines such as archeology and environmental science (Vasiliou & Economides, 2007).

Mobile learning is defined as using mobile devices such as cell phones, lap tops, pocket PCs, PC tablets, PDS and other handheld device in conjunction with wireless Internet network to enable multimedia communication using text, voice, video, and graphics data. M-learning allows student and faculty to exchange messages, sounds, pictures, and other rich communication among themselves using the Internet (Cavus & Ibrahim, 2009; Shen, Wang, & Pan, 2008; Vasiliou & Economides, 2007).

M-learning uses devices like portable audios, MP3, and PDAs containing learning content (Weekes, 2006). PDAs and smart phones have e-mail and web browsing functions as well as data transfer capabilities, which makes for powerful learning platforms (Wagner, 2005). One of the significant characteristics of m-learning is mobility that facilitates accessibility for learning environments, no matter when and where learners are. That is why a number of leading universities recently have shown an interest in building wireless network on campus to enhance students' learning (Salz, 2006).

M-learning builds new relationships and behaviors among learners who use information and personal computing devices (Alexander, 2004). Hardaker (2005) discussed the e-learning development as important issue of interest for world leaders. Many higher education institutions began to introduce a new system using m-learning. For example, the U.S. Military Academy at West Point, NY, installed the new version of Cranite's Wireless Wall Software Suite for wireless network in 2002 (PR Newswire, 2002). They created individual network connections so that they can readily implement a wireless local area network for their online curriculum (PR Newswire, 2002).

M-learning is expected to be an important learning channel as it allows for more active learning method allowing real-time interaction, exchange, feedback and discussion opportunities among students and faculty (Vasiliou & Economides, 2007). Studies done by the Learning and Skills Development Agency (Mobile learning inspires, 2005) show that a student's motivation for learning was greatly increased when they were provided with games, learning materials and learning tools, designed to be used on a range of portable devices such as mobile phones. Traditional classroom learning environment did not seem to suit these learners. However, they responded to new m-learning tools very positively. Students in the study were able to build higher self-esteem and enthusiasm for learning. The research supports the positive role of m-learning can play in higher education.

Advantages and Disadvantages of Mobile Learning

M-leaning provides many advantages for learners: equal opportunity access, ubiquitous connectivity, multigenerational users and uses, services for the mobile worker, and services for the mobile learner (Wagner & Wilson, 2005). M-learning provides opportunity for learning independent of time and space, and allows for greater freedom of movement that may be essential for certain learning experiences. With the use of m-learning, distance education can effectively incorporate students from different backgrounds with diverse learning styles and different skills including people who may have certain disabilities or specific learning difficulties. M-learning offers new opportunities to learners who rely on mobile computer solutions that other devices cannot provide, such as ability take pictures and share these in real-time with other learners. M-learning also provide learners the ability to use guided maps, or global positioning systems (GPS) necessary in field-based learning experiences such as for outdoor nature projects that require location-awareness (Vasiliou & Economides, 2007). Therefore, m-learning has greater potential than e-learning in terms of providing reach and accessibility. As mobile devices continue to evolve, educators are discovering new ways in which the functionality of the mobile devices can be applied to learning (Mikie & Anido, 2006). With increasing integration of wireless network, mobile devices and other networking technologies, m-learning would provide enhanced education and learning experience (Vasiliou & Economides, 2007).

However, there are also some limitations of m-learning that can be a barrier to its adoption. To be successful in m-learning environment, a learner has to be highly self-disciplined. Also, mobile devices have disadvantages such as a very small screen size. In addition, most of the available content is designed for the traditional PC-based web viewing. People who are using mobile devices have to be more concerned about security and resulting losses. According to Muir (2003), about 10 percent of mobile devices used by major organizations have serious security problems in protecting the data.

Wagner (2005) discussed three converging phenomena that is accelerating today's mobile-adoption curve. First, there are more wireless networks, services, and devices than ever before. For example, more and more schools and companies are building wireless networks for communication and training purposes. Second, consumers are demanding better mobile experiences than ever before. Third, people want "anytime, anywhere" connections more than ever before (Wagner, 2005). Currently, there are leading areas of m-learning: educational games, language instruction, and performance-support and decision-support tools (Wagner, 2005). In particular, downloading authentic learning materials plays a crucial role for language learners, so m-learning is being broadly used for language learning.

M-learning is becoming a new trend of learning and has many positive characteristics that may compensate for the limitations of the traditional type of learning. Therefore, studying m-learning trends, people's familiarity and awareness of this new channel of higher education and their awareness of available tools for m-learning will provide learners and educators a better insight for designing m-learning applications.

RESEARCH METHODOLOGY

Research Model

In order to answer the research questions, a written survey was developed based on the following model (Figure 2, see Table 1 for definitions).

Figure 2. m-Learning research model

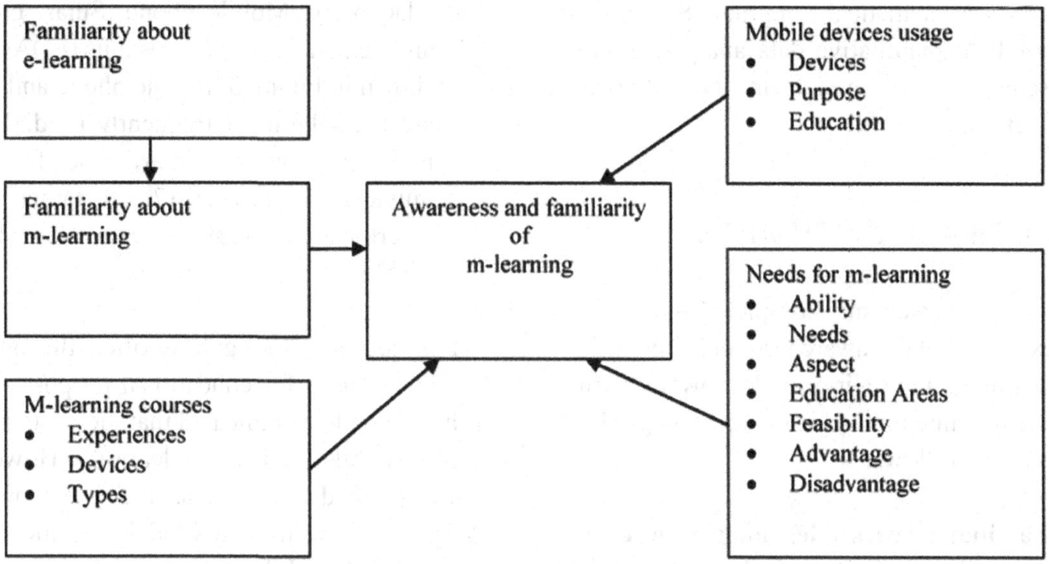

Table 1. Definitions of constructs used in the m-Learning research model

Constructs	Definitions
Familiarity about e-learning	The degree of familiarity with e-learning
Familiarity about m-learning	The degree of familiarity with m-learning
Mobile devices usage	The degree to which participants are using mobile device for educational purposes
m-learning courses	The degree to which participants are taking m-learning courses
Needs for m-learning	The degree to which participants are concerning with m-learning and needs

Research Process

- **Pilot study:** A survey based on research model in Figure 2 was developed (approved by Human Subject Committee of the university). A pilot study was conducted with an initial draft of the written questionnaire administered to five learners. They were randomly selected for validation of the items in the questionnaire. Primary purpose of this pilot study was to reduce any ambiguities in the questions. Based on the pilot study feedback, minor wording changes were made and survey was finalized.

- **Data collection:** A written paper-based survey was administered to 50 people with 47 valid respondents. Only those participants who were more than 18 year old could take part in the study. Twenty of the respondents (43%) were male, and twenty seven were female (57%). Majority of the respondents held either an associate degree or bachelor's, or were enrolled in a college course when the survey was conducted. Of all the respondents, twelve (25%) held a higher degree (master's and doctoral degree). As for ethnic background, the majority of respondents were Caucasians (40%), and fifteen were Asians (32%).

- **Data Analysis:** To analyze the survey responses, statistical program SPSS was used. A quantitative data analysis is presented for discussion in the following section.

RESULTS AND DISCUSSION

Forty seven participants completed the survey that examined their awareness and familiarity of m-learning, and their attitudes toward an innovative learning method using technology. The results are as follows.

- **Familiarity with e-learning & m-learning:** The majority of the respondents (83%) responded that they were familiar with the concept of electronic learning (e-learning). As for mobile learning (m-learning), 25% of the respondents said that they were aware of the concept of m-learning. It seems that the majority of the population (75%) from this study did not know what m-learning is. Among those who were familiar with e-learning, 31% responded that they knew the concept of m-learning. This may indicate that people who are already familiar with e-learning are more likely to know about m-learning.
- **Mobile devices:** The primary mobile devices frequently used these days are iPod, MP3 player, portable game devices, Blackberry, Mobile phone, Smart phone, and Personal Digital Assistants (PDAs). As shown in Figure 3, mobile phone and iPod are used the most frequently used. These mobile devices are primarily used for communication purpose (72%) rather than entertainment (11%) or education (11%) (Table 2).

For question asking how often the mobile devices are used for educational purpose, most of the respondents indicated that they usually do not use mobile devices for learning. However, 64% of the iPod users said that they use it for their education. It seems that iPod is the most frequently used mobile device for learning currently.

Regarding whether the respondents took a course or training that used mobile learning, 87% of the respondents said that they did not have any previous experience with this learning method. It appears that mobile devices are not yet being used for educational purposes in a systematic manner.

Awareness of M-Learning

As reported above, most of the respondents did not seem to be familiar with the concept of m-learning. It may be because it is rather new and an innovative way of learning which is very different from traditional learning. Nevertheless, the majority of

Table 2. The number of respondents who use mobile devices for the educational purpose

Mobile devices	Never	Rarely	Sometimes	Often	Very often
iPod	9 (29.0%)	2 (6.5%)	12 (38.7%)	3 (9.7%)	5 (16.1%)
MP3 player	9 (42.9%)	4 (19.0%)	4 (19.0%)	2 (9.5%)	2 (9.5%)
Portable game devices	12 (85.7%)	2 (14.3%)	N/A	N/A	N/A
Mobile phone	13 (61.9%)	2 (9.5%)	2 (9.5%)	2 (9.5%)	2 (9.5%)
Smart phone	3 (75.0%)	1 (25.0%)	N/A	N/A	N/A
PDAs	4 (57.1%)	N/A	1 (14.3%)	1 (14.3%)	1 (14.3%)
Others	2 (40.0%)	N/A	2 (40.0%)	1 (20.0%)	N/A

Figure 3. Frequently used mobile devices

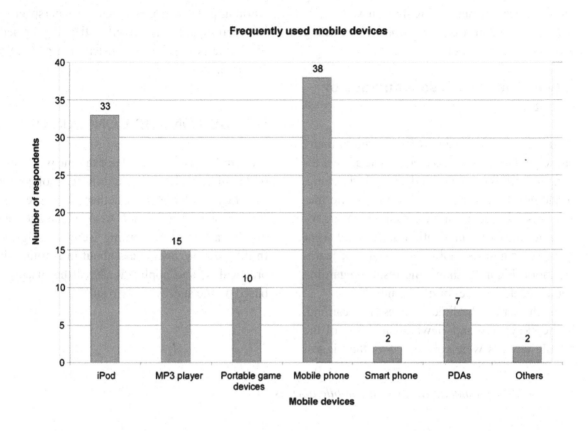

the respondents (98%) agreed that there is need for methods that facilitate learning any time and in any place. In particular, 32% responded that learning regardless of time and space is extremely important. Based on these responses, it is obvious that learners feel the need for the new type of learning which is always accessible to them regardless of time and space constraint.

With regard to the question asking whether the respondents could imagine learning using mobile devices, 75% expressed the possibility of m-learning with a positive attitude. Even though most of the respondents did not have a previous experience using mobile devices for education nor did they have a clear understanding of the concept of m-learning, results indicate that they have a positive feeling about m-learning and expect mobile devices to be useful learning tools.

As for the accessibility of learning material via mobile devices, 43% expressed a favorable response by saying that the mobile devices would be useful to access the learning materials. Regarding the use of mobile devices in the university setting, approximately half of the respondents (47%) expressed a favorable response for the possibility of communication by using mobile devices between faculty and students.

Educational Applications of M-Learning

Among different types of learning activities, listening to lectures by using mobile devices was considered the most useful educational activity. For collaborating with other students and watching lecture or training video, positive responses were reported. However, results indicate that using mobile devices for answering short answer exams is not very useful. Responses for other learning activities are shown in Figure 4.

Advantages and Disadvantages of M-Learning

Regarding the advantages of m-learning, many participants (45%) responded that it allows for greater flexibility of time and space for learning. In addition, the faster accessibility to new information was selected as an important advantage for m-learning. As for motivation, it does not seem that using a new technology motivates the learners more. Figure 5 shows the results regarding perceived advantages of m-learning.

With regard to the disadvantages of m-learning, limited keyboard and viewing capability of the mobile devices were considered as the biggest

problem. It appears that it is not easy to verify the learning process from the learner's perspective. The participants also pointed that higher self-discipline is required for m-learning as seen in Figure 6.

DISCUSSION AND CONCLUSION

This study was conducted to examine what kinds of learning tools using mobile technology are currently available and whether the learners are familiar with them or not. Also, advantages and disadvantages of m-learning were investigated. In this section, awareness about m-learning, its practicality, and applications will be discussed based on the survey study result.

Figure 4. Educational activities using mobile devices

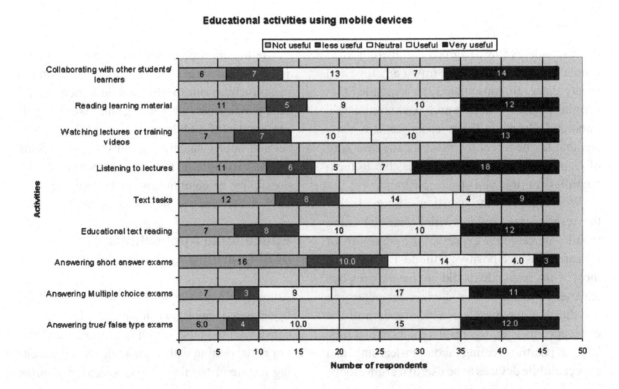

Figure 5. Advantages of m-learning

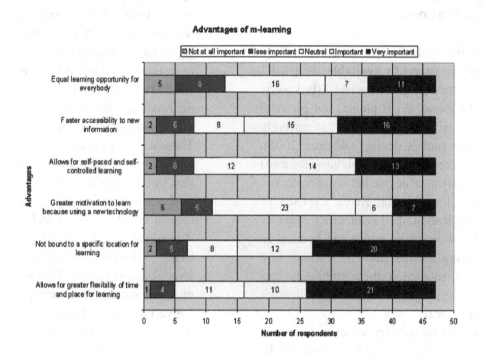

Figure 6. Disadvantages of m-learning

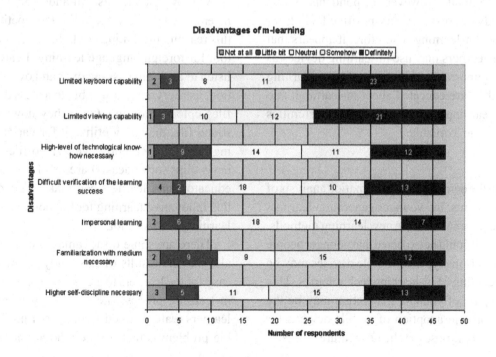

Findings of the Study and Their Implications

- **Learning tools using mobile technology which are currently available.** iPod, MP3 player, portable game devices, Blackberry, mobile phone, smart phone, and personal digital assistants (PDAs) are the currently available mobile devices (Weekes, 2006). Among these, the mobile phone is the most commonly used device but is not really being used for education. Rather it is used for communication. iPod is another frequently used mobile device which can be used as a learning tool. Because m-learning is a recent phenomenon, these mobile devices are not actively utilized yet in the instructional context.

- **Learner's familiarity about m-learning.** Based on the results reported in this study, there are not many people who are actually aware of m-learning. It seems that people still consider mobile devices only as a communication tool and not as a learning instrument. However, respondents of the study expressed a very positive feeling toward m-learning. Therefore, it appears that the learners may use m-learning devices as an important supporting tool for learning if they are educated about m-learning, and m-learning applications and opportunities become available.

Based on the demographic information analysis of the participants, the younger generation learners are more familiar with the new learning methods. Therefore, it could be expected that younger people who use various types of mobile devices may be most accepting of m-learning technologies. This demographic of younger generation may be the driving force in adoption of mobile devices for educational purposes in the near future.

- **Advantages and disadvantages found in implementing m-learning versus e-learning.** As seen the results, the most significant advantage of m-learning is to overcome the time and space constraints. Learners are able to easily access learning materials no matter where and when they are. It invites more people for learning. These days a great deal of information and knowledge is becoming available every day. In this situation, traditional education methods may be inadequate to take advantage of vast knowledge and incorporating it in higher education or training. We are living in the era of life-long education. In terms of continuous life-long education, m-learning could be a very practical alternative training tool to traditional methods of learning (Wagner, 2005).

There are various learning activities possible using mobile devices. Among them, listening to lectures (called podcasts) using mobile devices was indicated as the most useful educational activity by respondents. An added advantage of listening to lectures is the unlimited repetition. For this reason, m-learning could be used as a useful tool for foreign language learning. Learners can listen to a certain passage over and over. In addition, learners are readily able to access the media files uploaded online. Once they download the sound file, they may utilize it for various learning purposes. Recently even video files such as news clips (or vodcasts) are available online. If educators and learners can make a good use of this innovative learning tool, it could assist their learning process a lot.

There are some disadvantages of m-learning also. As the results of this study show, it is not easy for the learners to assess their learning using m-learning process, i.e., assessing whether the learners really learned a concept or not. Another big problem is that people who are not familiar with mobile devices may not understand the how to utilize m-learning. M-learning also requires a high standard of self-discipline by learners. If not, learners cannot focus on learning process since they are not in the physical instructional settings. In addition, there are some doubts about the possibility whether m-learning using a new technology can help learners stay motivated about their education and complete it. Also, inconvenience due to the small keyboard or tiny viewing screen may discourage people in the process of learning.

In spite of these disadvantages, m-learning could be a very useful learning tool if people are aware of mobile learning advantages and are educated in the use of pertinent mobile devices and tools. If they can control their learning, it allows for a self-paced learning. Therefore, it is clear that m-learning is one of the possible learning pedagogy that may be extensively used to provide accessible higher education to more people at affordable cost.

LIMITATION OF THE STUDY AND SUGGESTIONS FOR FURTHER RESEARCH

In this study, awareness of m-learning, people's attitude toward m-learning, currently available mobile devices, possible m-learning activities, and advantages and disadvantages of m-learning were surveyed and discussed. Since m-learning is a very recent phenomenon therefore level of awareness is still low. Also, there are very few well-developed m-learning pedagogies and materials currently available for educators to adopt easily in their curriculum. There is need for such applications and pedagogies to be developed and made widely available. However, mobile devices may be more frequently used for various purposes as well as for learning in the future as this technology matures. Thus, m-learning could be another education platform for people who may not have access to traditional higher education.

Another limitation of this study is the relatively small number of respondents. A future study with more respondents and with wider demographics diversity would provide even better understanding of the issues related to m-learning. According to the analysis of the participants' demographic information, those who have more familiarity with m-learning are younger college students. Therefore, a study that focuses on younger generation learners is recommended since this demographic uses more mobile devices. In addition, it would be interesting to study if the m-learning use for higher education attitudes differs by culture.

Overall, it is clear that mobile devices will play an increasingly important role in education and learning as more and more people worldwide continue to use these devices. M-learning success would be driven by collaboration among educators and students to design applications that reinforce advantages of m-learning, and minimize or eliminate the disadvantages.

REFERENCES

Alexander, B. (2004). M-learning: emerging pedagogical and campus issues in the mobile learning environment. *EDUCAUSE Center for Applied Research (ECAR) Bulletin,* (16).

Allen, E., & Seaman, J. (2007). Online Nation – Five Years of Growth in Online Learning. *The Sloan Consortium.* Retrieved March 15, 2008, from http://www.sloan-c.org

Barclay, K. H. (2001). *Humanizing learning-at-distance.* San Francisco, CA: Saybrook Institute.

Cardenas, K. (1998). Technology in today's classroom. *Academe, 84*(3), 27–29.

Cavus, N., & Ibrahim, D. (2009). m-Learning: An experiment in using SMS to support learning new English language words. *British Journal of Educational Technology, 40*(1), 78–91. doi:10.1111/j.1467-8535.2007.00801.x

Hardaker, G. (2005). Conference report. *Campus-Wide Information Systems, 22*(4), 247–248.

Hill, T. R., & Roldan, M. (2005). Toward Third Generation Threaded Discussions for Mobile Learning: Opportunities and Challenges for Ubiquitous Collaborative Environments. *Information Systems Frontiers, 7*(1), 55–70. doi:10.1007/s10796-005-5338-7

Holmberg, B. (1998). What is new and what is important in distance education. *Open Praxis, 1*, 31–33.

Hoppe, G., & Breitner, M. H. (2003). Business models for e-learning. In *Proceedings of E-Learning: Models, Instruments, Experiences, of Multi-Konferenz Wirtschaftsinformatik 2004*, Essen, Germany.

IBM Study Finds Consumers Prefer a Mobile Device Over the PC. (2008, October 22). Retrieved May 2, 2009, from http://www-03.ibm.com/press/us/en/pressrelease/25737.wss

Keegan, D. (1986). *The foundations of distance education*. London: Croom Helm.

Kolakowski, N. (2009, March 16). *Number of People Using Mobile Devices Doubles: comScore*. Retrieved May 2, 2009, from http://www.eweek.com/c/a/Mobile-and-Wireless/Number-of-People-Using-Mobile-Devices-Doubles-ComScore-879862/

Koo, Y. (2008). *Development of Mobile Learning Software. Unpublished master's capstone report*. Monterey Bay, CA: California State University.

Mikie, F., & Anido, L. (2006). Towards a standard for mobile e-learning. In *Proceedings of the Networking, International Conference on Systems and International Conference on Mobile Communications and Learning Technologies*.

Mobile learning inspires the hard-to-reach. (2005). *Education & Training, 47*(8/9), 681-682.

Muir, J. (2003). Decoding mobile device security. *Computer World*. Retrieved April 15, 2007, from http://www.computerworld.com/securitytopics/security/story/0,10801,82890,00.html

Muyinda, P. B. (2007). M-Learning: pedagogical, technical and organisational hypes and realities. *Campus-Wide Information Systems, 24*(2), 97–104. doi:10.1108/10650740710742709

PR Newswire. (2002, December 2). *U.S. military academy at West Point deploys Cranite's Wire(R) Software Suite 2.0*. New York: PR Newswire.

Nielsen Mobile. (July 2008). *Critical Mass: The Worldwide State of the Mobile Web*. Retrieved May 2, 2009, from http://www.nielsenmobile.com/documents/CriticalMass.pdf

Obringer, L. (2001). *How E-learning Works*. Retrieved March 18, 2008, from http://communication.howstuffworks.com/elearning.htm

Oh, C. H. (2003). Information communication technology and the new university: a view on eLearning. *The Annals of the American Academy of Political and Social Science, 585*, 134–153. doi:10.1177/0002716202238572

Porter, L. R. (1997). *Creating the virtual classroom: Distance learning with the Internet*. New York: John Wiley.

Prensky, M. (2004). *What Can You Learn from a Cell Phone? – Almost Anything!* Retrieved April 15, 2007, from http://www.marcprensky.com/writing/Prensky-What_Can_You_Learn_From_a_Cell_Phone-FINAL.pdf

Rosenberg, M. (2001). *E-learning*. New York: McGraw-Hill.

Salz, P. A. (2006). Learning to go. *EContent, 29*(3), 44.

Shen, R., Wang, M., & Pan, X. (2008). Increasing interactivity in blended classrooms through a cutting-edge mobile learning system. *British Journal of Educational Technology, 39*(6), 1073–1086. doi:10.1111/j.1467-8535.2007.00778.x

Slevin, J. (2000). *The Internet and society*. New York: Wiley.

Vasiliou, A., & Economides, A. A. (2007). Mobile collaborative learning using multicast MANETs. *International Journal of Mobile Communications, 5*(4), 423–444. doi:10.1504/IJMC.2007.012789

Wagner, E. D. (2005). Enabling Mobile Learning. *EDUCAUSE Review, 40*(3), 40–53.

Wagner, E. D., & Wilson, P. (2005). Disconnected. *T + D, 59*(12), 40-43.

Weekes, S. (2006). Listen and learn. *Training & Coaching Today*, 17.

This work was previously published in International Journal of Information and Communication Technology, Volume 6, Issue 3, edited by Lawrence A. Tomei, pp. 75-87, copyright 2010 by IGI Publishing (an imprint of IGI Global).

Chapter 23

An Empirical Study to Validate the Technology Acceptance Model in Explaining the Intention to Use Technology among Educational Users

Timothy Teo
Nanyang Technological University, Singapore

ABSTRACT

This study examines a sample (N=239) of pre-service teachers' self-reported intention to use technology. The Technology Acceptance Model (TAM) was used as a research framework in which findings contribute to technology acceptance research by demonstrating the suitability of the TAM to explain the intention to use technology among educational users. Using the structural equation modelling for data analysis, a good fit was found for both the measurement and structural models. Overall, the results of this study offer evidence that the TAM is effective in predicting pre-service teachers' intention to use technology. This paper concludes with a discussion of the limitations and recommendations for further study.

INTRODUCTION

Despite evidence showing technology to having an impact on educational practices and policies and subsequently have the potential to alter traditional definitions of education, the use of the computer in classrooms often remains peripheral and minimal and teachers do not appear to make effective use of technology for teaching (Zhao & Cziko, 2001). In many education systems, the teacher is a key influence to the effective use of technology in the educational system (Zhao, Tan, & Mishra, 2001) and plays a decisive role in determining computer use among their students (Teo, 2006). Hence, it is important to understand the factors that influence teachers' ability to cope with the pressures presented by the rapid advancements in educational technology and changes in educational policies.

While stakeholders in education expect teachers to engage technology in accordance with the belief that technology has an impact on students' learning, it must be borne in mind that teachers

DOI: 10.4018/978-1-61350-468-0.ch023

are affected by many variables that interact with each other that either facilitate or act as barriers to their use of technology. These include personal factors, such as computer self-efficacy (Gong, Xu, & Yu, 2004; Teo, 2008), technical factors, such as technological complexity (Teo, 2009; Thong, Hong, & Tam, 2002), and environmental factor, such as facilitating conditions (Ngai, Poon, & Chan, 2007; Teo, Lee, & Chai, 2008). The fact remains, that fostering technology acceptance among individual teachers is a big challenge for school administrators, technology advocates, and governmental agencies.

User acceptance refers to a willingness to adopt information technology for the tasks it is designed to support. For some long time, developers and procurers of technology could only rely on organizational authority to ensure that technology was used, in the case of many industrial/organizational contexts. However, the changing working practices in recent years among many organizations have enabled greater discretion among technology users. As such there is a need for these organizations to consider the dynamics of user acceptance and how this impacts on technology adoption and usage in their work environments. For this reason, technology acceptance has become an important topic and one of the most researched areas in the information science literature in recent years (Smarkola, 2007).

1.1. Technology Acceptance Model

In the last few decades, researchers have investigated how users' beliefs and attitudes affect their technology usage behaviours (e.g., Davis, 1989; Davis, Bagozzi, & Warshaw, 1989; Dishaw & Strong, 1998; Lederer et al., 2000; Moore & Bembasat, 1995; Straub, Keil, & Brenner, 1997; Taylor & Todd, 1995; Venakatesh, 2000; Venkatesh & Davis, 2000). Arising from these efforts, various theories and models emerged to explain technology acceptance. Of these models, the Technology Acceptance Model (TAM) by Davis (1989) is among the most popular. To a large extent, the TAM has been found to be a parsimonious model to explain technology adoption and usage in a variety of organizational contexts. In over two decades, the TAM has become a widely-used and tested model in technology acceptance research (Adams, Nelson, & Todd, 1992; Davis, Baggozi, & Warshaw, 1989; Lederer et al., 2000; Teo, Wong, & Chai, 2008; Venakatesh, 2000; Venkatesh & Davis, 2000; Venkatesh & Morris, 2000). Figure 1 shows the TAM.

The TAM contains two user beliefs that determine acceptance; perceived ease of use and perceived usefulness. Between these constructs, TAM suggests that perceived usefulness will be influenced by perceived ease of use, since users are more likely to use a technology when they perceive it to be easy to use. According to Davis

Figure 1. Technology acceptance model (Adapted from Davis et al., 1989)

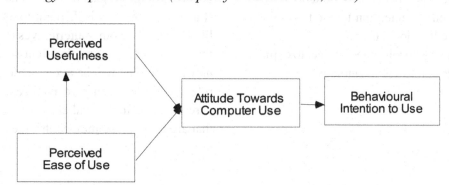

et al. (1989), the TAM was designed to explain the predictors of computer acceptance and usage behaviour across a wide range of computer technologies and user populations. He also intended the model to be parsimonious and generalizable. The appeal of the TAM is attributed to its simplicity and ability to model technology usage across different situations and types of technologies.

Despite being extensively tested and validated in the business and commercial settings, the application of TAM in education is limited. Among the educational users that have been included in technology acceptance studies, teachers (Zhao, Tan, & Mishra, 2001) and pre-service teachers (Teo, 2010; Teo, Wong, & Chai, 2008) form the large majority as they play a pivotal role in the integration of technology within the schools. A reason for the limited application of the TAM in education is the way teachers and pre-service teachers interact with technology. Generally, teachers and pre-service teachers tend to have more autonomy over which technologies to use and how they are used. Recent reviews of TAM studies have revealed a need to consider other settings in order to provide a more comprehensive and holistic view of technology adoption and usage (Lee, Kozar, & Larsen, 2003; Legris, Ingham, & Collerette, 2003).

The aim of this study is to assess the validity of the TAM when it is applied to in educational setting. The following research questions provide the direction of this study.

1. To what extent is the TAM suitable for use to explain the intention to use technology among educational users?
2. In what way do variables interact to explain the intention to use technology?

CONSTRUCTS IN THE TAM

2.1. Perceived Usefulness (PU)

The perceived usefulness of a particular system depends on the extent to which a system is perceived to enhance performance (Davis, 1989; Lederer et al., 2000). For example, if a technology, such as Blackboard, was perceived by the student to be an appropriate alternative to classroom instruction, it would have demonstrated its usefulness to the student as a useful tool. Davis et al. (1989) indicated that perceived usefulness influences attitude towards use. A positive perception of usefulness leans towards a positive attitude about the use of a technology. Recent works by Venkatesh and Morris (2000), Mathieson et al. (2001), and Teo (2009) provided evidence of a positive and significant relationship between perceived usefulness and attitude towards computer use.

2.2. Perceived Ease of Use (PEU)

Perceived ease of use is defined as the extent to which technology is believed to be free of effort (or easy to use) on the part of the user (Davis, 1989; Lederer et al., 1998). It is an individual's assessment that interacting with technology will be relatively free of cognitive burden. In other words, perceived ease of use reflects the facility with which an individual is able to interact with computers. The TAM suggests that a person's usage behaviours are shaped by the experiences with the technology (Agarwal & Karahanna, 2000). If a new technology is difficult to use, users are likely to explore other alternatives or stay with a familiar format (i.e., traditional classroom) and the new technology may be avoided altogether. The relationship between perceived ease of use and perceived usefulness indicates that technologies that are easy to use may contribute to increased usage.

2.3. Attitude towards Computer Use (ATCU)

Attitude towards computer use refers to the user's level of desire to use technology (Lederer et al., 1998). If a user perceives technology to be useful and easy to use, it is likely that the user's attitude towards that technology will be positive. The attitude towards use and behavioural intention relationship in the TAM suggests that people form intentions to perform behaviours towards which they have a positive affect (Davis et al., 1989). Consequently, a positive attitude towards computer use suggests a strong intention to use the technology.

2.4. Intention to Use (ITU)

Behavioural intention of use (ITU) is determined by the attitude towards computer use (Davis, 1989). If the attitude towards computer use is positive, users will form intentions to behave in a consistent manner. Similar to the attitude towards computer use and behavioural intention, the relationship between behavioural intention and actual usage implies that users with strong behavioural intention towards the technology use will, most likely, use that technology.

METHODOLOGY

3.1. Participants

Participants were 239 pre-service teachers enrolled at the National Institute of Education (NIE) in Singapore. They were enrolled in the one-year postgraduate diploma in education programme. Of these, 178 (74.5%) were female. Their mean age was 23.4 (SD=4.53). A large majority of the participants had access to a computer at home (87.0%) and the mean years of computer usage was 7.48 years (SD=4.11). The reported mean of daily computer usage was 3.37 hours (SD=2.41). Pre-service teachers were selected for this study because they were representative of technology users in education. Participants currently use technology for learning and assignment purposes as part of their teacher training and are expected be use technology when they enter the teaching profession upon completion of their teacher training. An educational user of technology is one who harnesses the affordances of technology for teaching and learning purposes although the actual use may not be confined within the physical confines of the school premises (e.g., e-learning). The sample in this study represented about 38% of the student population in the above-mentioned programme of study.

3.2. Measures

A survey questionnaire was administered to the participants who volunteered for this study. The instrument comprised 11 statements on perceived usefulness (PU) (three items), perceived ease of use (PEU) (three items), attitude toward computer use (ATCU) (three items), and intention to use (ITU) (two items). Participants gave their views to each statement on a five-point Likert scale, with from 1 = strongly disagree and 5 = strongly agree. The items and the sources where these items were adapted are listed in appendix 1.

3.3. Data Collection

Participants from various intact classes completed the survey questionnaire provided by this researcher. No rewards or course credit were given for participation. All participants were briefed on the purpose of this study and their rights not to participate in the study. All questionnaires were answered in the English language. On average, each participant took not more than 20 minutes to complete the questionnaire.

RESULTS

4.1. Data Analysis

The statistical analysis comprised two stages. In the first stage, descriptive statistics of the variables were performed. This was followed by assessments of the reliability and validity of the measure used in this study. At the second stage, the path model was tested by assessing the significance of the causal links between each pair of variables in the TAM.

4.2. Descriptive Statistics

The descriptive statistics of the measurement items are shown in Table 1. The mean values of all variables are above the mid-point of 3.0, ranging from 3.92 to 4.50. This indicates an overall positive response to the variables that are measured in this study. The standard deviations range from 0.60 to 0.64, indicating a narrow spread of scores around the mean. The values of the skewness and kurtosis for all variables are acceptable and suggest that the data can be regarded as normal for purposes of further analyses (Kline, 2005).

4.3 Convergent Validity

According to Fornell and Larcker (1981), an assessment for convergent validity includes establishing the item reliability of each measure and composite reliability of each construct. The item reliability of an item was assessed by its factor loading onto the underlying construct. Hair et al. (2006) suggested that an item is significant if its factor loading is greater than 0.50. As shown in Table 2, the eigenvalues of all constructs exceed 1.00 and the percent of cumulative variance explained of these four constructs was 77.50%. The factor loadings of all the items in the measure ranged from 0.77 to 0.89 (in bold). This exceeds the threshold set by Hair et al. (2006) and demonstrates convergent validity at the item level. The composite reliability of each construct was assessed using Cronbach's α. As shown in Table 3, the reliabilities of all the constructs ranged from 0.74 to 0.90 and regarded as fairly good. The final indicator of convergent validity is the average variance extracted which measures the amount of variance captured by the construct in relation to the amount of variance attributable to measurement error (Fornell & Larcker, 1981). Convergent validity is judged to be adequate when the average variance extracted for a construct equals or exceeds 0.50 (i.e., when the variance captured by the construct exceeds the variance due to measurement error). As shown in Table 3, the convergent validity is established for this study.

4.4. Discriminant Validity

This is assessed to measure the extent to which constructs differ. Discriminant validity is considered adequate when the variance shared between a construct and any other construct in the model is less than the variance that constructs shares with its measures (Fornell et al., 1982). The variance shared by any two constructs is obtained by squaring the correlation between the two constructs. The variance shared between a construct and

Table 1. Descriptive statistics of the six constructs

Variable	Mean	Standard Deviation	Skewness	Kurtosis
PU	4.22	.63	-.54	.55
PEU	3.92	.64	-.47	.55
ATCU	4.15	.60	-1.12	4.53
ITU	4.50	.60	-1.97	8.16

Table 2. Principal component analysis of the scale items

	PU	PEU	ATCU	ITU
PU1	**.778**	.194	.301	.190
PU2	**.895**	.192	.219	.093
PU3	**.856**	.136	.265	.143
PEU1	.175	**.817**	.153	.055
PEU2	.213	**.815**	.098	.095
PEU3	.064	**.832**	.252	.130
ATCU1	.294	.097	**.773**	.165
ATCU2	.198	.264	**.789**	.109
ATCU3	.253	.185	**.793**	.104
ITU1	.157	.090	.132	**.864**
ITU2	.128	.125	.138	**.863**
Total var. Expl.	2.448	2.253	2.190	1.635
% Var. Expl.	22.252	20.479	19.910	14.863

Extraction Method: Principal Component Analysis. Rotation Method: Varimax with Kaiser Normalization.
a Rotation converged in 6 iterations.

Table 3. Reliability and validities values of the measure

Construct (items)	α	AVE	PU	PEU	ATCU	BIU
PU (3)	.90	.71	(.84)			
PEU (3)	.82	.67	.41*	(.82)		
ATCU (4)	.81	.61	.59*	.45*	(.78)	
ITU (2)	.74	.75	.36*	.28*	.35*	(.87)

Notes:
(1) *p <.01
(2) AVE: Average Variance Extracted. This is computed by adding the squared factor loadings divided by number of factors of the underlying construct.
(3) Diagonal in parentheses: square root of average variance extracted from observed variables (items); Off-diagonal: correlations between constructs

its measures corresponds to average variance extracted. Discriminant validity was assessed by comparing the square root of the average variance extracted for a given construct with the correlations between that construct and all other constructs. Table 3 shows the correlation matrix for the constructs. The diagonal elements have been replaced by the square roots of the average variance extracted. For discriminant validity to be judged adequate, these diagonal elements should be greater than the off-diagonal elements in the corresponding rows and columns. Discriminant validity appears satisfactory at the construct level in the case of all constructs. This indicates that the each construct shared more variance with its items than it does with other constructs. The values in Table 3 show that there is discriminant validity in the data.

4.5. Test of the Measurement Model

Structural equation modelling (SEM) was used to assess the fit of the measurement model. SEM was chosen for its ability to examine a series of dependence relationships simultaneously, especially where there are direct and indirect effects among the constructs within the model (Hair et al., 2006). In this study, AMOS 7.0 (Arbuckle, 2005) was used with maximum likelihood estimation. In a SEM, sample size plays a key role in determining the reliability of the result. Hair et al. (2006) proposed that any study with five or fewer constructs, each with more than three items, and high item communality with.60 and higher, can adequately be estimated with sample size of 150. In this study, the sample size is 239 and this was considered adequate. However, although intention to use (ITU) comprised only two items, it has high alpha coefficient and AVE, indicating an acceptable level of convergent validity.

In using SEM, it is a common practice to use a variety of indices to measure model fit (Kline, 2005). In addition to the ratio of the χ^2 statistic to its degree of freedom, with a value less than 5 indicating acceptable fit, researchers recommended the use of the Normed Fit Index (NFI), Comparative Fit Index (CFI), Root Mean Square Error of Approximation (RMSEA), and Standardised Root Mean Residual (SRMR). Table 4 shows the level of acceptable fit and the fit indices for the research model in this study. The values of all indices fall within the recommended guidelines and indicate that the measurement model in this study has a good fit.

4.6. Test of the Structural Model

Figure 2 shows the resulting path coefficients of the research model in this study. The results of this study support existing TAM studies. Perceived ease of use significantly influenced perceived usefulness ($\beta = 0.47$, p < 0.001) and attitudes towards computer use ($\beta = 0.34$, p < 0.001). Perceived usefulness was found to be significant in influencing attitudes towards computer use ($\beta = 0.53$, p < 0.001) and attitudes towards computer use was found to be significant in influencing intention to use ($\beta = 0.49$, p < 0.001)

Perceived usefulness was found to be predicted by perceived ease of use, resulting in an R^2 of 0.216. This means that perceived ease of use explained 21.6% of the variance in perceived usefulness. Attitude towards computer use was predicted by perceived usefulness and perceived ease of use resulting in an $R^2 = 0.539$, suggesting that perceived usefulness and perceived of ease of use explained 53.9% of the variance in attitude towards computer use. The dependent variable, intention to use, was predicted by attitude towards computer use and indirectly by perceived usefulness and perceived ease of use, resulting in an R^2 of 0.237, indicating that these three variables explained 23.7% of the variance in intention to use. Figure 2 shows the structural model with the path coefficients.

Table 4. Fit indices for the measurement model

Model fit indices	Values	Recommended guidelines	References
χ^2	33.487, p < 444	Non-significant	Klem, 2000; Kline, 2005; McDonald and Ho, 2002
χ^2/df (deg. of freedom)	1.015	< 3	Kline, 2005
TLI	.99	=>.90	Klem, 2000; McDonald and Ho, 2002
CFI	1.00	=>.90	Klem, 2000; McDonald and Ho, 2002
RMSEA	.008 (.000,.048)	<.05 (good fit)	McDonald and Ho, 2002
SRMR	.026	<.05	Klem, 2000; McDonald and Ho, 2002

Figure 2. Path coefficient of the structural model

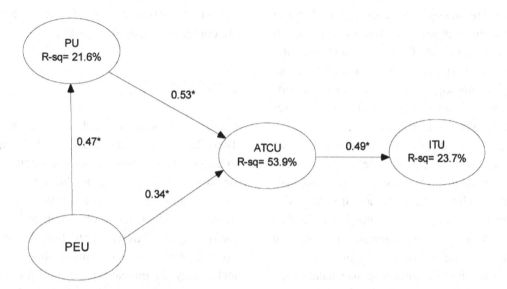

DISCUSSION

This study aims to assess the validity of the TAM to explain the intention to use technology among educational users. In addition, the extent to which the variables in the TAM contribute to the intention to use was also examined.

The results show that the TAM is a suitable model for use to examine the intention to use technology among educational users. It is found to be parsimonious and three core variables in the TAM, perceived usefulness, perceived ease of use, and attitude towards computer use explained 23.7% of the variance in intention to use. However, the variance explained in attitude towards computer use appeared to be greater (53.9%) with direct influences from perceived usefulness and perceived ease of use.

In addition, all paths coefficients in the model were significant. It was found that perceived usefulness and perceived ease of use, and attitude toward computer use were significant determinants of intention to use technology. This provided support to the adequacy of the TAM in representing the interaction among the variables in explaining

the intention to use technology. Among the path coefficients, those for PU → ATCU and ATCU → ITU were larger than the others. This finding is consistent with Bhattacherjee and Premkumar (2004) who cited PU as the main driving force behind the intention to use technology and when mediated by ATCU, PU and ATCU act as the two most important predictors of the intention to use technology. This view was supported by Mello (2006) who cited that, among other factors, a positive attitude towards ICT use was a desirable teacher attribute that contribute to a successful integration of technology in teaching and learning.

The findings from this study have implications to school administrators and teacher educators. Perceived usefulness and perceived ease of use are important user beliefs that decision-makers need to focus in order to encourage users' intention to use technology. However, the properties of perceived usefulness and perceived ease of use do not remain static. While users may perceive technology to be useful and easy to use at the adoption stage, they may soon experience limitations if they do not participate in continuing professional development to acquire more advanced skills and knowledge on the use of technology. This situation is more pressing for teachers who have to deal with students who are more experienced in the use of technology. Over time, such students may increase their expectations on their teachers to infuse technology into their lessons and consequently create insecurity and stress to the latter (Sugar, Crawley, & Fine, 2004).

In terms of attitude towards computer use, school administrators should design implementation strategies and place effective support structures to allow teachers to acquire successful experiences in the use of technology, in order that positive attitudes toward computer use could be cultivated among teachers. This in turn would reinforce teachers' intention to use technology over time. On the part of the teacher educators, it is important to ensure that pre-service teachers have access to technology in the curriculum and experience successes in the use of technology before they are posted to the schools. In the course of their training, pre-service teachers should be provided with the skills and experiences that will be relevant in their future job as a teacher. From the literature, pre-service teachers develop positive attitudes toward computer use when teacher educators integrated technology into their course work (Bai, 2006). Such integration include providing pre-service teachers with relevant information about how to use various technologies and providing a range of hands-on experiences.

From the teacher education perspective, although the TAM is adequate in explaining the intention to use technology among pre-service teachers in this study, there are other variables that influence the intention to use technology among pre-service teachers. Judge and O'Bannon (2008) noted that factors such as access to technology, mismatch of expectations among teacher educators in terms of technology and integration and the reward system, and the extent to which teacher educators work together, contribute to pre-service teachers' desire and intention to use technology. In essence, the authors stressed the

need for teacher educators to model technology use with a view to produce future teachers who are competent technology users.

LIMITATIONS

Parsimony is both a strength and weakness of the TAM. The low percentage (23.7%) of the variance in the intention to use technology among the participants in this study may be due to the exclusion of other significant variables in the TAM. Some of these variables may include subjective norms, facilitating conditions, and technical complexity (Teo, 2009). The issues surrounding the use of technology in education are multifarious and complex. Potential users, such as teachers, need to consider many of these issues together with their educational goals when they make decisions relating to technology integration for teaching and learning. Secondly, the data collected in this study was through self-reports and this may lead to common method variance, a situation where the true associations between variables are inflated, leading to inaccurate inferences.

CONCLUSION AND SUGGESTIONS FOR FURTHER STUDY

Although the findings of this study has provided some empirical support for the TAM as a parsimonious model with an ability to explain the intention to use technology, researchers should consider extending the TAM by considering other variables with a view to inspect possible increases in the explanatory powers of the TAM, to gain a more comprehensive understanding of the capability of the TAM in the educational context. This was concurred by Lee, Kozar, and Larsen (2003) who believed that extending the TAM by adding variables would allow a greater understanding of the TAM in terms of its applicability and relevance in various organizational contexts.

It is reasonable to expect the reliance and use of technology to increase in the future. In the educational setting, an extended TAM with additional variables such as subjective norm and facilitating conditions could be used a research to compare the intention to use technology between pre-service and practising teachers, or between teachers and students. This would allow us to gain insights into the deeper and more complex issues relating to educational uses of technology. Longitudinal studies may be conducted to trace the changes in the intention to use technology by pre-service teachers when they become practicing teachers. Finally, it is useful to examine whether there are discrepancies between self-reports and actual practice and, if these exist, to identify the factors that cause these differences.

REFERENCES

Adams, D. A., Nelson, R. R., & Todd, P. A. (1992). Perceived usefulness, ease of use, and usage of information technology: A replication. *Management Information Systems Quarterly, 16*, 227–247. doi:10.2307/249577

Agarwal, R., & Karahanna, E. (2000). Time flies when you're having fun: Cognitive absorption and beliefs about information technology usage. *Management Information Systems Quarterly, 24*(4), 665–694. doi:10.2307/3250951

Ajzen, I., & Fishbein, M. (1980). *Understanding attitudes and predicting social behaviour*. Englewood Cliffs, NJ: Prentice-Hall.

Arbuckle, J. L. (2006). *AMOS (Version 7.0)*. Chicago: SPSS.

Bhattacherjee, A., & Premkumar, G. (2004). Understanding changes in belief and attitude toward information technology usage: A theoretical model and longitudinal test. *Management Information Systems Quarterly, 28*(2), 351–370.

Compeau, D. R., & Higgins, C. A. (1995). Computer self-efficacy: Development of a measure and initial test. *Management Information Systems Quarterly, 19*(2), 189–211. doi:10.2307/249688

Davis, F. D. (1989). Perceived usefulness, perceived ease of use, and user acceptance of information technology. *Management Information Systems Quarterly, 13*(3), 319–340. doi:10.2307/249008

Davis, F. D., Bagozzi, R. P., & Warshaw, P. R. (1989). User acceptance of computer technology: A comparison of two theoretical models. *Management Science, 35*(8), 928–1003. doi:10.1287/mnsc.35.8.982

Dishaw, M. T., & Strong, D. M. (1999). Extending the technology acceptance model with task-technology fit constructs. *Information & Management, 36*(1), 9–21. doi:10.1016/S0378-7206(98)00101-3

Fornell, C., & Larcker, D. F. (1981). Evaluating structural equation models with unobservable variables and measurement error. *JMR, Journal of Marketing Research, 48*, 39–50. doi:10.2307/3151312

Fornell, C., Tellis, G. J., & Zinkhan, G. M. (1982). Validity assessment: a structural equations approach using partial least squares. In *Proceedings of the American Marketing Association Educators' Conference*.

Gong, M., Xu, Y., & Yu, Y. (2004). An enhanced Technology Acceptance Model for web-based learning. *Journal of Information Systems Education, 15*(4), 365–374.

Hair, J. F. Jr, Black, W. C., Babin, B., Anderson, R., & Tatham, R. (2006). *Multivariate Data Analysis* (6th ed.). Upper Saddle River, NJ: Prentice Hall.

Judge, S., & O'Bannon, B. (2008). Faculty integration of technology in teacher preparation: Outcomes of a development model. *Technology, Pedagogy and Education*, *17*(1), 17–28. doi:10.1080/14759390701847435

Klem, L. (2000). Structural equation modeling. In Grimm, L. G., & Yarnold, P. R. (Eds.), *Reading and understanding more multivariate statistics*. Washington, DC: American Psychology Association.

Kline, R. B. (2005). *Principles and practice of structural equation modeling* (2nd ed.). New York: Guilford Press.

Lederer, A. L., Maupin, D. J., Sens, M. P., & Zhuang, Y. (2000). The technology acceptance model and the World Wide Web. *Decision Support Systems*, *29*, 269–282. doi:10.1016/S0167-9236(00)00076-2

Lee, Y., Kozar, K. A., & Larsen, K. R. T. (2003). The technology acceptance model: Past, present and future. *Communications of the Association for Information Systems*, *12*, 752–780.

Legris, P., Ingham, J., & Collerette, P. (2003). Who do people use information technology? A critical review of the technology acceptance model. *Information & Management*, *40*, 191–204. doi:10.1016/S0378-7206(01)00143-4

Mathieson, K., Peacock, E., & Chinn, W. C. (2001). Extending the Technology Acceptance Model: The influence of perceived user resources. *The Data Base for Advances in Information Systems*, *32*(3), 86–112.

McDonald, R. P., & Ho, M.-H. R. (2002). Principles and practice in reporting structural equation analyses. *Psychological Methods*, *7*(1), 64–82. doi:10.1037/1082-989X.7.1.64

Mello, L. R. (2006). Identifying success in the application of information and communication technology as a curriculum teaching and learning tool. *Technology, Pedagogy and Education*, *15*(1), 95–106. doi:10.1080/14759390500435853

Ngai, E. W. T., Poon, J. K. L., & Chan, Y. H. C. (2007). Empirical examination of the adoption of WebCT using TAM. *Computers & Education*, *48*(2), 250–267. doi:10.1016/j.compedu.2004.11.007

Smarkola, C. (2007). Technology acceptance predictors among student teachers and experienced classroom teachers. *Journal of Educational Computing Research*, *37*(1), 65–82. doi:10.2190/J3GM-3RK1-2907-7U03

Sugar, W., Crawley, F., & Fine, B. (2004). Examining teachers' decisions to adopt new technology. *Journal of Educational Technology & Society*, *7*(4), 201–213.

Taylor, S., & Todd, P. A. (1995). Understanding information technology usage: a test of competing models. *Information Systems Research*, *6*(2), 144–176. doi:10.1287/isre.6.2.144

Teo, T. (2006). Attitudes toward computers: A study of post-secondary students in Singapore. *Interactive Learning Environments*, *14*(1), 17–24. doi:10.1080/10494820600616406

Teo, T. (2008). Assessing the computer attitudes of students: an Asian perspective. *Computers in Human Behavior*, *24*(4), 1634–1642. doi:10.1016/j.chb.2007.06.004

Teo, T. (2009). Modelling technology acceptance in education: A study of pre-service teachers. *Computers & Education*, *52*(1), 302–312. doi:10.1016/j.compedu.2008.08.006

Teo, T. (2010). A path analysis of pre-service teachers' attitudes toward computer use: applying and extending the Technology Acceptance Model in an educational context. *Interactive Learning Environments*, *18*(1), 65–79. doi:10.1080/10494820802231327

Teo, T., Lee, C. B., & Chai, C. S. (2008). Understanding pre-service teachers' computer attitudes: applying and extending the Technology Acceptance Model (TAM). *Journal of Computer Assisted Learning*, *24*(2), 128–143. doi:10.1111/j.1365-2729.2007.00247.x

Teo, T., Wong, S. L., & Chai, C. S. (2008). A cross-cultural examination of the intention to use technology between Singaporean and Malaysian pre-service teachers: an application of the Technology Acceptance Model (TAM). *Journal of Educational Technology & Society*, *11*(4), 265–280.

Thompson, R. L., Higgins, C. A., & Howell, J. M. (1991). Personal computing: toward a conceptual model of utilization. *Management Information Systems Quarterly*, *15*(1), 124–143. doi:10.2307/249443

Thong, J. Y. L., Hong, W., & Tam, K. Y. (2002). Understanding user acceptance of digital libraries: What are the roles of interface characteristics, organizational context, and individual differences? *International Journal of Human-Computer Studies*, *57*(3), 215–242. doi:10.1016/S1071-5819(02)91024-4

Venkatesh, V., & Davis, F. D. (2000). A theoretical extension of the technology acceptance model: Four longitudinal field studies. *Management Science*, *46*(2), 186–204. doi:10.1287/mnsc.46.2.186.11926

Venkatesh, V., & Morris, M. G. (2000). Why don't men ever stop to ask for directions? Gender, social influence, and their role in technology acceptance and usage behavior. *Management Information Systems Quarterly*, *24*(1), 115–139. doi:10.2307/3250981

Yuen, H. K., Law, N., & Chan, H. (1999). Improving IT training for serving teachers through evaluation. In Cumming, G., Okamoto, T., & Gomez, L. (Eds.), *Advanced Research in Computers and Communications in Education* (*Vol. 2*, pp. 441–448). Amsterdam: IOS Press.

Zhao, Y., & Cziko, G. A. (2001). Teacher Adoption of Technology: A Perceptual Control Theory Perspective. *Journal of Technology and Teacher Education*, *9*(1), 5–30.

Zhao, Y., Tan, H. S., & Mishra, P. (2001). Technology: teaching and learning: whose computer is it? *Journal of Adolescent & Adult Literacy*, *44*(4), 348–355.

APPENDIX: CONSTRUCTS AND ITEMS USED IN THIS STUDY

Construct	Item	
Perceived Usefulness (adapted from Davies, 1989)	PU1	Using computers will improve my work.
	PU2	Using computers will enhance my effectiveness.
	PU3	Using computers will increase my productivity.
Perceived Ease of Use (adapted from Davies, 1989)	PEU1	My interaction with computers is clear and understandable.
	PEU2	I find it easy to get computers to do what I want it to do.
	PEU3	I find computers easy to use.
Computer Attitudes (adapted from Thompson et al. 1991; Compeau and Higgins, 1995)		ATCU1
	Computers make work more interesting.	ATCU2
	Working with computers is fun.	ATCU3
I look forward to those aspects of my job that require me to use computers.	Intention to Use (adapted from Davies, 1989)	ITU1
	I will use computers in future.	ITU2

This work was previously published in International Journal of Information and Communication Technology, Volume 6, Issue 4, edited by Lawrence A. Tomei, pp. 1-12, copyright 2010 by IGI Publishing (an imprint of IGI Global).

Chapter 24
Problem–Based Learning in a Technical Course in Computing:
A Case Study

Eduardo Correia
Christchurch Polytechnic Institute of Technology, New Zealand

Ricky Watson
Christchurch Polytechnic Institute of Technology, New Zealand

ABSTRACT

Problem-based learning has been well-documented, from its early days in the teaching of medical professionals to its more recent use in other disciplines. It has been adopted in many educational institutions because it gives students a realistic problem and provides opportunities to translate knowledge into solutions. This article is a case study of this approach at a second-year technical course, in which members of the class were divided into groups and given a scenario concerning a fictitious organisation about to embark on a major upgrade to its existing and problematic networking infrastructure. The course consisted of two parts. The first group was provided with a set of virtual machines to upgrade, and the second group chose and implemented a major technology on this newly upgraded network. The authors outline how problem-based learning is used in this context in a way that informs the teaching of any technical computing course.

INTRODUCTION

By the time they reach the final semester of a two-year Diploma in Information and Communication Technology at the Christchurch Polytechnic Institute of Technology, students have completed most other courses on offer in the area of operating systems and networking. These courses usually follow a dual format of staff covering a particular topic and then students engaging in activities that illuminate, reinforce and clarify the topic. Students are able to understand a topic because the tasks confine, restrict and isolate areas of knowledge. It is an approach that ensures courses are well structured, comprehensive, and thorough, all important elements if students are to gain a basic

DOI: 10.4018/978-1-61350-468-0.ch024

mastery and understanding of the discipline. At the same time, this approach by definition splinters knowledge artificially into manageable constituent components that mask the real nature of a network as an intact, integrated, interconnected system. Problem-based learning can therefore be highly effective for more advanced studies because it creates "unified and dynamic wholes (from previously separated components) to effect the transformation of learning" (Beckwith, 1988, p. 4).

This article is a study on the use of the problem-based learning approach in a course called "Network Administration (Project)", which seeks this kind of "expanded view of purpose" (McDonald & Gibbons, 2009, p. 383), by giving students a scenario that provides an opportunity firstly to utilise skills learnt in a number of other courses and apply these skills in new ways and secondly to investigate and work with a range of systems and technologies with which they are not familiar and have not previously encountered in their studies. This shifts the focus to "authentic intellectual work" (Newmann, Bryk, & Nagoaka, 2001), the business of solving advanced, complex problems. Unlike other, more conventional courses, Network Administration (Project) portrays knowledge as rich and dynamic in all kinds of ways, what has been described as the "principle of multiplicity" (Koschmann, Kelson, Feltovich, & Barrows, 1998, p. 88), and the experience of teaching staff support the notion that problem solving is something that can be learnt (Jonassen, 2004).

Problem-based learning contains three major elements: focusing, from the start, on problems, making use of prior knowledge and seeking further relevant information, and interacting with others as part of a small group (Vardi & Ciccarelli, 2008). Network Administration (Project) encapsulates these three elements in a realistic scenario that is presented at the beginning of the course and is used all through it. The scenario raises a number of complex problems but lecturers and tutors deliberately offer no solutions. Teaching staff do address the class at certain points to clarify certain matters or announce what was expected in a particular task but no lectures take place and little conventional teaching occurs. Instead, students make use of two scheduled two-hour classes each week to work in groups, and teachers are present to clarify and support. The class are told, though, that teaching staff are to be considered managers who understood what was required at a high level but do not have specific technical expertise to resolve particular problems. This forces students to rely on their own initiative and resources, in keeping with full problem-based learning where "the nature of the problem guides and drives the entire learning experience (Ellis, Carswell, Bernat, Deveaux, Frison, Meisalo, 1999, p. 43). It ensures that learning is not restricted to the comprehension and application of certain knowledge but also extends to the more complex activities analysis, synthesis, and evaluation (Dennen, 2000).

THE SCENARIO: STARTING WITH THE PROBLEMS

The scenario for the course centres on a fictitious private tertiary educational institution called Progress College, with campuses in the three main metropolitan centres in New Zealand, Auckland, Wellington and Christchurch. The senior network administrators of Progress College have left quite suddenly, but it is well known that senior management are dissatisfied with evident deficiencies in performance and stability on the network, and that an independent study has found serious issues resulting from a blatant disregard for so-called "best practice". In terms of this scenario, each group in the class is the newly appointed team of network administrators tasked with resolving current issues and implementing a major upgrade. Teaching staff allocated to the course have the necessary technical skills but from the outset made it clear that they would be playing the role of senior managers who understood the issues at a high level but did not possess the technical skills to assist with specific problems. They would only help clarify whether a particular solution was feasible in terms of available resources or be consistent with the course objectives, but little beyond that.

Each group in the class was given the same set of eleven VMware Workstation virtual machines, including Ubuntu-based routers, domain controllers, domain member servers, and application servers (Figure 1). Each member of the group is asked to take a group of virtual machines and run it on his or her physical machine, but the class are not told anything about these machines, as it is their job to document the network. The three groups of virtual machines corresponded to where they were located (Auckland, Wellington and Christchurch), and if there are only two students in a group, the second student is expect to run both the Wellington and Christchurch set of machines. The virtual machines are distributed in this way to reduce the load on physical machines and to improve system performance. As the scenario states, the previous network administrators of

Progress College ignored principles of best practice, so students receive no accompanying documentation, with the exception of passwords of important user accounts.

The virtual machines are also poorly set up deliberately as a result of the scenario, with serious configuration errors and a demonstrable lack of good planning and design. There is a lack of a naming convention with no apparent indication as to the role of a machine on the network or its location. In one case, the name of the server is even deliberately misspelled, something that does unfortunately happen in live production networks! Students are informed that the Internet connection is in Auckland and that the other centres make use of this connection. This environment offers the opportunity to work on complex, open-ended problems, and this is preferable as issues can be addressed in a number of different ways (Kolodner, Hmelo, & Narayan, 1996).

The scenario for the course presents two major challenges: the first, to upgrade an existing net-

Figure 1. Progress college scenario network

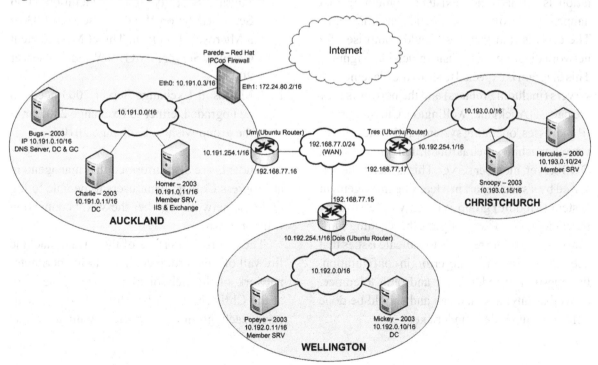

work that students are not familiar with, the second, to test and implement a selected technology on the upgraded network. A number of technologies are presented as options, and students can also, if they wish, suggest an alternative technology, which one student has done. As a result the course comprises of two basic parts: firstly, documenting and upgrading the current network and secondly, implementing a particular technology. This article does not definitively ascertain whether problem-based learning approach in this case leads students to remember more of what they learn in this course, but teaching staff believe that it does something that is consistent with other research in this area (Dochy, Segers, van den Bossche, & Gijbels, 2003).

PART ONE: DOCUMENTING AND UPGRADING THE CURRENT NETWORK

Students are first required to document a network that they are unfamiliar with and where documentation is virtually non-existent, something that happens all too often in production environments. The class is told that this should comprise of a network diagram using Visio, much like Figure 1. This diagram is expected to show the placement of servers (including routers) and the networks they are part of (Auckland, Wellington, Christchurch), IP addresses, operating systems and basic roles of various machines such as router, domain controller, DNS server, member server. This is then to be followed by a short report in a learning management system (Moodle) group Wiki only accessible by other members of the group and the teaching staff. The purpose of the report is to indicate issues that need addressing, including errors in configuration, the question of redundancy and fault tolerance, as well as anything that can and should be done before the upgrade is undertaken.

The students go on to actually upgrading the Progress College network. This involves upgrading all the Windows 2000 Server and Windows Server 2003 machines to Windows Server 2008 without losing any data. Before doing the upgrade, the students are asked to prepare the network for these major changes and make sure that all the machines function properly, wherever possible. The Progress College network upgrade has the following characteristics:

A. Brand new hardware is leased and Windows Server 2008 licences purchased, so an in-place upgrade is possible but not essential,

B. The Windows 2000 Server in Christchurch does not work and instead of fixing it, the group may decide to simply install a new machine in its place. If this is done, though, the objects for this server in Active Directory should no longer be present, otherwise other domain controllers will try to replicate to them.

C. A new firewall is to replace the IPCop firewall. This new firewall may be a Microsoft Internet Security and Acceleration 2006 Server (ISA) on Windows Server 2003 or a Microsoft Forefront Threat Management Gateway Server (TMG) on Windows Server 2008.

D. Microsoft Exchange Server 2003 needs to be upgraded, either to Exchange 2007 or, if the group wishes, Exchange 2010.

Students are also informed that management at Progress College want users to be able to log on to the network whether the WAN connection is up or down.

The external interface of the virtual machine firewall of each group connects to the perimeter network of the School of Computing network at the Christchurch Polytechnic. Teaching staff issue each group in the class with a unique publically registered domain name (1.procoll. info, 2.procoll.info, 3.procoll.info etc) and a public static IP address that is available on the Internet (165.84.198.221/25, 165.84.198.222/25, 165.84.198.223 etc). After the firewall and mail server are upgraded, users in the Progress College network are expected to still be able to send and receive actual emails and have authenticated access to the Internet. All groups in the class are required to complete the upgrade to the network approximately half way through the course, so that students can start implementing a significant technology at the same point in the course.

PART TWO: IMPLEMENTING A SIGNIFICANT TECHNOLOGY

Once the network has been upgraded, including the IPCop firewall to ISA or TMG, each group chooses a topic. The intention is for each topic to be unique to the group and once selected cannot be changed (unless there is a really compelling reason for the change). If some topics are, by nature, smaller and easier to implement than others, then related technologies can be deployed as well. Students document the implementation and testing of the technology of their choice, and ensure that they keep a log of both problems and solutions, including solutions that in the end did not work. Teaching staff suggest a number of technologies for Part Two.

GROUP WORK

The course focuses extensively on groups rather than individuals not only because that is how people mostly work in industry, but more importantly because it enables teaching staff to introduce larger, more complex problems. This is consistent with the findings of Lou, Abrami, and d'Apollonia (2001) that groups work better than individuals when the tasks are complex and

there is no or minimal feedback. Whereas groups usually comprise of five to seven people in most forms of problem-based learning, it was decided to make the groups for this course a minimum of two people and a maximum of three people, though later two students who were not present at that first class were permitted to work on their own. This departure from conventional problem-based learning practice was driven by the scenario, which demanded fewer people, and having one person responsible for each centre of the fictitious organisation made sense. It would ensure that everyone in the group contributed otherwise the group as a whole would suffer quite dramatically.

The other question teaching staff face is whether to place the students in groups or leave it instead to the students to decide who they wish to work with. The advantage of teaching staff doing this is two-fold: firstly, it is arguably more authentic because in the work place people generally do not get to choose who they work with and secondly it is possible to exercise greater control over the learning environment, thus avoiding the typical issues of self-selected student groups (McConnell, 2006). Teacher-selected groups, though, raise problems of their own (Webb, Nemer, Chizhik, & Sugrue, 1998). In the end staff decided to let the students form the groups themselves as this significantly reduces the risk of conflict that might impact negatively on learning, a factor especially important when the groups comprise of so few people. In addition due to the fact the groups are self-selected, students already know each other well from interactions in other courses, with the result that there is little time when the group is "less effective" because they are getting to "learn about each other" (McConnell, 2006, p. 26). It is gratifying that at least one study has found that in short-term projects for second-year students "allowing students to choose their own groups is best" (Richards, 2009, p. 2, 7).

While teaching staff do ask the class of eighteen students to form themselves into groups, two students were allowed to work on their own.

One wished to use the course to follow specific interests not shared by anyone else in the class; the other wished to preserve maximum flexibility, unhindered by other people's schedules. The former student was one of the top students in the class and completed all the requirements of the course; whereas the latter was granted extra time in order to complete the project. Most people prefer being part of a group and not to work on their own for the simple reason that if they do this, it would entail a significant increase in workload and reduce access to prior knowledge and experience. At the start of the course, teaching staff make it clear that people within a group should share information freely but that members of one group should not discuss matters with members of another, and it appears that students do follow these instructions. Still, in the first part of the course there is a risk that students will simply repeat the statements and activities of other groups. One way of avoiding this is to provide different scenarios and network environments to different groups. While this is an option, it does not appear to be necessary.

Most groups worked really well together, with members showing a high-level of engagement in activities, both during and outside class times, and this is consistent with studies that have shown problem-based learning to increase motivation among students (Pedersen, 2003). There were, though, two exceptions. One group of three students comprised of two older, more mature students and a younger student, who did not participate as much as he should have done. The older students took too much leadership and control and did not include the other student in enough of the group's activities. In the other group, one comprising of two students, one student appeared to lack interest and motivation, and simply let the other do much of the work on his own. This occurred in spite of teaching staff encouraging students to spread the workload evenly, wherever possible, and telling the class that all members of the group were expected to be aware of and familiar

with their scenario network and the changes that had been made to it. In future teaching staff may choose to employ other strategies such as posing a key question at the start of each class based on the scenario and asking students to discuss it in their groups and then making sure that everyone was participating (Vardi & Ciccarelli, 2008).

ASSESSMENT AND FEEDBACK

As the course only ran over seven weeks of teaching and comprised of 28 contact hours, it was decided to only have a single item of assessment. This single item of assessment consisted of an interview where the teachers of the course saw each group and asked the members of the group to demonstrate: that major network services continued to work after the upgrade; and how the technology they selected had been implemented and configured.

The students in each group were also asked open-ended questions such as "What was the most difficult part of the upgrade?" and "How did you contribute to the group?" As each group is required to maintain a wiki that keeps a record of their activities throughout the course, it was easy to see a history of the contributions of each member of the group, because the learning management system (Moodle in this case) also automatically recorded exactly when these contributions were made and by whom. As each member of the group only needed to be graded in terms of a "merit" (or distinction), a "pass" and an "NC" ("no credit"), it was a matter of judging the performance of the students in terms of these three broad categories. All groups were also asked what they would have done differently, if they were challenged in the same kind of way again. Most stated that they would give much more attention to planning before embarking on the migration, but that some of the lessons they learnt could only be gained through experience.

A short online survey was provided on the learning management system to students before they had done their assessments. Of the eighteen students in the class, fourteen responded. Both parts of the course were equally useful according to 50% of the students but fewer students showed a preference for the second part of the course, possibly because it was based on technologies with which they were unfamiliar. All the students considered the course to be either "excellent" or "good", with no students stating that the course was "satisfactory", "poor" or "very poor". All the respondents believed the course was relevant, with almost 80% stating that they strongly agreed that the course was relevant. However, a more sophisticated rubric for marking should be developed as it can better articulate how the final mark is reached and generate a higher level of consistency.

Students' comments reflected their appreciation for being given the freedom to resolve problems themselves and in their own way. There were a number of answers to the question "If there was one thing you would NOT change in this course, what would it be?" These included "Giving us the freedom to use whatever methods and ways to fix the problems at hand" as well as "The complexity of each task involved, and the small amount of help from the tutors". These indicated that students were grateful for the independence, freedom and ultimately trust placed in their ability to solve complex problems. Other comments, though, showed that some people did struggle to come to terms with this level of freedom. The last question was "If there was one thing you would change in this course, what would it be?" One wrote "More structure - at times we weren't sure exactly what we were meant to be doing - had to seek guidance from Ricky/Eddie". Another student indicated a definite preference for Linux and Macs, stating that he or she would replace the Windows machines with Linux or Macs "if possible", and a student did indicate that at times student machines struggled to cope with the demands of so many VMs simultaneously ("faster machines!"). Machines in this classroom have since been upgraded, but it is true that more of the work needed to be shifted from the Auckland site to the other two sites. A number of students, though, wrote that they would not change anything.

IMPROVEMENTS TO THE ENVIRONMENT

This was the first time this course was offered, and on reflection the network environment provided to students could have been a great deal more realistic. The Active Directory database contained over 7000 user accounts, something that was feasible through the use of a script that employed typical user names (not user 1, user 2 etc but something more like Susan Browne, Graeme Bell etc). The directory should have also contained computer accounts to reflect a more realistic view of the true number of objects that domain controllers would need to hold. The servers students were given could have also included a number of group policies, some linked to sites, some to the domain, and yet others to organisational units. These would have had a significant impact on the user environment, through security settings, login scripts and the installation of software. In future the following should also be considered for inclusion into the virtual machine networks given to students:

A. Adding shares with thousands of files so as to raise problems related to access permissions and disk quotas
B. Using custom server software (such as NAGIOS) for monitoring servers and services
C. Adding emails to mailboxes
D. Using roaming profiles
E. Introducing a more advanced firewall (such as ISA 2000) that would need an upgrade
F. Adding a database server using SQL.

Making these changes to the network environment provided to the class would give students more opportunities to deal with typical administration problems. It would entail performing more complete upgrades to newer technologies, and significantly increase the amount of data that needs to be migrated or changed in some way. This would make the network students work with reflect the kind of diversity and complexity typical of production environments.

CONCLUSION

The Network Administration (Project) course gives students ownership of a problem or task, supplies an authentic learning environment and provides opportunities for reflection, all key instructional principles according to Savery and Duffy (1996). It does this through three major types of activities: "engaging", "exhibiting" and "debriefing" (Thomas, 2009). Students engaged when they responded to the challenges of documenting the unfamiliar network, upgrading the machines on this network or (in Part two) implementing the selected technology. They exhibited when they shared their problems and solutions and demonstrated how things worked to other members of the group and teaching staff members, and they debriefed when they reflected on what they had done and what they had learnt on a group wiki on the learning management system. While it was gratifying to see students invest so much time and effort on engaging type of activities, they should have spent more time exhibiting and debriefing. One solution would be to ask students to write two formal reports, one on each part of the course, in this way prompting greater reflection on lessons learnt, and improving the quality of debriefing. Certainly, students did take responsibility for what they learnt, when they learnt it and how they applied that learning.

Teaching staff did not offer solutions directly or indirectly, and took care not to provide too much guidance, a problem common among expert tutors in problem-based learning environments (Silver & Wilkenson, 1991). Instead, students were granted a high level of independence and were able to seek and implement their own solutions, with students indicating in the short survey of the course that they appreciated the lack of help from teaching staff. Students needed to recall knowledge of technologies covered in other courses they had done in order to resolve some of the problems. This use of prior knowledge helped them make the most of the opportunities for learning provided by course-related activities (Krause & Stark, 2006). Other problems led students into new and unfamiliar territory, one filled with doubt, difficulty and uncertainty. It is important to preserve a certain lack of preparation. After all, it is this lack of preparation that generates the excitement and the uncertainty that is crucial in this course and gives it the relevance, the immediacy and the quality of a real-world environment. It is this quality that infuses problem-based learning in this particular course with a context that inspires curriculum and the way it is implemented (Taylor & Miflin, 2008), and makes it faithful to the original intent of problem-based learning as a curriculum rather than a teaching method (Barrows & Tamblyn, 1980). It also ensures students develop their skills in self-directed, independent learning, so important if they are to keep pace with ever-changing diverse, complex technologies.

A conventional approach to the teaching of technical courses in computing is not invalid or deficient, because it does promote consistency, stability and attention to detail, but problem-based learning actively explores linkages between ideas and the way things function in the real world with course content. It challenges students with the complexity, disorder, even anarchy of more realistic environments, important qualities of the learning environment that encourages what Marton and Säljö (1976) describe as "deep learning". The (virtual) environment provided did enable a negotiated group construction of knowledge that ensured learning went beyond that of the technologies themselves and onto the analysis of problems in context and the application of real solutions. While improvements can be made in a number of areas, it is important to resist at least in this technical course the "technological gravity" (McDonald & Gibbons, 2009) of the routine, the conventional and the predictable if the content is to connect meaningful knowledge with authentic practice.

REFERENCES

Barrows, H., & Tamblyn, R. M. (1980). *Problem-based learning: an approach to medical education*. New York: Springer.

Beckwith, D. (1988). The future of educational technology. *Canadian Journal of Educational Communication*, *17*(1), 3–20.

Dennen, V. P. (2000). Task Structuring for On-line Problem Based Learning: A Case Study. *Journal of Educational Technology & Society*, *3*(3), 329–336.

Dochy, F., Segers, M., van den Bossche, P., & Gijbels, D. (2003). The effects of problem-based learning: a meta-analysis. *Learning and Instruction*, *13*, 533–568. doi:10.1016/S0959-4752(02)00025-7

Duch, B., Groh, S., & Allen, D. (2001). *The power of problem-based learning*. Sterling, VA: Stylus Publishing.

Ellis, A., Carswell, L., Bernat, A., Deveaux, D., Frison, P., Meisalo, V., et al. (1999). Resources, tools, and techniques for problem based learning in computing. In *Proceedings of the ITiCSE'98*. New York: ACM ITICSE.

Jonassen, D. H. (2004). *Learning to solve problems: An instructional design guide*. San Francisco, CA: Pfeiffer.

Kolodner, J. L., Hmelo, C. E., & Narayan, N. H. (1996). Problem-based learning meets case-based reasoning. In *Proceedings of the 1996 international conference on Learning sciences* (pp. 188-195). Evanston, IL: International Society of the Learning Sciences.

Koschmann, T., Kelson, A. C., Feltovich, P. J., & Barrows, H. S. (1998). Computer-supported problem-based learning: A principled approach to the use of computers in collaborative learning. In Koschmann, T. (Ed.), *CSCL: Theory and practice of an emerging paradigm* (pp. 83–124). Mahwah, NJ: Lawrence Erlbaum.

Krause, U.-M., & Stark, R. (2006). Vorwissen aktivieren. In Mandl, H., & Friedrich, H. (Eds.), *Handbuch Lernstrategien* (pp. 38–49). Gottingen, Germany: Hogrefe.

Lou, Y., Abrami, P. C., & d'Apollonia, S. (2001). Small group and individual learning with technology: a meta-analysis. *Review of Educational Research*, *71*(3), 449–521. doi:10.3102/00346543071003449

Marton, F., & Säljö, R. (1976). On Qualitative differences in learning:Outcome and process. *The British Journal of Educational Psychology*, *46*, 4–11.

Marton, F., & Säljö, R. (2005). Approaches to Learning. In F. Marton, D. Hounsell, & N. Entwistle (Eds.), *The Experience of Learning: Implications for teaching and studying in higher education* (3rd Internet ed.). Edinburgh, UK: University of Edinburgh, Centre for Teaching, Learning and Assessment.

McConnell, J. J. (2006). Active and cooperative learning: further tips and tricks (part 3). *The SIGSCE Bulletin*, *38*(2), 24–28.

McDonald, J. K., & Gibbons, A. S. (2009). Technology I, II, and III: criteria for understanding and improving the practice of instructional technology. *Educational Technology Research and Development*, 57(3), 377–392. doi:10.1007/s11423-007-9051-8

Newmann, F. M., Bryk, A. S., & Nagoaka, J. (2001). *Authentic Intellectual Work and Standardized Tests: Conflict or Coexistence?* Chicago: Consortium on Chicago School Research.

Pedersen, S. (2003). Motivational orientation in a probelm-based environment. *Journal of Interactive Learning Research*, 14(1), 51–77.

Richards, D. (2009). Designing project-based courses with a focus on group formation and assessment. *ACM Transactions on Computing Education*, 9(1), 2:1-2:40.

Savery, J. R., & Duffy, T. M. (1996). Problem-based Learning: An Instructional Model and its Constructivist Framework. In Wilson, B. G. (Ed.), *Constructivist Learning Environments: Case Studies in Instructional Design* (pp. 135–150). Englewood Cliffs, NJ: Educational Technology Publications.

Silver, M., & Wilkenson, L. (1991). Effects of Tutors with subject expertise on the problem-based tutorial process. *Academic Medicine*, 66, 298–300. doi:10.1097/00001888-199105000-00017

Taylor, D., & Miflin, B. (2008). Problem-based learning: where are we now? *Medical Teacher*, 30(8), 742–763. doi:10.1080/01421590802217199

Thomas, L. (2009). From Experience to Meaning: The Critical Skills Program. *Phi Delta Kappan*, 91(2), 93–96.

Vardi, I., & Ciccarelli, M. (2008). Overcoming problems in problem-based learning: a trial of strategies in an undergraduate unit. *Innovations in Education and Teaching International*, 45(4), 345–354. doi:10.1080/14703290802377190

Webb, N. M., Nemer, K. M., Chizhik, A. W., & Sugrue, B. (1998). Equity issues in collaborative group assessment: Group composition and performance. *American Educational Research Journal*, 607–665.

This work was previously published in International Journal of Information and Communication Technology, Volume 6, Issue 4, edited by Lawrence A. Tomei, pp. 13-22, copyright 2010 by IGI Publishing (an imprint of IGI Global).

Chapter 25
Investigation into Gender Perception toward Computing:
A Comparison between the U.S. and India

Kittipong Laosethakul
Sacred Heart University, USA

Thaweephan Leingpibul
Western Michigan University, USA

Thomas Coe
Quinnipiac University, USA

ABSTRACT

A potential explanation for the decline of female participation in computing-related education and careers in the United States is the perception that computing is for males. In this regard, declining participation limits diversity in the IT workforce. Therefore, this paper investigates the impact of two psychological factors, computer anxiety and computer self-efficacy, on gender perception toward computing between American male and female students. The authors also investigate whether the same relationship is found in India, where, while computing is dominated by males, female participation is rapidly increasing due to global IT outsourcing.

INTRODUCTION

Computing has been perceived as a male domain for some time. When perceived as a specific gender domain, it can discourage the other gender from participating in computing-related activities, which impacts diversity and work productivity between male and female employees in computing-

related activities. In recent years, female participation in computing-related education and careers has declined in the U.S. One explanation for this problem is the female perception that computing is a male domain (Nobel, 2007; Leventman et al., 2004; Tahmincioglu, 2008). When computing is perceived as a male domain, it means that computing is perceived as an occupation-stereotyped

DOI: 10.4018/978-1-61350-468-0.ch025

male, males have higher computer self-efficacy than females, and males have lower computer anxiety than females (Rainer et al., 2003, p. 108). Tahmincioglu (2008, paragraph 12) reported that American females perceive computing as a male activity and a "geeky and nerdy" profession. According to Collis (1985), females tend to stereotype computer users – people who like computers are not socially or athletically-inclined. The decline of female participation reinforces male domination. When males dominate computing, they may be able to control computing-related activities by establishing behaviors that cause negative experiences for females, such as discrimination and the "glass ceiling" phenomenon (Rainer et al., 2003). This, in turn, discourages female participation even further.

Studies show that computer self-efficacy and computer anxiety are closely related to gender perception toward computing. However, no model has previously demonstrated the relationship between these three constructs. We believe that there is a relationship among these constructs which explains differences in perception between males and females. This study intends to develop a model that demonstrates these relationships.

Additionally, this study investigates whether our model holds across the U.S. and India; where, as in the U.S., computing is dominated by men (Dasgupta, 2004). Due to global IT outsourcing, computing has presented increased opportunities for both Indian men and women. Consequently, the number of Indian females in computing has been rising (Agarwal, 2005). We attempt to understand whether our model, which identifies the potential differences between American males and females, holds across both countries and also if the relationships among the psychological factors for Indian males and females offer insights toward decreasing gender stereotyping and/or increasing female participation in computing in the U.S.

THEORETICAL DEVELOPMENT AND RESEARCH HYPOTHESES

Gender Perception toward Computing

A gender-typed activity/occupation is defined as one where males or females are perceived as possessing different abilities, levels of ability, personality attributes, and/or interpersonal interaction styles (Astone, 1995, pp. 4, 8). Activities/occupations are described as either gender-type male or gender-type female (Astone, 1995, p. 4). Computing is widely perceived as a male domain. Based on the gender schema theory developed by Bem (1981), the gender difference in roles is mediated by cognitions as children encode and organize incoming information according to the definition of "male" and "female" behavior current and active in the society at that time.

Several studies find computing as a male domain. Wilder et al. (1985) determined that the computer was perceived to be more suitable for males. In a study with students in grades K-12, Smith (1986) found significant differences between males and females, with males having stronger beliefs in their ability and competencies in the use of computers. Rosen & Maguire (1990) found that women seem to suffer greater computer phobia than men. Using a gender stereotyping of computing scale to measure perceptions, Astone (1995) reported that, overall, computing was viewed as slightly feminine. Following Astone's study, Rainer et al. (2003) investigated how college students' gender perception toward computing had changed between the years 1995 and 2002. They found that computing was perceived as a female domain in 1995, but the perception had changed to a male domain in 2002. Hafkin and Taggart (2001) found that assumptions about gender and IT had already been established in developing countries. These assumptions may be determining the career paths in the IT sector; for example, women are perceived to be well represented in desktop publishing and software programming, but not in hardware design, operating systems, or computer maintenance (Hafkin & Taggart, 2001, p. 34). In a study of problems faced by Indian women working in the IT industry in Haryana, Godara (2007) interviewed one hundred women from fifteen IT organizations. The perception of a male-dominated society and gender discrimination was ranked second among seven identified problems.

Computer Anxiety

Computer anxiety is defined as "the tendency of an individual to be uneasy, apprehensive, or fearful about the current or future use of computers" (Igbaria & Parasuraman, 1989, p. 375). Heinssen et al. (1987) believed that resistance to and avoidance of computers results from fear, apprehension, and concern about looking stupid or damaging equipment. Several studies indicate a gender difference in computer anxiety. In studies of attitudes toward computers among college students, Dambrot et al. (1985) found some support for the contention that the gender gap in mathematics and science may extend to computers, implying computing to be a male domain. Temple and Lips (1989) reported that females were less comfortable and confident with computers than males. They also found that females had significantly less formal computer training and less intention to major in computer sciences. An explanation for this lack of confidence may be tied to their male peers' attitude that computing was more for males than females. Wilder et al. (1985) asserted that females felt significantly less comfortable than males in using computers. In a study of 270 undergraduates and 56 graduate students, Gilroy and Desai (1986) found that female college students had significantly higher computer anxiety than male students.

Based on these findings, individuals' perceptions that computing is more suitable to one gender over the other may be influenced by the difference of computer anxiety between genders. Most recent research indicates that computing is still a male domain and men have less computer anxiety than women. Thus, for men, the lower the computer anxiety, the stronger the perception that computing is more suitable to males than females. For women, the higher the computer anxiety, the stronger the perception that computing is suitable to males than to females. This leads to the following hypothesis.

H1.1: For men, computer anxiety will be inversely related to a gender-type male perception toward computing.

H1.2: For women, computer anxiety will be positively related to a gender-type male perception toward computing.

Computer Self-Efficacy

Self-efficacy refers to beliefs in one's capabilities to execute a course of action. Self-efficacy does not focus on the skill one has, but rather on judgments of what one can do with possessed skills (Bandura, 1997). Computer self-efficacy refers to "an individual's perceptions of his or her ability to use computers in the accomplishment of a task" (Compeau & Higgins, 1995, p. 191). Several studies indicate gender differences in computer self-efficacy. Collis (1985, p. 209) reported that male secondary school students were more positive about computer usage than females and more likely to express interest and pleasure in using a computer. Miura (1987) found that male undergraduates reported higher computer self-efficacy ratings than did females. Ogletree and Williams (1990) found that males had significantly more confidence in their ability to program computers than did females. Godara (2007) found that a lack of confidence in IT skills was found to be the most severe problem among Indian women in the IT industry.

Based on these findings, individuals' perceptions that computing is more suitable to one gender over the other may be influenced by the difference of perceived computer self-efficacy between genders. Alternatively, when individuals' computer self-efficacy increases, their gender perception toward computing would likely shift from favoring the opposite gender toward neutral or even toward their own gender. This leads to the following hypothesis.

H2.1: For men, computer self-efficacy will be positively related to a gender-type male perception toward computing.

H2.2: For women, computer self-efficacy will be inversely related to a gender-type male perception toward computing.

Based on these two hypotheses, our proposed model is depicted in Figure 1.

Females and the Computing Situation in the U.S. and India

Men dominate computing-related careers/educations in the U.S (Nobel, 2007, p. 1). The number of jobs in the IT professional workforce increased dramatically since 1983. Only 30 percent of these positions were occupied by women (Leventman et al., 2004, p. 1). Even more significantly, the number of women employed in computing and those who intend to major in computing-related degrees are actually on the decline (Tahmincioglu, 2008). Despite growing employment opportunities, women accounted for only 26.7 percent of computer and mathematical positions and 16.6 percent in all network and computer system administrators in 2006 (Nobel, 2007, p. 1). Women seem to have difficulty being accepted or accommodated in male-dominated IT fields (Tahmincioglu, 2008). For example, women may find it difficult to balance family and career because of the long work hours associated with IT positions.

Computing in India is also dominated by males (Dasgupta, 2004); however, Indian women are increasingly participating in computing-related occupations. Unlike in the U.S., there are indications that young women in developing countries are not as affected by the attitude that computing-related fields are not attractive fields to enter. Women comprise 30 to 50 percent of students in computer science and other natural sciences (including information technology) in a number of developing countries (Hafkin & Tag-

Figure 1. The proposed model

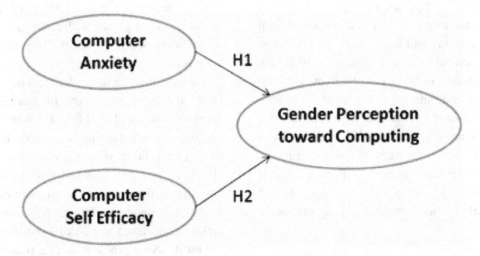

gart, 2001, p. 27-28). Additionally, within the IT sector, emphasis is on intellectual rather than physical resources. Therefore, the IT industry is considered to be an equal opportunity employer for men and women (Agarwal, 2005). As a result, Indian female participation rapidly increased from 18 percent of the IT workforce in 1998 to 36 percent in 2005. At least one-third of data processing jobs are expected to be held by women. Women comprised 35 to 65 percent of the workforce of many call centers. Although data entry does not require a college education, almost all the women in this industry are college educated.

With the opportunities in computing for both males and females in India, gender perception toward computing in India may not be as affected by computer anxiety and computer self-efficacy as in the U.S. In other words, the relationships between the psychological constructs for the U.S. may not be the same as those for India.

METHODOLOGY

The study tries to understand the factors influencing gender perceptions toward computing that is believed to be one of the reasons causing the decline of women participation in computing. The decision to participate in computing-related careers or others is most likely determined by students during their early academic years. Thus, using students that did not choose IT-related fields as their majors was suitable to the objectives of the study. We examined five samples of university students; four from the U.S. (244 students), and one from India (232 students). All samples were from four-year institutions that offer computing-related majors; namely, computer science, engineering, management information systems, and computer information systems. All respondents were business majors, but none were from IT-related business majors or concentrations.

The survey gathered data relating to student demographics and computer experience, including gender, age, school year, years of computer use, and the number of computer courses taken in college. The survey also contains three psychological constructs. These constructs include 1) Gender Typing Scale (Astone, 1995); 2) Computer Self-efficacy (Murphy et al., 1989); and 3) Computer Anxiety Rating (Heinssen et al., 1987).

Astone's Gender-Typing Scale (GTS) was developed to capture a perception of current gender roles in computing careers and activities. The scale measures how individuals perceive current gender roles in the technical and managerial aspects of computing, clerical and office uses of computers, and effective responses to computing. Our sample questionnaires employed two versions of the survey to mitigate survey-wording bias in the GTS section. The first version listed all GTS items as "female first"; for example, "I believe that more women than men seek careers in computing". The second version listed all GTS items as "male first". The first version's scores were subsequently reversed, so that all scores used and reported in the data analysis are in the "male first" direction.

The Computer Anxiety Rating Scale (CAR) was developed by Heinssen et al. (1987). The scale measures the level of anxiety toward computer use and confidence, enthusiasm and/or anticipation toward computer use (Harrison & Rainer, 1992). The Computer Self-Efficacy Scale (CSE) was developed by Murphy et al. (1989). For this study, the scale measures computer self-efficacy on two levels of computer skills: beginning computer skills and conceptual computer skills. All constructs were measured on a 5-point Likert scale, ranging from "1" meaning "strongly disagree"; to "5" meaning "strongly agree"; and "3" meaning "neutral".

Table 1. Demographic and computer experience

	American		Indian	
	Females	Males	Females	Males
	N=125 (Std Dev)	N=119 (Std Dev)	N=117 (Std Dev)	N=115 (Std Dev)
	Mean	Mean	Mean	Mean
1. Age	22 (4.73)	22 (5.05)	18 (0.99)	19 (1.70)
2. School years	3 (0.94)	3 (0.82)	2 (0.50)	2 (0.46)
3. Number of computer courses taken	2 (1.83)	2 (1.87)	1 (1.69)	1 (1.14)
4. Year of computer usage	12 (3.36)	11 (3.79)	4 (2.18)	3 (2.74)

RESULTS

Demographics and Computer Experience

Table 1 shows the demographic data of respondents as well as the frequency of productivity-software usage and online activities. Forty-nine percent of American respondents were male and 51 percent were female. Fifty-three percent of Indian respondents were male and 47 percent were female. Most American respondents were juniors, and most Indian respondents were sophomores. The average ages of American and Indian respondents were 22 and 19 years, respectively. American respondents have been using computers for 12 years, while their Indian counterparts have been using computers for 4 years.

Measurement Model Results

For a model to be compared across groups – American males/females and Indian males/females, we used the model comparison technique in SEM to develop the proposed model demonstrating the relationship among the three psychological factors (Figure 1). An assessment of the various levels of invariance across the study's four groups was necessary. Based on a configural invariance test, the results from a confirmatory factor analysis and a nested model from SEM showed satisfactory results. To ensure acceptable degrees of reliability and validity of the measurement model, certain items from the three constructs were removed from the four groups. Appendix A (Tables A1-A3) shows remaining items and the alpha reliabilities for GTS, CSE, and CAR after these adjustments. All alpha reliabilities ranged from 0.72 to 0.96, indicating acceptable reliability for the constructs.

Path Analysis

For the path analysis, a two-group comparison feature from AMOS 17 was used on the proposed model. A direct cross-sample comparison of paths allowed for analysis of the path differences across groups. Figure 2 and Figure 3 demonstrate all models of the four groups. Table 2 shows all fit indices of the four groups. All fit indices indicate a close fit threshold. Therefore, it can be concluded that the structural models fit the data well in all four groups. The results are presented in the next section.

Figure 2. Path estimates for American males and American females

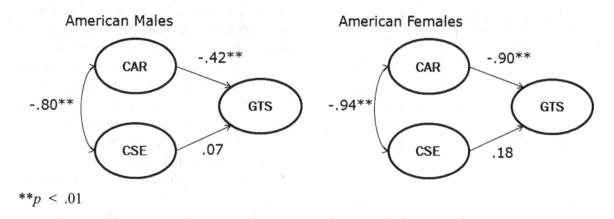

**p < .01

HYPOTHESES TESTING

Table 3 shows the results of the hypothesis tests. For American males, the SEM results indicate that the relationship between gender perception toward computing (GTS) and computer anxiety (CAR) is significant at the p <.01 level. Thus, H1.1 is supported. For American females, a path estimate (-0.90) between computer anxiety and gender perception toward computing is significant at the 0.01 level, but it has an inverse relationship. Thus, H1.2 is not supported. For both genders, the SEM results indicate that there is no empirical relationship between gender perception toward

computing (GTS) and computer self-efficacy (CSE). Thus, H2.1 and H2.2 are not supported for the American group. In addition, there is a significant inverse relationship between computer self-efficacy (CSE) and computer anxiety (CAR) at the p <.01 level for both American males and females.

As with their American counterparts, the SEM results indicate that there is a significant relationship between gender perception toward computing (GTS) and computer anxiety (CAR) at the p <.05 level for Indian males. Thus, H1.1 is supported. A path estimate (-0.28) between computer anxiety and gender perception toward

Figure 3. Path estimates for Indian males and Indian females

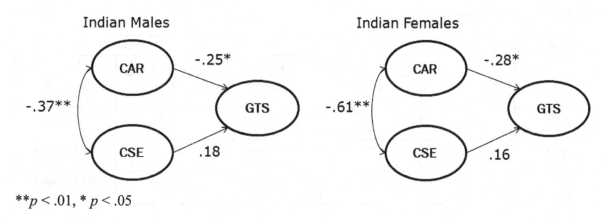

**p < .01, * p < .05

Table 2. Fit indices

Fit In-dices	Acceptable Range (Hair et al., 2006)	American Males	American Females	In-dian Males	Indian Fe-males
Cmin/DF	≤ 3:1	1.90	1.30	1.63	1.60
CFI	>.90	.98	.99	.95	.95
RM-SEA	<.08	.06	.04	.05	.06
NFI	>.90	.96	.97	.91	.93

computing is significant at the $p <.05$ level for Indian females, but it has an inverse relationship. Thus, H1.2 is not supported. In both groups, the SEM results indicate no significant relationship between gender perception toward computing (GTS) and computer self-efficacy (CSE). Thus, H2.1 and H2.2 are not supported for the Indian group. A significant inverse relationship between computer self-efficacy (CSE) and computer anxiety (CAR) is also found at the $p <.01$ level for both Indian males and females.

DISCUSSION

Based on demographics and computer experience (Table 1), the fact that Indian students used computers, on average, eight years less and took one less computer course than American students raises a question whether both samples would have comparable computing experience. Although this is a legitimate concern, these gaps may not necessarily indicate a big difference in computing experience between Americans and Indians. The difference in computer experience between the two samples depends on the type of computer activities and the content of computer courses that students from both countries take. As an extreme example, playing computer games does not amount to having more computing experience. The point, however, is that there is not enough information to determine whether both samples lack comparable computing experience, but there is enough information to conclude that both samples have basic computer experience and knowledge to participate in the study.

The hypothesis H1.1 is supported for American males. For American male students, their gender perception toward computing is influenced by their computer anxiety. The path estimate (-0.42) indicates that the higher the computer anxiety, the weaker the gender perception. However, a moderate path estimate means that getting over computer anxiety does not have that great of an impact on gender perception toward computing. Table 4 shows ranges of GTS, CAR, and CSE scores from all four groups. The range of American male students' CAR scores, 3.63-3.69[1], indicates medium-to-high computer anxiety. The range of

Table 3. Results of hypothesis tests

Hypothesis	Paths	U.S.		India	
		Path Estimates	Results	Path Estimates	Results
H1.1 (Male)	CAR → GTS	-0.42**	Supported	-0.25*	Supported
H1.2 (Female)		-0.90**	Not Supported	-0.28*	Not Supported
H2.1 (Male)	CSE → GTS	0.07	Not Supported	0.18	Not Supported
H2.2 (Female)		0.18	Not supported	0.16	Not Supported

$**p <.01, * p <.05$

their GTS scores, 2.64-2.95, leans toward neutral (3). Corresponding to their medium-to-high computer anxiety, American male students perceive that computing is suitable for not only males, but also for females.

The hypothesis H1.2 is not supported for American females. Contrary to the hypothesis, the path estimate (-0.90) indicates a strong inverse relationship between computer anxiety and gender perception toward computing. The range of their CAR scores, 3.58-3.73, indicates medium-to-high computer anxiety. The range of their GTS scores, 1.67-2.15, indicates a relatively strong perception that computing is not for males. Corresponding to their medium-to-high computer anxiety, American female students perceive that computing is more suitable for females than males. Compared to American male students, their computer anxiety levels are about the same, but American female students have a much stronger gender perception toward computing.

For Indian students, the hypotheses H1.1 and H1.2 are both supported. For Indian male students, the path estimate (-0.25) indicates a weak influence of computer anxiety on gender perception toward computing. The range of Indian males' CAR scores, 3.14-3.49, indicates moderate computer anxiety. In fact, their CAR scores are the lowest among the four groups. The range of GTS scores, 3.04-3.17, leans toward neutral. Corresponding to their moderate computer anxiety, Indian male students perceive that computing is suitable for both males and females. Similar to Indian male students, Indian female students' path estimate (-0.28) indicates a weak influence of computer anxiety on gender perception toward computing. The range of their CAR scores, 3.91-3.96, indicates high computer anxiety. In fact, their CAR scores are the highest among the four groups. The range of their GTS scores, 2.61-2.82, leans toward neutral. Corresponding to their high computer anxiety, Indian female students perceive that computing is not for one particular gender.

Based on the SEM results, hypotheses H2.1 and H2.2 are not supported for either the American or Indian groups (Table 3). While gender may have a strong influence on computer self-efficacy, computer self-efficacy does not have a direct impact on a gender perception toward computing. A significant inverse relationship between computer anxiety and computer self-efficacy, however, is found for all four groups. This finding is supported by a several studies (e.g., Thatcher & Perrewe, 2002; Webster et al., 1990; Fagan et al., 2004). Based on path estimates, this inverse relationship could be explained as increasing levels of computer self-efficacy resulting in decreasing levels of computer anxiety; correspondingly, increasing levels of computer anxiety result in decreasing levels of computer self-efficacy.

IMPLICATIONS

There are several implications based on our results. Researchers can now understand how computer anxiety influences gender perception toward computing for both American male and female students. Corresponding to their moderate computer anxiety, American male students perceive computing as an equal opportunity between males and females, while American female students perceive computing as a female domain. A possible interpretation for the finding that computer anxiety has a stronger influence on American female students than American male

Table 4. Ranges of GTS, CAR, and CSE scores

Construct	U.S.		India	
	Male	Female	Male	Female
Range of GTS scores	2.64-2.95	1.67-2.15	3.04-3.17	2.61-2.82
Range of CAR scores	3.63-3.69	3.58-3.73	3.14-3.49	3.91-3.96
Range of CSE scores	3.35-3.47	3.27-3.38	3.51-3.74	3.22-3.31

students is that female students, having higher computer anxiety, feel insecure about female roles in computing. It is likely that their survey answers contain bias about female roles in computing. Another possible reason could be explained by the paradox "We can, but I can't" (Collis, 1985) – that the typical female respondent feels that women in general are capable of computing, but that she as an individual is not competent or likely to be a computer user. While this paradox could explain why female non-IT-business students feel positively about the reality of female roles in computing, it is the individual female's computer self-efficacy that influences their gender perception toward computing. However, this study found no direct relationship between computer self-efficacy and gender perception toward computing. Nonetheless, a correlation between computer self-efficacy and computer anxiety provides a possible hint that computer self-efficacy may have a mediating relationship with gender perception toward computing through computer anxiety. To see a more complete picture of the relationship among these three psychological factors, further investigation to identify which factor (between computer anxiety and computer self-efficacy) would be a real antecedent of the phenomenon is needed. Our findings offer evidence that the decline of American female participation in computing during the last several years may be influenced by computer anxiety and a belief that they are not competent in computing.

A direct relationship between gender perception toward computing and computer anxiety is also found in the Indian group, but there is a different implication for this finding. Indian students' path estimates between computer anxiety and gender perception toward computing are weaker than those of American students, especially American female students. Indian students' computer anxiety does not have a strong influence on their gender perception toward computing as it does with American students. Indian male students show moderate computer anxiety and Indian female students show high computer anxiety, but both

groups perceive that computing was for males and females. The interpretation of this finding lies in the GTS, which captures a perception of current gender roles in computing-related activities. With increased use of computers within their education, Indian students developed a strong perception that both males and females had equal capability in computing. The GTS also captures how individuals perceive gender roles in current computing-related careers; which in this case, is the continuing increase of female participation in computing in India due to global outsourcing. Indian students' perception is thus likely to be influenced by their awareness of a large number of Indian women seeking computing-related jobs due to the impact of outsourcing on computing-related industries. These new opportunities allow Indians, especially Indian women, to not only create high income for their families, perhaps for the first time, but also raise their social status. These perceptions by Indian students must be strong enough not to be negatively impacted by any computer anxiety. An implication for this finding is that not only does computing skill, but also awareness of current gender roles in computing influence an individual's gender perception toward computing. The difference of findings between the U.S. and India also justify investigating other gender-related psychological profiles, such as culture and computer attitudes, which may affect the model.

Educational institutions in the U.S. should not only provide computing skills for students, but also create awareness of computing-related career opportunities. It is important to emphasize basic computer skills in addition to a fundamental knowledge of computing. This will strengthen computer self-efficacy and lessen computer anxiety; which, in turn, could influence the perception of computing toward being gender-neutral for American students, especially for females. One thing Americans could learn from Indians is that the awareness of career opportunities could also lessen individuals' gender perception toward computing and possibly encourage women to enter into computing-related fields. Unlike India, the U.S. has always had computing-related job opportunities for men and women, even though dominated by men. However, American women may not be well aware of job opportunities for women in computing-related fields. Further evidence of this lack of information toward opportunities for female participation can be found by the minimal discussion of computing-related job opportunities in introductory management information system courses. Using prominent female figures as examples of successful women in computing fields or inviting female guest speakers to computing-related classes could be effective tools to spark a stronger interest among female students in pursuing further education and computing-related careers.

LIMITATIONS

There are some limitations that should be understood before generalizing the results of this study to other contexts or audiences. First, the sample from the U.S. and India came from non-IT business majors, although we recognize that non-computing includes a wider range of education fields. While the focus of our sample is smaller, business still represents a wide variety of majors that students could choose from. Second, the Indian student sample came from a university located in the southern region of the country. According to Agarwal (2005), the concentration of IT companies in the southern region of India was higher than other regions of the country. Thus, it is likely that students in this region would have a much higher awareness of the opportunities for Indian women to work in computing-related fields than students from other regions. Although the findings from India may not be generalized for the whole country, they better represent gender perceptions toward computing in geographical areas where IT global outsourcing has a strong impact on the roles of Indian males and females in computing.

CONCLUSION

The persistent decline of female participation in computing in the U.S. prompts the need to examine the relationships between gender perception toward computing, computer anxiety, and computer self-efficacy for American male and female students. This study further examines whether these same relationships exist in India, where participation of females in computing has increased due to IT outsourcing. Our study concludes that the decline of American females in computing is likely to be influenced by their low computer self-efficacy. Efforts that increase computer self-efficacy and lower computer anxiety could encourage American female students to enter computing-related education. The findings from their Indian counterparts suggest further that the awareness of computing-related job opportunities for Indian women creates a strong perception of female roles in computing, which encourages female participation in computing-related fields.

This study provides evidence that individuals' gender perception toward computing is directly influenced by their computer anxiety and, possibly, indirectly influenced by computer self-efficacy. This relationship model is found in all four groups. It is highly probable that this relationship model could be extended to other countries due to its simplicity. However, the real value of the model comes from understanding the unique computing environment of different countries, such as an emphasis of computing in education and computing job opportunities. A country's unique computing environment affects the psychological constructs, and in turn, the degree to which these three constructs influence each other in explaining perception differences between males and females. Then, a guideline for improving gender perception toward computing for a specific country could be developed.

REFERENCES

Agarwal, R. (2005). *Digital technology and women employment: Employment dimensions in India.* United Nations Public Administration Network (UNPAN Report No. 023829). Retrieved from http://unpan1.un.org/intradoc/groups/public/documents/APCITY/UNPAN023829.pdf

Astone, M. K. (1995). *Gender stereotyping of computing.* Unpublished doctoral dissertation, Auburn University, Auburn, AL.

Bandura, A. (1997). *Self-efficacy: The exercise of control.* New York: W. H. Freeman.

Bem, S. L. (1981). Gender Schema Theory: A cognitive account of sex typing. *Psychological Review, 88*(4), 354–364. doi:10.1037/0033-295X.88.4.354

Collis, B. (1985). Psychological implications of sex differences in attitudes towards computers: Results of a survey. *International Journal of Women's Studies, 8*(3), 207–213.

Compeau, D. R., & Higgins, C. A. (1995). Computer self-efficacy: Development of measure and initial test. *Management Information Systems Quarterly, 19,* 189–211. doi:10.2307/249688

Dambrot, F. H., Watkins-Malek, M. A., Silling, S. M., Marshall, R. S., & Garver, J. A. (1985). Correlates of sex differences in attitudes toward and involvement with computers. *Journal of Vocational Behavior, 27,* 71–86. doi:10.1016/0001-8791(85)90053-3

Dasgupta, M. K. (2004, August). Information & communication technology for women's empowerment in India. *Information Technology in Developing Countries, 14*(2). Retrieved from http://www.iimahd.ernet.in/egov/ifip/aug2004/article4.htm

Fagan, M. H., Neill, S., & Wooldridge, B. R. (2004). An empirical investigation into the relationship between computer self-efficacy, anxiety, experience, support and usage. *Journal of Computer Information Systems, 44*(2), 95–106.

Gilroy, D. F., & Desai, H. B. (1986). Computer anxiety: Sex, race, and age. *International Journal of Man-Machine Studies, 25,* 711–719. doi:10.1016/S0020-7373(86)80084-0

Godara, V. (2007). E-business applications and information technologies: Providing new opportunities for women. *Business Review (Federal Reserve Bank of Philadelphia), 8*(1), 154–161.

Hafkin, N., & Taggart, N. (2001). *Gender, information technology, and developing countries: An analytic study.* Washington, DC: AED. Retrieved from http://www.usaid.gov/wid/pubs/it01.htm

Hair, F. J., Black, B., Babin, B., Anderson, E. R., & Tatham, L. R. (2006). *Multivariate data analysis.* Upper Saddle River, NJ: Prentice Hall.

Harrison, A. W., & Rainer, R. K. (1992). An examination of the factor structures and concurrent validities for the computer attitude scale, the computer anxiety scale, and the computer self-efficacy scale. *Educational and Psychological Measurement, 52,* 735–745. doi:10.1177/0013164492052003024

Heinssen, R. K. J., Glass, C. R., & Knight, L. A. (1987). Assessing computer anxiety: Development and validation of the computer anxiety rating scale. *Computers in Human Behavior, 3,* 49–59. doi:10.1016/0747-5632(87)90010-0

Igbaria, M., & Parasuraman, S. (1989). A path analytic study of individual characteristics, computer anxiety and attitudes toward microcomputers. *Journal of Management, 15*(3), 373–388. doi:10.1177/014920638901500302

Insight Magazine Releases, C. I. O. The Global Outsourcing Report. (2005, March 21). *CIO Insight*. Retrieved from http://www.ziffdavis.com/press/releases/050321.0.html

Leventman, P., Finley, M., & Brashler, P. (2004). *Gender equity in the U.S. information technology workforce. Annual Meetings of the American Sociological Association*. Retrieved from http://www.allacademic.com//meta/p_mla_apa_research_citation/1/0/9/6/8/pages109689/p109689-1.php

Miura, I. T. (1987). The relationship of computer self-efficacy expectations to computer interest and course enrollment in college. *Sex Roles, 16,* 303–311. doi:10.1007/BF00289956

Murphy, C., Coover, D., & Owen, S. V. (1989). Development and validation of the computer self-efficacy scale. *Educational and Psychological Measurement, 49*(4), 893–899. doi:10.1177/001316448904900412

Nobel, C. (2007, January 29). *Women in Technology: A call to action. InfoWorld*. Retrieved February 25, 2008, from http://www.infoworld.com/d/developer-world/women-in-technology-call-action-919

Ogletree, S. M., & Williams, S. W. (1990). Sex and sex-typing effects on computer attitudes and aptitude. *Sex Roles, 23*(11), 703–712. doi:10.1007/BF00289258

Rainer, R. K. Jr, Laosethakul, K., & Astone, M. K. (2003). Are gender perceptions of computing changing over time? *Journal of Computer Information Systems, 43*(4), 108–114.

Rosen, L. D., & Maguire, P. (1990). Myths and reliabilities of computer phobia: A meta-analysis. *Anxiety Research, 3,* 175–191.

Smith, S. D. (1986). Relationships of computer attitudes to sex, grade level, and teacher influence. *Education, 106,* 338–344.

Tahmincioglu, M. (2008, February 10). *Your career: Where are the women in tech? MSNBC*. Retrieved February 25, 2008, from http://www.msnbc.msn.com/id/23033748/print/1/displaymode/1098

Temple, L., & Lips, H. M. (1989). Gender differences and similarities in attitudes toward computers. *Computers in Human Behavior, 5,* 215–226. doi:10.1016/0747-5632(89)90001-0

Thatcher, J. B., & Perrewe, P. L. (2002). An empirical examination of individual traits as antecedents to computer anxiety and computer self-efficacy. *Management Information Systems Quarterly, 26*(4), 381–396. doi:10.2307/4132314

Webster, J., Heian, J. B., & Michelman, J. E. (1990). Computer training and computer anxiety in the educational process: An experimental analysis. In *Proceedings of the Eleventh International Conference on Information Systems* (pp. 171-182).

Wilder, G., Mackie, D., & Cooper, J. (1985). Gender and computers: Two surveys of computer related attitudes. *Sex Roles, 13,* 215–228. doi:10.1007/BF00287912

ENDNOTES

[1] For CAR (and CSE), corresponding to the 5-point Likert scale, "1" means very low computer anxiety (computer self-efficacy), "3" means medium computer anxiety (computer self-efficacy), and "5" means very high computer anxiety (computer self-efficacy).

APPENDIX A

Table A1. Remaining items for GTS, CAR, and CSE

GTS
GTS 1 - I believe that men answer computer questions better than women do
GTS 2 - I believe that more men than women use computers
GTS 3 - I believe that more men than women are more confident in computer use
GTS 4 - I believe that more men than women seek careers in computing
CAR
CAR 1 - I have avoided computers because they are unfamiliar and somewhat intimidating to me
CAR 2 - I dislike working with machines that are smarter than I am
CAR 3 - I feel insecure about my ability to interpret a computer printout
CSE
CSE 1 - I feel confident making selections from an onscreen menu
CSE 2 - I feel confident calling up a data file to view on the monitor screen
CSE 3 - I feel confident using a printer to make a "hardcopy" of my work
CSE 4 - I feel confident escaping/exiting from the program/software
CSE 5 - I feel confident copying an individual file

Table A2. American student groups - alpha reliabilities for GTS, CAR, and CSE

	American Males					American Females				
GTS	Mean	Std	Est	Var Ext	Cronbach	Mean	Std	Est	Var Ext	Cronbach
GTS 1	2.64	1.254	.840	.680	.890	1.88	1.247	.850	.670	.884
GTS 2	2.64	1.198	.780			1.67	1.177	.850		
GTS 3	2.95	1.171	.940			2.14	1.372	.900		
GTS 4	2.85	1.240	.640			2.15	1.173	.645		
CAR	Mean	Std	Est	Var Ext	Cronbach	Mean	Std	Est	Var Ext	Cronbach
CAR 1	3.63	2.220	.980	.954	.956	3.67	1.271	.980	.891	.960
CAR 2	3.69	2.138	.990			3.73	1.142	.950		
CAR 3	3.66	2.044	.960			3.58	1.281	.900		
CSE	Mean	Std	Est	Var Ext	Cronbach	Mean	Std	Est	Var Ext	Cronbach
CSE 1	3.45	1.339	.990	.933	.947	3.38	1.326	.980	.934	.956
CSE 2	3.35	1.286	.950			3.27	1.253	.930		
CSE 3	3.42	1.362	.960			3.30	1.315	.970		
CSE 4	3.47	1.320	.970			3.34	1.296	.980		
CSE 5	3.42	1.356	.960			3.34	1.251	.970		

Table A3. Indian student groups - alpha reliabilities for GTS, CAR, and CSE

	Indian Males					Indian Females				
GTS	Mean	Std	Est	Var Ext	Cronbach	Mean	Std	Est	Var Ext	Cronbach
GTS 1	3.04	1.496	.890	.674	.720	2.65	1.204	.870	.721	.920
GTS 2	3.15	1.653	.770			2.61	1.108	.830		
GTS 3	3.14	1.505	.830			2.76	1.252	.950		
GTS 4	3.17	1.425	.781			2.82	1.133	.730		
CAR	Mean	Std	Est	Var Ext	Cronbach	Mean	Std	Est	Var Ext	Cronbach
CAR 1	3.14	1.511	.790	.630	.794	3.96	1.290	.740	.617	.830
CAR 2	3.39	1.557	.760			3.96	1.084	.750		
CAR 3	3.49	1.366	.830			3.91	1.490	.860		
CSE	Mean	Std	Est	Var Ext	Cronbach	Mean	Std	Est	Var Ext	Cronbach
CSE 1	3.70	1.208	.790	.659	.739	3.31	0.896	.770	.662	.883
CSE 2	3.51	1.115	.900			3.26	0.970	.840		
CSE 3	3.53	1.232	.740			3.31	0.904	.740		
CSE 4	3.58	1.144	.850			3.29	0.933	.880		
CSE 5	3.74	1.209	.770			3.22	0.881	.830		

This work was previously published in International Journal of Information and Communication Technology, Volume 6, Issue 4, edited by Lawrence A. Tomei, pp. 23-37, copyright 2010 by IGI Publishing (an imprint of IGI Global).

Chapter 26
Emerging Trends and Technologies for Enhancing Engineering Education:
An Overview

Manjit Singh Sidhu
University Tenaga Nasional, Malaysia

Lee Chen Kang
University Tunku Abdul Rahman, Malaysia

ABSTRACT

Improving and enhancing education has been a prime goal for higher learning institutions that seek to provide better learning techniques, technologies, educators, and to generate knowledgeable students to fulfill the needs of industries. A significant area where improvements are required is in the engineering field. In this regard, one approach is to review the delivery and pedagogies used in current education systems. This paper examines the problems faced by staff and students in the field of Mechanical Engineering, which are found in the literature. Finally, the authors explore new technologies that could help enhance and promote the learning process of students experiencing problems.

INTRODUCTION

Education is the driving force of economic and social development in any country (Cholin, 2005; Mehta & Kalra, 2006; Manjit, 2007). Considering this, it is necessary to find ways to make education of good quality, accessible and affordable to all, using the latest technology available (Hattangdi & Ghosh, 2009).

The vast availability of technologies is becoming competitive and difficult to predict if it could improve the learning process. As such it would be beneficial to further research and review the options and benefits of present technologies.

DOI: 10.4018/978-1-61350-468-0.ch026

This paper deals with engineering education in the higher learning institution. Our focus is mainly targeted to mechanical engineering education since it was found in the previous studies that some first year undergraduates faced problems in understanding the concepts of engineering mechanics course (Scott, 1996; Gramoll, 2001; Manjit et al., 2002; Katarzyna, 2002; Manjit et al., 2005; Manjit et al., 2008). This subject is chosen because a number of academicians as reported in the literatures found that the main problem faced by students is visualization of dynamic motion of particles or rigid bodies.

COMMON PROBLEMS FACED BY ENGINEERING STUDENTS

Katarzyna (2002) reported the problems that first year undergraduates face while studying the Engineering Mechanics Dynamics course is the difference in understanding with regard to what is being taught in the classroom. Undergraduate students often expect a variety of teaching methods to be used in their learning. Although, in general, the lecture method is a common way of delivering knowledge to students, it treats all students on the same level of the basic acquired knowledge. However, in general most of these students do not bring to the course the same academic preparation (do not have the same motivation, interest, ability to learn/grasp) and come from different disciplines, remote regions with limited exposure to modern technology, have varying learning styles, and have different levels of proficiency in material learned at the foundation level. This results in different starting points, progress rates, and ultimately different levels of satisfaction, academic progress, and performance.

However, the aforementioned is not the only reason for difference among undergraduate student development in the same class. Students enrolling from the same foundation program but from different institutions and cultures are taught varying degrees of basic material, which they are required to know.

Finally, some entry-level undergraduate students do not have very strong grades in science and mathematics that makes certain engineering subjects difficult for them to comprehend and this discourages learning from taking place. As a result of this problem, if the lectures are too fast, this set of students may not be able to keep pace with the rest of the class thus the gap in their knowledge will only get wider as compared to the more advanced students. In this situation, some students are left out, and often the instructors are forced to find alternative methods (for example conducting extra classes) to help these students in understanding the subject matter. Since some students may take more time to understand the problem solving techniques and may require the lesson to be repeated several times before they understand, there is a need to study and understand the availability and benefits of newer technologies that could help them visualize and understand the engineering problems better. The emerging trends and benefits of new technologies are briefly addressed in the next sections.

Emerging Trends of Engineering Education

This section briefly describes present emerging trends in engineering education with regards to technology enhancements. In the current information society, there is an emergence of lifelong learners as the shelf life of knowledge and information decreases (Bhattacharya & Sharma, 2007).

In the past, it could take ample of time in finding text / information (from traditional libraries / textbooks). Today, with the availability of these materials in the form of digital multimedia on-line, a vast amount of related information could be reached through a personal computer with Internet connection via simple keywords search. People could easily access and gain knowledge via ICT (Information and Communication Technology) to keep pace with the latest developments (Plomp, Pelgrum, & Law, 2007). In such a scenario, education, which always plays a critical role in any economic and social growth of a country, becomes even more important. Education not only increases the productive skill sets of the individual but also his/her general knowledge. It gives him/her a sense of well being as well as capacity to absorb new ideas, increases his social interaction, gives access to improved health and provides several more intangible benefits (Kozma, 2005).

The availability of digital multimedia format materials such as text, sound, image, audio, video and animation has played a significant role in the way students learn, access and interact with information (Cairncross, 2002; Manjit, 2007). In addition the various kinds of ICT products available and have relevance to education, such as teleconferencing, email, audio conferencing, television lessons, radio broadcasts, interactive radio counseling, interactive voice response system, audiocassettes and CD-ROMs have been used in education for different purposes (Sharma, 2003; Sanyal, 2001; Bhattacharya & Sharma, 2007).

Cross and Adam (2007) listed four main rationales for introducing ICT in education as shown in Table 1.

The significance of these rationales (Table 1) can also be extended to engineering education. Other powerful ICTs including laptops wirelessly connected to the Internet, personal digital assistants, low cost video cameras, and cell phones have become affordable, accessible and integrated in large sections of the society throughout the world. It can restructure the learning process, promote collaboration, make education more widely available, foster cultural creativity and enhance the development in social integration (Kozma, 2005). It is only through education and the integration of ICT in education that one can teach students to be participants in the growth process in this era of rapid change (Bhattacharya & Sharma, 2007).

Table 1. Rationales for introducing ICT in education (Cross & Adam, 2007)

Rationale	Basis
Social	Perceived role that technology now plays in society and the need for familiarizing students with technology.
Vocational	Preparing students with jobs that require skills in technology.
Catalytic	Utility of technology to improve performance and effectiveness in teaching, management and many other social activities.
Pedagogical	To utilize technology in enhancing learning, flexibility and efficiently in curriculum delivery.

ICT can be used as a tool in the process of engineering education in the following ways:

- **Informative tool:** It provides vast amount of data in various interactive formats (multimedia) such as text, graphics, audio, video, and animation.
- **Situating tool:** It creates situations, which the student experiences in real life. Thus, simulation and mixed realities such as virtual reality and augmented reality are possible.
- **Constructive tool:** To manipulate the data and generate analysis.
- **Communicative tool:** It can be used to remove communication barriers such as that of space and time (Lim & Chai, 2004).

From the above, it can be seen that the use of ICT in education develops higher order skills such as collaborating across time and place and solving complex real world problems (Bottino, 2003; Bhattacharya & Sharma, 2007; Mason, 2000; Lim & Hang, 2003). Thus, ICT can be employed to prepare the workforce for the information society and the new global economy (Kozma, 2005; Manjit, 2008).

On the other hand while ICT technology is available, many academicians and psychologist are trying to study and improve the pedagogies for delivering quality education. For example by designing new user interfaces and patterns of interactions, employing specialized hardware and software technologies in teaching, designing teaching/learning models and creating/using new learning approaches such as blended learning (combination of face-to-face instruction with computer-mediated instruction) and game approach.

Technologies for Enhancing Engineering Education

Research has shown that the use of new technologies in engineering has the potential to enhance the learning process and provide engaging environment for the students. For example the use of following computer aided learning (CAL) packages:

- The work by Vaughan (1998) in the introduction of Fluids Mechanics course contains ten modules covering topics ranging from fluid statics to boundary layers. In addition to those modules, a laboratory simulation was also developed. This simulation consisted of six sections with experiments covering measurements of basic fluid properties, pressure and velocity measurements, applications of Bernoulli equation, applications of momentum equation, and pipe friction. By using an active learning approach, instructional technology can benefit students of varying backgrounds and skill levels. The students are able to view the same information from several perspectives, strengthening connections and transferability.

- The work by McMahon (2000) on Introduction to Materials Engineering CD-ROM multimedia-based course serves as both a comprehensive one-semester material education course for non-materials science and engineering majors. The course employs computer-presented tuto-

rials that can be utilized in several ways; as a replacement for classroom lectures in courses where the class meetings are devoted to studio-type active learning, as a supplement to classroom lectures that are illustrated by the animations provided, as a basic course in institutions where faculty from other branches of science or technology serve as coaches for specialized subjects such as materials science and engineering, or as a self-study course for those who must pursue the subject on their own.

- The work by Callister (2003) on an Introduction to Materials Science and Engineering CD-ROM contains eight dynamic learning modules where students can view and manipulate 3-D projections and activate animations that bring these concepts to life. In addition, students have the opportunity to improve their problem-solving skills and at the same time evaluate their progress.

- Recent work by Manjit (2007) on the development of technology-assisted problem solving (TAPS) packages were appreciated by first year undergraduate engineering students as it could help them visualize and understand the selected engineering problems better which were otherwise difficult to understand from the textbook alone.

A part from the use of CAL packages in engineering as mentioned above, new hardware technologies also helps significantly in enhancing the interaction process between the user and the software. Some of this hardware is explained in the next subsequent sections.

Graphics Tablet

A graphics tablet consists of a flat tablet and some sort of drawing device, usually either a pen or stylus. A graphics tablet may also be referred to as a drawing tablet or drawing pad. While the graphics tablet is most suited for artists and those who want the natural feel of a pen-like object to manipulate the cursor on their screen, non-artists such as engineering instructors may find it (Graphics Tablet) useful in their teaching as well. Figure 1 shows a demonstration of the graphics pen where important engineering concepts are being highlighted directly onto an image in the learning package.

Interactive White Boards

An interactive whiteboard (IWB) is a large interactive display that connects to a computer and projector. A projector projects the computer's desktop onto the board's surface, where users control the computer using a touch sensitive pen, finger or other device. Whiteboards enable teachers to support the range of learning styles of the learners in the class. The learners themselves feel empowered: The ability to visualize and recall the lesson supports learning; the range of resources that can be embedded within the IWB lesson software and the interactivity itself has engaged almost all of the learners and enhanced their progress (Cuthell, 2005). The board is typically mounted to a wall or on a floor stand as shown in Figure 2.

SOFTWARE TO INTERACT IN 3D ENVIRONMENTS

Another alternative to allow engineering students to visualize engineering problems is to design the engineering models (i.e. a piston, rod, robotic arm) using three dimensional (3D) modeling tools as its main interface environments. New emerging virtual reality (VR) tools could be used to develop user friendly 3D visual interactions which allow the user to enter text, see an animation in two and three dimensions, evaluate user input, and integrate multimedia attributes such as audio, video, animations, and graphics. In addition these VR tools improve productivity even more, as it can be used to construct highly interactive and quality materials that work perfectly with wide and narrow band-widths, regardless of the resolution of the monitors. Another powerful feature of these VR tools is that the 3D models could be interacted and visualized as stereoscopic views/images by wearing special 3D goggles. An example of a jet engine being interacted using VR software is shown in Figure 3.

Figure 1. An engineering learning package using a graphics tablet

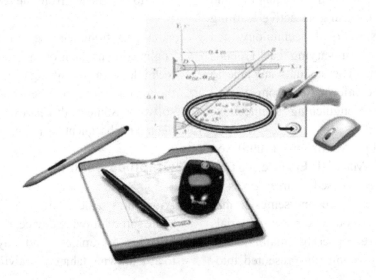

Figure 2. An engineering learning package projected onto an interactive white board

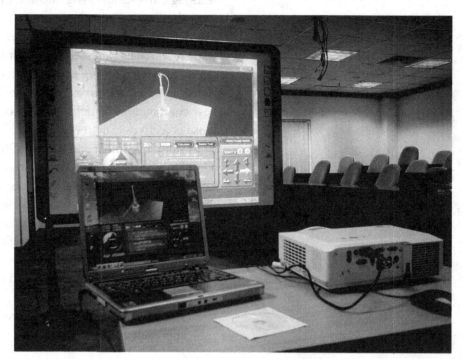

AUGMENTED REALITY

In general multimedia environments have offered new ways for learners to interact with various educational resources. Augmented reality (AR) is an emerging technology that overlays virtual objects onto real scenes that has potential to provide learners with a new type of learning material (Asai, 2005). The architecture of AR technology can be found in (Liarokapis, 2002, 2004).

AR has the ability to enhance real scenes viewed by the user, overlaying virtual objects over the real world, and works to improve the user's performance and perception of the world. Some advantages of using AR technology in teaching and learning include (1) the user can get three dimensional information based on a real scene, (2) the user can see objects from his/her viewpoint, and (3) the user can interact with both virtual and real objects wirelessly. With these advantages, some researchers have employed AR technology to develop their educational software for teaching and demonstration purposes (White, 2001; Lang, 2004; Asai, 2005; Liarokapis, 2004).

AR is now being used in engineering education, for example Liarokapis (2004), presents an educational application that allows users to interact with Web3D content using virtual and augmented reality. The study enables an exploration of the potential benefits of Web3D and AR technologies in engineering education and learning. Preliminary study found that by employing AR technology, students could understand more effectively through interactivity and multimedia content. An example of the study by Liarokapis is illustrated in Figure 4, where the user can interact with a 3D model of the object (i.e., Piston) and can compare it to real objects in a natural way.

Although AR has been used in education, its potential in education is just beginning to be explored and has not been practical enough to be used in educational environments due to its complex contents development approach (Manjit et al., 2009).

Figure 3. A 3D animated model

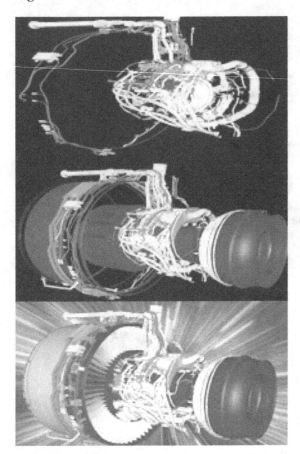

NEW APPROACHES IN LEARNING ENGINEERING

Blended Learning Approach

Blended learning may be phrased as a new education pedagogical approach that combines the use of electronic learning tools (such as email, software, and web-based support) and traditional classroom components to maximize teaching effectiveness. Brown et al. (1989) argued that the term blended learning is used to describe a solution that combines several different delivery methods, such as collaboration software, Web-based courses and knowledge management practices. Koohang (2006) and Lin (2008) claim that blended learning is a hybrid learning setting in which part of the learning activities and assignments are transferred from the face-to-face classroom to the distance learning environment. Based on these advantages, some research has stressed the importance of using a "blended learning approach", with clearly stated learning objectives and a selection of the best combination of delivery methods to meet those objectives (Smart & Cappel, 2005).

A study by Bullen and Russell (2007) on the adoption of a Blended learning approach to teaching first year engineering degree students has resulted in an improved student performance as measured by final examination results. In particular the study achieved greatest benefit through:

- The use of a weekly automated assessment scheme (WATS)
- Adoption of a just-in-time teaching approach

Although blended learning becomes more and more popular among higher education institutions (Howard & Remenyi, 2006), it is still at an early stage of development. As such, further research is required to see how exactly learning competencies are to be supported and encouraged in blended learning environments.

Game Learning Approach

Games are opening new potential for learning in formal situations and innovative ways and have been favored mainly by primary and secondary level of education. The main benefit for using a game approach in learning is motivation. Qualters et al. (2007), pointed that the use of interactive educational games can provide students with solid learning experiences. On the other hand serious games, blended with instructor-led and e-Learning training, could create high-impact social learning environments.

Today, some researchers are testing game learning approach for first year undergraduate Mechanical Engineering courses. For example

Figure 4. AR Visualization of a Piston (Liarokapis, 2004)

BEST Mechanics offers resources in statics, dynamics and the mechanics of materials. It provides interactive lessons and exercises, starting with fundamental topics and moving on to more advanced subjects. It includes Flash movies, examples and problems, games and a statics e-book. BEST Mechanics is a project from the Missouri University of Science and Technology. The website (http://web.mst.edu/~bestmech/) states that it is a work-in-progress.

Another study by Darling (2007) on the introduction of game based learning into the first year undergraduate syllabus of Mechanical Engineering was shown to be a great success. By using existing computing resources the students were able to work both individually and as a learning community based around their tutor group to design and test a virtual vehicle. An evaluation of the students engineering knowledge before and after the activity demonstrated significant learning gains while feedback from both the students and academic staff was very encouraging.

While the benefits of employing games approach in learning has been demonstrated in a number of studies, the challenges for providing a sufficient level of institutional support, both technical and pedagogic are insignificant. More studies may be required to test and see if game based learning approach is suitable for teaching in the higher learning institutions.

CONCLUSION

Mechanical engineering course subjects such as Mechanics Dynamics, combine a use of mathematics, schematic diagrams, and text descriptions. Frequently, students are unclear of basic principles of Engineering Mechanics Dynamics, and as such they do not know which mathematical relationships are to be applied in solving a particular problem. As such, this paper reviewed the feasibility of new ICT technologies that could be employed in teaching and learning of engineering.

ICT can enable wider access of information and knowledge, participation and interaction. Although such fundamental changes in the curriculum could take place and help transform the way students learn in many ways, this transformation may require new skills, capabilities and attitudes such as; are students and instructors prepared to use these technologies in their teaching and learning; are higher learning institutions committed to employ these new teaching aids.

The technologies reviewed in this paper include software such as CAL packages, virtual and augmented reality, 3D visual interactive software; hardware such as graphics tablet and interactive white board to enhance the problem solving skills and learning of students. New approaches to learning such as blended and game based learning were also reviewed.

It can be envisaged that the use of these technologies as replacement, or supplement to, human educators in engineering education would become widespread in the future. Such technology can be employed to demonstrate and correlate real life application and theory thereby promoting deep learning.

ACKNOWLEDGMENT

I would like to thank Dr. Kirandeep Kaur Sidhu for her constructive comments in writing and proof reading this paper. I am grateful to the College of Information Technology, University Tenaga Nasional, for providing an environment conducive to research.

REFERENCES

Asai, K. (2005). Augmented Instructions – A Fusion of Augmented Reality and Printed Learning Materials. In *Proceedings of the 5th IEEE International Conference of Advanced Learning Technologies* (pp. 1-3).

Bhattacharya, I., & Sharma, K. (2007). India in the knowledge economy – an electronic paradigm. *International Journal of Educational Management*, *21*(6), 543–568. doi:10.1108/09513540710780055

Bottino, R. M. (2003). ICT, national policies, and impact on schools and teachers' development. In *Proceedings of the 3.1 and 3.3 working groups conference on International federation for information processing (CRPIT '03)* (pp. 3-6). Darlinghurst, Australia: Australian Computer Society, Inc.

Brown, J., Collins, A., & Duguid, P. (1989). Situated Cognition and the Culture of Learning. *Educational Researcher*, *18*(1), 32–42.

Bullen, P. R., & Russell, M. B. (2007). *A Blended Learning Approach to Teaching First Year Engineering*.

Cairncross, S. (2002). *Interactive Multimedia and Learning: Realizing the Benefits*. Unpublished doctoral dissertation, Napier University, Scotland.

Callister, W. D. (2003). *Student Learning Resources. Materials Science and Engineering an Introduction*. New York: John Wiley & Sons Inc.

Cholin, V. S. (2005). Study of the application of information technology for effective access to resources in Indian university libraries. *The International Information & Library Review*, *37*(3), 189–197. doi:10.1016/j.iilr.2005.07.002

Cross, M., & Adam, F. (2007). ICT Policies and Strategies in Higher Education in South Africa: National and Institutional Pathways. *Higher Education Policy*, *20*(1), 73–95. doi:10.1057/palgrave.hep.8300144

Cuthell, J. P. (2002). *How do interactive whiteboards enhance learning?* Retrieved February 24, 2004, from http://www.virtuallearning.org.uk/iwb/Learning_theories.pdf

Cuthell, J. P. (2004). *Interactive whiteboards survey.* Retrieved May 22, 2005, from http://www.virtuallearning.org.uk/2003/whiteboards/survey.doc

Cuthell, J. P. (2005). Seeing the meaning. In *Proceedings of the impact of interactive whiteboards on teaching and learning (WCCE 05),* Stellenbosch, South Africa.

Darling, J. (2007). *Investigating the effectiveness and efficiency of games and game based learning communities to support students learning. TDF Evaluation report.* Retrieved May 2009, from http://www.bath.ac.uk/learningandteaching/recognition/tdf/case_studies

Gramoll, K. (2001). An Internet Portal for Statics and Dynamics Engineering Courses. In *Proceedings of the International Conference of Engineering* (pp. 1-6).

Hattangdi, H., & Ghosh, A. (2009). Enhancing the quality and accessibility of higher education through the use of Information Communication Technology. *International Journal of Educational Management, 21*(6), 1–12.

Howard, L., & Remenyi, Z. (2006). Adaptive Blended Learning Environments. In *Proceedings of the 9th International Conference of Engineering Education* (pp. 1-6).

Katarzyna, M. (2002). *Knowledge Representation, Content Indexing and Effective Teaching of Fluid Mechanics Using Web-Based Content.* Unpublished master's thesis, MIT, Cambridge, MA.

Koohang, A., Britz, J., & Seymour, T. (2006). Hybrid/Blended Learning: Advantages, Challenges, Design, and Future Directions. In *Proceedings of the Informing Science and IT Education Joint Conference,* Manchester, UK.

Kozma, R. (2005). National Policies That Connect ICT-Based Education Reform To Economic And Social Development. *Human Technology, 1*(2), 117–156.

Lang, U. (2004). Virtual and Augmented Reality Developments for Engineering Applications. In *Proceedings of the European Congress on Computational Methods in Applied Sciences and Engineering* (pp. 1-16).

Liarokapis, F. (2002). Multimedia Augmented Reality Interface for E-Learning (MARIE). *World Transactions on Engineering and Technology Education, 1*(2), 173–176.

Liarokapis, F. (2004). Web3D Augmented Reality to Support Engineering Education. *World Transactions on Engineering and Technology Education, 3*(1), 11–14.

Lim, C. P., & Chai, C. S. (2004). An activity-theoretical approach to research of ICT integration 13 in Singapore schools: Orienting activities and learner autonomy. *Computers & Education, 43*(3), 215–236. doi:10.1016/j.compedu.2003.10.005

Lim, C. P., & Hang, D. (2003). An activity theory approach to research of ICT integration in Singapore schools. *Computers & Education, 41*(1), 49–63. doi:10.1016/S0360-1315(03)00015-0

Lin, K. (2008). Building on Components into Traditional Instruction in Pre-Service Teacher Education: The Good, the Bad and the Ugly. *International Journal for Scholarship of Teacher and Learning, 2*(1).

Mason, R. (2000). From distance education to online education. *The Internet and Higher Education, 3*(1/2), 63–74. doi:10.1016/S1096-7516(00)00033-6

McMahon, C. J. (2000). *Tutorials for Introduction to Materials Engineering.* Merrion Media.

Mehta, S., & Kalra, M. (2006). Information and Communication Technologies: A bridge for social equity and sustainable development in India. *The International Information & Library Review, 38*(3), 147–160. doi:10.1016/j.iilr.2006.06.008

Plomp, T., Pelgrum, W. J., & Law, N. (2007). SITES2006 - International comparative survey of pedagogical practices and ICT in education. *Education and Information Technologies, 12*(2), 83–92. doi:10.1007/s10639-007-9029-5

Qualters, M. D., Isaacs, J., Cullinane, T., Laird, J., Mcdonald, A., & Corriere, J. (2007). A Game Approach to Teach Environmentally Benign Manufacturing in the Supply Chain. *International Journal for the Scholarship of Teaching and Learning, 2*(2).

Sanyal, B. C. (2001). *New functions of higher education and ICT to achieve education for all.* Paper presented at the Expert Roundtable on University and Technology-for- Literacy and Education Partnership in Developing Countries, International Institute for Educational Planning, UNESCO, Paris.

Schmidt, J. T. (2007). *Preparing Students for Success in Blended Learning Environments: Future Oriented Motivation & Self-Regulation.* Unpublished doctoral dissertation.

Scott, N. W. (1996). *A study of the introduction of educational technology into a course in engineering dynamics: classroom environment and learning outcomes.* Unpublished doctoral dissertation.

Sharma, R. (2003). *Barriers in Using Technology for Education in Developing Countries.* Washington, DC: IEEE.

Sidhu, M. S. (2007). *Development and Applications of Interactive Multimedia TAPS (Technology Assisted Problem Solving) Packages for Engineering.* Unpublished doctoral dissertation, Universiti Malaya.

Sidhu, M. S., Cheng, L. K., Der, S. C., & Omar, R. (2009). Augmented Reality Applications in Education. In *Proceedings of the Second Teaching and Learning Conference at UNITEN.*

Sidhu, M. S., & Ramesh, S. (2008). Virtual Worlds: The Next Generation for Solving Engineering Problems. In *Proceedings of the IEEE 8th International Conference on Computer and IT (CIT2008),* Sydney, Australia (pp. 303-307).

Sidhu, M. S., Ramesh, S., & Selvanathan, N. (2005). A Coach-Based Interactive Multimedia Tool For Solving Engineering Problem. *International Multimedia Cyberscape Journal, 3*(2), 28–36.

Smart, K. L., & Cappel, J. L. (2005). An exploratory look at students' perceptions of blended learning. *Issues in Information Systems, 6*(1), 149–155.

Vaughan, R. (1998). The Use of Multimedia in Developing Undergraduate Engineering Courses. *Journal of Materials, 5*(5). Retrieved February 2007, from www.tms.org/pubs/journals/JOM/9805/Voller/Voller-9805.html

White, M. (2001). A virtual Interactive Teaching Environment (VITE) Using XML and Augmented Reality. *The International Journal of Electrical Engineering Education, 38*(4), 316–329.

Chapter 27
Accessing ICT Enabled Content in Low-Income Countries:
Think Big, Start Small, and Scale Up

Solomon Negash
Kennesaw State University, USA

ABSTRACT

While the digital revolution has transformed the way many of us work and live, more than half the world's population lives in rural areas that have been shut-out of the digital transformation. Low-income countries have yet to realize the benefits from the digital revolution; therefore, a need exists for innovative and alternative models to overcome the lack of access to knowledge and learning. This paper examines the challenges faced by low-income countries in accessing ICT enabled content and proposes a Big-Small model where low-income countries can harness the ICT revolution. This paper concludes with a discussion on sustainability and future research directions.

INTRODUCTION

Access to content is the right to knowledge access (Rossini, 2007). Prior research indicates that ICT investment increases growth dividend (Roller & Waverman, 2001), facilitates economic growth (Waverman, Meschi, & Fuss, 2005), combats poverty (Calderon & Serven, 2004), and promotes expansion in economic activities (World Bank, 1991). ICT is also touted as a means for low-income countries to leapfrog out of their economic predicament (Murthy, 2001). Much of the literature

available about ICTs in a development context focuses on the digital divide. The emergence of the 'digital divide' (Brown, 2000) reflected the social and economic imbalance between high and low income countries.

In considering the digital divide, issues of access and connectivity are often the first level of focus. However, there are at least four dimensions of the digital divide – an *information divide* due to some people's inability to gain access to online information due to demographic characteristics; a *skills divide* related to computer specific capabili-

DOI: 10.4018/978-1-61350-468-0.ch027

ties; an *economic opportunity divide* related to the inability to receive training, education or employment opportunities; and a *demographic divide* related to certain people's inability to participate in electronic offerings (Molla & Al-jaghoub, 2007; Mossberger et al., 2003). This study focuses on skills and economic opportunity divide. Innovation in low-income countries can be hampered by the multi-prong challenges of the digital divide including access to the Internet, ICTs, and content (Rossini, 2007). These challenges are also highlighted by the World Bank Findings as the three pillars of the ICT revolution: connectivity, capacity, and content (Parakash, 2003).

The literature, when discussing low-income (developing) countries, includes countries like Brazil, China, India, and Mexico. Many of these countries have affordable Internet connectivity similar to high-income countries. Telephone rates are inversely correlated to content access, i.e., digital content is less accessible when telecommunication costs are high.

Over the last decade access to the Internet has markedly improved in low-income countries. For instance, in 2006 low-income countries accounted for nearly half of the Internet use; up from 36% in 2003 (UNCATD, 2006; UNCTAD, 2004). And as far back as 1997 most African countries, 48 of the 53 African countries, had Internet connectivity; the five exceptions were Congo, Equatorial Guinea, Gabon, Libya, Somalia, and Western Sahara. The primary reasons for these exceptions were either geopolitical isolation, as in the case of Libya and civil war as in the case of Somalia (Landweber, 1997). Therefore, country level Internet connectivity has been achieved around the world and it is not the primary challenge. The primary Internet connectivity challenge is connectivity to low-income or rural communities. Even in the United States, rural residents in 2003 lagged by half in broadband access compared to their urban counterparts; 9% households in US rural communities with broadband access compared to 22% for urban residents. By 2005 the broadband access gap in US rural and urban communities was 24% and 39%, respectively (Associated Press, 2005).

About half, 53%, of the world population in 2000 lived in rural communities from which 87% of them were from Africa and Asia (UN Population Division, 2001). These two regions have each 70% of their population in rural communities (UN Population Division, 2001). China and India, with their large population, account for 70% of the Asian rural population. China with 60% of its population, 800 million people, (Economist, 2007; China-Profile, 2007) and India with 70% of its population, nearly 700 million people, (Wikipedia, 2007; Press, 1999) account for the large proportion of the Asian rural community. When China and India are excluded the Asian rural population is much smaller. In contrast, over forty Sub-Saharan African countries have an average of 89% of their population in rural communities (World Bank, 2007b; Mbeki, 2005). Hence, content access models for low-income countries must consider the challenges in Sub-Saharan African countries.

This study is motivated by the research question: what ICT enabled models can be used to harness digital content access in low-income countries? The study evaluates the content access challenges in low-income countries and proposes a model for digital content access that can be implemented despite the challenges.

In the remainder of this paper, first, we set the context by discussing the availability of open education resources followed by content access challenges in low-income countries. We then propose the Big—Small ICT model for accessing content in low-income countries. We conclude with a discussion of sustainability and revenue model.

OPEN EDUCATION RESOURCES

Today, there is significant amount of educational content that is freely available digitally. Many groups including MERLOT, Connexions,

FLOSS4EDU and TESSA, MIT, UC Berkley, and Stanford University have opened their educational mega power to the public. MERLOT is reaching out to Africa through the MERLOT African Network initiative which provides FREE access to MERLOT content for African higher education institutions. The Connexions project is another example that started at Rice University and became a global source for open educational content. Success areas for the Connexions initiative were reported as modularized content; value to author, instructor, student; brand equity, content quality, user community, site usability; and revenue model (Dholakia, 2006).

Other platforms that are making a difference in Africa include Free/Libre and Open Source Software for Education (FLOSS4EDU), Qedoc Quiz Wiki, Teacher Education in Sub-Saharan Africa (TESSA), and the Global Text Project with its vision to deliver free online textbooks.

The MIT open courseware initiative has made 1800 courses freely available. UC Berkley's YouTube approach helps improve content access at all levels (Havenstein, 2007). The Stanford iTune initiative has also allowed public access to a wide range of lectures, speeches, debates and other university content (Tomassi, 2006). And "Twenty-five Nobel price-winning scientists are calling for the US government to make all taxpayer funded research papers freely available" (USA Today, 2004).

These pioneers have opened many educational opportunities including bring people back to the educational equation; reduce high cost of educational material; reduce time lag between production and use of learning; and enable re-use, re-contextualization, and customization, i.e. translation and localization (Baraniuk, 2007). And by and large, high-income countries have made the requisite infrastructure investments to tap into this freely available educational content. However, low-income countries face several challenges that hinder access. Researchers need to devise models that will avail the vast digital knowledge source to low-income and rural communities even when they don't have Internet connectivity.

CHALLENGES OF CONTENT ACCESS

The Hewlett Foundation, a pioneer in the open education repository (OER) movement, has identified four components in its OER approach: sponsor high quality open content; remove barriers, e.g., ICT barriers; understand and stimulate use, e.g., research & development, feasibility studies, and awareness creation; and equalize access, e.g., reach underserved communities (Atkins, Brown, & Hammond, 2007). In this section we outline the challenges of content access in Sub-Saharan Africa using the four components identified by the Hewlett Foundation.

High Quality Open Content

Open content refers to non-proprietary content that is freely available, often online. As indicated above many institutions have made educational content openly available. If low-income countries are to take advantage of the digital revolution they too must take part in both content authoring and content access. However, much of Sub-Saharan Africa is being challenged in accessing content, not to mention authoring. Direct measurement to assess country of origin for Internet content authoring is often difficult because content author may not reside in the same place as the computer (server) used to host the content. One potential surrogate measure for Internet content author countries is the number of Internet hosts registered by country. Giancarlo Livraghi (2007a, 2007b) reported 433,193,199 Internet host computers worldwide compared to 1,522,000 in Africa; Africa accounting for only 0.35% of the global Internet host computer count. Three African countries: South

Africa, Morrocco, and Egypt with 68.1%, 17.6%, and 5.9%, respectively, account for 91.6% of Africa's total Internet host computers. The remaining 50 African countries, combined, have only 127,445 Internet host computers, less than 0.03% of the worldwide count. In contrast, the United States has 230,600,000 Internet host computers, 53% of the worldwide count. The total number of Internet host computers in the 50 African countries is less than that of Turkey; a country that has less than 10% of Africa's population but has over 1.6 million Internet host computers. This indicates the dearth of content authoring in many African countries.

Africa's lack of content authoring poses a long term challenge. The issue is not lack of content but the personnel and ICT connectivity. The Brazilian Minister of Culture, Gilberto Gil, at the iCommons Summit in Rio in June 2006, challenged low-income countries to embrace their own cultural differences and diversity and to use ICTs to make their voices heard globally, projecting their own knowledge and culture into the international arena (Rossini, 2007). The Brazilian Minister invoked the term "tropicalism" (Rossini, 2007) to describe the need for countries in low-income countries to actively participate in content authoring. "Tropicalism" is a Brazilian term associated with the music revolution in the latter half of the 20th century where avant-garde musicians, artists, writers, and film makers identify themselves with a goal of breaking from its dependence on official patronage and ideological censorship to make film attractive to the public while still representing the interest of the people (Brazil, 2007). ICTs provide a workable venue for Africa to disseminate its unique content and join the spirit of "Tropicalism".

As researchers develop a model to open content access, content authoring should be an integral part of the model, i.e. rural communities need to engage in content authoring not just content access. As rural communities embrace the notion of content authoring and sharing, the OER concept of courseware for mining should permeate; the

Hewlett Foundation has "helped shift faculty perspective from this courseware is mine to this courseware is for (open) mining" (Atkins, Brown, & Hammond, 2007). The Connexions network, for example, has workable mechanism for creating and incorporating content to the knowledge repository for those with Internet connectivity. The proposed Big—Small model suggests to make this possible with or without Internet connectivity.

In addition to access challenge, low-income countries are faced with quality and sustainability of content (Atkins, Brown, & Hammond, 2007). While simultaneously promoting African content generation a mechanism for evaluating content has to be considered. A discussion of how to maintain the quality of open content is beyond the scope of this paper, suffice it to say that a review process and rating by readers should be integrally considered to maintain the quality and relevance of all content.

Content generation should also incorporate localization and contextualization challenges as well as shortage of trained personnel (Dzvimbo, 2005). Lessons learned from the OER movement should also be considered including re-use, where content is available in editable formats like wikis instead of view only formats like PDF; fragmentation, creating global repositories in lieu of the fragmented institution based OER repositories; and infrastructure cost (Baraniuk, 2007).

Remove Barriers: ICT Access Issues

Several factors create ICT barrier including Internet access, infrastructure, hardware and software acquisition, cost of ownership, and intellectual property. These issues, vis-à-vis content access, in Sub-Saharan Africa are discussed in this section.

Internet Access

Access to content and ICTs in advanced economies is focused at the individual level; for example, blackberries and i-phones that provide anytime/

anywhere access to the individual. This individual access is possible in high-income countries because the broadband Internet access needed to support these services is affordable for individuals.

Broadband Internet access, for example 6000 Kilo bit per second, in the United States is available at $33.00 dollars per month; cost for broadband access represents only 1.1% of per capita income. In contrast, per capita income for many of the Sub-Sahara African countries is below $1,000 (IMF, 2007). In Ethiopia, for example, broadband Internet access, defined as 256 Kilo bits per second—20 times slower than the example used in US, costs $100 per month after the recent 107% discount, $1,200 annually (ETC, 2005). Ethiopia, with its per capita income of $177 (IMF, 2007) broadband access is equivalent to 678.00% of per capita income, i.e. it will take the annual income of seven people to subscribe to a broadband access in Ethiopia. This price differential illustrates one of the reasons why Sub-Saharan African countries rank low in the ITU digital access index (ITU, 2003).

Infrastructure

Infrastructure is like the highway everyone loves to use but no one wants to pay for. Without a capable infrastructure many of the ICT revolution benefits cannot be realized. Paradoxically, many funding organizations do not want to pay for infrastructure. In many African countries ICT connectivity and content access challenges are compounded by the lack of electricity and high Internet access fees (Negash, 2006a; Parakash, 2003).

It has been shown that a critical mass in telecommunication investments, where the number of telecommunication infrastructure users is large enough to place downward pressure on prices, are needed before related economic developments are achieved (Roller & Waverman, 2001). Even if many of the infrastructure issues are to be addressed, reaching out to rural communities will take time. A framework that will address the

gamut of ICT challenges in Sub-Saharan Africa, from no Internet connectivity to full broadband Internet availability, with transition plan is needed.

Hardware and Software Acquisition

Complementary ICTs such as computers are not affordable for most Africans (Prakash, 2003). From a non-governmental organization (NGO) that has distributed over 3000 refurbished computers in Ethiopia, we learned that the average cost of a refurbished computer (Pentium IV, 2.4 GHz. Speed, with 256 RAM, with CD ROM and 17-inch CRT monitor) is around $400.00. This is significantly higher than the same computer available for under $150 in the U.S., a factor of 2.5 times higher cost in Ethiopia. These costs are not affordable for the average Ethiopian when considering the economic disparity of 20:1 between the U.S. and Ethiopia. For example, given the purchasing power of individuals in the US, i.e., 20 times higher than those in Ethiopia, a computer price of $400.00 for an Ethiopian is equivalent to a price tag of $8,000.00 for an American (400x20=$8,000) or looking it another way a computer priced at $150.00 in America should be available for $7.50 (150 / 20 = $7.50) for average Ethiopians to afford it. Of course it is unthinkable to expect U.S. residents to pay $8,000 for a refurbished computer. This price differential partly explains why personal computer penetration in countries with advanced economies like Japan, Korea, Canada, and United States are high at 78.2%, 77.9%, 66.8%, and 61.8%, respectively; and many of the African countries hover below 5% (ITU, 2003). If a similar level of digital revolution is expected in Sub-Saharan Africa, then we have to devise ways where computer prices are comparable, i.e., refurbished computers priced at $7.50.

One of the considerations for our Big—Small model is the cost factor per person: How do we reduce the cost of a computer per person to $7.50? One should think big and find innovative ways to achieve these price targets. The MIT $100 per laptop project is one such big thinking. Even the $100 per laptop price point is not affordable for Africans in rural communities. We don't anticipate computer prices to drop by a factor of 20 any time soon. Therefore while thinking about the big ideas we should have options to start small. For example, distributing hardware/software acquisition costs among many individuals by sharing them at a community center. Purchasing five computers, at $400 each, would cost $2000. If the five computers are installed at a community center or library and shared by 300 people, the cost per person can be reduced below the target price of $7.50. Hence starting small, by implementing community level ICT access, will achieve cost parity.

Total Cost of Ownership

As stated above, acquisition cost for hardware and software is financially challenging for rural communities, and much more when Total Cost of Ownership (TCO) is considered. According to the Gartner Group and Forester Research acquisition cost is only one-third of TCO (Total Cost, 2001). Total cost of ownership includes hardware and software acquisition, installation, training, support, maintenance, and infrastructure. A typical five-year TCO for a networked personal computer is 21% acquisition cost, 21% technical support, 13% administrative costs, and 45% end-user support (Total Cost, 2001). The single largest cost in TCO is end-user support which is comprised of initial training for end-users and ongoing operational support. These challenges are magnified in rural communities where basic keyboarding training and ICT awareness is lacking. The proposed Big—Small model accommodates cost effective end-user training. Users need a customer support center where they can get help for day-to-day operational issues. Establishing community centers in advance of individual level access will afford continuity for customer support. A community level approach will provide a long-term end-user training and support model.

Intellectual Property for Content

Software piracy is rampant in developing economies; most places in China, for example, Linux and Windows cost the same amount of money (Schafer, 2004). Regardless of economic capability intellectual property has to be respected at all times. Dalindyebo Shabalala from the Center for International Environmental Law (CIEL) in Geneva argues that low-income countries should have intellectual property standards tailored to their own circumstances (Shabalala, 2007).

The open education movement promises to disintermediate the scholarly publishing industry, in the process rendering some current business models not viable and inventing new viable ones, copy rights among them (Baraniuk, 2007). It will also change the way that we conceive of and pursue authorship, teaching, peer review, and promotion and tenure (Baraniuk, 2007). Low-income countries should incorporate digital intellectual property legislations in their laws (Shabalala, 2007). Copyright rules for content like the Creative Commons should also be integrated.

Awareness and Local Access

Lack of awareness ranks high in the challenges for the diffusion of OER in Sub-Saharan Africa. Kuzvinetsa P. Dzvimbo, the former Rector of African Virtual University (AVU), a program initiated by the World Bank in 1997, cited lack of awareness and access to resources as challenges when AVU attempted to disseminate the MIT open courseware to its partner universities (Dzvimbo, 2005).

A mechanism for accessing content locally, independent of Internet connectivity should be part of the long term solution. AVU, for example, used a mirroring server to make OER content available at the local level (Dzvimbo, 2005). Libraries that do not have Internet connectivity could access OER content from a local server that is periodically updated.

Equalize Access: Reaching Underserved Communities

Before individuals invest in ICT they need to know what benefits they can get from it. The potential beneficiaries, rural communities in this case, need to define the business need, and what they expect as an outcome. Defining what each member of the rural community can derive from ICT investments requires awareness about the tools. One way rural communities can gain quick benefits from ICTs is through Internet Intermediaries (James, 2004). Internet intermediaries use an intermediary person that inquires users' needs and identify potential solutions using the Internet, i.e. end users present their problems to the intermediary who then will search the Internet for alternative solutions on their behalf. Internet intermediaries may provide a logical transition in supporting rural communities (James, 2004). Intermediary and government based services can be achieved through community level ICT connections.

THE BIG—SMALL MODEL

The proposed Big—Small model was first published in 2005 as a model to help low-income countries access educational content through Information and Communication Technology (ICT) (Negash, 2005). This was an outgrowth from an action research at a non-governmental organization (NGO) in Ethiopia. The NGO focused on providing technology enabled library information access to underprivileged youth. The research paper was a result of the action research regarding the community based ICT center the NGO setup in Ethiopia in 2002. The center did not have Internet access at the time. Despite the lack of Internet access the center had five networked computers and stored digital library information on the local server. Patrons came to the center to access the digital information.

In 2006, the NGO connected its ICT center to the Internet and increased its networked computers eight fold, to forty computers. The number of patrons and level of service from the center increased correspondingly. By early 2009 the center was serving three-thousand patrons per month. Furthermore, in 2006 the NGO replicated its "small start" of five networked computers without Internet connection to two other locations. This study was informed by the experience from these installations. The Big-Small framework was later proposed as a viable investment for ICT enabled information access for developing economies (Negash, 2006b).

The Findings report from the World Bank recommended that Africa should engage in what it called "think big, start small, and scale up" approach to overcome its lack of access to knowledge and learning (Parakash, 2003). Internet and ICTs that have energized the digital revolution can serve as a catalyst (Waverman, Meschi, & Fuss, 2005) to help bridge the access gap.

Big thinking, big breakthroughs, and big ideas are rare and far in between. The same big results can be achieved by adding up smaller innovations. Most of the ICT revolution focus in the high-income countries has been to provide anyplace/anytime access to individuals. Miniaturized computing tools like blackberry, i-phone, and i-pod and Internet access to mobile devices are among the ICT revolution that provide individuals with information and network access anytime and anyplace. The same level of individual access is needed in low-income countries. We believe this should be the big idea to aim for ICT tools and Internet connectivity at the individual level. However, the culmination of high ICT development costs and low personal income levels in low-income countries, as discussed earlier, makes immediate implementation of this individualized approach a challenge.

While the challenges identified above including lack of trained personnel, weak economic strength, high hardware/software acquisition

Figure 1. The big-small model for ICT enabled content access

Connectivity

Level of Access

	Local	Network
Community	(1) Start Small	(2) Scale Up—A
Individual	(3) Scale Up—B	(4) Think Big

costs, lack of Internet connectivity, lack of access to content, and lack of content authoring persist in rural communities a unified framework that accounts for these challenges is needed. We propose such a framework called the Big-Small model-think big, start small, and scale up-for content and ICT access in low-income countries. The Big-Small model is depicted in Figure 1.

The *level of access* dimension in the framework consists of community and individual. Community refers to shared access from a common resource such as libraries or community centers. Individual refers to dedicated access to the individual at a residence or workplace. The *connectivity* dimension, local versus network, refers to the reach of information access. Local refers to information access within the local server. Network refers to information access from a wide area network including the Internet. In advanced economies Internet connectivity for individuals is prevalent shown as "Think Big" or Network—Individual in the 4th quadrant. In contrast, low-income countries (communities) do not own ICT equipments nor do they have Internet connectivity, hence should "Start Small" with Local—Community content and ICT access shown in the 1st quadrant.

The Big—Small content and ICT access framework has four quadrants. Low-income countries should evaluate their access status and enter the model at the appropriate level. For those without Internet connectivity the proposed framework can help them begin the Big-Small transformation immediately. The four quadrants are discussed below.

1st Quadrant - Start Small: in this quadrant users have Local-Community access, i.e. users that come to the community center can access information stored on the local server or workstations available at the community center. As described above, financial challenges limit individuals in low-income countries from getting access to the vast digital information. This framework proposes to re-direct the limited resources to community access investments. Community centers can reach large numbers of people, making the cost per person nominal, spreading the limited funds to reach more residents. Digital resources including books, journals, multimedia lessons, edutainment, and training programs can be downloaded and stored locally for dissemination. Community access increases ICT awareness. For example, teachers can get reference material for their classes, students can extend their research, and entrepreneurs can benefits from new training services. Community centers easily reach the younger generation addressing vital target groups proposed by Fillip: "Children and youths are a very appropriate target group for ICT initiatives" (Fillip, 2002, p. 4). Community centers can also be expanded to reach schools, community organizations, and other public institutions.

2nd Quadrant - Scale Up - A: The first Scale Up quadrant with Network-Community access is an extension of the 1st quadrant. Local area networks and computers, components of the 1st quadrant, have to be installed to make the 2nd quadrant feasible. As their financial means improve, low-income countries should strengthen their infrastructure to provide broadband connectivity at the community centers, increasing digital access to patrons. The community centers established in the 1st quadrant can provide support services for the 2nd quadrant. Once computers and ICT services are provided, end-user training becomes the next challenge, for example, training teachers on how to use the technology effectively (Fillip, 2002). The community centers established in the 1st quadrant can serve as resources for maintaining the network, providing training, and developing local content; leveraging the initial investment. The 2nd quadrant can also address end-users need through Internet intermediaries (James, 2004).

3rd Quadrant – Scale Up - B: The second Scale Up quadrant with Local-Individual access moves the level of access from community to individuals. This is an extension of the 2nd quadrant where community level Internet access is extended to individuals. Characteristics of the 3rd quadrant are when a critical mass of the local community is able to access most of the community center resources from work or home. The 3rd quadrant differs from the 4th quadrant in that all its end-user access goes through the community center, i.e., the individual is connected to the wide area network through the community centers. While this provides individuals greater access it does not incur the costs of connecting individuals to broadband services.

4th Quadrant – Think Big: in this quadrant users have Network-Individual access, i.e., end users have Internet access from home or work and can gain direct access to the global digital information. Characteristics of a community achieving 4th quadrant level can be signified by the critical mass of the local community having direct Internet access to the global

digital information, a corresponding decline in the number of Internet intermediaries will be observed.

Many rural communities may not advance beyond the 2nd quadrant. However, the Big-Small framework will avail access to the global digital information without having to advance beyond the Network—Community level. Many of the specialized needs from rural community may be satisfied through Internet intermediaries (James, 2004). Therefore despite the ICT challenges in low-income countries we posit that the Big—Small model allows them to participate in the digital revolution and spur economic activities.

SUSTAINABILITY

Sustainable development is a key goal of decision makers (Islam et al., 2003). Proposed sustainable models for educational programs include substitution model, partnership model, and segmentation model (Dholakia, King, & Baraniuk, 2006). Substitution models propose to fund the new open education program by using monies saved from the costly platforms that preceded the new project. While this is viable in high-income countries the low-income countries (communities) targeted in this study often do not have legacy infrastructures to replace, hence, the substitute model does not apply.

Partnership model proposes that rural communities attract new philanthropic and governmental funding. Economically strong partners can energize Africa's economy (Blyden & Davidson, 2005). Partnerships can give ICT development strong foundations. Success in ICT projects requires complementary skills including strong partner institutions, strong project manager, and an attitude to think big, start small, and scale up (Prakash, 2003). Partnership alone cannot lead to success. Strong local management and positive attitude are needed.

While partnerships are vital for initiating ICT projects, long-term success requires a revenue model for sustainability. Segmentation model proposes the creation of content that can be customized to add value that can be offered for a fee. The community undertaking the project should identify a revenue or cost-recovery model to sustain its projects. Partnerships can be coupled with endowments where the economically strong partner can establish an endowment to sustain the development. While the endowment retains its seed money the operation of the development project can be funded by the interest income from the endowment.

For the proposed Big—Small framework the partnership model may be the first step to jump start rural communities. As the rural community progresses in their Big-Small initiatives efforts should be focused to move from the partnership model to segmentation, endowment, and/or other appropriate revenue models (Dholakia, King, & Baraniuk, 2006).

CONCLUSION

This study has proposed a Big—Small model for ICT enabled content access in low-income countries. We recognize the challenges that hinder low-income countries from accessing the vast education resources available digitally. The high cost of ICT projects makes it difficult for low-income countries (communities) to take advantage of the digital revolution. The proposed Big—Small model provides a framework to start small while aiming big.

We encourage more research that allows low-income countries (communities) to transition despite the economic and human resource challenges. Further research is needed to test the proposed model, introduce new models, and evaluate sustainable models. Such endeavors help advance our collective understanding.

REFERENCES

Associated Press. (2006, February 26). *Rural broadband users close gap with cities: Pew survey notes increasing acceptance among people living in the country*. Retrieved March 1, 2006, from http://www.msnbc.msn.com/id/11581369/

Atkins, D. E., Brown, J. S., & Hammond, A. L. (2007). *A Review of the Open Educational Resources (OER) Movement: Achievements, Challenges, and New Opportunities*. Retrieved November 4, 2007, from http://www.hewlett.org/NR/rdonlyres/5D2E3386-3974-4314-8F67-5C2F22EC4F9B/ 0/AReviewoftheOpenEducationalResourcesOERMovement_ BlogLink.pdf

Baraniuk, R. G. (2007). Challenges and Opportunities for the Open Education Movement: A Connexions Case Study. In Iiyoshi, T., & Vijay Kumar, M. S. (Eds.), *Opening Up Education – The Collective Advancement of Education through Open Technology, Open Content, and Open Knowledge*. Cambridge, MA: MIT Press.

BEA. (2007). *US Government Bureau of Economic Analysis: Personal Income and Per Capita Personal Income by BEA Economic Area 2003-2005*. Retrieved November 25, 2007, from http://www.bea.gov/bea/regional/reis/scb.cfm

Blyden, B. K., & Davidson, I. E. (2005). Energizing Africa's emerging economy. *IEEE Power and Energy Magazine*, *3*(4), 24–31. doi:10.1109/MPAE.2005.1458227

Brazil: Cannibalism and Tropicalism. (2007). Retrieved November 25, 2007, from http://www.filmreference.com/encyclopedia/Academy-Awards-Crime-Films/Brazil-CANNIBALISM-AND-TROPICALISM.html

China-Profile. (2007). *China-Profile Analysis: Urban and Rural Population in China 1978 and 2002*. Retrieved November 22, 2007, from http://www.gerhard-k-heilig.com/cp/data/tab_rurpop_1.htm

Comcast. (2007). *Comcast Broadband Internet Access Plan.* Retrieved November 25, 2007, from http://www.whatisthis.com/broadband/comcast/

Dholakia, P. M. (2006). *What Makes an Open Education Program Sustainable?* Houston, TX: JGSM & Connexions, Rice University.

Dholakia, U. M., King, W. J., & Baraniuk, R. (2006). *What Makes an Open Education Program Sustainable?* The Case of Connexions.

Dzvimbo, K. P. (2005, October 27-28). The African Virtual University: A Strategic Approach to Open Educational Resources. In *Proceedings of the 2005 LINC Symposium*, Cambridge, MA. Retrieved November 28, 2007, from http://ocw.mit.edu/OcwWeb/web/home/home/index.htm

Economist. (2007). *Rural China: Missing the barefoot doctor.* Retrieved November 22, 2007, from http://www.economist.com/displaystory.cfm?story_id=9944734

ETC. (2005). *Ethiopian Telecommunication Corporation: ETC introduced sound tariff adjustments on its Internet Service Rates.* Retrieved November 15, 2007, from http://www.ethionet.et/publications/eNews/enews_june_17_2005.html

Fillip, B. (2002). Information And Communication Technologies (Icts) To Help Disadvantaged Groups Help Themselves. *Japan International Cooperation Agency (Jica) U.S.A. Office.* Retrieved February 23, 2006, from http://www.jica.go.jp/usa/topics/pdf/it.pdf

Havenstein, H. (2007). *UC Berkeley offers free course lectures on YouTube: Program launched this week offers 300 hours of videotaped courses and events. ComputerWorld.* Retrieved from November 4, 2007, from http://www.computerworld.com/action/article.do?command= viewArticleBasic&taxonomyId=13&articleId=9040959&intsrc=hm_topic

IMF. (2007). *International Monetary Fund: World Economic Outlook Database.* Retrieved November 25, 2007, from http://en.wikipedia.org/wiki/List_of_countries_ by_GDP_%28nominal%29_per_capita

Islam, S. M. N., Munasinghe, M., & Clarke, M. (2003). Corrigendum to "Making long-term economic growth more sustainable: evaluating the costs and benefits". *Ecological Economics, 47*(2/3), 149–166. doi:10.1016/S0921-8009(03)00162-9

James, J. (2004). Reconstructing the digital divide from the perspective of a large, poor, developing country. *Journal of Information Technology, 19,* 172–177. doi:10.1057/palgrave.jit.2000019

Landweber, L. L. (1997). *Mapping the Global Spread of the NET.* Retrieved from http://www.mundi.net/maps/maps_011/

Livraghi, G. (2007a). *Data-The Internet in Africa: Host Count.* Retrieved November 25, 2007, from http://gandalf.it/data/africeng.htm

Livraghi, G. (2007b). *Data on Internet Activity Worldwide: Host Count.* Retrieved November 25, 2007, from http://gandalf.it/data/data1.htm

Mbeki, M. (2005). *Underdevelopment in Sub-Saharan Africa: The role of the private sector and political elite. CATO Institute.* Retrieved November 22, 2007, from http://www.cato.org/pubs/fpbriefs/fpb85.pdf

Murthy, N. R. (2001). The ICT Revolution: Can Asia Leapfrog Poverty Barriers? In *Proceedings of the Role of IT in Poverty Reduction, the 34th Asian Development Bank Annual Meeting.* Retrieved November 28, 2007, from http:// www.adb.org/ AnnualMeeting/ 2001/ Seminars/ murthy_ paper.pdf

Negash, S. (2005, June 18-19). Library and Educational Access for Progress (LEAP): Information access as enabler for development. In *Proceedings of the Third International Symposium on Ethiopian Development Studies*, Addis Ababa, Ethiopia.

Negash, S. (2006a). ICT for Ethiopian Community Development. In Marshall, S., Taylor, W., & Yu, X. (Eds.), *Encyclopedia of Developing Regional Communities with Information and Communication Technology* (pp. 370–376). Hershey, PA: IGI Global.

Negash, S. (2006b, August 4-6). Information and Communication Technology (ICT) Investment in Economically Developing Countries. In *Proceedings of the Twelfth Americas Conference on Information Systems*, Acapulco, Mexico.

Prakash, S. (2003). *The African Virtual University and Growth in Africa: A knowledge and learning challenge. Findings, a publication of the World Bank*. Retrieved from http://www.worldbank.org/afr/findings

Press, L. (1999). A Client-Centered Networking Project in Rural India. *OnTheInternet, 5*(2), 36-38. Retrieved November 22, 2007, from http://som.csudh.edu/fac/lpress/devnat/nations/india/pondyoti.htm

Röller, L. H., & Waverman, L. (2001). Telecommunications infrastructure and economic development: A simultaneous approach. *The American Economic Review, 91*, 4. doi:10.1257/aer.91.4.909

Rossini, C. A. A. (2007). The open access movement: Opportunities and Challenges for Developing Countries. Let them live in interesting times. In *Proceedings of the Diplo Foundation Internet Governance Program*.

Schafer, S. (2004). Microsoft's Cultural Revolution; Battered by pirates and struggling to turn a profit, the brash American software giant is no longer trying to change China. Instead China's changing the company. *Newsweek International*, 46-49.

Shabalala, D. (2007). Towards A Digital Agenda for Developing Countries. Retrieved November 28, 2007 from http:// www.southcentre.org/ publications/ researchpapers/ ResearchPapers13. pdf

Tomassi, K. D. (2006). *Stanford on iTunes' is for Everybody*. Retrieved November 22, 2007, from http://www.forbes.com/2006/01/24/stanford-on-itunes_c x _kdt_ 06conncampus_ 0124 stanford. html

Total Cost of Ownership. (2001). Retrieved November 28, 2007, from http://www.widernet.org/projects/costofownership1.htm

UN Population Division. (2001). *World Urbanization Prospects: The 2001 Revision*. Retrieved from http://www.un.org/esa/population/publications/wup2001/WUP2001_CH2.pdf

Wikipedia. (2007). *Demographics of India*. Retrieved November 22, 2007, from http:// en.wikipedia.org/wiki/Demographics_of_India

World Bank. (2007b). *The Agenda for Agricultural-based Countries of Sub-Saharan Africa*. Retrieved November 22, 2007, from http://econ. worldbank.org/WBSITE/EXTERNAL/EXTDEC/ EXTRESEARCH/EXTWDRS/EXTWDR2008/0,contentMDK:21485080~isCURL:Y ~pagePK:64167689~piPK:64167673~theSite PK:2795143,00.html

This work was previously published in International Journal of Information and Communication Technology, Volume 6, Issue 4, edited by Lawrence A. Tomei, pp. 49-60, copyright 2010 by IGI Publishing (an imprint of IGI Global).

Chapter 28

The Role of Computer-Mediated Communication:
A Look at Methods for Delivering and Facilitating Training in Academic and Organizational Settings

Bolanle Olaniran
Texas Tech University, USA

Natasha Rodriguez
Texas Tech University, USA

ABSTRACT

The use of information technology to enhance classroom learning and deliver corporate training is the latest trend and focus of much research in the computer-mediated communication (CMC) and development industry. Technological advances continue to alter the various ways in which academic and organizational training is facilitated and conducted. This paper presents a review of the available literature and trends in CMC, specifically, CMC's theoretical approaches, types/roles, benefits/disadvantages, and contributions to academic institutions and corporate organizations. The authors also provide a discussion of future trends and implications in this subject.

INTRODUCTION

The use of computer-mediated communication (CMC) to enhance training in higher educational institutions and corporate organizations is the latest trend and focus of much research in the information technology and development industry. Researchers (Welsh, Wanberg, Brown, & Simmering, 2003) and practitioners (Olaniran, 2006, 2009; Wheeler, Byrne, & Deri, 2003) agree that technological advances continue to alter and redefine the various

ways learning and training is facilitated and conducted. CMC is a frequently utilized ICT system that "consists of electronically-mediated communication systems (i.e., e-mail, instant messengers, computer conferencing, and video-conferencing) that facilitate communication interaction among people" (Olaniran, 2006, p. 210). Although there are various estimates for growth in all aspects of CMC, it is apparent that academic institutions and corporate organizations will continue to increase the use of CMC in order to facilitate and deliver

DOI: 10.4018/978-1-61350-468-0.ch028

education and training. The aspect of quick access to information and knowledge without the constraints of time or geographic barriers makes CMC—along with its integrated learning environments, particularly eLearning—a highly valuable tool for higher education, as well as training in today's corporate work force (Olaniran, 1993).

As eLearning is strategically designed with implemented training programs, the system allows for acquisition of "the knowledge and skills needed to integrate sustainable practices into [our] day-to-day work," and lives (Wheeler et al., 2003, p. 96). According to Olaniran (1993), CMC is used as a "tele-meeting in which a computer serves as a 'meeting place' for participants" (p. 37). As organizations go global and maintain presence in geographically dispersed locations, training employees via CMC becomes essential. As a tool for gaining and providing necessary knowledge and skills, instructors can combine CMC tools with classroom applications to enhance, deliver, and facilitate training. Various research studies and articles continue to emerge to satisfy educational and organizational practices, such as the design, implementation, and use of CMC systems. This paper draws upon the available literature to provide a concise account of the role of CMC infrastructures and the nature of use within higher education and corporate organizations. Thus, a discussion of the following topics follows: (a) mainstream theories and approaches in CMC; (b) the role of different CMC infrastructures; and, (c) implications and future trends.

MAINSTREAM THEORIES AND APPROACHES IN CMC

Cues-Filtered Approach

Social presence theory (Short, Williams, & Christie, 1976) is frequently applied to CMC, although originally developed to describe teleconferencing. Walther (1995) explains social presence as "the feeling one has that other persons are involved in a communication exchange" (p. 188). During interactions, the degree of social presence is determined by the communication medium. If few cues and channels are available within a medium, then users are less likely to pay attention to other participants (Walther, 1995). Accordingly, because CMC lacks nonverbal cues, such as facial expression, hand gestures, as well as voice inflection and audio codes, it is assumed to be extremely low in social presence, especially in comparison to Face-to-Face (F2F) communication (Walther, 1995). According to Culnan and Markus (1987), a decline in the degree of social presence within a medium causes messages to become increasingly impersonal.

Other researchers, Sproull and Kiesler (1986), differentiate F2F from CMC with regards to information available in CMC in what they label as the 'lack of social context cues hypothesis.' Beyond the presence of participants, social context cues takes into consideration, "aspects of physical environment and nonverbal behaviors that define the nature of the social situation and actors' roles and relative status" (Walther, 1995, p. 188). According to Sproull and Kiesler (1986), when there is a lack of social context cues within a medium, the interactions grow increasingly uninhibited and this may lead to increased "flaming," cursing, aggressive, and intense language. Social presence theory and the 'lack of social context cues hypothesis' are related as both focus on the same causes and effects concerning the relational nature of CMC (Walther, 1995). Culnan and Markus (1987) categorize the two theories as the 'cues-filtered-out approach,' which indicates that any alterations to the nature of the messages or interpretation of them are effects, or outcomes due to the medium's structure. In other words, "such effects are inherent and constant" whenever individuals interact via computers (Walther, 1995, p. 188). According to Walther (1995), this interpretation is restricting and does not take into account the effects of other dynamics, including relationships, context, culture, conversational aspects, time, and so on.

It is assumed that the use of "equal time intervals" may create unintended effects and alter the experimental manipulation of media (Spears & Lea, 1992), as CMC systems require more messages to communicate the same amount of information and more time to exchange the same amount of messages in comparison to F2F. Early research in CMC supports the cues-filtered-out approach, specifically in group and interpersonal interaction contexts. Problems concerning early studies include limitations such as the use of short-term laboratory experiments with the inclusion of an F2F control group, or the use of long-term studies without the incorporation of a control group (Walther, 1995). Many other factors including the effects of time, relational communication, data gathering, nonverbal behaviors, and the exchange of social information were not taken into consideration (Walther, 1995). Thus, in response to the cues-filtered-out approach, Walther (1995) discusses his version of the social information processing theory.

Social Information Processing Theory

Social information processing theory (SIP), takes into account a variation of relational aspects of CMC. Walther (1995) proposes that the significant difference between CMC and F2F is due to the rate of transmission of information, rather than the capability of the media to send out the information. Among influential factors, studies noted varying "linguistic and typographic manipulations which may reveal social and relational information in CMC" (Walther, 1995, p. 190). Another factor, relational tone, is considered to change as a function of time in CMC. SIP, according to Walther (1995), integrates these factors and "refers to the way by which communicator's process social identity and relational cues (i.e., social information) using different media" (p. 190). Walther (1995)

suggests that if given plenty of time and message exchanges to allow relational development, then communication in later periods of CMC and F2F interaction will be similar.

At the same time, Olaniran (1994) alludes to the role of anticipation of future interaction (AFI) as crucial to positive relational mechanism. In other words, the degree to which individuals expect to engage in future interaction would influence positive relational messages. In earlier organizational literature, Fulk, Schmitz, and Steinfield (1990) use the term "social information processing" to illustrate a model of media choice, where "socially-constructed subjective assessments of media determine channel selection" (Walther, 1995, p. 190). Walther's (1995) interpretation uses SIP to explain how individuals process social information, and based on that information, communicate their relationships. The next theoretical approach dealing with CMC is the "adaptive structuration theory."

Adaptive Structuration Theory

Adaptive structuration theory (AST) developed as a response to group theory and critiques its traditional concerns a structurational perspective. DeSanctis and Poole (1994) note that AST "focuses on social structures, rules, and resources provided by technologies and institutions as the basis for human activity" (p. 125). The concept of structuration refers to, "the process of production and reproduction of social systems through the application of generative rules and resources" (Poole, Seibold, & McPhee, 1985, p. 76). AST contends that, over time, technology and social structures shape one another. Thus, technology influences users, and in turn, users influence technology by modifying it through the use of the technology, as well as the meanings users assign during social interaction. The AST model basically describes the interchange between information technologies (IT), social structures, and human communication (DeSanctis & Poole, 1994).

Social structures are embedded within institutions, for instance standard operating procedures, and provide the materials for preparing and accomplishing tasks, such as the development of a new information technology (DeSanctis & Poole, 1994). Structures are incorporated into the technology on behalf of the designer, who may choose to reproduce certain structures, so as to reflect the designer themselves, or they may be altered, improved, or integrated with other procedures, in turn creating new structures (DeSanctis & Poole, 1994). Structures are in technology and in actions. The two are joined in a "recursive relationship" where technology and action are repeatedly shaping one another (DeSanctis & Poole, 1994, p. 125). There are a variety of CMC infrastructures for facilitating and delivering training in higher education and corporate organizations. Thus, a look at current CMC infrastructures and their advantages and disadvantages is discussed next.

THE ROLE AND INFLUENCE OF CMC INFRASTRUCTURES

Asynchronous CMC vs. Synchronous CMC

Asynchronous CMC refers to an information technology system that is "pre-recorded" or available to students, instructors, and facilitators at any time of the day, "potentially from any location" (Welsh et al., 2003, p. 246). *Synchronous* CMC, on the other hand, requires all participants to be present in real-time, and it is sometimes referred to as 'live' computer-mediated communication (Welsh et al., 2003). CMC systems usually employed for research purposes are those in which participants are logged on to their computers at the same time, exchanging messages in "real time". While both asynchronous and synchronous CMC platforms seem to be very different from one another, some organizations and educational institutions use a de-

livery option called *blended learning*, which uses some combination of technology and classroom-based learning and has become a popular form for delivering training courses (Olaniran, 2008). According to Olaniran (2006), illustrating the difference between these media platforms (F2F, asynchronous and synchronous CMC) may help to explain the large amount of discrepancy between asynchronous and synchronous CMC structures found throughout the available literature.

Current research suggests there is no clear preference for synchronous or asynchronous CMC, yet the blending of both infrastructures for training is becoming increasingly apparent. After interviewing experts at Merck, Welsh et al. (2003) found that the biggest problem with the previous training program was information overload that leaves no time for management skills training. Therefore, Merck implemented a program that included web-based training (i.e., e-modules on various topics) and classroom-based training (i.e., interactive role playing and discussion) (Welsh et al., 2003). In order for blended learning to be successful, instructors must understand the various types of CMC tools, as well as efficiently and effectively implement these tools. The next section discusses asynchronous and synchronous CMC—as each platform is distinct.

Asynchronous CMC

Compared to other text-based CMC (i.e., IRC, chat), the use of e-mail continues to be the most common form of "CMC activity in interpersonal interaction" (Olaniran, 2002-2003, p. 206). McGugan (2002) describes an action research approach to CMC in which he focuses on one particular CMC system, WebCT—a type of virtual learning environment. WebCT, now referred to as Blackboard, is a "web-based course authoring and electronic communication system," where the majority of tools are asynchronous, with the exception of chat, discussion, and whiteboard

(McConnell, 2002, pp. 55-56). A basic principle of WebCT, or Blackboard, is to provide, "course designers with a set of individual tools that can be used in a variety of combinations, according to the requirements of particular courses" (McGugan, 2002, p. 31). Instructors and students can use Blackboard applications in a variety of ways, as they offer and allow for multiple learning and teaching methods (for full descriptions of the tools and uses, see McGugan, 2002).

Training can be facilitated and delivered via the Internet through eLearning technology, another type of CMC application. Courses in eLearning, according to Wheeler et al. (2003) "are offered to students for college credit, to employees for job training and skill development, to educators for professional development, and to individuals interested in particular topics and skills" (p. 96). Asynchronous eLearning tools vary in levels of complexity. For instance, less complex eLearning applications would include Microsoft PowerPoint slides posted by an instructor. Applications that are more complex require higher degrees of involvement on behalf of the learner, such as online learning simulations (i.e., "edutainment") that contain graphics, animation, video, and/or audio components (Hall, 1997). An appealing feature of eLearning is that courses are not constrained by instructors or physical classrooms where capacity is limited (Welsh et al., 2003). Organizations tend to consider eLearning when they are in need, or pressed, to deliver training to many people in a short amount of time. There are several methods and styles of eLearning courses that are in use by various organizations and these models include *Web-Assisted Instruction, On-line self-paced courses, On-line lectures, Guided Collaboration,* and *Digital Game-based Learning and Simulations.*

In a study about the emergent uses of eLearning, Welsh et al. (2003) found several organizations that successfully implemented training courses conducted through eLearning. One particular or-

ganization, Dow Chemical, created 'Interviewing Training,' that used several approaches to engage learners and maintain learner interaction in the course. The interactive approaches include simple hyperlinks or buttons to facilitate the learning experience, as well as comprehensive tests with multiple choice or 'drag and drop' questions. Once questions are answered, employees receive immediate feedback from the eLearning system regarding their answer choices. Learners are allowed to stop at any time, save, and return to finish the course, but total time to complete the course is two hours (Welsh et al., 2003). Because of this program, as well as other eLearning courses, Dow Chemical was awarded the ASTD's Excellence in Practice Award for Electronic Learning Technologies in 2001 (Welsh et al., 2003).

Some limitations associated with asynchronous CMC, as Branon and Essex (2001) note, include: "lack of immediate feedback, students not checking in often enough, length of time necessary for discussion to mature, and students feeling a sense of isolation" (p. 36). Dede and Kremer (1999) found that "asynchronous discussion provided richer, more inclusive types of interchange," but when compared to synchronous chat, needed additional time and offered significantly less social interaction (p. 4) (see appendix A for table of asynchronous tools with description). A discussion of synchronous CMC follows.

Synchronous CMC

Synchronous communication tools include: synchronous text, chat, audio-conferencing, video-conferencing, white boards, and much more. These collaboration tools are increasingly important components of online learning. Some synchronous CMC tools allow users to archive training courses and materials, making them available on-demand and on-time. Archiving is convenient for learners to store and access important information when needed. This tool is convenient for instructors, who can refer to archived information for class discussion, reuse of important information in later training sessions, and for accessing information on-demand. Another tool, synchronous chat, was found to be "useful for holding virtual office hours, team decision-making, brainstorming, community building, and dealing with technical issues" (Branon & Essex, 2001, p. 36). Some limitations associated with synchronous technology include: "getting students online at the same time, difficulty in moderating larger-scale conversations, lack of reflection time for students and intimidation of poor typists" (Branon & Essex, 2001, p. 36). Hines and Pearl (2004) note that although it may be more difficult to implement synchronous discussions, as compared to asynchronous discussions, "they have the advantages of providing a greater sense of presence and generating spontaneity" (p. 34). Welsh et al. (2003) discussed a complex type of synchronous learning that requires geographically dispersed employees to log into training sessions at a particular time, while guided by an instructor who "facilitates a discussion while showing slides or writing on a 'whiteboard' that appears on the computer screens of the learners" (p. 247). There are a full range of synchronous CMC tools available for training in the educational and corporate organizational contexts (see appendix B).

Synchronous CMC is faced with the major challenge of "resource availability," or what Olaniran (2006) describes as, "the degree to which the technology can be put together relatively easily and cheaply" (p. 217). Most higher education institutions and corporate organizations are able to incorporate asynchronous CMC tools and applications by making minor additions to their current training facilities. As one can see, synchronous CMC technology requires additional software and in some cases, hardware is also required (Olaniran, 2006).

IMPLICATIONS AND FUTURE TRENDS

Implications

The benefits of using CMC are obvious and can be highly beneficial for both, higher education and corporate organizations. One benefit of CMC that has gained considerable attention is the ability of instructors to track the progress of learners' activities, coursework, and mastery of course materials. Traditionally, it takes much effort to track such data, but through tools available in eLearning, the entire process of tracking and storing learner's progress can be automated (Welsh et al., 2003). This feature is beneficial when courses have a high number of learners where the instructor may not be able to keep up with each learner's progress, especially when they are dispersed across geographic boundaries. Both academic institutions and corporate organizations can benefit from eLearning by expanding services to learners across different regions and by ensuring that certain training and required courses are completed by employees via the Internet. As more companies in the United States turn to outsourcing, for example AT&T call centers in India, eLearning can be used to track progress of employees during training, as well as ensure that their employees overseas are providing quality customer care to their clients in the U.S and elsewhere around the globe. Today, Best Buy uses eLearning to track employee compliance, such as completion of the required safety courses and their scores to ensure proper certification (Welsh et al., 2003).

Tracking learners and employees implies that individuals are given freedom to complete courses at any time, from any location, regardless of whether instructors are present. Problems arise as organizations can never be sure the right person completed the course (Welsh et al., 2003). This is because when courses are on the Web and learners are given the freedom to complete them from the privacy of their own home, instructors can never be certain the appropriate individual is completing the necessary training. Another issue is that users could intentionally give deceitful responses to questions or engage in deceitful activity on the Web. Although progress, coursework, correct/incorrect responses, and completion can be tracked, there is no feature for detecting deceit, lies, and cheating from users. Another implication stemming from the ability to track progress is future growth of CMC tools—particularly eLearning applications and features. Thus, instructors may no longer be able to adequately keep up with learners' coursework and instead, rely on CMC technology to track progress.

Academic institutions and other organizations are turning to eLearning and other CMC applications (i.e., Blackboard, WebCT, Wiki) as a cost-saving measure. Specifically when organizations are looking to reduce high expenses associated with travel, classroom costs (i.e., printed materials), and necessary time spent off the job, eLearning becomes ever-more appealing. After implementing an asynchronous CMC system, Dow Chemical saved approximately $20 million on reduced time employees spent in training and saved $10 million, "due to a reduction in administrative time, cost of classroom facilities and facilitators, and cost of printed materials" (Welsh et al., 2003, p. 249). Although eLearning was successfully implemented as a cost-saving measure at Dow Chemical, this does not imply the same success for all organizations. Olaniran (2006, 2008) specifically criticizes the rush to implement eLearning as problematic. Therefore, each organization will require different materials, technology, systems development and implementation that are goal directed. Furthermore, the cost of developing and implementing highly interactive eLearning courses can run high; thus, cost savings are not fixed across contexts.

Studies about the nature of use and the effectiveness of CMC imply that several problems with the technology tend to deal with methods of implementation, which are often unclear. Additionally, requirements and expectations of students and instructors are sometimes unstated. For instance, studies focusing on e-mail imply that instructors should state clear and concise expectations and requirements for the use of e-mail within the course to prevent and alleviate problems. Eastman and Swift (2002) note similar problems with text-based CMC chat and use of chat rooms for training. In order to incorporate chat into the course effectively, there must be thorough implementation, support from the instructor, an established criteria for chatting (i.e., keeping group focus, informing learners about acceptable messages and effective participation), and finally promoting learner interactivity (Eastman & Swift, 2002). Moreover, when using synchronous technology requiring high-speed Internet connections (i.e., audio—or videoconferencing) the technical requirements and specifications should be outlined in detail (Olaniran, 2009). Furthermore, effective implementation of CMC must follow a systematic instructional design process that is suitable and tailored to each organization. This includes researching and testing which methods and tools work best for specific academic institutions and corporate organizations. A single design process, method of implementation, tools/applications, and training courses will not work for every organization.

FUTURE TRENDS

The first consideration for the facilitation of training via CMC, specifically within organizations, is to maintain programs that are culture and location-specific. It is important for organizations that have presence in several geographically dispersed locations to tailor their training program to individual regions. Microsoft, for instance, has several locations all over the world, meaning its employee's are distinct—separated by geographic boundaries and various cultures. Therefore, training at each location must be implemented and carried out with the consideration of the learners, geographic region, and cultural context. Dow Chemical found this true in its course when each location decided on its method of implementation and many locations neglected to enforce the company requirements. The locations that did enforce the training program often had issues because the messages delivered were not consistent and poorly communicated" (Welsh et al., 2003). Thus, Dow Chemical now offers the course entirely through asynchronous eLearning and avoids location-specific issues by providing each location with local classroom training after the web-based course is completed (Welsh et al., 2003). The classroom training is essential when location-specific problems arise and if needs are not met or ignored (Welsh et al., 2003). In essence, future work and research should explore blended learning approaches.

Future use and trends for delivering training can expect to see blended learning applications and methods—which have gained popularity in several organizations. For instance, American Airlines ticket and gate agent trainees were dropping out at a rate of 18% due to increased levels of information, such that trainees were overwhelmed during the classroom-based training course (Welsh et al., 2003). Increases in information, if not managed properly, may lead to information overload that results in unproductive and ineffective training, as individuals cannot retain information they are bombarded with (Welsh et al., 2003). To solve the problem, American Airlines turned to blended learning to manage information overload by offering part of the course asynchronously and part of it synchronously, "and only the most interactive part in the classroom" (Welsh et al., 2003, p. 248). The new training course, which combined self-paced asynchronous learning with classroom learning, met trainee's approval, reduced turnover rates,

and resulted in American Airlines winning the *American Society for Training and Development Excellence in Practice Award* for their solution (Welsh et al., 2003).

Changes among instructional methods and tools used to facilitate training will continue as corporate organizations and academic institutions are constantly changing and evolving. Future changes are expected as previous methods evolve or no longer work for certain organizations and new technologies and training methods constantly emerge. Phoenix Online believes that interaction with humans is much more important to success than learner interaction with digital content (Martinez, 2003). Consequently, Phoenix online keeps classes very small to alleviate drop-out rates and "offers its learners plenty of hand-holding, including round-the-clock tech support (Martinez, 2003, p. 1). Martinez (2003) found that half of all college and university freshmen enrolled in online courses drop-out because they are "unprepared for self-directed learning" (p. 2).

Research suggests CMC lacks appropriate personalized support (i.e., cues-filtered approach) to help learners manage their online experiences and motivate them to complete the course. Although research is inconsistent regarding learner attrition, most tend to list the following reasons for drop-out rates: demographics, ethnicity, family (problems), economics, experiences, background, finances, child care, distractions, job needs, and demands (Martinez, 2003). Methods should be developed in the near-future to manage attrition and retention issues as it affects different groups of learners.

One suggestion is the use of computer-mediated conferencing, which has much potential for training. This tool allows "increased group interaction, more equitable communication patterns, higher degrees of reflection, and time-and-place-independent discussions" (Hewitt, 2001, p. 208). The largest limitation with computer conferencing is the lack of support for convergent processes (e.g., strategies for communicating, learning models, etc.) (Hewitt, 2001). The following solutions for overcoming the lack of support for convergent processes and increasing future effectiveness were developed by Hewitt (2001): (1) Use a moderator to guide online discourse; (2) Assign tasks that require group synthesis; (3) Reject threaded systems in favor of linear systems; and, (4) Use synchronous technologies to support convergence (pp. 214-5). It is apparent that trainers/instructors will continue to play an integral role in training (Olaniran, 2006).

CONCLUSION

The goal of this paper was to present a comprehensive review of CMC and subsequently eLearning current trends. A description of several CMC tools were provided along with the advantages/disadvantages and benefits/drawbacks of each. The available research suggests that if properly implemented, technology can be used effectively and efficiently to deliver and facilitate education/training. Future trends require continuous efforts in research and analysis to evaluate and enhance CMC contribution to eLearning, as technology continuously changes. Notwithstanding, there is no doubt that CMC holds certain advantages for eLearning. However, attention to details in its implementation must be a priority. Thus organizations and academic institutions alike must consider training design, CMC infrastructure and support, managerial and technical support, and change management issues.

REFERENCES

Aldrich, C. (2003). *Simulations and the future of learning*. New York: Pffieffer/Wiley.

Bender, T. (2003). *Discussion-based online teaching to enhance student learning: Theory, practice, and assessment*. Sterling, VA: Stylus.

Branon, R. F., & Essex, C. (2001). Synchronous and asynchronous communication tools in distance education: A survey of instructors. *TechTrends*, *45*, 36–42. doi:10.1007/BF02763377

Cohn, E. R. (2002). *Instant messaging in higher education: A new faculty development challenge*. Retrieved March 30, 2009, from http://www.ipfw.edu/as/tohe/2002/Papers/cohn2.htm

Culnan, M. J., & Markus, M. L. (1987). Information technologies. In Jablin, F. M., Putnam, L. L., Roberts, K. H., & Porter, L. W. (Eds.), *Handbook of Organizational Communications: An Interdisciplinary Perspective* (pp. 421–443). Newbury Park, CA: Sage.

Dede, C., & Kremer, A. (1999). Increasing students' participation via multiple interactive media. *Inventio, I*. Retrieved March 31, 2009, from http://www.doit.gmu.edu/archives/feb98/dede_1.htm

DeSanctis, G., & Poole, M. S. (1994). Capturing the complexity in advanced technology use: Adaptive structuration theory. *Organization Science*, *5*(2), 121–147. doi:10.1287/orsc.5.2.121

Eastman, J. K., & Swift, C. O. (2002). Enhancing collaborative learning: Discussion boards and chat rooms as project communication tools. *Business Communication Quarterly*, *65*(3), 29–41. doi:10.1177/108056990206500304

Farmer, R. (2003). *Instant messaging-collaborative tool or educator's nightmare!* Retrieved March 30, 2009, from http://naWeb.unb.ca/poceedings/2003/PaperFarmer.html

Farrior, E. S., & Gallagher, M. L. (2000). An evaluation of distance education. *Topics in Clinical Nutrition*, *15*(4), 10–18.

Fetterman, D. M. (2002). Web surveys to digital movies: Technological tools of the trade. *Educational Researcher*, *31*(6), 29–37. doi:10.3102/0013189X031006029

Fulk, J., Schmitz, J., & Steinfield, C. W. (1990). A social influence model of technology use. In Fulk, J., & Steinfield, C. W. (Eds.), *Organization and Communication Technology* (pp. 117–140). Newbury Park, CA: Sage.

Gonzalez, C. L., & De Montes, L. S. (2001). Effective practices in distance education. *Computers in the Schools, 18*(2/3), 61–77.

Hall, B. (1997). *Web-based Training Cookbook*. New York: John Wiley and Sons.

Harrsch, M. (2003). RSS: The next killer app for education. *The Technology Source*. Retrieved March 30, 2009, from http://ts.mivu.org/default. asp?show=article&id=2010

Hewitt, J. (2001). Beyond threaded discourse. *International Journal of Educational Telecommunications, 7*(3), 207–221.

Hines, R. A., & Pearl, C. E. (2004). Increasing interaction in web-based instruction: Using synchronous chats and asynchronous discussions. *Rural Special Education Quarterly, 23*, 33–36.

Hughes, C., & Hewson, L. (2001). Structuring communications to facilitate effecting teaching and learning online. In Maddux, C. D., & Johnsons, D. L. (Eds.), *The Web in Higher Education: Assessing the Impact and Fulfilling the Potential* (pp. 147–158). New York: Hawthorne Press.

Hyman, A. (2003). Twenty years of ListServ as an academic tool. *The Internet and Higher Education, 6*, 17–24. doi:10.1016/S1096-7516(02)00159-8

Ingram, A. L., Hathorn, L. G., & Evans, A. (2000). Beyond chat on the internet. *Computers & Education, 35*, 21–35. doi:10.1016/S0360-1315(00)00015-4

Jung, I., Choi, S., Lim, C., & Leem, J. (2002). Effects of different types of interaction on learning achievement, satisfaction, and participation in Web-based instruction. *Innovations in Education and Teaching International, 39*, 153–162. doi:10.1080/14703290252934603

Martinez, M. (2003). High attrition rates in e-Learning: Challenges, predictors, and solutions. *The eLearning Developers' Journal*, 1-9. Retrieved February 23, 2009, from http://www. elearningguild.com/pdf/2/071403MGT-L.pdf

McConnell, D. (2002). *Implementing Computer Supported Collaborative Learning* (2nd ed.). London: Kogan Page.

McGugan, S. (2002). Asynchronous computer mediated conferencing to support learning and teaching: An action research approach. *Journal of Hospitality, Leisure, Sport and Tourism Education, 1*(1), 29–42. doi:10.3794/johlste.11.9

Olaniran, B. A. (1993). Integrative approach for managing successful computer-mediated communication technological innovations. *Ohio Speech Journal, 31*, 37–52.

Olaniran, B. A. (1994). Group performance and computer-mediated communication. *Management Communication Quarterly, 7*, 256–281. doi:10.1177/0893318994007003002

Olaniran, B. A. (2002-2003). Computer-mediated communication: A test of the impact of social cues on the choice of medium for resolving misunderstandings. *Journal of Educational Technology Systems, 31*(2), 205–222. doi:10.2190/576R-1NVK-M943-CJMP

Olaniran, B. A. (2006). Applying synchronous Computer-mediated communication into course design: Some considerations and practical guides. *Campus-Wide Information Systems, 23*(3), 210–220. doi:10.1108/10650740610674210

Olaniran, B. A. (2008). Human computer interaction and best mix of e-interactions and face-to-face in educational settings. In Kelsey, S., & St. Amant, K. (Eds.), *Handbook of Research on Computer Mediated Communication* (pp. 49–61). Hershey, PA: IGI Global.

Olaniran, B. A. (2009). Organizational communication: Assessment of videoconferencing as a medium for meetings in the workplace. *International Journal of Human Technology Interaction, 5*(2), 63–84.

Olaniran, B. A., & Austin, K. A. (2009). Web-assisted instruction in upper division communication studies curriculum: A theoretical and quantitative analysis. *Campus Wide Information Systems: The International Journal of Information & Learning Technology, 26*(1), 43–53. doi:10.1108/10650740910921555

Poole, M. S., Seibold, D. R., & McPhee, R. (1985). Group decision-making as a structurational process. *The Quarterly Journal of Speech, 71*, 74–102. doi:10.1080/00335638509383719

Prensky, M. (2001). *Digital game-based learning.* New York: McGraw-Hill.

Repman, J., Zinskie, C., & Carlson, R. D. (2005). Effective use of cmc tools in interactive online learning. *Computers in the Schools (The Hawthorne Press, Inc.), 22*(1/2), 57-69.

Richardson, W. (2004). Blogging and RSS—The "what's it?" and "how to" of powerful new tools for Web educators. *Multimedia & Internet at Schools, 11*(1), 10-13. Retrieved April 8, 2009, from http://www.infotoday.com/MMSchools/jan04/richardson.shtml

Riva, G. (2002). The sociocognitive psychology of computer-mediated communication: The present and future of technology-based interactions. *Cyberpsychology & Behavior, 5*, 581–598. doi:10.1089/109493102321018222

Short, J., Williams, E., & Christie, B. (1976). *The Social Psychology of Telecommunication.* London: John Wiley.

Spears, R., & Lea, M. (1992). Social influence and the influence of the "social" n computer-mediated communication. In Lea, M. (Ed.), *Contexts of computer-mediated communication* (pp. 30–65). Hemel Hempstead, UK: Harvester Wheatsheaf.

Sproull, L., & Kiesler, S. (1986). Reducing social context cues: Electronic mail in organizational communication. *Management Science, 32*, 1492–1512. doi:10.1287/mnsc.32.11.1492

Tiene, D. (2000). Online discussions: A survey of advantages and disadvantages compared to face-to-face discussions. *Journal of Educational Multimedia and Hypermedia, 9*, 371–384.

Vonderwell, S. (2003). An examination of asynchronous communication experiences and perspectives of students in an online course: A case study. *The Internet and Higher Education, 6*, 77–90. doi:10.1016/S1096-7516(02)00164-1

Walther, J. B. (1995). Relational aspect of computer-mediated communication: Experimental observations over time. *Organization Science, 6*(2), 186–203. doi:10.1287/orsc.6.2.186

Welsh, E. T., Wanberg, C. R., Brown, K. G., & Simmering, M. J. (2003). E-learning: Emerging uses, empirical results, and future directions. *International Journal of Training and Development, 7*(4), 245–258. doi:10.1046/j.1360-3736.2003.00184.x

Wheeler, K., Byrne, J., & Deri, A. (2003). eLearning and education for sustainability (EFS). *International Review for Environmental Strategies, 4*(1), 95–105.

APPENDIX A

Comparisons of Asynchronous Computer-Mediated Communications (CMC) Tools

Tool	Advantages	Disadvantages
E-mail	Beneficial for online peer response and immediate feedback; Minimal computer literacy needed; Attachment feature for submitting coursework privately; Instructors seem more readily accessible.	Accessibility of instructor; Instructor-centered methods may result; Dependence on instructors for information on the course that may be available on course Web site may result.
Listservs	Ease-of-use (EOU); Immediate response to discussions (messages are received through e-mail); All parties can speak in the same manner, regardless of level of technology and bandwidth access (equalizes discussions).	Sorting messages from e-mail and spam can be difficult; Multiple off-topic posts may dominate messages; Messages may be seen as temporary—quickly and easily deleted.
Discussion Boards	Can exchange written work, role-play, debate topics, and resources; Flexible tool, allowing several instructional strategies; Preferred by users with anxiety in F2F setting, lack self-confidence, struggle with language barriers	Inability to capture the richness of F2F; Difficult to assess participation; Failure to participate can occur; Critical thinking and focused learning does not naturally occur.
Blogs/ Weblogs	More cost-effective option (compared to other course management systems); Open, flexible nature that encourages discussion; Seen as vibrant, dynamic sources of content.	Slow uptake for adoption and use due to privacy, security, and access purposes; Flexible and informal nature disadvantage when it comes to maintaining focus and fostering critical thinking Complex structure may be confusing to instructors and learners alike.

APPENDIX B

Comparisons of Synchronous Computer-Mediated Communications (CMC) Tools

Tool	Advantages	Disadvantages
Chat	Multiple users meet in chat rooms at same time, regardless of location; Real-time communication; Able to give/receive immediate feedback; Immediacy of communication similar to F2F; Increased connectedness, greater development, and level of social relationships.	High level of technical requirements; Technical difficulties Users may lack needed typing skills to interact in a timely manner; Side conversations can be distracting; Possibility of information overload; Problems arise as group size increases.
Instant Message (IM)	Users can store list of contacts & system notifies them when someone is available for IM; Ability to block messages and users; College students found to favor IM as their preferred means of online communication; Allows for interaction/collaboration on projects, virtual conferences, remote guest speakers, class discussions, and prompt feedback; Sense of increased social presence among distant students.	Research has neglected to give attention to use of IM in higher education & in organizations; Slow embrace of the technology by faculty; "faculty nightmare," due to the increased expectations from users (e.g., being available at any time and adds to faculty workload); Chat rooms may be better than IM for extended discussions.
Audio- conferencing	Software programs can be used simultaneously with audio feeds to allow exchanges of information, files, or collaborative work; Can be a low-cost alternative to videoconferencing.	Difficulties with connectivity of technology; Difficulties with setting up the system and connecting to a conference; Detailed instructions are needed.
Video- conferencing	Ability to use higher level thinking in live F2F communication; Software programs can be used simultaneously with video feeds; Most resemblance to F2F interaction.	Difficulties with connections and setting up the system; Requires high-speed Internet connections for high-quality; detailed instructions needed.

This work was previously published in International Journal of Information and Communication Technology, Volume 6, Issue 4, edited by Lawrence A. Tomei, pp. 61-73, copyright 2010 by IGI Publishing (an imprint of IGI Global).

Chapter 29

Faculty Adopters of Podcasting:
Satisfaction, University Support and Belief in Podcasting

Jin Yang
University of Memphis, USA

ABSTRACT

Educators have started incorporating iPods for academic purposes and a growing interest exists in using podcasting as an educational tool. However, it remains uncertain whether podcasting will hit the critical mass and become an indispensable teaching tool for the classroom. In this regard, it is critical to evaluate the adoption experience of the faculty and identify the benefits and challenges encountered in the process. This paper derives its theoretical framework from two threads, the original model of the diffusion of innovation and the modified model in the organizational setting, which will help explore the phenomenon of podcast use at universities. This paper examines factors that might have a significant role in the faculty's experiential use of podcasting.

INTRODUCTION

Educators have been constantly testing technological tools to facilitate learning and teaching. For years, they have implemented a wide range of electronic devices and technological developments in classrooms: radio, closed circuit television and the Internet. E-learning pushes the use of technological tools to an unexpected higher level. In recent years, podcasting has become the buzzword on campus. CNN reports that iPods are "the most in thing among undergraduate college students" ahead of beer and facebook.com (CNN, 2006). It is easy to imagine students using the iPod to make up for lectures they missed, or to brush up on key concepts as the final exam approaches (Read, 2007). Professors of higher education are given a chance to meet students on their own turf.

Though some professors jumped on the bandwagon, "not everyone is sold on the utility of the podcast" (Vestal, 2007). It is uncertain whether podcasting will hit the critical mass and become a majority of professor's indispensable teaching kit in classroom. However, it is critical

DOI: 10.4018/978-1-61350-468-0.ch029

to evaluate faculty's adopting experience and identify the benefits and challenges encountered in the process. After all, faculty members are the podcasting adopters, users and practitioners. Their perception and their experience with podcasting will help develop models of applied podcasting practice and inspire continued innovations with the technology and determine the impact of podcasting on higher education.

LITERATURE REVIEW

Podcasting in Higher Education

Podcasting gained public attention in June 2005 when Apple released the iTunes 4.9 software with the addition of a podcast directory (Huntsberger & Stavitsky, 2007). Podcast download continues to increase with 19% of Internet users saying so in April of 2008, up from 12% of Internet users who said so in August 2006 (Madden, 2008). In November 2006, Podcast Alley cataloged 26,000 podcasts with more than 1 million episodes but in August, 2008, podcasts doubled to 43,000 with more than 2 million episodes (Madden, 2008). In promoting podcasts, universities are a strong participating force either with faculty producing podcasts or students developing podcasts (Madden, 2008). Almost all podcast portals have a category that specifically hosts and archives universities' podcasts. For instance, Podcast Alley has a category called University Channel that archives a collection of public affairs lectures, panels and events from academic institutions all over the world. On the iTunes Store, iTune U was created so that the public can find educational audio and video files from the top universities.

In elaborating the educational outcomes induced by digital technologies, Hoag et al. (2003) pointed to the benefits of engaged learning, increased access to class materials, asynchronous and synchronous communications and more interactions among students. Dennis et al.

(2003) added that the profound transformation through digital technologies lies in the extension of traditional boundaries of time and space, of interactions between students and teachers and the exponential growth of access to the resources. The initial research findings on podcasting seem to measure up to the positive speculations while others wonder whether these ubiquitous devices are really achieving educational goals. The so-called "iControversy" was coined to describe this concern (Vess, 2006, p. 479). Some educators reasoned that the podcasting has no inherent pedagogic values because "the pedagogical value of podcasts depends almost entirely on student motivation and the learning 'context' of the application" (McCloskey, 2007). Others speculated that "technology must remain subservient to pedagogy less we forget our educational mission" (Miller, 2006).

Good use of podcasting comes from the creative and well-thought planning of materials on podcasts. For example, University of Connecticut Psychology Professor David Miller used iCube, the recorded weekly one-hour discussion of course material or psychological topics when students met with him in his office (Campus Technology, 2007). Georgia College & State University Professor Deborah L. Vess did not want her graduate students simply listen to iPod lectures passively; instead, she created an application that relied on the student as producer of podcasts to foster an active learning environment (Vess, 2006). Such professors reported students had evaluated the use of podcasts positively.

As more instructors began to consider using podcasts to enhance online courses or supplement traditional classroom courses, some institutions (such as Duke University, Stanford and UC Berkeley) have taken a larger stride by implementing campus-wide initiatives to support podcasting practices. However, obstacles abound including technology know-how (Read, 2007); time, resources and IT staff expertise. The uncertainty about the potential impact of podcasting on higher education (Berger, 2007) makes it even more critical to ask what motivates pioneer faculty to adopt podcasting and what differentiates them from those who did not adopt the technology. The theory of innovation diffusion might provide some initial insight about the characteristics of these early faculty adopters.

Diffusion of Innovations

The theoretical paradigm of the innovation diffusion describes the process through which an innovation, perceived as a new idea, practice or object, spreads via communication channels over time among members of a social system (Rogers, 1995). For almost 50 years, many academic disciplines ranging from geography, political science to marketing have vigorously tested the validity and reliability of the diffusion model (Rogers, 2004). Studies of educational innovations can trace back to the early 1920s and 1930s when Columbia University's Teachers College researchers led by Paul Mort identified three findings: the best single predictor of school innovativeness is educational cost per student; a considerable time lag is required for the widespread adoption of new educational ideas; and, the pattern of adoption of an educational idea over time approaches an S-shaped curve (Rogers, 1971). After the 1950s, studies on educational diffusions shifted attention to teachers as adopters and educational change in less developed nations (Rogers, 1971). For instance, in 1968, the adoption of objective testing, classroom discussions, school libraries and audio-visual methods were studied in Thailand's local schools and researchers found an upward rather than downward flow of ideas in the bureaucratic system of Thailand (Rogers, 1971). Another outstanding educational innovation study conducted by Richard Carlson identified the opinion leadership patterns and variables correlated to innovativeness and characteristics of innovations in the diffusion of modern math among school superintendents (Rogers, 1971).

While the diffusion model mainly focuses on the procedure of how an innovation spreads and gets adopted, it also offers key factors that might influence the innovation diffusion. Perceived innovation's attributes, communication channels through which the message about an innovation is shared, the time span between the first awareness and the confirmation of an adoption decision and social system within which an innovation diffuses can all play a role in the innovation diffusion (Rogers, 1971; Singer, 2004).

At the early stage of the innovation diffusion, demographics seem to matter. The wealthier, better educated, and younger are frequently found to be associated with adopters (Rogers, 1995; Li, 2004; Atkin, Neuendorf, Jeffres, & Skalski, 2003; Fulk, 1993). Demographic factors were later broadened into individual influences in the study of new media's adoption by Rice and Webster (2002). Junior faculty members, a younger population of faculty on tenure track, may have to devote a considerable amount of time doing the triple missions of research, teaching and community services; therefore, they may not become the early adopters of podcasting as compared to senior faculty members.

Leonard-Barton and Deschamps (1988) suggested that those who perceive themselves as more innovative would be more likely to use an innovation. These innovative individuals not only tend to adopt a new medium earlier and use it more frequently, but also tend to use it more creatively (Rice & Webster, 2002) and have a greater ability to obtain information (Rice & Tyler, 1995). We all know that faculty's approaches to teaching vary significantly, which might be attributed to the individual characteristic of innovativeness. Some faculty members believe in the deep learning by focusing on students and changing students' conceptions while others want to focus on the transmission of knowledge (Trigwell, Prosser, & Waterhouse, 1999). Some employ new techniques and new ways of teaching while others keep to the traditional path of teaching. Hagner (2001) observed that the first-wave "entrepreneur" faculty always seeks out resources and the expertise to incorporate technology into the curriculum, but the second wave faculty members, though committed to quality education, were wary of new technologies only. The subtle difference between these two groups suggests the attribute of innovativeness is a possible factor that influences the diffusion of innovation of podcasting.

The diffusion of innovation studies also recognized the role of organizational influences in the diffusion (Zaltman, Duncan, & Holbeck, 1973). Researchers identified organizational attributes that might facilitate or inhibit the adoption of innovation such as the size of an organization or the specialization of an organization, functional differentiation and centralization of an organization (Moch & Morse, 1977). In studying the adoption of new information technologies in rural small businesses, researchers found that relative advantage of technology, top management support, organizational size, external pressure and competitive pressure are important determinants of the adoption of new information technologies (Premkumar & Roberts, 1999).

Podcasting use on campus is not simply a personal choice but a social phenomenon. Its developers, faculty members, are affiliated with institutions and its end users are a large body of student population. Moreover, the process of developing podcasting demands the coordination and cooperation from other sectors of the institutions. Therefore the campus-wide university support is essential for the successful adoption of podcasting.

Diffusion of innovation research also singled out attitudinal factors as predictors of the diffusion of innovation. For example, self-efficacy with regard to computer use was found to relate positively to the behavior of computer use (Compeau & Higgins, 1995). The attitude of faculty toward computers was found to be associated with the use and adoption of computers in teaching activities (Hoag et al., 2003). Those who perceive technology as an effective instruction tool were more

motivated to use it in classroom (Gueldenzoph & Guidera, 1999). Rogers (1995) argued that for those who faced a decision about adopting an innovation, the innovation itself had to be perceived as new or inclusive of relative advantages over whatever it is intended to supersede. Honey and Moeller (1997) concluded that a teacher's attitude toward technology and its role in the learning process determine the manner of its deployment with a positive attitude yielding constructivist and student-centered approaches and higher level of technology integration.

Podcasting use in higher education has a very short history, and the word of podcasting was announced as the word of the year by editors of the New Oxford English Dictionary only in 2005 (Skira, 2006). While podcasting technology sounds very promising because it is geared toward the student-centered teaching mode, the challenges and uncertainties of podcasting in the higher education setting remain. Therefore, the following four research questions are proposed in the study.

RQ1. What motivates faculty members to adopt podcasting in the curriculum?

RQ2. What content do faculty members place on podcasts?

RQ3. What obstacles and problems do faculty members encounter in the process of podcasting?

RQ4. What are significant predictors of faculty's podcasting satisfaction experience?

METHOD

This study utilized an online survey to collect information on faculty and their podcasting activities. It used three methods to locate podcasting faculty: iTunes U's listing of podcasting faculty, Google search outcomes of university Websites listing of podcasting faculty and a list of faculty podcasters provided by the Advanced Learning

Center of a Mid-South University. The three mixed methods yielded a sampling frame of 351 faculty members who were associated with podcasting.

The online survey was set up using the surveymonkey.com service. Four calls for taking the survey were made through the surveymonkey.com's email call service from November 16, 2007 to October 20, 2008. With some removals of faculty members due to their request or their indication that they were not the podcasting developers and some additions to the podcasting faculty list due to new search results, the final sample constituted a total of 318 faculty members.

Demographic attributes including age, gender and income were measured. Their academic attributes have included teaching positions (full professor to adjunct status), teaching disciplines (in what area do you teach), level of class (undergraduate, graduate or both), class size (how many students were in the podcasting class). Internet use was measured by asking how many years they have been using the Internet. Innovativeness was measured by using twenty different statements[1] on a 7-point Likert scale. A series of principal component factor analyses (with varimax rotation) were employed on the 20 statements to reduce data points. After deleting five variables that loaded with less than .60 factor loadings on any converged factor, four final components were retained and labeled: creative initiator (α=.86), non-doubter (α=.80), challenger(α=.75), peer leader (α=.70) (see Table 1 for details).

Table 1. Factor analysis for innovativeness

Variables		Factor Loadings			
		1	2	3	4
Creative initiator					
	Enjoy trying out new things	.74			
	Seek out new ways	.76			
	Frequently improve methods	.65			
	Creative in thinking and behaviors	.73			
	Not the last one to try new things	.62			
	Inventive person	.68			
	Find it stimulating to be original	.70			
Non-doubter					
	Cautious about new ideas (reverse coding)		.76		
	Suspicious of new (reverse coding)		.79		
	Rarely trust new ideas (reverse coding)		.73		
	Reluctant about new ways (reverse coding)		.68		
Challenger					
	Challenged by ambiguities (reverse coding)			.85	
	Challenged by unanswered questions (reverse coding)			.88	
Peer leader					
	Peers ask for advice and information				.85
	Feel oneself as an influential member of the group				.81
Variance explained*		39	11	10	7
Eigenvalue		5.8	1.6	1.4	1.1
*Given in percentages.					

To address RQ1, RQ2 and RQ3, one open ended question was asked of faculty members on their motivation, podcasting content and obstacles and problems respectively. RQ4 was addressed with one dependent variable of *satisfaction with podcasting* and four blocks of independent variables of *demographics, university support, attitude to podcasting* and *innovativeness*. Satisfaction was measured by asking how satisfied "you" are with the use of podcasting. The 5-point continuous response scale from *very unsatisfied* to *very satisfied* was used. University support was measured by one single question of how "you" would rate the university's support on a 5-point scale of supportiveness. Faculty's attitude to podcasting was measured using six different statements on a 7-point Likert scale.[2] The factor analysis (with varimax rotation) was employed on the six statements resulting in the deletion of two items with low reliability coefficients.[3] As a result, only one factor labeled as pedagogical attitude converged from this factor analysis (α=.78) (see Table 2 for details).

FINDINGS

A total of 109 faculty members responded to the survey with a response rate of 34%. A closer examination of the data resulted in the elimination of certain respondents who failed to complete at least 70% of the survey questions. The study only had 85 valid cases to analyze yielding a response rate of 27%.[4] The average length of time adopting podcasting was 16 months and faculty spent an average of more than 2 hours working on podcasting per week.[5] The average age of the pioneering podcasting faculty was 48, ranging from the youngest of 26 to the oldest of 70. In terms of gender, 27% of the faculty was female, 69% male and 4% did not specify their gender. Income wise, those earning below $34,999 accounted for 7%; between $35,000 and $49,999, 12%; between $50,000 and $74,999, 33%; between

$75,000 and $99,999, 11%; and above $100,000, 21%. Those who did not specify their income comprised about 17% (see Table 3 for details for faculty podcasters' profile).

RQ1. What Motivates Faculty Members to Adopt Podcasting in the Curriculum?

The open-ended responses to RQ1 were very diverse and thus classified into 12 categories. The most dominant motivation mentioned by faculty (37%) was "provide alternatives for students to learn," followed by 11% who said "engage and motivate students," then by 9% who said "review course materials." The coding process was to identify the primary motivation when multiple motivations were given (see Table 4 for details).

RQ2. What Content Do Faculty Members Place On Podcasts?

Fifty-three percent of the respondents indicated lecture, 17% extra-curriculum supplementary materials, 12% summaries, overviews or introductions, 7% guest speakers' talk or interviews, 5% mentioned class discussions, demonstrations of technical process and 7% did not specify what

Table 2. Factor analysis for attitude to podcasting

		Factor Loadings
Pedagogical attitude	Variables	
	Enhance Course content	.83
	Increase delivery efficiency	.76
	Engage students	.78
	Explore new ways of teaching	.75
Variance explained*		61
Eigenvalue		2.4
*Given in percentages.		

Table 3. Pioneering faculty podcasters' profile

Profiling Areas		Subcategories	Statistics
Demographic Areas			
	Gender	Male	69%
		Female	27%
		Missing	4%
		Total	100%
	Income	Below $34,999	7%
		Between $35,000 and $49,999	12%
		Between $50,000 to $74,999	33%
		Between $75,000 to 99,999	11%
		Above $100,000	21%
		Missing	17%
		Total	101%*
	Average Age		48 years
University Settings			
	Teaching positions	Full professors	28%
		Associate professors	17%
		Assistant professors	24%
		Instructors	12%
		Adjunct Faculty	9%
		Others	6%
		Missing	5%
		Total	101%*
	Teaching disciplines	Mass Communication	15%
		Psychology and Education	12%
		Biology, Chemistry, Biochemistry	11%
		Language, literature, classics, humanities	9%
		Art, Fashion and Design,	8%
		Computer Science and Information Science, digital technology	6%

		Math and Physics	6%
		Earth science and geography	5%
		Engineering	5%
		Theology and Anthropology	5%
		Health and Nutrition	5%
		Others	8%
		Missing	6%
		Total	101%*
	Level of Classes		
		Undergraduate	69%
		Both Graduate and Undergraduate	14%
		Graduate	12%
		Missing	5%
		Total	100%
	Class Size (mean=103)		
		8-25	39%
		26-50	11%
		51-100	14%
		101-300	16%
		301-500	7%
		Above 500	1%
		Missing	12%
		Total	100%
Podcast Use, Internet Use and Innovativeness			
	Average length of time using podcasting		16 months
	Weekly time spent on working on podcasts		129 minutes
	Average years of using Internet		14 years
	Innovativeness		6 on a scale of 1 to 7 **

* The total was not 100% due to the rounding error.
* * 1 representing least innovative and 7 most innovative

Table 4. Motivations to adopt podcasting in curriculum

Open-ended Answers		
	Provide alternatives for students to learn	37%
	Engage and motivate students	11%
	Review course materials	9%
	Take available opportunities	8%
	Keep up with new technology	7%
	Accommodate students' life styles	6%
	Experiment podcasting	6%
	Free up class time for class interaction and communication	5%
	Facilitate big classes	4%
	Make use of an effective tool	2%
	Archive course content	1%
	Participate in a large-scale project	1%
	missing	4%
	Total	101%*
*The total is not 100% due to the rounding error.		

Table 5. Podcasting content by faculty

Lecture	53%
Extra-curriculum materials	17%
Summaries, overviews or introductions	12%
Guest speakers' talk and interviews	7%
Class discussions and demonstrations of technical process	5%
Missing	6%
Total	100%

content was on podcasts. Again, only the primary content was coded for this study when multiple contents were mentioned by faculty (see Table 5).[6]

RQ3. What Obstacles and Problems Did Faculty Members Encounter in the Process of Podcasting?

The responses to obstacles and problems were classified into 11 categories. About 32% of the faculty indicated technical challenges and problems in using the podcasting, and 17% indicated time commitment as the obstacles to adopting podcasting. Other obstacles include reliance on others to get the podcasting done, motivate students to

use podcasts and legal issues and quality of the podcasting content. When multiple obstacles and problems were reported, only the most dominant one was coded for this study.[7] Unfortunately 31% of the faculty did not provide responses to this question (see Table 6 for details).

RQ4. What are Significant Predictors of Faculty's Podcasting Satisfaction Experience?

The study considered four areas that might account for faculty's satisfaction with the use of podcasting. The criterion variable was podcasting satisfaction experience. The independent variables entered into the regression equation were demographics, university support, innovativeness of faculty, and faculty's attitude to podcasting (see Table 7).

Demographics did not make any significant contribution to faculty's satisfaction with podcasting. University support was a significant positive predictor of faculty's satisfaction with podcasting explaining 18 percent variance of the satisfaction experience. All the four factors of innovativeness: initiator, non-doubter, challenger and peer leader did not turn out to be significant predictor of satisfaction. Lastly, pedagogical attitude to podcasting turned out to be a significant predictor of faculty's satisfaction with podcasting explaining 12 percent variance of the satisfaction experience.

DISCUSSIONS AND CONCLUSION

Attributes of the Pioneer Podcasting Faculty

The study had more male faculty podcasters than females. The income spectrum was a little skewed to the higher end. The average age of podcasting faculty adopters was the early middle age. All the university positions were fairly represented but there seems to be a pattern slanting from the highest end of full professors to the lowest end of adjunct faculty but assistant professors are the group that breaks the pattern and attempts to use podcasting more in this study. The faculty podcasters represented various disciplines but communication faculty constituted the largest. Majority of them were teaching undergraduate classes and the class size of 25 or less seemed to be the most common. The average years of using the Internet was 14 years and the average time spent on podcasting per week was around 2 hours. Most important of all, these faculty podcasters were a very innovative group of persons suggesting they are entrepreneurs.

Motivations

The adoption of podcasting is motivation driven. While task-oriented motivations such as freeing up class time, facilitating big classes, archiving course content, participating in projects are mentioned by faculty, pedagogy oriented motivations such as offering alternatives to learn and engaging students are prioritized by the faculty as the driving force. Some motivations are prompted by external sources such as university offering the opportunities, but some motivations origin from selves such as experimenting podcasting on its own. The diverse range of motivations revealed by faculty points to the various possibilities of integrating podcasting in class, but the central question faculty wants to address is still how to engage students using podcasting.

Podcast Content

There is some debate on whether faculty shall simply record their lectures on podcasts. University of Connecticut psychology professor David B. Miller argued that recording lectures was not particularly novel and students would benefit more if they were part of the podcast content development process such as participating in the recorded discussion (Campus Technology, 2007). Deubel (2007) observed that students develop literacy skills as they create podcasts because in creation they became more engaged with the materials. The early stage of using podcasting might explain why a majority of faculty members are simply recording lectures on podcasts. While it is not the best way to incorporate podcasting in curriculum, at least it is the starting point to gain valuable hands-on experiences. What is enlightening is some faculty members have already tested other content such as

Table 6. Obstacles and problems encountered in the adoption of podcasting

Open-Ended Responses	Percentage
Technical challenges and problems	32
Time commitment	17
Motivate students to use podcasts	6
Reliance on others	4
Legal issues (copyright concerns)	2
Investment returns	2
Pedagogical values of podcasting	2
Financial support	1
Extreme care with speech on podcasts	1
Passive learning	1
Quality of podcast content	1
Missing	31
Total	100

Table 7. Multiple regression analysis for predicting

Predictors		B	S.E.B	Beta	$\triangle R^2$
Podcasting Satisfaction Experience					
Attitude					.12**
	Pedagogical attitude	.23	.07	.37***	
Innovativeness					.07
	Initiator	-.00	.16	-.00	
	Non-doubter	.08	.16	.07	
	Challenger	.00	.07	.01	
	Peer leader	.09	.08	.16	
Support					.18**
	University support	.36	.11	.39**	
Demographics					.02
	age	.00	.01	.02	
	income	-.06	.06	-.12	
	gender	.11	.19	.07	
Final multiple R=.63, final R²=.40 *p<.05, **p<.01, ***p<.001					

lesson summaries, guest speaker talks, interviews and demos of processes. Once the faculty becomes more efficient with the use of the technology, the effort will be directed toward more creative and diverse podcast content.

Obstacles and Problems

Though one third of faculty of the sample did not provide feedback to this question on obstacles and problems, one third did indicate that technical challenge is the main obstacle encountered. Podcasting implementation is technically challenging and there are quite a few steps of developing the content and delivering it online. Technology adoption is always found to be concurrent with technical challenges. For instance, in a study on adoption of teaching aid technologies, Zimmerman and Yohon (2008) reported some faculties felt technologies were too complicated so that basic technology literacy training was in dire need. Time commitment is another main problem and

obstacle, followed by how to motivate students to use podcasts and reliance on others. Time is a commodity in short supply for higher education faculty and the faculty members tend to spend time on what is rewarded (Zimmerman & Yohon, 2008). Unfortunately, innovation adoption and technology use were not valued criteria for promotion and tenure decision (Zimmerman & Yohon, 2008), which might explain why faculty members pointed to time as an obstacle. Lastly, it would be a waste of resources if faculty's podcasts were not used by students. Therefore it might be important to place unique and essential course content on podcasts or make the use of podcasts as part of the final academic evaluation of students.

Factors Contributing to the Satisfactory Podcasting Experience

Individual influences such as demographics seemed to be less of a contributing factor to the podcasting use. While the early adoption of a certain innovation is usually influenced by demographic variables, several studies found out demographic variables were no longer playing an important role. Wei (2006) studied wireless Internet adoption among academics in 2004-2005 when wireless Internet was still considered the newly deployed technology and found that the demographic variables of age, gender, race, education did not contribute at all. This study provides further evidence that the old wisdom of the younger, male and the wealthy standing at the forefront of technology is not valid, at least not in the academic field.

What matters most in adoption of podcasting, however, is faculty's attitude toward podcasting, or specifically, the pedagogical attitude. Pedagogical attitude probes the pedagogical values that podcasting can bring to classes. The availability of podcasting can't mobilize faculty to adopt if faculty don't have faith in the pedagogical values in the first place.

Innovativeness dimensioned into initiator, non-doubter, challenger and peer leader did not end up as significant positive predictors of podcasting satisfaction experience. The previous findings on the predictability of innovativeness for the diffusion of innovation are always mixed. The study by Wei (2006) on wireless adoption among academics did not find being innovative predicted the adoption. However, Leonard-Barton and Deschamps (1988) pointed out those who perceive themselves as more innovative would be more likely to use an innovation. Rice and Webster (2002) found that the innovative individuals not only tend to adopt a new medium earlier and use it more frequently, but also tend to use it more creatively. Maybe in the academic environment, what matters is not how innovative faculty members are but how strongly they believe in podcasting. Even if a faculty member is not an innovative person, but if he believes strongly in the pedagogical values of podcasting as a teaching tool, he will mobilize every means to reach his goal.

Lastly, organizational influences have long been identified to either facilitate or inhibit the use of a particular communication medium (Rice & Webster, 2002). And the diffusion environment in which an innovation spreads not only matters in the initiating stage of an innovation, but also in the implementation stage and the evaluation stage. That is why university support is found to be the key predictor of the satisfactory experience. This finding aligns with other findings that when higher education faculty members adopt software (Zimmerman & Yohon, 2008) and wireless Internet (Wei, 2006), university support was always found to be significant.

In sum, for the colleges and universities that plan to integrate podcasting, the IT department and top administrators must ensure that the resources and support are sufficient, easily accessible and available for faculty. Though the faculty's attitude toward podcasting can't be changed overnight, the successful and satisfactory experiences of using podcasting will transform into a catalyst that provokes the enthusiasm of other faculty to explore podcasting. And there is no doubt that the effective use of podcasts in classes and subsequent positive academic performances demonstrated by students will eventually determine whether podcasting will become an essential teaching tool in higher education classrooms.

Issues and Concerns

This study raises several important issues for faculty and administrators to consider. Foremost is whether the university shall consider podcasting activity as a part of curriculum development for tenure promotion or merit pay increases since the time and effort invested in producing podcasts are tremendous. The current university policy that did not reward the podcasting practice might have a negative impact on the podcasting diffusion. Another significant concern with regard to the podcasts' impact on classroom is whether students' attendance at the class is still essential if all the missed lectures can be easily accessed via the podcasts. While it is at the faculty's discretion to determine what is appropriate to put on podcasts, students might choose not come to class if they realize that podcasts and class lectures are very similar. Redundant course content not only discourages attendance in class but also reduces the motivation to access and utilize the content. Lastly, if it is the faculty who produced the podcast content, obviously the faculty would have to own the right to podcast content. However, the university provided a great deal of resources and support to the production of podcasts; therefore the university has its share of effort in this final product of podcasts. The podcast ownership might be a tricky area to tackle with and university policy on ownership has to be laid out clearly.

Future research on podcast use on campus shall evaluate and compare faculty and students' perception of the podcasting and identify the essential IT support areas. Another significant research area to look into is whether the creative use of podcasts by faculty or students especially in terms of content is directly related to the satisfactory perception of podcasts. Eventually, the most significant question to ask is always what pedagogical values podcasts will bring for higher education.

REFERENCES

Atkin, D. J., Neuendorf, K., Jeffres, L. W., & Skalski, P. (2003). Predictors of audience interest in adopting digital television. *Journal of Media Economics, 16*(3), 159–173. doi:10.1207/S15327736ME1603_2

Berger, E. (2007). Podcasting in engineering education: A preliminary study of content, student attitudes, and impact. *Journal of Online Education, 4*(1), 1–6.

Bongey, S. B., Cizadlo, G., & Kalnbach, L. (2006). Explorations in course-casting: Podcasts in higher education. *Campus-Wide Information Systems, 23*(5), 350–367. doi:10.1108/10650740610714107

Cable News Network. (2006). *Apple surpasses beer on college campuses: Undergrads rate their iPods as more 'in' than beer*. Retrieved June 7, 2006, from http://cnn.com/2006/US/06/07/college.in.ap/index.html

Campus Technology. (2007). *2007 Campus technology innovators: podcasting*. Retrieved January 16, 2009, from http://campustechnology.com/articles/2007/08/2007-campus-technology-innovators-podcasting.aspx

Carr, C., & Devries, D. (1999). *HERI Faculty Survey*. Retrieved May 1, 2008, from http://www.gseis.ucla.edu/heri/web_examples/fullerton.pdf

Compeau, D. R., & Higgins, C. A. (1995). Computer self-efficacy: Development of a measure and initial test. *Management Information Systems Quarterly, 19*(2), 189–211. doi:10.2307/249688

Daniels, G. L., & Brozana, A. L. (2007, April). *Identifying correlates to and indicants of success in using downloadable audio as a journalism teaching tool*. Paper presented at the Broadcast Education Association Annual Conference, Las Vegas, NV.

Dennis, E. E., Meyer, P., Sundar, S. S., Pryor, L., Rogers, E., Chen, H. L., & Pavlik, J. (2003). Learning reconsidered: Education in the digital age. *Journalism & Mass Communication Educator, 57*(4), 292–317.

Dennis, E. E., Meyer, P., Sundar, S. S., Pryor, L., Rogers, E. M., Chen, H. L., & Pavlik, J. (2003). Learning reconsidered: Education in the Digital Age. *Journalism & Mass Communication, 57*(4), 292–317.

Deubel, P. (2007). Podcasts: where is the learning? *T. H. E. Journal*. Retrieved January 16, 2009, from http://www.thejournal.com/articles/20764_2

D&M Professional. (2007). Survey finds college students thirsty for podcasts to aid learning. *Pro Sound News*. Retrieved April 21, 2008, from http://www.prosoundnews.com/publish/news/Survey_Finds_College_Students_Thirsty_for_Podcasts_to_Aid_Learning_printer.shtml

Fulk, J. (1993). Social construction of communication technology. *Academy of Management Journal*, *36*(5), 921–950. doi:10.2307/256641

Gueldenzoph, L. E., Guidera, E., Whipple, D., Mertler, C., & Dutton, L. (1999-2000). Faculty use of instructional technology in the university classroom. *Journal of Educational Technology Systems*, *28*(2), 121–135. doi:10.2190/Q8B8-WC93-81CB-9Q0C

Hagner, P. (2001). *Interesting practices and best systems in faculty engagement and support*. Retrieved from http://net.educause.edu/ir/library/pdf/NLI0017.pdf

Hoag, A. M., Bhattacharya, S. S., Helsel, J., Hu, Y., Lee, S., & Lee, J. (2003). A literature review of computers and pedagogy for journalism and mass communication education. *Journalism & Mass Communication Educator*, *57*(4), 398–412.

Honey, M., & Moeller, B. (1990). *Teachers' beliefs and technology integration: different values and different understandings*. New York: Center for Technology in Eduation.

Huntsberger, M., & Stavitsky, A. (2007). The new 'podagogy': Incorporating podcasting into the journalism education. *Journalism & Mass Communication Educator*, *61*(4), 397–410.

Hurt, H. T., Joseph, K., & Cook, C. D. (1977). Scales for the measurement of innovativeness. *Human Communication Research*, *4*(1), 58–65. doi:10.1111/j.1468-2958.1977.tb00597.x

Kellum, G., & Hale, S. T. (2007). E-learning: educating the 21st century speech-language pathologists. *ASHA Leaders*, *12*(14), 24–25.

Leonard-Barton, D., & Deschamps, I. (1988). Managerial influence in the implementation of new technology. *Management Science*, *34*, 1252–1265. doi:10.1287/mnsc.34.10.1252

Li, S. C. S. (2004). Exploring the factors influencing the adoption of interactive cable television services in Taiwan. *Journal of Broadcasting & Electronic Media*, *48*(3), 466–483. doi:10.1207/s15506878jobem4803_7

Madden, M. (2008). *Podcast downloading. Pew Internet & American Life Project Memo*. Retrieved January 16, 2009, from http://www.pewinternet.org/pdfs/PIP_Podcast_2008_Memo.pdf

McCloskey, P. (2007). Consensus: Podcasting has no 'inherent' pedagogic value. *Campus Technology*. Retrieved April 21, 2008, from http://www.campustechnology.com/article.aspx?aid=49018

Miller, D. (2006, October 18). Podcasting at the University of Connecticut: Enhancing the educational experience. *Campus Technology*.

Miller, D. B. (2006). Podcasting at the University of Connecticut: Enhancing the educational experience. *Campus Technology*. Retrieved April 21, 2008, from http://www.campustechnology.com/article.aspx?aid=41255

Moch, M. K., & Morse, E. V. (1977). Size, centralization and organization adoption of innovations. *American Sociological Review*, *42*(5), 716–725. doi:10.2307/2094861

Premkumar, G., & Roberts, M. (1999). Adoption of new information technologies in rural small businesses. *Omega*, *27*(4), 467–484. doi:10.1016/S0305-0483(98)00071-1

Read, B. (2007). How to podcast campus lectures. *The Chronicle of Higher Education*, A32–A35.

Rice, R. E., & Tyler, J. (1995). Individual and organizational influences on voice mail use and evaluation. *Behaviour & Information Technology*, *14*(6), 329–341. doi:10.1080/01449299508914652

Rice, R. E., & Webster, J. (2002). Adoption, diffusion and use of new media in organizational settings. In Lin, C., & Atkin, D. (Eds.), *Communication Technology and society* (pp. 191–227). Cresskill, NJ: Hampton Press.

Rogers, E. M. (1971). *Diffusion of Innovation* (2nd ed.). New York: Free Press.

Rogers, E. M. (1995). *Diffusion of Innovation* (5th ed.). New York: Free Press.

Rogers, E. M. (2004). A prospective and retrospective look at the diffusion model. *Journal of Health Communication*, *9*, 13–19. doi:10.1080/10810730490271449

Rogers, E. M., & Shoemaker, F. F. (1971). *Communication of innovations*. New York: Free Press.

Singer, J. B. (2004). Strange bedfellows? The diffusion of convergence in four news organizations. *Journalism Studies*, *5*(1), 3–18. doi:10.1080/1461670032000174701

Skira, D. J. (2006). The 2005 word of the year: Podcasting. *Nursing Education Perspectives*, *27*(1), 54–55.

Trigwell, K., Prosser, M., & Waterhouse, F. (1999). Relations between teachers' approaches to teaching and students' approaches to learning. *Higher Education*, *37*, 57–70. doi:10.1023/A:1003548313194

Unsworth, L. (2008). Multiliteracies, e-literature and English teaching. *Language and Education: An International Journal*, *22*(1), 62–75. doi:10.2167/le726.0

Vess, D. L. (2006). History to go: Why iTeach with iPods. *The History Teacher*, *39*(4), 479–492. doi:10.2307/30037068

Vestal, S. (2007). Regions' universities test podcasting: Professors using new technologies to connect. *Knight Rider Tribune Business News*. Retrieved April 21, 2008, from http://proquest. umi.com/pqdweb?did=1222573261&sid=4&Fmt=3&clientld=37634&RQT=309&Vname=PQD

Wei, R. (2006). *Exploring predictors of adoption of wireless Internet among academics*. Paper presented at the annual meeting of the International Communication Association, Dresden, Germany.

Zaltman, G., Duncan, R., & Holbek, J. (1973). *Innovations & Organizations*. New York: John Wiley & Sons.

ENDNOTES

[1] These twenty statements were adapted from the innovativeness scale (IS) developed by Hurt, Joseph, and Cook (1977).

[2] These six statements were constructed to probe faculty's perceptions of podcasting use in classes from a pedagogical perspective. The scale was integrated with both positively and negatively worded items to avoid the response bias. A typical statement is: "I use the podcasting in the curriculum because I believe it will enhance my course content." The other variations were "increase the efficiency of the course content delivery," "engage students more with class materials," "service is made available on campus," "my colleagues are using it," and "provides a chance to explore new ways of teaching."

[3] The two deleted items are "my colleagues are using it" and "the technology is available on campus."

[4] Though the sample size of 85 is hardly representative of the podcasting faculty population across the U.S., we have to note that the podcasting faculty population is still

a minority group on campus. Moreover, the study was exploratory in nature which might justify the use of the limited sample size.

5   The maximum length of time adopting podcasting is 60 months (5 years) and the minimum is 1 month, and the median length is 12 months (1 year). Per week, the maximum time spent on producing podcasting is

13 hours and the minimum is 5 minute, and the median working time is 90 minutes.

6   The coding was done by the researcher and a GA after reaching a satisfactory agreement level of 80%.

7   The coding was done by the researcher and a GA after reaching a satisfactory agreement level of 80%.

This work was previously published in International Journal of Information and Communication Technology, Volume 6, Issue 4, edited by Lawrence A. Tomei, pp. 74-88, copyright 2010 by IGI Publishing (an imprint of IGI Global).

Compilation of References

Abel, R. (2005). Implementing best practices in online learning: A recent study reveals common denominators for success in Internet-supported learning. *EDUCAUSE Quarterly, 28*(3), 75–77.

Abrahamson, C. (1998). Storytelling as a pedagogical tool in higher education. *Education, 118*. Retrieved June, 27 2009 from http://www.questia.com

Adamich, T. (2006). CE cataloging and the school library as language set repository: using a MARC record for assessment. *Knowledge Quest, 35*(2), 73–78.

Adamich, T. (2007). Curriculum-based cataloging and the new metadata: cataloging beyond the world of MARC. In *Knowledge Quest, 35*(5), 66-71.

Adams, D. A., Nelson, R. R., & Todd, P. A. (1992). Perceived usefulness, ease of use, and usage of information technology: A replication. *Management Information Systems Quarterly, 16*, 227–247. doi:10.2307/249577

ADL. (2009). Retrieved from http://www.adlnet.org

Agarwal, R., & Karahanna, E. (2000). Time flies when you're having fun: Cognitive absorption and beliefs about information technology usage. *Management Information Systems Quarterly, 24*(4), 665–694. doi:10.2307/3250951

Agarwal, R. (2005). *Digital technology and women employment: Employment dimensions in India. United Nations Public Administration Network* (UNPAN Report No. 023829). Retrieved from http://unpan1.un.org/intradoc/groups/public/documents/APCITY/UNPAN023829.pdf

Ajzen, I., & Fishbein, M. (1980). *Understanding attitudes and predicting social behaviour*. Englewood Cliffs, NJ: Prentice-Hall.

Akbulut, A. Y., & Looney, C. A. (2007, October). Inspiring Students to Pursue Computing Degrees. *Communications of the ACM, 50*(10), 67–71. doi:10.1145/1290958.1290964

Aldrich, C. (2003). *Simulations and the future of learning*. New York: Pffieffer/Wiley.

Alexander, B., & Levine, A. (2008, November/December). Web 2.0 storytelling emergence of a new genre. *EDUCAUSE Review*, 40–56.

Alexander, B. (2004). M-learning: emerging pedagogical and campus issues in the mobile learning environment. *EDUCAUSE Center for Applied Research (ECAR) Bulletin*, (16).

Allen, R. (2001, Fall). Technology and learning: How schools map routes to technology's promised land. *ASCD Curriculum Update, 1-3*, 6–8.

Allen, I. E., Seaman, J., & Garret, R. (2007). *Blending in. The extent and promise of Blended Education in the United States*. Needham, MA: The Sloan Consortium.

Allen, E., & Seaman, J. (2007). Online Nation – Five Years of Growth in Online Learning. *The Sloan Consortium*. Retrieved March 15, 2008, from http://www.sloan-c.org

Almeda, M. B., & Rose, K. (2000). Instructor satisfaction in university of california extension's on-line writing curriculum. *Journal of Asynchronous Learning Networks, 4*(3), 180–195.

Alonso, F., López, G., Manrique, D., & Viñes, J. M. (2005). An instructional model for web-based e-learning education with a blended learning process approach. *British Journal of Educational Technology, 36*(2), 217–235. doi:10.1111/j.1467-8535.2005.00454.x

Aly, I., & Islam, M. (2005). Factors affecting oral communication apprehension among business students: An empirical study. *Journal of American Academy of Business, Cambridge, 6*(2), 98–103.

American Library Association. (2006) *Information literacy competency standards for higher education*. Chicago: American Library Association. Retrieved June 25, 2009, from http://www.ala.org/ala/acrl/acrlstandards/informationliteracycompetency.htm#iltech

American Nurses Association. (1994). *Scope of Practice for Nursing Informatics*. Washington, DC: American Nurses Publishing.

Anderson, C. (2007). *Preventing bad hires: The value of objective prehire assessment*. Retrieved April 13, 2009 from http:// download. microsoft.com/ download/f/2/b/ f2bde3bb-c982-4c5a-ae41-9300b6b8d413/Preventing_bad_hires.pdf

Anomi, E. E. (2007). *Student expectations of faculty in a nigerian lis school*. Library Philosophy and Practice. Retrieved 15 January 2008, from http://www. webpages. uidaho.edu /~mbolin / adomi.htm

Arbuckle, J. L. (2006). *Amos (Version 7.0) (Computer Program)*. Chicago: SPSS.

Arbuckle, J. L. (2006). *AMOS (Version 7.0)*. Chicago: SPSS.

Asai, K. (2005). Augmented Instructions – A Fusion of Augmented Reality and Printed Learning Materials. In *Proceedings of the 5th IEEE International Conference of Advanced Learning Technologies* (pp. 1-3).

Ashenhurst, R. (1972). Curriculum recommendations for graduate professional programs in Information Systems. *Communications of the ACM, 15*(5), 364–398. doi:10.1145/355602.361320

Aspden, L., & Helm, P. (2004). Making the connection in a blended learning environment. *Educational Media International, 41*(3), 245–252. doi:10.1080/09523980410001680851

Associated Press. (2006, February 26). *Rural broadband users close gap with cities: Pew survey notes increasing acceptance among people living in the country*. Retrieved March 1, 2006, from http://www.msnbc.msn.com/id/11581369/

Association of Mathematics Teacher Educators. (2008)... *Connections, 18*(1), 1–16.

Astone, M. K. (1995). *Gender stereotyping of computing*. Unpublished doctoral dissertation, Auburn University, Auburn, AL.

Atkin, D. J., Neuendorf, K., Jeffres, L. W., & Skalski, P. (2003). Predictors of audience interest in adopting digital television. *Journal of Media Economics, 16*(3), 159–173. doi:10.1207/S15327736ME1603_2

Atkins, N. E., & Vasu, E. S. (2000). Measuring knowledge of technology usage and stages of concern about computing: A study of middle school teachers. *Journal of Technology and Teacher Education, 8*(4), 279–302.

Atkins, D. E., Brown, J. S., & Hammond, A. L. (2007). *A Review of the Open Educational Resources (OER) Movement: Achievements, Challenges, and New Opportunities*. Retrieved November 4, 2007, from http://www. hewlett.org/NR/rdonlyres/5D2E3386-3974-4314-8F67-5C2F22EC4F9B/ 0/AReviewoftheOpenEducationalResourcesOERMovement_ BlogLink.pdf

Bailey, D. B., & Palsha, S. A. (1992). Qualities of the Stages of Concern Questionnaire and implications for educational innovations. *The Journal of Educational Research, 85*(4), 226–232.

Bailie, F. (2007). How a Technology Grant from the National Academy Foundation Has Begun to Make a Difference for Minority Students in an Urban High School. In C. Crawford et al. (Eds.), *Proceedings of Society for Information Technology and Teacher Education International Conference* (pp. 762-769). Chesapeake, VA: AACE.

Ball, C. T., & Pelco, L. E. (2006). Teaching Research Methods to Undergraduate Psychology Students Using an Active Cooperative Learning Approach. *International Journal of Teaching and Learning in Higher Education, 17*(2), 147–154.

Banaszewski, T. (2002). Digital storytelling finds its place in the classroom. *Information Today*. Retrieved February 12, 2009 from http://www.infotoday.com/MMSchools/jan02/banaszewski.htm

Bandura, A. (1986). *Social Foundations of Thought and Action: A Social Cognitive Theory*. Englewood Cliffs, NJ: Prentice-Hall.

Bandura, A. (1997). *Self-efficacy: The exercise of control.* New York: W. H. Freeman.

Baraniuk, R. G. (2007). Challenges and Opportunities for the Open Education Movement: A Connexions Case Study. In Iiyoshi, T., & Vijay Kumar, M. S. (Eds.), *Opening Up Education – The Collective Advancement of Education through Open Technology, Open Content, and Open Knowledge.* Cambridge, MA: MIT Press.

Barclay, K. H. (2001). *Humanizing learning-at-distance.* San Francisco, CA: Saybrook Institute.

Barrett, H. (2005). Storytelling in higher education: A theory of reflection on practice to support deep learning. In *Proceedings of the Technology and Teacher Education Annual Conference 2005* (pp. 1878-1883). Charlottesville, VA: Association for the Advancement of Computing in Education. Retrieved February 12, 2009 from http://electronicportfolios.com/portfolios/Kean.pdf

Barrett, H. (2006). *Researching and evaluating digital storytelling as a deep learning tool.* Retrieved February 12, 2009 from http://electronicportfolios.com/portfolios/SITEStorytelling2006.pdf

Barrows, H., & Tamblyn, R. M. (1980). *Problem-based learning: an approach to medical education.* New York: Springer.

Bates, T. (1986). Computer Assisted Learning or Communication: Which Way for Information Technology in Distance Education. *Journal of Distance Education, 1*(1), 41–57.

Bauer, J., & Kenton, J. (2005). Toward technology integration in the schools: why it isn't happening. *Journal of Technology and Teacher Education, 13*(4), 519–546.

Bausch, P., Haughey, M., & Hourihan, M. (2002). *We Blog: Publishing Online with Weblogs.* New York: John Wiley & Sons.

Baylor, A. L., & Ritchie, D. (2002). What factors facilitate teacher skill, teacher morale, and perceived student learning in technology-using classrooms? *Computers & Education, 39*(4), 395–414. doi:10.1016/S0360-1315(02)00075-1

Baylor, A. (1999). Intelligent agents as cognitive tools for education. *Educational Technology, 39*(2), 36–41.

BEA. (2007). *US Government Bureau of Economic Analysis: Personal Income and Per Capita Personal Income by BEA Economic Area 2003-2005.* Retrieved November 25, 2007, from http://www.bea.gov/bea/regional/reis/scb.cfm

Bear, G. G., Richards, H. C., & Lancaster, P. (1987). Attitudes towards computers: validation of a computer attitudes scale. *Journal of Computing Research, 32*(2), 207–219. doi:10.2190/1DYT-1JEJ-T8J5-1YC7

Bearden, W. O., Netemeyer, R. G., & Mobley, M. F. (1993). *Handbook of marketing scales.* Newbury Park, CA: Sage.

Becker, H. J. (2001). *How are teachers using computers in instruction?* Paper presented at the meeting of the American Educational Research Association. Retrieved May 25, 2008, from http://www.crito.uci.edu/tlc/FINDINGS/special3/ Boster, F. J., Meyer, G. S., Roberto, A. J., & Inge, C. C. (2002). *A report on the effect of the united streaming application on educational performance.* Farmville, VA: Longwood University.

Beckwith, D. (1988). The future of educational technology. *Canadian Journal of Educational Communication, 17*(1), 3–20.

Bem, S. L. (1981). Gender Schema Theory: A cognitive account of sex typing. *Psychological Review, 88*(4), 354–364. doi:10.1037/0033-295X.88.4.354

Benbasat, I., & Weber, R. (1996). Research commentary: Rethinking diversity. *Information Systems Research, 7*(4), 389–399. doi:10.1287/isre.7.4.389

Benbasat, I., & Zmud, R. W. (1999). Empirical research in Information Systems: The practice of relevance. *MIS Quarterly, 23*(1), 3–16. doi:10.2307/249403

Benbunan-Fich, R., & Hiltz, S. R. (2003). Mediators of the effectiveness of online courses. *IEEE Transactions on Professional Communication, 46*(4), 298–312. doi:10.1109/TPC.2003.819639

Benbunan-Fich, R., & Hiltz, S. R. (2002). *Correlates of effectiveness of learning networks: The effects of course level, course type, and gender on outcomes.* Paper presented at the 35th Annual Hawaii International Conference on System Sciences.

Bender, T. (2003). *Discussion-based online teaching to enhance student learning: Theory, practice, and assessment.* Sterling, VA: Stylus.

Berge, Z. L. (1995, January-February). Facilitating computer conferencing: Recommendations from the field. *Educational Technology*, 22–30.

Berger, E. (2007). Podcasting in engineering education: A preliminary study of content, student attitudes, and impact. *Journal of Online Education, 4*(1), 1–6.

Bhattacharya, I., & Sharma, K. (2007). India in the knowledge economy – an electronic paradigm. *International Journal of Educational Management, 21*(6), 543–568. doi:10.1108/09513540710780055

Bhattacherjee, A., & Premkumar, G. (2004). Understanding changes in belief and attitude toward information technology usage: A theoretical model and longitudinal test. *Management Information Systems Quarterly, 28*(2), 351–370.

Bielefeldt, T. (2001). Technology in teacher education. *Journal of Computing in Teacher Education, 17*(4), 4–15.

Biggs, J. B. (2003). *Teaching for Quality Learning at University* (2nd ed.). Buckingham, UK: SHRE and Open University Press.

Birbili, M. (2000). *Translating from one language to another. Social Research Update, 31.* Surrey, UK: University of Surrey.

Birx, E., Castleberry, K., & Perry, K. (1996). Integration of laptop computer technology into an undergraduate nursing course. *Computers in Nursing, 14*, 108–112.

Bitter, G. G., & Legacy, J. M. (2006) Using technology in the classroom (Brief version). Boston, MA: Allyn & Bacon.

Bloom, B. S. (1956). *Taxonomy of Educational Objective.* New York: Longmans.

Blyden, B. K., & Davidson, I. E. (2005). Energizing Africa's emerging economy. *IEEE Power and Energy Magazine, 3*(4), 24–31. doi:10.1109/MPAE.2005.1458227

Boase, K. (2008). *Digital storytelling for reflection and engagement: A study of the uses and potential of digital storytelling.* Retrieved February 12, 2009 from http://resources.glos.ac.uk/tli/lets/projects/pathfinder/index.cfm

Bond, C. (2007). Nurses' requirement for information technology: a challenge for educators. *International Journal of Nursing Science, 44*, 1075–1078. doi:10.1016/j.ijnurstu.2007.01.009

Bongey, S. B., Cizadlo, G., & Kalnbach, L. (2006). Explorations in course-casting: Podcasts in higher education. *Campus-Wide Information Systems, 23*(5), 350–367. doi:10.1108/10650740610714107

Bonifield, C., & Cole, C. (2007, June). Affective responses to service failure: Anger, regret, and retaliatory versus conciliatory responses. *Marketing Letters, 18*(1-2), 85–99. doi:10.1007/s11002-006-9006-6

Borgers, N., Hox, J. J., & Sikkel, D. (2004). Response effects in surveys on children and adolescents: the effect of number of responses options, negative wording, and neutral mid-point. *Quality & Quantity, 38*, 17–33.. doi:10.1023/B:QUQU.0000013236.29205.a6

Borgers, N., & Hox, J. J. (2000). *Reliability of responses in questionnaire research with children.* Paper presented at the Fifth International Conference on Logic and Methodology, Cologne, Germany.

Bottino, R. M., & Robotti, E. (2007). Transforming classroom teaching & learning through technology: Analysis of a case study. *Educational Technology & Society, 10*(4), 174–186.

Bottino, R. M. (2003). ICT, national policies, and impact on schools and teachers' development. In *Proceedings of the 3.1 and 3.3 working groups conference on International federation for information processing (CRPIT '03)* (pp. 3-6). Darlinghurst, Australia: Australian Computer Society, Inc.

Boyle, T., Bradley, C., Chalk, P., Jones, R., & Pickard, P. (2003). Using blended learning to improve student success rates in learning to program. *Learning, Media and Technology,* [REMOVED HYPERLINK FIELD]*28*(2-3), 165-178.

Brain, M. (1998). *Emphasis on teaching. What is good teaching?* Raleigh, NC: BYG Publishing, Inc.

Brandt, D. (2001). Information technology literacy: Task knowledge and mental models. [from the Academic Search Premier database.]. *Library Trends, 50*(1), 73. Retrieved July 20, 2009.

Branon, R. F., & Essex, C. (2001). Synchronous and asynchronous communication tools in distance education: A survey of instructors. *TechTrends, 45,* 36–42. doi:10.1007/BF02763377

Brazil: Cannibalism and Tropicalism. (2007). Retrieved November 25, 2007, from http://www.filmreference.com/encyclopedia/Academy-Awards-Crime-Films/Brazil-CANNIBALISM -AND-TROPICALISM.html

Brown, A. H., Benson, B., & Uhde, A. P. (2004). You're doing what with technology? An exposé on "Jane Doe" college professor. *College Teaching, 52*(3), 100–104.

Brown, J., Collins, A., & Duguid, P. (1989). Situated Cognition and the Culture of Learning. *Educational Researcher, 18*(1), 32–42.

Brown, D. (2003). Fitting workshops into faculty mores. In Brown, D. G. (Ed.), *Developing faculty to use technology: programs and strategies to choices and challenges.* Madison, WI: Atwood Publishing.

Brown, J. S., Collins, A., & Duguid, P. (1989). Situated Cognition. In R. W. Lawler & M. Yazdani (Eds.), *Artificial Intelligence and Education, 2,* 254-268.

Bruner, J. S. (1967). *On Knowing: Essays for the Left Hand.* Cambridge, Mass: Harvard University Press.

Brush, T., Glazewski, K., Rutowski, K., Berg, K., Stromfors, C., & Hernandez-Van Nest, M. (2003). Integrating technology in a field-based teacher training program: The PT3@ASU project. *Educational Technology Research and Development, 51*(1), 1042–1629.

Brusilovski, P., & Maybury, M. T. (2002). From adaptive hypermedia to the adaptive web. *Communications of the ACM, 45*(5), 30–33.

Brusilovsky, P. (1994). The Construction and Application of Student Models in Intelligent Tutoring Systems. *Journal of Computer and Systems Sciences International, 32*(1), 70–89.

Brusilovsky, P., & Henze, N. (2007). Open corpus adaptive educational hypermedia. In P. Brusilovsky, A. Kobsa, & W. Neidl (Eds.), *The Adaptive Web: Methods and Strategies of Web Personalization.* Lecture Notes in Computer Science. Springer-Verlag.

Bryman, A., & Cramer, D. (2001). *Quantitative data analysis with spss release 10 for windows: a guide for social scientists.* Philadelphia: Routledge: Taylor and Francis Group.

Bull, G., & Kajder, S. (2004). Digital storytelling in the language arts classroom. *Learning and Leading with Technology, 32*(4), 46–49.

Bullen, P. R., & Russell, M. B. (2007). *A Blended Learning Approach to Teaching First Year Engineering.*

Burch-Brown, C., & Kilkelly, A. (2003). Creative high-tech/low-tech teaching in an integrated teaching environment. In Brown, D. G. (Ed.), *Developing faculty to use technology: Programs and strategies to choices and challenges* (pp. 167–171). Madison, WI: Atwood Publishing.

Burnham, L., Miller, A., & Ray, L. (2000, March). *Putting the pieces together.* Paper presented at the International Conference on Learning with Technology, Does Technology Make a Difference? Temple University, Philadelphia.

Business Editors/Technology, E. F. W. (1998, June 8). Regrets, They Have a Few -- College Grads Re-Think Majors, Career Choices. *Business Wire, 1.*

Butler, M. B., Lee, S., & Tippins, D. J. (2006). Case-Based Methodology as an Instructional Strategy for Understanding Diversity: Preservice Teachers' Perceptions. *Multicultural Education,* 20–26.

Cable News Network. (2006). *Apple surpasses beer on college campuses: Undergrads rate their iPods as more 'in' than beer.* Retrieved June 7, 2006, from http://cnn.com/2006/US/06/07/college.in.ap/index.html

Cairncross, S. (2002). *Interactive Multimedia and Learning: Realizing the Benefits.* Unpublished doctoral dissertation, Napier University, Scotland.

Callister, W. D. (2003). *Student Learning Resources. Materials Science and Engineering an Introduction.* New York: John Wiley & Sons Inc.

Cambourne, B. (1995). Towards an Educationally Relevant Theory of Literacy Learning: Twenty Years of Inquiry. *The Reading Teacher, 49*(3), 182–190. doi:10.1598/RT.49.3.1

Cambourne, B. L. (1988). *The Whole Story: Natural Learning and the Acquisition of Literacy*. Auckland, New Zealand: Ashton-Scholastic.

Cameron, D., & Anderson, T. (2006). Comparing Weblogs to Threaded Discussion Tools in Online Educational Contexts. *Instructional Journal of Instructional technology and Distance learning, 2*(11). ISSN 1550-6908

Campbell, K. S., Mothersbaugh, D. L., Brammer, C., & Taylor, T. (2001). Peer versus self assessment of oral business presentation performance. *Business Communication Quarterly, 64*(3), 23–42. doi:10.1177/108056990106400303

Campbell, J., Kyriakides, L., Muijs, D., & Robinson, W. (2004). *Assessing teachers job effectiveness: Developing a differentiated model*. London and New York: RoutledgeFalmer.

Campus Technology. (2007). *2007 Campus technology innovators: podcasting*. Retrieved January 16, 2009, from http://campustechnology.com/articles/2007/08/2007-campus-technology-innovators-podcasting.aspx

Cardenas, K. (1998). Technology in today's classroom. *Academe, 84*(3), 27–29.

Cardis, P. (2006, July). Maximizing Referrals. *Professional Builder, 71*(7), 41–42.

Carmines, E. G., & McIver, J. P. (1981). *Analyzing models with unobserved variables: Analysis of covariance structures*. Thousand Oaks, CA: Sage.

Carnwell, R. (2000). Pedagogical implications of approaches to study in distance learning: developing models through qualitative and quantitative analysis. *Journal of Advanced Nursing, 31*(5), 1018–1028. doi:10.1046/j.1365-2648.2000.01394.x

Carr, C., & Devries, D. (1999). *HERI Faculty Survey*. Retrieved May 1, 2008, from http://www.gseis.ucla.edu/heri/web_examples/fullerton.pdf

Castelijn, P., & Janssen, B. (2006). *Effectiveness of Blended Learning in a Distance Education Setting*. Retrieved April 13, 2009 from http:// www.ou.nl/ Docs/ Faculteiten/ MW/MW%20Working%20Papers/gr%2006%2006%20castelijn.pdf

Castro-Schez, J. J., Castillo, E., Hortolano, J., & Rodriguez, A. (2009, February). Designing and Using Software Tools for Educational Purposes: FLAT, a Case Study. *IEEE Transactions on Education, 52*(1), 66–74. doi:10.1109/TE.2008.917197

Cavus, N., & Ibrahim, D. (2009). m-Learning: An experiment in using SMS to support learning new English language words. *British Journal of Educational Technology, 40*(1), 78–91. doi:10.1111/j.1467-8535.2007.00801.x

CEN/ISSS LTW. (2009). Retrieved from http://www.cenorm.be/isss

Centre for Excellence in Teaching and Learning in Reusable Learning Objects. (2005). *CETL FAQs*. Retrieved October 5, 2007 from http://www.rlo-cetl.ac.uk/faqs.htm

Chan, L. M. (1989). Inter-indexer consistency in subject cataloging. In *Information technology and libraries, 8*(4), 349-357.

Chandler, P., & Sweller, J. (1994). Cognitive Load Theory, Learning Difficulty and Instructional Design. *Learning and Instruction, 4*, 295–312. doi:10.1016/0959-4752(94)90003-5

Chao, T., Bulter, T., & Ryan, P. (2003). Providing a technology edge for liberal arts students. *Journal of Information Technology Education, 2*, 331–347.

Charniak, E. (1991). Bayesian networks without tears. *AI Magazine, 12*(4), 50–63.

Chen, N. S., Wei, C. W., Wu, K. T., & Uden, L. (2009). Effects of high level prompts and peer assessment on online learners' reflection levels. *Computers & Education, 52*(2), 283–291. doi:10.1016/j.compedu.2008.08.007

Chen, N. S. Kinshuk, Wei, C. W., Chen, Y. R., & Wang, Y. C. (2007). Classroom climate and learning effectiveness comparison for physical and cyber F2F interaction in holistic-blended learning environment. In *Proceedings of the 7th IEEE International Conference on Advanced Learning Technologies* (pp. 313-317).

Chen. (1986). Gender and computers: the beneficial effects of experience on attitudes. *Journal of Educational Computing Research, 2*, 265-282.

Cheon, M.J., Choong, Lee, C., & Grover, V. (1991). Research in MIS-points of work and reference: A replication and extension of the Culnan and Swanson study. *Data Base for Advances in Information Systems Journal, 23*(2), 21–29.

Chickering, A. W., & Gamson, Z. F. (Eds.). (1991). *Applying the seven principles for good practice in undergraduate education.* San Francisco, CA: Jossey-Bass Inc.

Chickering, A., & Ehrmann, S. C. (1996, October). Implementing the seven principles: Technology as lever. *AAHE Bulletin,* 3-6. Retrieved February 7, 2008 from http://www.tltgroup.org/programs/seven.html

Chin, W. W. (1998). The partial least squares approach to structural equation modeling. In G.A. Marcoulides (Ed.), *Modern Methods for Business Research* (pp. 295-336). Mahwah, NJ, USA: Lawrence Erlbaum Associates.

China-Profile. (2007). *China-Profile Analysis: Urban and Rural Population in China 1978 and 2002.* Retrieved November 22, 2007, from http://www.gerhard-k-heilig.com/cp/data/tab_rurpop_1.htm

Cho, K. (2006). Analysis of Intercultural Competency in the e-mail Exchange between Elementary School Students of Japan and Korea. *Journal of Japan Society for Educational Technology, 30*(1), 59–66.

Cholin, V. S. (2005). Study of the application of information technology for effective access to resources in Indian university libraries. *The International Information & Library Review, 37*(3), 189–197. doi:10.1016/j.iilr.2005.07.002

Chorus, C. G., Arentze, T.A., & Timmermans, H.J.P. (2008, January). A Random Regret-Minimization model of travel choice. *Transportation Research, 42*(1), -18.

Ciborra, C. U. (1998). Crisis and foundations: An inquiry to the nature and limits of models and methods in the Information Systems discipline. *The Journal of Strategic Information Systems, 7*(1), 5–16. doi:10.1016/S0963-8687(98)00020-1

Clark, D. (1998). Course redesign. Incorporating an Internet web site into an existing nursing class. *Computers in Nursing, 16,* 219–222.

Clarke, J. (2008). PowerPoint and pedagogy maintaining student interest in university lectures. *Contemporary Issues in Technology & Teacher Education, 56*(1), 39–45.

Clark-Ibanez, M., & Scott, L. (2008). Learning to teach online. *Teaching Sociology, 36,* 34–41. doi:10.1177/0092055X0803600105

Clay, M. (1999). Development of training and support programs for distance education instructors. *Online Journal of Distance Learning Administration, 11*(111). Retrieved June 19, 2008 from http://www.westga.edu/~distance/clay23.html.

Cohen, L., & Manion, L. (1994). *Research methods in Education.* (4th ed.). London: Routldege.

Cohn, E. R. (2002). *Instant messaging in higher education: A new faculty development challenge.* Retrieved March 30, 2009, from http://www.ipfw.edu/as/tohe/2002/Papers/cohn2.htm

Coley, R., Cradler, J., & Engel, P. K. (1997). *Computers and classrooms: The status of technology in U.S. schools. Policy Information Report.* Princeton, NJ: Educational Testing Service, Policy Information Center.

Collis, B. (1985). Psychological implications of sex differences in attitudes towards computers: Results of a survey. *International Journal of Women's Studies, 8*(3), 207–213.

Comcast. (2007). *Comcast Broadband Internet Access Plan.* Retrieved November 25, 2007, from http://www.whatisthis.com/broadband/comcast/

Compeau, D. R., & Higgins, C. A. (1995). Computer self-efficacy: Development of a measure and initial test. *Management Information Systems Quarterly, 19*(2), 189–211. doi:10.2307/249688

Conati, C., & VanLehn, K. (2000). Toward computer-based support of meta-cognitive skills: a computational framework to coach self-explanation. *International Journal of Artificial Intelligence in Education, 11,* 389–415.

Conati, C. A., Gertner, S., & VanLehn, K. (2002). Using Bayesian Networks to Manage Uncertainty in Student Modeling. *User Modeling and User-Adapted Interaction, 12,* 371–417. doi:10.1023/A:1021258506583

Conati, C. A., Gertner, S., VanLehn, K., & Druzdel, M. J. (1997). On-line student modeling for coached problem solving using Bayesian networks. In A. Jameson, C. Paris, & C. Tasso (Eds.), *Sixth International Conference on User Modeling* (pp. 231-242). New York: Springer.

Connolly, P. M., & Elfrink, V. L. (2002). Using Information Technology in Community-Based Psychiatric Nursing Education. *Home Health Care Management & Practice, 14,* 344–352. doi:10.1177/1084822302014005006

Conrad, D. (2004). University instructors' reflections on their first online teaching experiences. *Journal of Asynchronous Learning Networks, 8*(2), 31–44.

Cortazzi, M., & Jin, L. (2007). Narrative learning, EAL and metacognitive development. *Early Child Development and Care, 177,* 645–660. doi:10.1080/03004430701379074

Couger, J. D. (1973). Curriculum recommendations for undergraduate programs in Information Systems. *Communications of the ACM, 16*(12), 727–749. doi:10.1145/362552.362554

Council of Great City Schools. (2008). *Raising the Achievement of English Language Learners in the Seattle Public Schools.* Retrieved August 20, 2008, from http://www.cgcs.org/Pubs/Seattle_Bilingual.pdf

Courtright, K. E., Mackey, D. A., & Packard, S. H. (2005, April). Empathy among College Students and Criminal Justice Majors: Identifying Predispositional Traits and the Role of Education. *Journal of Criminal Justice Education. Highland Heights, 16*(1), 125–147.

Crable, E. A., Brodzinski, J. D., & Scherer, R. F. (1991). Psychology of computer use: XXII. Preliminary development of a measure of concerns about computers. *Psychological Reports, 69,* 235–236. doi:.doi:10.2466/PR0.69.5.235-236

Crawford, M. (2001). *Teaching contextually research, rationale, and techniques for improving student motivation and achievement in mathematics and science.* Retrieved March 5, 2009 from http://www.cord.org/uploadedfiles/Teaching%20Contextually%20(Crawford).pdf

Cronbach, L. J. (1951). Coefficient alpha and the internal structure of tests. *Psychometrika, 16,* 297–334. doi:10.1007/BF02310555

Cronbach, L. J. (1970). *Essentials of psychological testing* (3rd ed.). New York: Harper & Row.

Cross, M., & Adam, F. (2007). ICT Policies and Strategies in Higher Education in South Africa: National and Institutional Pathways. *Higher Education Policy, 20*(1), 73–95. doi:10.1057/palgrave.hep.8300144

Cuban, L. (2001). *Oversold and underused: Computers in the classroom.* Cambridge, MA: Harvard University Press.

Culnan, M. J., & Markus, M. L. (1987). Information technologies. In Jablin, F. M., Putnam, L. L., Roberts, K. H., & Porter, L. W. (Eds.), *Handbook of Organizational Communications: An Interdisciplinary Perspective* (pp. 421–443). Newbury Park, CA: Sage.

Curran, C. (2004) Strategies for e-learning in universities. *National Distance Education Centre and Dublin City University.* Retrieved June 15, 2009 from http://repositories.cdlib.org/cshe/CSHE-7-04/

Cushing, B. E. (1990). Frameworks, paradigms, and scientific research in Management Information Systems. *The Journal of Information Systems, 4*(2), 38–59.

Cuthell, J. P. (2002). *How do interactive whiteboards enhance learning?* Retrieved February 24, 2004, from http://www.virtuallearning.org.uk/iwb/Learning_theories.pdf

Cuthell, J. P. (2004). *Interactive whiteboards survey.* Retrieved May 22, 2005, from http://www.virtuallearning.org.uk/2003/whiteboards/survey.doc

Cuthell, J. P. (2005). Seeing the meaning. In *Proceedings of the impact of interactive whiteboards on teaching and learning (WCCE 05),* Stellenbosch, South Africa.

D&M Professional. (2007). Survey finds college students thirsty for podcasts to aid learning. *Pro Sound News.* Retrieved April 21, 2008, from http://www.prosoundnews.com/publish/news/Survey_Finds_College_Students_Thirsty_for_Podcasts_to_Aid_Learning_printer.shtml

Dambrot, F. H., Watkins-Malek, M. A., Silling, S. M., Marshall, R. S., & Garver, J. A. (1985). Correlates of sex differences in attitudes toward and involvement with computers. *Journal of Vocational Behavior, 27,* 71–86. doi:10.1016/0001-8791(85)90053-3

Daniels, G. L., & Brozana, A. L. (2007, April). *Identifying correlates to and indicants of success in using download-able audio as a journalism teaching tool.* Paper presented at the Broadcast Education Association Annual Conference, Las Vegas, NV.

Darling, A. L., & Dannels, D. P. (2003). Practicing engineers talk about the importance of talk: A report on the role of oral communication in the workplace. *Communication Education, 52*(1), 1–16. doi:10.1080/03634520302457

Darling, J. (2007). *Investigating the effectiveness and efficiency of games and game based learning communities to support students learning. TDF Evaluation report.* Retrieved May 2009, from http://www.bath.ac.uk/learningandteaching/recognition/tdf/case_studies

Dasgupta, M. K. (2004, August). Information & communication technology for women's empowerment in India. *Information Technology in Developing Countries, 14*(2). Retrieved from http://www.iimahd.ernet.in/egov/ifip/aug2004/article4.htm

Davenport, T. (1997, April). Storming the ivory tower. *CIO Magazine* (pp. 38-41).

Davis, F. D., Bagozzi, R. P., & Warshaw, P. R. (1989). User acceptance of computer technology: A comparison of two theoretical models. *Management Science, 35,* 982–1003. doi:10.1287/mnsc.35.8.982

Davis, F. D. (1989). Perceived usefulness, perceived ease of use, and user acceptance of information technology. *Management Information Systems Quarterly, 13*(3), 319–340. doi:10.2307/249008

Davis, F. D., Bagozzi, R. P., & Warshaw, P. R. (1989). User acceptance of computer technology: A comparison of two theoretical models. *Management Science, 35*(8), 928–1003. doi:10.1287/mnsc.35.8.982

Davis, G. B., Gorgone, J. T., Couger, J. D., Feinstein, D. L., & Longenecker, H. E. (1997). *IS'97 model curriculum and guidelines for undergraduate degree programs in Information Systems.* Association for Computing Machinery. Retrieved September 1, 2008, from http://www.aisnet.org/Curriculum/Is97.pdf

De Bra, P. (2004). Adaptive Web-based Educational Hypermedia. In M. Levene & A. Poulovassilis (Eds.), *Web Dynamics, Adaptive to Change in Content, Size, Topology and Use* (pp. 387-410).

De Corte, E. (1996). Changing views of computer supported learning environments for the acquisition of knowledge and thinking skills. In Vosniadou, S., De Corte, E., Glaser, R., & Mandl, H. (Eds.), *International perspectives on the designing of technology-supported learning environments* (pp. 129–145). Mahwah, NJ: Lawrence Erlbaum.

Dede, C., & Kremer, A. (1999). Increasing students' participation via multiple interactive media. *Inventio, I.* Retrieved March 31, 2009, from http://www.doit.gmu.edu/archives/feb98/dede_1.htm

DeLone, W. H., & McLean, E. R. (1991). Information systems success: The quest for the dependent variable. *Information Systems Research, 3*(1), 60–95. doi:10.1287/isre.3.1.60

DeLone, W. H., & McLean, E. R. (2003). The DeLone and McLean model of information systems success: A ten-year update. *Journal of Management Information Systems, 19*(4), 9–30.

Dennen, V. P. (2000). Task Structuring for On-line Problem Based Learning: A Case Study. *Journal of Educational Technology & Society, 3*(3), 329–336.

Dennis, E. E., Meyer, P., Sundar, S. S., Pryor, L., Rogers, E., Chen, H. L., & Pavlik, J. (2003). Learning reconsidered: Education in the digital age. *Journalism & Mass Communication Educator, 57*(4), 292–317.

Dennis, E. E., Meyer, P., Sundar, S. S., Pryor, L., Rogers, E. M., Chen, H. L., & Pavlik, J. (2003). Learning reconsidered: Education in the Digital Age. *Journalism & Mass Communication, 57*(4), 292–317.

Derntl, M., & Motschnig-Pitrik, R. (2005). The role of structure, patterns, and people in blended learning. *The Internet and Higher Education, 8,* 111–130. doi:10.1016/j.iheduc.2005.03.002

Derntl, M., & Motschnig-Pitrik, R. (2005). The role of structure, patterns, and people in blended learning. *The Internet and Higher Education, 8*(2), 111–130. doi:10.1016/j.iheduc.2005.03.002

Dershowitz, A. (1992). *Contrary to Popular Opinion*. New York: Pharos Books. Emery, C., Kramer, T., & Tian, R. (n.d). *Return to academic standards: challenge the student evaluation of teaching effectiveness*. Retrieved 10 January 2008, from http://www.bus.lsu.edu/ academics/ accounting/ faculty/lcrumbley/stu_rat_of_%20instr.htm

DeSanctis, G., & Poole, M. S. (1994). Capturing the complexity in advanced technology use: Adaptive structuration theory. *Organization Science, 5*(2), 121–147. doi:10.1287/orsc.5.2.121

DeShields, O. W. Jr, Kara, A., & Kaynak, E. (2005). Determinants of business student satisfaction and retention in higher education: applying Herzberg's two-factor theory. *International Journal of Educational Management, 19*(2/3), 128–139.

Deubel, P. (2007). Podcasts: where is the learning? *T. H. E. Journal*. Retrieved January 16, 2009, from http://www.thejournal.com/articles/20764_2

Dewey, J. (1938). *Experience and Education*. New York: MacMillan.

Dholakia, U. M., King, W. J., & Baraniuk, R. (2006). *What Makes an Open Education Program Sustainable?* The Case of Connexions.

Dishaw, M. T., & Strong, D. M. (1999). Extending the technology acceptance model with task-technology fit constructs. *Information & Management, 36*(1), 9–21. doi:10.1016/S0378-7206(98)00101-3

Dochy, F., Segers, M., van den Bossche, P., & Gijbels, D. (2003). The effects of problem-based learning: a meta-analysis. *Learning and Instruction, 13*, 533–568. doi:10.1016/S0959-4752(02)00025-7

Dowling, C., Godfrey, J. M., & Gyles, N. (2003). Do hybrid flexible delivery teaching methods improve accounting student learning outcomes? *Accounting Education: An International Journal, 12*(4), 373–391. doi:10.1080/0963928032000154512

Downes, S. (2004). Educational Blogging. *EDUCAUSE Review, 39*(5), 14-26. Retrieved October 26, 2009, from http://www.educause.edu/pub/er/erm04/erm0450.asp

Dralle, A. (2007). What instructional technology skills should new teachers possess? *VSTE Edge, 4*(7). Retrieved April 15, 2009, from http:// www.vste.org/ publications/ edge/ attach/ ve_0407/ edge_v4n7.htm.

Draude, B., & Brace, S. (2000). *Assessing the impact of technology on teaching and learning: student perspectives*. Murfreesboro, TN: Middle Tennessee State University. Retrieved May 21, 2007, From http://www.mtsu.edu/~itconf/proceed99/brace.htm1

Drennan, J., Kennedy, J., & Pisarski, A. (2005). Factors affecting student attitudes toward flexible online learning in management education. *The Journal of Educational Research, 98*(6), 331–338..doi:10.3200/JOER.98.6.331-338

Duch, B., Groh, S., & Allen, D. (2001). *The power of problem-based learning*. Sterling, VA: Stylus Publishing.

Duhaney, D. C. (2000). Teacher Education: Preparing Teachers to Integrate Technology. *International Journal of Instructional Media, 29*(1), 23–29.

Dyer, R. D., Reed, P. A., & Berry, R. Q. (2006). Investigating the relationship between high school technology education and test scores for algebra I and geometry. *Journal of Technology Education, 17*(2), 7–17.

Dzvimbo, K. P. (2005, October 27-28). The African Virtual University: A Strategic Approach to Open Educational Resources. In *Proceedings of the 2005 LINC Symposium*, Cambridge, MA. Retrieved November 28, 2007, from http://ocw.mit.edu/OcwWeb/web/home/home/index.htm

Eason, K. (1988). *Information technology and organizational change*. Bristol, PA.: Taylor & Francis.

Eastman, J. K., & Swift, C. O. (2002). Enhancing collaborative learning: Discussion boards and chat rooms as project communication tools. *Business Communication Quarterly, 65*(3), 29–41. doi:10.1177/108056990206500304

Economist. (2007). *Rural China: Missing the barefoot doctor*. Retrieved November 22, 2007, from http://www.economist.com/displaystory.cfm?story_id=9944734

Edyburn, D., Higgins, K., & Boone, R. (2005). *Handbook of special education technology research and practice*. Whitefish Bay, WI: Knowledge by Design, Inc.

Einarsson, G. (1972, August). An Advanced Course in Communication Systems Based on Case Studies. *IEEE Transactions on Education, 15*(3), 156–160. doi:10.1109/TE.1972.4320748

Ellis, A., Carswell, L., Bernat, A., Deveaux, D., Frison, P., Meisalo, V., et al. (1999). Resources, tools, and techniques for problem based learning in computing. In *Proceedings of the ITiCSE '98*. New York: ACM ITICSE.

Ertmer, P. (2005). Teacher pedagogical beliefs: The final frontier in our quest for technology integration? *Educational Technology Research and Development, 53*(4), 25–39. doi:10.1007/BF02504683

ETC. (2005). *Ethiopian Telecommunication Corporation: ETC introduced sound tariff adjustments on its Internet Service Rates*. Retrieved November 15, 2007, from http://www.ethionet.et/publications/eNews/enews_june_17_2005.html

Evans, E. (2005). Autonomous learning or social practice? Students' construction of technological literacy. *Journal of literacy technology, 5*(1), Retrieved July 20, 2009 from http://www.literacyandtechnology.org/v5/ellen_evans_05.pdf

Ezer, J. F. (2005). *The interplay of institutional forces behind higher ICT education in India*. Unpublished PhD dissertation, London School of Economics.

Fabry, D., & Higgs, J. (1997). Barriers to the effective use of technology in education. *Journal of Educational Computing, 17*(4), 385–395.

Fagan, M. H., Neill, S., & Wooldridge, B. R. (2004). An empirical investigation into the relationship between computer self-efficacy, anxiety, experience, support and usage. *Journal of Computer Information Systems, 44*(2), 95–106.

Falk, R. F., & Miller, N. B. (1992). *A primer for soft modeling*, Akron, OH: The University of Akron Press.

Farmer, J. (2004). *Communication dynamics: Discussion Boards, weblogs and the development of communities of inquiry in online learning environments*. Retrieved October 26, 2009, from http://incsub.org/blog/2004/communication-dynamics-discussion-boards-weblogs-and-the-development-of-communities-of-inquiry-in-online-learning-environments-of-inquiry-in-online-learning-environments

Farmer, R. (2003). *Instant messaging-collaborative tool or educator's nightmare!* Retrieved March 30, 2009, from http://naWeb.unb.ca/poceedings/2003/PaperFarmer.html

Farrior, E. S., & Gallagher, M. L. (2000). An evaluation of distance education. *Topics in Clinical Nutrition, 15*(4), 10–18.

Fasko, D. J. (2003, April). *Case Studies and Methods in Teaching and Learning*. Paper presented at the annual meeting of the Society of Educators and Scholars, Louisville, KY.

Fetter, M. (2009). Curriculum Strategies to Improve Baccalaureate Nursing Information Technology Outcomes. *The Journal of Nursing Education, 48*(2), 86–90. doi:10.3928/01484834-20090201-05

Fetterman, D. M. (2002). Web surveys to digital movies: Technological tools of the trade. *Educational Researcher, 31*(6), 29–37. doi:10.3102/0013189X031006029

Fill, K., & Ottewill, R. (2006). Sink or swim: taking advantage of developments in video streaming. *Innovations in Education and Teaching International, 43*(4), 397–408. doi:10.1080/14703290600974008

Fillip, B. (2002). Information And Communication Technologies (Icts) To Help Disadvantaged Groups Help Themselves. *Japan International Cooperation Agency (Jica) U.S.A. Office*. Retrieved February 23, 2006, from http://www.jica.go.jp/usa/topics/pdf/it.pdf

Finneran, K. (2000). Let them eat pixels. *Issues in Science and Technology, 1*(3), 1–4.

Fisher, W. (1985). The narrative paradigm: An elaboration. *Communication Monographs, 52*, 347–367. doi:10.1080/03637758509376117

Fisher, W. (1989). Clarifying the narrative paradigm. *Communication Monographs, 56*, 55–58. doi:10.1080/03637758909390249

Fjermestad, H. S. & Zhang, Y. (2005). Effectiveness for students: Comparisons of "in-seat" and aln courses. In S. Hiltz & R. Goldman (Eds.), *Learning Together Online: Research on Asynchronous Learning Networks* (pp. 39-79). London, UK: Lawrence Erlbaum Associates.

Flately, M. E. (2005). Blogging for enhanced teaching and learning. *Business Communication Quarterly*, 68(1), 77–80. doi:10.1177/108056990506800111

Flowers, T. A., & Flowers, A. L. (2008). Factors affecting urban African American high school students' achievement in reading. *Urban Education*, 43(2), 154–171. doi:10.1177/0042085907312351

Fornell, C., & Bookstein, F. L. (1982). Two structural equation models: LISREL and PLS applied to consumer exit-voice theory. *JMR, Journal of Marketing Research*, 19(4), 440–452. doi:10.2307/3151718

Fornell, C., & Larcker, D. F. (1981). Evaluating structural equation models with unobservable variables and measurement error. *JMR, Journal of Marketing Research*, 18(1), 39–50. doi:10.2307/3151312

Fornell, C., & Larcker, D. F. (1981). Evaluating structural equation models with unobservable variables and measurement error. *JMR, Journal of Marketing Research*, 48, 39–50. doi:10.2307/3151312

Fornell, C., Tellis, G. J., & Zinkhan, G. M. (1982). Validity assessment: a structural equations approach using partial least squares. In *Proceedings of the American Marketing Association Educators' Conference*.

Franz, D. P., Hopper, P. F., & Kritsonis, W. A. (2007). National Impact: Creating Teacher Leaders Through the Use of Problem-Based Learning. *National Forum of Applied Educational Research Journal*, 20(3), 1–9.

Franz, D., Pope, M., & Fredrick, R. (2005). Teaching preservice teachers to use mathematic-specific technology. In C. Crawford et al. (Eds.), *Proceedings of Society for Information Technology and Teacher Education International Conference 2005* (pp. 3462-3466). Chesapeake, VA: AACE.

Fredricksen, E., Pickett, A., Shea, P., Pelz, W., & Swan, K. (1999). *Factors influencing faculty satisfaction with asynchronous teaching and learning in the suny learning network*. Retrieved June 19, 2008 from http://www.aln-research.org/Data_Files/articles/full_text/fs-fredricksen.htm

Freire, P. (1994). *Pedagogy of the oppressed*. London: Continuum.

Fry, H., Pearce, R., & Bright, H. (2007). Re-working resource-based learning - a case study from a masters programme. *Innovations in Education and Teaching International*, 44(1), 79–91. doi:10.1080/14703290601081373

Fulk, J. (1993). Social construction of communication technology. *Academy of Management Journal*, 36(5), 921–950. doi:10.2307/256641

Fulk, J., Schmitz, J., & Steinfield, C. W. (1990). A social influence model of technology use. In Fulk, J., & Steinfield, C. W. (Eds.), *Organization and Communication Technology* (pp. 117–140). Newbury Park, CA: Sage.

Fulton, K., & Sibley, R. (2003). Barriers to equity. In Solomon, G., Allen, N., & Resta, P. (Eds.), *Toward digital equity: Bridging the divide in education* (pp. 14–24). Boston: Allyn & Bacon.

Gagne, R. M. (1987). *Instructional Technology: Foundation*. Hillsdale, NJ: Lawrence Erlbaum.

Gâlea, D., Leon, F., & Zaharia, M. H. (2003). E-learning Distributed Framework using Intelligent Agents. In M. Craus, D. Gâlea, & A. Valachi (Eds.), *New Trends in Computer Science and Engineering* (pp. 159-163). ISBN 973-9476-40-6

Gambill, S., Clark, J., & Maier, J. L. (1999). CIS vs MIS vs… : The name game. *Journal of Computer Information Systems*, 39(4), 22–25.

Gardner, D. G., Discenza, R., & Dukes, R. L. (1993). The measurement of computer attitudes: an empirical comparison of available scales. *Journal of Educational Computing Research*, 9, 487–507. doi:10.2190/DXLM-5J80-FNKH-PP2L

Garland, K. J., & Noyes, J. M. (2004). Computer Experience: a poor predictor of computer attitudes. *Computers in Human Behavior*, 20, 823–840..doi:10.1016/j.chb.2003.11.010

Garofalo, J., Drier, H., Harper, S., & Timmerman, M. A. (2000). Promoting appropriate uses of technology in mathematics teacher preparation. *Contemporary Issues in Technology and Teacher Education, 1*(1). Retrieved March 9, 2009 from http://www. citejournal. org/vol1/ iss1/ currentissues/ mathematics/article1.htm

Garrison, D. R., & Kanuka, H. (2004). Blended learning: Uncovering its transformative potential in higher education. *The Internet and Higher Education, 7*(2), 95–105. doi:10.1016/j.iheduc.2004.02.001

Garrison, D., & Kanuka, H. (2004). Blended learning: Uncovering its transformative potential in higher education. *The Internet and Higher Education, 7*(2), 95–105. doi:10.1016/j.iheduc.2004.02.001

Garrison, D. R., & Anderson, T. (2003). *E-Learning in the 21st century, A framework for research and practice*. New York: Routledgefalmer. doi:10.4324/9780203166093

Gay, G., Trumbull, D., & Mazur, J. (1991). Navigational Strategies and Guidance Tools for a Hypermedia Program. *Journal of Educational Computing Research, 7*(2), 189–202.

Gay, L. R., & Airasian, P. (2003). *Educational Research: Competencies for Analysis and Applications* (7th ed.). Upper Saddle River, NJ: Pearson Education.

Gefen, D., Straub, D. W., & Boudreau, M. C. (2000). Structural equation modeling and regression: Guidelines for research practice. *Communications of the Association for Information Systems, 4*(7), 1–30.

Geisert, P., & Futrell, M. (2000). *Teachers, computers, and curriculum: Microcomputers in the classroom*. Boston, MA: Allyn and Bacon.

Gen, M., & Cheng, R. (1997). *Genetic Algorithms and Engineering Design*. New York: John Wiley & Sons.

Georgina, D. A. (2008). *Technology Integration in Higher Education Pedagogy: Faculty Perceptions of Integration Skills*. Saarbucken, Germany: VDM & Co. KG, Org.

Geske, J. (1992). Overcoming the drawbacks of the large lecture class. *College Teaching, 40*, 151.

Gilroy, D. F., & Desai, H. B. (1986). Computer anxiety: Sex, race, and age. *International Journal of Man-Machine Studies, 25*, 711–719. doi:10.1016/S0020-7373(86)80084-0

Gils, F. (2005, February 17-18). *Potential applications of digital storytelling in education*. Paper presented at the 3rd Twente Student Conference on IT, University of Twente, Faculty of Electrical Engineering, Mathematics and Computer Science, Enschede, The Netherlands.

Giotopoulos, K. C., Alexakos, C. E., Beligiannis, G. N., & Likothanassis, S. D. (2005). Computational Intelligence Techniques and Agents' Technology in E-learning Environments. *International Journal of Information Technology, 2*(2), 147–156.

Girl, T., & Chong, L. (1998). Student teachers' perception of information technology and creativity. In Waas, M. (Ed.), *Enhanced learning: Challenge of integrating thinking and Information Technology into the Curriculum* (*Vol. 2*, pp. 584–591).

Glyer-Culver, B. (2003). *A Survey of Former Business Students (General Business, Management, Marketing, Real Estate). Summary Findings of Respondents District-Wide*. Sacramento, CA: Los Rios Community College, Office of Institutional Research.

Godara, V. (2007). E-business applications and information technologies: Providing new opportunities for women. *Business Review (Federal Reserve Bank of Philadelphia), 8*(1), 154–161.

Godwin-Jones, B. (2003). Emerging technologies Blogs and Wikis: Environments for on-line collaboration. *Language Learning & Technology, 7*(2), 12-16. Retrieved October 26, 2009, from http://llt.msu.edu/vol7num2/ emerging/default.html

Goel, S. (2006). Competency focused engineering education with reference to IT related disciplines: Is the Indian system ready for transformation? *Journal of Information Technology Education,* (5): 27–52.

Gong, M., Xu, Y., & Yu, Y. (2004). An enhanced Technology Acceptance Model for web-based learning. *Journal of Information Systems Education, 15*(4), 365–374.

Gonzalez, C. L., & De Montes, L. S. (2001). Effective practices in distance education. *Computers in the Schools*, *18*(2/3), 61–77.

Goodhue, D. L. (1995). Understanding user evaluations of information systems. *Management Science*, *41*(12), 1827–1844. doi:10.1287/mnsc.41.12.1827

Goodhue, D. L. (1998). Development and measurement validity of a task-technology fit instrument for user evaluations of information systems. *Decision Sciences*, *29*(1), 105–138. doi:10.1111/j.1540-5915.1998.tb01346.x

Goodhue, D. L., & Thompson, R. L. (1995). Task-technology fit and individual performance. *MIS Quarterly*, *19*, 213–236. doi:10.2307/249689

Goodson, I. F. (1988). *The making of curriculum: Collected essays.* London, UK: The Falmer Press.

Gordillo, S., Rossi, G., Moreira, A., Araujo, J., Vairetti, C., & Urbieta, M. (2006). Modeling and Composing Navigational Concerns in Web Applications: Requirements and Design Issues. In *Proceedings of LA-Web*.

Gorgone, J. T., Gray, P., Feinstein, D., Kasper, G. M., Luftman, J. N., & Stohr, E. A. (2000). MSIS 2000 model curriculum and guidelines for graduate degree programs in Information Systems. *Communications of the Association for Information Systems*, (3): 1–51.

Gorgone, J. T., Davis, G. B., Valacich, J. S., Topi, H., Feinstein, D. L., & Longenecker, H. E. (2002). *IS 2002 model curriculum and guidelines for undergraduate degree programs in Information Systems*. Association for Information Systems. Retrieved September 1, 2008, from http://www.acm.org/education/is2002.pdf

Grabe, M., & Grabe, C. (2008). *Integrating technology for meaningful learning* (5th ed.). Boston, MA: Houghton Mifflin Company.

Gramoll, K. (2001). An Internet Portal for Statics and Dynamics Engineering Courses. In *Proceedings of the International Conference of Engineering* (pp. 1-6).

Gribbons, B., & Herman, J. (1997). True and quasi-experimental designs. *Practical Assessment, Research & Evaluation*, *5*(14). Retrieved April 13, 2009 from http://PAREonline.net/getvn.asp?v=5&n=14

Gueldenzoph, L. E., Guidera, E., Whipple, D., Mertler, C., & Dutton, L. (1999-2000). Faculty use of instructional technology in the university classroom. *Journal of Educational Technology Systems*, *28*(2), 121–135. doi:10.2190/Q8B8-WC93-81CB-9Q0C

Gupta, U., & Houtz, L. (2000). High school students' perceptions of information technology kills and carrers. *Journal of Information Technology*, *14*(4), 2–8.

Gustafson, K. L., & Branch, R. M. (2007). What is instructional design? In R. Reiser & J. V. Dempsey (Eds.), *Trends and issues in instructional design and technology* (2nd ed., pp.

Gutek, G. L. (1988). *Philosophical and Ideological Perspectives on Education*. Englewood Cliffs, NJ: Prentice Hall.

Guttentag, S., & Eilers, S. (2004). *Roofs or RAM? Technology in urban schools*. Retrieved on October 26, 2008, from http://www.horizonmag.com/4/roofram.htm

Hafkin, N., & Taggart, N. (2001). *Gender, information technology, and developing countries: An analytic study*. Washington, DC: AED. Retrieved from http://www.usaid.gov/wid/pubs/it01.htm

Hagner, P. (2001). *Interesting practices and best systems in faculty engagement and support*. Retrieved from http://net.educause.edu/ir/library/pdf/NLI0017.pdf

Hahne, A. K., Benndorf, R., Frey, P., & Herzig, S. (2005). Attitude towards computer- based learning: determinants as revealed by a controlled interventional study. *Medical Education*, *39*, 935–943..doi:10.1111/j.1365-2929.2005.02249.x

Hair, J. F. Jr, Black, W. C., Babin, B. J., Anderson, R. E., & Tatham, R. L. (2006). *Multivariate data analysis* (6th ed.). Upper Saddle River, NJ: Prentice-Hall International.

Hair, F. J., Black, B., Babin, B., Anderson, E. R., & Tatham, L. R. (2006). *Multivariate data analysis*. Upper Saddle River, NJ: Prentice Hall.

Hair, J. F., Anderson, R. E., et al. (1998). *Multivariate Data Analysis*. Upper Saddle River, New Jersey, USA: Prentice Hall.

Hall, G. E., & Loucks, S. (1978). Teacher concerns as a basis for facilitating and personalizing staff development. *Teachers College Record, 80*, 36–53.

Hall, B. (1997). *Web-based Training Cookbook.* New York: John Wiley and Sons.

Hall, G., George, A., & Rutherford, W. (1979). *R & D Report No. 3032.* Austin, TX: University of Texas, Research and Development Center for Teacher Education.

Hallmark, J. R., Hanson, T. L., Padwick, G., Abel, D., & Stewart, P. (1993). *Communication apprehension remediation: The interaction effect of video self-observation and gender.* (Report No. CS508383) Miami, FL: Annual Meeting of the Speech Communication Association. (ERIC Document Reproduction Service No. ED363902).

Harasim, L. (2000). *Shift happens: Online education as a new paradigm in learning, internet and higher education special issue* (pp. 41-61). UK: Elsevier Science.

Hardaker, G. (2005). Conference report. *Campus-Wide Information Systems, 22*(4), 247–248.

Harley, D., & Maher, M. (2003). Technology enhancements in a large lecture course. *EDUCAUSE Quarterly, 26*(3), 27–33.

Harrison, A. W., & Rainer, R. K. (1992). An examination of the factor structures and concurrent validities for the computer attitude scale, the computer anxiety scale, and the computer self-efficacy scale. *Educational and Psychological Measurement, 52*, 735–745. doi:10.1177/0013164492052003024

Harrsch, M. (2003). RSS: The next killer app for education. *The Technology Source.* Retrieved March 30, 2009, from http://ts.mivu.org/default.asp?show=article&id=2010

Hasegawa, J. (2006). Practices for Real-time Distance Lecture Environments with Multimedia Supports. *Journal of Research Center for Distance Learning, 2*(2), 79–91.

Haskell, R. E. (1997). Academic Freedom, Tenure, and Student Evaluation of Faculty: Galloping Polls in the 21st Century. *Education Policy Analysis Archives, 5*(6). Huemer, M. (n.d). *Student Evaluations: A Critical Review.* Retrieved 15 January 2008, from http://home.sprynet.com/~owl1/sef.htm

Hattangdi, H., & Ghosh, A. (2009). Enhancing the quality and accessibility of higher education through the use of Information Communication Technology. *International Journal of Educational Management, 21*(6), 1–12.

Havelka, D. (2003). Students' beliefs and attitudes towards information technology. In *Proceedings of the ISECON*, San Diego, CA.

Havenstein, H. (2007). *UC Berkeley offers free course lectures on YouTube: Program launched this week offers 300 hours of videotaped courses and events. Computer-World.* Retrieved from November 4, 2007, from http://www.computerworld.com/action/article.do?command=viewArticleBasic&taxonomyId=13&articleId=9040959&intsrc=hm_topic

Hayashi, T. (2008, March). Regret aversion and opportunity dependence. *Journal of Economic Theory, 139*(1), 242. doi:10.1016/j.jet.2007.07.001

Hegney, D., Buikstra, E., Eley, R., Fallon, T., Gilmore, V., & Soar, J. (2007). *Nurses and information technology. An Australian Nursing Federation project funded by the Australian Government Department of Health and Ageing.* Commonwealth of Australia. Retrieved February 2, 2009, from http://www.anf.org.au/it_project/PDF/IT_Project.pdf

Heid, K. M. (1997). The technological revolution and the reform of school mathematics. *American Journal of Education, 106*(1), 5–61. doi:10.1086/444175

Heinssen, R. K. J., Glass, C. R., & Knight, L. A. (1987). Assessing computer anxiety: Development and validation of the computer anxiety rating scale. *Computers in Human Behavior, 3*, 49–59. doi:10.1016/0747-5632(87)90010-0

Hewitt, J. (2001). Beyond threaded discourse. *International Journal of Educational Telecommunications, 7*(3), 207–221.

Hill, J. R., & Hannafin, M. J. (2001). Teaching and learning in digital environments: The resurgence of resource-based learning. *ETR&D-Educational Technology Research and Development, 49*(3), 37–52. doi:10.1007/BF02504914

Hill, T. R., & Roldan, M. (2005). Toward Third Generation Threaded Discussions for Mobile Learning: Opportunities and Challenges for Ubiquitous Collaborative Environments. *Information Systems Frontiers*, 7(1), 55–70. doi:10.1007/s10796-005-5338-7

Hill, L. (2003). *Implementing a Practical e-Learning System*. Retrieved January 18, 2009 from http://agora. lakeheadu.ca/pre2004/december2002/elearning.html

Hiltz, S. R., & Wellman, B. (1997). Asynchronous Learning Networks as a Virtual Classroom Communication. *Journal of the Association for Computing Machinery*, 40(9), 44–49.

Hiltz, R. S., Kim, E., & Shea, P. (2007). Faculty motivators and de-motivators for teaching online: Results of focus group interviews at one university. In *Proceedings of the 40th Hawaii International Conference on System Sciences* (pp. 1-10).

Hines, R. A., & Pearl, C. E. (2004). Increasing interaction in web-based instruction: Using synchronous chats and asynchronous discussions. *Rural Special Education Quarterly*, 23, 33–36.

Hoag, A. M., Bhattacharya, S. S., Helsel, J., Hu, Y., Lee, S., & Lee, J. (2003). A literature review of computers and pedagogy for journalism and mass communication education. *Journalism & Mass Communication Educator*, 57(4), 398–412.

Hoffner, H. (2007). *The elementary teacher's digital toolbox*. Upper Saddle River, NJ: Prentice Hall.

Holmberg, B. (1998). What is new and what is important in distance education. *Open Praxis*, 1, 31–33.

Holsti, O. R. (1969). *Content Analysis for the Social Sciences and Humanities*. Reading, MA: Addison Wesley.

Honey, M., & Moeller, B. (1990). *Teachers' beliefs and technology integration: different values and different understandings*. New York: Center for Technology in Eduation.

Honig, H. (1997). Positions, power and practice: functionalist approach and translation quality assessment. *Current Issues in Language and Society*, 4(1), 15–19.

Hoppe, G., & Breitner, M. H. (2003). Business models for e-learning. In *Proceedings of E-Learning: Models, Instruments, Experiences, of Multi-Konferenz Wirtschaftsinformatik 2004*, Essen, Germany.

Horrigan, M. W. (2004, February). *Employment projections through 2012: Concepts and context*. Washington, DC: U.S. Bureau of Labor Statistics.

Houtz, L. E., & Gupta, U. G. (2001). Nebraska high school students' computer skills and attitudes. *Journal of Research on Computing in Education*, 33, 316–325.

Howard, L., & Remenyi, Z. (2006). Adaptive Blended Learning Environments. In *Proceedings of the 9th International Conference of Engineering Education* (pp. 1-6).

Howell, C. D. (2006). *Statistical Method for Psychology* (6th ed.). New York: Thomson Wadsworth Press.

Howland, J., & Wedman, J. (2004). A process model for faculty development: Individualizing technology learning. *Journal of Technology and Teacher Education*, 12(2), 239–262.

Huang, H. M., & Liaw, S. S. (2005). Exploring user's attitudes and intentions toward the web as a survey tool. *Computers in Human Behavior*, 21(5), 729–743.. doi:10.1016/j.chb.2004.02.020

Huba, M., & Freed, J. (2000). *Learner-Centered assessment on college campuses: Shifting the focus from teaching to learning*. Boston: Allyn and Bacon.

Hudiburg, R. A., Brown, S., & Jones, T. M. (1993). Psychology of computer use: XXXIX. Measuring computer users' stress: the computer hassles scale. *Psychological Reports*, 73(1), 923–929. doi:10.2466/pr0.1993.73.3.923

Hughes, C., & Hewson, L. (2001). Structuring communications to facilitate effecting teaching and learning online. In Maddux, C. D., & Johnsons, D. L. (Eds.), *The Web in Higher Education: Assessing the Impact and Fulfilling the Potential* (pp. 147–158). New York: Hawthorne Press.

Huntsberger, M., & Stavitsky, A. (2007). The new 'podagogy': Incorporating podcasting into the journalism education. *Journalism & Mass Communication Educator*, 61(4), 397–410.

Hurt, H. T., Joseph, K., & Cook, C. D. (1977). Scales for the measurement of innovativeness. *Human Communication Research, 4*(1), 58–65. doi:10.1111/j.1468-2958.1977.tb00597.x

Hyman, A. (2003). Twenty years of ListServ as an academic tool. *The Internet and Higher Education, 6*, 17–24. doi:10.1016/S1096-7516(02)00159-8

IBM Study Finds Consumers Prefer a Mobile Device Over the PC. (2008, October 22). Retrieved May 2, 2009, from http://www-03.ibm.com/press/us/en/press-release/25737.wss

IEEE. (2009). *LTSC.* Retrieved from http://ieeeltsc.org

Igbaria, M., & Chakrabarti, A. (1990). Computer anxiety and attitudes towards microcomputer use. *Behaviour & Information Technology, 9*(3), 229–241.. doi:10.1080/01449299008924239

Igbaria, M., & Parasuraman, S. (1989). A path analytic study of individual characteristics, computer anxiety and attitudes toward microcomputers. *Journal of Management, 15*(3), 373–388. doi:10.1177/014920638901500302

IMF. (2007). *International Monetary Fund: World Economic Outlook Database.* Retrieved November 25, 2007, from http://en.wikipedia.org/wiki/List_of_countries_by_GDP_%28nominal%29_per_capita

IMS. (2009). Retrieved from http://www.imsproject.org

INFOhio – The Information Network for Ohio's Schools and the Northwest Ohio Educational Technology Foundation. (2007). Overview of Social Studies alignment training (PowerPoint presentation). *Social Studies Alignment Training Resources, 1*(1), 9.

INFOhio -The Information Network for Ohio's Schools and the Northwest Ohio Educational Technology Foundation. (2007). Alignment criteria and process (PowerPoint presentation). In *Social Studies Alignment Training Resources, 1*(1), 6.

Ingram, A. L., Hathorn, L. G., & Evans, A. (2000). Beyond chat on the internet. *Computers & Education, 35*, 21–35. doi:10.1016/S0360-1315(00)00015-4

Insight Magazine Releases, C. I. O. The Global Outsourcing Report. (2005, March 21). *CIO Insight.* Retrieved from http://www.ziffdavis.com/press/releases/050321.0.html

Instone, L. (2005). Conversations beyond the classroom: Blogging in a professional development course. In *Proceedings of ASCILITE conference,* Brisbane, Australia.

International Society for Technology in Education (ISTE). (2000). *National Educational Technology Standards (NETS) for teachers.* Retrieved November 15, 2008 from http://cnets.iste.org/teachers/

International Society for Technology in Education. (2008). *National Educational Technology Standards (NETS•T) and Performance Indicators for Teachers.* Retrieved March 5, 2009 from http://www.iste.org/AM/Template.cfm?Section=NETS

International Society for Technology in Education (ISTE). (2000). *National Educational Technology Standards (NETS) for teachers.* Retrieved March 25, 2008, from http://cnets.iste.org/teachers/

International Society for Technology in Education. (2007). Retrieved August 23, 2008, from http://www.iste.org/Content/NavigationMenu/Professional_Development/Programming_ at_NECC/Summits1/20078/Digital_Equity_Summit/national-consideration-DE.pdf

Islam, S. M. N., Munasinghe, M., & Clarke, M. (2003). Corrigendum to "Making long-term economic growth more sustainable: evaluating the costs and benefits". *Ecological Economics, 47*(2/3), 149–166. doi:10.1016/S0921-8009(03)00162-9

ISTE. (2000). *National Education Technology Standards and Performance Indicators for Teachers.* Retrieved March 0, 2009, from http://cnets.iste.org/teachers/pdf/page09.pdf

Iyamu, E. O. S. (2006). Promoting group-based learning. *Research on Learning, 8*(2), 27–35.

Jacobs, G. (1992). Hypermedia and Discovery-Based Learning: A Historical Perspective. *British Journal of Educational Technology, 23*(2), 113–121.

Jacobsen, M., Clifford, P., & Friesen, S. (2002). Preparing teachers for technology integration: Creating a culture of inquiry in the context of use. *Contemporary Issues in Technology and Teacher Education, 2*(3). Retrieved July 15, 2009, from http://www.citejournal.org/vol2/iss3/currentpractice/article2.cfm

James, J. (2004). Reconstructing the digital divide from the perspective of a large, poor, developing country. *Journal of Information Technology, 19,* 172–177. doi:10.1057/palgrave.jit.2000019

Jenkins, A., Blackman, T., Lindsay, R., & Paton-Saltzberg, R. (1998). Teaching and research: Student perspectives and policy implications. *Studies in Higher Education, 23*(2), 127–141. doi:10.1080/03075079812331380344

Jin, S., & Bagaka, J. (2005). The role of teacher practices and classroom characteristics on the "digital divide" in students' usage of technology tools: A multilevel analysis. *Contemporary Issues in Technology & Teacher Education, 5*(3), 318–329.

Johnson, R. S. (2002). *Using data to close the achievement gap: How to measure equity in our schools.* Thousand Oaks, CA: Corwin Press.

Jonassen, D. H., Campbell, J. O., & Davidson, M. E. (1994). Restructuring the Debate: Learning with Media. *Educational Technology Research and Development, 42*(2), 31–39. doi:10.1007/BF02299089

Jonassen, D. H. (2004). *Learning to solve problems: An instructional design guide.* San Francisco, CA: Pfeiffer.

Jones, T., & Clarke, V. A. (1994). A computer scale for secondary students. *Computers & Education, 22,* 315–318..doi:10.1016/0360-1315(94)90053-1

Jones, G. (2006). The Skinny on Web 2.0. *InformationWeek.* Retrieved October 26, 2006, from http://www.informationweek.com/story/showArticle.jhtml?articleID=193001026

Joshua, M. T., & Joshua, A. M. (2004). Attitude of nigerian secondary school teachers to student evaluation of teachers. *Teacher Development, 8*(1), 67–80. doi:10.1080/13664530400200227

Judge, S., & O'Bannon, B. (2008). Faculty integration of technology in teacher preparation: Outcomes of a development model. *Technology, Pedagogy and Education, 17*(1), 17–28. doi:10.1080/14759390701847435

Jun, T., & Kim, J. (2008, May). A theory of consumer referral. *International Journal of Industrial Organization, 26*(3), 6623. doi:10.1016/j.ijindorg.2007.03.005

Jung, I., Choi, S., Lim, C., & Leem, J. (2002). Effects of different types of interaction on learning achievement, satisfaction, and participation in Web-based instruction. *Innovations in Education and Teaching International, 39,* 153–162. doi:10.1080/14703290252934603

Kajder, S., & Swinson, J. (2004). Digital images in the language arts classroom. *Learning and Leading with Technology, 31*(8), 18-9, 21, & 46.

Karampiperis, P., & Sampson, D. (2005). Adaptive learning resources sequencing in educational hypermedia systems. *Educational Technology & Society, 8,* 128–147.

Katarzyna, M. (2002). *Knowledge Representation, Content Indexing and Effective Teaching of Fluid Mechanics Using Web-Based Content.* Unpublished master's thesis, MIT, Cambridge, MA.

Kautto-Koivula, K. (1996). Degree-oriented adult education in the work environment. In P. Ruohotie & P. P. Grimmett (Eds.), *Professional Growth and Development: Direction, Delivery and Dilemmas* (pp. 149-188). Canada and Finland: Career Education Books.

Kay, R. (1993). An explanation of and practical foundations for assessing attitudes toward computers: the Computer Attitude Measure (CAM). *Computers in Human Behavior, 9,* 371–386..doi:10.1016/0747-5632(93)90029-R

Keaveney, S. M., Huber, F., & Herrmann, A. (2007). A model of buyer regret: Selected prepurchase and postpurchase antecedents with consequences for the brand and the channel. *Journal of Business Research, 60*(12), 1207. doi:10.1016/j.jbusres.2006.07.005

Keegan, D. (1986). *The foundations of distance education.* London: Croom Helm.

Keengwe, J., & Anyanwu, L. (2007). Computer Technology-infused Learning Enhancement. *Journal of Science Education and Technology, 16*(5), 387-393. Keengwe, J., Onchwari, G., & Wachira, P. (2008). The Use of Computer Tools to Support Meaningful Learning. *AACE Journal, 16*(1), 77–92.

Keengwe, J. (2007). Faculty Integration of Technology into Instruction and Students' perceptions of Computer Technology to Improve Student Learning. *Journal of Information Technology Education, 6,* 169–180.

Keengwe, J., Onchwari, G., & Wachira, P. (2008). Computer technology integration and student learning: Barriers and promise. *Journal of Science Education and Technology, 17*(6), 560–565. doi:10.1007/s10956-008-9123-5

Keengwe, J. (2007). Faculty Integration of Technology into Instruction and Students' perceptions of Computer Technology to Improve Student Learning. *Journal of Information Technology Education, 6*, 169–180.

Kellum, G., & Hale, S. T. (2007). E-learning: educating the 21st century speech-language pathologists. *ASHA Leaders, 12*(14), 24–25.

Kelly, G. (2008). A Collaborative Process for Evaluating New Educational Technologies. *Campus-Wide Information Systems, 25*(2), 105–113. doi:10.1108/10650740810866594

Kenny, A. (2002). Online learning: enhancing nurse education? *Journal of Advanced Nursing, 38*(2), 127–135. doi:10.1046/j.1365-2648.2002.02156.x

Kerlinger, F. N., & Lee, H. B. (2000). *Foundations of behavioral research* (4th ed.). Fort Worth, TX: Harcourt.

Kidd, T. T. (2009). The dragon in the schools backyard: A review of literature on the uses of technology in urban schools. *The International Journal of Information and Communication Technology, 5*(1), 88–102.

Kilov, H., & Sack, I. (2009). Mechanisms for Communication between Business and IT Experts. *Computer Standards & Interfaces, 31*, 98–109. doi:10.1016/j.csi.2007.11.001

Kirsch, I., Braun, H., Yamamoto, K., & Sum, A. (2007). *America's Perfect Storm: Three Forces Changing Our Nation's Future.* Princeton, NJ: Educational Testing Service.

Klem, L. (2000). Structural equation modeling. In Grimm, L. G., & Yarnold, P. R. (Eds.), *Reading and understanding more multivariate statistics.* Washington, DC: American Psychology Association.

Klemm, E. B. (2003). Cognitive load Criteria for Critical Evaluation and Selection of Web-Based Resources for Science Teaching. In *Proceedings of the Annual Meeting Report of National Association for Research in Science Teaching* (pp. 2-9).

Kline, R. B. (2005). *Principles and practice of structural equation modeling* (2nd ed.). New York: Guilford Press.

Koch, N. (2000). *Software Engineering for Adaptive Hypermedia Systems.* Unpublished doctoral dissertation, Ludwig-Maximilians-University, Munich, Germany. Retrieved from http://www.pst.informatik.uni-muenchen.de/ personen/ kochn/ PhDThesisNoraKoch.pdf

Koh, M. H., & Branch, R. M. (2004, October). *Online Learning Environments: A Report of an Instructional Design Case Event.* Chicago: Association for Educational Communications and Technology.

Kolakowski, N. (2009, March 16). *Number of People Using Mobile Devices Doubles: comScore.* Retrieved May 2, 2009, from http://www.eweek.com/c/a/Mobile-and-Wireless/Number-of-People-Using-Mobile-Devices-Doubles-ComScore-879862/

Kolodner, J. L., Hmelo, C. E., & Narayan, N. H. (1996). Problem-based learning meets case-based reasoning. In *Proceedings of the 1996 international conference on Learning sciences* (pp. 188-195). Evanston, IL: International Society of the Learning Sciences.

Koo, Y. (2008). *Development of Mobile Learning Software. Unpublished master's capstone report.* Monterey Bay, CA: California State University.

Koohang, A., Britz, J., & Seymour, T. (2006). Hybrid/Blended Learning: Advantages, Challenges, Design, and Future Directions. In *Proceedings of the Informing Science and IT Education Joint Conference*, Manchester, UK.

Koschmann, T., Kelson, A. C., Feltovich, P. J., & Barrows, H. S. (1998). Computer-supported problem-based learning: A principled approach to the use of computers in collaborative learning. In Koschmann, T. (Ed.), *CSCL: Theory and practice of an emerging paradigm* (pp. 83–124). Mahwah, NJ: Lawrence Erlbaum.

Kozma, R. (2005). National Policies That Connect ICT-Based Education Reform To Economic And Social Development. *Human Technology, 1*(2), 117–156.

Krathwohl, D. R., Bloom, B. S., & Masia, B. B. (1964). *Taxonomy of educational objectives: Handbook II: Affective domain.* New York: David McKay Co.

Krause, U.-M., & Stark, R. (2006). Vorwissen aktivieren. In Mandl, H., & Friedrich, H. (Eds.), *Handbuch Lernstrategien* (pp. 38–49). Gottingen, Germany: Hogrefe.

Krause, S. D. (2004). When blogging goes bad: A cautionary tale about blogs, email lists, discussion, and interaction. *Kairos, 9*(1). Retrieved October, 2009, from http://english.ttu.edu/kairos/9.1/binder.html?praxis/krause/index.html

Kulik, J. (2003). *Effects of using instructional technology in elementary and secondary schools: What controlled evaluation studies say*. Arlington, VA: SRI International.

Kurz, T. L., Middleton, J. A., & Yanik, H. B. (2005). A taxonomy of software for mathematics instruction. *Contemporary Issues in Technology & Teacher Education, 5*(2), 123–137.

Kvavik, R., & Caruso, J. (2005). *ECAR study of students and information technology: convenience, connection, control and learning*. Boulder, Co: Educause Center for applied Research. Retrieved May 5, 2007, from http://www.educause.edu/LibraryDetailPage/666?ID=ERS0506

Lai, S. Q., Lee, C. L., Yeh, Y. J., & Ho, C. T. (2005). A study of satisfaction in blended learning for small and medium enterprises. *International Journal of Innovation and Learning, 2*(3), 319–334. doi:10.1504/IJIL.2005.006373

Lambert, J. (2007). *Digital storytelling cookbook*. Retrieved March 1, 2009 from http://www.storycenter.org/cookbook.html

Lamshed, R., Berry, M., & Armstrong, L. (2002). *Blogs: Personal e-learning spaces*. http://www.binaryblue.com.au/docs/blogs.pdf

Landweber, L. L. (1997). *Mapping the Global Spread of the NET*. Retrieved from http://www.mundi.net/maps/maps_011/

Lang, U. (2004). Virtual and Augmented Reality Developments for Engineering Applications. In *Proceedings of the European Congress on Computational Methods in Applied Sciences and Engineering* (pp. 1-16).

Learning Technology Standards Committee. (2002). *IEEE Standard for Learning Object Metadata. IEEE Standard 1484.12.1*. New York: IEEE.

LeBlanc, G., & Nguyen, N. (1997). Searching for excellence in business education: an exploratory study of customer impressions of service quality. *International Journal of Educational Management, 11*(2), 72. doi:10.1108/09513549710163961

Lederer, A. L., Maupin, D. J., Sens, M. P., & Zhuang, Y. (2000). The technology acceptance model and the World Wide Web. *Decision Support Systems, 29*, 269–282. doi:10.1016/S0167-9236(00)00076-2

Lee, J. K., & Lee, W. K. (2008). The relationship of e-Learner's self-regulatory efficacy and perception of e-Learning environmental quality. *Computers in Human Behavior, 24*(1), 32–47. doi:10.1016/j.chb.2006.12.001

Lee, H., & Hollebrands, K. (2008). Preparing to teach mathematics with technology: An integrated approach to developing technological pedagogical content knowledge. *Contemporary Issues in Technology & Teacher Education, 8*(4), 326–341.

Lee, K. (2007). Online Collaborative Case Study Learning. *Journal of College Reading and Learning, 37*(2), 82–100.

Lee, Y., Kozar, K. A., & Larsen, K. R. T. (2003). The technology acceptance model: Past, present and future. *Communications of the Association for Information Systems, 12*, 752–780.

Lee, P. W. R., & Chan, F. T. (2007). Blended learning: Experiences of adult learners in Hong Kong. In J. Fong & F. L. Wang (Eds.), *Blended Learning* (pp. 79-87). Retrieved April 13, 2009 from http://www. cs.cityu.edu.hk/ ~wbl2007/ WBL2007_Proceedings_HTML/ WBL2007_PP079-087_Lee.pdf

Leeds, E., Raven, A., & Brawley, B. (2007). Primary traits of oral business presentation: translatable use for assessment in a virtual learning environment. *College Teaching Methods & Styles Journal, 3*(4), 21.

Leeds, E., & Maurer, R. (2009). Using digital video technology to reduce communication apprehension in business education. *INFORMS Transactions on Education, 10*(1).

Leedy, P., & Ormrod, J. (2001). *Practical research. Planning and design*. (7th Ed.) Upper Saddle River, NJ, USA: Merrill-Prentice Hall.

Legris, P., Ingham, J., & Collerette, P. (2003). Who do people use information technology? A critical review of the technology acceptance model. *Information & Management, 40*, 191–204. doi:10.1016/S0378-7206(01)00143-4

Leidner, D. E., & Jarvenpaa, S. L. (1995). The use of information technology to enhance management school education: A theoretical view. *MIS Quarterly, 19*, 265. doi:10.2307/249596

Lent, R. W., Brown, S. D., & Hackett, G. (1994). Toward a unifying social cognitive theory of career and academic interest, choice, and performance. *Journal of Vocational Behavior*, (45): 79–122. doi:10.1006/jvbe.1994.1027

Leonard-Barton, D., & Deschamps, I. (1988). Managerial influence in the implementation of new technology. *Management Science, 34*, 1252–1265. doi:10.1287/mnsc.34.10.1252

Leventman, P., Finley, M., & Brashler, P. (2004). *Gender equity in the U.S. information technology workforce. Annual Meetings of the American Sociological Association.* Retrieved from http://www.allacademic.com//meta/p_mla_apa_research_citation/1/0/9/6/8/pages109689/p109689-1.php

Li, N., & Kirkup, G. (2007). Gender and culture differences in Internet use: a study of China and the UK. *Computers & Education, 48*, 301–317. doi:10.1016/j.compedu.2005.01.007

Li, S. C. S. (2004). Exploring the factors influencing the adoption of interactive cable television services in Taiwan. *Journal of Broadcasting & Electronic Media, 48*(3), 466–483. doi:10.1207/s15506878jobem4803_7

Liarokapis, F. (2002). Multimedia Augmented Reality Interface for E-Learning (MARIE). *World Transactions on Engineering and Technology Education, 1*(2), 173–176.

Liarokapis, F. (2004). Web3D Augmented Reality to Support Engineering Education. *World Transactions on Engineering and Technology Education, 3*(1), 11–14.

Lieblich, A., Tuval-Mashiach, R., & Zilber, T. (1998). *Narrative research: Reading, analysis and interpretation.* Newbury Park, CA: Sage.

Light, R. J., Singer, J. D., & Willett, J. B. (1990). *By design: Planning research on higher education.* Cambridge, MA: Harvard University Press.

Lim, C. P., & Chai, C. S. (2004). An activity-theoretical approach to research of ICT integration 13 in Singapore schools: Orienting activities and learner autonomy. *Computers & Education, 43*(3), 215–236. doi:10.1016/j.compedu.2003.10.005

Lin, X., & Guan, J. (2002). Patient satisfaction and referral intention: Effect of patient-physician match on ethnic origin and cultural similarity. *Health Marketing Quarterly, 20*(2), 49. doi:10.1300/J026v20n02_04

Lin, K. (2008). Building on Components into Traditional Instruction in Pre-Service Teacher Education: The Good, the Bad and the Ugly. *International Journal for Scholarship of Teacher and Learning, 2*(1).

Littlechild, J. (2008, May/Jun.). What Motivates Clients to Provide Referrals? *Journal of Financial Planning*, 10–12.

Livraghi, G. (2007a). *Data-The Internet in Africa: Host Count.* Retrieved November 25, 2007, from http://gandalf.it/data/africeng.htm

Livraghi, G. (2007b). *Data on Internet Activity Worldwide: Host Count.* Retrieved November 25, 2007, from http://gandalf.it/data/data1.htm

Lomerson, W. L., & Pollacia, L. (2005, October). Declining CIS Enrollment: An Examination of Pre-College Factors. In *Proceedings of ISECON on EDSIG*, Columbus, OH (Vol. 22).

Looney, C. A., & Akbulut, A. Y. (2007). Combating the IS Enrollment Crisis: The Role of Effective Teachers in Introductory IS Courses. *Communications of the Association for Information Systems, 19*(1), 1–19.

Lou, Y., Abrami, P. C., & d'Apollonia, S. (2001). Small group and individual learning with technology: a meta-analysis. *Review of Educational Research, 71*(3), 449–521. doi:10.3102/00346543071003449

Lowry, M., & Johnson, M. (1999). Computer assisted learning: the potential for teaching and assessing in nursing. *Nurse Education Today, 19*, 521–526. doi:10.1054/nedt.1999.0390

Loyd, B. H., & Gressard, C. (1984). Reliability and factorial validity of computer attitude scales. *Educational and Psychological Measurement, 44*, 501–505.. doi:10.1177/0013164484442033

Loyd, B. H., & Loyd, D. E. (1985). The reliability and validity of an instrument for the assessment of computer attitudes. *Educational and Psychological Measurement, 45*, 903–908..doi:10.1177/0013164485454021

Luke, C. (2000). Cyber-schooling and technological change: Multiliteracies for new times. In Cope, B., & Kalantzis, M. (Eds.), *Multiliteracies: Literacy learning and the design of social futures* (pp. 69–91). New York: Routledge.

Madden, M. (2008). *Podcast downloading. Pew Internet & American Life Project Memo.* Retrieved January 16, 2009, from http://www.pewinternet.org/pdfs/PIP_Podcast_2008_Memo.pdf

Maes, J. D., Weldy, T. G., & Icenogle, M. L. (1997). A managerial perspective: Oral communication competency is most important for business students. *Journal of Business Communication, 34*(67).

Magolda, P. (2006). Critical fusion-technology and equity in secondary education. *AACE Journal, 14*(3), 287–311.

Mandel, N., & Nowlis, S. M. (2008, June). The Effect of Making a Prediction about the Outcome of a Consumption Experience on the Enjoyment of That Experience. *The Journal of Consumer Research, 35*(1), 9. doi:10.1086/527339

Marcel, K. (2002, December). Can law be taught effectively online? *JURIST.* Retrieved May 5, 2005 from http://jurist.law.pitt.edu/lessons/lesdeco2.php

Marcoulides, G., & Saunders, C. (2006). PLS: A Silver Bullet? *MIS Quarterly, 30*(2), iii–ix.

Marija, J. N. (1997). *SPSS 6.1 Guide to Data Analysis.* New Jersey: Prentice Hall.

Marra, R. M., Rodgers, K. A., Shen, D., & Bogue, B. (2009). Women Engineering Students and Self-Efficacy: A Multi-Year, Multi-Institution Study of Women Engineering Student Self-Efficacy. *Journal of Engineering Education, 98*(1), 27–38.

Marsh, H. W. (1986). Negative item bias in rating scales for preadolescent children: a cognitive phenomenon. *Developmental Psychology, 22*(1), 37–49..doi:10.1037/0012-1649.22.1.37

Martin, J., & VanLehn, K. (1995). Student assessment using bayesian nets. *International Journal of Human-Computer Studies, 42*, 575–591. doi:10.1006/ijhc.1995.1025

Martin-Blas, T., & Serrano-Fernandez, A. (2009). The role of new technologies in the learning process: Moodle as a teaching tool in Physics. *Computers & Education, 52*(1), 35–44. doi:10.1016/j.compedu.2008.06.005

Martinez, M. (2003). High attrition rates in e-Learning: Challenges, predictors, and solutions. *The eLearning Developers'Journal,* 1-9. Retrieved February 23, 2009, from http://www.elearningguild.com/pdf/2/071403MGT-L.pdf

Marton, F., & Säljö, R. (1976). On Qualitative differences in learning:Outcome and process. *The British Journal of Educational Psychology, 46*, 4–11.

Marton, F., & Säljö, R. (2005). Approaches to Learning. In F. Marton, D. Hounsell, & N. Entwistle (Eds.), *The Experience of Learning: Implications for teaching and studying in higher education* (3rd Internet ed.). Edinburgh, UK: University of Edinburgh, Centre for Teaching, Learning and Assessment.

Maruyama, G. (1998). *Basics of structural equation modelling.* Thousand Oaks, CA: Sage Publications.

Marwan, A. (2008). An Analysis of Australian Students' Use of Information and Communications Technology (ICT). *International Journal of instructional Technology and Distance Learning, 5*(11), 45-54.

Mason, R. (2000). From distance education to online education. *The Internet and Higher Education, 3*(1/2), 63–74. doi:10.1016/S1096-7516(00)00033-6

Massoud, S. L. (1991). Computer attitudes and computer knowledge of adult students. *Journal of Educational Computing Research, 7*, 269–291. doi:10.2190/HRRV-8EQV-U2TQ-C69G

Masthoff, J. (2006). The User As Wizard. In *Proc. of the Fifth Workshop on User-Centred Design and Evaluation of Adaptive Systems* (pp. 460-469).

Mathieson, K., Peacock, E., & Chinn, W. C. (2001). Extending the Technology Acceptance Model: The influence of perceived user resources. *The Data Base for Advances in Information Systems, 32*(3), 86–112.

Maxwell, J. R., Gilberti, A. F., & Mupinga, D. M. (2006). *Use of Case Study Methods in Human Resource Management, Development, and Training. Terre Haute.* IN: Indiana State University.

Mayo, N., Kajs, K., & Tanguma, J. (2005). Longitudinal study of technology training to prepare future teachers. *Educational Research Quarterly, 29*(1), 3–15.

Mayo, M., & Mitrovic, A. (2000). Using a probabilistic student model to control problem difficulty. In G. Gauthier, C. Frasson, & K. VanLehn (Eds), *the Fifth International Conference on Intelligent Tutoring Systems* (pp. 524-533). Berlin: Springer.

Mbeki, M. (2005). *Underdevelopment in Sub-Saharan Africa: The role of the private sector and political elite. CATO Institute.* Retrieved November 22, 2007, from http://www.cato.org/pubs/fpbriefs/fpb85.pdf

McBride, A. (2005). Nursing and the informatics revolution. *Nursing Outlook, 53*(4), 183–191. doi:10.1016/j.outlook.2005.02.006

McCloskey, P. (2007). Consensus: Podcasting has no 'inherent' pedagogic value. *Campus Technology.* Retrieved April 21, 2008, from http://www.campustechnology.com/article.aspx?aid=49018

McConnell, J. J. (2006). Active and cooperative learning: further tips and tricks (part 3). *The SIGSCE Bulletin, 38*(2), 24–28.

McConnell, D. (2002). *Implementing Computer Supported Collaborative Learning* (2nd ed.). London: Kogan Page.

McCormick, P. (1996). There's no substitute for good teachers. *U.S. Catholic, 61*(6), 46–49.

McDonald, R. P., & Ho, M.-H. R. (2002). Principles and practice in reporting structural equation analyses. *Psychological Methods, 7*(1), 64–82. doi:10.1037/1082-989X.7.1.64

McDonald, J. K., & Gibbons, A. S. (2009). Technology I, II, and III: criteria for understanding and improving the practice of instructional technology. *Educational Technology Research and Development, 57*(3), 377–392. doi:10.1007/s11423-007-9051-8

McDrury, J., & Alterio, M. (2003). *Learning through Storytelling in Higher Education.* London: Kogan Page.

McGettrick, A., Boyle, R., Ibbett, R., Lloyd, J., Lovegrove, G., & Mander, K. (2005). Grand challenges in computing: Education-A summary. *The Computer Journal, 48*(1), 42–48. doi:10.1093/comjnl/bxh064

McGugan, S. (2002). Asynchronous computer mediated conferencing to support learning and teaching: An action research approach. *Journal of Hospitality, Leisure, Sport and Tourism Education, 1*(1), 29–42. doi:10.3794/johlste.11.9

McMahon, C. J. (2000). *Tutorials for Introduction to Materials Engineering.* Merrion Media.

McMillan, J. H., & Schumacher, S. (1997). *Research in education: A conceptual introduction* (4th ed.). Don Mills, ON: Longman.

Meadow, D. (2003). Digital storytelling: Research-based practice in new media. *Visual Communication, 2*(2), 189–193. doi:10.1177/1470357203002002004

Mehta, S., & Kalra, M. (2006). Information and Communication Technologies: A bridge for social equity and sustainable development in India. *The International Information & Library Review, 38*(3), 147–160. doi:10.1016/j.iilr.2006.06.008

Mello, L. R. (2006). Identifying success in the application of information and communication technology as a curriculum teaching and learning tool. *Technology, Pedagogy and Education, 15*(1), 95–106. doi:10.1080/14759390500435853

Meyer, E., & Land, R. (2003). *Threshold Concepts and Troublesome Knowledge: Linkages to Ways of Thinking and Practicing within the Disciplines, ETL Project Occasional report 4.* Retrieved October 27, 2008, from http://www.ed.ac.uk/etl/publications.html

Michalewicz, Z. (1990). *Genetic Algorithms + Data Structures = Evolution Programs.* Berlin: Springer-Verlag.

Mikie, F., & Anido, L. (2006). Towards a standard for mobile e-learning. In *Proceedings of the Networking, International Conference on Systems and International Conference on Mobile Communications and Learning Technologies.*

Miles, M. B., & Huberman, A. M. (1994). *Qualitative data analysis.* Thousand Oaks, CA: Sage Publications.

Miller, D. (2006, October 18). Podcasting at the University of Connecticut: Enhancing the educational experience. *Campus Technology*.

Miller, D. B. (2006). Podcasting at the University of Connecticut: Enhancing the educational experience. *Campus Technology*. Retrieved April 21, 2008, from http://www.campustechnology.com/article.aspx?aid=41255

Ministry of Education. (1997). *Masterplan for Information Technology*. Singapore: Ministry of Education.

Mislevy, R. J., & Gitomer, D. H. (1996). The role of probability-based inference in an intelligent tutoring system. *User Modeling and User-Adapted Interaction, 5*(3-4), 253–282. doi:10.1007/BF01126112

Mitchel, M. (1996). *An Introduction to Genetic Algorithms*. Cambride, MA: MIT Press.

Mitchem, K., Wells, D. H., & Wells, J. G. (2003). Effective integration of instructional technologies (IT): Evaluating professional development and instructional change. *Journal of Technology and Teacher Education, 11*(3), 399–416.

Mitra, A. (1998). Categories of computer use and their relationships with attitudes toward computers. *Journal of Research on Computing in Education, 30*(3), 281–295.

Miura, I. T. (1987). The relationship of computer self-efficacy expectations to computer interest and course enrollment in college. *Sex Roles, 16*, 303–311. doi:10.1007/BF00289956

Mizukami, M. D. (2002, July). *Learning from Cases and Bridging Some "Theory-Practice" Gaps*. Paper presented at the annual world assembly of the International Council on Education for Teaching, Amsterdam.

Mobile learning inspires the hard-to-reach. (2005). *Education & Training, 47*(8/9), 681-682.

Moch, M. K., & Morse, E. V. (1977). Size, centralization and organization adoption of innovations. *American Sociological Review, 42*(5), 716–725. doi:10.2307/2094861

Mödritscher, F., Manuel Garcia-Barrios, V., & Gütl, Ch. (2004). The Past, the Present and the future of adaptive E-Learning. In *Proceedings of the International Conference Interactive Computer Aided Learning*.

Moffett, D. (2001). *Using the Internet to Enhance Student Teaching and Field Experiences*. Paper presented at the annual meeting of the Mid-Western Educational Research Association, Chicago.

More, C. (2008). Digital stories targeting social skills for children with disabilities. *Intervention in School and Clinic, 43*(3), 168–177. doi:10.1177/1053451207312919

Morehead, P., Li, L., & LaBeau, B. (2007). Digital storytelling: Empowering prospective teachers' voices as future educators. In C. Crawford et al. (Eds.), *Proceedings of Society for Information Technology and Teacher Education International Conference 2007* (pp. 634-635). Chesapeake, VA: AACE

Mouly, G. J. (1978). *Educational Research: the art and science of investigation*. Heinenmann. Boston: Allyn and Bacon.

Muir, J. (2003). Decoding mobile device security. *Computer World*. Retrieved April 15, 2007, from http://www.computerworld.com/securitytopics/security/story/0,10801,82890,00.html

Murphy, C., Coover, D., & Owen, S. V. (1989). Development and validation of the computer self-efficacy scale. *Educational and Psychological Measurement, 49*(4), 893–899. doi:10.1177/001316448904900412

Murphy, C. (1994, July 17-22). Curriculum-enhanced MARC (CEMARC): a new cataloging format for school librarians. In *Proceedings of the 23rd Annual Conference of the International Association of School Librarianship*, Pittsburgh, Pennsylvania (pp. 79-80).

Murthy, N. R. (2001). The ICT Revolution: Can Asia Leapfrog Poverty Barriers? In *Proceedings of the Role of IT in Poverty Reduction, the 34th Asian Development Bank Annual Meeting*. Retrieved November 28, 2007, from http:// www.adb.org/ AnnualMeeting/ 2001/ Seminars/ murthy_ paper.pdf

Muyinda, P. B. (2007). M-Learning: pedagogical, technical and organisational hypes and realities. *Campus-Wide Information Systems, 24*(2), 97–104. doi:10.1108/10650740710742709

Nash, J. B., & Moroz, P. A. (1997). An examination of the factor structures of the computer attitude scale. *Journal of Educational Computing Research, 17*(4), 341–356. doi:10.2190/NGDU-H73E-XMR3-TG5J

Natcha, P., Sasaki, N., & Yamada, T. (2006). Development of Self-learning and Collaborative Learning with Media-mix Utility. In *Proceedings of the Japanese Association for Education of Information Studies, 22nd Conference* (pp. 190-1).

National Center for Education Statistics. (2000). *Public school teachers' use of computers and the Internet.* Washington DC: U. S. Department of Education.

National Council of Teachers of Mathematics. (2000). *Executive summary: Principles and Standards for School Mathematics.* Retrieved March 5, 2009 from http://www. nctm.org/ uploadedFiles/ Math_Standards/12752_exec_pssm.pdf

National Research Council. (2000). *How people learn: brain, mind, experience, and school.* Washington, DC: National Academy Press.

NCATE/ITEA/CTTE Program Standards. (2003). *Programs for the preparation of technology education teachers.* Retrieved April 9, 2008, from http:// www.ncate.org/ ProgramStandards/ ITEA/ ITEAStandards.doc

Negash, S. (2006a). ICT for Ethiopian Community Development. In Marshall, S., Taylor, W., & Yu, X. (Eds.), *Encyclopedia of Developing Regional Communities with Information and Communication Technology* (pp. 370–376). Hershey, PA: IGI Global.

Negash, S. (2005, June 18-19). Library and Educational Access for Progress (LEAP): Information access as enabler for development. In *Proceedings of the Third International Symposium on Ethiopian Development Studies*, Addis Ababa, Ethiopia.

Negash, S. (2006b, August 4-6). Information and Communication Technology (ICT) Investment in Economically Developing Countries. In *Proceedings of the Twelfth Americas Conference on Information Systems*, Acapulco, Mexico.

Nelson, W., & Palumbo, D. B. (1992). Learning, Instruction, and Hypermedia. *Journal of Educational Multimedia and Hypermedia, 1*(3), 281–299.

Neuhauser, P. C. (1993). *Corporate Legends and Lore: The Power of Storytelling as a Management Tool.* New York: McGraw-Hill.

Newmann, F. M., Bryk, A. S., & Nagoaka, J. (2001). *Authentic Intellectual Work and Standardized Tests: Conflict or Coexistence?* Chicago: Consortium on Chicago School Research.

Ng, S. L. (2005, March). Subjective Residential Environment and its Implications for Quality of Life Among University Students in Hong Kong. *Social Indicators Research, 71*(1-3), 467. doi:10.1007/s11205-004-8032-0

Ngai, E. W. T., Poon, J. K. L., & Chan, Y. H. C. (2007). Empirical examination of the adoption of WebCT using TAM. *Computers & Education, 48*(2), 250–267. doi:10.1016/j.compedu.2004.11.007

NHSIA. (2001). Health informatics competency profiles for the NHS. In *Proceedings of the NHS Information Authority, Ways of Working with Information Programme*, Winchester, UK.

Nickell, G. S., & Pinto, J. N. (1986). The computer attitude scale. *Computers in Human Behavior, 2*, 301–306.. doi:10.1016/0747-5632(86)90010-5

Nielsen Mobile. (July 2008). *Critical Mass: The Worldwide State of the Mobile Web.* Retrieved May 2, 2009, from http://www.nielsenmobile.com/documents/CriticalMass.pdf

Nobel, C. (2007, January 29). *Women in Technology: A call to action. InfoWorld.* Retrieved February 25, 2008, from http://www.infoworld.com/d/developer-world/women-in-technology-call-action-919

Norman, D. A. (1986). Cognitive engineering. In D. Norman & S. Draper (Eds.), *User Centered Systems Design.* Hillsdale, NJ: Lawrence Erlbaum Associates.

Norman, K. L. (1991). *The Psychology of Menu Selection.* Norwood, NJ: Ablex.

Novitzki, J. (2000). Asynchronous learning tools in the traditional classroom: A preliminary study on their effect (IR No. 058-617). In *Proceedings of the International Academy for Information Management Annual Conference*, Brisbane, Australia.

Nunamaker, J. F., Couger, J. D., & Davis, G. B. (1982). Information Systems curriculum recommendations for the 80s: Undergraduate and graduate programs. *Communications of the ACM, 25*(11), 781–805. doi:10.1145/358690.358698

Nwankwo, B. (2006, September). NCC, DBI train 12,000 lecturers in ICT. *The Guardian, 27,* 35.

Nworgu, B. G. (1991). *Educational Research: Basic issues and methodology.* Ibadan: Wisdom Publishers.

O'Bannon, B. W., & Puckett, K. (2007). *Preparing to use technology. A practical guide to curriculum integration.* Boston, MA: Allyn & Bacon.

O'Reilly, T. (2005). *Compact definition. O'Rielly Radar.* Retrieved October 26, 2009, from http://radar.oreilly.com/archives/2005/10/web_20_compact_definition.html

Ober, S. (1987). The status of postsecondary business communication instruction--1986 vs. 1982. *Journal of Business Communication, 24*(49).

Ober, S., & Wunsch, A. P. (1983). The status of business communication instruction in postsecondary institutions in the United States. *Journal of Business Communication, 20*(5).

Obiakor, F. E., & Beachum, F. D. (2005). *Urban education for the 21st century: Research, issues, and perspectives.* Springfield, IL: CC Thomas Publishing.

Oblinger, D. G., & Oblinger, J. L. (2005). *Educating the Net Generation.* EDUCAUSE. E-book. Retrieved July 25, 2008, from http://www.educause.edu/educatingthenetgen

Obringer, L. (2001). *How E-learning Works.* Retrieved March 18, 2008, from http://communication.howstuffworks.com/elearning.htm

Ogletree, S. M., & Williams, S. W. (1990). Sex and sex-typing effects on computer attitudes and aptitude. *Sex Roles, 23*(11), 703–712. doi:10.1007/BF00289258

Oh, C. H. (2003). Information communication technology and the new university: a view on eLearning. *The Annals of the American Academy of Political and Social Science, 585,* 134–153. doi:10.1177/0002716202238572

Ohio Department of Education. (2007). *Data Driven Decisions for Academic Achievement (D3A2).* Retrieved October 15, 2007 from http:// www.ode. state.oh.us/ GD/ Templates/ Pages/ODE/ODEDetail.aspx?Page=3&Topic RelationID=55&Content=34940

Ohio Department of Education. (2007). *D3A2 overview.* Retrieved October 15, 2007 from http://www.d3a2.org/about.asp

Ojeme, S. (2007, July 24). Don Calls for improved ICT development. *Punch Newspaper* (p. 20).

Okiy, R. B., & Tiemo, P. A. (2007). The Nigeria communication Commission and the Digital Bridge Institute First South-South Zonal Advance Digital Appreciation workshop for tertiary institution. *Library Hi. Tech New, 24*(3).

Olaniran, B. A. (1993). Integrative approach for managing successful computer-mediated communication technological innovations. *Ohio Speech Journal, 31,* 37–52.

Olaniran, B. A. (1994). Group performance and computer-mediated communication. *Management Communication Quarterly, 7,* 256–281. doi:10.1177/0893318994007003002

Olaniran, B. A. (2002-2003). Computer-mediated communication: A test of the impact of social cues on the choice of medium for resolving misunderstandings. *Journal of Educational Technology Systems, 31*(2), 205–222. doi:10.2190/576R-1NVK-M943-CJMP

Olaniran, B. A. (2006). Applying synchronous Computer-mediated communication into course design: Some considerations and practical guides. *Campus-Wide Information Systems, 23*(3), 210–220. doi:10.1108/10650740610674210

Olaniran, B. A. (2009). Organizational communication: Assessment of videoconferencing as a medium for meetings in the workplace. *International Journal of Human Technology Interaction, 5*(2), 63–84.

Olaniran, B. A., & Austin, K. A. (2009). Web-assisted instruction in upper division communication studies curriculum: A theoretical and quantitative analysis. *Campus Wide Information Systems: The International Journal of Information & Learning Technology, 26*(1), 43–53. doi:10.1108/10650740910921555

Olaniran, B. A. (2008). Human computer interaction and best mix of e-interactions and face-to-face in educational settings. In Kelsey, S., & St. Amant, K. (Eds.), *Handbook of Research on Computer Mediated Communication* (pp. 49–61). Hershey, PA: IGI Global.

Olapiriyakul, K., & Scher, J. M. (2006). A guide to establishing hybrid learning courses: Employing information technology to create a new learning experience, and a case study. *The Internet and Higher Education, 9*(4), 287–311. doi:10.1016/j.iheduc.2006.08.001

Ololube, N. P. (2000). *An appraisal of workers perception of academic and professional training on Managers' job effectiveness in the oil exploration industry, A case of Dec oil and Gas.* Unpublished PGD thesis, Federal University of Technology Owerri, Nigeria.

Ololube, N. P. (2005a). Benchmarking the motivational competencies of academically qualified teachers and professionally qualified teachers in nigerian secondary schools. *The African Symposium, 5*(3), 17-37.

Ololube, N. P. (2005b). School effectiveness and quality improvement: quality teaching in nigerian secondary schools. *The African Symposium, 5*(4), 17-31.

Olson, G. B. (2005). Team-Working in the Real-World. In Sankar, C. S., & Raju, P. K. (Eds.), *Introduction to Engineering through Case Studies* (4th ed., pp. 221–266). Anderson, SC: Tavenner Publishers.

Olugbile, S. (2006, August 1). Old dons stum computer literacy. *Punch News* (p. 41).

Oppenheimer, T. (2003). *The flickering mind: The false promise of technology in the classroom and how learning can be saved.* New York: Random House.

Oppenheimer, T. (2003). *The flickering mind: The false promise of technology in the classroom and how learning can be saved.* New York, NY: Random House.

Oravec, J. A. (2003). Blending by blogging: Weblogs in blended learning initiatives. *Journal of Educational Media, 28*(2-3), 225–233. doi:10.1080/1358165032000165671

Orlikowski, W. J., & Baroudi, J. J. (1991). Studying Information Technology in organizations: Research approaches and assumptions. *Information Systems Research, 2*(1), 1–28. doi:10.1287/isre.2.1.1

Ornes, L., & Gassert, C. (2007). Computer Competencies in a BSN Program. *Research Briefs, 46*(2), 75–78.

Pan, C., Sivo, S. A., & Brophy, J. (2003). Students' attitude in a web-enhanced hybrid course: A structural equation modeling inquiry. *Journal of Educational Media and Library Sciences, 41*(2), 181–194.

Papadimitriou, C. (2003, July 2). MythematiCS: In praise of storytelling in the teaching of CS and Math. In *Proceedings of the International Conference on CS Education, ITICSE,* Thessaloniki, Greece.

Papert, S. (1993). *The children's machine: Rethinking school in the age of computer.* New York: Basic Books.

Papert, S. (1980a). Computer-based microworlds as incubators for powerful ideas. In R. P. Taylor (Ed.), *The Computer in the School: Tutor, Tool, Tutee.* New York: Teacher College Press.

Papert, S. (1980b). *Mindstorms: Children, Computers, and Powerful Ideas.* New York: Basic Books.

Papert, S. (1991). Situating Constructionism. In I. Harel & S. Papert (Eds.), *Constructionism.*

Parish, J. T., Berry, L. L., & Lam, S. Y. (2008, Feb.). The Effect of the Servicescape on Service Workers. *Journal of Service Research, 10*(3), 220. doi:10.1177/1094670507310770

Park, C., & Raven, A. J. (2006). Knowledge Management Systems Success at the Individual Level: Task Technology Fit Perspective. In *proceedings of the 37th annual meeting of the decision sciences institute* (pp. 30911-30916), San Antonio, TX: Decision Sciences Institute.

Parsad, B., & Jones, J. (2005). *Internet access in U.S. public schools and classrooms: 1994-2003 (NCES 2005-015). U.S. Department of Education.* Washington, DC: National Center for Education Statistics.

Pearl, J. (1998). *Probabilistic Reasoning in Intelligent Systems.* Los Altos, CA: Morgan Kaufmann.

Pedersen, S. (2003). Motivational orientation in a probelm-based environment. *Journal of Interactive Learning Research, 14*(1), 51–77.

Pereira, J. A., Pleguezuelos, E., Merí, A., Molina-Ros, A., Molina-Tomás, M. C., & Masdeu, C. (2007). Effectiveness of using blended learning strategies for teaching and learning human anatomy. *Medical Education, 41*(2), 189–195. doi:10.1111/j.1365-2929.2006.02672.x

Perez, J., & Murray, M. (2008, August). Keep Your IS Program Viable by Offering an IT Literacy Service Course: One Department's Response to Declining Enrollments. In *Proceedings of the AMCIS Conference*, Toronto, Canada.

Pfefer, J. (2002). Merging IT training with academia. In *Proceedings of the 30th annual ACM SIGUCCS conference on User services* (pp. 95-98).

Pinar, W. (2004). *What is Curriculum Theory?* New York: Lawrence Erlbaum Associates.

Pittaway, L., & Cope, J. (2007, April). Simulating Entrepreneurial Learning: Integrating Experiential and Collaborative Approaches to Learning. *Management Learning, 38*(2), 211–233. doi:10.1177/1350507607075776

Plomp, T., Pelgrum, W. J., & Law, N. (2007). SITES2006 - International comparative survey of pedagogical practices and ICT in education. *Education and Information Technologies, 12*(2), 83–92. doi:10.1007/s10639-007-9029-5

Plutsky, S., & Wilson, B. (2000). Study to validate prerequisites in business communication for student success. *Journal of Education for Business, 76*(1), 15.

Pole, C., & Lampard, R. (2002). *Practical social investigation. Qualitative and quantitative methods in social research.* Harlow: Printice Hall.

Poling, C. (2005). Building communication and collaboration among staff and students. *Leading & Learning with Technology, International Society for Technology in Education, 32*(6).

Polsani, P. (2003). Use and abuse of reusable learning objects. *Journal of Digital Information, 3*(4), 2–19.

Poole, M. S., Seibold, D. R., & McPhee, R. (1985). Group decision-making as a structurational process. *The Quarterly Journal of Speech, 71*, 74–102. doi:10.1080/00335638509383719

Pope-Davis, D. B., & Twing, J. S. (1991). The effects of age, gender, and experience on measures of attitude regarding computers. *Computers in Human Behavior, 7*, 333–339..doi:10.1016/0747-5632(91)90020-2

Pór, G., & Molloy, J. (2000). *Nurturing Systemic Wisdom Through Knowledge Ecology.* Systems Thinker.

Porter, B. (2005). *Digitales: The art of digital storytelling.* Denver, CO: Bernajean Porter Consulting.

Porter, L. R. (1997). *Creating the virtual classroom: Distance learning with the Internet.* New York: John Wiley.

PR Newswire. (2002, December 2). *U.S. military academy at West Point deploys Cranite's Wire(R) Software Suite 2.0.* New York: PR Newswire.

Prakash, V., & Lounsbury, J. W. (1984). The Role of Expectations in the Determination of Consumer Satisfaction. *Academy of Marketing Science, 12*(3), 1–17. doi:10.1007/BF02739316

Prakash, S. (2003). *The African Virtual University and Growth in Africa: A knowledge and learning challenge. Findings, a publication of the World Bank.* Retrieved from http://www.worldbank.org/afr/findings

Preece, J., Rogers, Y., Sharp, H., Benyon, D., Holland, S., & Carey, T. (1994). *Human-Computer Interaction.* Workingham: Addison-Wesley.

Premkumar, G., & Roberts, M. (1999). Adoption of new information technologies in rural small businesses. *Omega, 27*(4), 467–484. doi:10.1016/S0305-0483(98)00071-1

Prensky, M. (2001). *Digital game-based learning.* New York: McGraw-Hill.

Prensky, M. (2004). *What Can You Learn from a Cell Phone? – Almost Anything!* Retrieved April 15, 2007, from http://www.marcprensky.com/writing/Prensky-What_Can_You_Learn_From_a_Cell_Phone-FINAL.pdf

Press, L. (1999). A Client-Centered Networking Project in Rural India. *OnTheInternet, 5*(2), 36-38. Retrieved November 22, 2007, from http:// som.csudh.edu/ fac/ lpress/ devnat/ nations /india/ pondyoti.htm

Price, S., & Oliver, M. (2007). A framework for conceptualizing the impact of technology on teaching and learning. *Educational Technology & Sociology, 10*(1), 16–27.

Project Tomorrow-NetDay (2006). *Our voices, our future. Student and teacher views on science, technology and education.* National Report on NetDay's 2005 Speak Up Event.

Qualters, M. D., Isaacs, J., Cullinane, T., Laird, J., Mcdonald, A., & Corriere, J. (2007). A Game Approach to Teach Environmentally Benign Manufacturing in the Supply Chain. *International Journal for the Scholarship of Teaching and Learning, 2*(2).

Rainer, R. K. Jr, Laosethakul, K., & Astone, M. K. (2003). Are gender perceptions of computing changing over time? *Journal of Computer Information Systems, 43*(4), 108–114.

Rakes, G. C., & Casey, H. B. (2002). An analysis of teacher concerns toward instructional technology. *The International Journal of Educational Technology, 3*(1). Retrieved March 8, 2009 from http://www.ed.uiuc.edu/ IJET/v3n1/rakes/index.html

Ray, J. A. (2009). An Investigation of online course management systems in higher education: Platform selection, faculty training, and instructional quality. *International Journal of Information and Communication Technology Education, 5*(2), 46–59.

Razvi, S., & Allen, J. D. (2005, April). *The meaningfulness of case studies in an educational psychology class: Students' perspectives.* Paper presented at the annual meeting of the American Educational Research Association, Montreal, Canada.

Read, B. (2007). How to podcast campus lectures. *The Chronicle of Higher Education*, A32–A35.

Reece, M. J., & Gable, R. K. (1982). The development and validation of a measure of general attitudes toward computers. *Educational and Psychological Measurement, 42*, 913–916..doi:10.1177/001316448204200327

Reichgelt, H., Zhang, A., & Price, B. (2002). Designing an Information Technology curriculum: The Georgia Southern University experience. *Journal of Information Technology Education, 1*(4), 213–221.

Reichheld, F. (2006). The Microeconomics of Customer Relationships. *MIT Sloan Management Review, 47*(2), 73.

Reiger, R. C., & Stang, J. (2000). Education productivity; Labor productivity; Motivation (psychology). *Employees—Training of. Education, 121*(1).

Reinsch, N. L. Jr, & Shelby, A. N. (1997). What communication abilities do practitioners need? Evidence from MBA students. *Business Communication Quarterly, 60*(4), 7–29. doi:10.1177/108056999706000401

Repman, J., Zinskie, C., & Carlson, R. D. (2005). Effective use of cmc tools in interactive online learning. *Computers in the Schools (The Hawthorne Press, Inc.), 22*(1/2), 57-69.

Resnick, M. (1991). Xylophones, Hamsters, and Fireworks: The Role of Diversity in Constructionist Activities. In I. Harel & S. Papert (Eds.), *Constructionism*.

Rhodes, M. L., & Curran, C. (2005). Use of the human patient simulator to teach clinical judgment skills in a baccalaureate program. *Computers, Informatics, Nursing, 23*, 256–262. doi:10.1097/00024665-200509000-00009

Rice, R. E., & Tyler, J. (1995). Individual and organizational influences on voice mail use and evaluation. *Behaviour & Information Technology, 14*(6), 329–341. doi:10.1080/01449299508914652

Rice, R. E., & Webster, J. (2002). Adoption, diffusion and use of new media in organizational settings. In Lin, C., & Atkin, D. (Eds.), *Communication Technology and society* (pp. 191–227). Cresskill, NJ: Hampton Press.

Richards, D. (2009). Designing project-based courses with a focus on group formation and assessment. *ACM Transactions on Computing Education, 9*(1), 2:1-2:40.

Richardson, W. (2004). *Reading and blogging, Weblogg-Ed.* Retrieved October 26, 2009, from http://www. weblogg-ed.com/2004/03/31

Richardson, W. (2004). Blogging and RSS—The "what's it?" and "how to" of powerful new tools for Web educators. *Multimedia & Internet at Schools, 11*(1), 10-13. Retrieved April 8, 2009, from http://www.infotoday.com/ MMSchools/jan04/richardson.shtml

Riva, G. (2002). The sociocognitive psychology of computer-mediated communication: The present and future of technology-based interactions. *Cyberpsychology & Behavior, 5*, 581–598. doi:10.1089/109493102321018222

Rivera, J. C., & Rice, M. L. (2002). A Comparison of Student Outcomes and Satisfaction Between Traditional & Web Based Course Offerings. *Online Journal of Distance Learning Administration, 5*(3).

Robertson, I. T. (1991). *An evaluation of outdoor development as a management development tool.* MBA Dissertation. University of Edinburgh.

Robin, B. (2005). *Educational uses of digital storytelling. Main directory for the educational uses of digital storytelling* (Tech. Rep.). Houston, TX: University of Houston, Instructional technology Program. Retrieved February 12, 2009 from http://www.coe.uh.edu/digital-storytelling/default.htm

Roblyer, M. D., & Knezek, G. A. (2003). New millennium research for educational technology: A call for a national research agenda. *Journal of Research on Technology in Education, 36*(1), 60–71.

Roblyer, M. D. (2006). *Integrating educational technology into teaching* (4th ed.). Upper Saddle, NJ: Prentice Hall.

Rogers, E. M. (1995). *Diffusion of Innovation* (5th ed.). New York: Free Press.

Rogers, E. M. (2004). A prospective and retrospective look at the diffusion model. *Journal of Health Communication, 9*, 13–19. doi:10.1080/10810730490271449

Rogers, E. M., & Shoemaker, F. F. (1971). *Communication of innovations.* New York: Free Press.

Röller, L. H., & Waverman, L. (2001). Telecommunications infrastructure and economic development: A simultaneous approach. *The American Economic Review, 91*, 4. doi:10.1257/aer.91.4.909

Rosen, L. D., & Maguire, P. (1990). Myths and reliabilities of computer phobia: A meta-analysis. *Anxiety Research, 3*, 175–191.

Rosenberg, M. (2001). *E-learning.* New York: McGraw-Hill.

Rossi, G., Ginzburg, J., Urbieta, M., & Distante, D. (2007, July 16-20). Transparent Interface Composition in Web Applications. In *Proceedings of 7th International Conference on Web Engineering* (ICWE2007) (pp. 152-166), Como, Italy.

Rossini, C. A. A. (2007). The open access movement: Opportunities and Challenges for Developing Countries. Let them live in interesting times. In *Proceedings of the Diplo Foundation Internet Governance Program.*

Rovai, A. P., & Jordan, H. M. (2004). Blended learning and sense of community: A comparative analysis with traditional and fully online graduate courses. *International Review of Research in Open and Distance Learning, 5*(2). Retrieved April 13, 2009 from http://www.irrodl.org/index.php/irrodl/article/view/192/274

Royer, R., & Richards, P. (2007). Increasing reading comprehension with digital storytelling. In C. Montgomerie & J. Seale (Eds.), *Proceedings of World Conference on Educational Multimedia, Hypermedia and Telecommunications 2007* (pp. 2301-2306). Chesapeake, VA: AACE.

Rubio, D. M., Berg-Weger, M., & Tebb, S. S. (2001). Using structural equation modeling to test for multidimensionality. *Structural Equation Modeling, 8*(4), 613–626.. doi:10.1207/S15328007SEM0804_06

Ruchala, L. V., & Hill, J. W. (1994). Reducing accounting students' oral communication apprehension: Empirical evidence. *Journal of Accounting Education, 1*(1), 41–50.

Russell, T. (1999). *The No significant difference phenomenon.* Office of Instructional Telecommunications, North Carolina State University Chapel Hill, N.C.

Ryan, R. C. (2000). Student assessment comparison of lecture and online construction equipment and methods classes. *T.H.E. Journal, 27*(6).

Sagin Simsek, C. (2008). Students' attitudes towards integration of ICTs in a reading course: a case in Turkey. *Computers & Education, 51*, 200–211. doi:10.1016/j.compedu.2007.05.002

Salz, P. A. (2006). Learning to go. *EContent, 29*(3), 44.

Sanders, D. W., & Morrison-Shetlar, A. I. (2001). Student attitudes toward web-enhanced instruction in an introductory Biology course. *Journal of Research on computing in Education, 33*(3), 251-262.

Sandholtz, J. H., Ringstaff, C., & Dwyer, D. (1997). *Teaching with technology: Creating student-centered classroom.* New York: Teachers College Press.

Sankaran, S. R., Sankaran, D., & Bui, T. X. (2000). Effect of student attitude to course format on learning performance: An empirical study in web vs. lecture instruction. *Journal of Instructional Psychology, 27*, 66–74.

Santhanam, R., Sasidharan, S., & Webster, J. (2008). Using Self-Regulatory Learning to Enhance E-Learning-Based Information Technology Training. *Information Systems Research, 19*(1), 26–47. doi:10.1287/isre.1070.0141

Santrock, J. W. (2008). *Educational psychology* (3rd ed.). Boston.MA: McGraw-Hill Learning Solutions.

Sanyal, B. C. (2001). *New functions of higher education and ICT to achieve education for all.* Paper presented at the Expert Roundtable on University and Technology-for- Literacy and Education Partnership in Developing Countries, International Institute for Educational Planning, UNESCO, Paris.

Sarver, T. (2008, March). Anticipating Regret: Why Fewer Options May Be Better. *Econometric, 76*(2), 263.

Sauer, P. L., & O'Donnell, J. B. (2006). The Impact of New Major Offerings on Student Retention. *Journal of Marketing for Higher Education, 16*(2), 135–155. doi:10.1300/J050v16n02_06

Savander-Ranne, C., Lunden, O.-P., & Kolari, S. (2008, November). An Alternative Teaching Method for Electrical Engineering Courses. *IEEE Transactions on Education, 51*(4), 423–431. doi:10.1109/TE.2007.912500

Savery, J. R., & Duffy, T. M. (1996). Problem-based Learning: An Instructional Model and its Constructivist Framework. In Wilson, B. G. (Ed.), *Constructivist Learning Environments: Case Studies in Instructional Design* (pp. 135–150). Englewood Cliffs, NJ: Educational Technology Publications.

Sax, G. (2001). *Principles of educational and psychological measurement and evaluation* (5th ed.). Belmont, CA: Wadsworth.

Schafer, S. (2004). Microsoft's Cultural Revolution; Battered by pirates and struggling to turn a profit, the brash American software giant is no longer trying to change China. Instead China's changing the company. *Newsweek International*, 46-49.

Schiro, M. (2004). *Oral storytelling and teaching mathematics.* Thousand Oaks, CA: SAGE Publications.

Schmidt, W. H., McKnight, C. C., Houang, R. T., Wang, H. C., Wiley, D. E., Cogan, L. S., & Wolfe, R. G. (2001). *Why schools matter: a cross-national comparison of curriculum and learning.* Indianapolis, IN: Jossey Bass Publishing.

Schmidt, J. T. (2007). *Preparing Students for Success in Blended Learning Environments: Future Oriented Motivation & Self-Regulation.* Unpublished doctoral dissertation.

Schoech, D. (2000). Teaching over the internet: results of one doctoral course. *Research on Social Work Practice, 10*(4), 467–487.

Schrum, L. (1999). Technology professional development for teachers. *Educational Technology Research and Development, 47*(4), 83–90. doi:10.1007/BF02299599

Schrum, L., Burbank, M. D., Engle, J., Chambers, J., & Glasset, K. (2005). Post-Secondary educators' professional development: Investigation of an online approach to enhancing teaching and learning. *The Internet and Higher Education, 8*, 279–28. doi:10.1016/j.iheduc.2005.08.001

Schulman, A. H., & Sims, R. L. (1999). Learning in an online format versus an in-class format: An experimental study. *T.H.E. Journal, 26*(11), 54–56.

Schwarz, R. D., & Sykes, R. (2004, June). *Psychometric foundations of formative assessment* (pp. 1-4). Paper presented at the National Educational Computing Conference, New Orleans, LA. Retrieved October 5, 2007 from http://www.iste.org/Content/NavigationMenu/Research/NECC_Research_Paper_Archives/NECC_2004/Schwarz-Richard-NECC04.pdf

SCORM. (2009). Retrieved January 5, 2009 from http://www.adlnet.org/Technologies/scorm/

Scott, E. (2007). *No library resource left behind: linking your library collection to the Academic Content Standards (PowerPoint presentation). Tulare County.* Calif.: Office of Education.

Scott, E. (2007, July 12). *Follow-up questions - use of ClassroomClicks in Calif. Districts.* Personal e-mail correspondence.

Scott, N. W. (1996). *A study of the introduction of educational technology into a course in engineering dynamics: classroom environment and learning outcomes.* Unpublished doctoral dissertation.

Selwyn, N. (1997). Students' attitudes toward computers: validation of a computer attitude scale for 16-19 education. *Computers & Education, 28*, 35–41..doi:10.1016/S0360-1315(96)00035-8

Semich, G., & Runyon, L. (2002). Infusing technology in the classroom: Positive intervention makes the real difference in student learning. In C. Crawford et al. (Eds.), *Proceedings of Society for Information Technology and Teacher Education International Conference 2002* (pp. 1433-1437). Chesapeake, VA: AACE.

Sevdalis, N., Kokkinaki, F., & Harvey, N. (2008). Anticipating a regrettable purchase; Implications of erroneous affective forecasting for marketing planning. *Marketing Intelligence & Planning, 26*(4), 375. doi:10.1108/02634500810879287

Shabalala, D. (2007). Towards A Digital Agenda for Developing Countries. Retrieved November 28, 2007 from http:// www.southcentre.org/ publications/ research-papers/ ResearchPapers13. pdf

Sharma, R. (2003). *Barriers in Using Technology for Education in Developing Countries*. Washington, DC: IEEE.

Shashaani, L. (1997). Gender differences in computer attitudes and use among college students. *Journal of Educational Computing Research, 16*, 37–51..doi:10.2190/Y8U7-AMMA-WQUT-R512

Shea, P. J., Pelz, W., Fredericksen, E. E., & Pickett, A. M. (2002). Online teaching as a catalyst for classroom-based instructional transformation. In J.R. Bourne & J.C. Moore (Eds.), *Elements of quality online education: learning effectiveness, cost effectiveness, access, faculty satisfaction, student satisfaction* (Vol. 3). Needham, MA: Sloan Consortium.

Shelley, D. J., Swartz, L. B., & Cole, M. T. (2008). Learning business law online vs. onland: A mixed method analysis. *International Journal of Information and Communication Technology Education, 3*(1), 54–66.

Shelley, D. J., Swartz, L. B., & Cole, M. T. (2007). A comparative analysis of online and traditional undergraduate business law classes. *International Journal of Information and Communication Technology Education, 3*(1), 10–21.

Shen, P. D., Lee, T. H., & Tsai, C. W. (2008). Enhancing skills of application software via web-enabled problem-based learning and self-regulated learning: An exploratory study. *Journal of Distance Education Technologies, 6*(3), 69–84.

Shen, R., Wang, M., & Pan, X. (2008). Increasing interactivity in blended classrooms through a cutting-edge mobile learning system. *British Journal of Educational Technology, 39*(6), 1073–1086. doi:10.1111/j.1467-8535.2007.00778.x

Shen, P. D., Lee, T. H., & Tsai, C. W. (2007). Applying web-enabled problem-based learning and self-regulated learning to enhance computing skills of Taiwan's vocational students: A quasi-experimental study of a short-term module. *Electronic Journal of e-Learning, 5*(2), 147-156.

Shen, P. D., Lee, T. H., Tsai, C. W., & Ting, C. J. (2008). Exploring the effects of web-enabled problem-based learning and self-regulated learning on vocational students' involvement in learning. *European Journal of Open, Distance and E-Learning*, (1). Retrieved April 13, 2009 from http://www. eurodl.org/ materials/contrib/ 2008/ Shen_Lee_Tsai_ Ting.htm

Shneiderman, B. (1992). *Designing the User Interface* (2nd. ed.). Reading, MA: Addison-Wesley.

Short, J., Williams, E., & Christie, B. (1976). *The Social Psychology of Telecommunication*. London: John Wiley.

Shuman, L. J., Besterfield-Sacre, & McGourty, J. (2005). The ABET Professional Skills – Can They be Taught? Can they be Assessed? *Journal of Engineering Education, 94*(1), 41–56.

Shute, V. J., & Psotka, J. (1996). Intelligent tutoring systems: Past, Present and Future. In *Handbook of Research on Educational Communications and Technology* (pp. 1–99). New York: Scholastic Publications.

Sidhu, M. S., Ramesh, S., & Selvanathan, N. (2005). A Coach-Based Interactive Multimedia Tool For Solving Engineering Problem. *International Multimedia Cyberscape Journal, 3*(2), 28–36.

Sidhu, M. S. (2007). *Development and Applications of Interactive Multimedia TAPS (Technology Assisted Problem Solving) Packages for Engineering*. Unpublished doctoral dissertation, Universiti Malaya.

Sidhu, M. S., & Ramesh, S. (2008). Virtual Worlds: The Next Generation for Solving Engineering Problems. In *Proceedings of the IEEE 8th International Conference on Computer and IT (CIT2008)*, Sydney, Australia (pp. 303-307).

Sidhu, M. S., Cheng, L. K., Der, S. C., & Omar, R. (2009). Augmented Reality Applications in Education. In *Proceedings of the Second Teaching and Learning Conference at UNITEN*.

Silver, M., & Wilkenson, L. (1991). Effects of Tutors with subject expertise on the problem-based tutorial process. *Academic Medicine, 66,* 298–300. doi:10.1097/00001888-199105000-00017

Singer, J. B. (2004). Strange bedfellows? The diffusion of convergence in four news organizations. *Journalism Studies, 5*(1), 3–18. doi:10.1080/1461670032000174701

Singh, H. (2003). Building effective blended learning programs. *Educational Technology, 43*(6), 51–54.

Singleton, R. A., Jr., & Straits, B. C. (2005). *Approaches to social research.* New York, NY: Oxford University Press.

Sirvanci, M. (1996, October). Are students the true customers of higher education? *Quality Progress, 29*(10).

Skinner, E., & Hagood, M. (2008). Developing literate identities with English language learners through digital storytelling. *The Reading Matrix, 8*(2), 12–38.

Skira, D. J. (2006). The 2005 word of the year: Podcasting. *Nursing Education Perspectives, 27*(1), 54–55.

Slater, J. S., McCubbrey, D. J., & Scudder, R. A. (1995, September). Inside an Integrated MBA: An Information Systems View. *Management Information Systems Quarterly, 19,* 391–410. doi:10.2307/249601

Slaughter, L. A., Harper, B. D., & Norman, K. L. (1994). Assessing the Equivalence of Paper and On-line versions of the QUIS 5.5. In *Proceedings of the 2nd Annual Mid-Atlantic Human Factors Conference*, Washington, D.C.

Slevin, J. (2000). *The Internet and society.* New York: Wiley.

Smarkola, C. (2007). Technology acceptance predictors among student teachers and experienced classroom teachers. *Journal of Educational Computing Research, 37*(1), 65–82. doi:10.2190/J3GM-3RK1-2907-7U03

Smart, K. L., & Cappel, J. L. (2005). An exploratory look at students' perceptions of blended learning. *Issues in Information Systems, 6*(1), 149–155.

Smith, S. D. (1986). Relationships of computer attitudes to sex, grade level, and teacher influence. *Education, 106,* 338–344.

Smith, S. B., & Smith, S. J., & O'Brien, J. (2002). *Technology Innovation through Collaboration in a Teacher Education Program.* Retrieved August 11, 2008, from http:// thedigitalclassroom. com/ download/JCTE-Smith92604.pdf

Solidoro, A. (2007). *The digital storytelling: Multimedia creative writing as a reflective practice.* Retrieved February 12, 2009 from http:// www.filografia.org/ documents/ 1.%20Theoretical%20introduction/ 1.4%20Digital%20 Storytelling.pdf

Solvie, P., & Kloek, M. (2007). Using technology tools to engage students with multiple learning styles in a constructivist learning environment. *Contemporary Issues in Technology & Teacher Education, 7*(2), 7–27.

Sonnet, G., Fox, M. F., & Adkins, K. (2007, Dec.). Undergraduate Women in Science and Engineering: Effects of Faculty, Fields, and Institutions Over Time. *Social Science Quarterly, 88*(5), 1333–1356. doi:10.1111/j.1540-6237.2007.00505.x

Sorenson, R. L., Savage, G. T., & Orem, E. (1990). A profile of communication faculty needs in business schools and colleges. *Communication Education, 39*(2), 148–160. doi:10.1080/03634529009378797

Spark, J. J. (1983). *Distance Education: International Perspective.* London: St. Martin Press.

Spears, R., & Lea, M. (1992). Social influence and the influence of the "social" n computer-mediated communication. In Lea, M. (Ed.), *Contexts of computer-mediated communication* (pp. 30–65). Hemel Hempstead, UK: Harvester Wheatsheaf.

Spiro, R. J., & Jehng, J. (1990). Cognitive Flexibility and Hypertext: Theory and Technology for the Nonlinear and Multidimensional Traversal of Complex Subject Matter. In D. Nix & R. Spiro (Eds.).*Cognition, Education, and Multimedia: Exploring Ideas in High Technology.* Hillsdale, NJ: Earlbaum.

Spotts, T. (1999). Discriminating factors in faculty use of instructional technology in higher education. *Educational Technology & Society, 2*(4), 92–99.

Sproull, L., & Kiesler, S. (1986). Reducing social context cues: Electronic mail in organizational communication. *Management Science, 32,* 1492–1512. doi:10.1287/mnsc.32.11.1492

Standards, M. A. R. C. (n.d.). *Network Development and MARC Standards Office - Library of Congress.* Retrieved June 15, 2009 from http:// www.l oc.gov/ marc/ bibliographic/ bd521.html

Stevens, J. (1999). *Intermediate statistics* (2nd ed.). Mahwah, NJ: L. Erlbaum.

Strudler, N. (2003). Answering the call: A response to Roblyer and Knezek. *Journal of Research on Technology in Education, 36*(1), 72–76.

Student Evaluation of Instruction. (n.d.). Athens, OH: Ohio University. *Teacher Education Department.*

Sudzina, M. R., & Sudzina, C. M. (2003, June-July). *Insights into Successfully Teaching with Cases On-Line: The View from Both Sides of the 'Net.* Paper presented at the annual meeting of the World Association for Case Method Research and Case Method Application, Bordeaux, France.

Sugar, W., Crawley, F., & Fine, B. (2004). Examining teachers' decisions to adopt new technology. *Journal of Educational Technology & Society, 7*(4), 201–213.

Swan, K., Cook, D., Kratcoski, A., Lin, Y., Schenker, J., & Van't Hooft, M. (2006). Ubiquitous computing: Rethinking teaching, learning and technology. In S. Tettegah & Hunter (Eds.), *Educational and technology: Issues and applications, policy and administration,* (pp. 231-252). New York, NY: Elsevier.

Sweller, J., Van, J. M., & Paas, F. (1998). Cognitive Architecture and Instructional Design. *Educational Psychology Review, 10,* 251–296. doi:10.1023/A:1022193728205

Taber, N. (2008). Emergency Response: Elearning for Paramedics and Firefighters. *Simulation & Gaming, 39*(4), 515. doi:10.1177/1046878107306669

Tahmincioglu, M. (2008, February 10). *Your career: Where are the women in tech? MSNBC.* Retrieved February 25, 2008, from http://www.msnbc.msn.com/id/23033748/print/1/displaymode/1098

Talbot, L. (1995). *Principles and practice of nursing research.* St. Louis, MO: Missouri.

Taylor, S., & Todd, P. A. (1995). Understanding information technology usage: a test of competing models. *Information Systems Research, 6*(2), 144–176. doi:10.1287/isre.6.2.144

Taylor, D., & Miflin, B. (2008). Problem-based learning: where are we now? *Medical Teacher, 30*(8), 742–763. doi:10.1080/01421590802217199

Teclehaimanot, B. (2006). Technology Use in an Urban Setting: Implications for Schools Change. In C. Crawford et al. (Eds.), *Proceedings of Society for Information Technology and Teacher Education International Conference 2006* (pp. 1837-1847). Chesapeake, VA: AACE.

Temple, L., & Lips, H. M. (1989). Gender differences and similarities in attitudes toward computers. *Computers in Human Behavior, 5,* 215–226. doi:10.1016/0747-5632(89)90001-0

Teo, T., Lee, C. B., & Chai, C. S. (2008). Understanding pre-service teachers' computer attitudes: applying and extending the Technology Acceptance Model (TAM). *Journal of Computer Assisted Learning, 24,* 128–143.. doi:10.1111/j.1365-2729.2007.00247.x

Teo, T., & Noyes, J. (2008). Development and validation of a Computer Attitude Measure for Young Students (CA-MYS). *Computers in Human Behavior, 24*(8), 2659–2667.. doi:10.1016/j.chb.2008.03.006

Teo, T., Wong, S. L., & Chai, C. S. (in press). A cross-cultural examination of the intention to use technology between Singaporean and Malaysian pre-service teachers: an application of the Technology Acceptance Model (TAM). *Journal of Educational Technology & Society.*

Teo, T. (2006). Attitudes toward computers: A study of post-secondary students in Singapore. *Interactive Learning Environments*, *14*(1), 17–24. doi:10.1080/10494820600616406

Teo, T. (2008). Assessing the computer attitudes of students: an Asian perspective. *Computers in Human Behavior*, *24*(4), 1634–1642. doi:10.1016/j.chb.2007.06.004

Teo, T. (2009). Modelling technology acceptance in education: A study of pre-service teachers. *Computers & Education*, *52*(1), 302–312. doi:10.1016/j.compedu.2008.08.006

Teo, T. (2010). A path analysis of pre-service teachers' attitudes toward computer use: applying and extending the Technology Acceptance Model in an educational context. *Interactive Learning Environments*, *18*(1), 65–79. doi:10.1080/10494820802231327

Teo, T., Lee, C. B., & Chai, C. S. (2008). Understanding pre-service teachers' computer attitudes: applying and extending the Technology Acceptance Model (TAM). *Journal of Computer Assisted Learning*, *24*(2), 128–143. doi:10.1111/j.1365-2729.2007.00247.x

Teo, T., Wong, S. L., & Chai, C. S. (2008). A cross-cultural examination of the intention to use technology between Singaporean and Malaysian pre-service teachers: an application of the Technology Acceptance Model (TAM). *Journal of Educational Technology & Society*, *11*(4), 265–280.

Thatcher, J. B., & Perrewe, P. L. (2002). An empirical examination of individual traits as antecedents to computer anxiety and computer self-efficacy. *Management Information Systems Quarterly*, *26*(4), 381–396. doi:10.2307/4132314

The University of New South Wales (UNSW). (2003). *School of Biological, Earth and Environmental Sciences.* Retrieved 23 December 2007 from http://www.fbe.unsw.edu.au/fbeguide/teaching&learning/resources/LearningCommunity_180803.pd

Thomas, L. (2009). From Experience to Meaning: The Critical Skills Program. *Phi Delta Kappan*, *91*(2), 93–96.

Thompson, A. D., Schmidt, D. A., & Davis, N. E. (2003). Technology collaborative for simultaneous renewal in teacher education. *Educational Technology Research and Development*, *51*(1), 73–89. doi:10.1007/BF02504519

Thompson, A. D., Schmidt, D. A., & Davis, N. E. (2003). Technology collaborative for simultaneous renewal in teacher education. *Educational Technology Research and Development*, *51*(1), 73–89. doi:10.1007/BF02504519

Thompson, R. L., Higgins, C. A., & Howell, J. M. (1991). Personal computing: toward a conceptual model of utilization. *Management Information Systems Quarterly*, *15*(1), 124–143. doi:10.2307/249443

Thong, J. Y. L., Hong, W., & Tam, K. Y. (2002). Understanding user acceptance of digital libraries: What are the roles of interface characteristics, organizational context, and individual differences? *International Journal of Human-Computer Studies*, *57*(3), 215–242. doi:10.1016/S1071-5819(02)91024-4

Tiene, D. (2000). Online discussions: A survey of advantages and disadvantages compared to face-to-face discussions. *Journal of Educational Multimedia and Hypermedia*, *9*, 371–384.

Tobias, R. D. (1995). An introduction to partial least squares regression. In *SUGI Proceedings.* Retrieved August 1, 2008 from http://support.sas.com/rnd/app/papers/pls.pdf

Tomassi, K. D. (2006). *Stanford on iTunes' is for Everybody.* Retrieved November 22, 2007, from http://www.forbes.com/2006/01/24/stanford-on-itunes_c x _kdt_06conncampus_ 0124 stanford.html

Total Cost of Ownership. (2001). Retrieved November 28, 2007, from http://www.widernet.org/projects/costofownership1.htm

Trauth, E. M., Farwell, D. W., & Lee, D. (1993, September). The IS Expectation Gap: Industry Expectations Versus Academic Preparation. *Management Information Systems Quarterly*, 293–307. doi:10.2307/249773

Trawick-Smith, J. (2003). *Early childhood development: A multicultural perspective.* Upper Saddle River, NJ: Pearson Education, Inc.

Trigwell, K., Prosser, M., & Waterhouse, F. (1999). Relations between teachers' approaches to teaching and students' approaches to learning. *Higher Education*, *37*, 57–70. doi:10.1023/A:1003548313194

Tsuji, M., Taoka, F., & Teshima, M. (2002). A Comparative Analysis of International Distance Learning: ISDN VS. The Internet. In Murphy, D., Shin, N., & Zhang, W. (Eds.), *Advancing Online Learning in Asia* (pp. 201–210). Hong Kong: Open University of Hong Kong Press.

Tsuji, M. (2004). Issues of International Distance Learning. *International Journal of Computer, the Internet and Management, 12*(2), 201-8.

Tsuji, M. (2006). A Comparative Analysis of Distance Learning Methods: Lessons Learned from the Experiences of Osaka University. In K. Fukui (Ed.), *ESP e-Learning for Global Competency* (Frontiers Science Series No. 51, pp. 55-67). Tokyo: Universal Academy Press.

Tulare County. (Calif.) Office of Education. (December 2001- January 2002). Just a click away – Educational Resource Services Program Manager Elainea Scott and the new on-line Standards Resource Guide. In *The news gallery.* Retrieved October 12, 2007 from http://www.tcoe.k12.ca.us/PressRoom/NG2001_12/index.shtm

Tulare County. (Calif.) Office of Education. (2007) *Standards resource guide.* Retrieved October 12, 2007 from http://www.Classroomclicks.com/

Tulloch, J. B. (2000). Sophisticated technology offers higher education options. *T.H.E. Journal, 2*(4), 58–60.

Turban, E., Rainer, K. R., & Potter, R. (2003). *Introduction to Information Technology.* New York: John Wiley & Sons.

Turner, R. M., & Grizzaffi, K. (2003, May). *Creative Alternatives for Service Learning: A Project-Based Approach.* Paper presented at the annual meeting of the Campus Compact National Center for Community Colleges, Scottsdale, AZ.

Turoff, M. (1995). Designing a Virtual Classroom. In *Proceedings of the International Conference on Computer Assisted Instruction* (pp. 1-13).

U.S. Department of Education. (2000). *Teachers' tools for the 21st Century: A report on teachers' use of technology (NCES 2000-102).* Washington, DC: National Center for Education Statistics.

U.S. Department of Education. (2006). *Education Technology Fact Sheet.* Retrieved August 29, 2008 from http://www.ed.gov/about/offices/list/os/technology/facts.html.

UN Population Division. (2001). *World Urbanization Prospects: The 2001 Revision.* Retrieved from http://www.un.org/esa/population/publications/wup2001/WUP2001_CH2.pdf

University of Tennessee. (n.d). *Ideas and best practices for evaluating faculty teaching.* Retrieved 10 January 2008, from http://www.utc.edu /Departments/ fcouncil/ FacultyHandbook/ Appen/Teaching.pdf

Unsworth, L. (2008). Multiliteracies, e-literature and English teaching. *Language and Education: An International Journal, 22*(1), 62–75. doi:10.2167/le726.0

Uribe-Tirado, A., Melgar-Estrada, L. M., & Bornacelly-Castro, J. A. (2007). Moodle learning management system as a tool for information, documentation, and knowledge management by research groups. *Profesional de la Informacion, 16*(5), 468–474. doi:10.3145/epi.2007.sep.09

Vakhitova, G., & Bollinger, C. R. (2006). *Labor market return to computer skills: Using Microsoft Certification to measure computer skills.* Retrieved April 13, 2009 from http://gatton.uky.edu/faculty/Bollinger/Workingpapers/MSwagepaper11_06.pdf

Valdez, G. (2006). *Critical Issue: Technology: a catalyst for teaching and learning in the classroom. Learning Point Associate.* Retrieved June 12, 2007, from http://www.ncrel.org/sdrs/areas/issues/methods/technlgy/te600.htm

Van Raaij, E. M., & Schepers, J. J. (2008). The acceptance and use of a virtual learning environment in China. *Computers & Education, 50*, 838–852. doi:10.1016/j.compedu.2006.09.001

VanFossen, P. (1999, November 19-21). *Teachers would have to be crazy not to use the Internet!": Secondary social studies teachers in Indiana.* Paper presented at the Annual Meeting of the National Council for the Social Studies, Orlando, FL.

Vardi, I., & Ciccarelli, M. (2008). Overcoming problems in problem-based learning: a trial of strategies in an undergraduate unit. *Innovations in Education and Teaching International, 45*(4), 345–354. doi:10.1080/14703290802377190

Vasiliou, A., & Economides, A. A. (2007). Mobile collaborative learning using multicast MANETs. *International Journal of Mobile Communications*, *5*(4), 423–444. doi:10.1504/IJMC.2007.012789

Vaughan, R. (1998). The Use of Multimedia in Developing Undergraduate Engineering Courses. *Journal of Materials*, *5*(5). Retrieved February 2007, from www.tms.org/pubs/journals/JOM/9805/Voller/Voller-9805.html

Veen, W. (1993). The role of beliefs in the use of information technology: implications for teacher education, or teaching the right thing at the right time. *Journal of Information Technology for Teacher Education*, *2*(2), 1390–153.

Venkatesh, V., & Davis, F. D. (2000). A theoretical extension of the technology acceptance model: Four longitudinal field studies. *Management Science*, *46*(2), 186–204. doi:10.1287/mnsc.46.2.186.11926

Venkatesh, V., & Morris, M. G. (2000). Why don't men ever stop to ask for directions? Gender, social influence, and their role in technology acceptance and usage behavior. *Management Information Systems Quarterly*, *24*(1), 115–139. doi:10.2307/3250981

Vess, D. L. (2006). History to go: Why iTeach with iPods. *The History Teacher*, *39*(4), 479–492. doi:10.2307/30037068

Vestal, S. (2007). Regions' universities test podcasting: Professors using new technologies to connect. *Knight Rider Tribune Business News*. Retrieved April 21, 2008, from http://proquest.umi.com/pqdweb?did=1222573261&sid=4&Fmt=3&clientld=37634&RQT=309&Vname=PQD

Vonderwell, S. (2003). An examination of asynchronous communication experiences and perspectives of students in an online course: A case study. *The Internet and Higher Education*, *6*, 77–90. doi:10.1016/S1096-7516(02)00164-1

Vonderwell, S., & Peterman, F. (2008). Technology Integration and Community Mapping in Urban Education. In C. Crawford et al. (Eds.), *Proceedings of Society for Information Technology and Teacher Education International Conference* 2008 (pp. 2257- 2260). Chesapeake, VA: AACE.

Vose, M. F. (1998). *The Simple Genetic Algorithm: Foundations and Theory*. Cambridge, MA: MIT Press.

Vygotsky, L. S. (1978). *Mind in Society: Development of Higher Psychological Processes*. Cambridge, MA: Harvard University Press.

Wagner, E. D. (2005). Enabling Mobile Learning. *EDUCAUSE Review*, *40*(3), 40–53.

Wagner, E. D., & Wilson, P. (2005). Disconnected. *T + D*, *59*(12), 40-43.

Walmsley, B. (2003). Partnership-centered learning: The case for pedagogic balance in technology education. *Journal of Technology Education*, *14*(2). Retrieved April 13, 2009 from http://scholar.lib.vt.edu/ejournals/JTE/v14n2/walmsley.html

Walther, J. B. (1995). Relational aspect of computer-mediated communication: Experimental observations over time. *Organization Science*, *6*(2), 186–203. doi:10.1287/orsc.6.2.186

Wang, H. C., Chang, C. Y., & Li, T. Y. (2008). Assessing creative problem-solving with automated text grading. *Computers & Education*, *51*(4), 1450–1466. doi:10.1016/j.compedu.2008.01.006

Wardrope, W. J., & Bayless, M. L. (1994). Oral communication skills instruction in business schools. *Journal of Education for Business*, *69*(3), 132–135.

Webb, N. M., Nemer, K. M., Chizhik, A. W., & Sugrue, B. (1998). Equity issues in collaborative group assessment: Group composition and performance. *American Educational Research Journal*, 607–665.

Weber, R. (2004). Some Implications of the year-2000 Era, Dot-com Era, and Offshoring for Information Systems Pedagogy. *Management Information Systems Quarterly*, *28*(2), iii–xi.

Webster, J., & Hackley, P. (1997). Teaching effectiveness in technology-mediated distance learning. *Academy of Management Journal*, *40*(6), 1282–1309. doi:10.2307/257034

Webster, J., Heian, J. B., & Michelman, J. E. (1990). Computer training and computer anxiety in the educational process: An experimental analysis. In *Proceedings of the Eleventh International Conference on Information Systems* (pp. 171-182).

Weekes, S. (2006). Listen and learn. *Training & Coaching Today*, 17.

Wei, R. (2006). *Exploring predictors of adoption of wireless Internet among academics*. Paper presented at the annual meeting of the International Communication Association, Dresden, Germany.

Weisner, J., & Salkeld, E. (2004). Taking Technology into Schools: A dialogue between a preservice teacher and a university supervisor. *TechTrends*, *48*(3), 12–17. doi:10.1007/BF02763350

Weller, M., Pegler, C., & Mason, R. (2005). Use of innovative technologies on an e-learning course. *The Internet and Higher Education*, *8*, 61–71. doi:10.1016/j.iheduc.2004.10.001

Welsh, E. T., Wanberg, C. R., Brown, K. G., & Simmering, M. J. (2003). E-learning: Emerging uses, empirical results, and future directions. *International Journal of Training and Development*, *7*(4), 245–258. doi:10.1046/j.1360-3736.2003.00184.x

Wenglisky, H. (2006). Technology and achievement: The bottom line. *Educational Leadership*, *63*(4), 29–32.

Wepner, S. B., Tao, L., & Ziomek, N. M. (2003). Three teacher educators' perspectives about the shifting responsibilities of infusing technology into the curriculum. *Action in Teacher Education*, *24*(4), 53–63.

Wetzel, K. (2001). Toward the summit: Students use of technology. *AACTE Briefs*, *22*(6), 5.

Wetzer, I. M., Zeelenberg, M., & Pieters, R. (2007, August). Never eat in that restaurant, I did: Exploring why people engage in negative word-of-mouth communication. *Psychology and Marketing*, *24*(8), 661. doi:10.1002/mar.20178

Wheeler, K., Byrne, J., & Deri, A. (2003). eLearning and education for sustainability (EFS). *International Review for Environmental Strategies*, *4*(1), 95–105.

Whetstone, L., & Carr-Chellman, A. A. (2001). Preparing preservice teachers to use technology: Survey results. *TechTrends*, *46*(4), 11–17. doi:10.1007/BF02784820

White, M. (2001). A virtual Interactive Teaching Environment (VITE) Using XML and Augmented Reality. *The International Journal of Electrical Engineering Education*, *38*(4), 316–329.

Wikipedia. (2007). *Demographics of India*. Retrieved November 22, 2007, from http://en.wikipedia.org/wiki/Demographics_of_India

Wild, M. (1996). Technology refusal: rationalizing the failure of student and beginning teachers to use computers. *British Journal of Educational Technology*, *27*(2), 134–143. doi:10.1111/j.1467-8535.1996.tb00720.x

Wilder, G., Mackie, D., & Cooper, J. (1985). Gender and computers: Two surveys of computer related attitudes. *Sex Roles*, *13*, 215–228. doi:10.1007/BF00287912

Wiley, D. A. (Ed.). (2001). Connecting learning objects to instructional design theory: a definition, a metaphor, and a taxonomy. In *The Instructional Use of Learning Objects: Online Version*. Retrieved October 5, 2007 from http://reusability.org/read/chapters/wiley.doc

Williams, M. (2007). High cost of education. *Michigan Citizen*, *30*(1), 47.

Williams, J., & Jacobs. (2004). Exploring the use of blogs as learning spaces in the higher education sector. *Australasian Journal of Educational Technology*, *20*(2), 232–247.

Wilson, S. (2002). Development of a personal digital assistant (PDA) as point-of-care technology in nursing education. PDA cortex. *The Journal of Mobile Informatics*. Retrieved June 27, 2007, from http://www.pdacortex.com/pda_nursing_education.htm

Winn, W., & Snyder, D. (1996). Cognitive perspectives in pyschology. In Jonassen, D. H. (Ed.), *Handbook of research for educational communications and technology* (pp. 112–142). New York: Simon & Schuster Macmillan.

Winsor, J. L., Curtis, D. B., & Stephens, R. D. (1997). National preferences in business and communication education: A survey update. *Journal of the Association for Communication Administration (JACA)* (3), 170-179.

Wold, H. (1982). Soft modeling: The basic design and some extensions. In K.G. Joreskog & H. Wold (Eds.), *Systems under Indirect Observation 2.* (pp. 1-54). North-Holland, Amsterdam.

Woodrow, J. E. J. (1991). A comparison of four computer attitude scales. *Journal of Educational Computing Research, 7*(2), 165–187. doi:10.2190/WLAM-P42V-12A3-4LLQ

Yi, M. Y., & Davis, F. D. (2003). Developing and validating an observational learning model of computer software training and skill acquisition. *Information Systems Research, 14*(2), 146–169. doi:10.1287/isre.14.2.146.16016

Yildirim, S. (2000). Effects of an educational computing course on pre-service and in-service teachers: A discussion and analysis of attitudes and use. *Journal of Research on Computing in Education, 32*(4), 479–495.

Yin, R. K. (1994). *Case Study Research: Design and Methods.* (2nd ed.). Thousand Oaks, CA: Sage.

Young, A. T., Cole, J. R., & Denton, D. (2002) Improving technological literacy. *Issues in Science and Technology.* Retrieved April 13, 2009 from http://findarticles.com/p/articles/mi_qa3622/is_200207/ai_n9115217

Young, M. F. D. (1998). *The curriculum of the future.* London, UK: The Falmer Press.

Yuen, H. K., Law, N., & Chan, H. (1999). Improving IT training for serving teachers through evaluation. In Cumming, G., Okamoto, T., & Gomez, L. (Eds.), *Advanced Research in Computers and Communications in Education* (*Vol. 2*, pp. 441–448). Amsterdam: IOS Press.

Yun, J. H. (2003). Implementation of Video Conferencing System in Japanese Language Lesson for Distance Learning. In *Proceedings of the 2003 Conference proceedings, Society for Teaching Japanese as a Foreign Language* (pp. 189-94).

Yushau, B. (2006). The effects of blended e-learning on mathematics and computer attitudes in pre-calculus algebra. *The Montana Math Enthusiast, 3*(2), 176–183.

Z 39.50. (n.d.). *Network Development and MARC Standards Office - Library of Congress.* Retrieved June 15, 2009 from http://www.loc.gov/z3950/agency/

Zaltman, G., Duncan, R., & Holbek, J. (1973). *Innovations & Organizations.* New York: John Wiley & Sons.

Zapata-Rivera, J. D., & Greer, J. E. (2001). SModel server: Student modeling in distributed multi-agent tutoring systems. In J. D. Moore, C. L. Redfield, & W. L. Johnson (Eds.), In *Proceedings of the 10th International Conference on Artificial Intelligence in Education,* San Antonio, TX (pp. 446-455).

Zhang, A. M., Zhu, Y., & Hildebrandt, H. (2009). Enterprise Networking Websites and Organizational communication in Australia. *Business Communication Quarterly, 72*(1), 114–119. doi:10.1177/1080569908330381

Zhao, Y., & Cziko, G. A. (2001). Teacher Adoption of Technology: A Perceptual Control Theory Perspective. *Journal of Technology and Teacher Education, 9*(1), 5–30.

Zhao, Y., Tan, H. S., & Mishra, P. (2001). Technology: teaching and learning: whose computer is it? *Journal of Adolescent & Adult Literacy, 44*(4), 348–355.

Zhoa, Y., & Cziko, G. (2001). Teacher adoption of technology: A perceptual control perspective.

Zigurs, I., & Buckland, B. K. (1998). A theory of task/technology fit and group support systems effectiveness. *MIS Quarterly, 22*(3), 313–334. doi:10.2307/249668

About the Contributors

Lawrence A. Tomei is Senior Associate Provost for Academic Affairs and a professor in education at Robert Morris University. Born in Akron, Ohio, he earned a BSBA from the University of Akron (1972) and entered the US Air Force, serving until his retirement as a Lieutenant Colonel in 1994. Dr. Tomei completed his MPA and M.Ed. at the University of Oklahoma (1975, 1978) and Ed.D. from the University of Southern California (1983). His most recent articles and books on instructional technology include: Teaching Digitally: Integrating Technology into the Classroom (2001), Technology Facade (2002), Challenges of Teaching with Technology across the Curriculum (2003), Taxonomy for the Technology Domain (2005); and, Designing Instruction for the Traditional, Adult, and Distance Learner (2010).

* * *

Albert Akyeampong is an Instructor of Instructional Technology at the College of Education, Ohio University, Athens, Ohio. His research interests include: The Use of Instructional Technology in the Development and Delivery of Online/Distance Education, Free/Open Source Software, and 2.0 Technologies in Education.

Zerrin Ayvaz-Reis was born in Istanbul in 1958. She received her BSc degree in mathematics and astronomy in 1986, MSc degree in quantitative methods in 1990, and PhD degree in computer engineering in 1999, all from Istanbul University. She has taught courses on Software Engineering, Databases and UML (Unified Modeling Language). Her current research interests include Instructional Design, Computer Based Instruction, e-Learning, and Content Management System. Currently she is a faculty member in Instructional Computer Technologies department of Education Faculty in Istanbul University.

M. Erdal Balaban holds both a BSc and MSc in mathematics from Science Faculty of Hacettepe University in 1977. He continued his master degree at the Computer Science of Bosphorus University, his doctorate degree from Faculty of Business Administration at the Istanbul University, in 1983. He received his professor title in 1996 from the School of Business Administration at Istanbul University. He taught at Miller College of Business School, Ball State University, Indiana as a visiting professor in 2006-2007. His current research interests include Information Systems in Management. His primary teaching areas are Quantitative Methods and Management Information Systems.

Mamata Bhandar is based in Singapore and is an Assistant Professor at U21 Global. She has more than six years of experience in lecturing at the National University of Singapore. She also has industry experience in the software and manufacturing sectors. Dr. Bhandar obtained her PhD from the National University of Singapore in 2007. Her research interests are in knowledge management, specifically knowledge integration in the inter-organisational context, social capital and e-learning. Dr Bhandar's work has been published in the Journal of American Society of Information Systems and Technology (JASIST), Electronic Journal of Knowledge Management and the International Journal of Information and Communication Technology Education (IJICTE).

Joseph Blankson is an educational technology specialist and has experience teaching undergraduate and graduate courses in instructional technology and curriculum and instruction in both traditional face-to-face settings and online environments. Recently, he worked as a Continuing Medical Education Specialist (CME) –Technology at the Carle Foundation Hospital in Urbana, Illinois. Joseph is involved in the design, development, implementation, and evaluation of online courses for physicians. His conference presentations and publications focus on: integration of technology through curriculum development; faculty development in the use of technology for teaching and learning; developing effective computer based instructions; distance education and online course development; and issues surrounding access to technology.

Charlie C. Chen was educated at Claremont Graduate University and received the degree of PhD in Management Information Systems. Chen is an associate professor in the Department of Computer Information Systems at Appalachian State University. At present he is engaged in delivering a textbook project on supply chain management. His current research interests are project management and supply chain management. He is a member of Associations for Information Systems and Decision Science Institute. Chen is also a Project Management Professional (PMP) certified by the Project Management Institute. He has authored more than 40 refereed articles and proceedings and has presented at many professional conferences and venues. Chen has published in journals such as *Communications of Association for Information Systems, Behaviour and Information Technology, Journal of Knowledge Management Research Practice*, and *Journal of Information Systems Education*. Chen dedicates himself to be a transnational scholar and is a trip leader for a study abroad program in Asia (Japan and Taiwan).

Howard Clayton, an Associate Professor in the College of Business at Auburn University, is an expert on statistical methods with over 35 years teaching experience at both the K-12 and university levels. He has published many articles on statistical methods in journals. He currently serves as an evaluator on the research teams of three NSF funded grants, as well as an evaluator for the NSF sponsored Center for Advanced Vehicle Electronics (CAVE) at Auburn University.

Thomas Coe is an Associate Professor and Chair of the Finance Department at Quinnipiac University, Hamden, CT. He received his BSBA in Finance from the University of Akron (1984), his MBA from John Carroll University (1988), his MA in Economics (1992) and his PhD in Financial Economics (1994) from the University of New Orleans. Dr. Coe has participated published works relating to international financial markets and investments, personal financial planning, and financial education.

Michele T. Cole, J.D., PhD, associate professor of Nonprofit Management, Director of the Masters program in Nonprofit Management at Robert Morris University, Moon Township, PA. She received her J.D. from Duquesne University and her PhD from the University of Pittsburgh. Her research interests include effective online instruction, nonprofit sector curriculum development, legal issues in personnel management and application of business best practices and research to the nonprofit sector as well as the application of technology to learning strategies.

Eduardo Correia is a senior lecturer in the School of Computing at the Christchurch Polytechnic Institute of Technology in Christchurch, New Zealand. He worked for a number of years as a systems administrator and consultant, and has worked with VMware and virtualisation technologies since 2002. In 2003 with Ricky Watson he designed and implemented TechLabs, a network based on virtualisation used by the School of Computing for teaching. Dr Correia teaches courses in operating systems and networking, and holds a number of industry certifications, including Microsoft Certified Systems Engineer (MCSE) and a Microsoft Certified Technology Specialist (MCTS) in various areas.

Daniel Elemchuku Egbezor a Senior Lecturer in the Department of Educational Foundations at the University of Port Harcourt, Nigeria. He has written extensively in the areas of school effectiveness, teacher education, and curriculum reforms and has presented in national and international conferences. His publications have appeared in national and international journals, including chapters in books. His contact address is deegbezor@yahoo.com.

O.T. Emiri, B.LS and MSc in Library and Information Science, Delta State University, Abraka, Nigeria. He is currently with The University Library Delta State University Abraka (Delsu) . He is an associate Lecturer in the Deparment of Library and Information Science Delsu, Abraka. He has contibuted chapters in books and published articles in journals. His areas are Knowledge Mgt, ICT and Librarianship

Houbin Fang is a doctoral student in mathematics education in the Center for Science and Mathematics Education at The University of Southern Mississippi in Hattiesburg, USA. He received a Master's of Science of Instructional Technology at The University of Southern Mississippi and has an interest in applying technology application tools in the instruction of mathematics.

Teresa Franklin is Associate Professor of Instructional Technology at the College of Education, Ohio University, Athens, Ohio. Her research interests include: The integration of technology through curriculum development; handheld technologies in the higher education classroom; faculty development in the use of technology for teaching and learning; distance education and online course development; as well as issues surrounding access to technology.

David Georgina is an instructional designer at Minnesota State University, Mankato. His primary research interests are focused on integration of technology into pedagogy for Higher Education. His current research explores a content-first approach to faculty technology training in digital course conversion, and online learning environments.

Evelyn Gullett previously taught at the Department of Business and Technology, Webster University, St Louis, Missouri in the US. She combines her teaching experience with more than 23 years of international work experience. Her research interests include e-learning, organisational behaviour, change and development, work relationships, leadership application, training and development as well as qualitative research. Dr Gullett received her PhD in Human and Organizational Systems from The Fielding Graduate University, Santa Barbara, California. She holds an MA in Organizational Development and earned her MBA with a concentration in Human Resource Management and BA in Human Resource Development from Hawaii Pacific University.

Babita Gupta is a Professor of Information Systems at CSU Monterey Bay. Her research work appears in the Journal of Strategic Information Systems, CACM, Journal of Industrial Management and Data Systems, Journal of Information Technology Cases and Applications, and others. Her current research interests are in the areas of online privacy and security and use of RFID and biometrics.

Taralynn Hartsell is an Associate Professor in the Department of Technology Education at University of Southern Mississippi, USA. She teaches graduate courses in the Master's and PhD programs in Instructional Technology and Design. Her research interests include online learning, teacher education, and sociological and ethical perspectives in technology use.

Sherry Herron is an Assistant Professor in the Department of Biological Sciences and Director of the Center for Science and Mathematics Education at The University of Southern Mississippi, USA. She coordinates the Summer Math Institute that helps math teachers in the region learn how to integrate technology software and hardware into teaching.

D. Scott Hunsinger is an assistant professor of Computer Information Systems in the Walker College of Business at Appalachian State University in Boone, North Carolina, USA. He holds a PhD in Information Technology from The University of North Carolina at Charlotte. His research interests include IT certification, IT adoption, and group usage of technology. He has published articles in journals including *Journal of Information Technology Management, Journal of Information Technology Education, Information Systems Education Journal, Journal of Information Systems Applied Research, and Journal of Organizational and End User Computing.*

Youssreya Ibrahim is a Professor of Critical Care Nursing in Nursing Department, Faculty of Applied Medical Sciences, KSA. He has been involved as a Faculty staff member in the Faculty of Nursing, Mansoura University, Egypt for almost 15 years during which time he participated in the foundation of the Critical Care Nursing Department. Holding a Master and PhD degrees from Alexandria University in Critical Care Nursing, his research is focused on quality of nursing care in critical care units, as well as, application of information technology in the domain of critical care nursing. Dr. Ibraham has published some 20 scientific papers and supervised eight Master and PhD theses in this field. Administratively, he served as Vice-Dean at the Faculty of Nursing, Mansoura University, and nowadays is the Academic Supervisor of the Female Section at the Faculty of Applied Medical Sciences, Saudi Arabia. He has vast experience in quality assurance and accreditation programs both in Egypt and Saudi Arabia.

Nahed Kandeel is currently working as a lecturer in Critical Care Nursing Department, Faculty of Nursing, Mansoura University, Egypt. He holds a MSc and a PhD from University of Wales College of Medicine - School of Nursing and Midwifery Studies, UK, and worked as a member of administrative team of quality assurance and accreditation project at Faculty of Nursing from 2005 to 2009. He was a member of caring group, University of Maryland in 2008 and a member of Middle East Research Ethics Training Initiative (MERETI) group, University of Maryland, School of Medicine. Dr. Kandeel's major research interests focus on information technology education, research ethics and quality of nursing care in critical care units. His two research studies on information technology in nursing education have been presented in local conferences.

Lee Chen Kang is currently a lecturer in the Faculty of Information and Communications Technology, University Tunku Abdul Rahman, Malaysia. He received his BIT. (Hons) degree in Information Technology from the University of Tenaga Nasional, Malaysia in 2004 and Masters in Knowledge Management with Multimedia from Multimedia University 2007. He is currently a registered PhD. Candidate with Unievrsiti Tenaga Nasional, Malaysia.

Jared Keengwe is a faculty member at the University of North Dakota. His primary research interests include computer technology use and integration in higher education, constructivist pedagogy and meaningful student learning; and faculty professional development in teacher education programs. His current research explores faculty interactions in online learning environments and faculty diversity in higher education. His scholarly work has appeared in various journals including the Association for the Advancement of Computing in Education (AACE) Journal; the Journal of Science Education and Technology (JOST), and the Journal of Information Technology Education (JITE).

Benjamin Khoo completed his PhD (Information Systems) at the University of Maryland, Baltimore County. He is a member of two honor societies and was awarded the Phi Kappa Phi Dissertation Research Grant. He has published regularly in the major information systems journals. He is interested in both basic and applied research to further the effectiveness, usability, and ultimately the utility of information systems; and also the pedagogical issues related to these areas. Prior to becoming an academician, he was a member of the Technical Staff (Software Engineer) of a large telecommunication corporation.

Terry Kidd received his doctoral education training from the Texas A&M University and has previous graduate training in information systems, human resources development, and instructional technology. His research interests include e-learning and ICT innovation and its diffusion within an educational and community context to support teaching, learning, and human capital development. He has edited various books as the Handbook of Research on Instructional Systems Technology; the Handbook of Research on Technology Project Management, Planning, and Operations; Social Information Technology: Connecting Society and Cultural Issues; and Wired for Learning: An Educators Guide to Web 2.0.

Melih Kirlidog holds a BSc in Civil Enginering from Middle East Technical University, Turkey; an MBA (in MIS), and a PhD from University of Wollongong, Australia. He has worked as an ICT analyst and consultant for over twenty years in Turkey and Australia. His current research interests include intercultural ICT development and implementation, ICT in developing countries, Decision Support Systems, and community informatics. Since November 2002 he works as a full time academic in Department of Computer Engineering at Marmara University, Turkey.

Yangmo Koo holds a master's degree in management and information technology at California State University, Monterey Bay. He has been working with e-learning and mobile learning (m-learning) software development. He has extensive knowledge of research and development of computer aided language learning and has worked in the information technology field for four years.

Lydia Kyei-Blankson is an assistant professor in the Department of Educational Administration and Foundations at Illinois State University. She has expertise in research methods, applied statistics, and psychometrics and teaches graduate research methods and statistics courses. Her research interests investigate the underlying factors associated with student academic achievement. She is especially interested in technology use in education to improve student learning and achievement.

Judy Land is an assistant professor of accounting at North Carolina Central University. She currently teaches financial and intermediate accounting. Land's research interests are financial and international accounting, and her current research projects investigate earnings restatements and corporate governance. Land received her Bachelor's degree from Duke University, and her PhD in accounting from the University of North Carolina at Chapel Hill.

Kittipong Laosethakul is an Assistant Professor of Management Information Systems (MIS) at Sacred Heart University, Fairfield, CT. He received his BS in Mathematics from Chulalongkorn University in Bangkok, Thailand (1995), his MS in Management of Technology (MOT) from University of Alabama in Huntsville (1998), and his PhD in MIS from Auburn University (2005). His research interest covers electronic commerce subjects, gender-related issues in computing, and information technology in education environment.

Elke Leeds received the B.B.A degree from Loyola University of Chicago, the MBA from Kennesaw State University, and the PhD from Walden University in the management of information systems. She is currently an Assistant Professor of information systems (IS) in the Coles College of Business at Kennesaw State University. She is on the graduate faculty of the Coles MBA program, Executive MBA, and the Georgia Web MBA. She has published research papers in the *Informs Transactions on Education* (ITE), IEEE *Transactions On Professional Communication*, the *International Journal of e-Collaboration*, and the *International Journal of Applied Management and Technology*. Her current research interests include technology acceptance and fit, ethics in IT, communication technology, and communication skills in executive and engineering education.

Thaweephan Leingpibul is an Assistant Professor of Logistics and Supply Chain in the Haworth College of Business at Western Michigan University. He received his BSc in Food Science & Technology from Kasetsart University in Bangkok (1993), Thailand; his MBA from Missouri State University (2000), and his PhD from the University of Tennessee (2006). His research interests include logistics and supply chain, e-commerce, global outsourcing, demand management, food logistics and food supply chain.

Solomon Negash specializes in ICT for economically developing countries, e-learning, and business intelligence. He is the 2005 recipient of the distinguished eLearning award from his department and recipient of the 2007 Distinguished Graduate Teaching Award from his university. His work is published in Information & Management, Communication of the ACM, Psychology and Marketing, Communication of AIS, and at conference proceedings in the US, Canada, Spain, Ethiopia, Kenya, and Malaysia. Prof. Negash is the program coordinator for the Bachelor of Science in Information Systems (BSIS) program at Kennesaw State University.

Ugbomah Nwachukwu is a Lecturer in the Department of Intelligence and Security Studies, NOVENA University, Ogume, Nigeria. He has written papers in the areas of Sociology, Quality Education, Research Methodology, etc. His publications have appeared in national and international journals. His can be reached at ugnomahnwachukwu@yahoo.com.

Bolanle Olaniran is a professor & Interim Chair in the Department of Communication Studies at Texas Tech University, Lubbock Texas, USA.

Nwachukwu Prince Ololube is a Lecturer in the Department of Educational Foundations and Management, University of Education, Port Harcourt, Nigeria. He has written extensively in the areas of institutional management and leadership, school effectiveness, teacher effectiveness and quality improvement, and ICT in education. He has published in various international journals, chapters in books, and leading international conference proceedings. His contact address is ololubeprince@yahoo.com, ololube@ololube.com.

ChongWoo Park is an assistant professor of information technology at Georgia Gwinnett College in Lawrenceville, Georgia. He earned the BSc and MBA degrees from Korea University, the MSc degree from Syracuse University, and the PhD degree in computer information systems from the J. Mack Robinson College of Business at Georgia State University. Prior to his academic career, he was an IT consultant in Entrue Consulting Partners, the consulting division of LG CNS. His research interests include IT project management, technology adoption, knowledge management and systems, information seeking behavior, and IT use in education. His research has been published in journals including *Decision Sciences, Journal of the Association for Information Systems, IEEE Transactions on Engineering Management, and International Journal of Information and Communications Technology Education,* and presented at *Academy of Management Meeting, Americas Conference on Information Systems*, and *Decision Sciences Institute Meeting.*

Natcha Pavasajjanant received MA from Kyoto University of Education majoring in educational method and technology. She is currently a Ph.D. candidate at the Graduate School of Applied Informatics, University of Hyogo. The area of research is the design of teaching course with the use of ICT to develop distance education.

Avinash Rathod received his Bachelor of Medicine and Bachelor of Surgery (MBBS) from Andhra Medical College, NTR university of Health Sciences, India (2004) and a Master of Public Health (MPH) majoring in Epidemiology and Biostatistics from The University of Southern Mississippi, USA (2009). He is ECFMG (Education Commission for Foreign Medical Graduate) certified and wants to pursue a MD degree in future. His interest area is the statistical analysis of Research Data.

Arjan Raven is an associate professor of Management Information Systems. He received his PhD in Business Administration from the University of Southern California and additionally holds degrees in computer science from the University of Amsterdam and electrical engineering from the Utrecht School of Engineering. His current interests center around the fit of tasks and systems, and international development. Arjan has published in the *Journal of Organizational Computing and Electronic Commerce*, the *Data Base for Advances in Information Systems*, the *International Journal of Technology Management*, and the *Quarterly Review of Distance Education*. Arjan has consulted nationally and internationally with large companies in the areas of business process redesign and knowledge management.

Natasha Rodriguez is a graduate student in the Communication Studies Department at Texas Tech.

Chetan S. Sankar is Thomas Walter Professor of Management at Auburn University. He has received more than two million dollars from ten National Science Foundation grants to develop exceptional instructional materials that bring real-world issues into classrooms. He has won awards for research and teaching excellence from the Society for Information Management, NEEDS, Decision Sciences Institute, American Society for Engineering Education, American Society for Mechanical Engineering, International Network for Engineering Education & Research, and the Project Management Institute. He is the editor-in-chief of the Decision Sciences Journal of Innovative Education and the managing editor of the Journal of STEM Education: Innovations and Research.

Daniel J. Shelley, PhD, professor of education at Robert Morris University, Moon Township, PA. Shelley earned his BSc in Elementary Education from Penn State University in 1971. He completed a master's degree in Social Science with an emphasis in American History at Penn State in 1972. He earned his PhD in Education at the University of Pittsburgh in 1986. Shelley is also a certified Elementary Principal and a Curriculum Program Specialist. His research interests include enhancing pre-service teacher's skills and expertise in applying educational technology to their teaching, and the integration of technology into classroom teaching. He currently serves as the Director of the Southwestern region of the Pennsylvania Association for Educational Computing and Technology (PAECT). His classroom interests include robotics and instructional software and authoring. He has also written numerous articles and given presentations at national and international conferences on the integration of technology into classroom teaching.

Manjit Singh Sidhu is currently the Head of Graphics and Multimedia in the College of Information Technology, University Tenaga Nasional, Malaysia. He received his BSc. (Hons) degree in Computer Science from the University of Wolverhampton, UK in 1997 and Masters in Information Technology from University Putra Malaysia in 2000. He completed his Ph.D. in Computer Science from University of Malaya in 2007. He is a Chartered IT Professional and a member of the British Computer Society, a member of the Institute of Electrical and Electronics Engineers (IEEE), a member of the Malaysian Nasional Computer Confederation and Associate Fellow of the Malaysian Scientific Association. His research interests include user interface design approaches in multimedia and virtual reality applications.

Louis B. Swartz, J.D., associate professor of Legal Studies at Robert Morris University, Moon Township, PA. Mr. Swartz teaches Legal Environment of Business and The Constitution and Current Legal Issues at the undergraduate level and Legal Issues of Executive Management in the M.B.A. program. He received his Bachelors degree from the University of Wisconsin in Madison, Wisconsin (1966) and his Juris Doctorate from Duquesne University in Pittsburgh, PA (1969). He is the Coordinator of the Robert Morris University Pre-Law Advisory Program and a member of the Northeast Association of Pre-Law Advisers (NAPLA) and the Academy of Legal Studies in Business (ALSB). His research interests include online education, legal studies and business law.

Timothy Teo is an assistant professor at the National Institute of Education, Nanyang Technological University, Singapore. His research interests include ICT in education and teacher education. Timothy is also interested in applying statistical modeling techniques to study human attitudes, perceptions, and behavious, with special focus on technology-mediated teaching and learning.

Adobi Jessica Tiemo, Delta State University, Abraka – Nigeria, BSc Management from River State University Nigeeria. Msc Mgt Sc. Delsu Abraka, Nigeria. She is lecturering in the Dept of Bus Adm Delsu, Abraka, Nigeria. Her areas are Marketing, Management and ICT.

Pereware Aghwotu Tiemo, B.LS and MSc in library and information Science, Delta State University, Abraka, Nigeria. He has previously worked with The British Council Library, Ibadan and Lagos Office and aslo with Delta State University Library, Abraka. He is currently Senior Librarian and Head of Technical Services Niger Delta University, Wilberforce Island, Bayelsa State Nigeria. He has published various articles in reputable international and local journals. His areas are Internet, Computers, Information Management and Librarianship

Chia-Wen Tsai is an assistant professor in the Department of Information Management, Ming Chuan University. Dr. Tsai is one of the Editors-in-Chief of *International Journal of Online Pedagogy and Course Design*. He is also the Associate Editor of *International Journal of Technology and Human Interaction, International Journal of Information Communication Technologies and Human Development*, and *International Journal of Innovation in the Digital Economy*. He is interested in the online teaching methods and knowledge management

Andrew Egba Ubogu is a Lecturer in the Department of Geography at the Ahmadu Bello University of Zaria, Nigeria. He has written extensively in the areas of Transport Geography Pollution, GIS etc. His publications have appeared in national and international journals. His contact address is ubogu2001@ yahoo.com.

Patrick Wachira is a faculty member in mathematics and mathematics education at Cleveland State University, Ohio. His primary research and writing focus on the preparation of teachers to teach mathematics in a way that develops understanding facilitated by appropriate and effective integration of technology in teaching and learning.

Shuyan Wang is an Assistant Professor in Instructional Technology at The University of Southern Mississippi. Her research interests include the integration of technology throughout the curriculum, distance education, assessment, and electronic portfolios. Dr. Wang has published numerous book chapters and articles in national and international refereed journals.

Ricky Watson is a senior lecturer in the School of Computing at the Christchurch Polytechnic Institute of Technology in Christchurch, New Zealand. He worked for many years in industry as a systems administrator and consultant, and has worked with VMware and virtualisation technologies since 2001. In 2003 with Eduardo Correia he designed and implemented TechLabs, a network based on virtualisation used by the School of Computing for teaching. Mr Watson teaches courses in operating systems, networking, and programming, and holds a number of industry certifications, including Red Hat Certified Engineer (RHCE) and Microsoft Certified Systems Engineer (MCSE).

Jin Yang (Ph.D., Southern Illinois University, Carbondale) is an associate professor in the Department of Journalism at the University of Memphis. Her research interests have spanned new media communication and international mass communication. New media communication includes the impact on individuals, higher education and society, and international communication focuses on the cross-nation and cross-culture comparisons.

Hong Zhan is an assistant professor of Humanities and Communication in Chinese at Embry-Riddle Aeronautical University, Prescott. Her research interests include educational technology in foreign language instruction, online language instruction, and curriculum design for language program. Dr. Zhan has had numerous conference presentations and publications.

Index